A Social Psychology of Leisure

Second Edition

A Social Psychology of Leisure

Second Edition

Douglas A. Kleiber
University of Georgia

Gordon J. Walker
University of Alberta

Roger C. Mannell
University of Waterloo

Venture Publishing, Inc.
State College, PA

Production: Richard Yocum and George Lauer

Cover by StepUp Communications, Inc.

Manuscript Editing: Richard Yocum, Dan Threet

Library of Congress Catalogue Card Number 2011929715
ISBN-10: 1-892132-92-3
ISBN-13: 978-1-892132-92-5

Dedication

This book is dedicated to our wives, Pam, Janet, and Marg.

Table of Contents

Preface

In recent decades the social psychology of leisure has emerged as a prominent perspective for understanding the role and impact of leisure in people's lives. It is a dynamic field of study influenced by researchers in leisure studies and theories and research in the fields of psychology and sociology. There is a real interest in the practical applications of social psychology for understanding urgent social issues, and social psychological principles have been applied to improving arrangements for health, work, home life, and, of course, leisure.

An early systematic effort to examine the potential of social psychology for understanding leisure was provided by John Neulinger in the 1974 book, *The Psychology of Leisure: Research Approaches to the Study of Leisure.* In 1980, Seppo Iso-Ahola published *The Social Psychology of Leisure and Recreation*, the first textbook to map out the boundaries of the field and review the social psychological theory and research available at the time. Though a number of books and journal articles have been published since that time dealing with selected topics on the social psychology of leisure, there had not been a current and up-to-date textbook available until the first edition of *A Social Psychology of Leisure* was published in 1997. The first edition has been well received and used in many parts of the world. It has been translated into Japanese and Chinese and is widely cited.

This new edition builds on all of these earlier efforts and incorporates major new topics of research, innovative studies, and contemporary examples. It also advances from the first edition in several important ways. First, it makes more use of traditional social psychological topics such as conformity and persuasion, particularly in Chapter 9. Second, we have devoted the entirety of Chapter 10 to the subject of race, ethnicity, and culture, given the growing evidence for the influence of each on leisure behavior. And third, we have changed the focus of later chapters from benefits to outcomes, recognizing that leisure behavior may be both beneficial and harmful at times.

Those differences notwithstanding, we have continued with the general orientation that the social psychology of leisure is concerned with how people come to perceive time or behavior as free or discretionary, how they choose to fill and structure this discretionary time with behavior and experience, why they make these choices, and the implications of these choices for their happiness and personal growth. Finally, the social psychology of leisure is concerned with how leisure activity and experience is influenced by other people and by experiences in the other domains of life such as work, family, and community. The purpose of this book, then, is to provide the student with the opportunity to examine current social psychological theory and research about leisure behavior and experience. In other words, how do people's personalities and the social situations that they encounter during their daily lives shape their perceptions, experiences, and responses to leisure? In this book, we attempt to present the "basics" of the field—the core theories and findings that contribute to an understanding of leisure as it affects individuals' daily lives, as well as their use of leisure services.

A Social Psychology of Leisure is written to serve as a textbook for undergraduate students taking a course in the psychological and social aspects of leisure and recreation. It also provides for students in graduate courses a comprehensive introduction that should be supplemented by books and journal articles focusing on specific topics. Finally, especially as it has incorporated reference to newer literature, this volume is intended to serve as a sourcebook for leisure researchers in providing context and even direction when conducting studies that employ a social psychological approach. In Section One, The Nature of Social Psychology, two chapters deal with the social psychological approach and the evolution of an interest in leisure in social psychological research. In Section Two, Social Psychology of Leisure Essentials, four chapters explore the various meanings of leisure and how they are measured, the range of leisure experiences, and the role of freedom, motivation, needs, and self-determination in shaping leisure activity. In Section Three, Leisure and the Person, two chapters address personality, attitudes, and leisure identity, as well as age and gender as individual difference factors influencing leisure behavior and experience. In Section Four, The Social Context of Leisure, Chapter 9 approaches social influences in general and socialization in particular while Chapter 10 considers how race, ethnicity, and culture act as situational influences on leisure activity and experience. Finally, in Section Five, Identifying and Cultivating the Best of Leisure, Chapter 11 addresses the social psychological impacts of leisure in childhood and adolescence, Chapter 12 considers leisure impacts in adulthood, and Chapter 13 examines the theory and research that has been applied in practice to bringing out the more positive impacts of leisure across the lifespan.

The success of any text depends ultimately on its ability to communicate clearly to student readers and to spark interest in the field of study. We have attempted to present the material simply, without oversimplifying. Special attention has been given to selecting examples that illustrate basic principles and convey our enthusiasm for the field. This book will provide the reader with the necessary social psychological background material drawn from the fields of psychology and sociology. A previous course in social psychology is not required.

We have tried to maximize the clarity and interest level of the text. Many years of teaching undergraduate and graduate courses in this area have provided a testing ground for much of the material and the methods of presentation that appear in this book. In addition, many students and professors who used the first edition of *A Social Psychology of Leisure* have provided suggestions and comments about the book that we have attempted to take into consideration. We have attempted to avoid unnecessary technical terms. Many concrete examples are used, and where appropriate, topics are introduced through the use of scenarios highlighting various types of leisure behavior for students to analyze. These illustrations are used to raise questions about issues such as:

- How do individuals know when they are having a leisure experience?

- What is so special about leisure from a psychological perspective?

- Does leisure affect people's happiness and life satisfaction?

- Why do people sometimes seek danger and thrills during free time?

- Are some personality types better able to deal with leisure than others?

- Do certain child-rearing methods lead to greater leisure competency?

- How is leisure behavior similar and different across racial, ethnic, and cultural groups?

- Is there a positive side to "addiction" to activities such as online gaming?

- How do leisure attitudes develop and how can they be changed?

- Is leisure important for the development of intimate relationships?

- Are there gender differences in leisure perceptions and needs?

- Can leisure help people deal with stress?

- Are there effective ways to overcome social psychological barriers to leisure participation and satisfaction?

The bibliography at the end of the book is extensive. The discussion of each topic reflects attention to research and thinking found in the literature. We also have identified important studies that illustrate each issue, and these are examined in some detail. These studies also were selected to illustrate the various social psychological methods that can be used to answer questions that researchers, practitioners, participants, and students may have about leisure. By posing interesting leisure questions often found in the reader's own daily life and then demonstrating how researchers have attempted to answer these same questions, it is hoped that we can demonstrate the relevance, excitement, and methods of social psychological leisure research.

Finally, in this book we discuss the potential applications of the research reviewed. In some cases, these applications will have immediate implications for the provision of public and private leisure services in communities, tourism, park management, and private recreation businesses. However, there is another sense in which the book is applied. Not only can the information provided by a social psychology of leisure be used to more effectively plan leisure services, but also individuals, through an awareness of the social psychological dimensions of leisure, may be able to extend more control over their lives and better enjoy their own leisure. To this end, readers will constantly be asked to reflect on their own experiences and their personal observations of other people at leisure.

D. A. K.

G. J.W.

R.C. M

Acknowledgments

There are a number of people who deserve our thanks and whose interest and support have been greatly appreciated during the course of writing this edition.

For their comments on portions of the manuscript, we would like to thank University of Georgia graduate students Lisbeth Berbary, Rudy Dunlap, Nic Holt, Sunhwan Hwang, Mandy Jarriel, John Paul MacNeal, Joseph Pate, Heather Reel, Joe Wassif, and Clemson University graduate students Begum Aybar-Damali, Gena Bell, Dorinda Christian, Brian Krohn, Kirby Player, Preetha Sundareswaran, and Teresa Tucker.

Finally, on a personal note, our work on this book has occupied many nights and weekends and substituted for much of our own family leisure time. We are very grateful to our families, and in particular, Pam, Janet, and Marg, for their support and for enduring our mental and physical absences during this time. And as we said with the first edition, we promise not to do it again, at least not for a while.

Section One

The Nature of Social Psychology

1

Understanding Leisure with Social Psychology

Preview

This chapter introduces the reader to thinking about leisure from a social psychological perspective. We begin by looking at the need to study leisure and how social psychological thinking has influenced the provision of leisure services. Then we consider how the social sciences in general, through the scientific study of people's everyday behavior and experience, differ from other ways of understanding the lifestyles people lead and what makes their lives meaningful and happy. Next, several scenarios are presented that demonstrate how a social psychological approach can be used to better understand leisure issues. The social psychological approach used as a framework for this book is then described.

Social Science and the Quest for Happiness, Health, and the Good Life

People have always sought the formula for health and happiness. This search for the good life is as common today as at any time in the past—perhaps more so. Throughout history, people have looked to the values of the social groups of which they are members, the folk wisdom passed down to them from their elders, religion, and philosophy as sources for the answers to these questions. Beginning fairly early in the twentieth century, social scientists jumped into the fray in an attempt to provide answers as well.

A Question of Lifestyle: Juggling and Balancing the Demands of Daily Life

Whatever the source of ideas about health and happiness, the answers have often taken the form of a prescription for a particular way of living. Today these prescriptions are packaged as "lifestyle," and individuals are bombarded from all sides with suggestions for the best way to juggle and balance the various aspects of their lives. Daily newspapers feature lifestyle sections, weekly television series spotlight different and unique ways of living, and numerous self-help books on lifestyle appear on bookstore shelves. Lifestyle is typically described as a "total way of living" (Thirlaway & Upton, 2009; Veal 1993). Though not a new invention, people in previous generations, like fish in water, were immersed in their daily lives and for the most part oblivious to it; lifestyle alternatives were few for most people. While this lack of alternatives is still true for many people in different parts of the world, access to instantaneous electronic communication has created widespread awareness of lifestyle alternatives, even if these choices are not available to everyone.

Commercials urge people to create their own lifestyle—with the "right" products, of course. Television and magazines depict a whole range of ways to live. The food we eat, the manner in which we prepare and consume it, our clothes, our homes, the entertainment and leisure we enjoy, the work we do, and how we raise our children all define our lifestyle. If the number of newspaper articles and popular books written recently are any indication (e.g., Sandholtz, et al., 2002; Loflin & Musig, 2005), most people have come to believe that their lifestyles determine their health and happiness, and just as importantly, that they can *create* their own lifestyles through how they juggle and balance the work, family, and leisure aspects of their lives. Social scientists are studying the battle that people seem to be waging today to bring hectic lifestyles under control (e.g., Christiansen & Matuska, 2006; Gleich, 1999; Honore, 2004; McKenna & Thew, 2008), as well the impact various lifestyle choices may have on individuals and the larger society.

People-Watching as a Science

Science is responsible for many of the lifestyle choices that modern life allows. For many people, "science" suggests the *physical sciences,* such as physics, chemistry, and biology, and they can easily name a variety of inventions emerging from research in these sciences that have made modern life easier— for example, toasters, plastic bags, heart transplants, more resistant strains of plants, personal computers, and cellular telephones. Of course, some of these inventions have created difficulties as well. Current problems being addressed by physical and biomedical scientists are also well known, for example, global warming, bio-terrorism, nuclear waste disposal, AIDS, pandemics, and fossil fuel dependence. These changes and problems command the attention of scientists in a variety of fields, including those that study people per se.

The social sciences, such as psychology, sociology, and anthropology, have taken the popular pastime of "people-watching" and made a science of it. When asked to identify the kinds of inventions developed by social scientists, people often find it more difficult to come up with such a list. Yet social science has provided humanity with a number of inventions, such as psychotherapy, behavior modification, political polling, time management strategies, educational planning principles, and brainstorming. However, social science is probably better known for the types of problems it attempts to address, such as child abuse, poverty, neurosis, alienation in large cities, the pain and dysfunction of substance abuse, and unemployment. It also aims at the elimination of lifestyle diseases, such as heart disease, stress, obesity, and Type II diabetes, which can result from poor eating habits, smoking, an excess of sedentary activity (particularly media-based), and lack of exercise.

As people-watchers, everyone is an armchair social scientist, making predictions about the behavior of other people based on their own experiences. Everyone has theories about the best way to get a date, discipline children, organize a great party, keep New Year's resolutions, and approach the boss for a raise or a professor for a better grade—and we as individuals act on these theories. Social scientists, on the other hand, by carefully and systematically observing people in their homes, at work, at leisure, and even in psychological laboratories, attempt to provide a clearer and more objective picture of human behavior than we, as individuals, can hope to acquire on our own using our casual observations.

The social sciences have long been associated with the study of the types of human problems just mentioned. But during the latter part of this century, a shift has taken place. Social scientists are spending a great deal of time studying normal daily activities and the positive aspects of life as well. Altruism, creativity, humor, and quality of life are only a few of the subjects that have been addressed in the name of "positive psychology" (see Seligman & Csikszentmihalyi, 2000). More will be said about this shift in Chapter 2.

Much of this research by social scientists is being carried out in colleges and universities. Newer departments of health promotion, leisure studies, gerontology, consumer sciences, and family studies have emerged to provide answers to specific lifestyle issues and educate people to work in human service fields related to these. Like other sources of information and values in Western society, the solutions provided by social scientists are often controversial. However, the work of these social scientists is alerting society to important problems, sometimes confirming common sense understanding, sometimes severely challenging cherished ideas and beliefs. Hopefully, this research will contribute answers and raise social awareness about specific lifestyle issues so that people will be better able to manage their lives and more effectively support others as well. Accordingly, this book is intended to bring students of leisure and recreation, as well as parks and tourism, into that discussion with an enhanced understanding that will enable them to be more effective service providers, instructors, and researchers.

Why Study Leisure with Social Science?

We will explore the various meanings of leisure in Chapter 3 especially; but it should be recognized at the outset here that leisure is inherently associated with *lifestyle* and that people seem to have difficulty achieving lifestyle *balance*. As will be seen, some researchers have even suggested that an individual's leisure may have more impact on the quality of life than any other area of behavior and experience (see Kelly, 1996). Leisure has been described in a variety of ways. In fact, one of the longest-standing problems research-ers have had is agreeing on how to define and measure it. Leisure has been characterized as specific types of *activity* (e.g., attending a movie); as *time* free from obligations (e.g., the amount of time not spent in paid employ-ment and taking care of home, family, and oneself); as meaningful and sat-isfying *experience* (e.g., feelings of enjoyment, fun, excitement, relaxation, awe, belonging); or as some combination of activity, time, and experience. Any of these approaches to defining and measuring leisure can be useful, and the approach used often depends on what questions about leisure the researcher is trying to answer. Chapter 3 will examine the issues of leisure definition and measurement in some detail and provide some interesting examples.

As to why one should study leisure, many researchers do so simply because they are curious and would like to know more about why people choose to engage in the activities and pursue the experiences with which they fill their free time. Why do some people jump out of airplanes while others prefer quiet walks in the park? How is it that some friends never have enough time for the activities they constantly pack into their available free time, while others find their leisure empty and boring? What effects do these orientations have on other aspects of life? These and many other questions are fascinat-ing. Since leisure is based on free time or choice, most individuals have more personal control over what they do during their free time than at any other time during their daily lives. Consequently, for those researchers who make a profession out of people-watching, what people do for leisure may tell more about them—their innermost feelings, attitudes, beliefs, and per-sonality characteristics—than what they do in any other context. Leisure is fertile ground for learning more about other people as well as ourselves (Leckey & Mannell, 2000). It is the authors' hope that by reading this book and studying leisure behavior and experience, readers will become more aware of the factors that affect their own leisure, and consequently will be able to extend more control over this realm of their lives and better enjoy and benefit from it while developing ideas for positively influencing the lei-sure and lives of others.

Many who read this book will be studying in recreation and leisure stud-ies programs. Not only are you likely to be curious about leisure (both your own and others'), but you will be planning to enter the leisure services field, where you will be involved in developing and providing services and oppor-tunities that will enable others to make more of their leisure time. While lei-sure can be rewarding, it seems to be a problem for many people as well. To work with people and help them in developing meaningful and satisfying leisure, researchers and practitioners need to constantly study and examine people's leisure behavior and experience and the factors that influence them.

The resulting knowledge will hopefully sensitize leisure providers to such changing needs and better enable the provision of valued services and assistance.

Is Leisure a "Problem" to Be Studied with Social Science?

The use of non-work time and leisure in our society continues to raise highly significant questions both for the individual and for society. Society is facing major social transformations with the globalization of the economy and advancing technology that are creating radical changes in the way we as individuals work, the use of our non-work time, and the role of leisure in our lives. To make things even more exciting and perhaps complicated, there are many different views about how these changes in technology and economics are affecting the type of work individuals do, where they work, when they work, how much they work, and even if they work at all (see Haworth, 2004; Mannell & Reid, 1999).

What individuals do off the job, as leisure, and the lifestyles they lead are caught up in these same forces of change. Analysts who spend their time peering into the future are no more in agreement about what will happen with leisure than they are with work or the relationship between work and leisure (e.g., Hilbrecht, 2007; Lewis, 2003; McDaniels, 1990). There are even major differences of opinion about how much leisure and free time people actually have today, whether it is increasing or decreasing, and if it can play a positive or negative role in people's lives as the opportunities for work change (e.g., Robinson & Godbey, 1997; Schor, 1991, 1998). For many people, there is a distinct possibility of further growth in non-work time, though it may be unevenly distributed—with some actually working longer hours and others becoming underemployed or chronically unemployed. During the past few years, there have been policy discussions by governments, employers, and employee groups about the value and feasibility of job sharing and shorter work weeks in an attempt to distribute the work that is available to more people (e.g., Schor, 2005). These policies would result in more free time and possibly more leisure for many people.

The Organization for Economic Co-operation and Development (OECD) published a 2009 report examining the average amount of leisure time available in the eighteen of its member countries, including Canada and the U.S., for whom relatively recent time-use information was available (OECD, 2009). Leisure included hobbies, games, television viewing, computer use, recreational gardening, sports, socialising with friends and family, attending events, and so on (we will discuss the challenges of measuring leisure in Chapter 3). Leisure was found to occupy roughly one fourth of the time of the average working adult, or 5.76 hours out of the 24-hour day. If only waking hours are considered, leisure time is approximately one third of people's waking time. However, there are tremendous differences among people in their work and leisure lifestyle arrangements within and across countries. On the one hand, unemployment and part-time work have grown at the same time that the number of people working well beyond a forty-hour week has increased (Robinson & Godbey, 1997; Schor, 1998). Some of these latter individuals are doing so unwillingly; to keep their jobs, they have little choice as employers downsize and streamline their operations. Other people appear to be thriving on more work, though for some of these people work over-whelms life to the point of "workaholism" (e.g., Taris et al., 2008). On the other hand, for children, retirees, the underemployed, and the unemployed, leisure may account for much larger portions of their time and activity, though the quality of experience in all of that "free" time may give us pause about referring to it as leisure. These differences and problems make the study of leisure and how people deal with it a timely and important topic. Whether this time is idle, avoided, filled with pleasure, devoted to personal growth, used in the service of others, a source of frustration and anxiety, or used in ways that are personally or socially harmful is a matter of great aca-demic, political, and social interest. Thus, although leisure may not be a problem per se, its wide variety of manifestations suggests the full range of human experience.

Reaching the Potential of Leisure through Leisure Services

What individuals choose to do during their leisure may require few goods and services, involve no one but themselves and a few friends, and cost them nothing. However, there is an ever-increasing demand for public and private leisure services. These services are provided and influenced by numerous agencies at all levels of government, by professional and advocacy groups, and by private businesses. Leisure is big business as people spend money on travel, attending sport and cultural events, collectibles from stamps to paint-ings, and recreational goods from water bottles to sailboats. It is cultivated by governments for its contribution to economic growth. For example, many countries have developed strategies to promote tourism. The travel industry is the largest single industry in the world, and in 2008, the World Tourism Organization (WTO) estimated worldwide revenues to be about 944 billion U.S. dollars, or 30% of the world's exports of services (UNWTO, 2009). In recent years, people have shown greater concern and interest in leading healthier lifestyles. Governments have also been promoting healthier lifestyles in an attempt to reduce medical and healthcare costs, which have continued to grow beyond society's ability to pay. More and more, leisure has been sin-gled out as an important vehicle for promoting healthy lifestyles (Mannell, 2007). Consequently, local communities continue to build and manage recre-ational and cultural facilities. They provide programs for their citizens with the support of all levels of government. Public lands and forests continue to be acquired, protected as parks, and managed for recreational use and to promote healthy living (Kaczynski & Henderson, 2008). Reductions to recess and physical education in public schools have made public leisure services all the more important resources for physical activity.

As a consequence of the extensive resources being invested in leisure-service delivery systems by all levels of government and by the private and commercial sectors, there has emerged a need for skilled professionals and practitioners to plan, develop, and manage the various service systems. To help in this enterprise, scholars and researchers in leisure studies have been concerned with how individuals, groups, and society as a whole plan, organize, and use resources for leisure. The role of leisure in meeting the health and lifestyle needs of people in various types of employment, those working at home, families, retired adults, disadvantaged groups, persons with disabilities, and the unemployed is of continuing and growing interest. Researchers and practitioners are concerned about policies affecting public and private sector involvement in leisure-related matters such as sport, fitness, tourism, park and heritage development, and the arts.

Leisure services have also become "psychologized" to a great extent (Mannell, 1991). Many recreation providers are as concerned with the quality of the experiences provided by their recreational services as they are with the activities and settings they manage. This focus on the experience is evident in many consumer areas today. Research on consumer behavior in general has increasingly focused on the experience of buying in its own right, since consumers do more than simply attend to information to make purchasing choices (Pine & Gilmore, 1999). They also engage in imaginative and emotional consumption experiences. Pine and Gilmore note that businesses are increasingly inclined to orchestrate memorable experiences for their clients. The experience is the "value added" in marketing a product for companies such as Starbucks and IBM and, of course, with Disney, where the experience *is* the product. Parents have always sought enjoyable experiences for birthday parties, for example, and now companies such as "Pump It Up" specialize in creating such events. This growing focus on the nature of experience (Norman, 2004) is reminiscent of Toffler's prediction in his book *Future Shock* (1970) that no service will be offered to the consumer until it has been analyzed by teams of behavioral engineers to improve the quality of the experience it creates.

Of course, this notion of experience "engineering" smacks of manipulation, and is viewed by some critics as the antithesis of the freedom of choice, personal control, and spontaneity usually associated with leisure (e.g., Goodale, 1990). In the tourism and travel industry, for example, there are those who are very concerned with the lack of authenticity of many of the travel and tourism experiences available (e.g., Cohen, 1988; Franklin, 2006; MacCannell,

1973, 2001; Moscardo & Pearce, 1986; Urry, 2002). But many leisure service providers, particularly those in the private sector, have already developed theories or rules of thumb through trial and error to enhance the experiences of their customers and ensure a clientele willing to return again and again. For example, the formula for the success of theme parks is known and applied in designing and operating this type of leisure business, as noted by Cameron and Bordessa (1981). Success is based on structuring the leisure environment in such a way as to create or encourage predictably satisfying experiences (e.g., Sharpe, 2005). Regardless of how researchers and service providers feel about these issues, it has become apparent that an understanding of the psychological or experiential nature of leisure is important.

Leisure studies scholars draw on the knowledge and approaches of the social and management sciences, and the results of their research and thinking is disseminated in a wide array of national and international journals and conferences specializing in leisure studies. Most college and university recreation and leisure studies programs encourage their students to integrate and understand the interplay between "people," "resource," and "policy" issues. In other words, leisure studies courses require students to study individual and group leisure behavior as a function of social and cultural factors, the planning and management of natural and built resources for free time use, and policy/management issues associated with the provision of public and private leisure services. Social science can help formalize scientific planning and design principles that can provide the tools for those practitioners in the public and private service sectors who are involved with human behavior and experience during free time.

Social science research is devoted to understanding not only the antecedents and consequences of leisure choices, but also the factors that affect the quality and meaning of these choices. Hopefully, this knowledge will allow a better understanding of the problems people encounter in attempting to choose meaningful and enjoyable leisure; and while this knowledge may be applied in enhancing the management of human services, it may also be used to enable individuals to gain more control over their lives and better manage their own leisure.

Leisure and Social Psychology

Leisure has been studied from the perspectives of a variety of social science disciplines including sociology, anthropology, and economics (see Barnett, 1988, 1995; Chick, 1987, 1995; Peterson, Driver, & Gregory, 1988). Starting in the late 1960s, there has been a steady growth in the use of psychological, particularly *social* psychological, theory and research methods for developing an understanding of leisure (Argyle, 1996; Iso-Ahola, 1995; Mannell, Kleiber, & Staempfli, 2006).

From a psychological perspective, social psychologists attempt to understand how the actual, imagined, or implied presence of others influences the thoughts, feelings, and behaviors of individuals (Allport, 1968; Aronson, 2008) and this approach has been called "psychological social psychology" (Stryker, 1997) to distinguish it from sociological social psychology, which focuses more on group processes, ideological and political influences, and the social construction of meaning (see Mannell, Kleiber, & Staempfli, 2006). Mainstream psychological social psychology has been and continues to be primarily concerned with individuals' perceptions or construal of their social environment, recognizing that individuals can misperceive social and physical realities and that it is these perceptions, mistaken or not, that influence behavior and experience (Ross & Nisbett, 1991). Experimental research designs are widely used by psychological researchers, though field research methods have grown in popularity during the past twenty-five years.

Leisure researchers have only rarely used the experimental research methods of psychology. However, consistent with the social psychological approach in the field of psychology, there has been a focus on the leisure experience and behavior of the individual—in other words what she or he does and feels— and the factors that influence those actions and feelings. Also consistent with this perspective, researchers have been interested in the influence of *others* on leisure behavior and experience, based on the idea that the influences of others work through and interact with individual differences and psychological dispositions. Leisure also affords much in the way of privacy and solitude and thus relative freedom from the *direct* influence of others, but even there the thoughts, perceptions, and histories one brings to such situations— as well as the motivation for seeking out freedom and enjoyment— are products of social influence as well. Thus, as with other forms of human behavior, leisure behavior and experience are seen to be a function of the interplay of internal psychological dispositions (e.g., perceptions, feelings, emotions, beliefs, attitudes, needs, personality characteristics) and situational influences that are part of an individual's social environment (e.g., other people, group norms, human artifacts, and media). And, although the framework for this book has a strong psychological orientation, the increasing amount of research on leisure that is being done using sociological social psychological perspectives will also be considered in examining those processes.

The emergence of the social psychological study of leisure is not too surprising. Many researchers studying leisure have been committed to providing knowledge to practitioners who work with individuals to enhance their leisure participation and satisfaction. This "helping" orientation is a legacy of the parks and recreation movement, which began at the turn of the last century largely in response to the problems of industrialization and urbanization. The leisure service field is descended from this early movement and still has a responsibility for working with individuals to solve problems that are a result of both personal constraints and constraints imposed by their social environments. Thus, there has been substantial interest in understanding individual leisure behavior and experience as a function of the differences in needs, attitudes, and personality that individuals carry around with them, and the social contexts and situations that they encounter during their daily lives. The knowledge gained from this perspective will not only enable providers to more effectively market and promote leisure services and resources, it also offers the possibility of actually designing those services and resources to provide certain experiences for participants. Behavioral engineering of this sort raises a fundamental problem, however, that is somewhat problematic for some of the assumptions about leisure that we will explore throughout this volume: to the extent that leisure can be characterized as an experience of freedom, having it managed by others may threaten its very existence! Similarly, if leisure behavior is presumed to be a reflection of individual self-expression, how then does it survive social influence? In looking at leisure through the lens of social psychology, we are suggesting that such freedom and self-expression are nevertheless conditioned by social influence in varying degrees and are thus amenable to the good— and bad— ministrations of others.

We invite you, as the reader, to at least temporarily adopt this social psychological perspective in thinking about leisure and the various issues and problems that will be examined. We have found it to be a useful framework for our own thinking and understanding. Social psychology is a lively, dynamic field of enquiry. People *do* social psychology. So, before starting to examine the research on the social psychology of leisure, let's examine a "leisure problem" and observe firsthand social psychological thinking in action.

Social Psychology in Action: Old and New Scenarios

In the first edition of this book, we introduced the following story about a "video arcade." It was based loosely on real events that took place over thirty years ago. The playing of video games these days— while at least as controversial in some respects as we will see later— is far more likely to be done in homes, with one's personal computers and consoles, or in more informal settings with other personal digital devices. But the problems identified and discussed at that time, related to private leisure consumption in public spaces, may still apply today. You be the judge.

Kids Steal To Feed Video Habit, School Board Told

Educators and school board trustees want to zap students out of electronic game arcades and back into classrooms. Arcades have led to increasing problems of truancy, larceny, and young students being subjected to a poor environment, the trustees of the board of education were told Monday. "There's been a marked increase in the number of youthful offenders under the age of 16 who are pouring their ill-gotten gain into these machines," the deputy police chief told the committee. His comments were echoed by the principal of a local high school, who said students are "stealing from each other and from their parents" to feed their pinball and electronic game addictions.

Arcade owners have a habit of locating near schools to attract student business and as a result some youngsters are often late returning to class after lunch or don't come back at all, the principal said. He has discussed the problems with parents, police and other county principals, and called for a bylaw that would prohibit access to the arcades to children under 16 unless accompanied by a parent, restrict hours of business so they don't coincide with school times, restrict arcade locations and license the machines to control their number.

"I think you're all overreacting," said the operator of a local arcade. "This type of business is being harassed and has been for some time."

Did this scenario seem like something out of the past that would not be a problem today? Or can you think of similar issues that might concern school administrators and others today? How about when social networking is done by gang members in a local library in a way intended to provoke members of other gangs as happened recently in a southern U.S. city? "Expressing oneself" through Facebook or many other such websites would generally meet most definitions of leisure behavior, even though it may result in antisocial activity. Should the library find some way to ban social networking as a result? Is that reasonable? What are the risks if they fail to take such action?

A similar, and perhaps more obvious, example of such a use and misuse problem occurs where skateboarders practice inventive moves in spaces that were not intended for them. "Skaters"—skateboard aficionados—have been chased out of a lot of outdoor locations that might offer somewhat unconventional, challenging physical conditions to practice their boarding skills. There is some property damage that has been attributed to such activities, but at least as often it is the assumption that such "fugitive" activities bring with it criminal activities, particularly illegal drug use and trade, or even just the appearances of such that leads adults in charge to attempt to suppress this activity. Skaters often cultivate an unconventionality and have resisted being "co-opted" into skate parks that they consider too tame and mainstream and that often come with a cost to their freedom. Nevertheless, leisure services have often been asked to come up with solutions in "providing for" such individuals, or at least keeping them off the street.

Thus, problems of delinquency and antisocial behavior are sometimes associated with the leisure of adolescents and youth, whether or not such associations are justified. Questions about what prompts and influences such activities and what such activities lead to are among the many concerns of social psychologists. Another problem that has been connected with leisure is the sedentary behavior that leads to obesity, heart disease, and diabetes. These are the "lifestyle illnesses" of early and middle adulthood, often associated with television watching, snacking, and the lack of exercise, and will become more common in the future of such individuals because the relevant habits are being formed earlier in life. In fact, obesity in childhood has reached "epidemic" proportions (Surgeon General, 2006). Again, we may ask what are the factors that influence such sedentary behavior, or its more active alternatives, and how might they be influenced? These are also concerns of social psychologists (cf. Epstein, et al. 2006).

But Can We Call These Leisure "Problems"?

Was the arcade issue raised in the earlier edition a leisure problem? Is playing video games at the arcade considered leisure? And what about the skateboarding example? . . . leisure? . . . a leisure "problem"? There are a number of ways of defining leisure. In fact, one of the longest-standing challenges leisure researchers have had is agreeing on just exactly how to define and measure leisure. Leisure has been described at various times as an activity, as time free from obligations, as a meaningful and satisfying experience, or as some combination of these (e.g., Csikszentmihalyi, 1981). Leisure has also been defined both objectively and subjectively. In the case of objective definitions, the judgment is made based on what people are apparently doing whereas with subjective definitions, the question is, what are they feeling or experiencing? Most of us would probably agree that playing video games or skateboarding are leisure behaviors and recreational activities, and there probably would be consensus about this in many groups and societies. Also, the students in the newspaper stories participated in such activities during their free time (during lunch period and after school) and appear to find the activities meaningful and satisfying, even to the point of "addiction." Taken at face value, it seems plausible that the behavior discussed in both cases is leisure. We will return to this issue of defining and measuring leisure in Chapter 3.

It also appears that these behaviors may be regarded as problems by some. They are all at least presumed in some cases to be associated with negative outcomes: truancy, larceny, gang hostility and violence, and obesity. As will be seen, leisure problems often take the form of activities that may result in negative outcomes for the individual or society, but they are also reflected in barriers or constraints that prevent people from engaging in or experiencing satisfying leisure.

But we can also use the word "problem" more generally as a "research problem" and many of those in leisure research involve the study of the *benefits* of leisure as well. Can leisure be helpful in the coping process? If so, might it make a difference to one who is injured, ill, or who has lost a spouse? Do play and other activities in early childhood facilitate social development? How can we know? Might leisure activities be used to reduce inter-ethnic hostility or maybe even build a sense of community? The problems in this sense then are when and how leisure does contribute to adjustment, development, and well-being, a subject we will take up increasingly in the latter chapters of the book. But let us return to the questions that concerned us at the start and consider the ways we can approach them.

How Would You Approach These Problems?

Now, imagine that you are a leisure services practitioner working for the Department of Parks and Recreation in a community where one of the problem scenarios discussed above was occurring. Your department is approached by members of the city council seeking some assistance. Your director assigns you to look into the problem and asks you to provide her with some suggestions for recommendations that she can pass on to the city council. How would you approach this problem? What would you do first?

In the authors' courses, when we ask our students such questions, their first responses usually are suggestions to develop new recreational programs or interventions to combat the problems, that is, to provide "constructive" alternatives that will keep the youth out of trouble, or, in the case of sedentary activity, to keep them physically active. Recreation and human service students tend to be action- and solution-oriented. However, while this is admirable, there are other things one should do before stepping in with solutions.

First, let's be sure of the facts. Where exactly are the problems? Was there actually an increase in truancy and larceny in the school since the opening of the arcade in the earlier example? If so, was it due to the presence of the arcade and the fact that students play video games on its premises? Or was the problem that some people in the community felt that adolescents playing video games in a shopping mall is "bad," that is, that engaging in this activity is morally wrong, much like some people may feel that gambling or abortion are wrong while others do not. The problem, then, could be primarily one of a conflict of values—the values of adolescents who like to do certain activities and the providers of the technology and settings that are utilized in such activities versus the values of adults who see them as bad. In the original case, the link between video game playing or skateboarding and the deviant behavior associated with such activities may be irrelevant to this problem. We will return to this issue of values.

However, even if we could somehow move beyond an association between the activities and the problems to a determination that the activities are actually *causing* these problems in some cases, there would still be other questions to be addressed. Do video game playing, skateboarding, social networking, and television watching affect all youth in the negative ways considered? If not, why not? Which students are more "at risk"? There may be different solutions required for different students. These questions make the problems identified much more complex. The issue involves not only what is actually going on, but what different stakeholders think or perceive is happening and their value systems, which may be in conflict. This complexity is consistent with what most people know about human life from their own experience, and this is where a *social psychological approach* comes in handy.

The Social Psychological Approach

Can the Problems Be Studied With Social Psychology?

The social psychological approach is a scientific approach. Science is the application of the scientific method to answerable questions. The *scientific method* is simply a way of making observations or gathering information in a systematic way; it involves the use of controlled, systematic inquiry, and a logical and rational approach to explanation. Answerable questions are questions that can be answered by the use of the scientific method. While this reasoning sounds a bit circular, it simply means that the questions should have answers that can be arrived at by observing what is going on under various circumstances. As will be seen, a number of ways of observing what is going on are available with the social psychological approach. Sometimes the researcher carefully observes and records what is happening, or interviews or surveys the people involved. Sometimes the researcher may intervene and actually manipulate aspects of the situation under study and then observe what happens experimentally, either in a laboratory type setting or in the "field," that is, the actual social or natural environment. Sometimes the only way to gain some insight into the problem is for the researcher to re-create or simulate what goes on in the real world in a laboratory setting where the cause-and-effect relationships that may be at play can be more clearly examined.

If the problem cannot be answered through careful, systematic observation or the use of the scientific method, then approaches other than science may be necessary. An example of an unanswerable question for science is, "How many angels can dance on the head of a pin?" Many areas of human study and knowledge address questions for which science-based disciplines have no answers. Philosophy, art, literature, and religious studies are devoted to exploring not only some of the same questions addressed by the scientific disciplines, but also many issues that cannot be dealt with by the scientific approach.

Many of these latter issues involve values. The facts may even be quite clear and agreed upon, but we as individuals have to decide whether we are in favor or against a particular practice or course of action, and no amount of research is going to help us decide (e.g., abortion, ordination of homosexuals in the church, legalized gambling, the sale of alcohol on Sundays, and the appropriateness of children and adolescents using library Internet access to engage in provocative social networking). Novels are written, pictures painted, philosophical analyses presented, and religious and cultural standards called upon to provide answers to these questions for many people.

If we decide as individuals, practitioners, or researchers that an issue or problem can be clarified by observing or gathering further information, then we are ready to engage in social psychological analysis and research. We need to determine if there is, in fact, a problem. In the earlier video arcade case, did the facts support the connection between video game playing, and the truancy and larceny occurring in the school suggested by the newspaper story? Several types of information can be gathered to determine the facts. First, descriptive information is needed. Did incidents of crime in the school increase from the time the arcade opened? Did students from the school use their available "leisure time" to hang out in the arcade? Second, we would need still more information to determine if there was actually a relationship between the events, and more specifically a *cause-and-effect* relationship. Third, if there is evidence of a link, it would be useful to collect information that would clarify the *underlying linking mechanism*. That is, what are the social and psychological explanations for the link between playing at the arcade and the deviant behavior at school that might help to understand what actually took place and ultimately deal with similar problems?

This video arcade problem would have been amenable to more rigorous social psychological study and analysis if done at the time, though clearly the issue of what are appropriate recreation activities for adolescents has a value judgment component as well. At this point, we would have to go back to original records and see if sufficient information was available to establish correlations among the relevant behavioral variables. Perhaps the skateboard case would provide us with a more contemporary problem that we could study proactively. We could begin the study with an identification of where skateboarding occurs in the community and then do some careful observation to document trends in actual activity. At the same time, we might be able to get police data as to complaints and arrests in the area in which the activity takes place. If we observed no relationship between increases in skateboarding and registered complaints, it might be concluded that fears of such were unwarranted and that there was no "leisure problem" here. You might also speculate that the "problem" was really a conflict of values in the community over the appropriateness of children spending their leisure time skateboarding.

If an increase in skateboarding activity was indeed associated with an increase in criminal activity in the area, however, the problem would clearly warrant further study. As the researcher, you do not have enough information yet to conclude that skateboarding is causing or is in any way linked to the problems in the contiguous neighborhoods. The increase in skateboarding and illegal acts could simply be a coincidence. It may be different students who skateboard, on the one hand, and who are involved in delinquent activities, on the other. These latter problems could be due to other unidentified factors, such as the degradation of the built environment in a neighborhood that makes it more attractive to adventurous skateboarders as well as to those individuals who are emboldened by the obvious neglect to engage in such activities such as breaking windows in abandoned buildings. Both activities may simply be symptoms of other problems.

The next step in this social psychological research would be to collect information that would allow you to examine the presence or absence of a cause-and-effect relationship between skateboarding and illegal activities in the neighborhood, as well as develop some understanding of what the link might be.

Theory and Cause-and-Effect Relationships

How did the authorities cited in the original article explain the relationship between video arcade playing and school problem behavior? What was their *theory*? Theories are just explanations of how and why events are related. The theory suggested by the original newspaper article seems to be that the presence of the arcade provided *opportunities* and seduced students to engage in the *behavior* of playing video games, which in turn led to addiction and ultimately resulted in truancy and larceny. As we noted earlier, there was little or no evidence provided in the article to support this theory.

In the skateboarding example, let's assume for the moment that your research demonstrates that an increase in crime in a neighborhood does seem to have occurred simultaneously with the increase in skateboarding activity. However, given the number of skaters involved and the number of crimes committed, it could not be concluded that skating led to criminal activity in all cases or even any particular case. Clearly, if any skaters were involved in the criminal activities, not all of them were. This state of affairs is a more accurate reflection of what one would likely find and of the complexity of the human behavior that one typically encounters in one's daily life. Even with this knowledge, however, you do not yet have enough information to begin to understand why certain individual students seem to be adversely affected by the skateboarding subculture, let alone suggest a solution to the skateboarding "problem." The social psychological approach comes in handy at this point, and provides a useful framework for examining this redefined problem.

Social Psychological Ways of Looking at Problems

Throughout the development of psychology during the past century, competing views of how best to understand and predict people's behavior have been suggested. Within social psychology, these views can be roughly categorized into three types of approaches which differ according to the types of factors that are seen as the most useful for explaining a person's behavior and experience. These approaches differ according to the emphasis given to explanatory factors found in social situations (external factors) versus the person (internal psychological factors).

The Situation: Stimulus-Response Approach

B. F. Skinner was the best-known spokesperson for the stimulus-response (S-R) approach. He was an advocate of *behaviorism*, an extreme form of *situationism*. Behaviorism is not as popular as it once was as a framework for studying and explaining human behavior, but it is still applied in contexts where behavior management and "correction" is the purpose. Behaviorists argue that since people's attitudes, thoughts, feelings, and motives cannot be seen, attention should be directed to understanding the conditions that can lead to actual changes in behavior. Skinner felt that the science of human behavior would be better served if psychologists focused on what they could observe with their eyes—the circumstances or *stimuli* in the individual's environment that triggered the actual behavior, or *response,* itself, and the conditions or rewards that led to the reoccurrence of the behavior in these circumstances.

Situationism suggests that social situations or settings act as stimuli to elicit a response (behavior) and that this predictable response occurs because it leads to positive consequences or *rewards.* In other words, if a behavior in which a person engages under particular circumstances reliably produces a reward, then the likelihood that these circumstances will lead to the behavior in the future is quite high. Consequently, when using this approach, social psychologists do not need to rely on unseen mental or cognitive dispositions or processes such as attitudes, motives, personality traits, or emotions occurring within the individual to explain behavior.

If you as the researcher were to adopt this approach for understanding the connection between the video arcade and truancy and larceny, the skateboarding example or the other problems mentioned, you would develop explanations or theories that are restricted to identifying stimuli and rewards found in the social situations that are part of the students' daily lives. For example, you might theorize that the mere presence of other skateboarders stimulates the response of skateboarding. The rewards that maintain this behavior and perhaps result in it becoming excessive and even destructive to property might include the admiring words of peers. Skateboarding requires the resources of both time and money. You might theorize that these rewards are also responsible for students skipping school and stealing money. The reward for their deviant behavior is being able to continue to engage in the activity of skateboarding. This theory would be consistent with a cause-and-effect link between the presence of skateboarders, property destruction, and other delinquent behavior.

If you follow a strict situational approach, you might expect a large number of the students in the neighborhood to be at risk and respond similarly to the growth of skateboarding. However, connecting an increase in skateboarding to the inevitable destruction of property or other kinds of delinquent behavior is an "empirical question"; and if destructive behavior does not inevitably coincide with skateboarding or if destructive behavior occurs in the absence of skateboarding, then the association it tenuous at best.

How do you explain with situationism why some students have become involved while others have not? You might take a closer look at other aspects of the social environment of the students and attempt to identify additional situational influences that affect some students and not others. For example, in the case of the use of library Internet facilities that were used to promote antisocial gang-related messages, you could have proposed a theory that suggests that the mere availability of the Internet facilities is insufficient by itself to trigger the sending of gang-related messages. Perhaps, for the libraries' facilities to have stimulated such aggressive communications, there would have to have been a peer subculture present that encourages and rewards such behavior. In addition to the perpetrators being members of gangs that support this deviant behavior, you could have theorized that they are likely to come from families with restricted financial resources, making it necessary to use library facilities where home computers are not available. Additionally, the youth involved may not have part-time jobs or may not be involved in extracurricular school activities and, therefore, have so much free time on their hands that they are more susceptible to negative social influences. Finally, the nature of the Internet websites available through the library could also be examined for their influence as stimuli that prompt various kinds of social behavior.

The Person: Organism-Response Approach
Many people would look elsewhere than the social situation for an explanation of why some students are involved in this deviant behavior and others

are not. In fact, most people would want to know who these offending students were and something about them as individuals. Researchers who believe that differences among people can be measured and used to predict and explain why they behave as they do take a *person* or *organism-response (O-R) approach*. In contrast to situationism, the O-R approach is based on the assumption that people demonstrate stable and enduring differences in their needs, motives, attitudes, and personalities, independent of the situation, which lead them to behave consistently across a wide range of situations, yet differently from one another. Consequently, if you want to understand why some students are attracted to video games, skateboarding, social networking, and those activities that may be destructive or delinquent, you need to look for those characteristics that they carry around with them in their minds and that distinguish them from their more conventional and law-abiding peers.

A number of constructs have been used to identify and explain stable person differences, such as attitudes, needs, motives, and personality traits. These psychological dispositions may be learned, inherited, or a result of both types of influences. In the arcade example, what attitudinal or personality disposition could explain why some students gravitated toward the arcade while others did not, and why this activity leads to deviant school behavior for some? The same basic question could also be asked of skateboarders and those attracted to social networking as well as to gang activity and to other delinquent activities. Perhaps some adolescents have a greater need for excitement, what some researchers have called "sensation seeking." They may be more likely to be drawn to unconventional and risky activities—both legally recreational and deviant or delinquent—that satisfy their need for excitement. There are a large number of psychological *organismic*, or person, differences that could be identified that might explain why some students are more susceptible than others. For example, you could hypothesize that those utilizing library Internet sites for social networking—whether in relation to gangs or for other purposes—are more socially outgoing (extroverted) than others. Perhaps those with very negative attitudes toward authority are more susceptible to joining skateboarding groups than in doing leisure activities that involve adult supervision.

To test such *hypotheses*, you could administer personality tests to those involved and ask them to report on their various free time activities. Researchers have developed paper-and-pencil tests to measure a large number of personality traits and attitudes. You could see if the personalities and attitudes of those involved in the problematic activities differ from others who are comparable in other respects.

In spite of the fact that most people rely heavily on individual differences and personality to explain and understand other people's behavior as well as their own, research has shown that people tend to overestimate the power of person factors in explaining behavior (Aronson, 2008; Ross & Nisbett, 1991). In fact, people do not appear to behave as consistently in different situations as might be expected. People seen as "dishonest" are not dishonest in all situations, nor are "honest" people honest in all situations. A person's inflated belief in the importance of person factors for explaining behavior, together with the failure to recognize the importance of situational factors, has been termed the *fundamental attribution error* (Ross & Nisbett, 1991).

Consequently, today most personality and social psychologists have adopted a framework that looks for explanations of people's behavior and experience in the interaction of social situation and person factors.

The Situation by the Person: Stimulus-Organism-Response Approach

Approaches that take both the stimulus, or situation, and the organism, or person, into consideration to explain responses or behavior are called *interactionist*. The assumption underlying interactionism is that people's behavior and experience can be best understood by taking into account both the influence of the social situation (e.g., the presence and behavior of other people and other environmental conditions), and the influence of what people bring to the situation (e.g., perceptions, attitudes, motives, personality traits). The interaction of situation and person factors often results in different people perceiving or construing, and consequently responding to, the same objective situations quite differently. While interactionism may sound like a relatively straightforward idea, it turns out to be a complex notion with a number of versions. Not only can situation and person factors interact in different ways, but theorists differ in how they conceptualize the person factors.

An early and very influential perspective was succinctly expressed by Lewin (1935), in his classic statement that behavior is a function of the person and the environment, that is, $B = f(P, E)$. Lewin believed that it is not the person and the environment that determine behavior, but a person-environment unit—what he called the *life space*. From this perspective, the individual cannot be separated from the environment because "they interpenetrate one another in such a complex manner that any attempt to unravel them tends to destroy the natural unity of the whole and to create an artificial distinction between organism and environment" (p. 83). One way to understand this is with the idea of *construal*, which refers to the personal and subjective meaning that people attach to situations (Ross & Nisbett, 1991). Social psychologists taking this approach assume that a person's understanding of situations is the result of an active, constructive process, rather than a passive reception and registering of the situation. Consequently, the impact of any "objective" situation depends on the personal and subjective meaning that the individual attaches to that situation. To predict the behavior of a given person successfully, one must be able to comprehend her or his construal of the situation—that is, the manner in which the person understands the situation as a whole. In the case of the video arcade problem from years past, for example, had this approach been utilized, authorities would have tried to develop an idea of how those involved were thinking and feeling about the arcade and school settings.

Since Lewin's statement, social psychological researchers who adopt the interactionist perspective have differed in the extent to which they feel that situation and person factors can be separated for study. On the one hand, some are interested in the general processes of social perception and construal common to all people—that is, the way people come to interpret their social environments and other people's behavior. In their research and analyses of behavior, these researchers are careful to assess how the people they are studying perceive and interpret surrounding social contexts. On the other hand, other researchers are interested in how the relatively stable personality, motivational, and attitudinal differences that people carry around with them affect both how they perceive the social situations that they encounter and, in turn, how they respond to them. The following illustration from the skateboarding problem would be an example of interactionism of the latter type. Students who are members of peer groups that value skating expertise (social situation influence) might be more likely to be get into trouble in the neighborhoods where the activity takes place. However, only a small percentage of these adolescents typically do get into trouble. Let's also say that a small portion of the students who are assessed as sensation seekers get involved (person influence), but, again, not everyone who has a high need for sensation gets involved with skating. Neither situation nor person factors by themselves seem to explain very effectively the deviant behavior of concern. However, if you were to examine sensation seekers who are also members of peer groups who value skating and find that a very high percentage of them engage in property destruction and other kinds of deviant behavior at school or in the neighborhoods, you would have a *situation by person interaction* and, perhaps, a much better explanation of the behavior in question.

This scenario exemplifies only one type or form of interactionism, that is, the *additive model of interactionism* (Endler, 1983). The behavior and experience of the individual are seen to be dependent on three sources of influence: situations, persons, and their interaction. As noted previously, there was a small independent influence of the situational influence—a peer group. Also the person variable, the sensation seeker, had a small independent influence. However, it was only when these situation and person variables both were present or interacting that they have a strong influence on behavior.

Other types of interactionism differ in the way that the situation and person are seen to interact or influence a person's experience and behavior (Diener,

Larsen, & Emmons, 1984). For example *reciprocal* interactionism (Bowers, 1973; Pervin, 1968) is a more dynamic model. Reciprocal interactionism has been studied by researchers who believe in the importance of identifying and measuring stable individual differences (e.g., personality traits, needs, attitudes). It predicts that there is a relationship between personality and the situations people naturally choose to be in most of the time. In everyday life, people usually have some freedom of choice over the types of situations in which they spend time. It might be expected that personality variables have an influence on this choice (Mischel, 1977). It also could be expected that in their everyday lives people, when not constrained by situational demands, would choose to spend their time in the kinds of settings that are most congruent or compatible with their personalities (Emmons, Diener, & Larsen, 1986).

This model has some interesting implications for leisure researchers. In fact, a leisure researcher might expect that what people do during their leisure more accurately reflects their personalities than activities done at any other time in their daily lives, given the greater freedom to choose and fewer constraints operating in their social environments (Kulka, 1979; Pervin, 1968). High-sensation seekers may choose to spend more time in more adventurous and exciting activities and experience them more positively as a consequence of this "congruency" between their personalities and the situation. Consequently, person variables may be seen to operate at least twice. People choose to seek out specific situations and to avoid others based on differences in their personalities, and once in these situations person variables may influence their behavior and experience.

One final note on interactionism—sometimes the situation may have more influence on a person's behavior and experience, and at other times person factors may be more influential. It has been demonstrated that the effects of personality on behavior are likely to be greatest when situational influences are weak and less restrictive in terms of the possible behaviors that may be exhibited (e.g., Buss, 1989; Mannell & Bradley, 1986; Monson, Hesley, & Chernick, 1982; Price & Bouffard, 1974). For example, there may be circumstances in which being part of a social group or having friends who do social networking online may overpower personality differences such that even relatively more introverted individuals become involved. When outside the peer group context, personality differences may have a stronger influence on participation or nonparticipation in this activity.

In the above discussion, the various leisure problems identified have not been solved. But hopefully, the reader has arrived at a clearer understanding of social psychological thinking and analysis in action. Also, as the leisure services practitioner in this situation, you should have a better idea of where to look for answers and what types of information gathering might be useful in understanding the problem and developing effective solutions. The chapter will now be concluded by more formally defining social psychology and the social psychology of leisure.

Pinning Down the
Social Psychology of Leisure

Social psychology is the scientific study of the behavior and experience of individuals in social situations. The social psychology of leisure can be identified in much the same way, with leisure being the behavior and experience of specific interest. The activity problems introduced demonstrated that social psychology is different from other types of knowing, including other social sciences and areas of psychology, because of its focus on the influence of social situations on the individual. Consequently, the social psychology of leisure is *the scientific study of the leisure behavior and experience of individuals in social situations.*

The social psychology of leisure involves scientific study. As we discussed, there are many approaches to understanding how people think, feel, and behave. One can learn about human behavior from novels, films, history, and philosophy. What makes social psychology different from these artistic and humanistic endeavors is the use of social science. It applies the scientific method of systematic observation, description, and interpretation to the study of people.

The social psychology of leisure focuses on the *individual*. Many other disciplines also employ scientific techniques to study human behavior: anthropology, economics, political science, and sociology. All of these disciplines along with social psychology are called social sciences. They differ in the aspects of human behavior that are of primary concern. The level of analysis sets social psychology apart from other social sciences. Sociology, for instance, classifies people in terms of their nationality, race, socioeconomic class, and other social factors. Sociologists are more interested in how collectives of people, such as small groups, organizations, institutions, and societies as a whole operate. Social psychology is concerned with how individuals behave in and perceive their social world: how they learn about it, remember what they experience in it, and appraise and evaluate it.

The social psychology of leisure involves the study of experience and behavior. Experience is a general term that refers to the awareness of the individual. What a person perceives, feels, learns, or remembers—in a word, her or his *experience*—is often inferred from behavior. Researchers can also observe experience by communicating with people, that is, having people tell them what is on their minds. Behavior is comprised of those actions of the person that researchers can see and observe. However, even here a full understanding of behavior can only be achieved when a researcher knows what it means to the person who performed it. Consequently, the researcher will be interested in both leisure behavior and experience as defined "objectively" by outside observers and "subjectively" by the individual herself or himself. *Leisure*, itself, is challenging to define. There is no universally accepted way of defining leisure. Definitions and measurements will vary depending on the nature of the leisure issue or problem of interest. We will tackle defining leisure in Chapter 3.

The phrase "in social situations" refers to the social contexts in which most human behavior occurs. During the course of people's daily lives, they are constantly moving from one social context to another. Social situations refer to other individuals, groups, the institutions of family, work and church, cultures and subcultures, and even the products and creations (artifacts) of human activity, such as films, books, and the built environment, that influence one's experience and behavior.

Finally, we would like to remind the reader that social science can never be completely value free. Many scientists today do not believe that any kind of science can ever be completely unbiased and objective. And indeed how could it be? Science is a human enterprise. Certainly social scientists choose what and how to study; their choices are influenced by their personal perspectives and values. However, good social science is the effort to shake ourselves free of preconceptions, or at least become aware of them, and more clearly see, even if never perfectly, what is going on around us as observers. We turn now to the story of how those values and purposes have gradually taken shape in an emerging social psychology of leisure.

2

The Social Psychology of Leisure: Story of a Growing Field of Study

Preview

In this chapter, we discuss more about social psychology, the way leisure has been treated in mainstream social psychological research, and the emergence of the social psychology of leisure in the field of leisure studies. We begin by looking briefly at the history, development, and the types of questions that have been asked by social psychologists, pointing out also that while they have come primarily from the field of psychology, social psychologists in sociology have also contributed and are increasingly doing so. Next, we examine the roots and emergence of the social psychology of leisure itself and the extent to which it is developing into an international field of study.

Social Psychology's Heritage

Beginnings

The social psychology of leisure is not a recognized subfield of either psychology or sociology proper; it is the offspring of leisure studies itself. Many scholars in leisure studies whose work could be considered psychological or social psychological might not label it as such themselves; and while much of the research found in leisure studies is not based on psychological or social psychological theory and research methods, a significant amount of it has been.

Several books, including the first edition of this book, have provided varying descriptions of the psychology and social psychology of leisure as a field of study—*The Psychology of Leisure* (Neulinger, 1974, 1981), *The Social Psychology of Leisure and Recreation* (Iso-Ahola, 1980a), *The Social Psychology of Leisure* (Argyle, 1996), and *A Social Psychology of Leisure* (Mannell & Kleiber, 1997). It is apparent that the social psychology of leisure continues to be a work in progress; there are significant gaps in knowledge that these authors bridge with mainstream social psychological theory and research that is untested in leisure contexts. Also, the stories told by these books about the social psychology of leisure rely primarily on psychological perspectives and tend to ignore the contributions of sociology to the subject.

Given that social psychology is located at the peripheries and intersection of the fields of psychology and sociology, it also has a sociological counterpart. Broadly speaking, sociologists devote their efforts to understanding social phenomena that have effects on individuals and psychologists specialize in identifying the mechanisms or mental processes through which social phenomena have their effects (Thoits, 1995). Increasingly, leisure research is being informed by these perspectives. As we noted in the previous chapter, this book draws both on psychological and sociological social psychology, and leisure researchers vary in their grounding in these fields.

Psychological Approaches

Psychology as a scientific field of study was created in the last quarter of the nineteenth century and has its roots in Western Europe and North America. Social psychology as a recognizable subfield did not get underway until sometime later. Psychology is the science of mental processes and behavior and their interaction with the environment, and psychologists study the processes of perception, thinking, learning, cognition, emotions, motivations, personality, abnormal behavior, interactions between individuals and with the environment. The field is allied with the physical sciences in the study of perception and brain-behavior relationships and with anthropology and sociology in the study of social influences on behavior. Social psychology emerged out of this latter "alliance."

While not everyone agrees about who founded social psychology (Farr, 1991), generally two individuals are credited with completing the first social psychological research, American psychologist Norman Triplett and French agricultural engineer Max Ringelmann. Ringelmann is notable for identifying a phenomenon that came to be called "social loafing"—the tendency of individuals to put forth less effort when they are part of a group. For example, when he had a group of men pull on a rope, they each pulled less hard than when pulling alone. Ringelmann's research was conducted in the 1880s, though not published until 1913 (Ringelmann, 1913). Triplett (1897–1898) published the first research article in social psychology at the end of the nineteenth century. The issue that Triplett was studying continues to be of interest today. Interestingly, the recreational and sporting activity of cycling was the subject of this first published social psychological study, though the focus was on the performance of the rider rather than the experience or meaning of the activity to the participant. As mentioned in Chapter 1, the meanings of leisure activity and experience have typically been prioritized by leisure researchers. What made this a social psychological study was the fact that Triplett wanted to know what influence cycling with another person, rather than alone, would have on the speed of cycling. The study was also important because it demonstrated that complex social processes, in this case social influence, could be studied scientifically.

These isolated studies reported by Triplett and Ringelmann did not create social psychology as a distinct subfield of psychology. Writers of the first three textbooks in social psychology, the English psychologist William McDougall (1908) and Americans Edward Ross (1908) and Floyd Allport (1924), did much to distinguish a social psychological approach from other psychological approaches and establish the boundaries of the subfield by identifying the topics, issues, and theories that they regarded as its subject matter—an area of psychology concerned with social influences on individual behavior.

Early Theory and Research

Social psychology was given a great boost through the research of a number of psychologists. One of the first important contributors was Muzafer Sherif. He was quite innovative and frequently controversial. In 1936, Sherif published a very influential study of social influence. Participants in this research observed a visual illusion (the *autokinetic effect*)—a dot of light that was actually stationary but that people see as moving. Watching alone in a darkened room, participants differed considerably in their individual estimates of the light's movement. When they watched together in groups, however, their estimates of the light's movement eventually converged. The location of the light itself never changed, but members of these groups would soon come to see the light move in the same way, that is, they developed shared norms or rules for how the light apparently moved. Sherif and other researchers have used this technique to study such processes as how groups develop and pass on norms to new group members, and the influence of the status or prestige of group members on norm development. Like Triplett's research, the research of Sherif was important for the development of social psychology because it demonstrated that it is possible to study complex behavior like social influence and norm formation in a rigorous, scientific manner.

Another important contributor to social psychology, as we have already noted, was Kurt Lewin. As we mentioned in the last chapter, Lewin's (1935) *field theory* specifies that behavior is a function of the interaction between the person and the environment, that is, $B = f(P, E)$. Lewin also influenced the field with his strong interest in the application of social psychology to the analysis and solution of social problems. During the Second World War, Lewin completed some of the first social psychology of health behavior research, including how to promote more economical and nutritious eating habits (Lewin, 1947). Today, applied social psychology flourishes. Social psychological theory and research informs practitioners in areas such as advertising, business, education, environmental protection, health policy, law, politics, public policy, religion, sports and, of course, leisure.

Expansion and Enthusiasm

Following World War II and during the 1950s, the whole field of psychology grew dramatically, particularly in the United States (Benjamin, 1986). Increased government funding was available for teaching and research in universities on a whole range of issues. One of the most dramatic areas of growth was in the subfield of social psychology. There was tremendous enthusiasm and optimism that social science research and, in particular, social psychological research could help with the solutions to a wide range of social issues facing society. Major contributors carried out research in topic areas that are still of great significance, and in turn, they trained new generations of social psychologists. For example, researchers studied prejudice and stereotyping (e.g., Allport, 1954), conformity and person perception (e.g., Asch, 1956; Shachter & Singer, 1962), cognitive dissonance and social comparison (e.g., Festinger, 1954, 1957), attribution and balance theory (e.g., Heider, 1958), attitudes and persuasion (e.g., Hovland, Janis, & Kelley, 1953) and social exchange (e.g., Thibaut & Kelley, 1959).

This growth and enthusiasm continued into the 1960s. Social psychologists considered how people thought (Kelley, 1967) and felt (Schachter, 1964) about themselves and others. They studied interactions in groups (Moscovici & Zavalloni, 1969) and social problems such as why people fail to help others in distress (Latane & Darley, 1970) and the extent to which people will obey the directions of others (Milgram, 1963, 1965). They examined aggression (Bandura, 1973), the psychological impact of physical attractiveness (Berscheid & Walster, 1974), and stress (Glass & Singer, 1972), among many other things. The famous "epinephrine" study of Shachter (1964) demonstrated that with ambiguous emotions, people look for social cues to determine what exactly they are feeling.

Overcoming a Crisis of Confidence

Not all social psychologists were confident of the success of social psychology. There came a time when some thought of it as being in crisis (e.g., Elms, 1975). Many of the disagreements among social psychologists during this period can be understood as a reaction to the dominant research method used—the laboratory experiment. Those who questioned the laboratory method maintained that certain practices were unethical (Kelman, 1967), that experimenters' expectations influenced their research participants' behavior (Orne, 1962; Rosenthal, 1966), and that the theories being tested in the laboratory could not be applied to understanding behavior outside the laboratory in daily life or different cultures (Gergen, 1973). Social psychology was also criticized for trying to be too scientific and experimental, relying on *logical positivism*, the philosophical assumption that researchers can "get to the bottom of things," finding the essential facts about human nature just as is done in biology, chemistry, and other "hard" sciences. This criticism came from social scientists who see human behavior as constantly changing as society changes. As will be seen, some sociological approaches to social psychology use an "interpretive" approach to deal with this type of criticism.

Though these issues continue to be debated today, social psychology has been able to progress as a result of a better understanding of its strengths and weaknesses. The debate on ethics has led to more rigorous and uniform standards for research. Greater attention is being given to the limitations and possible biases of frequently used research methods. Laboratory experiments continue to be done, but there has been a gradual acceptance of a wider variety of research methods (Houts, Cook, & Shadish, 1986). It has been recognized that different topics require different kinds of approaches. Research techniques range from the laboratory experiment to interviews and naturalistic observation. Each technique is seen as having unique advantages and disadvantages, and any single topic can benefit from being investigated by a number of approaches. Laboratory research on leisure has been infrequent, but as we will see in Chapter 3, a variety of research approaches have been used in social psychological leisure research.

Mainstream social psychology has been and continues to be concerned with individuals' perceptions or construal of their social environment, recognizing however that social and physical realities can be misperceived and that it is these perceptions, mistaken or not, that influence behavior and experience (Ross & Nisbett, 1991). Experimental research designs are widely used by psychological researchers, though other field research methods have grown in popularity during the past 25 years.

Social psychology today continues to be a dynamic field. Though certain ideas remain important to how social psychologists explain people's behavior, theories and approaches change and evolve, and go in and out of popularity. For example, important theories about attitudes and attitude change were developed and tested in the 1950s. In the 1960s, consistency theories dominated. They were developed to explain the motivating power of inconsistencies among a person's cognitions (i.e., beliefs, attitudes, and values) or between cognitions and actions, what is called *cognitive dissonance*, which can actually lead to changes in beliefs, attitudes, or behavior (Berkowitz & Devine, 1989). *Attribution theory* emerged in the 1970s, helping to explain the kinds of causal explanations people give for the events in their lives and the effects these causal inferences have on their social behavior (Weiner, 1986). Beginning in the late 1970s and continuing to the present, *social cognition* (the study of how people perceive, remember and interpret information about themselves and others) has proven very influential (Augustinos, Walker, & Donaghue, 2006; Devine, Hamilton, & Ostrom, 1994). Theories have also been advanced to explain people's behavior in a more holistic manner by accounting for emotions and motivations, on the one hand, and cognitions, on the other (e.g., Boggiano & Pittman, 1992; Power & Dalgleish, 2007).

Also, the new millennium has seen the growth of *positive psychology* (e.g., Seligman & Csikzentmihalyi, 2000; Robbins, 2008), a recent branch of scientific psychology that studies the factors that enable individuals and communities to thrive. This approach gets away from the pathological and victimological aspects of psychology and turns instead to valued subjective experience such as hope, wisdom, creativity, future mindedness, courage, spirituality, responsibility, and perseverance. With respect to the past, it addresses well-being, contentment, and satisfaction. Enjoyment, creativity, and happiness are the concerns of the present, and hope and optimism, the future. At the individual level, positive psychology examines positive traits such as the capacity for love, courage, and interpersonal skill, while at the group level it deals with civic virtues such as responsibility, nurturance, altruism, civility, tolerance, and industriousness. With respect to intervention, the focus is on prevention and the cultivation of human strengths, resilience, self-regulation, and protective factors. Positive psychology assumes that human beings are self-organizing and self-directive organisms.

Like many social sciences, social psychology has also been open to the criticism that its theories and research findings may not have adequately dealt with gender and that the field was dominated by men. However, women have had a strong influence on the field since its beginnings (Johnston & Johnson, 2008). An interest in women and gender issues emerged in the 1960s and has continued. Some time ago, Berscheid (1992) noted that there is a growing number of women in the field. In fact, in many countries, women now out-number men in the field (Skinner & Louw, 2009). As will be seen later in the chapter, social psychology has also become much more international and diverse.

The new diversity in social psychology is reflected by the many applied areas to which social psychologists contribute research and theory. The value of social psychology for understanding contemporary life has been recognized by psychologists and non-psychologists alike. Many fields (e.g., business, education, health, social work, journalism, recreation) now require courses in social psychology for their students. Many researchers trained in professional or applied disciplines, though not social psychologists, have substantial research training in the social psychological approach, its theories, and research meth-ods. For many years now social psychology has found itself "hyphenated to reflect its alliances with other areas of psychology and fields outside of psy-chology: social-development, social-clinical, social and physical realities, social-personality, social psychology and law, social-health, social-organiza-tional, social-educational, social-environmental, and social-community" (Berscheid, 1992, p. 531). Social psychologists became "the vanguard of the movement to extend the boundaries of traditional psychology into the realms vital to contributing solutions for real-world problems—the areas of health, ecology, education, law, peace and conflict resolution, and much more" (Zimbardo, 1992, p. xiv).

Sociological Approaches

Sociological social psychology includes research on social structure and per-sonality, small groups research, and symbolic interactionism (Thoits, 1995). Interpretivist or constructionist perspectives such as symbolic interactionism and phenomenology, which have much in common, and grounded theory, which evolved from symbolic interactionism (Robrecht, 1995), have been the sociological approaches most commonly adopted in the study of leisure. For example, with symbolic interactionism, the ways in which people define reality and how beliefs are related to actions are explored. Reality is viewed as being created by people who attach meaning to situations. These meanings are expressed by symbols such as words, objects, and events, and these symbolic meanings are the basis for actions and interactions. Symbolic meanings are different for each individual, though they may be shared by groups and transferred to new members by socialization (Fine, 1993). Most interactionists advocate the systematic collection of data through in-depth interviewing and observing people's behavior as they go about their everyday life.

Treatment of Leisure in Mainstream Psychology

Social psychologists have been interested in what they consider the *basic social psychological processes* that underlie all human behavior across all types of social situations and settings. For example, the processes of conformity, aggression, interpersonal attraction, or attitude change operate in all social situations, such as work, leisure, education, or health contexts. However, a number of specialized areas have evolved, for example, the social psychology of work (Argyle, 1990), the social psychology of health (Rutter & Quine, 1994), and the social psychology of leisure (Argyle, 1996; Iso-Ahola, 1995). In these subfields, not only have major social psychological theories been applied to understanding the issues of interest, but theories specific to these subfields have been developed.

Mainstream social psychology itself, has paid relatively little attention to leisure since its inception over a century ago. However, as we suggested in our brief historical overview of social psychology, researchers have occasionally studied the social processes that interested them in leisure and play contexts. For example, William McDougall (1908), in the first textbook on social psychology, identified play as a basic human instinct or tendency. A few years later, G. T. W. Patrick (1916) wrote a leisure-related book, *The Psychology of Relaxation*. In his social psychology text, Floyd Allport (1924) argued that leisure serves as a form of need compensation—compensation for oppressive work. Since the emergence of these early works, a number of social psychological studies have been reported that have implications for understanding leisure, though their focus was not to study leisure specifically.

Social Influence on Cycling and Football Spectators

Leisure settings have provided a useful testing ground over the years for numerous studies of basic social psychological processes. The 1898 bicycle experiment reported by Triplett and referred to earlier in this chapter is a good example. He was a bicycle enthusiast and a social scientist. On the basis of his own experience, he theorized that cyclists ride faster over a given distance when in the presence of other riders than when alone, even when the cyclists in both situations are trying to perform their best. To test his theory, he devised an experiment in which some riders, randomly selected, attempted to cycle as fast as they could alone while others cycled in the presence of other cyclists.

Triplett found that those individuals who performed in the presence of others cycled five seconds per mile faster than lone cyclists. He described this phenomenon as the *dynamogenic* or *rabbit effect*. The influence of the presence of other people on performance has continued to interest researchers and today this phenomenon is known as the *social facilitation effect* (Zajonc, 1965). However, Triplett's study was not an attempt to understand cycling as a leisure behavior, but rather to examine or discover an underlying principle of general human behavior—the influence of other people on an individual's performance. Nevertheless, as the earliest example of basic social psychological research, it introduced the study of the influence of competition on performance, a subject of great interest to those concerned with recreational sports.

A second research study that can be used to illustrate the use of leisure contexts to examine general social psychological principles was based on a rather infamous college football game (Hastorf & Cantril, 1954). A Dartmouth and Princeton football game, played during the 1940s between the two rival schools, was billed as a grudge match. It was called the dirtiest and roughest game in the history of the two schools. Dartmouth was out to get Princeton's all-American, Dick Kazmaier, and eventually did, as he was forced to leave with a broken nose. A player on the other team had his leg broken, and there were fist fights throughout the game.

In this study, the researchers showed film clips of the game to students from each school some months later. The objective for the students was to spot infractions of the rules. Students from both schools observed and reported twice as many violations by players from the opposing team during this study, demonstrating the way in which *social perception* can be influenced by group membership or reference group loyalty.

Social Perception and Group Behavior at Camp

The *Robbers' Cave Studies* of Muzafer Sherif and his associates (Sherif, Harvey, White, Hood, & Sherif, 1961) were carried out in the leisure setting of a summer camp to study general social psychological principles. These studies took place at Connecticut, New York, and Oklahoma camps. Sherif and his colleagues selected psychologically normal 9-year-old to 13-year-old boys from middle-class backgrounds. The boys were randomly assigned to two groups. Each group was sent to different areas and facilities at the camps and for the first week were unaware of the presence of the other group.

The researchers used the boys' involvement in camp and outdoor recreation activities to study the formation of norms and leadership in groups. Eventually, the two groups of boys were made aware of each other and a series of competitive games were staged. The researchers observed the impact that this intergroup competition had on the group norms and leadership structures that had already developed. For example, they found that in some groups norms for toughness evolved to the point where the boys would not report injuries to camp counselors. Also, the leadership structure of the groups often changed. Now that the tasks facing the groups shifted from noncompetitive and friendship-oriented activities to competing successfully and winning against other groups, different boys, often those with good athletic skills and toughness, became the leaders.

Sherif and his research team also built experiments into the camping experience through the use of games. To study how group membership affected perceptions of other people, the researchers had the boys participate in a game that required them to estimate the number of beans collected by themselves and the other boys. They were asked individually to judge how many beans each of the other boys had collected in the game. The researchers found that both group membership and the leadership structure of the groups influenced these perceptions. For example, the boys tended to judge boys who were members of their own group, the in-group, as more competent at the task than members of an out-group. Also, the higher the status of a boy in his own group, the more competent at this task he was judged to be by the other group members. These judgments were actually unrelated to how well each of the boys had done at the task.

Finally, the researchers were interested in the impact of getting these, by now, antagonist groups of boys involved in cooperative activities. They found that by presenting the boys with a common problem that required them all to work together, for example, finding a leak in the camp waterline that came down from the surrounding hills, the boys eventually decreased their competitiveness, aggressiveness, and dislike of the members of other groups. Establishing such a *superordinate goal*, which required cooperation for its achievement, worked better than rewards and church sermons.

Rewards in the Playroom and Altruism at the Beach

Social psychologists continue to use leisure settings or situations to study basic social psychological processes. The first major study of intrinsic motivation and the factors that undermine it, the *overjustification effect*, involved studying children playing with colored markers in a preschool "play room" (Lepper, Greene, & Nisbett, 1973). As we will present in a later chapter, these researchers found that rewarding children to do things that they already enjoy can reduce their motivation to engage in activities for the enjoyment and personal satisfaction they offer. This demonstrated that rewards can have the effect of turning play into work.

A study of altruism or helping behavior by Moriarity (1975) took place in a leisure setting on a beach with sunbathers. In this study, a confederate of the researcher would spread out her blanket and put an expensive radio on it near an unsuspecting sunbather. A short time later, the confederate would get up and leave for a few minutes. After leaving, a second confederate of the researcher would approach, grab, and "steal" the first confederate's radio. The researcher then observed how the sunbather reacted. In some cases, the first confederate would ask the sunbather to watch her possessions. As one might expect, getting a commitment from the sunbather was more likely to result in this person engaging in some kind of helping behavior. Only 20 percent of the bystanders attempted to help when they had made no commitment to do so, whereas 95 percent intervened when the commitment had been established. When individuals feel personal responsibility, they are significantly more likely to act in an altruistic way.

Emergence of Personality during Leisure

The last example we will present is based on two studies reported by Ed Diener, Randy Larsen, and Robert Emmons (1984). In these studies, the researchers did not start out with any particular interest in leisure, nor were they interested in contributing to a social psychological understanding of leisure. However, their research examined certain social psychological processes that underlie human behavior, and interestingly, they found that these processes were more likely to be seen in recreational contexts. Essentially, they found that people's personalities were more likely to influence their behavior and experience in recreational settings. For example, they measured how outgoing and extroverted the university students in their study were. They then had these students carry diaries with them every day for a number of weeks. The students recorded their activities, the different social settings in which they became involved and how they felt when involved (moods). When the researchers analyzed this information, they found that the students' personalities were more likely to affect the choice of activities and settings in which they participated during their leisure. For example, in recreational situations extroverts were more likely to choose to be involved in social activities and introverts in solitary activities. Such differences did not appear in other contexts such as work. Extroverts also had more enjoyable experiences when with other people than when alone, whereas those students who were more introverted experienced greater enjoyment in solitary activities. This personality difference in choice of activities and level of enjoyment was not found for non-recreational situations. It would seem that the effect of personality on behavior and experience is likely to be greatest when situations are less restrictive and allow greater freedom of choice. Of course, freedom of choice is central to notions of leisure.

These types of studies, though not carried out to further knowledge of leisure behavior per se, do provide an idea of how the basic social psychological principles of human behavior can be used to explain leisure behavior. A number of studies referred to in this book will be of this sort and contribute to the understanding of not only leisure but behavior in general. The last study mentioned, however, suggests that there may exist social psychological principles that are more likely to operate in leisure contexts.

Treatment of Leisure in Mainstream Sociology

Although the first pioneering works that explore the role and meaning of leisure in the life of society can be placed in the late nineteenth to early twentieth century (e.g., Thorstein Veblen's *The Theory of the Leisure Class* in 1899), the beginnings of truly systematic social science research, primarily sociological, began in the late 1920s. Sociologists examined leisure as a social phenomenon rather than as a moral issue, an object of social reform, or a management issue.

For example, Lynd and Lynd (1929, 1937) examined the structure of everyday community life based on well-designed surveys and thorough observation. In addition to examining people's work, family life, community activities, and religious practices, the Lynds' research provided extremely interesting insights into the changing patterns of leisure involvement and attitudes during a 10-year period. Lundberg, Komarovsky, and McInerny's (1934) sociological study attempted to examine leisure behavior as part of the social structure of U.S. society. Leisure behavior and community participation were examined as a function of social class, race, ethnicity, political affiliation, family structure, and community recreation institutions (Zuzanek, 1982).

Sociologists continued to contribute to the study of leisure. The Chicago Center for the Study of Leisure, established in the 1950s, served as a catalyst for social science research on leisure phenomena. Examples of this work include the study of leisure as part of more general trends of social and cultural change (e.g., Riesman's *Lonely Crowd*, 1950), the relationship between leisure and social stratification (e.g., Smigal, 1963), and socio-cultural meanings of leisure behavior (e.g., de Grazia, 1964). Some commentators have argued that the sociology of leisure has not lived up to the exciting expectations created during the 1950s and 1960s (Zuzanek, 1982) and that there has been a lack of theory building and conceptual linkage with mainstream sociology (Godbey, 1988), though efforts have been made more recently (Mannell, Kleiber, & Staempfli, 2006).

To some extent, though, sociology developed new interest in leisure as it gave more attention to social psychology, particularly among those espousing symbolic interactionist and grounded theory perspectives. Like psychologists, sociological researchers have typically been interested in more basic social psychological phenomena such as social roles, self-presentation, and socialization. However, this research has provided rich detail about specific leisure activities and the groups of individuals who participate in them. For example, in his classic study, *Street Corner Society*, William Foote White (1943) "hung out" with a gang of young Italian men as a participant observer and made many of his observations during the gang's free time activities. From among these observations, he noted that group structure and status in the gang influenced leisure behavior. On several occasions, he observed that when the members of the gang bowled competitively against one another, their scores matched their social status and leadership positions in the gang regardless of their actual bowling skills and, in turn, their bowling scores reinforced and maintained their gang status.

The research and theorizing of Gary Alan Fine is an especially good example of symbolic interactionism in research on leisure and of social psychological research on leisure within mainstream sociology. Following extensive field work involving participant observation and informal interviews, Fine (1987) published a fascinating account of a group of pre-adolescents playing summer little league baseball and the shared meanings they developed about girls, morality, and adult control in their lives. He also studied a group of older youth who developed a subculture around role-playing fantasy games such as *Dungeons & Dragons* (Fine, 1983). The extensive research on amateurs, hobbyists, and volunteers involved in what sociologist Robert Stebbins referred to as *serious leisure* (1982, 1992a, 2001b, 2007) is another good example of this type of sociological social psychology. Stebbins interviewed musicians, collectors, and career volunteers, among others, who demonstrated high levels of commitment to and identification with their activities, putting forth great effort and sacrifice, persevering in the face of obstacles, and gaining enduring benefit from the activities and from identifying with like-minded others. We will return to this work in Chapter 4 and throughout later chapters.

Psychological and sociological perspectives on social psychology exist as "two solitudes," divided more by their different epistemological assumptions than by the human social behavior in which their practitioners are interested (Matalon, 1999). Factors such as disciplinary egocentrism and institutional barriers have also limited communication between psychological and socio-logical perspectives on social psychology (see Stephan, Stephan, & Pettigrew, 1991). However, in leisure studies, the two perspectives appear to coexist reasonably well.

Social Psychological Approaches in Leisure Studies

Not surprisingly, there has been at least as much written about leisure-related issues and phenomena by people in the recreation and leisure studies field as by those outside of it (Barnett & Wade, 1988; Zuzanek, 1982, 1991). As community and government agencies became more involved in leisure ser-vices, and university programs in recreation and leisure studies developed, particularly in the United States and Canada, recreation practitioners, educa-tors, and researchers contributed to the development of applied recreation research dealing with the management and provision of leisure services. Much of this early work attempted to justify and promote the need for leisure services and resulted in a great deal of uncritical, highly speculative, and moralistic writing about the benefits of these services. These types of publications found their way relatively quickly into the curricula of the newly emerging univer-sity recreation degree programs of the time and to a large extent contributed to the formulation of the social philosophy of the recreation profession (Kelly, 1988; Zuzanek, 1982). What was called for, though, was a more scientific approach to understanding leisure, and leisure scholars began turning to the social sciences, and psychology in particular, for direction.

From the mid-1960s to the early 1970s, research studies using social psychological concepts began to appear in the literature of recreation and lei-sure studies. Deliberate attempts to develop and promote a social psychology of leisure emerged in the 1970s (see Iso-Ahola, 1980a, 1988; Mannell, 1984a). With his 1980 textbook, *The Social Psychology of Leisure and Recreation*, Seppo Iso-Ahola contributed to the development of the social psychology of leisure by identifying theory and research from mainstream social psychol-ogy that had very direct relevance for understanding leisure behavior. This widely used book also demonstrated that in spite of the small amount of social psychological research done on leisure at the time, there were many interesting questions to be studied and good potential for further development.

Early Efforts

Among the subjects of emerging interest, leisure researchers gave special attention to the psychological effects of leisure on the individual, in particu-lar personality development (Iso-Ahola, 1980a). Authors have long claimed that play and recreation are good for children since they promote a sense of justice, decision-making ability, self-control, perseverance, and initiative, as well as social skills such as kindness, friendliness, and tolerance. However, as Iso-Ahola noted, while leisure philosophers and writers have suggested such effects in the past, little theory development and research was carried out before the 1970s.

Some of the earliest empirical work that can be labeled social psychological was done by researchers in the United States interested in understanding why people participate in outdoor recreation. Interest in the motivations and satisfactions associated with outdoor recreation emerged in the 1960s and blossomed in the 1970s. Early studies (e.g., Bultena & Taves, 1961; Burch 1965, 1969; LaPage, 1974) found diverse motivations for participation in camping and wilderness use.

Maturation of the Field

The founding of the *Journal of Leisure Research* in 1969 gave an important push to the development of the social psychology of leisure in North America. Although it was not exclusively psychologically oriented, the journal did provide an outlet for contributions in this area (Iso-Ahola, 1995). Early published research on leisure used such social psychological concepts and approaches as attitudes (e.g., Brown, 1970; Heberlein, 1973; Neulinger & Briet, 1969), motivation and satisfaction (e.g., Bultena & Klessig, 1969; Burch, 1969; Mercer, 1973), group behavior (e.g., Field & O'Leary, 1973; West & Merriam, 1970), environmental influences (e.g., Knopp, 1972; Witt & Bishop, 1970), socialization (e.g., Bishop & Chace, 1971; Kelly, 1974; Yoesting & Burkhead, 1973) and interactionism (e.g., Bishop & Witt, 1970). A number of studies were also published that began to explore social psychological strategies for measuring leisure (e.g., Bishop, 1970; Bull, 1971; Kelly, 1973; Witt, 1971).

In the 1970s, Driver and his associates began laying a more systematic social psychological foundation for the study of motivations in outdoor recreation (e.g., Driver, 1976; Driver & Brown, 1975; Driver & Toucher, 1970). To better understand why people choose to participate in particular activities, the rewards they receive from participation and the factors that enhance the quality of the experience derived from participation, a psychological approach was proposed where recreation was defined as "an experience that results from recreation engagements" (Driver & Tocher, 1970, p. 10) and leisure was basically regarded as free time.

Calls for the systematic development of social psychological approaches for the study of leisure emerged early in the 1970s. Driver (1972) argued for the potential contributions that social psychology could make to recreation resource management. John Neulinger, in his book *The Psychology of*

Leisure (1974), also argued for the importance of psychology for studying and understanding leisure. Like Driver and his associates, Neulinger argued that the subjective nature of leisure requires the theories, methods, and tools of psychology if it is to be studied effectively. Neulinger's well-known book was the first written on the psychology of leisure and he contributed substantially by outlining important issues that could be studied. He also drew the attention of researchers to a variety of social psychological theories and research areas that had relevance to the study of leisure. For example, Neulinger suggested that the psychological concepts of *time perception, boredom, sensory deprivation, locus of control, perceived freedom,* and *intrinsic motivation* might prove useful for understanding leisure. He also advocated a "person-environment" interaction approach for the study of leisure experiences (p. 110), and for the use of laboratory experiments. In subsequent chapters, you will discover that a number of these suggestions have been picked up and explored by leisure researchers.

As noted, a great deal of the research and theory in the psychological study of leisure has been done from a social psychological perspective (Ingham, 1986; Iso-Ahola, 1995, Mannell, 1984a). In 1978, the first Psychology/Social Psychology of Leisure session was held in Miami, Florida, and organized by Seppo Iso-Ahola as part of the Leisure Research Symposium associated with the National Recreation and Parks Association. This symposium session is now a major annual meeting place of researchers working in the social psychology of leisure area. The other sessions, such as management, human development, therapeutic recreation, and sociology have also become "psychologized" with the frequent reporting of studies focusing on social psychological constructs (Iso-Ahola, 1995).

Another significant contribution to the development of a social psychology of leisure, as suggested earlier, was provided by Iso-Ahola with the publication of his 1980 textbook, *The Social Psychology of Leisure and Recreation.* As an introductory textbook for several generations of students, it contributed to the definition of the boundaries of the emerging field and provided students with an idea of what it is like to examine leisure from a social psychological perspective.

There was a 17-year gap between the publication of the Iso-Ahola textbook and the next textbook—the first edition of this book (Mannell & Kleiber, 1997). However, a great deal of social psychological leisure research had occurred between the publication of these two textbooks. In 1980, two edited books on the psychology and social psychology of leisure were published (Iso-Ahola, 1980b; Ibrahim & Crandall, 1980). Phillip Pearce published a textbook on the social psychology of tourist behavior in 1982. A number of edited works reviewed significant advances in the field. Gaétan Ouellet edited a special issue of the journal *Society and Leisure* in 1984 on the social psychological study of leisure. In the same year, Peter Stringer edited a special issue of *Annals of Tourism Research* on the social psychology of tourism. Most of the chapters in Michael Wade's edited book the following year, *Constraints on Leisure* (1985), were social psychological analyses of leisure, as were many of those in Edgar Jackson and Thomas Burton's 1989 edited book, *Understanding Leisure and Recreation*. Also, the major journals in the field of leisure studies began to publish a great deal of research done from a social psychological perspective, with articles on benefits, constraints, ethnicity, discrimination, family, and health, among other subjects that lend themselves to this approach.

Ongoing Developments

Research on leisure motivation and satisfaction in the outdoor recreation area has continued and has been extended to many types of leisure behavior (see Manning, 1999; Mannell, 1999). Tinsley and his colleagues contributed to early theorizing about leisure needs and motives and their systematic measurement (e.g., Tinsley & Kass, 1980), and this work continues to be relevant to understanding the psychological benefits experienced by people in a variety of leisure settings (Tinsley, Tinsley, & Croskeys, 2002). Innovative research methods and concepts have led to advances in researchers' ability to conceptualize, measure, and understand leisure experiences and states, as well as behavior, from a psychological perspective (see Dattilo & Kleiber, 1993, 2002; Mannell & Dupuis, 1994; Mannell & Iso-Ahola, 1987; Samdahl, 1991; Shaw, 1985a; see also Chapter 3). Coupled with these developments, considerable research has been done in the area of understanding the role that perceived freedom and intrinsic motivation play in leisure (see Barnett, 1991; Iso-Ahola, 1989; see also Chapters 5 and 6). Individual differences in leisure behavior and personality were barely addressed in the early years, with a few exceptions (e.g., Driver & Knopf, 1977; Iso-Ahola, 1976; Kleiber, 1979), but with the development of leisure-specific personality constructs, it became an active area of study (see also Iso-Ahola, 1995; Kleiber & Dirkin, 1985; and Chapter 7). Early interest in measuring leisure attitudes cooled but was subsequently regenerated around the issue in how to influence and change leisure attitudes (Manfredo, 1992; see also Chapter 13). Interest in leisure socialization and the influence of life cycle changes on leisure developed fairly early (see Kleiber & Kelly, 1980; Osgood & Howe, 1984) and has been maintained (Freysinger, 1990; Kleiber, 1999), albeit with greater attention to the role of leisure in childhood and adolescent development in particular (e.g., Hutchinson, Baldwin, & Caldwell, 2003; Witt & Caldwell, 2005; see also Chapters 8, 9, and 11).

Interest in leisure and aging has also expanded (e.g., Burnett-Wolle & Godbey, 2007; Freysinger, 2005; Kleiber, McGuire, Aybar-Damali, & Norman, 2008), as has concern for the relationship between work and leisure, and how people organize and balance the work, leisure, and family domains of their lives (see Freysinger, 1994; Kabanoff & O'Brien, 1986; Kirchmeyer, 1993; Mannell & Reid, 1999; Shaw, 1992, 2001b; see also Chapters 8, 9, and 12). Early interest in the relationship between leisure and health has become a major area for leisure theory development (Iwasaki & Mannell, 2000b; Kleiber, Hutchison, & Williams, 2002) as has the impact of life events such as caregiving (Dupuis, 2000) and disability (Hutchinson, Loy, Kleiber, & Dattilo, 2003) on leisure and health.

The subject of gender has also captured increasingly more attention over recent decades in various areas of social science. Leisure studies has been no exception (Henderson, Hodges, & Kivel, 2002). An interest in the socio-cultural and cross-cultural dimensions of leisure and ethnicity as they affect leisure is starting to mature as well (Stodolska & Yi, 2003; Walker, Deng, & Dieser, 2005; see also Chapter 10). From a social psychological perspective, age, gender, and ethnicity are individual difference factors that, along with personality, interact with situational influences to influence behavior and experience.

In North American leisure studies, frameworks such as *leisure benefits* (Driver & Bruns, 1999) and *leisure constraints* (Jackson, 2005) have provided a means of organizing thinking about whole areas of social psychological research as they apply to leisure phenomena and services. In the case of constraints, the focus of the research has expanded to include the identification of factors that encourage leisure involvement (i.e., affordances and facilitators) and the *negotiation* strategies employed by people to overcome constraints. Constraints models are becoming more social cognitive and the psychological mechanisms of negotiation and motivation are being tested with more sophisticated statistical modeling approaches. Interpretive social psychological approaches have been useful in identifying the meanings and context of constraints (see Jackson, 2005).

An increasing number of leisure researchers have utilized interpretive sociological approaches to leisure and there appears to be wide acceptance of their use (Mannell, Kleiber, & Staempfli, 2006; Weissinger, Henderson, & Bowling, 1997). Theory and research emerging from this perspective have added insights in traditional areas of inquiry and expanded the areas of interest to include research on the leisure behavior and experience of individuals in the context of women's health (Parry & Shinew, 2004), romantic relationships (Herridge, Shaw, & Mannell, 2003), resistance and empowerment (Green, 1998), and body image and identity (Frederick & Shaw, 1995).

Social Psychology of Leisure
as an International Field of Study

Until the 1970s, European leisure studies was predominantly sociological. But in 1979, John Haworth, a British psychologist, argued for more attention to the role of the individual as an active agent in creating his or her "existence and future" within the "leisure sphere" (p. 53). He appeared to be reacting to what he saw as an overemphasis on institutional and societal influences on leisure behavior. A later review of psychological contributions to the study of leisure by another British psychologist (Ingham, 1986, 1987) suggests that "the major thrust of psychological contributions to the study of leisure has come from the United States" and that "few psychologists in the United Kingdom profess to an interest" (Ingham, 1986, p. 256). But this has changed to some extent; psychologist Michael Argyle published *The Social Psychology of Leisure* in 1996, and even sociologists in Britain give more attention to the generation of meaning in the context of leisure.

Based on our discussion of the psychology and social psychology of leisure thus far, most references to early contributions to this subfield are primarily North American and to a lesser extent British. To what extent has the social psychological study of leisure reached further? There are several ways to look at this issue. Debates within the mainstream of American social psychology itself are instructive.

Over half a century ago, after the Second World War, there began what has been called an American "colonization" of Western European social psychology and its influence has spread to many other countries as their scholars have become interested in studying social influences on individual behavior (van Strien, 1997). The sheer volume of American research has been almost overwhelming and the primary theories and approaches used have been American. This globalization of social psychology within the discipline of psychology is reflected by an increasing proportion of authors from outside the United States publishing in the premier U.S.-based journals (e.g., Quiñones-Vidal, Lozpez-García, Peñarañda-Ortega, & Tortosa-Gil, 2004). However, there has been some recent interest in the extent to which different regions or localities are developing their own indigenous social psychologies that reflect their values and traditions. Some analysts have suggested that a "decolonization" has been occurring that involves an effort to achieve a cross-fertilization of American and non-American perspectives. There have been substantial efforts to make social psychology texts relevant outside of North America in Britain, Europe, and Australia by including data from these countries (Demitrakis, 1997; Vaughan & Hogg, 1995), though it is not clear that this strategy has led to new perspectives or theories.

There has been some advocacy for the development of indigenous social psychologies. For example, in a recent edited volume, the simple transference of social psychological ideas and research findings from the American-European to Asian contexts is questioned (Markus & Kitiyama, 1991; Yang, Hwang, Pedersen, & Daibo, 2003). There appears to be growing recognition that the development of indigenous social psychologies might help researchers identify cultural bias and better adapt social psychology to the international and multicultural community. For example, Sinha (2003) suggests that the field of social psychology in India is moving toward indigenization by integrating ancient Indian wisdom and more contemporary folkways with the Western psychological tradition, which may contribute to a better understanding of Indian realities. He argues that the international community of social psychologists can facilitate this integration by being constructive in its critique of the process. However, at the present time, there would appear to be no recognized coherent and well-articulated indigenous psychological social psychologies, nor have these developments influenced mainstream (North American) social psychology. While constructionist sociological social psychology research is unlikely to inhibit the emergence of unique local social psychological perspectives, Cook (2000) suggests that sociological social psychologies have not addressed the challenge of becoming more cross-cultural.

With respect to the social psychology of leisure, there is very little evidence that alternative indigenous non-Western leisure social psychologies are emerging at the present time, either psychological or sociological. However, some interest is being shown in the psychological study of leisure by scholars in other countries where the tradition has not previously been established. For example, Murray and Nakajima (1999) and Santos, Ribeira, and Guimarães (2003) have adapted standardized measures of leisure motivation and leisure stress coping developed by North American researchers for use in Japan and Portugal respectively. Also, Mannell and Kleiber's (1997) book on the social psychology of leisure was selected by Japanese leisure researchers for translation into Japanese in 2004. The topic of national, cultural and ethnic differences in the social psychology of leisure will be taken up more completely in Chapter 10.

Conclusion

The psychological study of leisure is primarily social psychological and includes post-positivist psychological and constructionist sociological approaches. This pluralism appears to be healthy, and researchers using these perspectives often study similar phenomena, resulting in a profitable cross-fertilization of insights and understanding. For example, multiple perspectives and mixed methods have been particularly valuable in the development of theory and research on leisure constraints. There has also been substantial growth in studies of gender and, in particular, the discovery of differences in the meaning of leisure for women and its potential role in resisting cultural stereotypes and constraints on various aspects of life. Researchers are also giving more attention to ethnic and cultural diversity in leisure behavior and experience and are moving beyond simple descriptions of differences and similarities to developing improved understanding and explanations. The growth in the use of mainstream social psychological constructs, theory, and sensitizing concepts, and the development of social psychological theory indigenous to leisure studies itself are both encouraging developments.

Section Two

Social Psychology of Leisure Essentials

3

Social Psychology Approaches for Studying Leisure

Preview

In the study of leisure, one of the most active debates has been about the nature of leisure itself. The story of the quest to understand leisure from a social psychological perspective is partly a tale of the ways that researchers have attempted to translate various philosophical, historical, and common-sense notions of leisure into social psychological constructs that can be defined, observed, measured, and studied scientifically. From a social psychological perspective, there is no single way to conceptualize and define leisure. Different approaches have their advantages as well as limitations. Some strategies work better for certain types of questions researchers and practitioners want answered, and different strategies are more useful for others. In this chapter, we will present a typology that identifies and classifies approaches for defining, observing, and measuring leisure and then look at how researchers have used various research methods to study leisure, given these different approaches. As will be seen, researchers have been truly inventive in their attempts to explore and understand the social psychological nature and dynamics of leisure. They have used a wide range of research methods that include surveying and interviewing people, time-budget diaries, experience sampling, and field and laboratory experiments. Recent attention has also been given to less common methods based on visual methods that include photo-elicitation and analysis of the photographs and drawings people create to express their leisure experiences.

Social Psychological Ways of Studying People

As already noted, today social psychology is primarily based on a social cognitive perspective that stresses the importance of not only looking at explanations or theories that account for the influence of external influences on behavior and experience, but at the ways people perceive and interpret their environment. According to this view, it is important that research methods are used to look within individuals, particularly at their cognitive and emotional processes, in order to understand their behavior and experience. As we saw in the previous chapter, Kurt Lewin (1935) argued that the environment which influences human actions is not a set of physical characteristics and events but the life space of people, that is, the environment and what it means to them. People actively construct or make sense of the situations in which they find themselves. For example, Lewin pointed out that a landscape consisting of hills and valleys, trees and bushes, and open spaces would be a very different environment to soldiers in combat than to a group of friends on a picnic, and would influence behavior and experience in different ways.

In social psychology and other social science disciplines, the development and evaluation of explanations or theories about people's behavior and experience are based on empirical research. "Empirical" means based on observation and requires the use of various strategies or methods for gathering information or data. Psychological and social psychological explanations require the use of psychological attributes such as personality traits, attitudes, values, moods, emotions, etc. However, no psychological attribute can ever be directly observed. It can only be inferred on the basis of what we can see of people's behavior, that is, what they say and do. If we observe that an individual does not play Internet poker or visit the local casino during her free time, we might start to think that this person holds certain attitudes toward gambling. Consequently, we might predict that she would also be opposed to buying lottery tickets. We are guessing that something called an attitude toward gambling exists and accounts for the stability of her behavior across a variety of situations. This gambling attitude is a "hypothetical construct." In their explanations, social psychologists make extensive use of hypothetical constructs; that is, variables that are presumed to exist and that can be used to explain behavior. We cannot see a hypothetical construct like an attitude. It is not a tangible thing. Many experiences (e.g., fun, enjoyment, relaxation, contemplation, flow) and even behaviors (e.g., running in the park, cooking, Internet activity) that are thought to be leisure, and the factors hypothesized to influence them (e.g., attitudes, needs, personality traits) are based on hypothetical constructs. We cannot see fun although facial expressions can be used as indicators of the experience. Use of the Internet might be work, leisure, or neither depending on factors that are hypothetical constructs such as goals of the activity, sense of freedom in participating, needs being satisfied, etc.

To return to attitudes toward gambling, if they do actually exist, and most people believe they do, how can we observe and even measure them? Social psychological researchers who study people's behavior including leisure use various psychological attributes to explain leisure behavior and experience. How can we observe a leisure attitude, a negative attitude toward authority, a playful personality trait, or a video game addiction? In order to be able to define a hypothetical construct in a quantifiable way, social psychologists often employ *operational definitions*, that is, they define the construct in terms of the operations used to measure it. Thus, in one study, leisure attitude may be defined and measured in terms of how many leisure activities people were engaged in during the past week. In another study, a leisure attitude might be operationally defined in quite a different manner (e.g., how much effort one makes to go to the movies with a spouse during a week filled with work and family responsibilities). Social psychologists also ask people to self-report their attitudes, often by having them rate on a paper-and-pencil scale the extent to which they like or enjoy leisure activities.

Social psychological research methods used for making observations can be divided into two types: (1) nonexperimental and (2) experimental. If non-experimental methods are used, no effort is made to influence the conditions under which the people being studied respond. For example, researchers might wish to study the relationship between IQ and attending the arts and they measure both in a survey distributed to members of a community. However, even if IQ and attending the arts are found to be positively related or correlated, the data will not provide any clues about cause and effect. Having a higher IQ might enable people to enjoy and consequently attend the arts more frequently, or conversely, attending the arts might lead to an increase in IQ. In addition to surveys, other types of nonexperimental methods are used and include archival research, case studies, questionnaires (closed- and open-ended), various types of interviews varying from completely unstructured to structured and observational studies.

With the experimental method, the researcher deliberately assigns study participants randomly to two (or more) groups and does something, what is called the treatment (independent variable), to one group and not the other. Then the researcher measures the effect of the treatment by comparing the two groups' behavior or experience (dependent variable) to see if they differ. To ensure that it is the treatment that caused the difference, the experiment is designed to treat the two groups exactly the same except for the treatment, that is, to exclude extraneous variables. For example, as we will see later in the chapter, in a laboratory experiment, a researcher gave one group of participants more choice than the other in choosing a game to play and measured the influence of having different amounts of choice on the quality of the experience they derived from playing. He found some interesting differences. In social psychology, though not in the study of leisure, the laboratory experiment has and continues to be the most frequently used research method, though field experiments such as the one described in the previous chapter on helping behavior at the beach are sometimes used as well. It should be noted that longitudinal studies where researchers follow and observe the same group of people over time also can help in sorting out what causes what.

The Challenge of Defining, Observing, and Measuring Leisure

Like many psychological constructs, leisure can be defined in many ways, making it easier or more difficult to observe and measure. In the scenarios examined in Chapter 1, the reader faced the challenge of deciding whether playing a video game in an arcade, skateboarding, and social networking on library computers were leisure behaviors and experiences. Deciding what is and what is not leisure is an ongoing issue with which researchers must deal. Before they can look at the factors that affect people's leisure and how leisure in turn affects people, they must have some sense of what it is, what it looks like, and how to observe or measure it.

Most people with some interest in leisure, at one time or another, have tried their hand at defining it. Finding a way to define, observe, and measure leisure has been the holy grail of leisure scholars and there continues to be interest in defining leisure generally (e.g., Kelly, 2009) or specific types such as serious and casual leisure (e.g., Stebbins, 1997). Some observers over the years have felt that coming up with a definition of leisure is about as unattainable as finding the Holy Grail and that little progress has been made (Sessoms, 1986). The difficulties of defining leisure and deciding what it is, as well as observing and measuring it, have long been regarded as a significant challenge to progress in the study of leisure.

It is easy to see why this assessment has been made. Many definitions of leisure abound. Researchers and theorists often view leisure as participation in recreational or cultural activities such as sports, hobbies, and dance. Leisure also is identified by the setting in which it is experienced, such as parties, theaters, and parks. It is described as time free from obligation, the freedom to do whatever one wants to do, or as simply doing something for its own sake. Certain feelings or experiences are considered leisure. A sense of freedom, relaxation, fun, enjoyment, and even intense concentration have been said to characterize leisure. To make matters more complicated, people have been heard to say that their work can be leisure!

However, as we will explain in this chapter, a great deal of thinking and research has increased researchers' ability to observe, measure, and study leisure from a social psychological perspective. We will examine a number of strategies that they have used to confront this challenge. A typology describing four key approaches used by researchers to define and decide what constitutes leisure will be described. Based on these approaches, researchers have studied the leisure of people from many walks of life. They have had them respond to questionnaires and surveys, they have observed and interviewed people in settings where leisure takes place, and they have tracked and monitored people as they engage in leisure and non-leisure activities during daily life. Researchers have even involved people in experiments in the psychological laboratory and in the field to study leisure.

A typology of research approaches for defining, observing, and measuring leisure is presented in Figure 3.1 (see p. 58). The typology with its classification scheme has two principal dimensions. The first is the type of phenomena being considered as leisure. Two types of social psychological phenomena are identified—objective and subjective (Neulinger, 1974; Ellis & Witt, 1991; Lawton, 1993). Objective definitions and approaches to observation and measurement equate leisure with certain types of activities, settings, and/or time. Leisure can be defined and measured as behavior, i.e., as something people do. It also can be defined by setting, i.e., by people's immediate social and physical environment and what is going on in it. In contrast, according to subjective definitions, leisure is associated with the occurrence of certain types of mental states, attitudes, emotions, cognitions, perceptions, meanings, needs satisfied, and/or experiences.

Type of Phenomena	Definitional Vantage Point	
	External	Internal
Objective	**Behavioral-Observer** Approach	**Behavioral-Participant** Approach
Subjective	**Experiential-Observer** Approach	**Experiential-Participant** Approach

Descriptions of Approaches	
Behavioral-observer approach:	**Behavior of the participant** is defined by the **researcher/observer** as leisure or non-leisure on the basis of the activity in which the participant is engaged or the setting or time period in which it is embedded.
Experiential-observer approach:	**Experience, satisfaction, or meaning** associated with an episode is defined by the **researcher/observer** as leisure or non-leisure.
Behavioral-participant approach:	**Behavior of the participant** is defined by the **participant** as leisure or non-leisure on the basis of the activity in which he/she is engaged or the setting or time period in which it is embedded.
Experiential-participant approach:	**Experience, satisfaction, or meaning** associated with an episode is defined by the **participant** as leisure or non-leisure.

Figure 3.1 Research Approaches to Defining and Measuring Leisure

The second way to distinguish among leisure definitions, observations, and measures is according to the definitional vantage point taken by the researcher when studying leisure. In other words, regardless of whether the researcher is studying behavior, settings, or mental states, what is defined as leisure can be based either on the viewpoint of the researcher (external) or that of the person being studied (internal).

Typology of Approaches for Defining, Observing, and Measuring People's Leisure

Type of Leisure Phenomena: Objective and Subjective

When leisure is defined as "what people do," researchers have used measures based on the activities in which the people studied participate and the amount of time they spend engaged in these activities. This approach generally involves observing and measuring the number of specific activities (e.g., skiing, watching a movie, doing crossword puzzles) or general categories of activities (e.g., social, sport, cultural) participated in by individuals, the frequency of participation in these activities, and the amount of time they are involved. Leisure can also be defined according to the setting or environment likely to support activities or evoke experiences thought to be leisure. Tennis courts, beaches, and theaters are among the more obvious settings for leisure. It is often difficult to disentangle leisure activities and settings. Some activities can only occur in specific settings. For example, a party or visiting a park can be viewed as both leisure activities and settings for leisure. Consequently, leisure settings are frequently not distinguished from leisure activities, though the importance of distinguishing between the impact of settings and activities has been noted (Manning, 1999). Deem (1986) and Henderson (1990a) suggested that activities and settings can be thought of as "containers" for what people define or experience as leisure.

When leisure is defined in terms of what people think and feel, it is treated as a subjective phenomenon. In this case, researchers make observations or use measures that reflect people's mental experience while engaged in leisure activities and the satisfactions or meanings derived from these involvements. The mental world of leisure is populated by conscious experiences including emotions, moods, satisfactions, cognitions, attitudes, and beliefs. Of course, these phenomena are hypothetical constructs—they can't be seen directly. While they can be inferred from behavior, researchers often "observe" them based on what people tell them about their experiences. Such self-reports can be obtained in interviews or by using questionnaires with standardized rating scales.

In Figure 3.1, when the type of phenomena under study is objective, we have called it a "behavioral" approach to definition, and when subjective, an "experiential" approach. These ways of defining, observing, and measuring leisure are not in conflict or competition. Questions about leisure require the use of a variety of approaches. A full understanding of leisure often requires that researchers simultaneously use both of these approaches. For example, assume that a team of researchers is interested in the relationship between people's leisure and their ability to cope with the daily stress in their lives. Also assume they have a theory that suggests that people who are more actively involved in leisure are more immune to stress, that is, they experience less stress and consequently less illness. In order to study this relationship, leisure and stress need to be measured. Consider leisure. If these researchers measure leisure as an objective phenomenon or behaviorally, they could observe how many activities people are participating in, the types of leisure settings they encounter during their daily life, how frequently they participate or how much time they are involved in these activities and settings. If they also have a way of measuring stress, they could then see if those people who have greater leisure are less stressed.

However, it is quite possible that this objective approach to defining, observing, and measuring leisure would provide an incomplete picture. If the researchers also knew what the people being studied were experiencing when they were involved in leisure activities and settings—how enjoyable, challenging, relaxing, and satisfying they are—researchers might have a better idea of the impact that these leisure involvements have on people's ability to cope with stressful events in their lives. This approach treats leisure experientially or as a subjective phenomenon.

Definitional Vantage Point: External and Internal

You have probably noticed that although we have suggested that leisure has been defined by researchers in terms of people's behavior, the setting in which the behavior takes place and their mental experience, we have not identified how researchers decide whether a behavior, setting, or experience is leisure or something else. In other words, who decides?

In the social psychological study of leisure, who decides what leisure is depends on the definitional vantage point used by the researcher in a particular study. The definitional vantage point can be external or internal to the person or people being studied. In the typology in Figure 3.1, the external and internal vantage points are called the "observer" and "participant" approaches, respectively. If an external vantage point is adopted, what constitutes leisure is determined by the researcher as observer and is based on viewpoints other than those of the individual or people being studied.

External definitions of leisure are typically based on what people in a social group or society actually agree to be leisure, and researchers often share these beliefs if they are members of the same group or society. When studying people who are members of societies or groups that differ from their own, researchers must first develop an understanding of what leisure is for these social collectives. In a sense, the researcher predetermines or imposes a definition of leisure on the people being studied and hopefully this is informed by a thorough knowledge of the social groups to which the people being studied belong or identify.

This approach is not quite as dictatorial as it sounds. Researchers may be interested in how an individual becomes involved in activities typically seen as leisure in that person's social group or culture, what keeps them involved, and the psychological, spiritual, and other costs and benefits of their involvement. They may or may not ask them if they view the activities as leisure. For example, Stebbins (1992b) examined these types of issues in studies of people singing in a barbershop quartet and Parry (2009) studied cancer survivors involved in dragon boat racing. They did not explicitly ask the people in their studies if these activities were leisure or something else. Other researchers, as well as leisure service providers, may be interested in how accessible certain leisure opportunities are for the members of a group or community. These leisure opportunities likely consist of the activities (e.g., youth sports), settings (e.g., skateboard parks), and experiences (e.g., appreciation of beauty in an art gallery) generally seen by the people living in this community to be leisure, and that are made available through the efforts of both public and private leisure service agencies. Consequently, it makes sense to use an external, socially derived definition of leisure in studying these types of equity issues.

However, if an internal vantage point is adopted by the researcher, the definition of leisure is based on the perception or construal of the behavior, setting, or experience as leisure by the individuals being studied. In other words, the researcher leaves it up to the individuals in the study to determine if an activity, setting, or experience is leisure for them personally. An early study by Johnson (1978) demonstrates this distinction between what we have called the external and the internal vantage points or observer versus participant definitions. Adults and their children were often found to have very different ideas about whether a particular physical setting, such as a park or an alleyway, was a recreation or non-recreation space. Thinking back to the skateboard scenario in Chapter 1, it's quite possible that the youth were less likely to experience leisure when skating in a skateboard park provided by the city than when doing so in non-designated recreation spaces such as the outside stairs and ramps of public buildings. By using the individual's own definition of leisure, researchers often feel that they will get a more accurate picture of how much leisure people feel they have and what is meaningful to them. In turn, this may allow a clearer understanding of how leisure impacts their lives. Personal definitions of leisure can be expected to be influenced by and consistent with the values and beliefs of the group and society of which people are members. However, while externally and internally based definitions of leisure are frequently in agreement, they can be and often are at odds, as was the case of the skateboarders and the adults in their community.

This idea of the internal vantage point is an important one for the social psychology of leisure. As we saw in Chapter 1, social psychologists studying all types of behavior and experience attach a great deal of importance to how individuals perceive or construe their own behavior, the behavior of others, and the situations in which they find themselves. Construal is an important idea for understanding all aspects of human behavior and experience and the influence of the social environment. Ross and Nisbett (1991) have stated that:

> [the] impact of any "objective" stimulus situation depends upon the personal and subjective meaning that the actor attaches to that situation. To predict the behavior of a given person successfully, we must be able to appreciate the actor's construal of the situation—that is, the manner in which the person understands the situation as a whole. (p. 11).

The social psychological perspective is based on a belief in the importance of taking into account both socially derived or external, as well as personal or internal definitions of behavior, settings, and experiences to fully understand human behavior (Barone, Maddux, & Snyder, 1997).

Let's return to the skateboarding example we discussed in Chapter 1. An external definitional vantage point could be adopted based on the knowledge that skateboarding is a popular recreational activity and skateboarding parks are leisure settings for many adolescents. In fact, it would be fairly safe to say, at least in North America, that skateboarding and skate facilities are seen by most people as leisure behavior and settings, respectively. If researchers surveyed the adolescents who lived in the community about their leisure by sending them a questionnaire that asked them to indicate how frequently or how much time they spent doing this activity in this setting, researchers would likely feel confident they were getting valid information about the adolescents' leisure. This strategy would be a relatively quick and inexpensive way in which to measure how much of the adolescents' leisure was spent skateboarding.

However, observers cannot be absolutely certain that skateboarding is experienced as leisure for each of the adolescents or even for a particular adolescent each time he or she participates. If researchers are trying to understand the impact that skateboarding has on the daily lives and school experience of these adolescents, they may feel it is important to adopt a research strategy that allows them to measure the extent to which each of the adolescents construes skateboarding as leisure.

Of course, researchers can also examine the subjective nature of leisure from both external and internal vantage points. Experiences of fun and enjoyment are subjective leisure phenomena and often taken as signs that people are engaged in leisure. However, not all individuals may construe themselves to be engaged in leisure simply because they are enjoying themselves. For some individuals, leisure might be better indicated by other feelings such as relaxation, escape, or even excitement.

In actual practice, a combination of the four approaches classified in the typology shown in Figure 3.1 (p. 58) is often used for determining if someone is engaged in leisure. These four approaches have been labeled the behavioral-observer, behavioral-participant, experiential-observer, and experiential-participant approaches. If a researcher were to observe a person in a skate park engaged in skateboarding (objective phenomenon) and overheard this individual say she was having a good time (subjective phenomenon), the observer would likely assume that this engagement was leisure for that person. Of course, the observer could confirm the observation and external definition by approaching the skateboarder and asking if she felt that what she was doing was "leisure"—adopting an internal definitional vantage point.

Social psychological approaches for conceptualizing, observing, and measuring leisure have advanced. Approaches have been developed that utilize not only objective and subjective phenomena when studying the leisure of individuals, but that also define leisure from external and internal vantage points. In the remainder of this chapter, we will examine research methods that not only illustrate these four approaches to definition but that have been used to further a social psychological understanding of leisure.

Definitions and Research Methods Used in the Social Psychological Study of Leisure

Experimenting on Leisure

In scientific research, whether the natural or social sciences, an experiment is an empirical approach to acquiring data about the world and a method of investigating causal relationships among variables. As already noted, experiments, particularly laboratory experiments, are widely used by social psychologists to study many types of human behavior and experience. However, experiments have been used relatively rarely to study leisure, particularly in the laboratory.

Field experiments are a bit more common. Field experiments have the advantage that outcomes are observed in a natural setting rather than in a contrived laboratory environment. However, field experiments suffer from the possibility of contamination since experimental conditions cannot be controlled with as much precision and certainty as in the lab.

Field Experiments

In the experimental study of leisure, field settings have ranged from popular outdoor recreation areas to bars. For example, Stoep and Gramann (1987) examined the impact of personally delivered messages given to youth groups hiking a park's trails. The "depreciative behavior" (e.g., damage to park monuments and cultural features) committed by youth groups as measured by time-lapse photography at four locations along the trail was less for those youth who received the messages than those who did not. This depreciative behavior was leisure behavior as defined by the researchers and consequently could be classified as a *behavioral-observer* approach to definition and measurement. More recently, Vitterso and his colleagues (2004) examined the impact of encountering snowmobiles on the quality of the leisure experiences of cross-country skiers in recreation areas—an *experiental-observer* approach. In a field study conducted in the leisure setting of a bar, nonverbal social interaction was examined. Women who were confederates of the researcher varied the length of time they held eye contact with fellow male bar patrons from less than a second up to four seconds. The influences on the men's responses were noted. Longer duration of eye contact was associated with duration of the returned glance and greater frequency of smiling (Gueguen et al., 2008). This nonverbal social behavior in the bar is leisure as defined by the researchers—a *behavioral-observer* approach.

Other leisure field studies have examined the success of interventions to improve people's leisure. For example, Backman and Mannell (1986) randomly assigned 44 residents of a seniors' residence to three different treatment groups and one control group that received a leisure education program, a recreation activity exposure program, and combination of these programs or no program. They found that the greatest increases in positive attitudes toward leisure and in recreation behavior occurred for the group receiving the combination program. Searle et al. (1995) randomly assigned older adults to an experimental (treatment) group and a control group. The treatment group (13 people) participated in an extensive leisure education program. Fifteen older adults were in the control group that did not participate in the program. Participants in the experimental group came to experience higher levels of control over their leisure, leisure competence, and life satisfaction and reduced levels of boredom when compared to the control group. Leisure was thus defined and measured in a variety of ways in these field studies; in field experiments and studies like those just reviewed, the researcher typically defines what constitutes leisure.

Laboratory Experiments

Although the experiment, particularly the laboratory experiment, has not been used frequently to study leisure behavior and experience, early in the development of the social psychology of leisure some researchers were advocating its use (Bishop & Witt, 1970; Iso-Ahola, 1979a; Mannell, 1979; Neulinger, 1974). Leisure experiments have been reported (e.g., Mannell & Bradley, 1986), and there is some continued use of experimental designs. However, few studies bring people into a laboratory and create conditions where people's actual leisure behavior and experience are examined.

A more common type of leisure experiment that is not quite a laboratory study nor a field study involves creating treatments by presenting study participants with hypothetical scenarios where they are asked to imagine themselves in different situations and then indicate how they think they would behave, feel, or react. For example, Bishop and Witt (1970), in one of these *thought experiments*, had their study participants imagine being in different situations that were described to them (e.g., "you have just gotten results from the biggest exam of the year and you have either failed or not done as well as you expected to do"). The participants were then asked to select what they would do from a variety of alternatives (e.g., watch TV, take a nap, play games, sit and relax). Bishop and Witt designed the experiment so that they could observe differences in leisure choices based on the different personality characteristics of the participants (which they measured) as well as the different situations the experimenters asked them to imagine. The researchers found that neither personality nor the situation accounted for what type of leisure activity the participants thought they would engage in. It was the interaction of personality and the situation that determined their imagined leisure behavior. A behavioral-observer (or imagined behavioral) approach was used to define leisure.

Iso-Ahola (1979a) used a similar experimental approach to study the characteristics of experiences that people define as leisure. He asked the people in his study to imagine themselves experiencing different amounts of freedom of choice and different types of motivation and goals while participating in an activity—an activity that he did not name or identify. He found that the participants were more likely to define their involvement as leisure when they imagined themselves experiencing more choice, felt they were doing an activity for its own sake and perceived their goal was not to accomplish anything beyond enjoying themselves. According to the typology presented in Figure 3.1, Iso-Ahola used an *experiential-participant* approach to define leisure since it was the participants who decided this experience was leisure.

More recently, this experimental approach has been used effectively by McCarville and his colleagues to study the responses of people in a variety of leisure service settings. For example, Bernier and McCarville (2005) randomly assigned their study participants to four groups and presented those in each group with one of four hypothetical scenarios in which an individual named Chris spent the day at a ski center that offered a 100% money-back guarantee that the experience would be a good one. Chris was described either as having visited the center earlier with plans to return (high-relationship scenario) or as being a first-time visitor with no plans to return (low-relationship scenario). The price of the day package (lift tickets and rentals) was set at either $35 (low-material-gain scenario) or $125 (high-material-gain scenario). Each of the groups was presented with one of the four possible combinations of these variables, that is, there were four treatment groups with each receiving one combination of the high or low versions of each message. Participants in the study answered a series of questions about the likelihood that Chris would fraudulently invoke the guarantee to obtain a refund. As predicted, the potential for material gain and the extent of the relationship with the leisure service both influenced participants' predictions that Chris would act in a fraudulent manner. Those in the low relationship/high material gain group were most likely to feel that Chris would ask for a refund. In this study, it is not as clear that leisure is the objective or subjective phenomenon being studied. Rather leisure, skiing at a ski center, is the context in which a participant's response to a service provider is examined. Perhaps it could be argued that taking advantage of the money-back guarantee is itself an aspect of Chris's skiing experience and leisure behavior. In this is the case, Chris's leisure response, the extent of his fraudulent behavior, is a leisure behavior as defined by the researchers—a behavioral-observer definition or approach.

Of course, we can ask if the study participants or people in general would actually behave in the ways the study participants thought Chris would. Clearly, these types of experiments based on hypothetical situations and responses are highly artificial. However, researchers would be the first to suggest that their findings would need to be confirmed by observations and experience in the actual settings being simulated. Yet these findings do provide interesting and useful insights on leisure behavior and experience that would be very difficult to observe and study systematically in their natural settings. These types of studies also provide preliminary information about whether various theories or explanations of people's leisure behavior might have some validity before heading out and gathering data in natural settings.

There have also been a few studies reported on leisure behavior and experience that have used the more traditional social psychological laboratory experiment. For example, Mannell (1979), Mannell and Bradley (1986), Tang (1986) and Iwasaki and Mannell (1999) have examined the behavior and experience of study participants engaged in recreational activities (e.g., playing

games) in the laboratory. In these studies, participants with different personality traits or orientations (e.g., internal versus external locus of control, Type
A versus Type B behavior, intrinsic versus extrinsic leisure motivation) have
been put in different experimental conditions (e.g., level of choice, perception of a task as work versus leisure, controlling versus autonomy-supportive
environment) to examine the effects on the level of enjoyment, intrinsic satisfaction, and psychological absorption or flow experienced in an activity.

Anatomy of a Leisure Experiment

To illustrate how leisure might be studied with a laboratory experiment and
the challenges of defining and measuring leisure in this context, we will
describe an early study reported by Mannell (1979). The laboratory was used
to create or simulate a period of free time in which a game was played. With
the use of the laboratory, the researcher was able to: (1) engineer a period of
"free time" during the course of the experiment that the participants would
perceive, at least within certain limits, was their own time and separate from
the "obligatory" activities under study; (2) manipulate the independent variables, that is, vary the setting; (3) hold constant all other features of the
physical and social environment for all participants in the study; (4) measure
the dependent variables used to operationalize the type of leisure experience
of interest; and (5) disguise the purpose of the experiment so that the participants would behave as normally as possible.

The amount of freedom participants had in choosing a game to play during
the free time period and the competitiveness of the game were the independent
variables and were manipulated. It was predicted that those participants who
had greater freedom of choice and were in a more competitive situation would
become more psychologically involved or absorbed in the game than participants who were given no choice and put in a less competitive situation.

The participants in the study were 60 university students. An appointment
was made with each individual to visit and participate in a "learning experiment." Each participant was randomly assigned to one of four treatment conditions (see Figure 3.2, p. 68): (1) low choice of game/low competitive game;
(2) low choice of game/high competitive game; (3) high choice of game/low
competitive game; (4) high choice of game/high competitive game. Consequently,
15 students participated in each one of these four sets of conditions, and they
were randomly assigned to ensure any differences in their experiences and
behaviors were due to the different treatments and not pre-existing differences.

Each participant arrived and was met individually by a graduate research
assistant. The laboratory consisted of two adjoining rooms. In the first room,
all participants performed a tracking task requiring them to follow a moving
light on a screen with a pencil-like wand. Whenever they lost contact with
the light the electronic equipment made a beeping sound and recorded a

miss. The participants were led to believe that their performance on this task was the major focus of this "learning" study. They were asked to remove their watches and all jewelry, supposedly to prevent interference with the electronic equipment in the laboratory. However, the real purpose was to collect their watches and prevent them from keeping track of how much time they were involved in playing a game in the "free time" phase of the experiment in the second room.

They performed the tracking task for five minutes, then were ushered into the second room of the laboratory which was furnished to look like a waiting room with comfortable furniture and pictures and posters adorning the walls. In this adjoining room, the participants were told that the people in the study waited for various lengths of time before returning to perform again on the tracking task. Every effort was made to encourage the participants to feel that what happened in this waiting or "free time" period had nothing to do with the actual purpose of the experiment. Once in the waiting room, those participants who had been assigned to either of the two high choice conditions were told by the graduate student assistant that her advisor, whose experiment this was, was allowing her to ask them to help her by choosing to play one of two games she was developing for people who were hospitalized and by filling out an evaluation form while they were waiting for the next phase of the experiment. It was stressed that they were under no obligation to play. In addition to the choice of playing one of the two games, the high choice participants could choose to sit and read magazines. Actually, the two games were just one game packaged in two different boxes with different names to create the perception of choice. Using only one game ruled out the possibility that differences in psychological involvement or absorption among the experimental groups could be due to the difference in the games. Participants in each of the low choice conditions were made aware of these alternatives but were told that they had to play a specific game since the other one had been fully tested and evaluated. Also, they were not given the choice of sitting and reading.

Freedom of Choice	Competitiveness of the Game	
	Low	High
Low	15 participants	15 participants
High	15 participants	15 participants

Figure 3.2 Experimental Conditions in Leisure and Flow Study

The research assistant demonstrated the game. The game itself allowed the participants to pace themselves, and required them to create a series of patterns on specially designed cards and then match them from memory using a tray of red and white cubes. Participants in each of the two high competitive conditions were instructed to record their scores and place them in an envelope that they would be required to sign so that comparisons could be made with the other participants' scores. Participants in the low competitive conditions were instructed to record their scores, but that these would not be collected and used by the experimenter.

The participants were then left to play the game for 30 minutes. Following this "free time" period, they were taken back to the first room of the laboratory where they completed scales used to assess their level of psychological involvement or absorption in the game. Absorption was operationalized in two ways. The first was as perceived time duration. High levels of involvement or absorption result in people experiencing time as passing very quickly (Csikszentmihalyi, 1975, 1990). By measuring the length of time the participants perceived that they had spent playing the laboratory game during the standard time period of 30 minutes, the researchers were able to measure their experience of "time going quickly." A time-duration scale was devised, consisting of two horizontal lines displayed on a sheet of paper (see Figure 3.3a, p. 70). The participants were instructed that the top line represented the time they had spent performing on the 5-minute tracking task when they arrived at the laboratory. They were requested to draw a line through the second, longer horizontal line at a point that represented their estimate of the time duration of the waiting (free time) period. The assumption was that the shorter the time duration was judged, the more absorbing the experience during the free time period.

The second measure of involvement or absorption was the participants' focus of attention or level of concentration on the game. Focus of attention was measured by testing the participants' memories of the features of the waiting room environment. A situational memory test was devised consisting of 10 five-item multiple choice questions (see Figure 3.3b, p. 71). It was assumed that the less the study participant remembered about the waiting room, the greater the focus of attention and absorption in the game. Two additional trials on the tracking task (to ensure the participants perceived the learning task as the central purpose of the study) were followed by a partial debriefing to determine if they had any suspicions about the hypotheses or actual purpose of the study. None of the participants suspected the real nature of the experiment. A month later, a full debriefing was given to the participants and the purpose and deceptions involved in this study were discussed.

As predicted, participants in the high choice and high competitive conditions became more psychologically involved and absorbed with the game than those in the low choice and low competitive conditions. In Figure 3.4, p. 72, it can be seen that those participants who perceived they had more choice in playing the game remembered less about the waiting room environment, that is, they were more focused and involved in the game. The same was true of those participants in the high competitive conditions. Out of the ten items they were asked to recall, on average the high choice/high competitive participants only correctly identified one feature of the waiting room. In comparison, the low choice/low competitive group on average recognized three features of the waiting room. These participants clearly did not become as fully involved in the game. The time duration estimates followed the same pattern. A rough conversion of the time scores (centimeters) into minutes suggests that the low choice/low competitive participants perceived the duration of the 30-minute waiting period reasonably accurately, that is, about 29 minutes in length. The participants in the high choice/high competitive condition experienced the 30-minute period to be only about 10 minutes in duration.

The author argued that the study demonstrates that perceiving a leisure activity as freely chosen does have a highly significant influence on the quality of a leisure or recreational experience. The competitiveness of leisure activities also influenced the leisure experience.

Leisure or not?

What makes this study a leisure experiment? Are you persuaded that leisure was studied in the experiment? The author claims to have measured and studied factors (amount of choice, competitiveness) that influence one aspect of the leisure experience (psychological involvement or absorption). Did the author operationalize and measure leisure using any of the four options suggested

---

Time Duration Scale

Two lines are displayed below. The shorter line represents the *amount of time* you spent performing on the pursuit rotor learning task before the waiting period. *Please draw a vertical line through the second longer line to indicate your estimate of the amount of time you spent in the waiting room.*

|———————————|

Time performing on the pursuit rotor

|——————————————————————————————

Time spent in the waiting room

Figure 3.3a Time Duration Scale (adapted from Mannell, 1979)

Waiting Room Situational Memory Test

For each of the following questions about the waiting room, *circle* the correct answer. If you don't remember, please circle *e*.

1. *What type of flooring did the room have?*
   a. tile
   b. hardwood
   c. carpet
   d. scatter rugs
   e. don't remember

2. *How many windows did the room have?*
   a. 1
   b. 2
   c. 3
   d. 4
   e. don't remember

3. *What did the curtains on the window look like?*
   a. solid color
   b. flowered pattern
   c. checkered pattern
   d. vertical stripes
   e. don't remember

4. *How many posters were on the wall?*
   a. 2
   b. 3
   c. 4
   d. 5
   e. don't remember

5. *What was the predominant color in the poster above the game table?*
   a. blue
   b. red
   c. green
   d. yellow
   e. don't remember

6. *What was the year and month on the calendar above the coffee table?*
   a. October 1976
   b. December 1976
   c. August 1977
   d. January 1978
   e. don't remember

7. *How many bookcase shelves were filled with books?*
   a. 0
   b. 1
   c. 2
   d. 3
   e. don't remember

8. *How many pencils were in the cup of the game table?*
   a. 1
   b. 2
   c. 3
   d. 4
   e. don't remember

9. *What did the painting in the sitting area depict?*
   a. a ship
   b. fruit
   c. portrait of a man
   d. flowers
   e. don't remember

10. *What was written on the blackboard?*
    a. a date (14/02/78)
    b. an arithmetic sum (2+2=4)
    c. a time (12:45 p.m.)
    d. a temperature (67°)
    e. don't remember

Figure 3.3b Waiting Room Situational Memory Test (adapted from Mannell, 1979)

by the typology described in Figure 3.1 (p. 58)? Like most research, not everyone is going to agree with the way leisure is defined, operationalized, and measured. Let's examine the case for the researcher having in fact measured and studied leisure in this experiment.

First, is psychological involvement or absorption in an activity an important dimension of leisure experiences? As will be discussed in the next chapter, this aspect of human experience has been called "flow" (Csikszentmihalyi, 1975) and has come to be seen as an important dimension of human experience and a characteristic or type of leisure experience. Csikszentmihalyi (1990) and others have argued that flow experiences are our best, most complete sources of enjoyment. Of course, in judging the success of the researcher in studying this aspect of a leisure experience, we would have to also agree that his measures were actually indicators of psychological involvement or flow. Flow is a hypothetical construct—it cannot be seen directly. The study participants' memory of the features of a room and their drawing a longer or shorter line segment may seem like odd indicators of a leisure experience but the researcher provides a logical reason for the connection. If we were to agree for the moment that psychological involvement or flow is a characteristic of

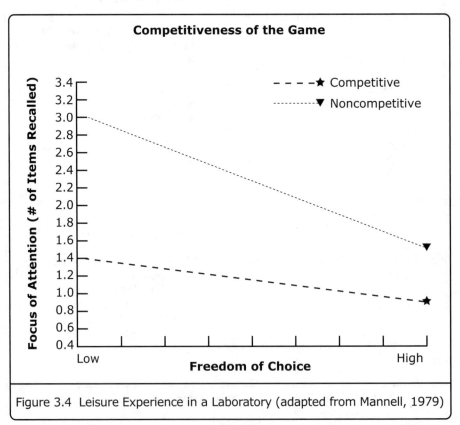

Figure 3.4 Leisure Experience in a Laboratory (adapted from Mannell, 1979)

some leisure experiences and was measured in this study, according to the definitional typology presented in Figure 3.1, the type of leisure phenomena studied would be characterized as subjective or experiential.

Second, with respect to the definitional vantage point, it is clear that it is the researcher, and not the participants, who defined this experience of flow as leisure. Consequently, an external definitional vantage point was adopted in this study. However, we do not know if those participants who experienced higher levels of flow would have been more likely to describe their experience during the laboratory free time period as leisure. This definition and measure of leisure can be classified as using an *experiential-observer* approach.

Inventories and Surveys: Remembering and Reporting Leisure Behavior and Activity

The most frequent research method used in leisure research has been the survey. As part of the survey, the most common approach to measuring leisure has been the leisure behavior inventory. An inventory is comprised of a list of activities and respondents are asked to indicate if they have participated in these activities and usually how often during a specified time period (e.g., week, month, season, year), or to rate their relative frequency of participation on a scale of 0 to 3 (see Figure 3.5, p. 74). Surveys designed for leisure research are also used to gather socio-demographic, and other types of leisure and non-leisure information. In the former case, researchers have used surveys to also measure things that prevent or constrain people's leisure participation as well as other aspects of leisure behavior and experience (Mannell & Iwasaki, 2005). In the case of non-leisure information, quality of life, work, and family information may be collected.

Researchers typically design custom inventories to suit their research purposes and the lifestyles of the people they are studying. For example, skateboarding is not likely to be included in the list of activities used to measure the leisure participation of people who are frail. Consequently, the types and numbers of activities vary substantially from study to study. While this tailoring of leisure behavior inventories provides flexibility, the lack of widely used, standardized scales can make it difficult to compare findings between studies (Mannell & Dupuis, 1994).

A customized leisure behavior inventory was developed by Ragheb (1980) and included in a survey questionnaire to study the influence of a variety of attitudinal and socio-demographic factors on the leisure participation of 383 adolescents and adults in the southern United States. Many researchers continue to be interested in measuring people's level of overall leisure participation (e.g., Hawkins et al., 2004) and sub-types of leisure behavior such as recreational sport (e.g., Alexandris & Carroll, 1997). They typically modify and

Indicate the number of times you participate or engage in each of the following activities during a typical week. Write your answer on the line provided.

_____ Listening to records, stereo, tapes
_____ Reading books for pleasure
_____ Reading magazines and newspapers
_____ Walking the dog or pet
_____ Fitness exercise (e.g., jogging, aerobics, walking, weight-training)

In the following list, circle the number of those activities in which you have participated *at least once during the last year.*

1   Taking a vacation trip
2   Visiting a national or regional park
3   Visiting a fair or festival
4   Visiting an art gallery
5   Attending a live theater performance (e.g., drama, comedy, musical)
6   Attending a rock concert
7   Attending a sporting event (e.g., baseball, football, hockey)
8   Dining out at a restaurant
9   Going to the movies
10 Visiting a public library
11 Attending a club meeting
12 Working for a church group or charity
13 Taking general interest or art courses

For each of the physical activities listed below rate how frequently you participated during the last year. If you "never" participate in the activity circle the "0." If you participated "infrequently" circle the number "1." If you participated "occasionally" or "frequently" circle the numbers "2" or "3" respectively. In the case of seasonal activities (e.g., water-skiing) rate your frequency of participation on the basis of when the activity could be engaged in.

0   1   2   3   Swimming
0   1   2   3   Water-skiing, surfing, scuba diving
0   1   2   3   Playing tennis, squash, other racquet sports
0   1   2   3   Golfing
0   1   2   3   Bowling
0   1   2   3   Team sports (e.g., baseball, football, ice hockey)
0   1   2   3   Gardening
0   1   2   3   Fishing or hunting
0   1   2   3   Camping or visiting a private cottage

Figure 3.5 Typical Leisure Behavior Inventory Items—*What Items Would You Include?*

borrow items from published inventories such as Ragheb's. For example, Heintzman and Mannell (2003) did so to help them examine the relationship between the leisure styles and spiritual health of the 248 people they surveyed. The original leisure behavior inventory developed by Ragheb consisted of 41 activities. The participants in this study were asked to indicate their frequency of participation in each activity by selecting one of the following alternatives: 1 = "never," 2 = "seldom," 3 = "some" of the time, 4 = "often," and 5 = "very often." For the analysis of the information collected with the inventory, the leisure activities were examined individually and grouped by the researcher into six categories: mass media, social activities, outdoor activities, sports activities, cultural activities, and hobbies (see Figure 3.6, p. 76). These ratings provided a score on each activity for each participant, ranging from 1 to 5. Also, the researcher was able to calculate an average score for each category of activity and an overall leisure participation score for each participant by averaging the ratings of the activities in each category and the ratings for all 41 activities respectively. With these measures of leisure, Ragheb was able to determine that individuals who were more active were also more satisfied with their leisure. This relationship was strongest for hobbies and cultural activities. Gender and educational differences were also found in levels of leisure participation.

Leisure behavior inventories and, as we will see, time diaries rely heavily on what we have called the external definitional vantage point and the *behavioral-observer* approach. In spite of their utility, they fail to consider the way individuals construe these activities and the subjective meanings that they associate with them. Researchers typically assume that specific activities have a common meaning or are defined as leisure by everyone in the study. However, activities that constitute leisure are likely to differ by culture and subculture, gender, age, and perhaps even personality. Also, the same individual may view an activity to be leisure on one occasion and something else on a second occasion. Knowing what the people being studied personally define as leisure, rather than relying on researcher-imposed judgments, may in some circumstances provide a more sensitive approach to measuring the quantity and quality of leisure experienced.

This ability may be particularly important when researchers are interested in understanding individual behavior and how involvement in the same activities and settings can have a different impact on various individuals, their quality of life, well-being, work, and so on. For example, Stebbins (1983) defined the activities involved in being an amateur magician as a type of leisure ("serious leisure")—an external vantage point perspective. However, his observations and interviews with practitioners of this leisure activity made it clear that the participants sometimes experienced their activities as very work-like when rehearsing and practicing, having to perform when ill, or, when the time pressures from other domains of their lives were heavy. However, at other times, particularly during a good performance, the activity was described as leisure at its best.

As we will see, the ability to determine whether people see the activity and setting in which they are involved as leisure (with its various meanings) is an integral part of qualitative research and a variety of direct observation methods. However, researchers have experimented with behavioral inventories to allow the assessment of leisure behavior from the internal definitional vantage point of the participant. Researchers often allow respondents to identify and record activities that they perceive to be leisure, which are not included on the list provided by the researcher. Participants may also be asked to write in their most frequent, important, or favorite leisure activities.

Time Budgets and Diaries: Only So Much Free Time in a Week

The measurement of leisure time could be done by following people around with a stopwatch and recording the amount of time they spend involved in

Mass Media	Cultural Events
Watching TV	Attending concerts, singing, etc.
Reading newspapers or magazines	Attending ballet, opera, dance
Going to movies	Visiting art museums
	Folk or square dancing
	Attending theater
Sports Activities	**Outdoor Activities**
Spectating at sports events	Picnicking
Fitness activities (e.g., jog, swim)	Fishing, hunting
Team sports (e.g., softball, soccer)	Gardening
Individual sports (e.g., golf, fencing)	Day outings (e.g., zoo, museums)
Dual sports (e.g., tennis, squash)	Hiking
	Boating
	Nature study
	Camping
Social Activities	**Hobbies**
Visiting friends	Painting, drawing, sketching
Entertaining friends	Woodwork, furniture refinishing
Dating	Collecting (e.g., stamps, coins)
Attending parties	Needlework, sewing, knitting
Social dancing	Floral arranging, plant care
Indoor game parties	Weaving, pottery, sculpture
	Photography, movie-making

Figure 3.6 Example of Grouping of Leisure Activities into Larger Categories (adapted from Ragheb, 1980)

leisure activities and settings. Perhaps a trench coat and dark sunglasses would be useful as well! This method would be similar to "time-and-motion studies" done in industrial settings where the amount of time spent on various tasks by workers is studied by direct observation (Robbins, Bergman, Stagg, & Coulter, 2003). However, this approach would be time-consuming and rather intrusive. Instead, researchers have asked people on survey questionnaires to estimate how much time they spend engaged in leisure during a specified period of time, for example, the past day, month, or year. More typically, researchers have people record in a diary the sequence and duration of the activities in which they engage over a specified period, most typically the 24-hour day. This time-diary or time-budget approach allows the researcher to estimate the amount of time that the participant spends in various daily activities including leisure (Zuzanek & Box, 1988). Other researchers (e.g., Moss & Lawton, 1982; Zuzanek, 2005) have collected time-use data by asking respondents to recount the activities and time duration of involvement from the previous day. In a study reported by Zuzanek and Smale (1992), this information was collected in a telephone interview. Again, the definition of what is leisure is typically determined by the researcher. Consequently, the time-diary or budget approach has primarily involved the use of an external definitional vantage point and leisure is measured as a behavior, that is, as an objective phenomenon. This is the *behavioral-observer* approach (see Figure 3.1, p. 58).

Time-budget studies have been used since the 1920s, though wider use has been made of them during the past 40 years (Mannell, 2003). They have been used to examine how much time people in different segments of society and at different life cycle stages spend at paid work, leisure, housework, and family obligations; how these patterns change from workdays to weekends, and, more recently, how time-use effects the experience of time pressure, stress, and health (e.g., Michelson, 1999; Robinson, 1977; Short, 2005; Szalai, 1972; Zuzanek, 1980).

In its simplest form, the time diary requires participants to record the main activities in which they engage during the course of the day and when they engage in these activities (see Figure 3.7, p. 78). Other types of information may also be requested (e.g., if doing two things at once, indication of the secondary activity, where the activity was done, and with whom). Following the completion of the study, the researcher then sums up the time spent in various types of activities to measure the amount and proportion of time the participants spent in these activities during their daily lives. Typically, respondents carry the diaries for one or two weekdays and one weekend day. The entries can be weighted to provide time-use estimates for a complete week of 168 hours. Sometimes a typical weekday and weekend day are described from

Day Filled Out: Mon   Tue   Wed   Thur   Fri   Sat   Sun

Date: _____

Evening: page 3

What was the main thing you were doing?	Time began	What else were you doing?	Where?	With whom?
	6:10			
	6:20			
	6:30			
	6:40			
	6:50			
	7:00			
	7:10			
	7:20			
	7:30			
	7:40			
	7:50			
	8:00			
	8:10			
	8:20			
	8:30			

Figure 3.7 Example of a Time Diary Page

the data. An extensive activity-classification scheme that continues to be influential was developed by an international group of researchers for use in analyzing large time-budget studies (Szalai, 1972). This type of time-budget classification scheme is typically based on distinctions between economically motivated behavior (e.g., work for pay), biologically or physiologically determined behavior (e.g., sleep, eating, personal hygiene), and family role-oriented and house maintenance activities (e.g., childcare, house chores). Leisure is sometimes defined as the time left over but typical leisure activities are also described in this scheme (e.g., sport, television viewing, religious activities).

Traditional time-budget study using a behavioral-observer approach
The use of time-budget data to examine leisure defined as an objective phenomenon and from an external definitional vantage point is illustrated by a study reported by Zuzanek and Smale (1992) on the "rhythms of the week." From this study, we also can see how time-budget research can provide a detailed picture of how people structure their time and daily lives and how leisure fits with the rest of life. The researchers were interested in how time spent engaged in leisure and other activities varied across the days of the week. They also wanted to know how participation time in these activities was influenced by being employed, married, or having small children, and if this impact differed for men and women. Data for these analyses came from a national study carried out by the Canadian government in 1986. The time-budget data were collected over the telephone. A total of 9,946 households all over Canada were randomly dialed by a computer, and individuals 15 years of age and older who answered were interviewed. In addition to demographic characteristics, the respondents provided information on their time use for a 24-hour period encompassing a randomly selected day from the previous week. They reported the primary activity in which they were involved, the total duration of each activity in minutes, where the activity took place, and with whom they were involved. This information was recorded on a time-diary form by the interviewer. Activities identified by the respondents were classified into 1 of 99 activity types. Zuzanek and Smale then grouped these activities into the general categories of work, domestic activities, childcare, personal care, and leisure. They also specifically examined the leisure activities of dining out and television viewing. The amount of time in minutes each respondent spent engaged in these types of activities was calculated.

For the sample as a whole, the researchers found time spent in leisure activities was relatively similar from Monday to Thursday, then, as would be expected, increased on Friday and was highest on Saturday and Sunday. Saturdays and Sundays differed substantially, however. Saturdays were days of domestic work and shopping as much as they were days of leisure.

Much of Saturday's leisure was taken up with outings. In comparison, Sundays were days of sleep, rest, family contacts, childcare, and mostly passive leisure. For men, this meant watching television.

Employed mothers seem to be the major losers when it comes to leisure, particularly on Sundays. When time at paid work, domestic work, and childcare were added together, employed mothers with small children reported 2 to 2.5 hours greater workloads, a half-hour less sleep, and 1 to 2 hours less leisure compared to mothers at home on workdays. This difference decreased on Saturdays, but increased again on Sundays, when employed mothers reported 1.5 hours higher overall workloads, and 2 hours less leisure time than mothers at home. When employed mothers were compared with employed fathers, workloads balanced out on workdays. However, they had about a half-hour less leisure per workday. This difference was amplified on the weekend days. Employed fathers reported workloads which are 1 to 1.5 hours lower than those reported by employed mothers, and their leisure exceeded that reported by employed mothers by 2 to 2.5 hours per weekend day. Employed mothers with small children were the only group who increased rather than reduced their domestic work and childcare on weekends relative to workdays. Employed women with small children appear to have less opportunity than other groups, including employed men with small children, for the break in a busy week that leisure provides. In other words, being employed, married, and having young children amplified the difference between the amount of leisure available to men and women.

Of course, it would be interesting to see if this difference remained if an internal definitional vantage point was adopted in defining leisure. It is possible that the women with small children in this study may have defined childcare on Sundays as leisure. For example, Bella (1989) has theorized that some of the time that women spend in role-related activities and caring for family members may be experienced as leisure. She argued that there are significant differences in the way men and women define leisure that are due to their different social roles.

Modified time budget using a behavorial-participant approach

Shaw (1984) introduced an innovative way of using the time-diary method to simultaneously measure leisure behavior, setting, and time from both external and internal definitional vantage points. In effect, with the use of a modified time-budget diary, she compared the results of behavioral-observer and behavioral-participant approaches by studying the amount of leisure time a group of 60 married couples had during the course of a normal week in their lives. These study participants filled out the time diary on a typical weekday and weekend day. After the completion of the time diaries, during a follow-up interview, her research participants were asked to classify all the activities they had listed in their diaries as "work," "leisure," "a mixture of work and leisure," or "neither work nor leisure." Though not a frequently used research approach, a few subsequent studies have added a column to the time diary respondents fill out. In this column, the respondents are asked to check one of the four categories used by Shaw to indicate their definition of the activities they are recording in their diaries (e.g., Mannell & Reid, 1996).

In Shaw's study, the activities recorded in the diaries were categorized using the 37 activity codes from the multinational time-budget study mentioned earlier (Szalai, 1972). Shaw then grouped these activities further into five main types: paid work, housework and household obligations, childcare, personal care, and leisure. In other words, leisure was defined from an external vantage point (*behavioral-observer* approach). However, Shaw was also able to define and measure leisure from the internal vantage point of her respondents (*behavioral-participant* approach). Not only was she able to compare the extent to which her respondents' internal perceptions corresponded to the external definitions used by time-budget researchers, but she was also able to determine if the people in her study encountered situations where they perceived externally defined "non-leisure" activities and settings as leisure.

In this study, Shaw found significant differences in the amount of leisure reported by her respondents when their internal psychological definitions of leisure were used compared to the use of the external activity definitions. Fourteen percent of the externally defined leisure activities were judged as something other than leisure. Studying and participation in religious, community, and cultural organizations were frequently not defined as leisure, and even active sports, reading the paper, and social events were not always defined as leisure. However, reading a book was defined as leisure 100% of the time. Interestingly, 35% of all work and obligated activities were actually defined as leisure. While paid work and home chores were rarely perceived to be leisure, activities such as eating, childcare, and gardening were rated as leisure quite frequently.

Shaw also found differences in what was seen as leisure by men and women. The men in her study were much more likely than the women to perceive externally defined obligated activities as leisure. Cooking, shopping, and childcare were defined as leisure more often by males. Shaw suggests that men feel less obligated and more freedom of choice with respect to these activities than do women. The women in the study perceived a few externally defined leisure activities, such as gardening and social events as leisure more often than men.

One final point that Shaw's study illustrates is the fact that the same individual can perceive the same activity differently at different times—an activity whether externally defined as leisure or non-leisure can be perceived as leisure on one occasion and non-leisure on another. For example, 22.1%

of the respondents perceived their paid work activities as leisure on one occasion and work on another. The same was found for home chores (37.5%), television (12%), cooking (69.1%), and childcare (85.3%).

The implications of using definitions of leisure based on the external or internal vantage point is nicely demonstrated in a follow-up analysis of her data (Shaw, 1985b). The 60 married couples studied were randomly selected from working- and middle-class areas of Halifax, Nova Scotia, Canada, with the criterion that the husband worked full-time. The women in the study were full-time employed, part-time, or not employed outside the home (33 employed, 27 housewives). The mean age of the respondents was 39.6 years; 19 couples had children over 18 years of age, 41 couples had at least 1 child at home, 21 couples had at least 1 preschool child. The paid employment engaged in by the men varied from unskilled blue collar to professional work. Over half the women were employed in clerical and sales occupations.

Given the assumption that having leisure is important to the quality of life, Shaw argued that it is important to determine if different groups in society have equal access to leisure, much as society is concerned about whether people have equal access to employment, education, and health services. In this analysis, she wanted to determine if the men and women in her study had access to equal amounts of leisure time. Additionally, Shaw was interested in the effects that employment status, time devoted to employment, and family workload had on the availability of leisure time. It should be noted that the research reported on gender differences in leisure-time use has and continues to typically define leisure from an external vantage point (e.g., Bittman, 1999; Blanke & Corneliben, 2005) and as we suggested earlier may be insensitive to what men and women see as leisure. However, Shaw's time-budget data allowed her to also define leisure activities and time from the internal vantage point of her respondents. Interestingly, these later studies show that time-use differences between men and women have not changed significantly.

In Shaw's study, when using their perceptions of leisure, no significant difference in the leisure time available to the men and women (men's mean= 6.37 hours, women's mean=6.02 hours) was found for weekdays. However, a highly significant difference between the leisure time available to men and women (men's mean=11.77 hours, women's mean=8.10 hours, a difference of 3.67 hours) was found on weekend days.

Female and male respondents who had high family workloads, as defined by the number and age of their children and spouses who worked longer hours, were found to have significantly less leisure time available. The impact was, however, much greater for women. For example, having a wife with a high workload decreased leisure time on a weekend day by 2.15 hours for men, whereas women having a husband with a high work load decreased leisure time by 4.88 hours. Also, husbands' work time was found to negatively impact on wives' leisure time during the week, but wives' work time did not impact on husband's leisure time during the week.

Interestingly, in spite of the fact that women and men do differ on the frequency with which they see various activities as leisure, both the *behavior-observer* and *behavior-participant* approaches to defining leisure demonstrated that women have inequitable access to leisure. Shaw's findings on female-male differences were very similar to those reported some years later in the study we examined by Zuzanek and Smale (1992) and these gender differences seem to be continuing into the 21st century (Kay, 2000). Recent time use analyses of younger and older adolescents suggest that these gender differences also exist in adolescence and become stronger as adolescents get older and are about to become young adults (Hilbrecht et al., 2008).

Experience Sampling Method: Leisure Experience in Everyday Life

A large portion of people's leisure behavior and experience are embedded within the everyday activities that make up their lives. As we have seen, time-budget or time-use research has the advantage of allowing leisure to be examined in the context of the other activities that comprise people's daily lives. Another related research method is the experiential sampling method, or ESM, that was developed to monitor not only what people do during their everyday lives but to measure the psychological states and experiences that accompany daily activity (Hektner, Schmidt, & Csikszentmihalyi, 2007; Larson & Csikszentmihalyi, 1983). This method is used to uncover the regularities in perceptions and feelings of happiness, self-awareness, concentration, and other characteristics of conscious experience in various settings, including work and leisure.

Typically, study participants carry electronic pagers or wear digital watches that provide a random signal seven to nine times throughout the day for a period of one week. At each signal (typically an audible beep), the respondents take out a booklet of brief questionnaires (experiential sampling forms, or ESF) and complete a series of open- and closed-ended items indicating their current activity, the social and physical context of their activity, and their psychological state (see Figure 3.8, pp. 84 and 85).

Though the ESF has been modified across studies, the types of variables and scales included have been fairly standard. The ESF includes items that require respondents to: write in the time of the pager signal and the time that they actually filled out the ESF (usually, the questionnaire data are dropped if too much time elapses between the signal and response); write down what they were thinking about at the time of the signal; record the main thing/activity they were doing; check on a list who they were with;

Experiential Sampling Form   Page 1 of 2

Date: _____ Time beeped: _____ am/pm Time filled out: _____

As You Were Beeped:

What were you thinking about? _____
_____

What was the main thing you were doing? _____
_____

Who were you with?   ☐ Spouse/Partner   ☐ Alone
                      ☐ Your Children   ☐ Other _____
                      ☐ Friends/Neighbors   _____

How well were you concentrating? _____
_____

Was it hard to concentrate? _____
_____

Were you in control of the situation? _____
_____

How much did you like what you were doing? _____
_____

Describe How You Felt As You Were Beeped:

	Very	Quite	Some	Neither/ Not Sure	Some	Quite	Very	
Alert	—	—	—	—	—	—	—	Drowsy
Happy	—	—	—	—	—	—	—	Sad
Irritable	—	—	—	—	—	—	—	Cheerful
Energetic	—	—	—	—	—	—	—	Tired
Upset	—	—	—	—	—	—	—	Calm
Active	—	—	—	—	—	—	—	Passive
Worried	—	—	—	—	—	—	—	Carefree
Excited	—	—	—	—	—	—	—	Bored
Confused	—	—	—	—	—	—	—	Clear
Relaxed	—	—	—	—	—	—	—	Harried
Good	—	—	—	—	—	—	—	Bad

Figure 3.8a Experiential Sampling Form (ESF) (adapted from Zuzanek & Mannell, 1993)

Experiential Sampling Form Page 2 of 2

0 1 2 3 4 5 6 7 8 9

Did you feel lonely when beeped?

— — — — — — — — — —

Not at all Maybe Very much

Challenges of the activity:

— — — — — — — — — —

Low High

Your skills, knowledge, or competence in the activity:

— — — — — — — — — —

Low High

Do you wish you had been doing something else?

— — — — — — — — — —

Not at all Maybe Very much

How free were you to choose this activity?

— — — — — — — — — —

Not at all Very much

Did you do it primarily: ☐ for your immediate enjoyment or pleasure
☐ because it was good for you
☐ for the benefit of others
☐ because you had to
☐ because there was nothing else to do

At this moment, would you feel like watching TV?

— — — — — — — — — —

Not at all Maybe Very much

Why/Why Not? _____

_____

★★★★★★★★★★★★★★★★★★★★★★★★★★★★★★

Great thoughts, wisecracks

Figure 3.8b Experiential Sampling Form (ESF) *(cont'd)* (adapted from Zuzanek & Mannell, 1993)

rate several items that measure the level of psychological involvement in the activity (e.g., level of concentration, personal skills and challenge, perception of the passage of time); rate mood states on semantic differential scales assessing affect and arousal; and indicate the reasons or motivations for participation. Some researchers have included additional scales or items on the ESF that require respondents to rate their feelings of self-esteem when signaled (Wells, 1988), the extent to which the activity was leisure for them (Samdahl, 1988), willingness to engage in alternative activities (Mannell & Zuzanek, 1991), and time pressure and stress (Hilbrecht et al., 2008).

The ESM has been used to address a number of leisure-related research questions. Studies have examined the intrinsic satisfactions resulting from participation in recreational compared to non-recreational activities (Graef, Csikszentmihalyi, & Gianinno, 1983), the meaning and quality of experiences derived from the leisure activities engaged in by adolescents (Kleiber, Caldwell, & Shaw, 1993; Kleiber, Larson, & Csikszentmihalyi, 1986; Larson, Gillman, & Richards, 1997; Suman, Deepali, & Larson, 2002; Mannell et al., 2005), leisure activities as a context for social relationships (Larson, Mannell, & Zuzanek, 1986), the influence of freedom of choice and intrinsic motivation on leisure experiences (Mannell, Zuzanek, & Larson, 1988; Samdahl, 1988), and the relationship between enduring involvement and flow in leisure and non-leisure activities (Havitz & Mannell, 2005).

In an early study of leisure using the ESM, Kleiber et al. (1986) collected data that allowed them to identify those leisure activities and settings in which adolescents experienced the most positive moods and became most psychologically involved. A sample of 75 male and female high school adolescents volunteered to participate in the study. Over the course of the study week, the students responded to 69% of the signals or beeps. The total number of self-reports or ESFs completed was 4,489.

The activities engaged in by the adolescents when they were signaled were determined by their response to the question: "What was the *MAIN* thing you were doing (as you were beeped)?" When analyzing this data, these responses were coded into 15 basic activity categories. The mood or affective properties of their experiences were measured by having them rate how happy/sad, irritable/cheerful, lonely/sociable, and angry/friendly they were feeling. These ratings were later combined by the researchers for an affect score. The involvement or flow dimension of the experience was measured by having the adolescents rate the level of concentration and challenge they experienced in the activity. The extent to which they perceived themselves free to participate in the activity and the extent to which they were motivated to participate by interest in the activity itself (intrinsic motivation) and not something else (extrinsic motivation) were measured on similar scales.

Figure 3.9 shows the frequency with which the adolescents were involved in the 15 basic types of activities over the course of a typical week in their lives. Figure 3.10 (p. 88) summarizes the average levels of freedom, affect, concentration, and challenge they experienced in the three major activity categories created by further classifying the 15 activities into production, maintenance, and leisure. As can be seen, those activities defined as leisure by the researchers were experienced as more positive and free. However, when considering the involvement indicators of concentration and challenge, a different picture emerges. Leisure activities had only slightly higher levels of concentration and perceived challenge than maintenance activities and considerably lower levels than productive activities. The researchers point out that these findings are consistent with the view that leisure is relaxing but it also suggests that the leisure activities of adolescents rarely require much in terms of effort and attention or what might be called psychological involvement or flow. If, as suggested by the researchers, activities that more frequently generate psychological involvement or flow do contribute to personal growth and development, then the typical leisure of adolescents should perhaps be a concern.

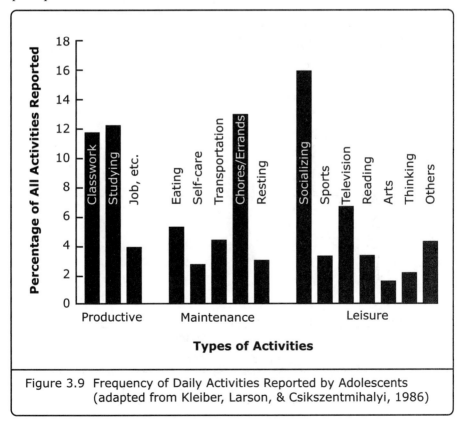

Figure 3.9 Frequency of Daily Activities Reported by Adolescents
(adapted from Kleiber, Larson, & Csikszentmihalyi, 1986)

However, it may not be as bad as it seems. When the researchers examined different types of leisure activities, they found evidence for two categories of leisure experience. One, *relaxed leisure*, was found in the leisure activities of socializing, watching television, reading, and listening to music, as well as the maintenance activities of eating and resting. The authors suggest that this type of leisure provides pleasure without high levels of involvement. The second category of leisure experience was associated with the set of activities that included sports, games, artwork, and hobbies. These activities were also experienced as freely chosen, intrinsically motivated, and very positive, yet also as *challenging and demanding of effort and concentration* rather than relaxing. These differences in the capacity of adolescents' leisure activities to produce psychologically involving experiences has been confirmed in subsequent ESM studies (Larson, 2005; Mannell et al., 2005), and the implications for leisure's role in the health and psychological development of adolescents are explored later in this book.

The experience sampling method is a useful technique to monitor the experiences accompanying activities that researchers judge to be leisure

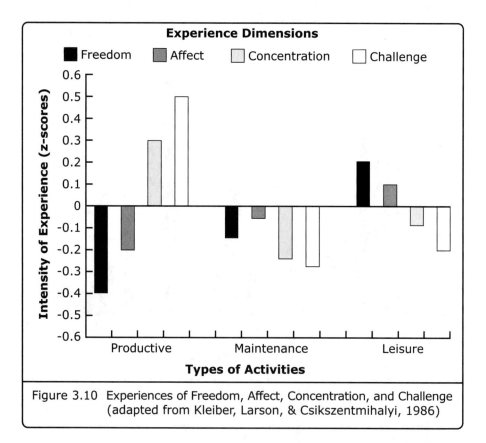

Figure 3.10 Experiences of Freedom, Affect, Concentration, and Challenge (adapted from Kleiber, Larson, & Csikszentmihalyi, 1986)

(e.g., sport, artwork, television viewing, socializing). Kleiber and his colleagues (1986) used an external definitional vantage point. They used both *behavioral-observer* and *experiential-observer* approaches to decide which activities and experiences were leisure for the adolescents in their study. In one of the few studies that has used the ESM with an internal definitional vantage approach to defining and operationalizing leisure, Samdahl (1988) examined the leisure experience of her study participants. She included items on the ESF that asked her respondents to rate on 7-point Likert scales (1 *"Strongly disagree"* to 7 *"Strongly agree"*) the extent to which they construed their activities as leisure. Similar to other ESM researchers, Samdahl used an ESF that also required her respondents to indicate their moods, perceptions of freedom or constraint, motivation, and so on.

The participants were 18 women and men from a variety of backgrounds, between the ages of 18 and 60, who volunteered to participate in the week-long study. These individuals completed 695 ESFs in response to the "beeps" emitted by the electronic pagers they carried. Samdahl was able to demonstrate that when people perceived that they had chosen to participate in an activity independently of the expectations of other people (low role constraint) and they felt that they were expressing their true selves (high self-expression), they were more likely to construe and rate the activity or situation as "leisure" and experience positive moods (see Figure 3.11, p. 90).

Naturalistic Observation: Leisure in Its Natural Habitat

Probably the most obvious method to use in studying leisure is the way most people gather information every day of their lives. In other words, if one wants to know about an individual's leisure, why not just go "where it's happening" and watch it happen? A growing number of researchers are doing just that. Rather than examining the full range of people's leisure activities, these types of studies have typically focused on the individual's involvement in specific leisure activities. This trend is due to the greater interest researchers are showing in how people become involved in or are recruited into leisure activities, why they drop out or remain involved, why some people develop an ongoing, career-like commitment to the activity, and the ways in which involvement in the activity impacts other areas of people's lives, and their health and well-being.

Direct observation may take the form of in-depth interviews, participant observation, case studies, or some combination of these methods. These approaches are often termed "field research" (Creswell, 2009). In a sense, social psychologists do field research whenever they observe or participate in ongoing social situations and try to understand the behavior they observe, whether in a leisure setting or some other setting. Information collected through direct observation can be quantitative or qualitative. Quantitative leisure data resulting from direct observation would be converted into numerical form, such as the number of activities participated in, the frequency of participation in an activity, or the observable consequences of participation. Few such studies have been reported. The earlier discussed studies by Stoep and Gramann (1987) on young hikers in a park and Gueguen et al. (2008) on nonverbal communication in a bar would be examples, as is a study by Dumas and Laforest (2009). These latter researchers carried out an observational study in 11 public skate parks involving 388 days of observation. They observed the frequency of injuries and the types of social and physical interactions among the youth who were engaging in skateboarding.

However, most of the leisure research using direct or participant observation has been qualitative. This qualitative field research produces data that are not reduced to numbers. Written notes are made by the researcher describing what the people being observed are doing or saying. The basic tools of field research are a notebook or field journal and a pencil. If possible, qualitative researchers take notes as they are observing. When this is not feasible, notes are written as soon as possible afterward. Notes typically include both empirical observations and interpretations of them. In other words, researchers record what they "know" has happened as well as what they "think" has happened. In field research, it is also appropriate for the researcher to take a more active role than passive observer; consequently, the researcher may question or interview the people being studied. Researchers' notes may also consist of a record of these unstructured interviews, including the questions and responses.

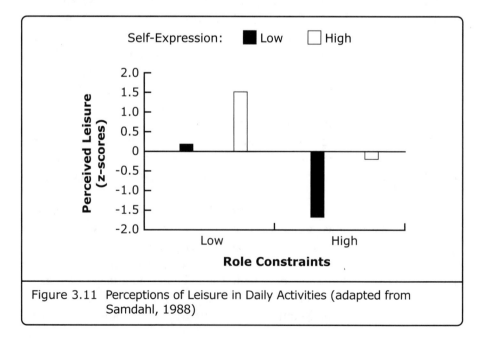

Figure 3.11 Perceptions of Leisure in Daily Activities (adapted from Samdahl, 1988)

Robert Stebbins has used direct observation in many studies of people engaging in leisure, particularly to explore and develop his theory of *serious leisure*, a topic we take up at length in the next chapter. He has studied participants in various types of sport (baseball, football), art (music, theater), variety art (magic, stand-up comedy), science activities (archaeology, astronomy), and hobbies (barbershop singing) (see Stebbins, 1992a, 1992b, 1992c, 2001a). In so doing, Stebbins has taken an external definitional vantage point in defining what constitutes serious leisure. The various activities he has labeled serious leisure and chosen to study may or may not be perceived as leisure by the participants. He also recognizes that the participants likely do not see their participation in these activities as leisure all the time (1992a, pp. 3–6).

Stebbins' (1993) research on amateur magicians provides a good example of the direct observation approach. Thirty amateur magicians ranging in age from 16 to 73, and living in Calgary, Alberta, Canada, were observed over a 1-year period. The study participants were interviewed but only after approximately eight months of participant observation of all social aspects of the practice of magic, which included performances, monthly gatherings, and executive committee meetings of an amateur magicians' association, its annual banquet, a festival, television taping sessions, and informal gatherings of magicians whenever these occurred. He also used unstructured interviews to gain further insights into the participants' behavior and experience. The participant observations and interviews provided a rich and detailed picture of what amateur magicians do, the various settings in which they pursue their activity, and the amount of time they invest in the activity. In addition to developing an understanding of the nature of this leisure activity, Stebbins was able to gather information about how the participants became interested in and committed to regular participation. He was also able to determine the psychological rewards and costs of participation, as well as the impact of this type of leisure involvement on their other leisure involvements, and the work and family domains of their lives (Stebbins, 1992a, p. 17).

The strength of direct observation lies in the ability of the researcher to provide rich detail about all aspects of the activity under study. Also, direct observation, like the time diary and ESM, gives researchers a sense of how these activities are embedded in the contexts of daily life and other activities. Another advantage of direct observation is related to the opportunity that it affords the researcher to develop an understanding of what these activities mean to the participant (Creswell, 2009) and to determine if they are, in fact, leisure from the internal vantage point of the individual.

With direct observation, the researcher is able to study only a relatively small number of individuals, who are typically not randomly selected. Therefore, care must be taken in generalizing the research findings to other individuals or groups. Also, in-depth, direct observation can be extremely time-consuming for the researcher and field research observations are very personal. Consequently, they can be difficult for other researchers to confirm or replicate. A variety of strategies are available to help field researchers using direct observation assess the reliability of their observations (Creswell, 2009). These limitations or challenges are well-recognized among those researchers using direct observation and are more than made up for by the detailed descriptive information obtained on the activities and how they are connected to other aspects of the participants' lives. As Stebbins and many other researchers using qualitative approaches have suggested, direct observation provides an excellent opportunity to explore new issues and develop new ideas and theory that can guide future research.

Interviews: Dialogues on Leisure Behavior and Experience

As Stebbins did in his research on serious leisure, researchers often use interviews when they are directly observing people to gain further insights into their behavior and experience. For example, Fine (1983, 1987), in two well-known studies, observed and interviewed young male adults engaged in role-playing games and boys who played little league baseball. Although observational studies have been relatively rare in the study of leisure, leisure researchers are increasingly using interviews, particularly semi-structured interviews, to explore and develop an understanding of some aspect of people's leisure. For example, studies have been reported examining mothers' roles in developing their daughters' leisure attitudes, values, and behaviors (Shannon & Shaw, 2008), amateur artists who become volunteers in leading an art organization and develop it as a serious leisure career (Bendle & Patterson, 2009), adolescents' views of playfulness as a personality characteristic (Staempfli, 2007), the influence of discrimination against American Muslims after September 11, 2001 on their leisure behavior (Livengood & Stodolska, 2004), the factors that influence the social and psychological costs and benefits of being involved in a community garden group (Glover, 2004), and traveling retirees' perceptions of tourism and travel and the place of tourism in retirement (Nimrod, 2008c).

The semi-structured interview is typically used in qualitative research and lends itself to understanding leisure behavior and experience from the perspective of the individual. In other words, leisure is defined from an internal definitional vantage point. While a structured interview has a formalized limited set of questions, a semi-structured interview is flexible, allowing new questions to be introduced during the interview in response to the dialogue with the person being interviewed. The researcher in a semi-structured interview generally explores a variety of interrelated themes. The specific topics explored during the interview are thought out in advance and usually an interview guide is prepared, which is an informal "grouping of topics and

questions that the interviewer can ask in different ways for different participants" (Lindlof & Taylor, 2002, p. 195). This flexibility helps the researcher
adapt the questions to the responses of the people being interviewed (Creswell,
2009). For example, in a study of women's leisure within heterosexual
romantic relationships (Herridge et al., 2003), questions such as the following were included in the interview guide: "How do you typically spend your
leisure time?" "How much leisure time do you spend with your partner?" "How
do the two of you decide how you are going to spend your leisure time
together?" "How does your partner spend his leisure time?" "How do you
feel about how you spend your leisure time?" The interview guide was pilot
tested for the usefulness of the questions and their wording with women not
involved in the final study. However, some researchers use interviews that
are not even this structured. For example, in Glover's (2004) community
garden study, he gave only one initial prompt, "Tell me the story of your
community garden," and the study participants led the "conversations." He
interrupted only periodically to help clarify or probe deeper for greater detail
and let the participants reply in the form of long stories.

In terms of the use of this type of research methodology for defining
leisure and leisure-related concepts, all four types of definitions and approaches
to observation can be found, although the use of interviews to establish an
internal vantage point is common. For example, Gunter (1987) asked university students to describe both their most memorable and typical leisure
experiences—an *experiential-participant* approach. He then analyzed these
stories to discover if the leisure experiences that stood out in their minds
shared a common set of characteristics or attributes. The most common
attributes were: a sense of *separation* from the everyday world; *freedom of
choice* in one's actions; a feeling of pleasure, or *pleasurable involvement* in
an event; *spontaneity*; *timelessness*; *fantasy* (creative imagination); a sense
of *adventure* and *exploration*; and *self-realization*.

The importance of taking individual definitions of leisure into account
(internal vantage point) and looking at the factors that influence whether
something is construed as leisure is nicely demonstrated in an interview
study reported by Henderson (1990). She carried out 1- to 3-hour life-history
interviews with women who were 60 or more years old and had lived on a
farm for the majority of their married lives. The interviews were carried out
in the participants' homes, and they were asked to reflect on their total lives.
Henderson was interested in understanding the types of activities and the
social and physical settings that were seen by this group of women as leisure,
as well as how changes over the lifespan affect these perceptions. She found
that these women, who had worked hard all their lives, typically found leisure-like experiences in their work and family obligations, even though they
saw themselves as having had little or no leisure. At first glance, an outside

observer may not have judged their involvements to be leisure. However, the women had found opportunities to experience freedom of choice, enjoyment and satisfaction in a variety of activities, social settings, and physical locations—what Henderson called *"containers for leisure."* For example, many family obligations and community activities with other women had elements of leisure for the study participants, even though they involved work-like activities. The home was also found to be a primary location or container for leisure.

Conclusion

Sometimes it is difficult to get excited about definitions of concepts and research methods when we just want to know the facts and get explanations about an area of human behavior like leisure about which we are curious. Hopefully, this chapter has demonstrated that the ways in which we define and study leisure are intimately tied to the ways in which we come to understand leisure. Social psychological knowledge about people's leisure is not static. It is continually being challenged, modified, and expanded by researchers. It is important that we appreciate where this knowledge comes from and can critically evaluate it on the basis of our own experience and knowledge of how researchers work. Studying leisure with social psychology is an exciting enterprise, as will become apparent in the following chapters, where a wide variety of issues are discussed and explored.

As we have seen, one way the definitions, observations, and measures used by researchers to study people's leisure can be understood is according to whether they are based on external, socially derived views of what constitutes leisure or the internal vantage point of the participant. Social psychologists studying all types of behavior and experience attach great importance to how individuals perceive or construe their own behavior, the behavior of others, and the situations in which they find themselves. Advances have been made in modifying traditional measures of leisure to allow researchers to assess what people construe as leisure. Survey research using behavior inventories and time diaries have dominated leisure research in the past, leading leisure to be defined by activities, settings, and time. These approaches also focus on people's leisure style, that is, the full range of leisure activities in which people engage. There has been a growth in studies of single specific activities, and a corresponding growth in the number of studies reported using direct observation and interview methods. Researchers using behavior inventories and time-diary methods have also typically used external definitions of what constitutes a leisure activity or setting. However, some innovative approaches have been developed to assess whether the individuals being studied are in agreement with researcher definitions and construe the activities, settings, or time periods in which they are involved as "leisure." Surveys with behavior inventories can be designed to allow respondents to identify and record activities that they perceive as leisure that are not included on the list provided by the researcher. The time-diary method can also be used to simultaneously measure leisure behavior, settings, and time from both external and internal definitional vantage points.

This measurement capability is important because the activities that constitute leisure for various groups of people are likely to show cultural and subcultural, gender, age, and possibly attitudinal and personality differences. And the same individual may view an activity to be leisure on one occasion and something else on a second occasion. Knowing what the people being studied personally define as leisure, rather than relying on researcher-imposed judgments, provides a more sensitive approach in some cases for assessing the quantity and quality of leisure experienced and may better allow researchers to establish the relationship between leisure and other aspects of people's lives, such as mental health, quality of life, work, successful retirement, and so forth.

In this chapter, objective and subjective approaches to the definition, observation, and measurement of leisure from both external and internal vantage points have also been illustrated and discussed. Social scientists in general are making increasing use of interviews, direct observation, case studies, logs, diaries, and the experience sampling method. This trend is certainly the case in the study of leisure. A growing amount of research using a wide variety of research methods has been focused on understanding the nature of leisure experiences in people's daily lives.

The importance of understanding leisure from the perspective of the individual leisure participant is not lost on leisure service professionals. They cannot structure, "engineer," or provide leisure experiences directly. As a practitioner, one is limited to fostering, encouraging, and facilitating meaningful leisure experiences through the management of the recreation environment and setting, and the provision of concrete activities and opportunities. Leisure service providers can also help people develop the skills and attitudes necessary to allow them to take advantage of these opportunities. Hopefully, the social psychological research reviewed in this book will help leisure service professionals understand the personal and social situational factors that not only affect the quality of leisure experiences but the links between the objective environments they manage and the way they are construed and perceived by the individual participant.

We have reached the end of our discussion of the principal types of methods used by researchers studying the social psychological dimensions of leisure. As you explore the ideas you will encounter in subsequent chapters, look for how leisure is being defined and the types of observations and measures researchers are using. The difficulties of defining leisure, as well as deciding how to observe and often measure it, have long been held up as the major challenges and impediments to progress in the study of leisure. Some still feel that leisure researchers have made little progress. However, as we have seen, it no longer seems justified to criticize the field of leisure studies for a lack of advancement in conceptualizing, observing, and measuring leisure; new methods and approaches will undoubtedly be proposed.

For example, a special issue of the *Journal of Leisure Research* edited by Stewart and Floyd (2004) focused on the use of visual approaches (e.g., photographs, photographing, and drawing) to gather information and gain fresh insights into leisure behavior and experience. They pointed out that visual imagery has had a long but understated history in leisure research. Photographs have been frequently used to measure the scenic quality and visual attraction of leisure and tourism environments and visual images have been useful in studying visitor perceptions of the social and physical dimensions of these environments. Researchers have explored the influence of photographs on memories of tourist experiences. Photography also has provided a way of studying children's leisure and their use of leisure environments. Photo-elicitation research, that is, photographs taken by study participants themselves, have been used to stimulate conversations or stories about their experiences and perceptions of leisure environments and activities as they attempt to make sense out of what they have captured.

Drawings, as a type of visual image, are more removed from reality and have been seen as having the potential to allow people to express their perceptions, feelings, and the meanings they associate with leisure. In her study of children from various cultural backgrounds participating in an international camping program, Yuen (2004) employed self-directed drawings as a way for children to communicate aspects of their leisure experiences. Yuen argues that such drawings evoke more details about children's experiences than children not using drawings. She also suggested that the uniqueness of each child's drawing is matched by distinctive stories told by each child.

There also are leisure researchers who argue that in addition to the use of new methods to help generate insights into leisure behavior and experience, the use of stories, poems, and other expressive forms may be better or at least additional ways of communicating findings to enhance research's impact on leisure policy and practice (Parry & Johnson, 2007). Parry and Johnson go on to suggest that an increasing number of researchers desire to be systematic in studying people's behavior and experience, but at the same time more literary in the expression of the findings of such research, with the use of evocative writing techniques and other forms of creative expression. For example, Dupuis and her colleagues have carried out highly rigorous research on the experience of having a family member with Alzheimer's disease and the impact on leisure and leisure's role in dealing with this traumatic event. Their findings have been published in scientific research journals (e.g., Dupuis & Smale, 2000) and have also contributed to the creation of a theatrical play called "I'm Still Here" that is used to help families cope and practitioners work more effectively with people who have Alzheimer's to maintain the quality of their leisure and life. Doing leisure research can be an exciting enterprise!

Leisure Experience

Preview

Chapter 3 has given us both a variety of leisure definitions and meanings and different ways to study them. What we do in this chapter—preferring a somewhat more subjective perspective—is identify some of the *experiences* most commonly associated with leisure. But because we need a starting point, we will define leisure for this purpose as a distinguishable *context* of relative freedom wherein preferred immediate experience has priority over instrumental outcomes. If this sounds suspiciously like free time, it is, in a sense. But as was suggested in the previous chapter, "free" should not simply be equated with choice or the lack of obligation but rather with the absence of worry and with a sense of opportunity and possibility. When time is really felt as free, when it is distinguishable from other blocks of time taken up by obligatory or necessary actions, the meaning of leisure as a context can be understood. The question we will attend to here, then, is this: what are the experiences that are sought in that context? We are thus taking an external vantage point in defining leisure the way we do for this chapter, but we emphasize subjective meanings to bring leisure fully to life here, and will rely to a great extent on internal vantage points in identifying and describing those experiences.

So what is leisure to you, experientially? We asked you to help us define it in the last chapter, but if you go along with our working definition for this chapter, what is it you *feel* and *think* when you are doing just what you want to do in your free time?

Seeing leisure simply as the *context for* the variety of experiences that occur during free time allows us to define things more clearly for purposes of both research and practice. But is there nothing to say about the feeling of leisure per se, the emotion that is experienced when leisure is recognized as being at hand, as it is apprehended? Recall the point that time available may be beset with emotional difficulties and may even be a burden to those without the resources to act effectively. Perhaps the experience of freedom that one feels at the onset of a leisure episode—whether pausing to rock on the porch or putting the hang-gliding equipment in the van—continues to be felt over the duration of the activity that is recognized, at least in retrospect, as an opportunity for gratifying experience.

In this chapter, we will consider such experiences as excitement, flow, and relaxation as being among those most commonly sought in and through leisure, and we will examine how they are incorporated into activities that come to be taken more and more seriously. We then recognize that leisure and recreation are experienced more broadly in the context of people's lives and generally incorporate points of attention to past and future time perspectives. Finally, we introduce the concept of *savoring,* which utilizes self-awareness to add depth to a leisure experience. But let us begin with the properties that define experience in general.

Properties of *All* Leisure Experiences

Jessica has just had a "learning experience." She was looking forward—with some trepidation—to her trip to the remote part of the province, having been invited by her friend, Bree, and her family to join them. Jessica had never been camping and in fact was a bit afraid of the idea of "wilderness." But she was very close with Bree and was willing to embrace the "adventure" of it. A struggle with climbing the first day and putting up the tent that night, with little sleep to follow, didn't do much to make her more comfortable. Kayaking was also on the agenda for the next day and she was really worried about that. However, things improved and she began to like it all and even picked up the kayaking skills to the point that she found herself getting lost in the moment and feeling refreshed as a result. She was even able to offer a few tips to Bree's younger brother after a while. Jessica also liked the family's practice of allowing each the personal space and time alone for reading or whatever. She found a rock near a stream that was a perfect place for sitting quietly and letting her mind wander. But there were still moments when she was ready for the trip to be over. The prospect of encountering wild animals—however unlikely—was not appealing to her and some of the rafting parties that came through were very rowdy and even a bit obnoxious toward Bree and her. But now, days after returning, she was mostly feeling very good about herself, having "survived" the adventure and remembering fondly some of the fun with the family, the kick she got out of mastering the kayak and, of course, her special rock.

Jessica's story here is not unusual. Most leisure episodes or encounters involve a range of feelings and cognitions, the essence of experience. Leisure experiences, whether occurring in settings simulated, virtual or real, authentic or artificial, have come to be seen perhaps not only as important but as the primary aspects of leisure and recreational behavior. Many researchers believe that to understand the impact of leisure on health, well-being, and other domains of daily life, they not only need to be able to assess what people do in and as their leisure but also what they are experiencing while they do it and then how they make sense of, or construe, the experience.

Immediate conscious experience is the experience of the present moment. The metaphor "stream of consciousness" used by William James (1890) aptly describes mental experience and suggests that conscious states are perceived as both continuous and constantly changing. The stream of consciousness can be described as "the flow of perceptions, purposeful thoughts, fragmentary images, distant recollections, bodily sensations, emotions, plans, wishes, and impossible fantasies . . . . [it] is our experience of life, our own personal life, from its beginning to its end" (Pope & Singer, 1978, p. 1).

A number of properties have been proposed by theorists and researchers as important features to measure when studying the experiences accompanying leisure engagements. In Table 4.1, these properties have been listed and described. Also, studies in which these properties have been examined and the types of research methods used are noted. Moods that reflect positive and negative feelings or emotions have been most frequently measured when studying the experiences accompanying leisure. The levels of intensity, relaxation, arousal, or activation felt by the individual have also been assessed. Only a few studies have actually attempted to assess the cognitive components of the experience, that is, what people are actually thinking or imagining, when engaged in leisure. These include the experience sampling method studies referred to in Chapter 3 (e.g., Csikszentmihalyi & Larson, 1982; Mannell, 1993; Mannell et al., 1988; Samdahl, 1992) as well as studies of changing moods in recreation experiences (e.g., Borrie & Roggenbuck, 2001). In addition to these basic emotional and cognitive features of conscious experience, other properties that have been suggested or studied include perceptions of how quickly time is passing and how self-conscious or self-aware people are when engaged in a leisure activity or setting. Also, the levels of absorption or concentration, feelings of competence, interpersonal relatedness, and sense of freedom experienced have been measured. Finally, intrinsic motivation, to which we turn in more depth in the following two chapters, has also been measured in experience sampling studies of leisure.

Good and Optimal Leisure Experiences

By observing and measuring those properties of leisure experience, one can begin to get an idea of the quality of the experiences people have while in various leisure settings and while engaged in various leisure activities. Ideally, this may allow participants, or those providing leisure services, to make leisure experiences even better. Good leisure experiences may better contribute to well-being and happiness. However, this raises a rather important question: "What *is* a good leisure experience?" Is it characterized by more positive moods, greater intensity, a relaxed feeling, the experience of time going quickly or slowly, greater absorption, lesser or greater self-consciousness, or something else?

The best tourist experiences have been characterized as having special qualities. For example, the ultimate travel experience has been compared to a religious experience and to be the result of pilgrimage, where the tourist

Table 4.1   Immediate Conscious Experience Approach: Properties of Leisure Experiences and Examples of Research

Property	Description	Studies & Techniques
Emotions, moods	Affective component of experience, typically seen to vary along a positive-negative dimension, though research suggests that there may be independent positive and negative dimensions to our experiences (e.g., affection, elation vs. anxiety, sadness).	**On-site survey:** Hammitt (1980); Hull, William & Young (1992); Hull & Michael (1995); Hull, Michael, Walker & Roggenbuck (1996); Jones (2008); McIntyre & Roggenbuck (1998); More & Payne (1978) **Laboratory:** Mannell (1979); Mannell & Bradley (1986) **ESM:** Chalip, Csikszentmihalyi, Kleiber & Larson (1984); Csikszentmihalyi & LeFevre (1989); Delespaul, Reis & DeVries (2004); Ellis, Voelkl & Morris (1994); Evans & Haworth (1991); Havitz, Morden & Samdahl (2004); Kleiber, Larson & Csikszentmihalyi (1986); Mannell, Zuzanek & Larson (1988); Samdahl (1988, 1991, 1992) **Qualitative:** Lee, Dattilo & Howard (1994)
Arousal, activation, relaxation	Feelings of mental and physical activation or arousal seen to vary in intensity (e.g., alert-drowsy, active-passive, energetic-tired, excited-bored).	**On-site survey:** Hammitt (1980); Hull, Michael, Walker & Roggenbuck (1996); McIntyre & Roggenbuck (1998); More & Payne (1978) **ESM:** Delespaul, Reis & DeVries (2004); Graef, Csikszentmihalyi & Gianinno (1983); Mannell, Zuzanek & Larson (1988); Zuzanek & Mannell (1993a, 1993b) **Qualitative:** Lee, Dattilo & Howard (1994)
Cognitions	Ideas, beliefs, thoughts, and images.	**On-site survey:** Jones (2008); Stewart (1992) **ESM:** Borrie & Roggenbuck (2001); Csikszentmihalyi & LeFevre (1989); Larson, Mannell & Zuzanek (1986) **Qualitative:** Lee, Dattilo & Howard (1994)
Time duration	Characteristic of involvement in an activity. Perception of how much time has passed during participation in an activity or context. The perception may or may not correspond to the actual amount of clock time that has passed. The more involved the faster time is perceived as passing.	**Laboratory:** Mannell (1979); Mannell & Bradley (1986) **ESM:** Ramos & Folkers (1994)

Table 4.1 Immediate Conscious Experience Approach: Properties of Leisure Experiences and Examples of Research (cont'd)

Property	Description	Studies & Techniques
Concentration, focus of attention, absorption	A characteristic of involvement in an activity. The more involved and more absorbed, the narrower the focus of attention, the higher the level of concentration and the less aware the participant is of anything else than the activity engaged in.	*On-site survey:* Hammitt (1980) *Laboratory:* Mannell (1979); Mannell & Bradley (1986) *ESM:* Kleiber, Caldwell & Shaw (1993); Kleiber, Larson & Csikszentmihalyi (1986); Mannell, Zuzanek & Larson (1988)
Self-consciousness, self-awareness, ego-loss	A characteristic of involvement. More involved, less self-concious, and self-aware the participant. Ego-loss is the loss of awareness of one's sense of self when highly involved in an activity or context.	*ESM:* Samdahl & Kleiber (1989); Samdahl (1991)
Sense of competence	Feeling of the participant that they are knowledgeable or skilled in the activity.	*ESM:* Csikszentmihalyi & Larson (1984); Csikszentmihalyi & LeFevre (1989); Ellis, Voelkl & Morris (1994); Graef, Csikszentmihalyi & Giainno (1983); Mannell, Zuzanek & Larson (1988) *On-site survey:* McIntyre & Roggenbuck (1998); Priest (1992)
Sense of freedom	The feeling of freedom that may accompany participation in an activity or event.	*On-site survey:* Hull, Michael, Walker & Roggenbuck (1996) *ESM:* Csikszentmihalyi & Graef (1980); Kleiber, Caldwell & Shaw (1993); Kleiber, Larson & Csikszentmihalyi (1986)
Sense of interpersonal relatedness	Perception that an activity or context will lead to the enhancement of relationships between participants.	*On-site survey:* McIntyre & Roggenbuck (1998) *ESM:* Borrie & Roggenbuck (2001); Delespaul, Reis & DeVries (2004); Havitz, Morden & Samdahl (2004); Walker & Wang (2009)

searches for something less tangible than the trip itself and more rewarding than just being there (Cohen, 1979a). The search for this ultimate tourist experience has also been described as a quest. MacCannell (1976) referred to it as a quest for authentic experiences; Cohen (1979b) called it a quest for center; Meyersohn (1981) suggested it is a quest for meaning; and Przeclawski (1985) considered it a quest for values. Stebbins (2005, p. 79) has more recently described such experiences as *epics*, meaning harrowing experiences of heroic proportions that a recreationist finds unpleasant at the time (sometimes because of a serious injury), but that takes on great import afterwards. Not unlike de Grazia, Cohen (1979a, p. 194) suggested that these more profound modes of experience are hard to realize for all but a select few.

Considering such elite and exotic experiences to be "good" may stretch our sense of good leisure experiences too far, but most people would probably be comfortable with the idea that a higher quality leisure experience would be associated with more positive and less negative moods. However, even here there is not complete agreement. For example, some leisure may be accompanied by negative moods at the time of participation due to the difficult challenges, such as Stebbins suggested, the effort required, or other conditions in the setting, such as poor weather. But there seems to be general agreement that leisure is mostly experienced as pleasant in anticipation, in actualization and in recollection (Mannell, 1980; Stebbins, 1992a; Tinsley & Tinsley, 1986). It seems quite likely that good leisure experiences can take on many shapes and forms and that there is a need for researchers to explore leisure experiences and states based on a wide variety of properties and using a number of different measures.

What constitutes a legitimate leisure experience may be debatable still, but the view that good leisure leads to an *optimal experience* has been a prevalent theme in theory and research. Optimal experiences are states of high psychological involvement or absorption in activities or settings (Csikszentmihalyi & Csikszentmihalyi, 1988). From this perspective, a high-quality leisure experience is seen to be similar to a variety of highly involving psychological states, for example, peak or mystical states, flow, and intense sport experiences (Kleiber & Dirkin, 1985; Mannell, 1980, 1993). Maslow's (1968) notion of *peak* experience and Csikszentmihalyi's (1975, 1990) concept of *flow* have been particularly attractive conceptualizations for leisure researchers, since they identify a variety of features or characteristics of conscious experience that can be used to define and measure optimal experiences, experiences that also have some grounding in mainstream psychology in the study of attention and absorption (e.g., Quarrick, 1989; Roche & McConkey, 1990; Tellegen & Atkinson, 1974).

Maslow (1968, p. 73) described peak experiences as "moments of highest happiness and fulfillment" often achieved through nature experience, aesthetic perception, creative movement, intellectual insight, orgasmic experience, athletic pursuit, and the like. Csikszentmihalyi (1975, 1990, 1997) asserted that flow is the experience of deep involvement that individuals frequently seek in their various activities and that leisure and play activities and settings can be excellent sources of flow. However, participation in leisure activities and settings does not guarantee that flow will be experienced. The appropriate choices must be made and certain conditions must be present in the activity or setting for such an experience to occur.

Common Leisure Experiences

Have you ever looked at a person's face and drawn a conclusion about that person's mood? Of course you have; we all have. And psychologists have made a regular study of how emotions and moods are readily detectable in those who do not intentionally attempt to avoid such impressions (Eckman & Friesen, 2003). Certainly smiles and frowns are dead giveaways. Other emotions and experiences are not so clearly detected, but for starters we might suggest that leisure has three or four very common "faces." There is of course the smiling face of fun, mirth, and sociability. And there is a face of calm and peacefulness, where facial muscles are relaxed and the body posture conforms as well. Excitement, too, is recognizable, as is the concentration and focused attention of intense absorption. These each represent distinguishable experiences that are regularly sought and embraced as leisure. But they are quite different experiences after all, aren't they?

There are those among leisure scholars (e.g., Tinsley & Tinsley, 1986) who see "pure" leisure, or *the* leisure experience, as being essentially that of one particular experience—flow. This concept was introduced in the previous chapter—and will be more closely examined—but clearly there are others as well. Being focused "in the moment" or present-centered is a component of flow as we have discussed, but leisure may also incorporate a sense of anticipation of something to come or of recollection of something from the past, in a more reflective process. When such experiences—of anticipation and recollection are positive, we can also speak of "savoring," to describe the experience, as two psychologists (Bryant & Veroff, 2007) have recently done. We will have more to say about this also later in the chapter. And as noted in the last chapter, a greater degree of emotional intensity or passion may be reflected in leisure that is "serious" while casual dispassionate dispositions also characterize much leisure experience.

Interest and Excitement

Consider the appeal to a young child of a sailboat that passes by along the beach for the first time in her experience. The appeal of the movement of the boat and the thought of actually being in it and perhaps even controlling it is intriguing. As has already been suggested and will become abundantly clear in Chapter 6, leisure activity is intrinsically motivated. The activity is attractive for what it offers and provides in terms of experience and needs no other reward. But as with the beginning apprehension of leisure discussed above, initial and continuing involvement in an activity is a subject of emotional experience as well. *Interest* is clearly a basis of intrinsic motivation, but it also has emotional properties (Izard, 1977; Silvia, 2008). Psycho-physiologically, it follows the course of optimizing one's operating level of arousal. When arousal is too high it leads to stress and anxiety; but when it is too low it is associated with boredom and is unpleasant as well. This Yerkes-Dobson model of optimal arousal was also established as an explanation for why people play (Ellis, 1973; see Figure 4.1). Pushing back on the environment in a playful way brings arousal back up to a moderate, optimal level. But it also reflects optimal information flow, which is the basis of interest as well.

This basis of intrinsic motivation will be discussed further in Chapter 6, but suffice it to say here that the response to the pull of interesting information

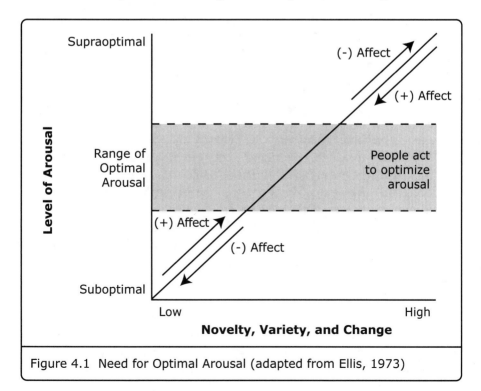

Figure 4.1 Need for Optimal Arousal (adapted from Ellis, 1973)

about possibilities for action is invigorating, even if it is simply a matter of watching or reading about something. Interest is what has been called a "knowledge emotion" (Silvia, 2008)—along with confusion, surprise, and awe—and it is one of the key orienting and activating aspects of leisure involvement. It occurs when one encounters novel, challenging, or aesthetically pleasing activities or objects that promise the satisfaction of basic needs (Deci, 1992). It may itself be stimulated by activities that have some connection to one's existing dispositions and interests, as a kind of extensive process of self-discovery, or it may come about in response to attractive images that are entirely new, such as seeing someone else obviously enjoying an unfamiliar activity (Kleiber, 1999, 2004). But in any case, it brings on focused attention and a desire for more involvement.

Interest is exciting in a minimal but critical way. When activities or objects attract attention and interest, it is appropriate, physiologically speaking, to say that they are exciting in that they raise arousal. But *excitement* is also arousal extended to upper levels just short of anxiety and fear and maybe even crossing that line on occasion. Psychologist Daniel Berlyne spoke some time ago about the *arousal-jag* experience that attracts people to activities that are thrilling (Berlyne, 1960, see also Zillmann & Vorderer, 2000). Hang gliders and race car drivers may gain control over highly arousing and even dangerous conditions as they go, but it is the "rush" associated with being at or over the edge of optimal that makes it appealing for some. Nor must one go to such extremes for excitement. Driving into an unfamiliar city or entering a crowd of concertgoers can also be as exciting as it is appealing and interesting.

Reading a murder mystery, riding a rollercoaster, guiding a raft down a raging river, or watching the conclusion of a tightly contested soccer match, are among other leisure events that seem to elicit this kind of emotional experience. Excitement may share the intensity and the focused attention of flow experience, to which we turn next, but even higher levels of arousal may be sought where there is no emphasis on performance and control is surrendered to a great extent. Risk or adventure recreation takes advantage of some degree of danger and the elevated arousal that is associated with it to capture attention, but by gaining control of the situation a further and deeper sense of involvement is created that brings about a special sense of competence and pleasure and may generate deeper engagement in the experience as a result (Ewert & Hollenhorst, 1989; Jones, Hollenhorst, & Perna, 2003; Pohl, Borrie, & Patterson, 2000; Priest, 1992).

Flow

In Chapter 3, we described earlier experiments conducted at the University of Waterloo (Mannell, 1979, 1980; Mannell & Bradley, 1986) that attempted to reconstruct leisure in the laboratory by manipulating perceived freedom and intrinsic motivation (topics that we will return to in some depth in the next two chapters). While one might wonder how freedom could be captured in the laboratory setting, where behavior is manipulated, it is clear that the participants in the experiment felt closer to having the experience of leisure when they were afforded more choice. Similarly, they were more intrinsically motivated—liked the experimental activity more—when they were so absorbed in it (playing board games) that they lost some track of time and the conditions of the environment around them. Thus, the experience was presumed to be flow-like.

Csikszentmihalyi (1975) originally developed his theory of *flow* on the basis of extensive interviews with people engaged in their most enjoyable leisure (including rock climbers, basketball players, recreational dancers, chess players) and work (surgeons). The model provides insight into how the activities of everyday life come to be invested with meaning and experienced as optimal. Episodes that provided intensely absorbing experiences, where challenges roughly match participants' skills, and in which the participants lost track of time and awareness of themselves, were best remembered and experienced as most rewarding. Csikszentmihalyi's subsequent studies have led him to suggest that these flow experiences are "the best moments of people's lives" and "occur when a person's body or mind is stretched to its limits in a voluntary effort to accomplish something difficult and worthwhile" (Csikszentmihalyi, 1990, p. 3). *Enjoyment* is largely the experience of flow in Csikszentmihalyi's view, and it can be differentiated from pleasure accordingly:

> Pleasure is the good feeling that comes from satisfying homeostatic needs such as hunger, sex, and bodily comfort. Enjoyment, on the other hand, refers to the good feelings people experience when they break through homeostasis—when they do something that stretches them beyond what they were—in an athletic event, an artistic performance, a good deed, a stimulating conversation. Enjoyment, rather than pleasure, is what leads to long-term growth and personal happiness (Seligman & Csikszentmihalyi, 2000).

So what is flow, exactly? How does it come about, and how do we know if and when we are in it? In his 1990 book, *Flow*, Csikszentmihalyi distinguished between characteristics of flow and conditions that bring it about. The experience of flow, of being very absorbed in an activity, is characterized by the merging of action and awareness, concentration on the task at hand, a sense of control (*exercising* control versus being in control), some risk and uncertainty, loss of self-consciousness, and alteration of time sense (faster or slower). The conditions that are most likely to bring flow about are challenging activity, clear goals and feedback, and the capacity for concerted attention. When these conditions are in play, the individual has the psychological experience of being in a zone of present-centered competence, no longer attending to self or extraneous factors such as time or the surrounding environment. But the matching of challenges and skills, at a fairly high level for the individual is necessary to achieve this experience. When they are out of balance—as Figure 4.2 suggests—boredom or anxiety result. And when both challenge and skills are suboptimal, apathy is the result.

In his earlier work, Csikszentmihalyi (1975) summarized the basic features and operation of his flow theory with a simple diagram where skills and challenges where compared as co-acting dimensions (see Figure 4.3). Assume that the diagram represents an involvement in a leisure specific activity, for example, a new video game. The two most theoretically important dimensions of the experience, challenges and skills, are represented on the two axes of the diagram. The letter C represents Christie, a girl who has just purchased a video game she has never played. The diagram shows Christie at four different points in time. When she starts playing (C1), Christie has limited knowledge and skills for this particular game, and the major challenge she faces is getting the game character she controls with her controller to move in the direction she wants. This is not a very difficult feat, but Christie is likely to enjoy it because the difficulty is just right for her rudimentary skills in the new game. So at this point she will probably be in flow. But she cannot stay there for long. After a while, if she keeps practicing, her skills will improve, and then she will grow bored with just being able to control

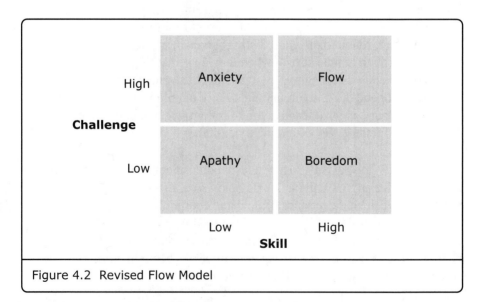

Figure 4.2 Revised Flow Model

the character (C2). Also, being an experienced video game player, she likely realizes that there are harder challenges for her than just moving the character around on the screen—at which point, she will feel some anxiety (C3) concerning her "poor" performance.

Neither boredom nor anxiety is a positive experience, so Christie will be motivated to return to the flow state. How is she to do it? Glancing again at the diagram, one sees that if she is bored (C2) and wishes to be in flow again, Christie has essentially only one choice: to increase the challenges she is facing. (She also has a second choice, which is to give up playing altogether—in which case C would simply disappear from the diagram.) By setting herself a new, more difficult goal that matches her skills—for instance, to avoid the traps and pitfalls that are blocking her mission in the game and to move onto the next level—Christie would be back in flow (C4). If Christie is anxious (C3), regaining flow requires that she increase her skills. Theoretically, she could also reduce the challenges she is facing, and thus return to flow somewhere near where she started (C1).

The diagram shows that both C1 and C4 represent situations in which Christie is in flow. Although both are enjoyable, the two states are quite different in that C4 is a more complex experience than C1. It is more complex because it involves greater challenges and demands greater skills from

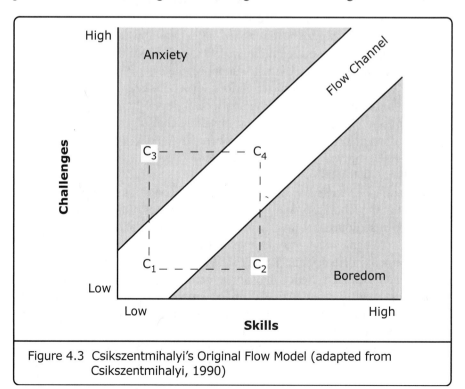

Figure 4.3 Csikszentmihalyi's Original Flow Model (adapted from Csikszentmihalyi, 1990)

the player. But C4, although complex and enjoyable, does not represent a stable situation, either. As Christie keeps playing, either she will become bored by the stale opportunities she finds at that level, or she will become anxious and frustrated by her relatively low ability. So the motivation to enjoy herself again will push her to get back into the flow channel, but now at a level of complexity even higher than C4.

Csikszentmihalyi (1990, p. 75) regarded this dynamic feature of flow activities as the basis for their contribution to psychological growth and discovery. One cannot enjoy doing the same thing at the same level for long. People grow bored or frustrated, and then the desire to enjoy themselves again pushes them to stretch their skills or to discover new opportunities for using them. Therein lies the reason for the attractiveness of video games for participants. Because of the multiple levels of difficulty of the games, no sooner has the player succeeded in mastering one set of tasks than she or he is faced with a new, more challenging level of difficulty. While sports and games provide good opportunities for this constant matching of challenges and skills, the interactive nature of computer-based games allows this challenge-skill matching process to occur over and over automatically.

But Csikszentmihalyi changed the earlier continuum model—where it appeared that flow could occur at even low levels of challenge if skills were similarly low—to the four-quadrant model shown in Figure 4.2, p. 110) because evidence from experience sampling studies indicated that the "low-low" condition was experienced with low affect and low intrinsic motivation (Csikszentmihalyi & Csikszentmihalyi, 1988, p. 261). And thus he referred to that condition as *apathy*. Evidence supports the case that even though the model may be applied to people at various levels of skill, one must have a sense that his or her skills are being applied at a level slightly higher than average for oneself and in relation to comparable challenges to become deeply absorbed in an activity. The model has been validated in a number of investigations, including two studies of whitewater kayaking adventure experience (Jones et al., 2000, 2003).

Mannell (1979, 1980) demonstrated that the conditions of flow can be generated in the laboratory and that the characteristics of flow can then be measured. In so doing, the investigators showed that experiences accompanying leisure engagements vary in level of flow or absorption. Flow is also the central element in Tinsley and Tinsley's (1986) theory of leisure experience and its benefits. In their theory, they agree that the experiences accompanying leisure activities can vary in level of involvement; however, they regard pure leisure, what they call "the leisure state," as occurring only when an intense flow experience is achieved.

Other theorists, including Csikszentmihalyi himself, do not equate flow states with leisure states since it has been demonstrated that flow experiences can occur in a wide variety of activities and settings, including those associated with work. On the one hand, it seems reasonable to hypothesize that there may be more potential for achieving flow states in leisure than other domains. The greater freedom allowed by leisure to select and control individual activities should allow one to maintain or achieve a match between challenges and skills. On the other hand, if people regularly select relaxing and passive involvements devoid of challenges for their leisure, these choices will not likely promote the experience of flow. In fact, studies of adult workers (Bryce & Haworth, 2002; Csikszentmihalyi & LeFevre, 1989; Delle Fave & Massimini, 2003) and retired older adults (Mannell, Zuzanek, & Larson, 1988) have indicated that flow is experienced at least as frequently and often more frequently in work or obligatory, nonwork tasks than in leisure. The participants in all those studies most commonly chose passive activities for leisure, while the things they "had to do" frequently were more challenging and demanding of higher levels of skill. Nevertheless, when work is actually enjoyable in a flow-producing way, people are inclined to say "my work is my leisure," adding to the view that flow-type enjoyment is an expected and desirable form of leisure experience, even if it is relatively uncommon. Csikszentmihalyi and his colleagues and other researchers have in fact studied flow in a variety of contexts, including surgery, teaching, and management, but as an essential experience of enjoyment, they look to leisure, with its freedom of choice and self-direction, as the most promising context for flow.

Relaxation

Like flow, relaxation may be considered a common, prototypical leisure experience, more common than flow and excitement in fact, especially in association with leisure (Kleiber, Caldwell, & Shaw, 1993; Mobily, 1989; Shaw, 1985a). And consider its differences from those experiences. Reminiscing with a friend, while sitting in rocking chairs on the front porch, and hang-gliding over the California coast would seem not to fit together in the same category. At least they would be at opposite ends on a continuum of arousal.

Relaxation is often a matter of bringing arousal down rather than up (see Figure 4.1 on p. 107) and often involves disengaging from more stimulating or stressful circumstances. Many people look to leisure to escape the pressures of their everyday lives (e.g., Stebbins, 1997, 2001, 2007; Watkins & Bond, 2007). There is a sense of freedom that comes from disengaging from required activities associated with work, school, and family life; and exercising freedom from other demands often affords the freedom to act in particular ways. Engagement in particular activities where attention is fully invested has the effect of perpetuating a sense of disengagement from ordinary life (Kleiber, 1985). In that sense, the diversion created in the reverie of the person rocking on the porch differs only in degree and intensity from that produced in taking to flight off a rocky cliff.

This particular way of realizing leisure may be more characteristic of males than females in most cultures, however (Bella, 1989). For females, at least those involved consistently in nurturing others, such disengagement is neither as possible nor as necessary for creating enjoyable engagement. Leisure for mothers and grandmothers, in Western cultures anyway, has often been that which can be engaged in while taking care of the family. Nevertheless, in one study, women were as likely as men to identify *separateness* as central to satisfying leisure experience (Gunter, 1987). Furthermore, both men and women often find a way to attend to home and family in the context of leisure. Whether leisure is created by finding a distinct change in focus or is combined with role responsibilities, it is the sense of self-expression that gives it its meaning to a great extent. In contrast, where conditions of deprivation and fear are prevalent, leisure is nearly impossible to create, regardless of role relations.

If leisure is constructed around a sense of freedom, however, what should we make of those free time activities that require a commitment to a schedule or that bring about some degree of stress or discomfort? Freedom and enjoyment might predictably be threatened under these conditions. Being a group member of an organization usually entails scheduled meetings and some role responsibilities. Many activities and many vacations that are freely initiated and begun with great enthusiasm meet with difficulties and frustrations. Does leisure end at the point that a person has a flat tire on the road to a national park or when the horse is pulling stubbornly against the reins of a would-be rider? Or what about the feeling of not wanting to attend yet another meeting despite being one of the group's initial organizers? The experience obviously changes at such points. In some sense, the "spell" of leisure—at least that associated with an easy, relaxed attitude of mind—is broken. Nevertheless, leisure is rather labile in accommodating a wide range of experiences.

The idea of surrendering demonstrates a degree of trust and faith, and indeed comfort, with one's surroundings. To have leisure is simply to relax in many cases. This is the essence of Josef Pieper's views on leisure. For Pieper (1952), relinquishing the affairs of everyday mundane reality, at least temporarily, and being at peace allows one to give fuller attention to spiritual matters and to devotion. Such devotion does not require effort, in Pieper's view, but is instead the result of relaxed openness and appreciation of the gift of life. Leisure was for Pieper, first of all, an attitude of mind whereby one's humanity is celebrated and affirmed, a condition of the soul that is receptive and effortless.

While Pieper's view may not be very consistent with other contemporary understandings of leisure, even beyond its theological underpinnings, the contrast of leisure with effort can be found in everyday language. To do something "leisurely," according to dictionary definitions, means to do it "casually" or in an easy, relaxed manner that an abundance of time available might allow. Similarly, the suggestion that you respond "at your leisure" is an invitation to respond in a relaxed, unhurried manner when time and occasion affords the opportunity. More generally, though, relaxation is created in disengaging from action, and it is treasured, even necessary, in compensating for an existence that feels rushed and demanding (See Kleiber, 2000, for further discussion of this point.). Nevertheless, it can offer more than just emotional adjustment. Leisure as relaxation is likely to have a temporal quality defined by what was left behind and what will follow. It is often a pausing in one's life to gain perspective, to register appreciation, and simply to experience the here and now.

In *Freedom and Destiny*, psychoanalyst Rollo May (1981) discussed the significance of the *pause* as a critical element of freedom and creativity. The pause, which is more commonly represented in Eastern than Western thought, signifies what is *not* rather than what is. The pause signifies appreciation and opportunity; it is time pregnant with possibility. But it also represents a kind of resistance in interrupting "the rigid chain of cause and effect":

In the person's life response no longer blindly follows stimulus. There intervenes between the two our human imaginings, reflections, considerations, ponderings. Pause is the prerequisite for wonder. When we don't pause, when we are perpetually hurrying from one appointment to another, from one "planned activity" to another, we sacrifice the richness of wonder (p. 167).

May suggests that musicians are especially aware of the power of pauses in giving notes meaning and clarity. He links the pause to creativity more directly in seeing it as "inviting the Muses" where painters, poets, and other artists put themselves in a position of "readiness for the 'lucky accident'." The pause takes advantage of the capacity to appreciate. In everyday thought, reflection requires pausing, and yet pauses can last for longer as in a weekend, a vacation, or a sabbatical. But May also notes that the American sense of leisure does not make particularly good use of the pause—in some contrast to Europeans as well as people in non-Western cultures—preferring to define the freedom of leisure in the action that can occur, in movement and becoming rather than in contemplation and being. This may begin to explain why the writing of Josef Pieper, which portrays leisure as a receptive rather than an active state, has received so little attention in North American leisure studies. Creativity and even meaning are casualties of this orientation in May's view. More positively he suggests that the letting be or letting happen that one does in wandering an unfamiliar city or "wasting time" in some other way, "may turn out to be the most significant thing one can do." The significance comes in the reflection it affords for making meaning and charting direction.

As May suggests, other cultures do not appear to have quite the same problems with relaxation that Americans do. Studies done on "ideal affect" by Jeanne Tsai and colleagues (Tsai, Knutson, & Fung, 2006) with students from Asia and the U.S. indicate that compared with American students, those from Hong Kong have a lower preference for high arousal positive affect (e.g., excitement) and a higher preference for low arousal positive affect (e.g., calm). More will be said about these cultural differences in Chapter 10.

Fun, Sociability, and "Casual Leisure"

Common as they are, interest and flow, excitement and relaxation are only some of the variations in leisure experience, and have been considered here mostly without regard to context. Clearly what one is doing and with whom one is doing it will have an influence on experience. The word "fun" even implies some degree of sociability according to some (Podilchak, 1991a,b). And leisure is often associated with that kind of experience and with the absence of serious concerns. As we will see shortly, leisure can be quite serious, but so much of free time is spent in casual social interaction, it would be a mistake to dismiss it as unimportant. Robert Stebbins (1982, 1992) regarded all such activities as "casual leisure" and distinguished them from those forms of leisure involvement where people are intensely invested and committed, whether involved interactively with others or not. The virtues of casual leisure are that people are generally relaxed, feel comfortable, and are mostly happy, but such activities typically lack the intensity and depth of involvement of serious leisure and therefore lack much of what such activities provide (Stebbins, 1997, 2001).

Taking Leisure Seriously

Have you ever gotten so involved with an activity that you have neglected some other aspects of your life? Did you defend yourself in that case with the argument that the activity was very important to you, a part of your identity in fact? What was that activity, and how did you come to get so deeply "into" it? Leisure experience often extends beyond the immediate and deeper than the casual. In considering the course of serious investment in leisure activity, it is possible to do an etiology of leisure experience that is developmental, starting with the arousal of interest, the experimental engagement in learning about a subject or making preliminary attempts to execute its requisite skills, the acceptance of being a novice in the activity, the experience of committing to learning more about it, and finally the experience of committing seriously to the activity. Much of this process has been analyzed and discussed in the research on "specialization" and on "serious leisure."

Serious Leisure

In Robert Stebbins' (1982, 1992) work on serious leisure, weekend musicians, mushroom collectors, amateur astronomers, and barbershop singers, among others, described their activities as being intensely enjoyable and flow-like. He thus defined serious leisure as the systematic pursuit of an amateur, hobbyist, or volunteer activity that participants find so substantial and interesting that, in the typical case, they launch themselves on a career centered on acquiring and expressing its special skills, knowledge, and experience (Stebbins, 1992). However, the interviews also revealed that pain, discomfort, and personal sacrifice are common to these activities and that commitment to the group often brought conditions that were quite work-like with respect to practice, event schedules, and the like. As leisure activities become more serious in their importance to an individual, inconveniences such as flat tires and social constraints such as membership dues and meetings are often accepted as parts of the whole. Furthermore, a sense of commitment and obligation can even enhance the experience of enjoyment (Stebbins, 2000). This happens in two ways: (1) the kind of commitments reflected in belonging to an organization or being a member of a family can serve to structure experience as something special, around which life can be organized; and (2) if something is risked or staked in an activity, the intensity of absorption is often deepened. Taking lessons or buying equipment is the kind of stake that has been referred to as a "side bet" (Becker, 1960); it raises the level of commitment and, as a result, increases the intensity of involvement and often the level of performance as well. And despite obligation and commitment, the action is still acknowledged as voluntary and discretionary (see also Buchanan, 1985).

To illustrate the idea of a stake, consider the game of basketball. One can shoot baskets in the driveway, but an organized basketball game with spectators and with relative position in a league to be determined by the outcome of the game puts much more at stake. Or, compare harmonizing with a group of friends on the street corner with performing at a festival in front of hundreds of people. Such conditions can be sobering in the same way that setting off on a hang glider can be, and the casual spontaneity and playfulness of such activities are sacrificed in the interest of cultivating a point of attention that optimizes performance. To the extent that attention is more completely focused, however, the intensity of experience and the resulting enjoyment is also maximized. That such intense experience may fit within the context of leisure is supported by the fact that they are embedded within a personal framework of choice and self-expression (Shamir, 1988).

The second way in which commitment can facilitate the experience of leisure and enjoyment is in structuring ongoing experience. This is also paradoxical because responding to a set of requirements reflects the relinquishing of choice in the matter, and choice is the freedom most commonly associated with leisure. But freedom should not be equated with choice; nor is it always a reflection of control. Abandoning choice with ongoing consent for involvement is an aspect of commitment that deepens the experience (Harper, 1986). More will be said about issues of freedom and motivation in the next two chapters.

So, commitment—reflected in effort, voluntary obligation, and perseverance—is a critical part of serious leisure. But Stebbins found other characteristics in his study of those who seemed to take leisure activities seriously, including *identification* with the activity and others who participate seriously, a *unique ethos*, that is, a "social world" shared with fellow participants, and the sense of *enduring benefits*, such as enhanced self-esteem, that derive from participation. These qualities are uniformly found among the three types of participants he studied: amateurs, hobbyists, and volunteers (Stebbins, 1992). And researchers have subsequently established the characteristics of serious leisure among quilters (Stalp, 2006), "Shag" dancers (Brown, 2007), sea cadets (Raisborough, 2007), living history interpreters (Hunt, 2004), show dog owners (Baldwin & Norris, 1999; Gillespie, Lefler & Lerner, 2002), athletes of various kinds (e.g., Collison & Hockey, 2007; Jackson, 1992; Major, 2001), and even among spectators (Gibson, Willming, & Holdnak, 2002; Madrigal, 2006). A scale has even been developed to measure serious leisure, with items such as "If I encounter obstacles in [activity], I persist to overcome them," and "I value interacting with others who are also involved with [activity]" (Gould, Moore, McGuire, & Stebbins, 2008).

Specialization

The idea of enduring involvement and of having a "career" of sorts with an activity also brings up the related subject of *specialization*, one of the most regularly researched areas in leisure studies. In continuing with an activity, participants typically will either transcend the novice stage and move forward to higher levels of competence and commitment and involvement with others in the activity or will drop out (Bryan, 1977, 2000; Scott & Shafer, 2001). McFarlane (2001) identified four stages in the specialization progression:

awareness, adoption, continued involvement, and commitment. Similarly, with respect to the social worlds of participation, Unruh (1980) suggested that there are strangers, tourists, regulars, and insiders in nearly every social world.

A relatively small percentage of novice or neophyte participants continue toward specialization. As with other serious leisure participants, those specializing in an activity seek out new challenges and solutions in their activities related to rules, limits, settings, and time constraints. Research has also demonstrated that activity specialists are more inclined to have setting preferences (Scott & Thigpen, 2003), to be attached to certain spaces and places (Bricker & Kerstetter, 2000), and to have more specifications for appropriate resource conditions (Shafer & Hammitt, 1995), among other things. Specializing can occur in any number of activities, social worlds, and sub-worlds. There are online interactive game players for example, who restrict their attention to one particular game and become extremely competent in that game, creating a social world around it (Holt & Kleiber, 2009). Activities that have been the targets of specialization research include birding (McFarlane, 1994; Scott & Thigpen, 2003), hunting (e.g., Miller & Graefe, 2000), and vehicle-based camping (McIntyre & Pigram, 1992).

Specialization theory then is very much about serious leisure in dealing with complex leisure activities that offer something of a career to participants. However, it doesn't go quite as far as Stebbins' work on amateurs, hobbyists, and volunteers in considering how the experience locates participants in a wider social world. Arguably this is an important part of the experience. Specialization theory and research also tends mostly to focus on people's behavior without delving very far into the nature of the experience of deeper involvement with an activity.

Situational and Enduring Involvement

Specialization depends first of all on *involvement*, the extent to which people engage cognitively, emotionally, and behaviorally with an activity, a product, a place or destination, or a service. Involvement is further defined as an unobservable state of motivation, arousal, or interest evoked by a particular stimulus or situation, which has drive properties (Havitz & Dimache, 1997). Leisure researchers have referred to serious leisure activities as high investment or *high involvement* activities (Mannell, 1993; Kelly et al., 1987) and have recognized the importance that they have to personal identity and quality of life. Identifying with a particular activity, product, place, or service gives it identity "salience" (Shamir, 1992).

Involvement can be situational and temporary in the deepening of interest, but only enduring involvement has implications for identity. Reviews of research on involvement (e.g., Havitz & Dimanche, 1997, 1999; Havitz & Mannell, 2005; Kyle, Graefe, Manning, & Bacon, 2004; McIntyre, 1989) describe cognitive, affective, and behavioral aspects of enduring involvement, specifically with respect to *attraction* (importance and pleasure associated with the activity), *centrality* (value relative to other domains such as occupation), and *self expression* (the extent to which identity is reflected therein). In measures of enduring involvement items addressing attraction to a particular activity are tied to the inherent appeal of the activity itself, such as "deep sea fishing is important to me," "deep sea fishing interests me," "deep sea fishing is one of the most enjoyable things I do," "deep sea fishing is pleasurable," and "I really enjoy deep sea fishing." Centrality is reflected in items such as, "a lot of my life is organized around deep sea fishing," "deep sea fishing plays a central role in my life," and "my life is organized around deep sea fishing." Self-expression items include such things as, "when I participate in deep sea fishing, I can really be myself," "you can tell a lot about a person by seeing him (her) deep sea fishing," and "when I participate in deep sea fishing others see me the way I want them to see me." (See Kyle et. al., 2007, for more on the measurement of involvement.)

Attachment to places also reflects similar shades of psychological and enduring involvement. For example, in a study of the relationship between leisure activity involvement and place attachment among hikers along the Appalachian Trail (Kyle, Graefe, Manning, & Bacon, 2004), the investigators found that the self-expression and attraction dimensions of activity involvement predicted whether one would identify personally with the section of the trail where the hiking took place. But in an ethnographic study of people who had returned repeatedly to an agricultural fair in Pennsylvania, Kyle and Chick (2007) found that those most attached to the activity pointed to the associations with family and friends as the critical factor rather than the place or activity itself. Measures of activity involvement appear to miss this factor (see also Kyle & Chick, 2002), but it is clearly relevant to the identification and unique ethos aspects of serious leisure. Studies of loyalty to products, services, destinations, and activity—the tendency to use or visit them again—also demonstrate a connection to enduring involvement, specialization, and serious leisure (e.g., Iwasaki & Havitz, 2004).

Must Leisure Experience Always Be Pleasant?

We have suggested that leisure is defined in part by the experience that is sought or preferred, but in fact a far wider range of emotions are associated with leisure activities and thus must be considered part of leisure experience. In discussing excitement, we spoke about the case when fear is built into an activity, like amusement park rides; it is the dissipation of fear that brings the pleasurable sense of relief. Indeed, entertainment or art engagements may frequently create temporary increases in negative moods and decreases in positive moods—such as a tragedy viewed at the theatre or a horror movie (Mannell, 1980; Zillmann & Vorderer, 2000). But that fear is an intrinsic aspect of the activity, while in some other activities fear is an unanticipated and unwelcome emotion, tolerated at best as a necessary evil or discouraging altogether. There is a certain amount of fear, for example, that accompanies destination travel and hiking—particularly for women—on national park trails (cf. Bialeschki, 2005; Coble, Selin, & Erickson, 2003). Encounters with others in recreation environment—built as well as natural—may result in conflict, if only as a result of limited carrying capacity. Indeed, with high expectations for preferred experience, unpleasant encounters and competition for resources is inherently frustrating and may lead to hostility, aggression, and violence.

As we noted earlier, a desire for preferred experience may not always be realized. Flow may be interrupted; *boredom* may follow as things get repetitive, or *anxiety* may be raised by happenings that are unexpected or the appearance of others whose presence is unwanted. The co-participation with others can be stressful when competition is unwanted, resources are limited or solitude is sought. Commitment may deepen loyalties and contribute to serious leisure as noted above, but when it is demanded of participants, a sense of obligation may quite literally turn off the tap of good feelings (Gillespie et al., 2002; Stebbins, 2000, 2007).

Even passionate attachments to serious leisure activities can turn sour and become unpleasant (Vallerand et al., 2007). Guilt may also be another unwelcome concomitant of serious leisure, as it often is with workaholism. And obsessiveness can come to accompany serious leisure passions in ways that are costly to one's sense of self and relationships (Stenseng, 2008). The neglect of family and of other social responsibilities, and even of other aspects of one's own development, are common costs of serious leisure according to Stebbins (1992b, 2005). Indeed, Stebbins (2005) reported on three "cost" categories of serious leisure: *disappointments*, from high expectations when anticipated outcomes and benefits aren't realized; *dislikes*, when others don't behave as desired or conditions are constraining rather than facilitating of the activity; and *tensions*, such as interpersonal friction. Similar to the greater distress with crowding that comes to those with higher levels of activity involvement and place attachment (Kyle et al., 2004), serious devotees of an activity are more easily bothered by less than optimal conditions. Indeed, conflict in recreation settings has been a consistently researched topic, especially by resource management specialists, for many years (e.g., Jacob & Schreyer, 1980; Schneider, 2000; Vaske, Needham, & Cline, 2007).

Anxiety and boredom have been discussed as the imbalance in skills and challenges that undermine the prospects of flow, and, as we have already noted, flow accounts for relatively little of leisure experience. Anxiety is also reflected in the fear discussed above and in the stress associated with a sense of inadequate skill or preparation for a particular activity. Choosing more manageable activities or enhancing self-efficacy may work to reduce anxiety. Boredom may arise from being both overskilled for a given challenge or from failing to find or seek appropriate challenges. In any case, boredom is very common in free time, particularly in adolescence, and often leads to self-injurious behavior, such as drug abuse or promiscuous sexual activity, in the interest of raising arousal to a more optimal level.

Boredom may also be more common in some people based on particular aspects of their personality, as we will see again in Chapter 7. Extroverts are more susceptible to boredom because they have a higher arousal threshold. But it has been proposed that boredom for some people is especially associated with leisure, that is, they find free time boring in and of itself and/or the available alternatives unappealing. Iso-Ahola and Weissinger (1990) developed a personality test called the *Leisure Boredom Scale* to measure this leisure-specific trait by having people rate how well such items as the following describe them: "For me, leisure time just drags on and on," and "During my leisure time, I almost always have something to do" (second item is scored the reverse of the first item). Their research showed that people who score higher on these types of items are less likely to perceive themselves as socially competent, are less likely to be able to entertain themselves, have lower self-esteem, are less positive toward leisure, and are less likely to be involved in a variety of leisure activities.

In one study (Iso-Ahola & Crowley, 1991), substance abusers were found to score higher on leisure boredom. Interestingly, though, they were also more likely to go to rock concerts and engage in physical recreation than nonabusers. The authors concluded that, "Because of their personality predisposition toward sensation seeking and low tolerance for constant experiences, substance abusers presumably prefer active leisure lifestyles. But if leisure activities fail to satisfy their need for optimal arousal, leisure boredom results and drug use may be the only alternative" (p. 260) (see also Caldwell, Darling, Payne & Dowdy, 1999; Wegner, Flisher, Muller, & Lombard, 2006.).

Experience Changes during Leisure Engagements

Leisure engagements, that is, activities that are organized within and for the purpose of leisure, may involve a variety of different meanings and experiences that may change during the course of the engagement (e.g., Hull, Stewart, & Yi, 1992; Watkins, 2000; Watkins & Bond, 2007). One of the first studies to attempt to monitor on-site leisure experiences was reported by More and Payne (1978). The leisure activity and setting studied by these researchers was a day trip to one of three wildlife sanctuaries near several cities in Massachusetts. While at these nature centers, the participants viewed nature exhibits, picnicked, observed wildlife, and hiked. The moods accompanying this engagement were measured by having the visitors fill out a *survey questionnaire* when they entered and then again when they left the park. Besides asking for background information about the participants, the questionnaire contained a mood adjective checklist which required respondents to indicate on a 4-point Likert scale the extent to which each of 33 adjectives described how they were feeling at the moment. In this study, the leisure experience was defined as the change in visitors' moods over the course of their visit to the nature center.

More and Payne predicted that negative moods (e.g., aggression, anxiety) would decline and positive moods (e.g., elation, vigor) would increase based on the theory that visitors to natural areas from cities should experience temporary escape from the pressures and tensions of urban life. They found that negative moods did decrease significantly; however, they also found positive moods decreased (see Figure 4.4, p. 124). The researchers suggested that the participants arrived in high spirits with very positive moods and low levels of negative moods in anticipation of the outing, and that they likely chose to leave the park when they had had enough and were feeling tired and less enthusiastic. They added that the findings indicated that the on-site experience is just the "tip of the iceberg," the most visible part of the total leisure episode, and that what goes on before and after the event needs to be taken into consideration.

In a more recent study of 111 urban hikers (Lee & Shafer, 2002), all participants said that their objective was to have an "enjoyable experience," but they varied considerably in the meanings they sought with respect to challenge, satisfaction, absorption, and personal growth. This was largely due to personality differences, or what the authors regarded as "fundamental sentiments," such as being adventurous or meditative. These sentiments then interact with the impressions one gets along the way and affects satisfaction with the experience accordingly. Asking participants to recollect five events that occurred along the way, such as seeing fish and meeting others on the trail, and rate feelings at the time, the investigators determined that affect (pleasure and satisfaction with the activity) increased as a function of how well it fit with one's more fundamental sentiments (see also Lee, Shafer, & Kang, 2005).

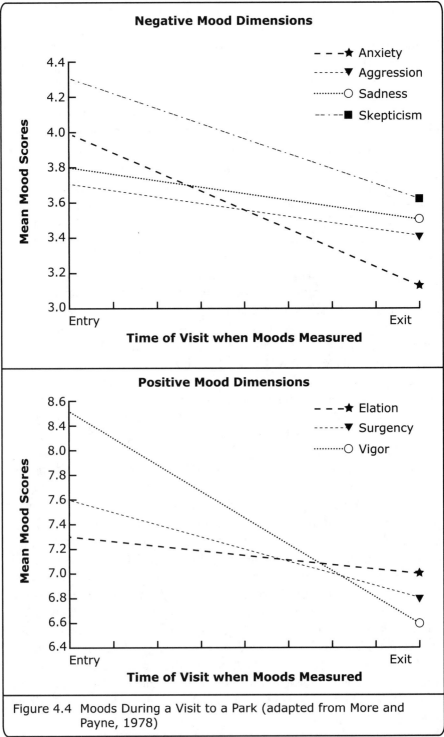

Figure 4.4 Moods During a Visit to a Park (adapted from More and Payne, 1978)

Extending the Range of Leisure Experience: From Anticipation to Recollection

We are inclined to think about leisure activities having a discrete beginning and an end: the start and end of a ballgame, opening the coin collection and putting it away, starting down the trail and coming out at the desired location. But the experience of leisure around such activities is always more complicated and usually begins sooner and ends later, often years later. We have already talked about some of the behavioral and emotional aspects of the experiences that are generally sought in leisure, but other kinds of experience surround those, and while they involve aspects that may be more cognitive than that associated with overt behavior, they may be equally as intense. The glimmer of excitement that comes with the idea of partaking of an event should be recognized as leisure experience, as would the eager anticipation and even the dutiful planning to make it occur. When the activity proper has been completed, the pleasure of recollection and reminiscence may be either private or social. Of course, the evaluation of mishaps associated with the event or of disappointments in aspirations not being realized would fall into a realm of emotion more associated with regret, and such memories may be relinquished as failing to meet anyone's definitional test of leisure unless, of course, they can be enjoyed, even laughed at, in retrospect.

Researchers have come to recognize leisure and recreation events as typically involving a *multi-phase experience* (Clawson & Knetsch, 1966). According to Clawson and Knetsch, the phases include:

(1) anticipation—a period of imagining and planning the trip or event;
(2) travel to—getting to the recreation site;
(3) on-site—the actual activity or experience at the site;
(4) travel back—the return trip home; and finally
(5) recollection—the recall or memory of the activity or experience.

In a fairly early study on the subject, Hammitt (1980) examined all of the five phases of the recreation experience by measuring the moods of 61 students during a trip to Mud Lake Bog (a small marsh) in Michigan. The *anticipation phase* moods were measured after students had received a 1-hour lecture on their upcoming trip to the bog environment. Moods for the *travel to* phase were measured when the bus arrived at the bog, *on-site* moods were assessed part of the way through their presence at the site, and *travel from* moods were assessed when the students returned to the buses. The *recollection* phase was measured two days after the bog trip. Levels of positive moods tended to increase during the "anticipation" and on into the "on-site" phases of the recreation experience, but then rapidly declined during the "travel from" phase. Negative moods showed the opposite trend. In conclusion, Hammitt pointed out that there is a need to consider many recreation engagements as a "package deal; all parts having a potential role" (p. 114). Depending on the length or nature of the leisure activity—for example, vacations and going to the movies would be quite different—the various phases may take on greater or lesser importance in shaping leisure experience.

Subsequently, the *Journal of Leisure Research* devoted a special issue to the subject of multiphasic recreation experiences (1998, Vol 30, No. 4) with articles addressing experience changes in adventure activities (McIntyre & Roggenbuck), multi-day competitive events (Hultsman), trail users (Walker, Hull, & Roggenbuck), wilderness activities (Patterson et al.), and vacations (Vogt & Stewart). Among the challenges facing research on this subject is the need for methods that are flexible, that don't rely on single observations, and are sensitive to change, such as experience sampling. Additionally, a more general recognition that leisure is contextual in meaning and not always easily managed for a particular experience outcome is needed (Norman). More recently, Borrie and Roggenbuck (2001) demonstrated that in spite of high and low points in an extended leisure encounter, there was no evidence that leisure is ever felt as lost along the way.

Savoring

The old adage that we should "stop and smell the roses" seems especially appropriate in this fast-paced world. As suggested in the section on relaxation, we may not be inclined to pause in our daily life or in our ambitious plans to reflect on what is or will be taking place. Recently, that process has been examined in a book on the positive side of life called *Savoring*. The authors consider savoring to be a process by which people "bring about, appreciate and enhance positive experiences in life" (Bryant & Veroff, 2007). It is further characterized by sharing with others, memory building, self-congratulation, comparing ("It doesn't get any better than this."), sensory and perceptual sharpening, absorption, behavioral expressiveness, temporal awareness, and counting blessings. Savoring is similar to flow in that it is a positive experience, but it is different in being about *considering* the experience rather than being in the experience itself. It may come immediately after flow or the other experiences we have been discussing. The authors consider it the positive equivalent of *coping,* which is about managing negative experiences. And while it is mostly about being in the present, savoring also applies to positive anticipation of the future and pleasurable reminiscence about the past. Savoring is made more likely, though, where other demands are not pressing, and that makes it a common leisure experience.

People differ in the capacity to savor, however; dwelling in the moment and luxuriating about the good things in life past, present, and future is more characteristic of some than others. And we will return to this subject in the chapter on personality and individual difference factors influencing leisure. But it is important to recognize it here as a common leisure experience, occurring whenever someone is appreciating, cherishing, enjoying, and relishing what is currently taking place, has taken place, or will take place in the future. As with flow, it is not just about pleasure but instead encompasses a higher-order awareness or reflective discernment on the part of the individual.

Of course, while savoring is positive in emotional tone, it may not always be interpersonally salubrious and in fact may interfere with being in the moment more completely, i.e., experiencing flow. Gloating over a victory in tennis would likely be considered a rude example of savoring. And pointing out that "this is fun" in an activity might have a way of undoing the fun. Mindful savoring may interfere with sexual experience, for example. But Bryant and Veroff point out that savoring occurs with a wide variety of activities such as eating and drinking, religious activity, intellectual pursuits and conversations, and finding oneself in beautiful natural settings. Reminiscence and storytelling are common ways of savoring the past, and they can be promoted either informally or formally.

Summary and Conclusion

In the end we can conclude that there is no single leisure experience. Whether defining leisure from an external or an internal vantage point, as discussed in Chapter 3, we come up with a variety of experiences that are commonly associated with leisure. These include feelings of intrigue or interest, excitement, flow, relaxation, and just plain old fun. Most of these feelings are positive, but we know also from research that leisure engagements or episodes may encompass a range of negative emotions as well, including fear, frustration, anger, anxiety, and boredom. When people take activities seriously, they may get so involved as to not only experience flow in the short term but through further specialization to turn it into an identity-defining preoccupation. Finally, it is important to note that experiences are also associated with places and people that further define the experiences and their meaning, as does the broader social and political climate. In subsequent chapters, with our interactionist framework, we will address what characteristics individuals bring to leisure activities and how they are shaped by the social context. We turn next to a more careful consideration of the subjects of freedom and motivation, the most fundamental conditions of leisure experience.

Leisure Needs

Preview

As we learned in the previous two chapters, researchers have found a variety of meanings and experiences that distinguish leisure from other realms of human activity. This chapter addresses the preconditions of these meanings and experiences. The two preconditions that have turned up repeatedly in the leisure studies literature and that are central to a social psychological understanding of leisure are *perceived freedom* and *intrinsic motivation*. We begin this chapter by describing a time-honored framework that unites these two attributes. We then examine the concept of leisure needs and how one need in particular—the need for autonomy—is associated with both perceived freedom and intrinsic motivation. We return to the concept of intrinsic motivation in the next chapter, where we compare and contrast it with other types of motivation before describing a contemporary framework that combines needs and motivations and demonstrates how leisure motivation leads to leisure participation.

Maybe you have wondered why people participate in various leisure activities. The authors have also pondered these mysteries. Why do usually reasonable friends jog 10 kilometers (6.2 miles) every day during their lunch hour regardless of summer heat waves or winter blizzards? Why is it that on many pleasant evenings during the summer months, adolescent vandals, under cover of darkness, "recreate" by throwing park benches into a nearby lake (where the next morning, parks and recreation personnel fish them out with the same unfailing regularity)? Why does a teen spend 10 straight hours online in an interactive video game—missing meals and other normal activities—playing with people he has never even met before? Why do people climb rocky cliffs alone and unassisted, increasing the risk to their health and well-being? Why do the people in the next campsite in a tranquil wilderness area play their radio late into the night? Why does the 10-year-old girl on the baseball team who strikes out every at-bat come to each game with great enthusiasm, while one of the more highly skilled players acts like he wishes to be someplace else in spite of personal success? One way researchers attempt to answer these "why" questions is by identifying the various needs and motivations that *push* people to seek out specific leisure activities and experiences. John Neulinger was among the first leisure researchers to do so.

Neulinger's Paradigm

In Neulinger's (1974, 1981) book *The Psychology of Leisure*, he developed a framework he called a *leisure paradigm*. This model, resulting from the cross-classification of perceived freedom and intrinsic and extrinsic motivation, was concerned with identifying and, in a sense, predicting when an activity or episode would be construed as some type of leisure or non-leisure by the participant (see Figure 5.1).

Neulinger held that the primary defining criterion of leisure was *perceived freedom*. As we learned earlier, a number of leisure researchers have also proposed perceived freedom (or similar notions) as a central defining element of leisure (e.g., Gunter & Gunter, 1980; Iso-Ahola, 1999; Kelly, 1972; Parker, 1971). Neulinger (1981) defined perceived freedom as "a state in which the person feels that what she or he is doing is done by choice and because one wants to do it" (p. 15). Neulinger argued that everyone knows the difference between doing something because one "has to" and doing something because one "wants to." He pointed out that whether such a perception is true freedom or only the *illusion* of freedom is irrelevant because in human behavior even illusions have real consequences (an important point to which we will return shortly). Perceived freedom, as used by Neulinger and other authors, is equated with free choice, which suggests that to have leisure people must perceive that the social setting provides more than one option for action.

The other criterion in Neulinger's framework is the *type of motivation* that underlies the decision to participate in an activity. Based on early notions of *intrinsic* motivation (Deci, 1971; Lepper, Greene, & Nisbett, 1973), he distinguished between intrinsic and *extrinsic* motivation. For the purpose of his paradigm, Neulinger described motivation as being intrinsic when the rewards for participation are "seen as coming from engaging in the activity itself" (1974, p. 17). Motivation was labeled *extrinsic* when the activity is engaged in primarily because it leads to rewards external to the activity itself, such as money, grades, recognition, and awards (see also Chapter 3).

Perceived Freedom	Type of Motivation	
	Extrinsic	Intrinsic
Constrained	**Pure Job**	**Pure Work**
Free	**Leisure-Job**	**Pure Leisure**

Figure 5.1 Neulinger's "Leisure Paradigm" (adapted from Neulinger, 1981, p. 18)

The cells in Neulinger's typology represent four basic ways an activity can be experienced or perceived on the basis of how much freedom of choice and the type of motivation (intrinsic versus extrinsic) people perceive they had when becoming involved in an activity. Because Neulinger theorized that perceived freedom is the primary and critical determinant of what is perceived as leisure, the two cells that represent activities that are freely chosen are both seen as leisure and the other two cells as non-leisure. When an activity is perceived to be freely chosen and motivated for intrinsic reasons, Neulinger called it *pure leisure*. At the opposite extreme, there are activities that are experienced as least leisure-like or *pure job*. The individual has no choice about participating and is motivated by extrinsic reasons. The typology also provides a description of involvements which are neither pure leisure nor pure job. When people have little or no choice about participating but are intrinsically motivated, activities are experienced as *pure work,* work that is enjoyable regardless of its consequences or conditions. Neulinger felt that activities that are engaged in for extrinsic reasons but are freely chosen can be experienced as leisure, a *leisure-job,* in his terms. According to Neulinger, leisure-jobs include much of what is commonly referred to as recreation, such as when a person exercises to maintain her health or plays poker for the sake of winning the pot (but not because she actually needs the money). Before concluding this section, we should note that Neulinger's paradigm has not been utilized very much in recent years, partly because it has been apparent that the picture is more complex and that a variety of needs must to be considered as influential in the construction of leisure. However, we introduce it here because it does provide a preliminary framework for our analysis and a way to think about the needs that bring people to leisure.

Needs

Origins of Needs

Where do needs come from? Common practice has been to divide needs into those that have their basis in people's inherited biological nature (that is, the physiological needs essential for survival) and those that they learn or acquire through their interactions with the social environment (that is, psychological needs, some of which also increase the likelihood of survival).

Physiological Needs

Considerable agreement exists about basic physiological needs, since these are founded upon "tissue deficits" or biochemical imbalances in the body (e.g., hunger, thirst, rest). There is also recognition that, as with many other animals, human beings' brains are governed by the need to have a certain, optimal level of information flow and stimulation, as was discussed in Chapter 4. When stimulation falls below a certain threshold, one will seek novel, incongruous, or challenging circumstances to raise arousal to an optimal level. If arousal exceeds that level, however, measures will be taken to reduce it. Our choice of behavior and activity at any given moment is in part a function of the activity's ability to elicit different levels of arousal.

This *need for optimal arousal* is an important reason for a great deal of exploration (Berlyne, 1971), play (Ellis, 1973), and other forms of leisure activity (Iso-Ahola, 1980a). It also explains the nature of boredom and how this condition can lead a person toward activities that will increase his or her arousal and stimulation. The more novel, incongruous, challenging, or uncertain the outcome of the involvement, the more arousing are the activities. For example, if a person is under-aroused, or bored, she or he is more likely to seek out leisure activities or settings that are new, challenging, or maybe even risky (e.g., hiking a new trail, playing at a higher level of difficulty in a computer game, going to a casino). If a person is over-aroused, he or she is more likely to seek out leisure activities or settings that are familiar, relaxing, and predictable (e.g., visiting a nearby park, watching a favorite movie).

This is not to say these physiologically based needs operate without respect to learning and culture. Weber, Hsee, and Sokolowska (1998), examined traditional proverbs in China ("If someone has never left his home, he cannot be a great person") and the United States ("A bird in the hand is worth two in the bush") to determine if there were cultural differences in risk-taking. In the first part of their study, these researchers found that Chinese proverbs advocated *greater* risk-taking than American proverbs. However, in the second part of their study, they found that this was true for financial but not social decisions. Weber and colleagues believed this outcome reflected the importance of social harmony in Chinese culture and therefore the greater likelihood that a person would be economically "cushioned" by significant others if he or she made a poor investment and "fell." From a leisure perspective, a greater tolerance for economic risk-taking in conjunction with the "cushion hypothesis" could help explain the higher than average number of Chinese North Americans who report having gambling problems. Thus we see the interaction of nature and nurture, of the organism (person) and the situation, in determining even physiological needs, and this is reflected in all domains of life, including leisure.

Psychological Needs

Less agreement exists about psychological needs. Some researchers have tried to list all psychological needs (Murray, 1938), while others have tried to identify what they believe are the most important psychological needs (Deci & Ryan, 2000), and still others have tried not only to single out "core" psychological needs but also to arrange them in some sort of order or framework. Murray's (1938) comprehensive inventory, for example, included among others needs: achievement, affiliation, aggression, autonomy, deference, dominance, harm avoidance, nurturance, order, play, sex, and understanding. In contrast, Fiske (2003, 2004) believes there are five core psychosocial needs: belonging, understanding, controlling, enhancing self, and trusting others, with belonging being the most overarching of these. Deci and Ryan (1985; 2000) are even more succinct than Fiske, holding that there are three core needs that are essential for people's psychological growth and well-being: the *need for autonomy* (which involves freedom to initiate one's behavior, typically through personal choice and control); the *need for competence* (which involves effective functioning and, in turn, the desire to seek out and conquer ever bigger challenges); and the *need for relatedness*. Relatedness refers to the need for people to feel that: (1) they are loved by and connected to others, (2) those others understand them, and (3) they are meaningfully involved with the broader social world in which they live (Deci & Ryan, 1991, p. 243). Ryan and Deci (2000, 2002) refer to the above as "basic needs theory."

Basic needs theory holds that these three needs are inborn or innate and therefore common to all humans (although they can and do vary across people to some extent). Of these three, autonomy is often considered the most important, in part because it and competence are always pertinent whereas relatedness is not (for example, if you have chosen to play a video game by yourself, or go on a solo hike, this need is not relevant.) Finally, these three core psychological needs may subsume other more secondary needs. Fiske (2004), for example, has proposed that the needs for control, understanding, and self-enhancement all fall under the need for relatedness, but this is likely due to her focusing more clearly on social motives. We will discuss the need for autonomy more in the second half of this chapter, when we examine the leisure concept of perceived freedom, and we will discuss this need as well as the need for competence and relatedness in the next chapter, when we examine how these three core psychological needs affect motivation.

Arguably, Maslow (1968) developed the most well-known needs framework (see Figure 5.2). Maslow theorized that everyone possesses five need categories that are arranged in a hierarchy of importance. At the lowest level are physiological needs, followed in order by safety and security needs, belongingness and love needs, ego and esteem needs, and self-actualization. Once lower-level needs are satisfied, needs at the next highest level emerge and influence behavior. The levels of the need hierarchy are not rigidly separated but overlap to some extent. Thus, it is possible for a higher-level need to emerge before a lower-level need is completely satisfied. In fact, Maslow suggested that average adults in Western societies have satisfied about 85% of their physiological needs, 70% of their safety needs, 50% of their social needs, 40% of their self-esteem needs, and 10% of their self-actualization needs. Although Maslow never collected data to support these estimates, research suggests that lower-level needs are indeed satisfied more than higher-level needs (Steers & Porter, 1991).

Although Maslow's theory has a great deal of appeal, it has proved difficult to test (Steers & Porter, 1991; Wahba & Bridwell, 1976). There is no clear evidence showing that human needs can be separated into five distinct categories or that these needs are structured into any special hierarchy. Apparently, higher-level needs can influence behavior even when lower-level needs are largely unfulfilled, as is often seen in people dealing with deprivation or disability. However, Maslow's framework has been widely adopted by theorists and planners who are interested in improving social conditions. For example, his hierarchy has provided a theoretical basis for work-organization-improvement programs such as participative management, job enrichment, and quality of work-life projects (Cherrington, 1989). According to the theory, an organization must use a variety of factors since people will be at different levels of the need hierarchy.

While empirical support for Maslow's hierarchy is weak, his highest need, the need for self-actualization, has been the focus of some leisure research. Maslow (1970) defined self-actualization as a person's full use and exploration of his or her talents, capacities, and potentialities. Csikszentmihalyi and Kleiber (1991) argued that leisure offered unique conditions for self-actualization unavailable in other, more constrained domains (such as paid employment), in part because "involvement in an activity must be deep, sustained, and disciplined to contribute to an emerging sense of self" (p. 94).

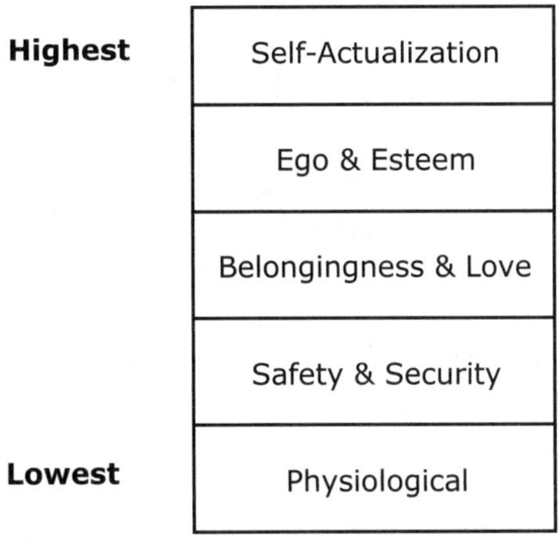

Figure 5.2 Maslow's Hierarchy (adapted from Maslow, 1968)

They then proposed that self-actualization is related to flow experiences in that, for example, when the self disappears during flow it reappears afterward stronger than ever, and this is what being self-actualized implies (Csikszentmihalyi, 1975, 1993). The deep, sustained, and disciplined involvement described by Csikszentmihalyi and Kleiber is also one of the qualities of serious leisure (Stebbins, 2005, 2007), and therefore it is not surprising to find that self-actualization is identified as a personal benefit of serious leisure. Finally, self-actualization has also been linked with certain leisure settings, particularly wilderness (Roggenbuck & Driver, 2000; Young & Crandall, 1984).

A study of psychological priorities of American college students (Sheldon, Elliot, Kim, & Kasser, 2001) indicated that self-esteem was ranked highest, followed by a rough equivalence among relatedness, autonomy, and competence in the next place, followed by pleasure/stimulation, physical thriving, self-actualization/meaning, security, and popularity/influence, with these five not being significantly different from each other, and then finally luxury. Although self-esteem's top ranking seems to conflict with Deci and Ryan's (1985, 2000) contention that autonomy, competence, and relatedness are the core psychological needs, some researchers have proposed that self-esteem can be considered to be an aspect of competence (Sheldon et al., 2001). On the other hand, Greenberg, Pyszczynski, and Solomon's (1986) *Terror Management Theory* proposes that self-esteem functions to buffer people from death anxiety, which suggests that this need may be distinct from other core needs. Regardless, it is worth adding that a group of South Korean students ranked Sheldon and colleagues' (2001) 10 needs somewhat differently than their American counterparts did, an issue we will return to in Chapter 10.

Leisure Needs

How Many *Leisure* Needs Are There?

At least two inventories have been developed based on the idea that leisure activities can satisfy Deci and Ryan's (1985, 2000) three core psychological needs (that is, autonomy, competence, and relatedness) as well as a variety of other easily "expressed" needs. Tinsley and Kass (1978) found that the 44 needs that they measured could be reduced to eight types (i.e., self-expression, companionship, power, compensation, security, service, intellectual aestheticism, and solitude). Driver's 39 *Recreation Experience Preference Scales* (Driver, 1976) have been reduced to 19 categories, 8 that research has shown are important to recreationists using natural and wilderness areas (Rosenthal, Waldman, & Driver 1982). These include exploration, escaping role overload, general nature experience, introspection, exercise, being with similar people, seeking exhilaration, and escaping physical stressors. Driver, Tinsley, and Manfredo's (1991) inventories each measure a large number of needs, but if leisure is a more limited realm of life it makes sense that it would be shaped by, and satisfy, a smaller set of needs. In spite of the large number and types of expressed needs reported in various studies of leisure behavior and the different names used to label them, there is some agreement about the relatively small number of basic types that operate (Tinsley, 1984).

A Leisure Needs Model

In contrast with these need inventories, Iso-Ahola (1982, 1989) has suggested that the reasons people participate in leisure can be reduced to two basic dimensions—escaping and seeking (see Figure 5.3). According to Iso-Ahola, these two forces simultaneously influence people's leisure behavior. On the one hand, leisure activities are engaged in because they provide novelty or change from daily routine and stress. By *escaping* the everyday environment, a person can leave behind his or her personal and/or interpersonal worlds. The personal world refers to escape from one's own problems, troubles, difficulties, and failures, and the interpersonal world refers to other people, such as coworkers, friends, and family members. An individual can escape both worlds simultaneously. He suggests that escape is a powerful leisure need due to the constraining nature of a person's life, particularly her or his work. Escape is also based on the need for optimal arousal; individuals are constantly trying to escape from under-arousing and over-arousing conditions.

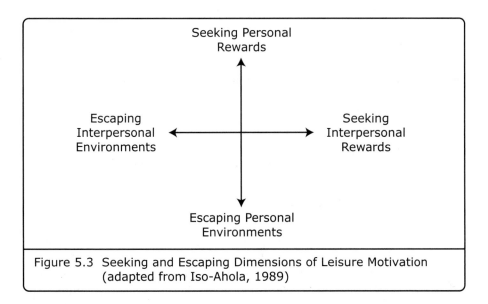

Figure 5.3 Seeking and Escaping Dimensions of Leisure Motivation (adapted from Iso-Ahola, 1989)

The other dimension is the tendency to *seek* psychological need satisfactions from participation in leisure activities. The satisfactions that people may seek through leisure can also be divided into personal and interpersonal types. Personal satisfactions consist mainly of self-determination, sense of competence, challenge, learning, exploration, and relaxation. On the other hand, people often want to engage in leisure activities for social contact and connectedness. Iso-Ahola (1989) suggests that both the seeking and escaping needs are forms of intrinsic motivation, a topic that we will discuss more fully in the next chapter.

In a study of a group of sightseeing tourists participating in a guided tour of Washington, DC, Dunn Ross and Iso-Ahola (1991) found that the reasons for participating in the tour could be classified according to the seeking and escaping dimensions of Iso-Ahola's model. Participants were primarily energized by *knowledge seeking* and opportunities for *social interaction*. However, there was evidence of an escape dimension, in that the tourists also wanted to escape their troubles, work, and other responsibilities by participation in the tour. A more recent study (Snepenger, King, Marshall, & Uysal, 2006) also supported Iso-Ahola's model, with these researchers finding that tourism experiences (e.g., going to the Superbowl) were driven more by personal escape and personal seeking than in more typical recreational experiences (e.g., going to a high school football game). In spite of these two studies' results, it remains to be seen how useful it is to reduce leisure needs to only these two dimensions.

Are Some Needs Satisfied *Only* during Leisure?

Can you think of any needs that can only be satisfied in leisure? Is leisure, itself, a basic "human need"? That is not such a new or unusual idea. In 1908, McDougall proposed that people are born with an instinct to play that directs their behavior; and more recently, Ohler and Nieding (2006) suggested that evolutionary theory could be used to explain animal play generally and human computer-game playing specifically.

Nevertheless, leisure research has not led to the discovery of needs that can only be met through what a person does during leisure. The forces operative in other areas of an individual's life also influence the activities chosen in and as leisure. For example, Reid and Mannell (1993) asked a large group of working people to rate the extent to which they typically satisfied 16 needs in both their work and their leisure. Most of the respondents reported that all of these needs were satisfied to some extent in both work and leisure, though the needs for self-esteem and achievement were met to a greater degree in work and the needs for social interaction and escape were met to a greater degree in leisure. In an experience sampling method study (Ryan, Bernstein, & Brown, 2010) composed of 74 American workers, the needs for autonomy, competence, and relatedness were all less satisfied during work than non-work activities. Ryan and colleagues added, however, that because they did not differentiate between the various types of non-work activities that exist (e.g., leisure versus "self-maintenance" such as grooming and grocery shopping), their findings may actually have underestimated the role of non-work need satisfaction. Finally, Walker and Wang (2009) had 35 Chinese/Canadians respond to a watch alarm that was randomly programmed to ring once every two hours, seven times a day, for 12 days. When the alarm rang, participants reported what activity they were doing, whether it was work, leisure, both, or neither (cf. Shaw, 1984), and how well their core psychological needs for autonomy, competence, and relatedness were being satisfied. As shown in Table 5.1, these researchers found that when people were alone, autonomy was satisfied the most during leisure and the least during neither (e.g., doing household chores, driving to work), whereas competence was satisfied the most during work and the least during neither. In contrast, when people were with others, autonomy and competence were satisfied the most during leisure and the least during work. In summary, although these studies collectively do not make the case that all needs can be satisfied through leisure, they do demonstrate that some needs are more readily satisfied during leisure than at other times, depending to some extent on the social context (i.e., whether one is alone or with others).

Before we conclude this section we want to point out that leisure may not only be the best context for *satisfying* certain needs, it may at times also be the best context for *ignoring* certain needs, including some of those basic needs identified by Deci and Ryan, Fiske, and others. We have already noted that relatedness is not always relevant (such as when we choose to hike alone), and *not* being in control may be desirable in some leisure situations, such as with some wilderness hikers as we will see shortly. And the need for

Need	Social Setting	
	Alone	**With Others**
Autonomy	Satisfied most during leisure	Satisfied most during leisure
	Satisfied least during neither	Satisfied least during work
Competence	Satisfied most during work	Satisfied most during leisure
	Satisfied least during neither	Satisfied least during both
Relatedness	Not applicable	Satisfied most during leisure
	Not applicable	Satisfied least during work

Table 5.1 Need Satisfaction (adapted from Walker & Wang, 2009)

understanding (cognition) may also be suppressed in some cases. Using a *Need for Cognition* scale developed earlier (Cacioppo & Petty, 1982), Henning and Vorderer (2001) discovered that students who had a low need for cognition watched more television, which led them to conclude that "people with nothing to do are likely to escape with television depending on how unpleasant they find what is left for them to do (namely thinking) when they have nothing else to do" (p. 117). The need to maintain self-esteem (cf. Tesser, 1988) may also be abandoned through leisure. Baumeister (1991) posited that the perceived frequency of embarrassing, humiliating, and degrading experiences would lead to lower self-esteem which, in turn, would lead to a desire to "escape the self" through various, often addictive, behaviors. Besides masochism, meditation, spirituality, and alcohol use and abuse (all of which have been linked to leisure at one time or another), Baumeister also identified two types of leisure activities that can be used to escape the "burden of selfhood:" (1) participation in leisure activities, particularly those likely to result in flow experiences (Csikszentmihalyi, 1990); and (2) watching leisure activities, particularly those involving mental focusing and de-individuation (such as concerts or sporting events). Unfortunately, research on escaping core needs through leisure is currently limited, but this area seems worthy of further attention in the future.

Leisure Needs, Activities, and Settings

At the beginning of this chapter, we stated that researchers often attempt to answer "why" questions (e.g., why do people jog in blizzards, rock climb alone, and play baseball even if they always strike out?) by identifying the various needs and motives that *push* people to seek out specific leisure activities, settings, and experiences. At first glance, the focus of these explanations appears to be internal to the person. However, on closer scrutiny, the answers to these "why" questions have both *person* and *situational* components, and therefore require an *interactionist perspective* to be understood. Thus, besides the forces within people that *push* them to engage in certain behaviors, researchers are also interested in the characteristics of leisure activities and settings that *pull* people to select them rather than others.

For example, John has several physiological and psychological needs that are currently aroused, such as feeling a need to be connected with other people (need for relatedness), feeling like he needs to have accomplished something (need for achievement), and needing to get away from the frenzied nature of his job (need for reduced arousal). Based on these needs, what would you recommend he do during his leisure this coming weekend? Where should he go and what should he do? Is there a single, specific leisure activity or experience that will best provide a "package of satisfactions" to meet his needs (i.e., relatedness, achievement, and reduced stimulation rather than, say, self-expression and increased stimulation), or are there a wide variety of activities and settings available to him? Many people would be quite prepared to counsel John and make suggestions based on the belief that leisure activities and settings do differ in their ability to satisfy specific needs.

Iso-Ahola (1999), for example, described how two activities—television watching and physical exercise—could satisfy a person's aroused needs. According to Iso-Ahola, the frequent and widespread use of television is likely a response to people's need for escape (from daily stress and over- and under-stimulation) in combination with providing them with an illusion of choice and control. For example: Which TV channel? Watch it now or record it? Watch it and another channel picture-in-picture? Watch it for how long? What volume level? More bass or less? But Iso-Ahola added that:

> Selecting television watching gives them an easy way to feel limited autonomy and control, and this may be psychologically sufficient. The sense of autonomy derived from television watching, however, becomes illusory because it does not make people feel good about themselves psychologically; at best this activity helps only partially to fulfill their most basic human need: a need for autonomy (Deci & Ryan, 1991). . . . Even though the sense of autonomy may be limited because it (television watching) is not what people would really like to do, it nevertheless is powerful; in fact, so powerful that it may mask and hinder people from pursuing the fulfillment of their other innate (psychological) needs, such as needs for personal competence and social interrelationships. (p. 37)

In contrast, while the need for autonomy could at least partially be satisfied by *not* exercising, by freely choosing to engage in exercise we can satisfy this need at least equally as well (and much more than while watching television, Iso-Ahola argues); we can still fulfill our need for escape (from daily stress and over- and under-stimulation); and we can also satisfy our core needs for competence (by running harder routes or quicker times) and relatedness (by running with a partner or as part of a club; assuming we *want* to be with others, which, as we have discussed, is not always the case).

Iso-Ahola's (1999) in-depth discussion of these two leisure activities is useful for at least three reasons. First, it demonstrates that similar and different types of relationships can exist between different kinds of needs, activities, and settings. Second, it clearly links Deci and Ryan's (1991, 2000) social psychological theory of basic needs (with the need for autonomy being preeminent) with research that has found that perceived freedom is the primary attribute of leisure (and so the key component in most leisure theories, including Neulinger's paradigm). Third, it highlights the illusory nature of need satisfaction and why, as a result, we typically speak of *perceived* freedom during leisure. Because of the importance of the last two of these three, we examine each in greater detail in the rest of this chapter.

Perceived Freedom and Control in Life and Leisure

Perceived Freedom

To quickly review, Neulinger (1981) and others (e.g., Gunter & Gunter, 1980; Iso-Ahola, 1999; Kelly, 1972; Parker, 1971) held that the primary defining criterion of leisure was *perceived freedom*. Perceived freedom for Neulinger was "a state in which the person feels that what she or he is doing is done by choice and because one wants to do it" (p. 15). While freedom is a complex phenomenon that includes political, social, and philosophical dimensions, one of its most important components is the subjective experience or perception of acting voluntarily. People in their daily lives perform thousands of acts. Each of these acts is experienced as being more or less compulsory, more or less voluntary (see also Lefcourt, 1973; Presson & Benassi, 1996).

Imagine, for example, you are caring for two young children. They have had their breakfast and while you are cleaning up the dishes they gravitate to the television. They are now deeply engrossed in a television program. It's a beautiful day, and you want them to go outside and play in the nearby park. Experience tells you that, depending on how you approach the children, you may be in for some conflict and a poor start to a potentially pleasant day. You may also end up with children who are less than enthusiastic about an activity they typically enjoy. How do you handle this situation? What are your options? You could tell the children that they "must go outside and play." They may resist, argue, perhaps refuse, or at best drag themselves out of the house with the look of martyrs, only to return within minutes to report that there is nothing to do.

In an effort to avoid this outcome, you may resort to what is sometimes called "reverse psychology." You can tell the children that though it is a beautiful morning and their friends are likely already at the park, they "cannot go out and play right now." Sometimes this strategy actually works and the children might lose interest in the television program and lobby you to let them go and play at the park. In this case, you "reluctantly" give in and let them "have their way." Unfortunately, it doesn't take children very long to develop immunity to this strategy. If the children are experienced with adults and their ways, they are likely to look at you with contempt and perhaps even pity.

There is another strategy that you can consider. Though requiring the children go outside and play, you could allow them to decide for themselves when they will do so, at least, within certain limits. You tell them that they have to go outside and play, but they can watch another half-hour of television before they go out, or they can go outside now and come in before lunch to watch the television. If the play at the park is an attractive option, and you remind them of this, they may go along with this suggestion. On the other hand, this may not work, either, and then you will have to decide whether to use your authority as an adult and dictate what they do.

The children's behavior and reactions in this hypothetical situation and the strategies for dealing with them revolve around the importance of having *choice* and feeling in *control*. When an authority figure tells someone that they have to do something, such as "you have to go out and play," she or he restricts their choices. This may result in individuals feeling that they have little control over what is going on, and it prevents them from feeling that they are the "cause" or "origin" of their own behavior. The need for self-determination is reflected in the children's resistance to doing what they are told and in their less-than-enthusiastic response to the request that they go outside and play in the park.

When you used reverse psychology, you were attempting to take advantage of the children's desire for self-determination. By appearing to restrict or eliminate the option of going outside to play in the park, you expected them to react negatively and try to increase the amount of choice and control they have by lobbying to do what has been forbidden. Of course, the children will eventually come to realize that they are being controlled and really have no choice. Consequently, they are not likely to experience their behavior as self-determined. At this point, the strategy loses its effectiveness.

With the final strategy, you are attempting to give the children a feeling of choice that will hopefully allow them to feel that playing in the park is self-determined behavior. Obviously, the amount of choice available to the children is somewhat limited by the guidelines and conditions you have established. You have effectively constrained their behavior. However, it may be sufficient to allow the children to feel some control over the situation and consequently react positively to your request to go out and play in the park.

Perceived freedom, as used by Neulinger and others, is equated with free choice, which suggests the idea that to have leisure, people must perceive that the social setting provides at least more than one opportunity for action. This type of perceived freedom has been called *decision freedom* (Steiner, 1970). Social psychologists have in general assumed that the experience of freedom is an attribution people make about their behavior (see Brehm & Brehm, 1981; Schwartz, 2000; Steiner, 1970; Wortman, 1975). Perceived freedom is not an all-or-nothing condition. In fact, in most situations, people are likely to be constrained in some way so that they typically feel only *relatively* free or free within certain limits. Though an individual may have the afternoon off to do as she or he wishes, in actual fact, choices for leisure are likely constrained to some extent by the time available, finances, recreational skills, and the availability of friends. Indeed, some constraints actually define activities and allow them to happen, such as the rules of a game that limit freedoms (e.g., where a tennis ball can be legitimately served) and make the game possible and enjoyable (McGuire & Norman, 2005; Shogan, 2002).

Regardless, two key questions remain: "Is perceived freedom an important dimension of people's everyday experience?" and "Do people distinguish leisure from non-leisure activities and settings as a function of perceived freedom?" Perceived freedom's importance is nicely demonstrated by a study conducted by Csikszentmihalyi and Graef (1980). They studied a sample of 106 working men and women from the Chicago area with the experience sampling method over the course of a typical week in their lives. Respondents were asked to record the main activity they were engaged in when signaled and how free they felt to participate. The percentage of the time people perceived their actions to be freely chosen varied greatly between activities. As one might expect, work was rated as the least freely chosen activity. Only 15% of the time was it experienced as voluntary. Activities experienced as freely chosen most frequently were sports and games (90% of the time). As can be seen in Figure 5.4, leisure activities were experienced much more frequently as freely chosen, though there were interesting gender differences. Males rated most activities as more voluntary, especially cooking and childcare. The only activities for which this trend was reversed and women felt greater freedom of choice were in leisure settings outside the home (e.g., movies, restaurants), and during informal social gatherings. Idling, watching television, and reading were activities in which gender differences were least noticeable in terms of perceived freedom.

Control

In the social psychological literature, a variety of terms identify the human desire for freedom and control. Theories have been proposed suggesting that a sense of freedom or control is a fundamental need and essential to health and well-being. As noted earlier, Fiske (2004) considers control one of our core social needs. In 1968, deCharms proposed that people are all motivated by the desire to be masters of their own fate, and that people strive to be *causal agents* or the *origins* of their behavior. In fact, exercising control is satisfying in itself. All humans want to understand their world and to exercise control over their environment; otherwise they would not survive. As Lefcourt (1973, p. 424) noted, having a sense of control "has a definite and positive role in sustaining life."

Ellen Langer (1983) suggested that people have such a strong need for control that it leads them to perceive that they have control and freedom of choice even when they do not. In her book *The Psychology of Control,* Langer suggested that people need to feel they can control the important events in their lives, and she argued that most people are unrealistically optimistic about the future and tend to exaggerate the amount of control they have over uncontrollable life events. She found that even bright, well-adjusted university students delude themselves by believing they can control the outcomes of games of chance. When the students she was studying played cards against a competitor, they bet more money when their competitor seemed nervous rather than confident, even though they were aware that the winner was determined purely by chance. When the participants in her study played a lottery, they were more reluctant to sell their ticket after choosing the number themselves than after receiving an assigned number, even though it did not improve their chances of winning (Langer, 1975). Langer's work has been well-supported, with a review of 53 separate experiments leading the two researchers to conclude that "illusion of control effects have been found across different tasks, in many situations, and by numerous independent

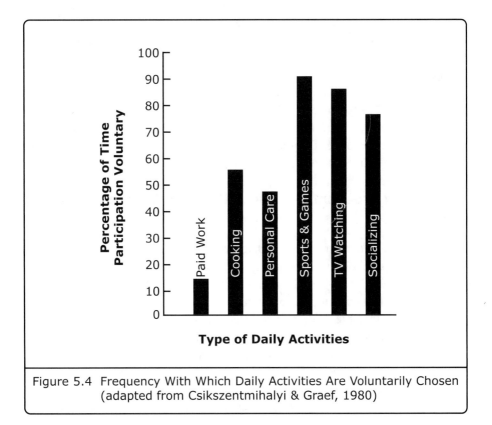

Figure 5.4 Frequency With Which Daily Activities Are Voluntarily Chosen (adapted from Csikszentmihalyi & Graef, 1980)

researchers" (Presson & Benassi, 1996, p. 306). A more recent, non-experimental study with undergraduate students led another group of researchers to a similar conclusion: specifically, that Langer's illusion of control "is still today a robust phenomenon that can be observed even in the context of a very simple computer program that users try to control (and believe that they are controlling) over the Internet" (Matute, Vadillo, Vegas, & Blanco, 2007, p. 176).

On the other hand, there may be times when people gain control by recognizing and adjusting to their circumstances. According to Weisz, Rothbaum, and Blackburn (1984) there are two types of control: primary and secondary. Primary control occurs when individuals enhance their rewards by *influencing* existing realities. In contrast, secondary control occurs when individuals enhance their rewards by *accommodating* to existing realities. From a leisure perspective, Scherl (1989) argued that while some wilderness visitors want to demonstrate their control over nature (e.g., by cutting down trees to build a lean-to) most visitors prefer to adjust to nature (e.g., by covering their sleeping bag with fallen leaves). Additionally, Weisz and colleagues also identified different types of secondary control, but of these, vicarious secondary control may be the most pertinent to leisure studies. Although generally conceived in terms of adapting so as to align with significant others, they believed that some Zen activities (e.g., archery, flower arranging, and visiting gardens) could "give the perceiver a feeling of complete identification with the focal object or event" (Weisz et al., 1984, p. 962). Thus, there could be a relationship between this type of secondary control and some of the leisure attributes we described in the previous chapter (see also Kleiber, 1985). Fiske (2004) also points to cultural differences on this dimension; trusting and giving up primary control to others is more common in Asian, African, and Latino societies (Fiske & Depret, 1996), where families especially are a source of secondary control.

Theories of Freedom and Control and Their Implications for Leisure

Psychological Reactance and Substitutability

The "reverse psychology" example used earlier, where getting kids to play outside in spite of their other inclinations was the objective, was based on an understanding that any kind of coercion is likely to be resisted, even if it would be otherwise agreeable. If perceived freedom and control are so important, it should come as no surprise that a threat to, or the elimination of, freedom can have negative psychological consequences. Brehm (1966) suggested that a threat to or loss of freedom generates a state of motivational arousal he called *psychological reactance,* which results in attempts to regain the freedom. According to this theory, individuals have a set of specific behavioral freedoms—actions, thoughts, and feelings—which they exercise to varying degrees. When a specific freedom is eliminated or threatened, the individual will evaluate that freedom more favorably and be motivated to re-establish it (Brehm, 1966; Brehm & Brehm, 1981), the so-called "forbidden fruit" phenomenon. For example, 16-year-old Rachel's parents restrict her from going out with certain friends because of their reputations for getting into trouble. How strongly she will react depends on several factors according to reactance theory. First, the more she has learned to expect to have this particular freedom, the more psychological reactance will be experienced as a result of the threat to or elimination of it. Rachel will experience greater reactance if she has been with these friends regularly rather than only occasionally. Second, her reaction to the threat, or to the actual elimination of this behavioral freedom, is stronger if this freedom is perceived as important. She is likely to experience greater psychological reactance if these friends are a major source of approval and relatedness for her. Third, if her parents forbid any involvement with these friends, she will experience greater reactance than if they identify specific activities to avoid. Finally, if the threat to this freedom is likely to negatively impact on her other activities, then reactance will be greater than if there was no such impact. In other words, psychological reactance will be greater if socialization with these particular friends is also the primary context for involvement in a variety of other leisure activities.

Brehm described several common consequences of experiencing psychological reactance. The threatened or eliminated behavioral freedom can become more attractive to the individual. In the previous example, forbidding or threatening the opportunity to socialize with particular friends may result in the adolescent wanting to interact with them even more than she currently does. Driscoll, Davis, and Lipetz (1972) found that the more interference in a romantic relationship there was by parents, the more in love the couples were. On the other hand, if people are coerced into engaging in an activity, it can reduce its attractiveness. For example, Wright, Wadely, Danner, and Phillips (1992) found that matchmaking and arranging blind dates for friends can backfire. Motivated to preserve the freedom to make their own romantic choices, prospective partners may become less attractive to each other than they would have without outside encouragement. And if parents actually approve of an adolescent's choice of romantic partners, they might be wise not to be too enthusiastic about it, lest their approval be regarded as imposing and interfering.

An individual can also demonstrate psychological reactance by engaging in direct attempts to restore the threatened or eliminated option, or compensate for the loss by pursuing related behaviors. In the case of the prohibited friends, the adolescent may sneak out to hang out with them or attempt to persuade his parents that they are not so bad, to restore this freedom. Failing that, the individual may develop totally new friendships that offer something of those that he was denied.

Restrictions on activities are perhaps the most common kinds of threats to recreation freedom, whether due to the risk the activity poses to the individual or the impositions it imposes on others or on the environment. Examples include skateboarding in areas not intended for skateboarding, hunting for a species that is beginning to be endangered, or being under a doctor's orders to give up a preferred sport that is seen as the cause of a chronic back problem. Iso-Ahola (1980a) suggested that a person with a wide variety of leisure skills is much better equipped to handle threats to recreational freedom. Iso-Ahola subsequently expanded this idea into the *Theory of Substitutability* and suggested that people will be less willing to replace one leisure activity for another when the external "pressure for substitution of leisure behaviors gives rise to psychological reactance" (Iso-Ahola, 1986, p. 371). A study by Sutton and Ditton (2005) lends support to Iso-Ahola's theory, as they found that Texas anglers interested in catching a trophy fish would be less willing to fish for another species if, for example, a natural resource agency decided stocks of the originally sought-after fish were too low. It is worth noting, however, that Sutton and Ditton also found that the vast majority (86%) of their anglers reported that other species would provide acceptable substitutes.

In its application to leisure, psychological reactance theory offers a way to "predict the arousal of negative affect when the individual has limited choice, which potentially could interfere with the individual's ability to enjoy and become involved in an activity" (Mannell & Backman, 1979, p. 301). Feeling that you had little choice in the decision to participate would also reduce the attractiveness of the activity. Some support for this hypothesis was provided by the experiment described in Chapter 3, which simulated a period of free time in the laboratory and manipulated the freedom of choice subjects had to play a game. As predicted, the participants were found to have less positive and psychologically involving experiences when they perceived they had less choice than other participants.

From a more applied perspective, Kyle, Absher, and Chancellor (2005) looked at whether psychological reactance theory could help explain people's reaction to increasing recreation fees at a U.S. National Forest. As they expected, people with lower incomes reported experiencing higher levels of psychological reactance, whereas people with higher incomes reported experiencing lower levels of reactance. Kyle et al. held that these results occurred because visitors with lower incomes had fewer options (such as going to another park) and, therefore, they experienced more intense negative emotions than those with higher incomes.

Learned helplessness

Another important social psychological theory based on the belief that freedom and control are important for human functioning is the theory of *learned helplessness*. According to Abramson, Garber, and Seligman (1980) and others (Witt & Ellis, 1985), if perceived freedom occupies one end of a continuum, then learned helplessness, a phenomenon in which experience with uncontrollable events creates passive behavior toward subsequent threats to well-being (Seligman, 1975), occupies the opposite end. In one study, dogs that received a series of electrical shocks over which they had no control later failed to escape from additional shocks by crossing a barrier into a compartment where no shocks were delivered (Maier & Seligman, 1976). Those that had not received uncontrollable shocks quickly learned to avoid the subsequent shocks by crossing over. Similarly, human subjects exposed to inescapable bursts of noise failed to protect themselves in a later situation where noise could be easily avoided (Hiroto, 1974).

Seligman (1975) argued that these findings indicate that both animals and humans exposed to uncontrollable or inescapable negative events come to believe that control is not possible, and therefore, stop trying to exert control. Childhood or adult socialization experiences and social environments where repeated failure occurs and which lead people to attribute these uncontrollable events to their own personal failings are thought to be a source of low self-esteem and depression, that is, learned helplessness.

Because it appeared to have such significant consequences for learning, adaptation, and mental health, Seligman and his colleagues turned their attention to efforts to counteract or prevent the effects leading to learned helplessness. They found that animals and humans alike could be "immunized" to learned helplessness, by learning effective responses to negative stimuli that are initially presumed to be inescapable (Seligman, 1991). A kind of directive therapy thus led to a condition that the researchers called "learned optimism." This kind of treatment has important implications for the practice of therapeutic recreation, where learning that one's actions can bring about enjoyment, despite conditions associated with disability and aging, helps to reduce depression and leads to more general kinds of empowerment (e.g., Searle, Mahon, Iso-Ahola, Adam Sdrolias, & van Dyck, 1995, 1998).

The theory of learned helplessness can be applied to understanding participants' reactions in other leisure settings. Iso-Ahola (1977, 1980a, 1980b) suspected that participation in Little League Baseball may induce learned helplessness as a result of young players being exposed to failure and subsequent feelings of lack of control. He concluded that a team's repeated failure could, under some conditions, contribute to the development of learned helplessness. If players attribute their failure to a lack of personal ability or control, their enjoyment of the activity is reduced and they are likely to withdraw. If the problem becomes compounded by repeated exposure to failures and uncontrollable events, such as striking out repeatedly, a state of generalized helplessness may be the consequence. This learned helplessness might influence involvement in other leisure or even non-leisure activities.

Today, in many communities, leisure service providers have developed a variety of strategies to minimize these negative effects of children's organized sports. Noncompetitive recreational leagues that de-emphasize winning and stress skill development and fun are common. Preseason practices, followed by player drafts to allow the formation of better balanced teams, have also been implemented. As Iso-Ahola (1980b) suggested, the most obvious solution would be to remove competition from leisure activities entirely. However, he points out that such solutions are unrealistic. While competition and winning can be de-emphasized, elimination altogether is unlikely. In fact, even if society were to cease declaring people winners and losers, they would still continue to "compete" by using subjective criteria and standards. People, whether children or adults, seem to have a need and desire to evaluate their personal abilities relative to those of others (Festinger, 1954). Subtle and indirect social comparison can be as powerful as a direct failure in creating the perception of incompetence or helplessness.

People learn to deal with failure by using a variety of psychological strategies and consequently avoid developing feelings of learned helplessness. If one watches children who play on a losing team, it can be seen that they often are able to focus on their own personal successes and skill development, and attribute the failure to the team as a whole or to other players. Effective coaching might also take the direction of cultivating learned optimism in such cases, such as through attribution retraining, where failure is attributed to effort and other circumstances rather than to one's abilities (Dweck, 1999; Weiner, 1985). People can also learn to put winning and losing into perspective when confronted with a failure. The importance of the leisure activity in which failures are experienced can be minimized and the importance of leisure activities in which the individual is proficient can be emphasized (Iso-Ahola & Mannell, 1985). Too much winning is not good either, however. People are not likely to develop strategies for coping with failure if they are not occasionally exposed to it (Iso-Ahola, 1980b, p. 199). This topic of socialization into leisure activities will be taken up again in Chapter 9.

Learned helplessness theory also helps in understanding the psychological challenges that institutionalized older adults and people with disabilities may face in enjoying meaningful leisure (Dattilo & Kleiber, 1993; Iso-Ahola, 1980a; MacNeil & Teague, 1987). Both the disability itself and other people's reactions to it may lead persons with disabilities to perceive themselves to be helpless. This can reduce their efforts, their sense of recreational freedom, and thereby the possibility of achieving success in subsequent leisure engagements. In a study of older adults who were residents in a nursing home, Shary and Iso-Ahola (1989) demonstrated that these feelings of helplessness and lack of control can be reversed. They provided one group of residents with an orientation session that stressed the importance of the residents taking responsibility for making leisure choices that affected their daily lives at the facility. This group was given a choice over the type, scheduling, and length of a variety of leisure activities in which they could participate during the course of the study. A second group of residents, the control group, participated in similar activities but were not sensitized to the importance of taking responsibility and control of their lives in the facility, and they were not given opportunities to make choices or assume any responsibility over situations during the leisure activities. At the end of the study, the group that was encouraged to take control of their leisure perceived themselves to be much more competent, had higher levels of self-esteem, and enjoyed their leisure participation much more than did the control group—that is, they had learned not to feel helpless.

The development of highly realistic electronic games could also, potentially, help reduce the likelihood of learned helpless among people with disabilities. For example, Weiss, Bialik, and Kizony (2003) had young adults with severe cerebral palsy snowboard *virtually*, catch virtual balls, and play goalie in a virtual soccer game. Study participants reported that all three virtual reality experiences were highly enjoyable, but given the opportunity all preferred playing soccer. "The ability to make choices and to indicate preferences," according to the researchers, "is a first step toward the achievement of a sense of independence and responsibility" (p. 339). The long-term outcome, they believed, could be a reduction in their participants' perceptions of learned helplessness.

Summary

Generally, the need for a sense of freedom and control is thought to be important or common to all people. However, there are theories that suggest that the need for freedom and control varies in strength among people as a result of socialization experiences and personality. For example, Burger (1992) has proposed a *need for control* that he describes as a personality trait. In other words, some people have a high need for control, whereas for others this need is much less important. As we will discuss in the chapter on leisure and personality (Chapter 7), researchers have examined these types of individual differences and their influence on the ability to experience leisure.

Limits to Freedom and the Politics of Control

The translation of the concept of leisure into the social psychological construct of perceived freedom has stimulated leisure research and provided a bridge to the extensive work in general social psychology. The use of definitions, measures, research strategies, and theories from these social psychological areas of inquiry has provided a basis for building an improved understanding of leisure, and provides useful ideas to help people experience more mean-ingful leisure. Given the importance of perceived freedom, it is no surprise that leisure, at its best, can provide a context that promotes extremely mean-ingful and psychologically powerful activities and experiences. It is also worth acknowledging that leisure researchers have taken these ideas and applied them to understanding and improving the quality of people's activi-ties and experiences in leisure contexts.

It should be noted that there have been criticisms in leisure studies of an over-reliance on social psychological interpretations of such an important idea as *freedom*, particularly in conceptualizing freedom as "free choice" or "decision choice," as has typically been done in leisure theory and research. Perceived freedom can be viewed as ongoing experience and even an out-come of leisure experience (Harper, 1981, 1986; Kleiber, 1985). It might also be useful to distinguish between the different meanings of freedom suggested by the terms "freedom from" and "freedom to" (Bregha, 1980; Sylvester, 1985). It has been suggested that *freedom from* refers to the absence of duress, coercion, and interference, and *freedom to* involves willful choice and action on the part of the individual. These two types of freedom could have quite distinct implications for an individual's behavior and experience during leisure.

The idea that maximizing freedom through maximizing choice will lead to improved well-being has also been reconsidered in recent years. For exam-ple, there is a limit to the number of choices one can reasonably be able to consider at one time (e.g., having to decide between numerous university courses) without feeling either burdened or anxious about not making the "right" decision (Iyengar & Lepper, 1999). Moreover, research suggests that some people may feel *worse* than other people as their options increase (Schwartz, 2000; Schwartz, Ward, Monterosso, Lyubomirsky, White, & Lehman, 2002). For example, how would you respond to the following questions: (a) "When I watch TV, I channel surf, often scanning through the available options even while attempting to watch one program"; (b) "When shopping, I have a hard time finding clothing I really love"; and (c) "Renting videos is really diffi-cult; I'm always struggling to pick the best one" (Schwartz et al., p. 1182). If you strongly identified with all three statements you are likely a "maximizer," whereas if you strongly rejected all three as being like you, you are likely a "satisficer." Schwartz and colleagues found that maximizers were generally less satisfied with their choices than satisficers and, importantly, maximization was negatively associated with happiness, optimism, self-esteem, and life satisfaction and positively associated with depression, perfectionism, and regret.

The absence of choice can certainly compromise a sense of freedom, but it does not follow that many choices enhance that experience. Social psychologists have determined that beyond an optimal number, choices are experienced as burdensome in decision-making situations (Steiner, 1970). A trip down the aisles of a large grocery store may be a sufficient reminder of that, but the information overload that many feel in choosing among television channels or websites is more clearly leisure-related. In fact, making the decision is what feels liberating in such cases.

The opportunity for "ongoing consent" in a decision, according to William Harper (1986), makes choice largely irrelevant to the meaning of freedom in leisure. Freedom is "undergone," in Harper's view, as one is drawn into an activity and acts in accord with it. This kind of surrendering to the activity relinquishes any choice to do otherwise in the interest of committing fully. Studies of recreation trip engagements support this idea. Considering various choices and options is associated with relatively low positive affect, whereas enthusiasm rises once the decision has been made (Hammitt, 1980). Such surrender occurs most readily when the activity is immediately compelling, as might be the case with whitewater rafting. But it may also come about as a consequence of other commitments, such as caring for one's grandchildren. A sense of obligation would seem to make such activities extrinsically rather than intrinsically motivated, but making a commitment can have the effect of putting one in a better position to relax and surrender to whatever happens.

Research also suggests that maximizing freedom through maximizing choice could differ across socio-demographic groups. In a "reactance" study, for example, Snibbe and Markus (2005) found that middle-class participants liked their choice of pens less when they were constrained by an experimenter, whereas working-class participants did not change their liking for their pen choices. In a related study, Stephens, Markus, and Townsend (2007) discovered that people from working-class backgrounds "are relatively more likely to make and prefer choices that produce similarity to others and that people from [middle-class] backgrounds are relatively more likely to make and prefer choices that produce differences from others" (p. 825). Because these differences in the structure and importance of autonomy, choice, and perceived freedom are even more pronounced when Western countries are compared with Eastern countries, this topic will be examined in much greater detail in Chapter 10.

Constraints, too, may be beneficial in limiting the "field of play"—both in the sense of games and in life more generally—and thus allowing one a better sense of important objectives, priorities, and relationships with others. In discussing "serious leisure" activities such as some hobbies and amateur activities, Robert Stebbins (2000) notes that obligations that limit freedoms in some respects are generally willingly met in the spirit of agreeable commitment. Similarly, Kleiber, McGuire, Aybar-Damali, and Norman (2008) proposed that factors that keep people from participating in or enjoying recreation activities later in life may actually be beneficial and even life-enhancing. We will outline leisure constraints theory briefly in the next chapter, and we will discuss the idea of *beneficial constraints* more fully in later chapters.

Finally, some have suggested that the social psychological approach has tended to divert people from considering important *value-based* ethical issues such as the nature of their responsibilities when making leisure choices (Sylvester, 1985). Goodale (1990) has even suggested that by defining leisure as perceived freedom and emphasizing the importance of people's subjective impressions, researchers and leisure service practitioners have tended to ignore the sometimes negative *objective conditions* in people's lives that may limit their ability to experience meaningful and rewarding leisure, the result being that insufficient attention is being given to developing the strategies needed to correct these conditions. We will give further attention to the situational conditions that influence leisure experience in Chapters 9 and 10, but unless researchers develop an understanding of how people come to perceive and interpret the objective conditions of their lives with respect to freedom and leisure, the potential of interventions to change those objective conditions cannot be understood or anticipated.

Understanding recreationists' needs, including their need for autonomy (perceived freedom) or their other psychological needs, provides only a partial understanding of why they participate in a particular leisure activity. In Chapter 6, therefore, we explore the concept of intrinsic motivation and compare and contrast it with other types of motivation, before describing a contemporary theory that combines needs and motivations to better explain leisure participation. In the next chapter, we also briefly outline two other theories—the theory of planned behavior (Ajzen, 1991b) and leisure constraint theory (Crawford & Jackson, 2005)—that provide us with further insight into why people, for example, jog during heat waves and blizzards, rock climb alone and unassisted, and strike out every at-bat but still love to play baseball.

Leisure Motivations

Preview

So, how do we go from leisure needs to leisure participation? What brings you from feeling a need for some aspect of leisure to actually making a move in that direction? Motivation is the intervening factor. As we have already noted, in the view of many scholars leisure has two principle attributes: perceived freedom and intrinsic motivation. We discussed perceived freedom in the previous chapter and turn our attention now to intrinsic motivation. Intrinsic motivation involves interest, enjoyment, and action taken solely for its own sake. But the picture is more complicated than this. The need for freedom and autonomy is also reflected in the internalization of goals and purposes that are initially *extrinsically* influenced, and this applies to leisure behavior as well. Thus, this chapter will begin by comparing and contrasting intrinsic motivation with other types of motivation before describing a contemporary framework, *self determination theory (SDT)*, that explains how other purposes—often established or presented by other people—become internalized. Two motives, extrinsic-integrated and intrinsic, frequently reported during leisure are discussed in detail. Factors that influence perceived freedom and intrinsic motivation are also identified, and the implications for promoting participation and enhancing enjoyment are discussed. Finally, this chapter will conclude with an elaboration and revision of the SDT model that integrates many of the key concepts we have described in the first half of this book with those we will discuss in the second.

Motivation

In the previous chapter, we said that researchers often try to answer "why" questions—why, for example, people jog during heat waves and blizzards, rock climb alone and unassisted, throw park benches into a nearby lake, and strike out every at-bat but still love to play baseball—by identifying the various needs that compel people to seek out specific leisure activities and experiences. But what actually moves people toward action is their motivation. While needs (at least core needs like competence and, even more so, autonomy) are almost always relevant and therefore relatively stable, motivations can and do vary across contexts. For example, people are motivated to rock climb for a variety of reasons, including to win a competition, because their partner pressures them to do it, because they feel guilty if they don't, because they feel it is important to their health, or because they simply find climbing interesting and enjoyable in and of itself. Moreover, though most leisure activities likely involve more than one motivation, the main reason a person climbs can change over time. Changes in attention to, and satisfaction of, core needs may be one reason for this change in motivation, but there are others. Before we look at how and why these changes occur, however, further background on the different types and forms of motivations and their potential organization is necessary.

Intrinsic and Extrinsic Motivation

Motivation concerns energy, direction, and persistence (Ryan & Deci, 2000). Energy and persistence can be directed toward a number of domains, including university courses, paid employment, household chores, and, most importantly for us, leisure activities. Originally it was thought that there were two types of motivation: *intrinsic* motivation, where an activity is interesting, enjoyable and rewarding in and of itself, and *extrinsic* motivation, where an activity is rewarding for external reasons, such as getting paid, receiving awards, or gaining recognition. Extrinsic motivation can even be experienced as an ulterior motive. Have you ever, for example, gone to a movie you didn't want to see but you went because you wanted to be with that special person? Or have you ever participated in a sport because you thought it might result in a college scholarship, connections for getting a job, or a job promotion itself? Some universities, in fact, now offer classes that not only teach you how to play golf but also how to successfully "network" with clients and bosses while playing golf!

In their investigation of experience in daily life described in Chapter 5, Graef, Csikszentmihalyi, and Gianinno (1983) examined whether intrinsic and extrinsic motivation really were important dimensions of people's everyday experiences. The investigators asked study participants two questions thought to measure whether they were either intrinsically or extrinsically motivated ("How much do you wish to be doing something else at this moment?" was one). Overall, 22% of the participants' daily experiences were intrinsic, although as Figure 6.1 (p. 158) shows, percentages varied from 3% during paid work, to 18% during household chores, to approximately 40% during leisure activities in general.

The findings of Graef et al. supported Neulinger's (1974, 1981) framework and advanced our understanding of leisure motivation, but concerns persisted. Graef and colleagues found that in 40% of their cases people's answers suggested they were simultaneously intrinsically and extrinsically motivated. Additionally, around this same time other social psychologists were also encountering problems with how intrinsic and extrinsic motivation were conceptualized. Originally, researchers believed that the two types of motives were additive, meaning that intrinsic motivation and extrinsic motivation could be summed, resulting in total motivation. But subsequent studies revealed that when people who were intrinsically motivated were then extrinsically rewarded, their levels of intrinsic motivation often decreased (Deci & Ryan, 2008). (This problem, called *overjustification*, will be discussed further shortly.) Because of these conceptual difficulties, in the mid-1980s social psychologists began to examine intrinsic and extrinsic motivation more closely.

Variations of Intrinsic and Extrinsic Motivation

Deci and Ryan (1985, 1991; Ryan & Deci, 2000) identified four approaches to characterize intrinsic motivation. First, intrinsically motivated behaviors can occur in the absence of any apparent external reward. Accordingly, when people are in *free-choice* situations, that is, situations where they can freely choose among behavioral alternatives, it is assumed that what they choose to do is more intrinsically motivated. Second, intrinsically motivated behaviors are engaged in out of *interest* and *enjoyment,* as was discussed in Chapter 4. It is the experience of interest in an activity that pushes people to become involved in it, whereas enjoyment impels them to stay involved, and this is why interest and enjoyment are frequently measured to indicate the presence of intrinsic motivation. Third, intrinsically motivated activities are frequently *optimally challenging* and often result in absorbing experiences such as flow (Csikszentmihalyi, 1990). Consequently, "when people are intrinsically

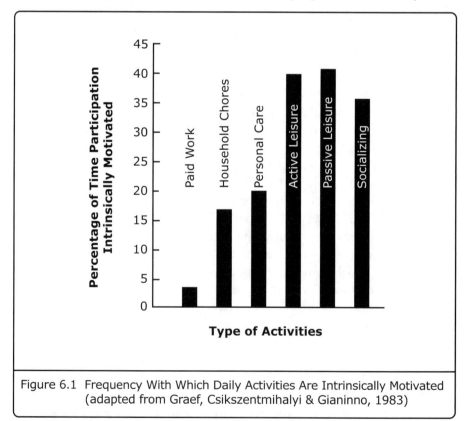

Figure 6.1 Frequency With Which Daily Activities Are Intrinsically Motivated (adapted from Graef, Csikszentmihalyi & Gianinno, 1983)

motivated they will seek out and attempt to conquer optimal challenges" (Deci & Ryan, 1991, p. 242). And fourth, intrinsically motivated behaviors are fostered by the three innate psychological needs we discussed in the previous chapter—autonomy, competence, and relatedness.

In the same way our understanding of intrinsic motivation was refined, so too was it expanded. Vallerand and Losier (1999), for example, proposed there are three forms of intrinsic motivation: toward knowledge, toward accomplishment, and toward experiencing stimulation. Intrinsic motivation toward knowledge involves participating in an activity because you find it pleasurable to learn something new or to learn more about it. A climber, for example, might say that she scales cliffs because she enjoys learning new moves. Intrinsic motivation toward accomplishment involves participating in an activity because you find pleasure in trying to reach new goals and in outdoing yourself. In this case, a climber might say she scales cliffs because she enjoys mastering difficult skills. Finally, intrinsic motivation toward experiencing stimulation involves participating in an activity because you find certain sensations associated with it pleasurable. In this last case, a climber might say she scales cliffs because she enjoys doing exciting things, such as leaping from one hold to another, or rappelling down the rope after reaching the top.

Research also suggests that the importance of these three forms of intrinsic motivation may differ, with implications for continuing involvement. A study (Sarrazin, Vallerand, Guillet, Pelletier, & Cury, 2002) of female handballers, for example, found that their primary motivation for playing was intrinsic stimulation, followed by intrinsic accomplishment, and then by intrinsic knowledge. Interestingly, when the researchers re-examined their participants 21 months later, they learned that approximately one-quarter of the women had quit the sport. When they compared the "dropout" players with the "persistent" players, Sarrazin and colleagues found that the dropouts had originally reported significantly lower levels of all three forms of intrinsic motivation, with accomplishment being particularly low. These findings suggest that, when it comes to intrinsic motivation, feeling stimulated may be the primary motive for playing a sport, but feeling you aren't accomplishing what you hoped or wanted to may be the primary motive for quitting it.

Deci and Ryan (1991; Ryan & Deci, 2000) proposed that extrinsic motivation can take several different forms as well. *External motivation* refers to behaviors that are controlled by factors clearly external to the individual, like the promise of a reward or the threat of punishment. Running to win awards or avoid punishment (e.g., your coach says you can't compete in the race if you don't come to practice) would be examples of external motivation. *Introjected motivation* refers to activities that are driven by internal pressures, wherein actions are controlled by what one feels one *ought* to do rather than in response to the need for autonomy, competence, or relatedness. In spite of the fact that these pressures are internal to the person, such behaviors are said to have an external perceived locus of causality because the source of their motivation (the "shoulds" of parents for example) is external to the person's sense of self. It is introjected regulation that is operating when people participate because it makes them feel virtuous with respect to others or because they would feel guilty if they did not. *Identified motivation* refers to activities that are done neither for rewards like money or trophies (i.e., external motivation) nor out of real and genuine interest (i.e., intrinsic motivation), but because the person believes they are important and worthwhile. Running because you believe it is healthy to exercise, or deciding to weight-train, not because your coach wants you to nor because it is interesting and enjoyable in itself, but because you believe your times will improve, are examples of identification. *Integrated motivation* results from internalizing an activity or behavior so completely that it becomes a major part of "who you are" as a person. For example, when one of the authors was conducting a focus group with some mountain bikers, he asked one person how he would respond if he was at a party and someone said to him "What do you do?" The participant replied, "I'd tell them I was a mountain biker. But it's a stupid question." When the author asked why the question was stupid, the mountain biker replied, "Because I wouldn't be at a party unless it was with other mountain bikers."

Finally, Deci and Ryan (1985) proposed there may be situations when both intrinsic motivation and extrinsic motivation are absent. *Amotivation*, therefore, "is a state in which people lack the intention to behave.... [likely because] they lack either a sense of efficacy or a sense of control with respect to a desired outcome" (Deci & Ryan, 2000, p. 237). Not knowing why you continue to run every day, day after day, is an example of amotivation.

Self-Determination Theory

Around the same time Neulinger (1974, 1981) was developing his leisure paradigm with its emphasis on perceived freedom, another social psychologist, Edward Deci, was conducting research on the factors that influence intrinsic motivation. Over the next decade or so, while Neulinger's focus shifted more towards leisure and quality of life issues, Deci and a colleague, Richard Ryan, began formulating a behavioral framework they called *self-determination theory* (SDT). We have already introduced many of their propositions and findings, but the theory is so compelling in its implications for understanding leisure behavior that we consider it further here. SDT includes several mini-theories. The *basic needs theory*, which we have already discussed, holds that autonomy, competence, and relatedness are innate human needs. *Organismic integration theory* (OIT) is primarily concerned with how the variations in motivation discussed in the previous section are organized with respect to one another. And *cognitive evaluation theory* (CET) addresses how a person who is currently intrinsically motivated can become extrinsically motivated, and vice versa.

According to organismic integration theory, individuals attempt to transform socially prescribed norms or standards into personally endorsed values or "self-regulations" (Deci & Ryan, 2000). This process, called internalization, is not either/or in nature but rather is variable in degree; how well we internalize something depends on how well our core needs are fulfilled. Competence and relatedness are the most easily satisfied because before a norm can be internalized a person has to be able to recognize and comprehend it, and because norms are typically learned from significant others, a sense of closeness likely already exists. Thus, satisfying the need for autonomy is essential, and how much an activity involves "a full sense of volition and choice" (Deci & Ryan, 2000, p. 237) largely determines how autonomous or "self-determined" it is.

Of the different motives that exist, Deci and Ryan (2000) propose that intrinsic motivation is the "poster child" or prototype for self-determined activity and as such is the standard against which all of the others should be compared. Amotivation is the exact opposite of intrinsic motivation because it is lacking in energy, direction, and persistence, and so extrinsic motivation falls in between. As we have already learned, however, there are different kinds of extrinsic motivation and, not surprisingly, they all vary in how autonomous they are: from external (the least self-determined), to introjected, to identified, to integrated (the most self-determined). Even though integration is the most self-determined extrinsic motivation, because it is not done for its own sake, a gap between integrated and intrinsic motivation is shown in Figure 6.2 (p. 162).

Two questions immediately arise when we look closely at Deci and Ryan's (1985, 2000) motivational framework. First, from a theoretical perspective, does research support this motivational sequencing? Second, from a practical perspective, does differentiating among these motives really add anything to our understanding of leisure?

To answer the first question, Ryan and Connell (1989) conducted a pioneering study of why elementary school children did their homework. The researchers found that identification was the major reason but, more importantly, that external, introjected, identified, and intrinsic motivations were sequenced as theorized. At the time of their study, little was known about integration or amotivation, and so these motivations were not investigated, but other studies have included one or both. Baldwin and Caldwell (2003), for instance, developed a scale to measure adolescents' motivations during free time. Baldwin and Caldwell's findings also supported the proposed sequencing, although their study excluded internalization because they felt adolescents were not developmentally capable of this type of motivation. However, in a study of recreational and competitive college athletes that included all six motivations (Mallett et al., 2007), the SDT framework's structure was once again supported.

In contrast, Walker and Wang (2008) proposed dividing both introjected motivation into "reward" (e.g., "I would feel prideful") and "punishment" (e.g., "I would feel guilty") dimensions and external motivation into reward (e.g., "Others will think more positively about me") and punishment (e.g., "Others would be ashamed of me") dimensions. Statistical analyses conducted with a sample of Canadian students largely supported this restructuring, and subsequent analyses uncovered significant differences between introjected reward and punishment and external reward and punishment when leisure motivations were compared. The latter finding also helps answer our second question as it suggests that, from a practical perspective, differentiating among motives does improve our understanding of leisure. Further support for this proposal can be found when all of the motivations in Walker and Wang's study are scrutinized (see Figure 6.3).

Walker (2008) conducted a follow-up study of these same seven motivations and amotivation, but with a sample of 35 Chinese-Canadians and using the experience sampling method. Participants completed a diary seven times a day for 12 days when a randomly scheduled watch alarm rang. The diary

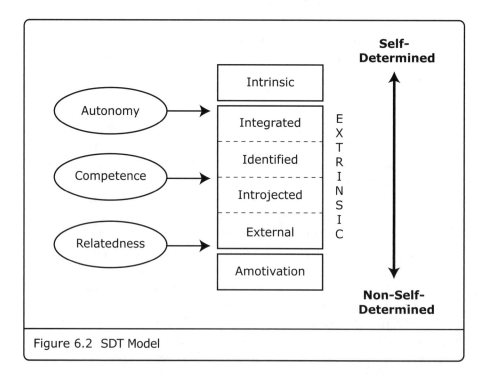

Figure 6.2 SDT Model

asked them to report what activity they were doing and to rate a set of items regarding their motivations for doing it. Walker subsequently classified the activities into four categories—work-related, unpaid work, self-care, and leisure—and then compared his participants' motivations for each. Key motivational differences across these four categories are reported in Table 6.1 (p. 164). Walker then reclassified his leisure category into four subgroups— socializing, watching television, other passive (e.g., reading a book), and other active (e.g., playing a sport)—and compared his participants' motivations for each. Key motivational differences across these four leisure categories are also reported in Table 6.1. In summary, there appear to be important motivational differences across everyday life domains as well as within the leisure domain itself.

After reading about these Chinese-Canadian participants' leisure and non-leisure motives, do you think they are similar or different than yours? For instance, which motivation (intrinsic, integrated, identified, introjected, external, or amotivated) would you say always (or almost always) explains why you go to school, go to your job, watch television, listen to music, or play sports? Can you think of a different motivation that might sometimes explain why you do each of these activities? Or what about a motivation that you would say never (or almost never) explains why you do each of these activities? These are important questions because, as we will learn in Chapter 10, ethnicity and culture can affect an individual's motivations. Indeed, as we will see in the next section, and then further in Chapters 9 and 10, motivations are greatly influenced by socialization.

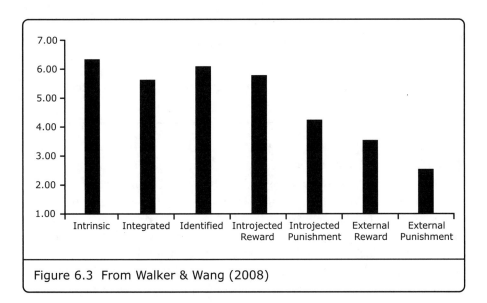

Figure 6.3 From Walker & Wang (2008)

Table 6.1 Differences in Motivations Across and Within Categories (Walker, 2008)	
Motivation	Differences
Intrinsic	Overall, higher during leisure than during self-care, with both of these being higher than work-related. During leisure only, higher when watching television than when socializing or doing other passive activities.
Integrated	Overall, equally high during leisure and self-care, with both of these being higher than during work-related and unpaid work. During leisure only, no differences among four types of leisure.
Identified	Overall, equally high during work-related, unpaid work, and self-care, with all of these being higher than during leisure. During leisure only, other passive activities higher than other active activities and watching television.
Introjected Reward	Overall, higher during work-related than during leisure and unpaid work, with self-care being lowest. During leisure only, higher during socializing and other passive activities than during watching television.
Introjected Punishment	Overall, highest during work-related and lowest during leisure and self-care. During leisure only, socializing highest and watching television lowest.

Social Learning, Social Cognition, and the Self

Motivations are shaped by environmental circumstances and socialization and are subject to general learning or "reinforcement" principles (Bandura, 1974). Much of learning, even social learning, is about responding to consequences, to reward and punishment. Reinforcement theory (James, 1890; Skinner, 1971) thus casts motivation in terms of *approach* to rewarding consequences and the *avoidance* of aversive consequences. People are motivated to avoid pain and discomfort, isolation and humiliation, etc., and to approach rewarding circumstances, those that bring the "goods" of society, both tangible and intangible, such as approval of others. This applies to an extensive range of animal and human behavior, including leisure activity. To use a leisure example, a child may practice the violin to please his mother and gain permission to watch his favorite television program that she has made contingent upon his practice. Or a young woman may join a book club principally because of the influence the others in the group have to further her career. Using SDT principles, both are apparently extrinsically motivated to some degree, at least at the start of their involvement, but through introjection and identification the activities may become internalized and thus more self-determined in time.

When the activity itself seems less important than what one might desire as a result of participation, motivation is more extrinsic than intrinsic, as we noted earlier. In fact, though, intrinsically motivated activity, such as the favorite television program, may serve as the reward for less enjoyable activity. As another example, the loving reactions of cherished parents may be the principal source of children's willingness to try a new activity. Or the admiration a child has for her older sister may lead her to adopt the same activity in the interest of being like her, gaining her affection or even appropriating some of the satisfaction she obviously gains from participating in the activity. This is the principle of *modeling* that is also one of the more prominent social learning principles (Bandura, 1986). However, if the rewards for engaging in the activity are more external to the experience of the activity itself, then it is clearly extrinsically motivated, motivated by achieving some desired consequence or end state, even if it is the affection of a big sister.

In talking about motivation, especially that which is intrinsic and apparently innate, it is not surprising to find that comparisons are often drawn to the motivation of animals, even with respect to leisure experience. Thus animals are arousal avoidant at times where relaxation is needed and at other times seek to raise arousal to an optimal level, often through play. This is essentially the analysis that Ellis (1973) provided in his foundational book *Why People Play* (see Chapter 4). However, human motivation is also different from that of other animals in some important respects: (1) the capacity to evaluate action against standards of worth; and (2) the capacity to reflect on one's capacity to execute courses of action (Caprara & Cervone, 2000).

Because humans are capable of reflecting back on the past and considering the future, they can, in effect, motivate themselves. They can push and pull themselves and do so based on their experience. The setting of goals clearly reflects the perception of the future and the capacity of forethought. The main point here is to recognize some amount of *volition* in human motivation, where standards of performance may be considered, one's action may be evaluated against those standards, and new actions taken in response to that assessment. Motivation thus often has a lot to do with how you *think* about what you do and this involves your sense of self (cf. Dweck, 1999; Fiske, 2004).

Motivation theories that focus on beliefs and expectations (including those about oneself) reflect the constant interplay between environmental demands and the way the individual processes information about the self and the world, what social psychologists refer to as *social cognition* (e.g., Aronson, 2008). People's actions reflect the framework or schemata they use in understanding the world, their expectations of what will happen if they act in particular ways, and the degree to which they believe they can attain their goals. They are in fact motivated by the goals they set.

Goal setting is found in a variety of leisure activities, especially those in which greater understanding or greater skills are sought. This is particularly true when leisure activities become "serious" (Stebbins, 2005). Taking activities seriously typically requires effort, perseverance, and a willingness to endure some discomfort to achieve a goal. This type of motivation appears to differ from that associated with immediate gratification, pleasure, and hedonism, phenomena often associated with leisure. The model of motivation that applies in learning a new activity and refining skills—in composing or performing music, for example—seems to apply more to work than to leisure and begs the question of intrinsic motivation. But goals can be compatible with leisure and with intrinsic motivation. Indeed, the flow that comes from deep absorption in an activity—clearly driven by optimal experience needs—is often facilitated by having goals that give structure and purpose to the activity (Csikszentmihalyi, 1990). In this regard, achievement motivation researchers (e.g., Duda, 1989; Dweck, 1999; Dweck & Elliott, 1983; Nicholls, 1984) make a distinction between *task-oriented* and *ego-oriented* achievement motivation. The former is reflected when a person cares mostly about responding to the challenges implicit in the task at hand, such as when a batter in batting practice experiments with a grip to make better contact with the ball. Ego-orientation reflects the extent to which the same batter seeks to have more hits than anyone else on the team. Both require and benefit from goals, but a task-orientation facilitates concentration on the action and is more likely to be in tune with its intrinsically enjoyable aspects.

Task-oriented activity is closer to being intrinsically motivated and more commonly associated with "growth motives." Maslow's (1968) hierarchy once again appears relevant to understanding how the self is incorporated in the realization of leisure. Self-actualization places the self in an evaluative role regarding the patterns of expressiveness that are most personally meaningful and most consistent with one's essential character, while still accommodating the prospect of evolution of the self. Maslow's theory incorporates the self and social cognition and fits that broader category of *humanistic* psychologies that emphasize the realization of human potentials (see also Rogers, 1961).

These theories help social psychologists understand how and why people strive to make their lives meaningful and make an important distinction between the "true self," where people feel authentic, and the "false self," when they are essentially living their lives as others would have them live it, never really feeling as if they are themselves. Humanistic psychology emphasizes the *potential*s of individuals as critical aspects of their personalities that may or may not be developed. The relatively new "positive psychology" movement revisits these aspects of human behavior and motivation and more clearly defines the conditions and circumstances for their realization (Seligman & Csikszentmihalyi, 2000; Lopez, 2008). Self-determination theory (Ryan & Deci, 2000) is very much a part of the positive psychology movement.

In considering the place of a future orientation—to achieve desired consequences—in leisure, we will see shortly that concentration on extrinsic rewards can be threatening to intrinsic motivation; but distal goals that are part of self-realization create a structure for growth and achievement that can be created without sacrificing intrinsic satisfaction and enjoyment.

Integrated Extrinsic and Intrinsic Motivation

Because high levels of perceived freedom are frequently reported during leisure and the basic needs for autonomy, competence, and relatedness are particularly well served in leisure, it is not surprising that the two most self-determined motivations, integrated and intrinsic, are commonly reported during leisure. Consequently, a great deal of research has been conducted on these two motivations—in the leisure field because they are so common and in other fields (i.e., paid work, education) because they are so *un*common yet highly valued and important to growth and achievement. Less autonomous motivations, such as exercising because of identification with others who perceive its health benefits (e.g., Wilson, Rodgers, Blanchard, & Gessell, 2003) or introjection of parental or cultural values about participation in family activities (e.g., Walker & Wang, 2008) may also be associated with leisure, as noted earlier. But leisure is clearly more about intrinsic and integrated extrinsic motivation, and so we turn our attention to them in particular.

Integrated Extrinsic Motivation

Integrated motivation results from the complete internalization of extrinsic regulation. With respect to running, such integrated regulation is different from that experienced by people who participate because they feel that they *should* exercise (i.e., introjection), or for health reasons (i.e., identification), or because their friends are pressuring them to do so (i.e., external). They are well aware, for example, that there are health benefits and their friends would disapprove if they stopped. They may even occasionally receive awards for their participation in competitive races. However, they also feel that their participation is highly self-determined. This was the point Neulinger (1981) was making about the "leisure-job" category in his leisure paradigm (see Figure 5.1, p. 131), and what Iso-Ahola (1979a) meant when he stated that perceived freedom is the "critical regulator" of something being perceived as leisure. When integrated motivation exists, people will likely continue to run even if friends turn to new activities and awards for participation are no longer available. They will likely continue to experience it as leisure activity because of the choice they exercise.

Support for these ideas comes from several areas of research. For example, research in educational settings has shown that when people are more fully engaged in learning, whether through intrinsic or integrated motivation, they report greater interest in assigned material, higher levels of enjoyment of the material, more understanding, and greater flexibility in utilizing newly acquired information (Csikszentmihalyi, 1990; Rigby, Deci, Patrick, & Ryan, 1992). Stebbins' (1992a) notion of "serious leisure" is a good example of leisure behavior that is often motivated by integrated motivation. He found that the amateur musicians and variety performers he studied often received payment for their performances and participated in their "leisure" in what could be seen as controlling conditions (e.g., required rehearsals, performances at required times and places). However, these activities were still experienced as leisure, even though participants acknowledged and honored their "obligations" to their fellow participants.

In a study of older adults using the experience sampling method (Mannell, Zuzanek & Larson, 1988), high intrinsic interest was often experienced in activities under the control of integrated motivation. When signaled, the older adults rated the amount of choice they had perceived in selecting their current activity and whether they had been intrinsically or extrinsically motivated to participate. On the basis of these ratings, the researchers classified the activities reported during the study week into four types according to Neulinger's paradigm. Ratings were also completed that allowed the measurement of how intrinsically interesting the activities experienced during participation were. *Intrinsic interest* was defined as the extent to which the activity was optimally challenging or a "flow experience" and enjoyable (see Deci & Ryan, 1991, p. 242). An activity was considered optimally challenging or flow-producing when the respondent rated it as being above average in challenge and their skills in the activity were also rated as above average (see Csikszentmihalyi & LeFevre, 1989). Enjoyment was assessed by having the older adults rate how "happy/sad" and "cheerful/irritable" they were feeling when participating in the activity.

The intrinsic interest experienced in the activities comprising each of the four leisure/non-leisure types is shown in Figure 6.4. The activities classified as leisure-job according to the Neulinger typology were experienced as the most intrinsically interesting, that is, they were experienced most frequently as flow and as the most enjoyable. These leisure-job activities appear to fit the definition of activities under integrated motivation. They were extrinsically motivated and yet freely chosen allowing a sense of self-determination.

A surprising finding of this study was that the older adults more frequently experienced flow in activities that were extrinsically motivated (see Figure 6.4). Pure-job activities produced as many flow experiences as pure leisure, and leisure-job activities were experienced as flow significantly more frequently than pure leisure activities as noted above. When the researchers examined the differences in the types of activities that were classified as extrinsically and intrinsically motivated, they found some interesting differences. The pure leisure of the older adults more frequently consisted of passive leisure

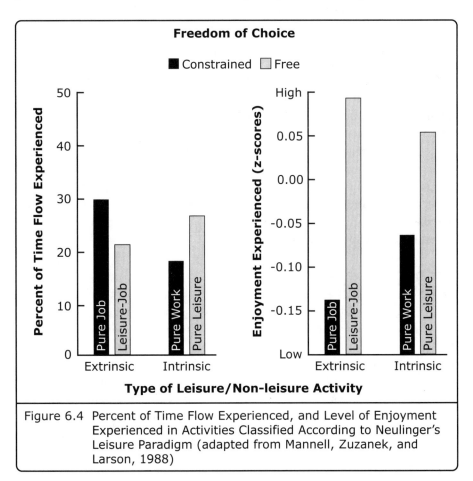

Figure 6.4 Percent of Time Flow Experienced, and Level of Enjoyment Experienced in Activities Classified According to Neulinger's Leisure Paradigm (adapted from Mannell, Zuzanek, and Larson, 1988)

activities, such as relaxing, reading, watching television, and listening to music. In comparison, leisure-job activities were frequently more demanding activities such as hobbies, volunteering, caring and playing with grandchildren, and exercise. The extrinsic motivation associated with these latter activities included the obligation and commitment they felt either to others through their volunteer and family care activities or to their own health and personal development, in the case of exercise activities and hobbies. It appears that when the older adults internalized and integrated extrinsic regulation of their activities, as with the leisure-job activities, they were more likely to experience flow and enjoyment. In fact, they seemed to "benefit" from this integrated regulation. They felt self-determined (perceived freedom of choice) and yet their sense of obligation and commitment "pushed" them into activities that were more challenging and demanding of their skills than the ones they often chose for pure leisure. They also experienced as much enjoyment in the leisure-job activities as in the pure leisure activities (the slight difference indicated was not statistically significant). In a follow-up analysis of this study, those older adults who had more of these experiences reported higher levels of life satisfaction (Mannell, 1993).

The older adults experienced flow as frequently in the pure-job activities as they did in the pure-leisure activities. These extrinsically motivated pure-job activities seemed to "push" the respondents to become involved in more demanding activities, resulting in higher levels of flow. Nevertheless, the research participants regarded such activities as less enjoyable than others, reflecting the impact of obligation and again demonstrating the importance of feeling that one's behavior is self-determined. This finding is similar to Csikszentmihalyi and LeFevre's (1989) discovery that flow experiences occurred more often during work than during leisure. Both studies' outcomes may have been because having clear goals and structure is an important condition for flow experiences to occur.

Intrinsic Motivation

As we learned earlier, self-determination theory is composed of mini-theories (Deci & Ryan, 2000), two of which (basic needs theory and organismic integration theory) have already been described. The third, *cognitive evaluation theory* (CET), is primarily concerned with how a person who is currently intrinsically motivated can become extrinsically motivated or vice versa. We begin with a discussion of the danger of rewards, praise, and extrinsic regulation on intrinsic motivation followed by a discussion of how parents and others (including recreation practitioners) can foster intrinsic motivation, primarily through the securing of autonomy and perceived freedom.

The Danger of Rewards, Praise, and Extrinsic Regulation in Leisure

It is common for people to strive for external rewards. In fact, rewards frequently are a part of leisure activities and contexts. Trophies and prizes are awarded for participation and good performance in children's and adults' leisure activities. Rewards are used by parents to encourage participation in those leisure activities that they feel are good for their children. But what happens to their intrinsic motivation once these rewards are no longer available? When people are rewarded for listening to music, playing games, or volunteering, their behavior can become *overjustified*, that is, they may begin to attribute their participation to extrinsic incentives rather than to the intrinsic interests with which they had previously approached the activity. Research has suggested that such overjustification can be dangerous. The introduction of extrinsic rewards tends to undermine people's experience of self-determination and induce a shift in *perceived locus of causality* from internal to external (deCharms, 1968), and consequently their motivation from intrinsic to extrinsic. People come to construe their participation as due to receiving a reward, which reduces their interest in the activity. This problem, the *overjustification effect*, has been demonstrated in numerous experiments (see Amabile & Hennessey, 1992; Deci & Ryan, 1985; Lepper & Greene, 1979).

Mark Lepper and his colleagues (Lepper, Greene, & Nisbett, 1973), for example, gave children attending a preschool a chance to play with colorful felt-tipped markers—a chance most of them couldn't resist. By observing how much time the children spent on the activity, the researchers were able to measure their interest in the activity, that is, their intrinsic motivation. Two weeks later, the children were divided into three groups, all equal in their initial level of intrinsic motivation. One group of children was simply asked if they would draw some pictures with the markers. The second group was told that if they used the markers, they would receive a "Good Player Award" (a certificate with a gold star and a red ribbon). In the third group, the children were not told they would receive the reward for drawing pictures but after they had finished drawing were given the same award as the children in the second group.

About a week later, the teachers placed the markers and paper on a table in the classroom while the experimenters observed through a one-way mirror. Since no rewards were offered, the amount of free time the children spent playing with the markers reflected their intrinsic motivation. The results were as predicted. Children who had previously expected and received a reward for their efforts were no longer as interested in the markers as they had been. Children who had not received a reward maintained their interest. Those who had unexpectedly received the reward, having played with the markers without the promise of reward, also remained intrinsically motivated (see Figure 6.5, p. 172).

The paradox that rewards undermine, rather than enhance, intrinsic motivation has been observed in numerous settings with children and adults. If an individual accepts money for a hobby or leisure activity, before she or he knows it, what used to be play can come to feel like work. In general, settings that are experienced as *autonomy supportive* (i.e., encouraging self-determination and choice) have been shown to maintain or enhance intrinsic motivation, whereas social situations that are *controlling* (i.e., experienced as pressure to perform in specific ways) have been found to undermine intrinsic motivation. In fact, it is not only material rewards and "good player" awards that create a controlling social setting. Situations where the motivation for participation is due to threats of punishment, obligations, evaluations, deadlines, and imposed goals can also undermine or reduce intrinsic motivation. This broad set of factors that can create controlling conditions comprise a process called *extrinsic regulation* (Deci & Ryan, 1991).

The overjustification effect can have serious implications for how classroom teachers use rewards (as well as bribes and threats and other "consequences") to shape improved study habits, how business managers use incentives to increase worker productivity, how parents motivate their children, how coaches encourage their players, and how leisure service providers get the people with whom they work to become engaged and maintain their involvement in leisure activities. For example, most parents want their children to become involved in leisure activities that not only give them enjoyment but

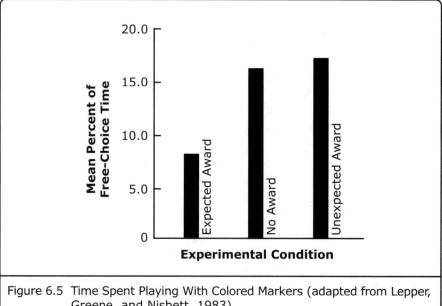

Figure 6.5 Time Spent Playing With Colored Markers (adapted from Lepper, Greene, and Nisbett, 1983)

also provide a variety of benefits, such as exercise, intellectual stimulation, physical skill development, and opportunities to develop friends and social skills. They would like their children to become intrinsically motivated to participate in these types of activities so that they do not have to coerce, bribe, or otherwise influence them to participate. By fostering intrinsic motivation to participate, parents, teachers, and coaches increase the likelihood that children will maintain their involvement in these types of activities as they develop and become independent. Consequently, they may be better prepared when on their own to seek and select personally rewarding and meaningful pursuits when they have free time available.

Does this mean that all types of rewards and extrinsic regulations will undermine the development and maintenance of intrinsic motivation? Is there no role for rewards in developing intrinsic motivation to participate in a leisure activity where none previously existed? Should rewards always be avoided? No, not necessarily. If a person is not intrinsically motivated to start with, then a reward cannot hurt because the behavior could not become "overjustified." If the reward is not offered before an individual decides to participate, then participation is likely to be seen as being under the individual's own control and the reward perceived as a *bonus*, rather than as a *bribe*. For example, as part of an experiment, university students were paid to play a laboratory game (Bradley & Mannell, 1984). Before deciding to play the game, students in one experimental condition were told that they would receive a monetary reward if they participated. The results of the experiment showed that they perceived the reward to be a bribe for playing. Students in a second group were offered the same reward after they had already decided to play the game. They were found to perceive the reward as a bonus for their participation. In a later phase of the experiment, when they had a free-choice period and could choose from among a variety of activities, this second group chose to play the original game more frequently and for longer periods of time than the first group, who had perceived the reward to be a bribe. When the reward was seen as a bonus for participation, it did not interfere with the students' feelings of self-determination and their intrinsic interest in the activity. Research has demonstrated that intrinsic interest in an activity can often be maintained by fostering autonomy-supportive conditions that allow people to feel their behavior is self-determined, even in the face of extrinsic rewards and other forms of external control (e.g., Harackiewicz, 1979; Ryan, Mims, & Koestner, 1983). We will discuss autonomy-supportive environments more shortly, but first we need to look at how another kind of reward—one that is less concrete than ribbons, medals, certificates, or trophies—influences intrinsic motivation.

Although praise is mostly assumed to be beneficial (Carnegie, 1964), Henderlong and Lepper (2002) argued that it can have both positive and negative effects on children's intrinsic motivation. After conducting a comprehensive literature review, these researchers proposed that five factors affected whether praise either enhanced or undermined intrinsic motivation. First and most importantly, the praise has to be perceived as being sincere. Thus parents, coaches, or instructors who use sarcasm as a "motivational tool" may in fact be having the opposite effect. Second, the praise has to be high but realistic. Telling a 10-year-old climber, for example, that she is the best in the world could actually undermine her intrinsic motivation. Third, the praise should focus more on effort or process than ability. Therefore, it is better to say, "You found a good way to climb that route" than "You must be a great climber." Fourth, praise that provides positive information about a person's competence without comparing it to that of another ("You're a much better climber than Kelly") will enhance intrinsic motivation for a longer period of time. Lastly, informational praise ("You did that last move very well") is more enhancing than controlling praise ("You did that last move very well, as you should"). Importantly, Henderlong and Lepper cited numerous studies that found controlling praise is more detrimental for females than males. Also noteworthy is that praise is seldom provided in some cultures (Chinese and Japanese, for example), because it is viewed as being harmful to a child's character if it is given too often (Henderlong & Lepper, 2002).

Fostering Perceived Freedom and Intrinsic Motivation in Leisure

Based on our discussions of freedom of choice and intrinsic motivation, certain guidelines can be suggested if parents and other caregivers want to maximize the likelihood of, for example, children voluntarily going out and playing at the park and experiencing the activity as intrinsically interesting leisure. Generally, feelings of self-determination need to be fostered by providing opportunities for personal choice and control; using rewards with care to avoid perceptions of external control and bribery; involving the children in the decision-making process; taking their perspective and showing care for them, not just their behavior; and encouraging the internalization and integration of extrinsic regulation when it is part of the setting. These factors all contribute to the creation of an *autonomy-supportive environment*.

As parents, teachers, coaches, instructors, and leisure service providers, caregivers can foster intrinsic interest in activities by providing people with such an autonomy-supportive environment (see Csikszentmihalyi & Rathunde, 1998; Grolnick & Ryan, 1989; Larson, 2000; Rathunde, 1988; Ryan & Deci, 2000). Two studies help demonstrate how this type of environment can foster interest in leisure and also be fostered in leisure settings. Sharp, Caldwell, Graham, and Ridenour (2006) were curious about how parental influence and individual motivation affected adolescents' experiences of interest in leisure in general. These researchers measured whether grade 7, 8, and 9 students felt their parents knew what they did during their leisure (*parental knowledge*), and also whether their parents interfered too much with or were overly controlling of their leisure (*parental control*). They also measured how much the students were "*self-regulated*" (a combination of introjected and identified motives) and *amotivated* with their leisure, and whether the students found their leisure experiences interesting or boring. Results indicated that parental knowledge directly and positively impacted adolescents' interest in leisure while parental control directly and negatively impacted their interest. Parental knowledge also had a positive effect on self-regulated motivation, which in turn positively affected interest in leisure, whereas parental control was related to amotivation which in turn negatively affected interest in leisure. Sharp and colleagues concluded: "It may be that adolescents who perceive their parents as too controlling and intrusive in their free time feel less competent and efficacious more generally and are less likely to explore different kinds of activities and develop a sense of their interests and talents" (p. 369).

In contrast, in Gillard, Watts, and Witt's (2007) study, parental influence was absent because the parents themselves were absent! These researchers examined how internally motivated (a combination of intrinsic and identified motives), externally motivated, or unmotivated adolescent girls were before they attended a Girl Scout camp; how well their needs for autonomy, related-ness, and competence were satisfied by other Scouts, the camp counselors, and the camp's activities while they were there; and how interested they were in the camp shortly before they left for home. Two major findings emerged: first, peers' and even more so counselors' satisfaction of the girls' needs for autonomy, relatedness, and competence had a positive effect on camp inter-est; second, above and beyond need satisfaction, if the Scouts were internally motivated before they arrived at camp, they were even more interested before they left for home, whereas if they were unmotivated beforehand they were less interested before they left, above and beyond need satisfaction. Among Gillard and colleagues' practical recommendations were that camps focus on building internal motivation before camp begins by, for example, having open houses where staff can learn more about potential attendees' current interests, and by soliciting information from campers' families about homesickness or other concerns before campers arrive. The researchers also recommended that, once the girls arrived at the camp, autonomy could be facilitated by providing information about options and actions, acknowledging feelings, incorporating campers' perspectives into activities, and providing structure and guidance that explain why certain behaviors are encouraged or discour-aged. Relatedness could be fostered by hiring skilled and caring counselors,

learning more about campers' backgrounds and interests, and having counselors model expected and desired behaviors. Competence could be facilitated by organizing activities to maximize skill-building and by providing
effective and positive feedback (Gillard et al., p. 157; see also Eisenman, 2007;
and Grossman & Bulle, 2006).

The last item suggests that hiring skilled and caring camp counselors can
result in a more autonomy supportive environment and therefore in more intrinsically motivated campers. But a more direct approach is also possible, through
social contagion (Wild, Enzle, Nix, & Deci, 1997). Wild and colleagues divided
undergraduates into two groups: the first was told that the instructor teaching
them a new magic trick was being paid (and so was extrinsically motivated),
whereas the second was told that the instructor teaching them the same trick was
a volunteer (and so was intrinsically motivated). Both groups rated the instructors' skill levels the same, but the volunteer-instructor group reported they enjoyed
the lesson more, enjoyed performing the trick more, and were more interested
in learning other tricks, than the paid-instructor group. That the first group
became "infected" with intrinsic motivation after being taught by an instructor who was also intrinsically motivated is inspiring (and suggests who we
really want to hire are skilled, caring, *and* intrinsically motivated counselors).
But the results of the second part of the study were even more compelling
because, after both groups voluntarily taught other undergraduates the trick
they had learned, these second-generation learners differed even more than
their student instructors. Specifically, second-generation learners taught by
students who had learned from the intrinsically motivated instructor reported
they enjoyed performing the trick much more and were much more interested
in learning other tricks than second-generation learners taught by students
who had learned from the extrinsically motivated instructor. Thus, if a coach,
instructor, or counselor who is intrinsically motivated "infects" you, then
those you teach will likely "catch" an even stronger dose of intrinsic motivation than you did.

In conclusion, leisure frequently involves intrinsic and integrated extrinsic
motivation, both of which are evoked by conditions that enhance a person's
sense of autonomy, competence, and interpersonal relatedness. Leisure can also
be viewed as an autonomy-, competence-, and relatedness-supportive environment in and of itself. This is the essence of leisure's power and attraction.

Motivation and Its Relationship to Other Factors Affecting Participation

We are now halfway through our examination of the social psychology of
leisure, and it seems like a good time to integrate some of the information we

have already learned as well as to introduce some of the topics we will examine in the remainder of the book. With regard to the former, we have discussed leisure in terms of participation in certain activities (Chapter 3) and the immediate conscious experiences (Chapter 4) that happen concurrently. In the latter chapter, we also identified specific attributes that could result in a person interpreting her or his activity or experience as leisure rather than non-leisure. Because these phenomena are concerned with the "here and now," they differ from needs (Chapter 5) and motivations (Chapter 6), which are theorized to precede them. Based on Haggar, Chatzisarantis, and Harris' (2006) research, Figure 6.6 (see p. 178) provides a visual representation of the causal relationships amongst these concepts.

As the reader will have noticed, this figure also includes six new psychological concepts: personality, *the theory of planned behavior* (TPB; Ajzen, 1991b), intention to participate (part of TPB), constraints, constraint negotiation, and encompassing everything else, socialization, and socio-cultural factors. Based on Haggar and colleagues' and others' work (e.g., Ajzen, 1991b; Crawford, Jackson, & Godbey, 1991; Hubbard & Mannell, 2001; Walker & Virden, 2005), each of these factors also affects leisure participation in a certain causal order, with three of these concepts (TPB, constraints, and constraint negotiation) being discussed briefly below, while two others (personality and socialization) are discussed in detail in the next few chapters.

According to TPB (Ajzen, 1991), an individual's *behavior* is largely dependent on his or her *intention* to perform that behavior, which in turn, is determined by: (1) the person's *attitudes* toward the behavior, both affective ("Is it enjoyable or unenjoyable?") and instrumental ("Is it wise or unwise?"); (2) the *subjective norms* he or she believes significant others have concerning the behavior, both injunctive ("Do they approve or disapprove?") and descriptive ("Do they actually do it or not?"); and (3) his or her perception of whether the behavior can be performed (i.e., *perceived behavioral control*), both in terms of self-efficacy ("Is it easy or difficult?") and *controllability* ("Do I have a little control or a lot?"). The theory of planned behavior has helped explain people's participation in numerous leisure activities, including hunting (Hrubes, Ajzen, Daigle, 2001), dancing (Pierro, Mannetti, Livi, 2003), boating, biking, climbing, jogging, and beach activities (Ajzen & Driver, 1991, 1992), and even playing the lottery (Walker, Courneya, & Deng, 2006).

In the same way that the theory of planned behavior has helped explain why people participate in certain leisure activities, leisure constraint theory (Crawford & Jackson, 2005) has helped explain why they either do not participate or do not do so to the degree or in the manner they had hoped. According to Crawford and Godbey (1987) there are three types of constraints: (1) *intrapersonal* constraints, which are individual qualities that affect the formation of leisure preferences (ability, for example); (2) *interpersonal*

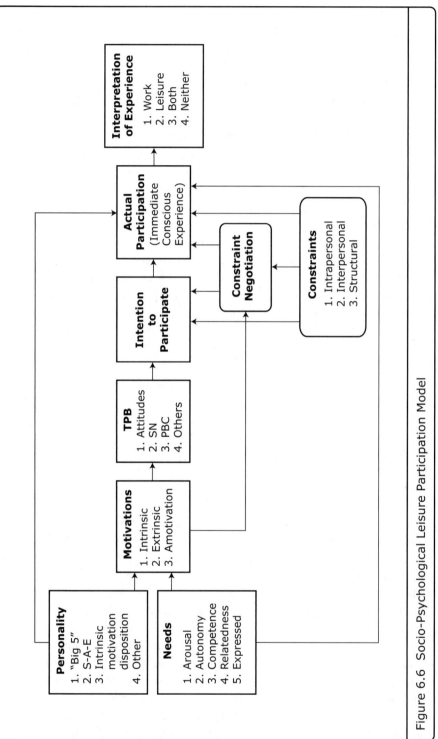

Figure 6.6 Socio-Psychological Leisure Participation Model

constraints, which are social factors that affect the formation of leisure preferences (friends, for instance, who prefer other activities); and (3) *structural* constraints, which occur after leisure preferences are formed but before actual leisure participation takes place (lack of time and money being the most often mentioned). Considerable research attention has focused not only on recreationists' constraints to leisure but also how they "negotiate" these constraints (see Jackson, 2005, for a comprehensive review of leisure constraints research).

Finally, as we will learn in Chapter 9, how a person is socialized can affect his or her participation in leisure as well as many of the other leisure concepts shown in Figure 6.6. Socio-cultural factors can also be influential, and although we have chosen to discuss age and gender throughout our book, we will examine the effects of age, gender, race, ethnicity, and culture on leisure in more detail in Chapters 8, 9, and 10. Before we do so, however, it is necessary to examine the influence of *personality* on leisure.

Leisure and the Person

7

Personality, Attitudes, and Indentity as Personal Influences on Leisure

Preview

What is personality? Does your leisure reflect your personality? Would the people who know you agree? Could they predict the leisure activities you would choose to participate in during your free time? How are your leisure interests different from those of others? Are they always different or only sometimes different? Do the things that you do during your leisure affect your personality and the way you see yourself? These are questions that make leisure a matter of personality.

In previous chapters, we have tried to make it clear that behavior generally, and leisure behavior in particular, comes about through the interaction of individual dispositions and situational influences. In this chapter, we will focus on the former, that is, those factors in individuals that cause them to behave consistently across a wide range of situations and react differently to the same situation than others do. Of course, age, gender, ethnic background, and educational history are among the many factors that will also play a role in influencing behavior. We will look at age and gender in particular in the next chapter. The primary interest in this chapter, however, is in the set of personal characteristics that make people unique, that is, their personalities and individual needs. It is also worth noting that that leisure activity may have a formative role to play in the evolution of personality, especially as it relates to identity and the development of individual potential. But that issue will be addressed in Chapters 11 and 12. Our concern here in this chapter is with how personality influences leisure activity.

The Nature of Personality

Brenda Epperson is a 45-year-old divorcée who has the reputation of being "everywhere" in town. Her friends call her "the mayor" since she seems to know and be friendly with almost everyone she meets; and whether it's in the grocery store, a coffee house, or a restaurant, she will have something engaging to say to those she encounters. Sheila Belichek is the same age as Brenda, single, with a similar educational background, but in contrast to Brenda, Sheila prefers to spend her free time reading mystery novels and doing some writing of her own. As has been established in previous chapters, there may be many factors that contribute to these differences in leisure behavior. To the extent that Brenda's and Sheila's patterns of behavior are internally consistent and distinctive, however, social psychologists are likely to regard these patterns as reflective of their *personalities*.

The term "personality" is often used in everyday conversation. As with the cases of Brenda and Sheila above, when people make statements such as "John isn't really good-looking, but he has a nice personality," they typically use the term to denote the manner in which a person acts across a variety of situations. Psychologists use the term to describe not only an individual's reputation—the way the person acts and is known socially—but also the "internal processes" that create that reputation. From this perspective, personality refers to the "enduring patterns of thought, feeling, and behavior that are expressed in different circumstances" (Hogan, 1987).

Theory and research on personality have been devoted to two separate aspects of those "enduring patterns." The first is what such patterns indicate about the "structure" of personality. Personality here refers to the *organization* of enduring patterns of thought, feeling, and behavior. Pervin (1990) characterizes this focus on intra-individual integration as follows:

> What is distinctive about personality is the focus on the person as a system, thereby involving the interplay between consistency and diversity, stability and change, and integration and conflict, as well as the study of people in a variety of contexts and over a long enough time period for patterns to emerge, in their private world of thought and feeling as well as in their public behaviors (p. 726).

The second task has been to study the way people resemble and differ from one another, that is, their *individual differences*. Thus, people are grouped as being higher or lower on various aspects of personality, many of which are reflected in leisure behavior, as we shall explain shortly.

Personality and Identity

The structure and organization of personality have been approached in various ways over the years. Among the more important structural dynamics of personality is the function of self-awareness. Being able to reflect on the consistency and mutability of one's own behavior is distinctly human and has a great deal of influence on other behaviors, such as planning and self-regulation. This ability is, in turn, the source of information that allows us to form a general picture of ourselves, a self-conception or self-schema, that includes internal consistencies and inconsistencies, differences from and similarities with others, and plans and goals for the future. This self-conception is also referred to as one's identity (see Schlenker, 1984; Stryker, 1987, 2000). In Chapters 11 and 12, when we discuss social psychological consequences of leisure, we will explore the manner in which choices made in the interest of enjoyment and self-expression during leisure influence the formation of personal identity and personal growth. But here, toward the end of this chapter, we will examine identity and self theories—and the related research—in terms of how it influences leisure choices.

The most common understanding of identity in psychology is that it is a "personal theory of self." Erik Erikson's writing has been an influential source for theory and research on identity, taking into account socio-cultural as well as psychodynamic factors. He included in identity "a conscious sense of individual uniqueness, . . . an unconscious striving for continuity of experience, and . . . a solidarity with a group's ideals" (1968, p. 208.) and pointed out that it demonstrates "both consistent sameness within oneself (selfsameness) and a persistent sharing of some kind of essential character with others" (1980 [1959], p. 102). And while this is a fair characterization of the nature of identity, its substance is a "multiplicity" of feelings, values, tastes, personal characteristics, beliefs, interests, social roles, and social group memberships to which a person is more or less committed (see, for example, Harter, 1990; Rosenberg & Gara, 1985).

Identity can be characterized by its personal (private) and social aspects and by qualities of cohesion, authenticity, and domain salience. It is also dynamic in "pushing" individuals in alternating opposite directions ("dialectically"—cf. Freysinger, 1995; Iso-Ahola, 1980a; Kleiber, 1999), at times toward more differentiation of self or more integration, toward greater individuation or social accommodation and identification with others, and toward more exploration of alternatives or more commitment to specific options. Toward the end of the chapter, these will be explored in more detail with respect to implications for leisure activity and experience.

Trait, Temperament, and Need Constructs

Trait, temperament, and need theories use everyday language to describe personality. Trait theories of personality have been largely derived from the words people use to classify themselves and others in their everyday lives—adjectives like "shy," "devious," "manipulative," "open," or "friendly." *Traits* are emotional, motivational, cognitive, and behavioral tendencies that constitute underlying dimensions of personality on which individuals vary. According to Allport (1955), who developed the trait-approach to personality, the concept of trait has two separate but complementary meanings. On one hand, a trait is an observed tendency to behave in a particular way. On the other, a trait is an inferred underlying personality disposition that generates this behavioral tendency. Presumably, a tendency to be cheerful (an observed trait) stems from an enduring pattern of internal processes, such as a tendency or need to experience positive affect, to think positive thoughts, or to wish to be perceived as happy (an inferred disposition). *Temperament* is akin to trait, in that both are enduring characteristics of the individual. Temperaments contrast with traits slightly, though, in being more about the how or "style" of behavior, related to general affect, energy, and attentional patterns, while traits refer more to dispositions toward action (Caprara & Cervone, 2000).

Emotionality, activity, and sociability are commonly considered temperaments (Buss & Plomin, 1984), but these are often regarded as traits as well. *Needs* are also often studied as traits when they are dispositional rather than situationally aroused. Murray's basic needs model (1938; e.g., achievement, affiliation, aggression, autonomy, deference), introduced in Chapter 5, is an example of this approach. Murray also included the *need for play* as a personality factor; that is, some people have more of it than others.

Trait theories provide the basis for most of the work on personality in leisure studies, though aroused needs and motives have also been studied in relation to particular leisure activities, as was suggested in Chapter 5. Researchers have attempted to predict leisure behavior based on individual differences, as will be demonstrated shortly. Leisure behavior may also *contribute* to the development of some aspects of personality, particularly with respect to identity formation as noted above. But this is a subject for our outcomes chapters.

So what describes *you* as a person? Are you kind? Anxious? Aggressive? Exuberant? Extroverted? Conscientious? Do any of those characteristics come into play in directing your leisure choices and experiences? Literally hundreds of personality factors have been found to differentiate individuals in a somewhat permanent way and across most, if not all, situations. But a lot of these factors are somewhat interchangeable. Can a person who is outgoing also be regarded as extroverted? Is nervousness the same thing as anxiousness? In recent years, the study of personality has been able to reduce the vast array of personality characteristics to five fundamental factors: extroversion, agreeableness, conscientiousness, neuroticism, and openness to experience (Costa & McCrae, 1985, 1988; Costa, McCrae, & Dye, 1991; Degman, 1990; McCrae & Costa, 1999; McCrae & John, 1992). While the names of these factors vary somewhat among researchers, the 5-factor model (FFM or "Big 5") appears to be basic to all personality measures. But other factors—whether or not they can be incorporated in the five or not—have guided much of the leisure research done on personality, even leading to the development of leisure-specific dispositions. Our goal here, then, is to describe these various personality factors with a focus on determining their relevance to leisure behavior and leisure experience, a subject we will take up again shortly.

Where Do Personality Traits Come From?

The interactionist framework employed here recognizes stable individual difference, or "person" factors, as interacting with situational, or "environment" factors in directing behavior. Thus, even though individuals must interpret what the environment affords them in terms of action possibilities or how those possibilities are constrained, one's personality provides a relatively permanent set of dispositions influencing both those interpretations and the choices and decisions for action one takes. Nevertheless, the stability of these dispositions is a matter of some controversy in the study of personality. To what extent has your personality changed in the last few years? Have your friends and relatives always seen you as the same? What does growing older hold for you and them?

Part of the answer to those questions lies in where traits come from in the first place. If they are "learned," that is, the result of imitation, modeling, and response to the rewards and punishments of social life, they are more likely to change as environmental conditions change, than if they are the expression of genetically derived tendencies. But if a trait doesn't change much over the life course and is relatively resilient in the face of a variety of environmental conditions, how would researchers know if it was determined by one's genetic makeup or by some compelling experiences in early childhood?

One approach to that problem is to compare people with their "next of kin." The more similar they are to the ones who are blood relatives, the more likely it might appear that traits have been inherited. But be careful here! People who are genetically most similar are also most likely to have shared a similar "family" environment. If you are more like your mother than her sister (your aunt), it could be because you share more of your mother's genes, or it could be because she raised you and "passed on" some of her characteristics to you in the process. One of the few ways to sort out the *heritability* of traits from their environmental sources is to compare people with the same genetic background who are reared together with those who are reared apart. Fortunately for research purposes—if not for the twins themselves—a substantial number of twins have been separated at birth and raised in different environments. If they are very similar despite this separation, it is an argument for the power of their genes (heritability) in determining that similarity.

Most studies of twins have been conducted to address the nature-versus-nurture debate on the origins of intelligence. Relatively few psychologists have argued for the heritability of much of personality—except perhaps in activity level and aggressiveness. This has been due in part to the general abandonment of trait psychology in recent decades. But with the re-emergence of attention to personality, there is renewed interest in the question of the heritability of traits. In a now classic study by Tellegen and his associates (1988), the personality characteristics of twins reared apart and together were examined. Using the Multidimensional Personality Questionnaire, 11 primary scales and 3 higher order factors were studied for monozygotic and dizygotic twins. Monozygotic (one egg) are "identical" twins and share more genetic makeup than dizygotic (two egg) or "fraternal" twins. The study addressed three factors—positive emotionality, negative emotionality, and constraint—which compare closely to three of the "Big 5" traits described earlier: extroversion, neuroticism, and conscientiousness. Table 7.1 shows the average correlations for each group. The fact that the correlations for monozygotic twins reared apart are not much lower than monozygotic twins reared together and yet are much higher than dizygotic twins reared together reflects the heritability of those personality dimensions.

Zuckerman (1979, 1994) also studied twins in his research on sensation-seeking—the tendency to seek stimulation and excitement and welcome some risk—finding similarly that identical twins are more alike with respect to sensation-seeking than fraternal twins even when reared apart. Zuckerman concluded from this research that nearly one half of the variability in the sensation-seeking trait was attributed to heredity, the same figure arrived at by Tellegen and associates (1988) with respect to the personality characteristics they assessed.

In general, however, it is important to recognize that even if as much as 50% of the variability in some aspects of personality can be attributed to genetic differences, the rest of the variability is attributable to other sources. There have certainly been many social scientists who have asserted that environmental influences have at least as much influence in determining personality, and, while the studies reviewed above emphasize the impact of genetics, environmental influences shape personality in a variety of ways. For example, of the many environmental factors influencing personality, facing adversity in life, such as a debilitating illness or injury, can be especially influential in developing such characteristics as persistence, resilience, or, on the less positive side, pessimism in one's personality (Caprara & Cervone, 2000).

Table 7.1 Correlations on Three Personality Factors Between Different Types of Twins (Reared Together and Apart) (adapted from Tellegen et al., 1988, p. 1035)

Types of Twins & Socialization Experience				
	MZA*	DZA	MZT	DZT
Positive emotionality	0.34	-0.07	0.63	0.18
Negative emotionality	0.61	0.29	0.54	0.41
Constraint	0.57	0.04	0.58	0.25

* MZA = monozygotic twins reared apart (n=44)
  DZA = dizygotic twins reared apart (n=27)
  MZT = monozygotic twins reared together (n=217)
  DZT = dizygotic twins reared together (n=114)

Why Should Personality Characteristics Affect Leisure Behavior in Particular?

While we have already considered a number of different meanings of leisure, the special relevance of personality to leisure becomes most apparent when leisure is considered a context for self-expression, where an individual is most likely to feel like her or his "true self." In an experience sampling study referred to in Chapter 2, Samdahl (1988, 1992) asked 18 young adults to carry a pager for a week to sample their experience of leisure and non-leisure. When they were "beeped" (according to a random schedule), they were to stop and indicate what they were doing at the time, with whom they were doing it, and what their subjective experience was on a variety of dimensions. They were asked to what extent they would regard a particular occasion as leisure and also whether they felt irritable, relaxed, comfortable, and so forth, and, perhaps most importantly, how much what they were doing was an expression of their "true self." Samdahl found that regarding a situation as leisure was highly associated with feeling like one's true self, especially in informal social situations. "The opportunity to be truly self-expressive and accepted for who you really are," she concluded, "may be one factor that makes informal social interaction an important leisure context" (1992, p. 28).

The point is that in leisure people generally want to feel free to be themselves; common feelings of being controlled by others or by situational demands are generally far less than in other social settings. Even if one interacts with others (and surely much if not most of leisure experience is social) and chooses to "go by the rules" (of a game, a dance, or an organizational meeting) the experience of leisure is sustained to the extent that the situation is relatively unimposing, thereby allowing individuals to "be themselves."

Personality traits are more likely to be influential in casual situations than in situations where there are clear demands and expectations, such as is common in work settings. Traits become more important when the social situation is familiar, informal, or private; when instructions are nonexistent or general; and when choice is considerable. The demands of the social situation become more important than traits when the opposite conditions (noted in parentheses) apply (Buss, 1989). Diener, Larson & Emmons (1984) make a similar argument, as noted earlier (see Figure 7.1).

Support for this idea was demonstrated in an experimental laboratory study of leisure and flow by Mannell and Bradley (1986). They found that when the social setting was highly unstructured and there were few guidelines and expectations for behavior, as in many leisure settings, the participants' personalities (in this case, their locus of control) had a greater influence on their behavior and experience in playing a game than when they were in a more regulated setting. Whatever situational factors come into play, leisure choices and experiences are influenced, at least to some extent, by stable individual differences. In this chapter, we are especially concerned with those individual difference characteristics or traits that seem to lead people to behave in relatively consistent and predictable ways. So, let's turn now to how individual differences in personality come to influence leisure behavior in the first place. We will consider which personality factors are correlated with leisure behavior, which ones are likely to influence leisure behavior, which are commonly studied in leisure research, and finally, the characteristics of individuals that seem distinctly linked to certain patterns of leisure behavior.

Traits more influential than situations when...

- Settings are familiar, informal, or private

- There is little or no instruction

- Choice and freedom are considerable

Situations more influential when...

- Settings are novel, formal, or public

- Instructions are detailed and complete

- There is little or no freedom or choice

Figure 7.1 Traits vs. Situations

Personality Factors and Their Apparent Influence on Leisure Activity and Experience

The various relationships between personality and leisure interests and activities is a tempting subject for researchers. This is partly due to their apparent ease of measurement. Personality traits are typically assessed by having people fill out "paper-and-pencil tests" that require them to rate the extent to which a series of statements describe them (see Figure 7.2, pp. 192 and 193, for an example of a leisure-specific personality test developed by one of the authors). On the basis of these ratings, how strongly they exhibit a particular trait is determined. Personality-trait research on leisure has also been popular because of the assumption that there are stable individual differences that explain leisure behavior and preferences. The differences have been seen as useful for predicting leisure interests and even for "target marketing" to potential program participants or resource users.

Self-As-Entertainment Scale

Most people have periods of free time ranging from a few moments during the course of their daily activities to large amounts of vacation time. The following statements reflect how different people feel about their free time and how they use it. Please respond as quickly and accurately as possible by indicating the extent to which each of the statements describes you.

	Doesn't Sound Like Me	Sounds A Little Like Me	Sounds A Lot Like Me
1. I have an active imagination.	1 2	3 4	5
2. I like to go places where there is lots to do.	1 2	3 4	5
3. I can make almost anything fun for myself.	1 2	3 4	5
4. I find at this stage of my life that there is not enough to occupy my free time.	1 2	3 4	5
5. When I have to wait for something, I usually get so engrossed in my thoughts that I fail to notice the time.	1 2	3 4	5
6. My most enjoyable vacations are those where I go someplace new.	1 2	3 4	5
7. Filling my free time is a problem for me.	1 2	3 4	5
8. If something I have planned is canceled, I have difficulty finding an enjoyable substitute.	1 2	3 4	5
9. I am good at entertaining myself.	1 2	3 4	5
10. I like to go out a great deal.	1 2	3 4	5
11. I enjoy relaxing and letting my mind wander.	1 2	3 4	5
12. If I have a free day, I prefer to go somewhere away from home.	1 2	3 4	5
13. When I have time on my hands, I usually find someone to spend it with.	1 2	3 4	5
14. I am a person who likes to go to new places.	1 2	3 4	5
15. I am never at a loss for something to do.	1 2	3 4	5
16. I am good at thinking of things to do with my free time.	1 2	3 4	5
17. I often have a difficult time deciding what to do with my free time.	1 2	3 4	5

Figure 7.2 Self-As-Entertainment Scale (adapted from Mannell, 1984, 1985) *continued on next page*

Self-As-Entertainment Scale

	Doesn't Sound Like Me		Sounds A Little Like Me		Sounds A Lot Like Me
18. I am good at thinking of fun things to do.	1	2	3	4	5
19. I remember my good times by the places I've been.	1	2	3	4	5
20. My life would be dull without my daydreams.	1	2	3	4	5
21. I often use my imagination to entertain myself.	1	2	3	4	5
22. I have too much time on hands.	1	2	3	4	5
23. I am good at making up games.	1	2	3	4	5
24. My favorite activities require me to use my knowledge and skills.	1	2	3	4	5
25. When I am bored, I go someplace where there are things happening.	1	2	3	4	5
26. I like teaching myself to do new activities.	1	2	3	4	5
27. I often feel there is nothing to do.	1	2	3	4	5
28. It doesn't matter where I am, I enjoy myself.	1	2	3	4	5

Subscale Composition:

Self Mode refers to a person's physical and/or cognitive skills and ability to find or create challenging and interesting pursuits with which to fill their free time (includes items 3, 4, 7, 8, 9, 15, 16, 17, 18, 22, 23, 24, 26, 27, and 28—items 4, 7, 8, 17, 22, and 27 are reverse coded).

Environmental Mode refers to a person's capacity to fill their free time with interesting and enjoyable pursuits by actively seeking out places or environments and other people. These people or places in turn impose structure and determine the content of their free time for them (includes items 2, 6, 10, 12, 13, 14, 19, and 25).

Mind-Play Mode refers to a person's capacity to fill their free time by turning inward and using imagination and fantasy (includes items 1, 5, 11, 20, and 21).

Figure 7.2 Self-As-Entertainment Scale (adapted from Mannell, 1984, 1985) *continued from previous page*

For example, some early research on personality and leisure was driven in part by managers' desires to identify the reasons why recreationists chose their sites and activities. Escape, affiliation, achievement, exploration, and social recognition were some of the personality-based needs identified that managers could use to distinguish between recreationists (Driver & Knopf, 1977). It was hoped that this personality-based information might then be used to tailor leisure services and programs to give users what they wanted (Knopf, 1983).

General Approaches to Research on Leisure and Personality

If you have been reading this book from front to back, the topic of motivation is not new to you; we have covered the needs aspect of it in Chapter 5 and intrinsic motivation per se in Chapter 6. But we reconsider it here because individuals are often defined by differences in motivation, and these differences are important to leisure experience. Implicit in this idea is the distinction between *motivational dispositions* and *aroused motives* (Hilgard, 1962). The motives that are generally important to people are called motivational dispositions and the assumption is that this set of motives differs from one person to another. In this case motives are essentially personality traits. For example, a person may be generally more achievement-oriented and have a higher need for adventure than her best friend. However, not all of a person's important motives are likely to operate and influence behavior at the same time. When a person's needs are active, social psychologists call them *aroused motives* or *manifest needs* and these are situationally-determined as well.

With a more general approach to personality-based leisure interests, Allen (1982) administered the *Personality Research Form* (Jackson, 1974), an instrument used to measure Murray's 20 personality "needs," and a leisure interest inventory to 212 undergraduates. Fifty-one leisure interests were then reduced to nine leisure interest factors through factor analysis, and seven of the nine factors were found to correlate with 12 of Murray's 20 personality needs. Of special interest were the correlations between athletic and outdoor interests and the need for dominance, and between an interest in mechanical activities and the need for autonomy. Driver and Knopf (1977) used this same measure of personality to find that while personality was only modestly related to the *choice* of outdoor recreation activity, it was a stronger predictor of the *extent* of participation. Male nature-trail walkers and back-country hikers had a higher than normal need for autonomy.

The use of another measure, the *Edwards Personal Preference Schedule*, also based on Murray's needs, in a study of participation in selected outdoor recreation activities, revealed a number of significant relationships (Moss & Lamphear, 1970). Hunters, for example, were found to be more dominant, traditional, and dogmatic than non-hunters (Moss & Lamphear, 1970), but again the correlations, though statistically significant, were only modest.

Part of the criticism of earlier research on personality and leisure is that personality measures have often been used as part of a "fishing expedition" to find anything at all that is related to activity participation. It has also become clear that participation alone is not likely to reveal much about personality; people participate in the same activity for a wide variety of reasons, and the same people may participate for different reasons at different times. An example from a British researcher is as telling as it is unusual:

> The choice of leisure-time pursuits is a function of many variables. . . Collecting birds' eggs has been given as an example of acquisitive or competitive needs, scientific or outdoor interests, or just an aesthetic interest in the shape or color of eggs (Nias, 1977).

Looking beneath the behavior to personality-based needs may not be particularly revealing. Backpacking, to pick a more common example, attracts some participants who characteristically seek high stimulation and others who search for escape and solitude (Knopf, 1983). Williams, Ellis, Nickerson, and Shafer (1988) found a variety of motives (achievement, leadership, nature, escape from social pressure and escape from physical pressure) for participation in outdoor pursuits in general. And a British study of personality correlates of Internet use among young adults found few substantial relationships between extraversion, neuroticism, psychoticism, loneliness, and self–esteem associated with being online (Hills & Argyle, 2003). Still, there have been a variety of associations between specific traits and specific activities in the research. A study of chess players (Avni, Kipper, & Fox, 1987) established that they were more nonconventional than others and had a higher need for order. An earlier study of fantasy-game playing in adolescence found that those playing more often had higher scores on introversion than norm groups (Douse & McManus, 1983). A higher level of television watching has also been found among those with a lower need for cognition (Henning and Vorderer, 2001), as noted in Chapter 5.

Much of the research on personality in relation to leisure behavior has focused on sports. For example, Ogilvie (1968) reviewed findings that indicated that athletes were more likely to be more extroverted and risk-taking than nonathletes and higher in self-assertion, tough-mindedness, self-sufficiency, and forthrightness. But Schurr, Ashley, and Joy (1977) pointed out that individual sport participants may be different from team sport participants in that regard. In their study of 865 male athletes, individual sport participants were more self-sufficient and less dependent than team sport participants. They also suggested that sports that are more "directly" competitive, such as wrestling and basketball, are likely to involve participants who are different from those who prefer "parallel" competition, such as baseball or tennis.

Elite athletes have been shown to have more perfectionist tendencies than nonathletes according to one study (Dunn, Causgrove Dunn, & Syrotuik, 2002), but the investigators in this study found that the maladaptive (neurotic) element of perfectionism was associated with having an ego (competitive) orientation to the sport, whereas the conscientiousness component was associated with being more task oriented.

On the other hand, a meta-analysis of research on the so-called "iceberg" profile among elite athletes—where low scores on tension, depression, confusion, anger, and fatigue and high scores on vigor are presumed to be associated with high success—reveal little support for the profile (Rowley, Landers, Kyllo, & Etnier, 1995). Most of this earlier work was done on male athletes, and while comparisons on the basis of sex alone have not shown significant personality differences associated with *elite sport* involvement (Williams, 1978), it is clear that women face a very different socialization process with respect to sport, as will be discussed further in Chapter 8. When it comes to more casual, recreational sport involvement, there is evidence that personality is predictive of sport involvement for females but not so much for males (e.g., Kleiber & Hemmer, 1981). Perhaps because sport involvement is more expected for males, it is one of those cases—for males, anyway—where the situation matters more than the personality.

In some cases the causal direction has been turned around to see whether and how extensive activity involvement might influence personality. Sport research in particular has been directed by efforts to identify personality differences between athletes and nonathletes, with differences presumably caused by participation in sport activities. However, this mostly correlational research has usually failed to establish the dynamics of the relationships; that is, it failed to provide evidence for how participation in sport activities actually causes personality to develop. Another problem has been the failure to include social-setting factors when predicting behavior. But let's turn to the "Big 5" and what research has to say about their influence on leisure activity and experience.

The "Big 5" and Leisure

As noted above, factor analyses of various traits and motivational dispositions have resulted in the general isolation of five fundamental factors: extroversion, agreeableness, conscientiousness, neuroticism, and openness to experience (McCrae & Costa, 1999). These dispositions have been related to a wide variety of behaviors, many of them leisure-related such as music preferences (Rentfrow & Gosling, 2003) and inclinations toward alcohol and tobacco use (Malouff, Thorsteinsson, Rooke, & Schutte, 2007; Malouff, Thorsteinsson, & Schutte, 2006).

Extroversion includes such traits as assertiveness, gregariousness, excitement seeking, and positive emotionality, and it predicts capacity to master daily activities and be engaged in multiple activities (Caprara & Cervone, 2000). An earlier word for extroversion was "surgency," reflecting all those characteristics that put one into *action*. People who are high on extroversion are "high energy" people, to use a more common expression. It is easy to imagine then that this dimension might be a prime predictor of those who do a lot of different leisure activities, who engage in the same activities more intensely than others, or who engage in activities that can provide high levels of stimulation like whitewater rafting. Extroversion has been shown to have a physiological base. Eysenck (1967) first proposed that extroverts have "high cortical inhibition" and thus low baseline cortical arousal, thereby creating a "stimulus hunger" that leads them to seek out stimulation externally. In contrast, introverts have low thresholds of arousal and thus require less stimulation to stay at an optimal level of activation.

Given these characteristics, an element of risk in activities would be more appealing to those higher on this dimension, as would be the case for contact sports. Athletes are typically higher on extroversion than nonathletes (e.g., Hughes, Case, Stuempfle, Evans, 2003; Kane, 1972; Kirkcaldy & Furnham, 1991; Ogilvie, 1968; Schurr, Ashley, & Joy, 1977; see also Browne & Mahoney, 1984, for a review), particularly those in high-endurance sports (Egloff & Gruhn, 1996) and other high-adventure activities such as mountain climbing (Egan & Stelmack, 2003). Exercisers are higher on extroversion than non-exercisers, especially those who exercise with others (Courneya & Hellsten, 1998) and exercise for weight control (Davis, Fox, Brewer, & Ratusny, 1995). Brandstätter (1994) found that, compared to introverts, extroverts more often used the freedom of leisure for more highly stimulating and social activities. By contrast, people who spend a lot of time playing computer fantasy games (e.g., Dungeons & Dragons) have been found to be less extroverted than the norm (Douse & McManus, 1983). Extroversion is also associated with boredom in leisure (Barnett & Klitzing, 2006) and with higher alcohol consumption (e.g., Cook, Young, Taylor, & Bedford, 1998), but it is unclear whether it is the gregarious aspect or the excitement-seeking aspects of extroversion that is more important to the relationship or perhaps a combination of both. In a Swedish study of 14-year-olds in a central city, adventurousness (made up of impulsivity and thrill seeking) was associated with attendance at a teen center and with more norm-breaking activity, but only in interaction with peer influence (Person, Kerr, & Stattin, 2004).

Tourism patterns have also been associated with this cluster of characteristics. Plog (1972) contrasted the "allocentrics" who seek out unstructured and exotic travel from the "psychocentrics" who prefer familiar venues. Smith (1990a) found only partial support for Plog's allocentric/psychocentric model.

But by combining measures of activation, introversion, and locus of control, Nickerson and Ellis (1991) were able to elaborate the model for the purpose of predicting destination preferences, travel companions, interaction with local cultures, and degree of activity. Introversion, the opposite of extroversion in this study, proved to be a significant predictor of tourism styles.

Agreeableness, the most "prosocial" of the "Big 5," includes such characteristics as trust, straightforwardness, and altruism and is contrasted with hostility, indifference, and self-centeredness. Those with high levels of this trait would be likely to welcome the social aspects of leisure and perhaps use the context of leisure to serve others, as in volunteer work or coaching and teaching in youth recreation programs. High-risk recreation participants are also apparently oriented toward higher levels of sociability (Schrader & Wann, 1999). And this may be a particularly important characteristic to have in staying socially integrated in later life (Reis & Gold, 1993; see also Lawton, 1994). On the other hand, seeing leisure as an opportunity for self-indulgence and escape would likely be the orientation of those who are low on this factor. But there is little research in this area to support such speculation. In one study (Driver & Knopf, 1977), nature-trail walkers were significantly lower than average on a measure of affiliation, but whether that is a reflection of an orientation toward escape and self-indulgence or merely a preference for solitude is not at all clear.

The third member of the "Big 5" is *conscientiousness*. According to McCrae and John (1992), the factor conscientiousness is defined by such components as order, dutifulness, achievement striving, self-discipline, and deliberation. Others (e.g., Goldberg, 1981) associate it with conventionality. A person with high scores on this dimension is organized, responsible, and reliable, whereas one who is low on this factor is likely to be impulsive and oriented toward immediate gratification. Those high on this factor might be expected to embrace the goal-orientation and work ethic that characterize more serious leisure activities (Stebbins, 1992a), such as being a member of an amateur astronomers' club. Serious athletes reflect this to some extent in having higher levels of perfectionism (Dunn et al., 2002) as noted above. On the other hand, those who are high on this factor may have some difficulty being spontaneous and accommodating companions. Compulsiveness or orderliness may hinder a person from "letting go." The limited research on this factor has shown a correlation with exercise adherence, particularly that which is scheduled and highly intense (Courneya & Hellsten, 1998). Competitive chess players also appear to have a high need for order, but the fact that they are also low on conventionality (Avni, Kipper, & Fox, 1987) challenges the integration of these two aspects as the essence of this factor.

Neuroticism, the fourth factor, represents the general tendency to experience distress. It is defined by such components as anxiety, hostility, depression, and self-consciousness. Emotional stability would appear to be the converse. It is reasonable to assume that one high in neuroticism would have some difficulty achieving the depth of involvement necessary for fulfilling enjoyment. Recall that flow is associated with a loss of self-consciousness and the absence of anxiety. Neuroticism may also be associated with the psychopathological condition of *anhedonia*, the inability to experience pleasure. In a study of 73 German adults (Kirkcaldy, 1989), neuroticism was associated with dislike of playful leisure activities. Athletes have been shown to be low in neuroticism (Kane, 1972; Schurr, Ashley, & Joy, 1977), as have skiers, skydivers, and scuba divers (Martin & Myrick, 1976). Schill, Beyler, and Sharp (1993) used ideas related to this dimension to develop a measure of what they called the "self-defeating personality." They found that people high on this measure reported less pleasure and enjoyment from individual and social activities than those who were low on the measure. According to the authors, this orientation is attributable to the tendency to discount the positives in one's life, an orientation that would likely make one resistant to attempts to introduce recreation therapeutically, in spite of the need for such. Nevertheless, neuroticism may have some advantages; it has been associated with a higher level of adherence to exercise programs (e.g., Courneya & Hellsten, 1998), especially those that are devoted to weight control (Davis, Fox, Brewer, & Ratusny, 1995).

The fifth and final factor in the Big 5 group is *openness to experience*, having to do with aesthetic sensitivity, the need for variety, and unconventional values (McCrae & Costa, 1987, 1999). It is also called the "intellect" dimension, though it is independent of intelligence, because it tends to incorporate openness to new ideas, flexibility of thought, cultural interest, and educational aptitude. It would thus be likely that people high on this dimension would be disposed to reading, attending classes, and generally participating in high-culture activities to a greater extent than others. But whether openness to experience is the same as intellectualism has been the subject of some debate. While it has been commonly associated with cultural orientation, it is also used to describe a particular attentional style associated with such things as absorption potential and hypnotizability (Swanson, 1978). As such, it is probably negatively related to boredom proneness, which has been found to be negatively associated with the potential for absorption (Seib & Vodanovich, 1998). The dimension of "sentience," the tendency to be attuned to one's senses, would seem to combine both aspects. In the study by Driver and Knopf (1977) referred to earlier, nature-trail walkers were particularly high on this dimension. And the characteristic was regarded by Reis and Gold (1993) as being most likely to lead to developing more nonwork friendships in later life—a result that also enhances life satisfaction. While it is not generally correlated with sport participation, ultra marathoners have been found to be high on this trait as well (Hughes, Case, Stuempfle, & Evans, 2003).

There are other personality dimensions or traits that, in spite of the alleged inclusiveness of the Five Factor Model, seem to fall outside of it. Or perhaps they represent two or more factors in combination. Because they have been studied so frequently with respect to leisure however, we will consider them here. These are locus of control, attentional style, sensation seeking, the Type-A behavior profile, playfulness, shyness, the autotelic personality, and boredom proneness.

Other Personality Traits Associated with Leisure

Locus of Control

As discussed in Chapter 5, various theories assume that everyone has a need for freedom and control (Burger, 1992). However, people differ in how much freedom and control they believe they actually have in their lives. Julian Rotter (1966) called this personality dimension *locus of control*. People with an *internal* locus of control believe they largely control their outcomes, and those with an *external* locus of control believe that luck, the environment, or powerful others are responsible for their outcomes. In 1968, deCharms describes this essential difference in perceptions of control in terms of people who are *origins* and *pawns*. Rotter developed the I-E Scale to measure locus of control. A great deal of social psychological research has been done with this scale, and locus of control appears to be an important personality dimension along which people differ (Lefcourt, 1976, 1982). It also has significant implications for physical and mental health across the lifespan (Heckhausen, 1999), particularly with respect to coping capacity.

With respect to leisure, Neulinger (1974, p. 16) suggested that perceptions of freedom, and consequently leisure, could be a function of stable personality differences such as locus of control. He argued that the more freedom of choice and control that people characteristically feel they have in their lives, the more likely they are to experience leisure in a given situation. Using the locus of control scale (I-E Scale) developed by Rotter, researchers have attempted to examine the relationship between locus of control and leisure behavior. If, in fact, leisure involvements are characterized by greater opportunities for freedom of choice, then people who believe that they have more control in their lives should prefer or feel more positive about these involvements.

In an attempt to examine whether internals and externals react differently to having choice in leisure settings, Mannell and Bradley (1986) conducted a laboratory experiment. Similar to the Mannell and Backman (1979) study described in Chapter 3, a "free-time" period was created in the laboratory.

The 80 undergraduate students who participated in the experiment completed the I-E Scale and were classified as internals and externals. Of particular interest to the present discussion of personality and leisure is the behavior and experience of the study participants when they played a game in conditions that provided very few guidelines for how they played—a very open-ended, unstructured "leisure setting." In this part of the experiment, conditions were created in the laboratory that led half of the internals and half of the externals to perceive that they had no choice in playing a laboratory game. The other half of the internals and externals were led to believe that they had a great deal of choice in the game they played, as well as whether they played at all during the free time period. The extent to which the participants had "flow experiences" while playing the game was measured using the "time duration" and "situational memory" measures discussed in Chapter 3. As predicted, the internals experienced higher levels of flow when they perceived they had greater freedom of choice, whereas the externals experienced slightly less flow when they perceived greater freedom of choice while playing the game (see Figure 7.3, p. 202).

The results of this research suggest that to understand leisure behavior, not only do the actual opportunities for choice available in the leisure setting need to be considered, but also individual differences in how much control and freedom people typically feel they have in their lives must be examined. These individual differences may influence how people perceive the actual choice available to them, and consequently, it may modify their leisure experience. For example, if you generally feel that you have little control over the things that happen to you, then it is unlikely that being in a situation where you have little or no choice will create much discomfort or psychological reactance to interfere with your experience. In contrast, too much freedom of choice may be overwhelming or threatening for externals. However, if you have an internal locus of control, you would be likely to desire a wider range of options.

In a study of sport participation among college students (Kleiber & Hemmer, 1981), the fact that females involved with sport were more internal in their locus of control than other females, and more internal than the males in the study regardless of their level of sport involvement, was interpreted as indicating that females in sport needed to feel especially internally directed to be able to forge their own way in a realm traditionally dominated by males. Those with an internal locus of control are also more likely to be adventurous in their style of travel and more likely to travel to exotic places than those with an external locus of control (Nickerson & Ellis, 1991).

Surprisingly though, internals seem to have a less positive attitude toward leisure than those with a more external locus of control. In a study of a group of college students (Kleiber, 1979), positive attitudes toward leisure were modestly correlated with an external rather than an internal locus of control. In spite of expectations to the contrary, internals were less likely to see leisure as "good" than externals and less likely to believe that living a life of leisure could be worthwhile.

The preliminary explanation that was entertained for these results was that students with a higher internal locus of control were more likely to be achievement-oriented and work-oriented, and more likely to see leisure as being the opposite (i.e., associating it with laziness and sloth). But a subsequent study of a different group of people, including both students and nonstudents (Kleiber & Crandall, 1981), with work ethic measured and controlled for, yielded results that were not significantly different from the first study. Those with an internal locus of control, even if they were not very work-oriented, were no more likely to embrace leisure than those with an external locus of control. In fact, among the female students in the sample, the opposite was true;

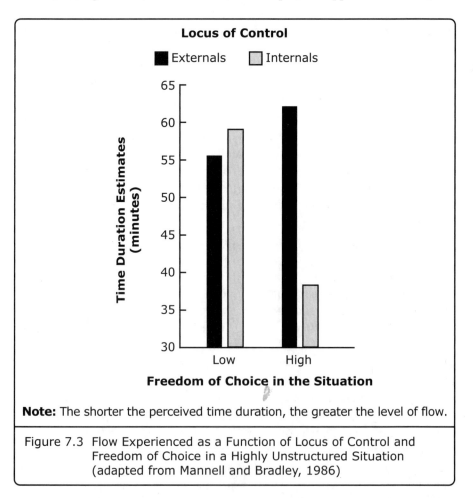

Note: The shorter the perceived time duration, the greater the level of flow.

Figure 7.3 Flow Experienced as a Function of Locus of Control and Freedom of Choice in a Highly Unstructured Situation (adapted from Mannell and Bradley, 1986)

those who were more external were more likely to value leisure. Perhaps, as the authors argued, those who feel less able to control their circumstances are more content to "give in" to the forces around them and when those conditions are benign, as in the circumstances of leisure, this type of person is especially appreciative. Obviously, more research is needed with this personality variable.

Sensation Seeking

A trait sometimes related to extroversion in the "Big 5" family is *sensation seeking*. Like extroversion, it is the tendency to pursue stimulation and take risks to bring about optimal experience (Zuckerman, 1979, 1994), but it isn't defined by the social interest that is found in extroversion. Components of Zuckerman's *Sensation Seeking Scale* (SSS) include thrill and adventure seeking, experience seeking, disinhibition, and boredom susceptibility. According to Zuckerman, high sensation seekers tend to participate in more adventurous, intense activities and prefer a greater variety of activities. In contrast, individuals who are predisposed to avoid stimulation are likely to prefer more familiar leisure situations (Barnett & Klitzing, 2006). And while most athletes are high on this characteristic—in line with its association with extroversion as discussed above—runners, even ultra-marathoners, score low on measures of this characteristic (Hughes, Case, Stuempfle, & Evans, 2003).

Participating in high-risk recreational activities, such as skydiving or whitewater canoeing, is clearly associated with high scores on sensation-seeking measures (Robinson, 1992; Schrader & Wann, 1999). Robinson recognized a high need for stimulation in individuals preferring recreation activities involving some risk, but he pointed out that other personality variables, as well as certain life circumstances, had collectively more influence in leading one to high-risk recreation.

Attentional Style

People have been found to differ in how they process information; this is referred to as *attentional style*. Some of this was implied in our earlier discussions of extroversion and openness to experience. But the way in which attention is deployed or directed—independent of one's excitability or orientation to experience—may be implicated in leisure experience. This is particularly true with respect to the ability to get into flow, which requires that limited attentional capacity be allocated to some sources of stimulation at the expense of others, and this capacity differs between individuals (Keele & Hawkins, 1982). Being able to "tune out" spectators and become absorbed while playing in a baseball game comes easier to some than others and makes flow-type experience more likely. The propensity for *absorption* is thought to be a stable personality characteristic (Roche & McConkey, 1990; Tellegen &

Atkinson, 1974). Using a measure called the *Tellegen Absorption Scale* (TAS), high-scoring and low-scoring subjects were found to have different electro-encephalographical (EEG) patterns in response to competing secondary tasks (i.e., potential distractions) (Davidson, Schwartz & Rothman, 1976). Those with higher TAS scores were better able to ignore secondary stimulation. This ability has also been associated with hypnotic susceptibility (Davidson, Goleman, & Schwartz, 1976) and with intrinsic motivation (Hamilton, 1981).

The fact that introverts score higher on tests of absorption than extroverts (Thackeray, Jones, & Touchstone, 1974)—presumably because the latter are more attuned to external stimuli—suggests some advantages for introverts in their leisure experiences. Though extroverts may be more oriented to a highly stimulating environment, introverts are likely to get more deeply involved in what they are doing. Also relevant to this discussion is Mehrabian's work on individual differences in *stimulus screening* (1976). People who are better at screening out stimulation have a greater potential for becoming absorbed and are less likely to be distracted once activities have begun. Nonscreeners, on the other hand, may potentially get more out of simple activities in a less confusing environment, approaching such activities "with a passion" (Mehrabian, p. 31). The possibility that such attentional styles may be nurtured, rather than being genetically "hard wired" in the individual, is intriguing with respect to its implications for leisure skill development and education, and in particular for management of clients with attention deficit disorder.

Type-A Behavior

In examining the lifestyles of people with a history of hypertension and other forms of coronary heart disease (CHD) in the 1970s, physicians came to the conclusion that there are factors besides inherited constitution, diet, and smoking that are implicated in the course of the disease (Friedman & Rosenman, 1974). In fact, they argued that the "hurry sickness" found in many highly achievement-oriented people is a better predictor of heart ailments than those other factors. In their research, people with *Type-A behavior*, as it was called, showed an incidence of CHD at least 4 times that of their opposite, *Type-B personalities*. Investigators in the 1980s compiled a large number of studies of Type-A people that consistently demonstrated several characteristic tendencies among these unleisurely people. These include hyperaggressiveness leading to competitiveness, insecurity leading to achievement striving, time urgency, the incessant struggle against time, and hostility leading to impatience with others (Friedman & Ulmer, 1984). Type-A people commonly do more multitasking, whereas Type-B people do not. Type-B people, who make up only about 10% of the population in contrast to a larger number of Type-As and combinations of the two, do things more patiently and in keeping with their own natural rhythms. The Type-B person does not feel challenged or threatened to the same extent as Type-A people do and thus does not experience the Type-A's typical insecurity and hostility. Type-Bs have, in fact, been found to be more responsive to relaxing stimuli (Strube, Turner, Patrick, & Perrillo, 1983) than Type-As. Subsequent research has not provided such strong support for a Type-A-CHD connection (Myrick, 1995), but it is still recognized as a personality profile that can have serious implications for health problems caused by stress (Wrzeniewski, Wonicki, & Turlejski, 1988).

The relationship between Type A/B behavior and leisure has not been thoroughly investigated, but there have been a few important studies and many indications from other research. A study of married adults revealed a negative relationship between Type-A tendencies and involvement in relaxing activities (Becker & Byrne, 1984). Kircaldy, Shephard, and Cooper (1993) found British police officers who were Type-As to be, in general, less likely than others to be involved in leisure activities. Among college students, on the other hand, Type-As have been found to attend more live concerts than Type-Bs (Tang, 1988), take more competitive and aggressive approaches in experimental game situations (Van Egeren, Sniderman, & Ruggelin, 1982), and show a pattern of accumulating as much leisure activity experience as possible. Weissinger and Iso-Ahola (1987) studied college students and working adults to examine the relationship between Type-A tendencies and participation in 12 selected leisure activities. Using the *Jenkins Activity Survey for Health Prediction* (Jenkins, Zyzanski, & Rosenman, 1979), these investigators found that Type-As reported significantly more overall participation than Type-Bs, especially in outdoor activities, competitive sports, fitness activities, and home-related, job-related, and school-related activities.

In an intriguing experimental study of Type-A and Type-B personality types, Tang (1986) used a personality questionnaire to measure undergraduate students' Type-A/Type-B orientation. Then, one at a time, the participants in the study were taken into a laboratory room and randomly assigned to either a "work task" or a "leisure task" condition. The same anagram task (participant is given a set of letters and asked to make an English word) was used in both conditions. However, in the work condition, the task was described as similar to work (such as that done by an editor or librarian). In the leisure condition, the same anagrams were described as similar to leisure activities such as crossword puzzles and playing *Scrabble*. After performing the anagram task, the participants were given a choice of engaging in one of three tasks during a free-choice period. One of these tasks was an anagram-solving task similar to the one they had just completed. The participants were then left alone for 15 minutes and the amount of time they spent engaged in the tasks was recorded through a one-way mirror. As can be seen in Figure 7.4 (p. 206), Type-B people spent less time during the free-choice period engaging in the anagram activity when they perceived it to be "work" than did

Type-A participants. When the task was labeled "leisure," there was a tendency for Type-Bs to spend more time on the task than Type-As. Tang suggests that the results may be taken to mean that Type-As "tend to spill over their coronary behavior pattern to leisure activities" and that "there is no difference between work and leisure" (p. 8) for these people. On the other hand, Type-Bs appear to distinguish and "prefer leisure over work" (p. 8). Tang concludes that it is not clear if Type-As' participation in leisure activities is a blessing or a curse. Type-As' leisure activity might either help them to relieve stress or might contribute to premature death due to coronary heart disease given their tendency to get highly involved in whatever they do.

In reviewing medical opinion on *workaholism*, Pietropinto (1986) likened it to Type-A behavior. "At the core of the workaholic's obsession with performance is a neurotic need for love and acceptance" (p. 94). According to a survey of physicians, workaholics' typical approach to leisure is first to fill it with work (49%), second to follow a hectic schedule of varied leisure activities (33%), and third to engage in competitive sports or games.

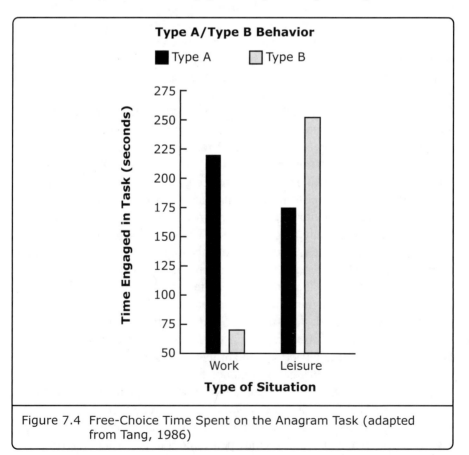

Figure 7.4 Free-Choice Time Spent on the Anagram Task (adapted from Tang, 1986)

The connection of Type-A behavior to workaholism also relates to a study of individual differences in the ability and inability to "switch-off" from work (Cropley & Millward, 2009), which the investigators link to *rumination*, the tendency to go over the past and worry about the future (see also Martin & Tesser, 1996). Cropley and Millward found that while work pressures themselves may contribute to rumination, people in the same types of positions and with the same types of stresses (all mid-level managers in their study) differ in terms of whether they ruminate about work and to what extent it interferes with their leisure. Ruminators as a group, according to the study's authors, were more inclined to be overcommitted to work, to have a live-to-work rather than a work-to-live philosophy, to be more extrinsically than intrinsically motivated, to be more inclined to have intrusive thoughts about work and trouble with work boundaries, more inclined to withdraw in social situations and more inclined to consider leisure unfulfilling and burdensome.

Playfulness

Playfulness is a personality construct that has been measured reliably in relation to childhood, adolescence, and adulthood, though somewhat differently for each age group. Studies of playfulness in relation to child development (Barnett, 1990; Barnett & Kleiber, 1982, 1984; Glynn & Webster, 1993; Lieberman, 1977) have identified cognitive, physical and social spontaneity, sense of humor, and manifest joy as the central factors. These studies have revealed important relationships with developmental indicators. Liebermann described the playful child as showing "bubbling effervescence" and "glint-in-the-eye" behavior and as demonstrating higher levels of creativity. Interestingly, the relationship between playfulness and creativity was found to be different for boys and girls (Barnett & Kleiber, 1982). Playful boys were no more likely to be creative than less playful boys when intelligence was controlled; whereas for girls, a positive relationship between playfulness and creativity was found. The explanation offered for the difference was that boys in North America are generally expected to be playful, so their level of playfulness does not necessarily reflect the fluidity and independence of their thought processes—factors associated with creativity. On the other hand, when girls, who may not be encouraged to be playful, exhibit high levels of playfulness, it is much more likely to reflect underlying personality processes that, in fact, are related to creativity. Such speculation needs to be tested further, but it suggests another way in which personality characteristics can interact with previous socialization and the demands of the social environment.

Playfulness researchers (e.g., Lieberman, 1977) speculated that playfulness in adolescence would take the form of more emphasis on intellectual curiosity and humor rather than on physical spontaneity. Indeed, a continuing emphasis on the physical spontaneity aspect of playfulness might be maladaptive in some respects, being associated with restlessness in settings such as school, where opportunities for overt physical self-expression are generally confined to periods of recess and locations such as the gymnasium. Perhaps as a result, physical spontaneity has been de-emphasized in the study of playfulness in adolescence. Items such as "I like to clown around" and "By being playful it is easier to get along with people" were used in a measure developed for a study of playfulness and coping in adolescence (Staempfli, 2007). Staempfli found only limited evidence of the influence of playfulness on coping using this measure, and much of its impact on mental health appeared to be mediated by one's sense of satisfaction with leisure in adolescence. However, since the scale developed for that study was uni-dimensional, it may not have been sensitive to the variations in playfulness which may have been associated differently with the dependent measure of coping and mental health.

Research on playfulness in adulthood shows that it is an aspect of personality that still has meaning, regardless of the fact that it isn't associated directly with play behavior. In focus groups with more than 600 college students, Barnett (2007a) determined that the meanings (adjective descriptors) most associated with playfulness broke down into factors of *gregariousness* (cheerful, happy, friendly), *uninhibited* (spontaneous, impulsive, and unpredictable), *comedic* (clowns around, jokes/teases, funny) and *dynamic* (active, energetic). These findings led her to define playfulness—for adults—as "the predisposition to frame (or reframe) the situation in such a way as to provide others (and possibly oneself) with amusement, humor, and/or entertainment" (p. 955). She also found that that these meanings were also associated—though only moderately—with being creative, and unlike the case with childhood playfulness, no substantial gender differences in meanings or functional relationships were found.

Other research on playfulness in adulthood has used different items and measures and has found somewhat different factors, some related to attitudes toward fun (e.g., Shen, Chick, & Zinn, 2009). And qualitative studies of playfulness in later life appear to emphasize unconventionality and fun, as with members of the "Red Hat Society" (e.g., Yarnal, 2006; Yarnal, Chick, & Kerstetter, 2008), while leaving as an issue the question of whether the "players" in adulthood were also players in their past. In any case, more research is needed on these different measures and their associations with indicators of development, social competence, mental health, or other kinds of leisure behavior.

Time Orientation

There is considerable evidence now that people differ consistently in terms of time orientation, being characteristically more present-, past- or future-oriented (Zimbardo & Boyd, 1999). Using a specially developed time-orientation measure (ZTPI), Zimbardo and his colleagues differentiated a past orientation that was positive, with the bias to interpret the present in terms of a warm sentimental view of the past (e.g., "I like family rituals that are regularly repeated"); a negative past-orientation, having a bias to think about the present in terms of an unhappy or stressful past (e.g., "I think about the good things that I have missed out on in life"); a hedonistic present-orientation, where the present is treated with a "devil-may-care" preference for self-indulgence and risk taking (e.g., "I often follow my heart rather than my head"); a fatalistic present-orientation, which reflects an external locus of control and a sense that life may be hopeless (e.g., "Often luck pays off better than hard work"); and a future-orientation that interprets the present in light of goals and rewards (e.g., "I believe that a person's day should be planned ahead each morning"). Most of their work and the work of others using this measure in this area has focused on adolescents and young adults and has identified an association between low future-orientation and high present-orientation with self-indulgent and delinquent activities, lower achievement, and academic motivation. A high future time orientation, on the other hand, has been associated with academic performance and achievement motivation.

However, being present-centered is also essentially about being in the moment and is arguably more consistent with a positive attitude toward leisure. For one thing, it would be necessary to allow complete absorption in an activity such as is associated with flow. Also, as noted above in our discussion of Type-A behavior, worry about the future is associated with maladaptive rumination that keeps one from relaxing in the present (Martin & Tesser, 1996). Unfortunately, leisure research has not given much attention to this personality characteristic in examining the links between time orientation, leisure attitude, and experience.

In one of the few studies on the subject, Shores and Scott (2007) did not attempt to assess whether time orientation was associated with attitude toward leisure or toward the tendency to achieve flow, but they did examine the relationship between the five time orientations referred to earlier with preferred recreation experiences and desired recreation benefits. In so doing, they found that a hedonistic present-time orientation was associated with a preference for risky leisure activities, while a future-orientation was more highly related to a preference for using recreation to test competence, improve physical fitness, and bring the family closer together. The ZTPI measure used in their study has been criticized for having an inherently conventional bias in its future-orientation-items and for using present-orientation-items that were essentially unconventional and antisocial (Keen, 2007). So perhaps it is understandable that in the Shores and Scott study, a future-orientation was associated with an *instrumental* orientation toward recreation, that is *using* recreation intentionally to achieve other benefits. Nevertheless, this was a valuable study for setting the stage for research on this important leisure-relevant dimension of personality.

Time orientation also appears to change with age or, to the extent that it remains stable, to have different adaptive values at different points in the life course. Carstensen and colleagues (Carstensen, Isaacowitz, & Charles, 1999) did a series of studies that suggested that it is adaptive for older people to put more emphasis on the present than the future as they move into later life. A more limited time horizon typically makes people more intent on living in and for the moment. Such an orientation is associated with a more positive emotional tone and enhanced subjective well-being in later life. While these researchers found that a future orientation was by contrast generally more adaptive for younger people—as expressed, for example, in giving more emphasis on meeting new people than enjoying old friends—when the future time frame was foreshortened for them in some way, as by serious illness or an impending graduation, priority was given more to present-centered enjoyment.

The Autotelic Personality

To the extent that people can be characterized as "types," as in Type-A, present-centered, and playful people, a type most intimately related to leisure is the *autotelic personality* discussed by Csikszentmihalyi (1975, 1990). Autotelic means that the purpose of an activity lies in the activity itself. Some activities—and many typical leisure activities—are rewarding enough in themselves to need no other justification or external reward. Thus, as was discussed in earlier chapters, they are intrinsically motivating. Usually, such activities work that way when they provide an appropriate level of challenge that matches well with a person's skill level, thus allowing the experience of "flow." But some people are able to create such internal satisfaction with activities or situations that are not intrinsically motivating to most other people or to themselves initially. The *autotelic person* is one who is able to find intrinsic interest and enjoyment in almost everything he or she does. Such people are able to create leisure-like experience in unleisure-like circumstances. Consequently, boredom and anxiety are less common for them because they are able to find or create optimal levels of challenge in almost any activity or setting by reinterpreting the challenge to fit their interests and skills. This may mean finding something to manipulate or play with, cognitively or physically, in an otherwise boring situation (e.g., creating a mind game while waiting in line) or managing a more difficult situation by attending only to certain elements of it (e.g., focusing on a particular repetition in a complicated piece of music). It is likely that some of the characteristics discussed above, such as attentional style, are important to the autotelic personality. While the autotelic personality hasn't been measured directly, an "intrinsic leisure motivation" scale was developed by Weissinger and Bandalos (1995) to measure the extent to which people expected to be intrinsically motivated in leisure. And Barnett (2006; Barnett & Klitzing, 2006) used the *Work Preference Inventory* to assess an orientation toward intrinsic motivation in terms of self-determination, curiosity, enjoyment, interest, and task involvement. They found that higher scores on this measure predicted interest in sports and performing arts but not health/fitness, outdoor, or aquatics activities among a culturally diverse group of undergraduates. Still, it might be used in conjunction with other measures to approximate an assessment of the autotelic personality.

Shyness

A final example of a personality trait that may influence leisure behavior and experience is *shyness*. Shyness shares some of the characteristics of introversion, contrasts with sensation seeking, and, in the extreme, may be pathologically associated with social anxiety (see Crozier, 2001; Zimbardo, 1990). Shyness has multiple properties, some of which may facilitate or interfere with certain leisure experiences (Lee & Halberg, 1989). In a study of 94 undergraduate students, researchers found that people who were diagnosed as being chronically shy scored low in perceived freedom in leisure as measured by the *Leisure Diagnostic Battery (LDB)* (Witt & Ellis, 1984). These individuals' perceptions of having little freedom and control in leisure suggests that they may have difficulty experiencing leisure and finding satisfaction in leisure, particularly in social situations. This interpretation is consistent with other research on shyness that suggests that people who are shy may feel they lack control in their lives and have low social competence (e.g., Leary & Atherton, 1986).

Leisure-Specific Personality Dispositions

Leisure researchers have not always been satisfied with the personality traits derived from mainstream psychology as explanatory constructs. There has also been the suspicion that leisure is such a distinct and ubiquitous context that it brings out different characteristics than other situations. This has led some researchers to conceptualize leisure-specific dispositions that might prove to be more useful than general personality traits in describing and predicting leisure behavior (see Kleiber & Dirkin, 1985; Mannell, 1984b). These measures have been generated primarily for leisure research, and their application to other areas of human behavior has yet to be explored.

Self-As-Entertainment Capacity

The capacity or ability of people to fill their free or discretionary time with activity (i.e., mental, physical, or social) that is personally satisfying and perceived as appropriate has been discussed as *Self-as-Entertainment* (SAE), or the ability to entertain oneself (Mannell, 1984b). Individuals high on this characteristic perceive a match between the time they have available and their ability to use it. They do not experience time as "hanging heavily on their hands" and are less likely to regard leisure as boring. Nor are they likely to feel that they are wasting time in their leisure. Individuals low on this trait, on the other hand, perceive that they have too much free time and that there is frequently "nothing to do." A 28-item measure of this characteristic (introduced earlier in the chapter, see Figure 7.2, pp. 192 and 193) has been developed. Three "modes" of self-as-entertainment underlie the items: self, environmental, and mind-play. The central construct is measured by the "self" mode, that is, the extent to which people perceive they can successfully structure their own free time. The "environmental" mode reflects the extent to which people fill their free time by going places or by seeking out other people. Finally, the "mind-play" mode refers to the extent to which people are able to use fantasy and imagination to fill their time.

Several studies have been reported that support the scale's reliability and validity with undergraduate students and nonstudent adults (Ellis & Yessick, 1989; Mannell, 1984b, 1985; Iso-Ahola & Weissinger, 1990). Barnett and Klitzing (2006) found it a strong predictor (inversely) of boredom in free time. Self-as-entertainment capacity would be another close approximation to the autotelic personality orientation and might be used with the measures of intrinsic motivation to more clearly operationalize it.

Intrinsic Leisure Motivation Personality Disposition

Weissinger and Iso-Ahola (1984) proposed that some people are more oriented to engage in and experience leisure as intrinsically motivated than other people. Weissinger developed the *Intrinsic Leisure Motivation* scale to measure this individual difference, and the research she did with it indicated that it is reliable and potentially useful (see Weissinger & Bandalos, 1995). People with high scores on the scale are characterized as having a strong desire for self-determination, competence, deep involvement, and challenge while engaging in leisure pursuits. In one study, Iso-Ahola and Weissinger (1987) found that people who had a high score on the scale were much less likely to experience boredom during their leisure. Weissinger has suggested that the *Intrinsic Leisure Motivation* scale could be used to study how people come to see leisure as having the potential to be intrinsically rewarding. As we suggested earlier, it might be a reasonable measure of at least part of the autotelic personality. It also could be a useful tool in leisure education and leisure counseling as well as in therapeutic recreation practice for identifying people who may have difficulty experiencing leisure.

Perceived Freedom in Leisure

Neulinger (1981, 1986) developed the *What Am I Doing Scale* (WAID) to measure the amount of perceived freedom people experience in leisure during a specific period of time in the course of their daily lives. This instrument has received only limited use (e.g., Ellis & Witt, 1984; Hultsman & Russell, 1988). A more widely used measure is the LDB, developed by Witt and Ellis (1984), from which a shorter version has also been developed (Witt & Ellis, 1985). The LDB assesses the extent to which people generally feel that their leisure is freely chosen. Perceiving freedom in leisure is felt to affect people's ability to use play and recreation to attain leisure and the benefits associated with it.

Several studies have been reported that suggest that the level of perceived freedom in leisure as assessed by the LDB is related to people's ability to experience meaningful and satisfying leisure. As noted earlier, Lee and Halberg (1989) found that people who were diagnosed as being chronically shy scored low in perceived freedom in leisure as assessed by the LDB. Adolescents scoring high in perceived freedom in leisure were found to participate more frequently, to have more positive attitudes toward leisure, and to be more satisfied with their leisure roles (Munson, 1993). They also participated more in volunteer and community service activities and found these activities more satisfying.

Leisure Boredom

Boredom is a general condition of mind that people experience to greater or lesser degrees depending on their circumstances and also their personality. As noted earlier, extroverts are more susceptible to boredom because they have a higher arousal threshold. But it has been proposed that for some people, boredom is especially associated with leisure, that is, they find free time boring in and of itself, or the available alternatives unappealing. Iso-Ahola and Weissinger (1990) developed a personality test called the *Leisure Boredom Scale* to measure this leisure-specific trait by having people rate how well such items as the following describe them: "For me, leisure time just drags on and on" and "During my leisure time, I almost always have something to do" (second item is scored the opposite of the first item). Their research has shown that people who score higher on these types of items are less likely to perceive themselves as socially competent, are less likely to be able to entertain themselves, have lower self-esteem, are less positive toward leisure, and less likely to be involved in a variety of leisure activities.

More recently, Barnett and Klitzing (2006) sought to identify how boredom in free time was associated with personality, gender, race, and ethnicity in a large sample of college students. The investigators determined that boredom susceptibility, though almost a personality trait itself, was associated with a variety of different personality and motivation factors in patterns that varied somewhat by gender, race, and ethnicity as well. As noted earlier, free time boredom was associated with lower levels of extroversion and intrinsic motivation orientation.

In another study (Iso-Ahola & Crowley, 1991), substance abusers were found to score higher on leisure boredom. Interestingly, though, they were also more likely to go to rock concerts and engage in physical recreation than non-abusers. Iso-Ahola and Crowley concluded that, "Because of their personality predisposition toward sensation seeking and low tolerance for constant experiences, substance abusers presumably prefer active leisure lifestyles. But if leisure activities fail to satisfy their need for optimal arousal, leisure boredom results, and drug use may be the only alternative" (p. 260). However, a more recent study of South African teenagers (Wegner, Fisher, Muller, & Lombard, 2006) failed to find an association between substance abuse and leisure boredom.

Boredom proneness or boredom susceptibility may be a stable personality factor in some respects. It might be the other end on the continuum of capacity for absorption and openness to experience (cf. Seib & Vodanovitch, 1998). But in general, treating boredom as a stable individual difference factor that predicts leisure activity and experience may be less appropriate than looking at boredom in free time as a *consequence* of the interaction or personality and circumstances. We will return to this idea in Chapters 9 and 11.

The research on all of the leisure specific needs discussed in this section is limited. In particular, their discriminant validity—whether they are truly measuring something different than more general (non-leisure focused) measures that are similar—remains a question. Perhaps, though, if these leisure specific orientations have limited value as enduring personality traits, they may be better understood as leisure attitudes.

Attitudes toward Leisure and Specific Leisure Activities

One type of psychological disposition that we have not discussed thus far is attitude. Attitudes are learned for the most part and can change rapidly under certain circumstances. But they also represent the enduring value structure of individuals and how those values are applied. Only a limited amount of research has been done on leisure attitudes, but research has shown that they are amenable to influence and change, a subject we will take up again in Chapter 13. In fact, attitudes have been seen as so important that attitude-change theories and strategies have been developed and applied to a wide range of lifestyle behaviors, including health and exercise behavior (e.g., Hagger, Chatzisarantis, & Harris, 2006; Manfredo, 1992).

Is idleness the devil's workshop? Should the length of the workweek be reduced? Are people on welfare entitled to leisure? Should cultural activities such as the ballet or public television be supported with tax dollars? Is participation in organized sports a good way for children to spend their leisure? Is being on a social networking site all evening a good use of time? Is bungee jumping a safe and worthwhile leisure pursuit? Is downhill skiing an appropriate leisure activity for people without the use of their legs? Your answers to these questions reflect your attitudes toward various aspects of leisure, which may also impact your own leisure behavior and experience. Leisure itself may be unappealing to some. A strong Protestant work ethic may be associated with a view that leisure is frivolous, trivial, and even decadent. If what people do is judged entirely in terms of that which is accomplished or produced, much of leisure is likely to be regarded as relatively worthless. Such an ethic may stand in the way of leisure participation and enjoyment. There is also the question of who, if anyone, is "entitled" to leisure. Those who work at home, but do not earn a wage—as with many mothers, for example—may be less likely to see leisure as something that they deserve (Henderson, 1991b; Henderson & Bialeschki, 1993). Similarly, those who are retired or unemployed may have some difficulty if they have come to regard enjoyment as something that must be "earned" by socially sanctioned productive work. Such attitudes, which incorporate both self-perceptions and social norms, may be very influential with respect to leisure behavior and experience, and they may be relatively enduring individual characteristics.

Although there are various approaches to attitudes, social psychologists generally agree that attitudes vary in level of intensity from mild to extreme (Petty & Cacioppo, 1986; Zanna & Rempel, 1988). "Like," "dislike," "love," "hate," "admire," and "detest" are the kinds of words people use to describe their attitudes, and attitudes can be measured. The easiest and most often used method to assess a person's attitude about something is to simply ask. For example, a researcher could ask someone how positive or negative they feel about the role leisure plays in people's lives today, about people who retire early, or about a specific activity like opera. Although self-report is straightforward, attitudes are sometimes too complex to be measured with a single question. Responses can be influenced by wording, the context, and other extraneous factors. Consequently, researchers often use multi-item questionnaires called attitude scales, which come in various forms. The most popular is the Likert scale, named after its inventor, Rensis Likert (1932). In this technique, people are presented with a list of statements on an attitude object and are asked to indicate on a multiple-point scale how strongly they agree or disagree with each statement. Their total attitude score is calculated by summing their responses to all the items. Researchers often create their own attitude scales to meet the needs of their specific research study; however, there are many standardized attitude scales that have been developed. Several such scales have been developed to measure attitudes toward leisure in general. For example, the *Leisure Ethic Scale* (Crandall & Slivken, 1980) is comprised of ten items (see Figure 7.5). Ragheb and Beard's (1982) 24-item *Leisure Attitude Scale* has also been used.

As noted above in our review of work on locus of control as a leisure-related personality variable, the relationships between leisure ethic and work ethic and between leisure attitudes and personality are complex (Kleiber, 1979; Kleiber & Crandall, 1981). A positive attitude toward leisure (positive leisure ethic) may be somewhat suspect among those who feel effective at controlling their own environment and believe strongly in the values of goal setting,

---

This scale measures your attitudes toward lesure. By this we mean how you feel about your leisure, your recreation, or the things you do in your free time. Please answer as quickly and accurately as possible by indicating whether you agree or disagree with each of the following statements.

	Completely Disagree	Moderately Disagree	Moderately Agree	Completely Agree
1. My leisure time is my most enjoyable time.	1	2	3	4
2. I admire a person who knows how to relax.	1	2	3	4
3. I like to do things on the spur of the moment.	1	2	3	4
4. I would like to lead a life of complete leisure.	1	2	3	4
5. Most people spend too much time enjoying themselves.	1	2	3	4
6. I don't feel guilty about enjoying myself.	1	2	3	4
7. People should seek as much leisure as possible in their lives.	1	2	3	4
8. I'd like to have at least two months vacation a year.	1	2	3	4
9. Leisure is great.	1	2	3	4
10. It is good for adults to be playful.	1	2	3	4

Note: All items are scored 4 points for "completely agree" to 1 point for "completely disagree," except for item five, which is reversed.

Figure 7.5 Leisure Ethic Scale (adapted from Crandall & Slivken, 1980)

hard work, and achievement. But stated values about work and leisure are often ideological and normative and may not reflect one's appreciation of leisure activity and experience. And the links between attitude toward leisure and leisure behavior remain to be more clearly examined.

Indeed, it should not be assumed that negative leisure attitudes always constrain behavior in any case. In fact, research has demonstrated that the link between attitudes and behavior is far from automatic (see Eagly & Chaiken, 1993). Having a negative attitude toward television viewing does not mean that one does not watch television. Conversely, holding positive attitudes toward spending more leisure time with family, exercising regularly, or traveling to exotic places does not necessarily mean that a person does those things. However, researchers have identified conditions under which attitudes are linked to behavior. One key factor is the *level of generality and specificity* of the attitude and behavior of interest. Attitudes affect behavior only when attitude measures closely match the behavior in question. Research on a wide range of issues has supported this principle (Ajzen, 1991b). To illustrate, assume that researchers are trying to use attitudes to predict whether people will visit a museum sometime within the next two years. Attitudes might be measured in a series of questions ranging from very *general*, such as "How do you feel about museums?" to very *specific*, such as "How do you feel about visiting a museum during the next two years?" Because the latter type of question is more specific and deals with intentions, it would be more likely to predict actual museum visiting behavior.

The link between one's attitudes and one's actions must also be placed within a broader context. Attitudes are only one determinant of behavior. This limitation formed the basis of Fishbein's (1980) *theory of reasoned action*, which Ajzen (1991) then expanded and called the *theory of planned behavior (TPB)*, as discussed to some extent in Chapter 6. This latter theory states that attitudes influence behavior through a process of deliberate decision making and that their impact is limited by subjective norms (what others think about the issue or activity), perceived behavioral control (one's locus of control with respect to the issue or action), and actual controllability of the situation (what anyone can do under the circumstances). Figure 7.6 (p. 218) illustrates these dynamics (although perceived behavioral control does sometimes affect behavior directly, for which we might expect a direct line between the two). For example, if everyone Janice encounters feels and expects that she can no longer be an active sports person because of a diving accident she had, she is less likely to look for opportunities for physical activity in her leisure. Further, if Janice no longer feels confident in her athletic ability, she is less likely to plan to try something like adapted downhill skiing, even though she feels quite positive about the idea. This disability and the subsequent loss in confidence are examples of intrapersonal constraints in the scheme described in Chapter 6, but the reactions and attitudes of others make it about interpersonal constraints as well. We will address such things more fully in Chapter 9.

Generally, previous research has found a positive but rather modest relationship between leisure attitudes, on the one hand, and overall leisure participation and satisfaction, on the other. More recently, though, as noted in Chapter 6, theory of planned behavior models have been applied to a variety of leisure activities (Ajzen & Driver, 1991, 1992; Haggar, Chatzisarantis, & Harris, 2006; Hrubes, Ajzen, & Daigle, 2001; Pierro, Mannetti, & Livi, 2003; Walker, Courneya, & Deng, 2006) to enhance predictive precision. Ajzen and Driver (1991, 1992) in particular demonstrated the theory's ability to predict leisure intentions and behavior. Consistent with the theory, intentions to perform five different activities (e.g., spending time at the beach, outdoor jogging, mountain climbing, boating, and biking), together with perceptions of behavior control, were shown to predict the extent to which respondents engaged in these activities over a 12-month period.

To summarize, attitudes toward a person, object, or behavior do not always correspond to actions because other factors must be taken into account. However, when attitudes are strong and specific to a particular behavior, they can constrain or motivate leisure behavior. The question then becomes, "How are leisure attitudes changed so that they are not intrapersonal constraints to leisure participation?" We will deal with this question in Chapter 13 and return now to the ways personality influences leisure through the organization of identity.

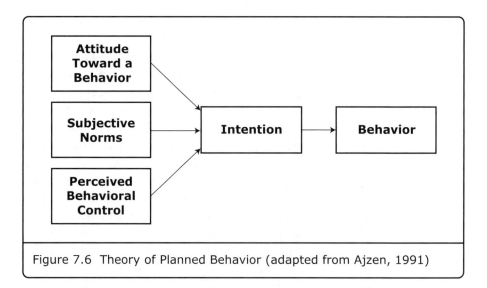

Figure 7.6 Theory of Planned Behavior (adapted from Ajzen, 1991)

Identity and Leisure

Personal Versus Social Identity

Personal identity is a product of internal consistencies and inconsistencies with one's past, differences and similarities one has with others, and plans and goals for the future. A colleague shared a profile of one of his doctoral students that seems to illustrate some of these properties. The student insists that there was never anyone among her family and friends who saw her as even going to college, much less continuing on to do graduate work, but her desire to express aspects of herself that were not valued (or even acknowledged) by the others in her world led her along and gave her a basis for transforming the way she views herself. Reflected therein is both her uniqueness relative to others and the sense of future that she envisioned as a product of her own doing, independent of the others in her early experience.

Social identity, on the other hand, is derived from *identification* with others; one may be an Asian-American, a brick mason, a Girl Scout, or a senior citizen among many other possible group identities. Identities are embedded in families (son, daughter, wife, cousin), neighborhoods (next-door neighbor, United Way volunteer), schools (teacher, student, clerk, custodian), and economic institutions (preferred customer, dealer, secretary), as well as gender, race, and ethnic groups, rather than being defined in opposition to them (Heath & McLaughlin, 1993; Stryker, 1987, 2000). We will take up matters of gender, race, and ethnicity in Chapters 8, 9, and 10, but it is important to recognize their powerful influence on identity and personality here. Group identity may also include former roles such as ex-wife or ex-athlete, and it may reflect *assigned* conditions such as physically disabled, heterosexual, or multiracial. But identifications must ultimately be recognized and accepted by the individual to be significant, and some social categories that could be used to describe someone may not be personally meaningful. For example, being a Capricorn or a resident of Crestview Heights, may not be particularly defining for a person. As with personal traits, social categories have to be "owned" personally and recognized socially to be part of one's social identity. Finally, we note that identities are also shaped around places—where someone is from and to what extent one is attached to a particular geographical location. (e.g., Williams, 2002).

Identity Characteristics

Coherence

While the multiplicity of personal and social elements might suggest separate selves, as in multiple personalities, the various characteristics one has are organized into one self. Disparate elements in one's identity can be accommodated, at least until they come into conflict, but they must be integrated into a coherent whole to be a part of one's enduring identity (Baumeister, 1995). The coherence of identity is sometimes threatened by its complexity, however. In asking adolescents to describe themselves, Susan Harter (1990) reports the response of a 15-year-old who demonstrates the ambivalence of relating to parental imperatives ("study!") and friends' demands ("be popular!"), which in turn conflict with a boyfriend's exhortations ("relax!"); if she responds to all of them, she also feels "phony" as a result.

The issue of coherence becomes particularly difficult when life events interrupt a person's understood life story. Imagine the questions about who you are subsequent to an automobile accident that leaves you paralyzed or if you had been married for 20 years and your spouse suddenly dies. In such cases, the "illness" is not only about physical changes or role changes but about a loss of self as defined by available interests and activities (e.g., Kleiber et al., 1995). And even in the case where the disruption is relatively minor on the surface—as with a stress fracture for a distance runner—if the activity has had a great deal of *salience* to the individual's identity, as with serious leisure activities, coherence may be threatened (e.g., Collinson & Hickey, 2007).

Salience of Interests and Concerns

Domains of interest, such as political ideology, religious beliefs, vocations and avocations, and roles, also vary in their *salience* both across individuals and for the same individual at different points in time. Sheldon Stryker argued that role identities are organized into a self-conception according to a hierarchy of salience (Stryker, 1987). The higher the salience, the more important the role and the higher the probability that various situations will be seen as opportunities to perform that role. Also, in addition to roles, if a person identifies with a particular object, activity, or place, it has salience for him or her.

Leisure identities may be more or less salient in a person's constellation of role identities, as Shamir (1988, 1992) and others have established. They become more salient, according to these researchers, to the extent they involve expression and affirmation of the individual's talents or capabilities and provide a degree of social recognition and affirmation of his or her central values. Leisure-identity salience is motivating to further involvement and typically leads to greater commitment to the activity and greater comfort in contexts in which the activity occurs. For example, to a person for whom the role of scout leader is particularly salient, any social situation, regardless of the presence of children or other scout leaders, is likely to be seen as an opportunity to discuss scouting and scouts. Or a salient domain may vary in terms of the characteristics reflected at any given point in time (e.g., moving from flamboyant guitarist performing in club venues to teacher of classical techniques).

Authenticity

Aspects of identity may also feel more or less *authentic* to a person. Authenticity is conditioned partly by real or perceived external demands to behave in anything other than a natural way, partly in finding and responding to one's inner characteristics and potentials, and partly as a matter of comfort or "fit" with the immediate environment. Erikson (1968) associated core identity with "the real me," the sense of being deeply and intensively active and alive, "an invigorating sameness and continuity" (p. 19). Alan Waterman offered a similar view in his work on personal expressiveness (Waterman, 1990, 1993a, 1993b). In Waterman's view, people default on their potential when forced to by environmental demands (for survival), social pressures, pleasurable distractions, or lack of will. The total absence of personal expressiveness results in "identity pathologies" including *diffusion*, where one is not seeking (such as being distracted by meaningless pleasures), and *disguise*, where chosen identity components are determined by external contingencies such as status and wealth, for example, without considering one's potentials.

The question of whether some components of identity vary with respect to authenticity has also been considered by Ralph Turner (1978, 1987). But in contrast with Waterman, Turner associated authenticity more with being *comfortable* in social situations than with being aligned with one's unique potentials. Just as Waterman did, Turner noted that situational identities are often negotiated bargains, rather than reflections of commitment and authenticity, and that people feel least themselves in institutionally defined contexts such as school, church, or work.

When Turner asked students to identify when and where they felt most truly themselves, the majority indicated that they felt that way when being with others in "casual and personal conversation, in a purposeless encounter without sexual overtones" (p. 132). While the "true self" was also often associated with resisting institutional constraints, it is this "customary" everyday self that seems most comfortable and authentic to people in Turner's view.

This customary self is situated largely through what Norman Denzin referred to as "self-lodging," which is "translating features of one's own identity into the selves, memories and imaginations of others" (Denzin, 1970, p. 127). Denzin regarded self-lodging as a motive, since—in contrast to the need to present oneself in a certain way—it makes the self "unproblematic." People feel most authentic in contexts of relative freedom from external expectations, where companionable others allow them to relax and feel comfortably themselves. Denzin noted that self-lodging is indicated by nicknames, dress and speech styles, and gestures that contribute to a sense of belonging. While such circumstances imply an identity that is at least temporarily stable and coherent, *dislodging* can also take place. Being spurned by a lover or fickle friends is unsettling to identity, making it problematic again. And thus the process of identity formation is likely to begin again and again. In fact, one's identity will evolve and change throughout the lifespan.

One leisure context that may be particularly challenging to identity authenticity is tourism. Both the tourist, who is often in a very different context from those with which she/he is familiar and comfortable, and the "receiving culture," which may be presenting itself to attract tourists or to heighten tourist experience, encounter questions of authenticity. (For details, see MacCannell, 1992, Urry, 2002, and Franklin, 2006.)

Dialectics of Identity Formation

Identity formation is motivated in some cases, then, by a search for authenticity, for one's true self, while at other times and for other people it is driven by the need for stability and for being a more consistent and predictable member of society. But whatever motivates the search for and formation of identity, the process itself has considerable complexity.

Identity formation is first of all age-related, emerging in early adolescence in conjunction with the cognitive changes that allow for abstract thought. In Piaget's view, the transition from concrete to formal operations enables one to consider abstractions such as truth and beauty and to form hypotheses and theories, even a theory of oneself. The difficulty in the early stages—and herein lies the first part of the problem—is in shaping a theory that is both accurate and useful. Given that a sense of self is initially constructed almost entirely in response to the reactions of others, having a stable view is extremely unlikely because of the constant flow of new and contradictory information. Indeed, the ability to consider oneself from the viewpoint of others initially leads to the misconception that one is in fact the continuous subject of others' attention. The "imaginary audience," (Elkind, 1981), evoked as a result, is a source of the self-consciousness that is notoriously disconcerting in adolescence. Such self-consciousness is disruptive to both performance and enjoyment.

With age and experience, *differentiation* of the self occurs, allowing more understanding and control over the sources of information that are used for self-definition. The example discussed earlier of the 15-year-old girl in conflict over how she should act with her parents, peers, and boyfriend demonstrates such differentiation (in spite of the challenge that it creates for coherence). But Harter (1990) also notes that identity becomes more internally determined with age, giving increasing importance to traits, wishes, and emotions.

Identity is constructed through both differentiation and *integration*. Identity itself is an indication that integration has taken place, that a coherent, unified sense of self has been formed out of disparate characteristics. But differentiation creates the characteristics that are to be organized in the first place. Creating and recognizing distinctions in experience is the basis of differentiation. Differentiation allows a person to see oneself more precisely as well as more abstractly—as tolerant, kind, and sensitive, for example, rather than simply as a nice person. And information is used selectively to create a self-image that is as positive as possible under the circumstances.

Still, discrepancies in self-perception arise and create pressure and distress wherever a unified, coherent sense of self is sought (McAdams, 1997). Adolescents distinguish "false" from "true" selves insofar as they feel they have to impress others, try out new behaviors, or accommodate to the demands of intolerant adults. Even the 15-year-old that Harter interviewed noted that "I can only be my true self with my close friends," contrasting them to her parents who still treat her "like a kid" (Harter, 1990).

Discrepancies caused by status and relationship conflicts in early and middle adolescence give way to those that come with role interpretation as one moves into adulthood. Interpreting the role of parent, for example, often reflects both differentiation and integration in adjusting to that role alone. A friend who recently became a first-time parent has resisted embracing the role as she has observed others do it. She struggles with wanting to be more than the role of mother requires yet also tries to be successful within the role. She does what she can to avoid being categorized as a "typical mom" (e.g., dragging pictures of the child out of her purse at predictable points and letting conversations with other mothers digress into endless child comparisons); and yet she has found herself working on her singing and storytelling with the child so that she can be a "good mom."

As the principal processes of identity formation, *identification* and *individuation* also operate dialectically. Marilyn Brewer (1991) points to a principle of *optimal distinctiveness* in describing the way individuals identify with groups. Being like others brings the sense of being part of a collective, but it is meaningful to identity only where that collective is distinguishable from others. The need to be connected with others is satisfied within groups, while the need to be distinctive is satisfied in intergroup comparison. For example, adolescents are often criticized for conforming so much, and yet in identifying so closely with peers they are usually distinguishing themselves from adults or from other peer groups (Brown, 1990). Individuation in identity formation generally centers around the establishment of distinctiveness, but this is as likely to occur in relations with others as in separating from them, a point which is generally neglected in research on identity. One's identity may be found and/or elaborated in relating to others in intimate ways.

Exploration and *commitment* also operate dynamically and dialectically in identity formation, working to define a person with respect to the various domains that are encountered in the course of growing up. Exploration has been referred to as "a period of struggle or active questioning in arriving at identity decisions regarding goals, values, and beliefs," while commitment involves "the making of relatively firm choices regarding identity elements and engaging in significant activity directed toward the implementation of those choices" (Waterman, 1993b, p. 148). The interaction of these processes results in four possibilities according to James Marcia (1980; see Figure 7.7). *Identity achievement* requires both exploration and commitment. Exploration in the absence of commitment—a common condition in adolescence—results in what Erikson and Marcia refer to as *moratorium*, a delay in the process of making decisions. Where commitments are made in the absence of exploration—often the result of simply internalizing values, beliefs, and wishes of parents—identity formation is at least temporarily *foreclosed*. And without either exploration or commitment, a person remains *diffused*, "uninvolved in the process of finding someone to be and sometimes even uninvolved in the process of finding something to do" (Waterman, 1993b, p. 149). These *statuses*, as Marcia calls them, apply to each domain a person experiences. Also assumed to some extent here is that people are producers of their own development and that, with some degree of freedom, they take steps to find themselves in whatever domains are particularly salient to them. Perhaps leisure affords some of the freedom necessary for exploration and in some cases for commitment as well.

In sum then, the processes, dynamics, and structures of identity influence behavioral choices and experiences in work, family, and other contexts, but they have their greatest play in the context of leisure where relative situational freedom is expanded. That leisure experiences might then influence identity, particularly through exploration and commitment, is a theme to be picked up again in Chapter 11.

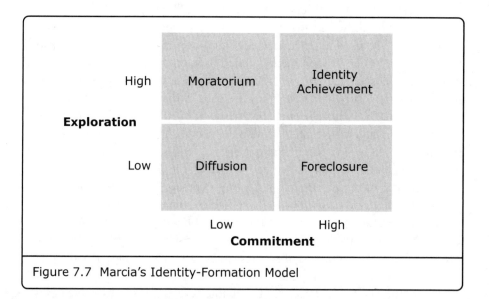

Figure 7.7 Marcia's Identity-Formation Model

Interactionism and Other Issues of Personality and Leisure

In this chapter, we have shown that one of the ways social psychologically oriented researchers have attempted to understand leisure is by looking inside of people for the causes of their leisure behavior and experience. General personality dispositions that are useful in explaining a wide range of human behavior have also been found to have relevance to leisure behavior. Leisure-specific personality dispositions have been identified and they, too, show some promise. Identity, as an organizing structure of personality, has also been shown to direct leisure in some ways. However, it is worth reminding ourselves that researchers cannot "see" personality dispositions and traits or identity dialectics; these can only be inferred from what people do and say. Personality dispositions, traits, and attitudes are hypothetical constructs, that is, they are terms and ideas that represent an individual's enduring character. These can be relatively stable and to some extent their importance and relevance varies from one person to another. As we have seen, these differences among people are related to how they use and experience their leisure.

As plausible and attractive as personality explanations of leisure are, it is important to note that personality does not act in a social vacuum. No matter how different they are from each other, people are influenced by the various social settings and social roles that they move in and out of during their daily lives. If a professor encounters the president of her university at a social reception, she may act differently than if she was in a restaurant lounge with longtime friends. A middle-aged man behaves differently with his children as the coach of their soccer team than when fishing with them during a family vacation. Sometimes the influence of the situation is so strong that one's personality appears to have little influence on one's behavior. On the other hand, where there is little structure and few expectations in a situation, a person's behavior may be strongly influenced by her or his personality.

The importance of the interaction of personality and social situation was demonstrated in the experiments by Tang (1986) and Mannell and Bradley (1986), described earlier in this chapter. In the former case, the behavior and experience of the participants could only be understood when both social situation (work-versus-leisure context) and personality dispositions (Type-A versus Type-B) were taken into account. In the latter study, the influence of the amount of choice available in the social setting on game-playing behavior and flow experience was moderated by the locus of control of the participants.

Sometimes the interaction between personality and social situation is even more subtle, as we saw in Chapter 2. Recall that Diener, Larsen, and Emmons (1984) found that people's personalities were more likely to influence their choice of activities in leisure settings than work settings, and that engaging in activities that were consistent with personality dispositions (e.g., social activities are consistent with being extroverted) led to more enjoyment of the activities. However, this only occurred when people were in a leisure setting, not a work setting. This form of interaction is called "congruence," and there appears to be an advantage in doing things where there is congruence between personality and the activity demands of the situation. In studies of teachers, engineers, physicians, and lawyers (Melamed & Meir, 1981; Melamed, Meir, & Samson, 1995), personality factors did not cause these people to choose different activities, but those respondents whose leisure and work provided opportunities that were congruent with their personality-based psychological needs reported higher levels of well-being. In other words, if a person with an orientation to be investigative, social, or enterprising was regularly involved in activities judged to have similar characteristics, he or she was less likely to be anxious, sick, or depressed—a finding that we will return to in Chapter 13.

Interactionism is prominent in leisure research and practice. Ellis and Yessick (1989) stressed the practical importance of considering the individual's status on such variables as perceived freedom, intrinsic motivation, and self-as-entertainment when providing and assessing the effectiveness of therapeutic recreation interventions. Recreationists' intentions to obey rules in outdoor recreation areas have been shown to depend on both personality and situational factors (Gramann & Bonifield, 1995). And we can offer still other examples, such as a study of Outward Bound in Australia, where managed experience reduced the impact of neuroticism on moods states (Fry & Heubeck, 1998); or an investigation of recreation center attendance where peer influence interacted with adventurousness to lead to more inappropriate sexual activity (Person, Kerr, & Stattin, 2004); or in the way sensation seeking interacts with social aspects to have different outcomes in high-risk recreation settings (Robinson, 1992).

Conclusion

In concluding this chapter, then, it should be noted that although it appears that personality "causes" or directs leisure behavior and experience (at least to some extent), the relationship implied is clearly more complicated. Personality dispositions and traits themselves are a function of social experience as well as innate predispositions. Leisure-specific personality dispositions, motives, and needs are strongly influenced by the socialization process and a variety of social factors. Also, it is likely that frequent and intense experiences with certain kinds of leisure activities have the effect of shaping personality characteristics that in turn determine behavior not only in leisure but in other settings as well.

For example, a person who grows up hunting and fishing alone and comes to enjoy the incumbent solitude of that activity may learn to be somewhat introverted with respect to interacting with people in other areas of life. Such speculation, however, clearly needs the benefit of further research. In completing this unit on individual differences, we turn now to Chapter 8 on the influence of age and gender.

Age and Gender as Determinants of Leisure Behavior and Experience

Preview

In the previous chapter we considered individual differences in personality—in traits, temperaments, needs, attitudes, and identity. In this chapter, our focus is on age and gender, two factors that are equally defining for individuals and, as a result, for leisure. We might have given our attention to race, ethnicity, and culture here as well, but we will consider them primarily as contextual/situational influences in Chapter 10. This may seem somewhat arbitrary in that just as race and ethnicity have an effect on leisure as socio-cultural factors, age and gender are socially constructed to a great extent as well; that is, what it *means* at a particular point in time and space to be of a certain age or to be male or female is socially constructed. Nevertheless, we examine them here as somewhat enduring sources of difference in leisure behavior and experience, with some attention to how they are interpreted situationally and how they have changed over time.

With respect to age, there are many contrasting ideas about what it means to grow up and grow older. Some of them involve clear misconceptions; others are stereotypes that may have some truth but are clearly overgeneralizations. It is clear, though, that age is differentiating. There are dramatic differences in people of different ages; 12-year-olds are different as a group from 50-year-olds and "twentysomethings" are usually pretty different from those in their forties. Age does have its behavioral and attitudinal correlates: most children play, most teenagers seek to align with friends, most people have children before the age of 40, most people retire sometime after age 60, and most older people are more conservative than most younger people. There are many other consistencies associated with aging as well. Models of development that have been focused exclusively on childhood have given way to those suggesting that people pass through a series of stages over the entire lifespan/life course[1] in somewhat predictable ways. What should become clear in this chapter is that aging is not only a biological process. Being a certain age brings about certain experiences just as, for example, being at work in a corporation brings about specific experiences. In the next chapter, we will consider how age-related contexts—such as family and work—influence leisure behavior, but in this chapter we examine whether age differences are stable enough to hold up across situations and consequently constitute relatively enduring individual differences.

Other factors define the individual, of course. These include gender, culture, race, and disability, among other things. While there may be biologically based characteristics associated with such factors, for the most part they are constructed in interaction with the norms and values of society that give shape

---

[1] These terms have slightly different connotations, but differ mostly because lifespan is used in psychology and life course in sociology. We will use them interchangeably.

to expectations for how people differing in gender, culture, race, and disability behave. Of those factors, we will focus especially on gender; gender differences in leisure behavior are pronounced and relatively enduring, whatever their source. To be a girl or a woman is to encounter leisure in quite different ways than boys and men do, even in societies that are putting ever-decreasing emphasis on gender differences. These may be powerful influences, applying in many if not most situations. They also interact with situational influences, such as how women realize leisure (or don't) in the parenting role. Indeed, such differences are often a reflection of differences in opportunities and social expectations. The way in which situations, social units, and cultures influence leisure will be addressed in the next unit, in Chapters 9 and 10. But for our purposes in this chapter, as we did with personality in Chapter 7, we will treat age and gender in terms of their stable, determining influence when other factors are held constant.

Leisure Activity and Experience over the Lifespan

Imagine you have kept a record of your leisure behavior during the past year, the types of activities and the frequency of participation, and you put this record in a time capsule. Or better yet, you travel to the future in a time machine and observe yourself 5, 10, and 20 years from now. If you are a young adult, you could even go 50 or 60 years into the future. What would your future leisure style look like as compared to the past year? Would you be doing the same types of things with the same frequency? Would you have dropped some activities and added new ones? As you look "back from the future," do you think that you would have been able to predict your leisure style based on what you did in the "present"? Would there be a pattern to the changes that occurred in your leisure style as you aged? Would this pattern be similar to that of your parents or your friends? What is it about growing older that leads to these changes? Would you find that your leisure helped you deal with these changes?

Development is not completed when one leaves adolescence. For most, it is a process that occurs over the entire lifespan and applies to nearly all areas of human behavior. Development is not simply the accumulation of interests, abilities, and experiences; it is *systematic and predictable change by which people become qualitatively different in some way from what they were before, even as they maintain other aspects of themselves.* Leisure shows some important relationships with age. Knowing how old people are, especially if researchers have some clues as to the history that they share with other members of their age cohort, may allow the prediction of leisure interests and leisure activities. However, it should also be clear by now that leisure behavior is in many cases resistant to the influences of age; it is as if leisure is the one context in which people have permission to *not* "act their age." The control that leisure affords may give it special significance as a source of meaning in the personal life narrative that people write for themselves as they grow up and older.

Development involves three types of influences: (1) normative age-graded influences, (2) normative history-graded influences, and (3) non-normative life events (Baltes, Cornelius, & Nesselroade, 1980). Stage theories, such as those of Eric Erikson (1963) and Jean Piaget (1962), address the first type, normative age-graded influences. These theories describe *ontogenetic changes*, changes that may even be "species-specific" and biological in origin; that is, they apply to everyone, even if there are variations in how they influence people's behavior. The emergence of "object permanence" in infants and "self-consciousness" in adolescents are examples. Presumably, such changes should be found across cultures and historical periods. Other age-graded influences include predictable life events such as graduation from high school at age 17 or 18, taking a first full-time job sometime in the twenties, and retiring somewhere around age 65. These changes are more dependent on social expectations and norms and apply to most but not all members of a given society (in this case, most industrialized Western societies). These changes are both expected and accepted by others, thus making them "the thing to do at the time."

The second type of developmental influence, normative history-graded, involves a form of evolutionary change associated with significant historical events, such as the worldwide depression in the 1920s and '30s, the Vietnam War in the 1960s for Americans, or secular trends such as changes in attitudes toward women. Often, what appear to be inevitable, stage-related changes, such as retirement from work in the late fifties or early sixties, are more the result of living at a particular time in a particular culture than being attributable to any universal human ontogenetic pattern. Leisure-behavior patterns may be susceptible to normative history-graded influences as well. For example, McPherson (1991) pointed out that a fondness for dancing characterizes people who grew up in the 1920s to a greater extent than other *cohorts* (groups of people of similar age and who have had similar "historical" experience), while those going through their formative years in the 1970s and '80s are more likely to be a part of the "fitness boom." People who grew up during the economic depression of the 1930s have been shown to place less value on leisure than those of other cohorts (Elder, 1974). Ekerdt (1986) points to the emergence of a "busy ethic" among this group, an action orientation that "legitimates the leisure of retirement, defends retired people against judgments of senescence, and gives definition to the retirement role" (p. 243). In other words, leisure is all right for this cohort group only if it is used "productively."

All generational theory is of this type. To the extent that boomers are different from "the greatest generation," the "me-generation," "X" and "Y" generations, or the "millenials," there are generational effects that may endure even with age (Howe & Strauss, 1997). We will give more attention to such influences when we turn to situation/contextual influences in the chapters to come.

Finally, development is influenced by non-normative life events, such as a divorce, disability, or a new job, where the changes experienced by people are precipitated more by unexpected life circumstances than by biological, social, or large-scale cultural changes. In this case, it is certainly more difficult to predict the impact of such changes, but leisure activities are often altered as a result. For example, Hormuth (1984) found that being transferred to a new location because of a job is likely to be seen as an opportunity to reinvent oneself to some extent, to "try on new hats," and to establish some new relationships and activity patterns. We will deal with these situational influences in the next chapter as well.

During adulthood, life events (both normative and non-normative), social expectations, and role responsibilities (such as being a parent, worker, or volunteer) have more influence on adult behavior, including leisure behavior, than ontogenetic changes. Nevertheless, there are some changes that are consistent enough across people, cultures, and historical periods to suggest some inevitability. It takes a critical perspective on development and an appreciation of longitudinal research to begin to understand the nature of changes over the life course and to sort out their causes. In this chapter, we examine how leisure behavior changes over the life course. Still, let us begin with what we know about age differences in leisure and offer some suggestions as to why those differences occur.

As children grow and adults age, leisure interests, activities, and meanings change. Changes in leisure behavior are a reflection of other developmental changes. Leaving the question of the impact of leisure experience on developmental processes for later chapters, the concern in this chapter is with the changes in leisure behavior that are more or less predictable over the lifespan. Of course, predictable changes also provide some indication as to the function and value of leisure experience as well. If the leisure activities of newly married couples, for example, are predictably more home-based than when the partners were single, it speaks to the effect of an important role transition, but it also hints at the significance of leisure in the establishment and maintenance of those relationships. Nevertheless, it is with the changes themselves that we concern ourselves in this chapter, starting with evidence of patterns of change that take all or most of the lifespan into account and then turning to those which apply specifically to the periods of childhood, adolescence, and adulthood.

Lifespan Changes

One of the most thorough, widely cited, and now classic studies of variations in leisure activity across the lifespan was done in 1972 at the University of Houston, in a survey of 1,441 people between the ages of 20 and 94. The survey was stratified according to gender, ethnicity, and two occupational statuses. This investigation showed that overall leisure activity level was negatively associated with age (see Figure 8.1), and that, with very few exceptions, most individual activities showed this same pattern. In other words, the older the person, the less likely she or he was to be found on the ski slope, dance floor, or movie theaters, among other places. In fact, even participation in relatively sedentary activities such as socializing, playing games, and engaging in hobbies was shown to be less frequent in older age groups. Activities done outside of the home and those requiring physical exertion and high intensity of involvement showed the highest negative correlation. This negative relationship between activity and age appears to have held up over time as well (e.g., Agahi, Ahacic, & Parker, 2006).

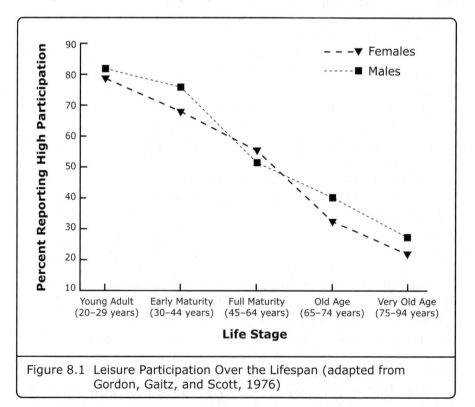

Figure 8.1 Leisure Participation Over the Lifespan (adapted from Gordon, Gaitz, and Scott, 1976)

If we use the entire lifespan as our frame of reference, the relationship would not show such a precipitous decline. Children and adolescents must develop skills and establish some degree of independence from parents en route to broadening their leisure horizons. Seppo Iso-Ahola (1980a) suggested a curvilinear relationship, with one's leisure repertoire reaching a peak in early to middle adulthood and declining thereafter (though it should be pointed out that this is just what people are able to do rather than what they actually do, as we will see shortly.) Still, it was his view that as adults age there is a decline in the number of personal leisure resources (i.e., skills) available that corresponds to the apparent decline in the number of leisure activities in which they engage.

Subsequent research provided additional support for this general assumption. In a study of 3,927 households in Alberta, Canada (Iso-Ahola, Jackson, & Dunn, 1994), researchers found that the number of adults who indicated they had started new activities within the last year decreased steadily over three successive adult-aged cohorts, leveling off with groups who had already retired. The number "replacing" activities (dropping one but starting another) also declined as a function of age. But while this research involved the respondents in considering their own changes, it is still cross-sectional in nature, comparing different groups on the same behavior at the same point in time. An alternative interpretation—that different age groups may be different for other reasons, such as the experience they have shared within a cohort over time—must also be entertained. For example, with respect to the negative correlation between reading and age reported in the Houston study, it may well be that the older cohorts who were surveyed *never* read as much as the younger cohorts, even when they were young. This becomes a plausible explanation when one considers the great improvements in access to education of younger cohorts compared to those born 60 years ago or more. Indeed, a more recent 16-year longitudinal study of a group of people over 60 showed an increase in reading over this period (Stanley & Freysinger, 1995).

Longitudinal research is necessary to establish changes in the same individual or the same cohort over time. Longitudinal studies of the leisure patterns of older people in fact give a rather different picture than most cross-sectional studies. The prevailing evidence suggests continuity of interests rather than decline (Cutler, 1977; Lounsbury & Hoopes, 1988; Iwasaki & Smale, 1998; Lee & King, 2003; Palmore, 1981; Scott & Willits, 1989; Singleton, Forbes, & Agwani, 1993). And one longitudinal study even showed an *increase* in activity involvement from early adulthood to middle age (Freysinger & Ray, 1994), perhaps reflecting a reduction in other role responsibilities.

Longitudinal studies help with the problem of interpreting change to some extent, but they still leave us with a "cohort problem" if we don't consider multiple cohorts at the same time. Even if a cohort has changed in a consistent way, the changes may not apply to a cohort that has had a dramatically different life history. Wars and economic depressions, for example, have clearly had an effect on the cohorts who have endured them, as was suggested earlier. People who survived the Depression in the late 1920s and early 1930s have been less willing to abandon themselves to immediate gratification and self-indulgence than those who have grown up with relative economic security (Elder, 1974). More than any other in recent history, this cohort has been oriented toward staying busy and being productive in the later phases of their lives. As we implied earlier, the association of particular cohorts with certain leisure activities, attitudes, or interests, such as the dancing and gaiety of the Roaring 20s or the "digital divide" that distinguishes current younger from older cohorts, is an important caveat to keep in mind in any discussion of the influence of age on leisure (see following text block).

More sophisticated studies that follow several age groups over time would offer clearer indications of the relative influence of age and history on leisure activity, but even then we would still be left with the problem of interpreting the meaning of the changes observed. Changes in overt activity can mean

The Cross-Sectional Data Interpretation Problem

Studies like that of Gordon, Gaitz, and Scott (1976), which compare different age groups on their frequency of leisure participation, are called cross-sectional studies because they assess types and rates of participation across different segments of society, age being just one criterion used to classify people (gender, race, social class, and geographic location are examples of others). With respect to developmental studies, age group differences, especially if they show a linear progression, make it tempting to assume that getting older leads to the difference or "change" observed, whether positive or negative. But age differences may be associated with all those influences referred to earlier; that is, though it may be that getting older brings certain inevitable changes, it is possible that older people differ from younger people not because they are older but because they have lived through a different historical period. Younger people may be more like other members of their young age cohort than they are members of older cohorts not so much because they are younger but because they share a certain set of experiences. For example, will you and your friends engage in leisure activities similar to those of your parents when you are their current age? Will you be as active or inactive? Younger people have had electronic media and entertainment equipment such as video games, televisions, VCRs, and computers available to them for most of their lives. Children are now growing up with the Internet and social networking. Do the different opportunities and constraints that people experience early in life cause them to exhibit consistently different leisure behaviors and orientations as they grow older?

different things to different people. A decline in involvement in stock-car racing, for example, might signal the end of interest in the activity for one person while for another interest is simply transferred to some other aspect of the activity, such as teaching others to drive. Or it may be that the meanings that were sought in the activity, to test one's skills in a competitive context for example, are found in an alternative activity such as coaching a youth league basketball team.

Leisure researchers concern themselves primarily with changes in overt activity, but leisure interests, values, and orientations may also be influenced by developmental change. One of the orientations that apparently changes substantially over the life course is interest in change itself. Experimentalism is much more common among youth than their elders. Indeed, experimentalism and an orientation to change seem to be characteristic of younger age groups. Taking an evolutionary perspective on this, younger cohorts must have the flexibility necessary to adapt to whatever changes come their way and to move into new niches, while older generations are responsible for providing as much stability and security in the environment as they can to afford the young a context in which to explore, experiment, and survive (Brent, 1978). The well-known "generation gap" between newer and older cohorts is partly attributable to this phenomenon. Seppo Iso-Ahola (1980a) offered a hypothetical profile of the relative strength of preferences for novel versus familiar leisure forms over the life course, as depicted in Figure 8.2. It is noteworthy that, if the suggestion is valid, older people are more like young children than they are like young adults in their greater preference for familiarity. On the other hand, generational change suggests something different

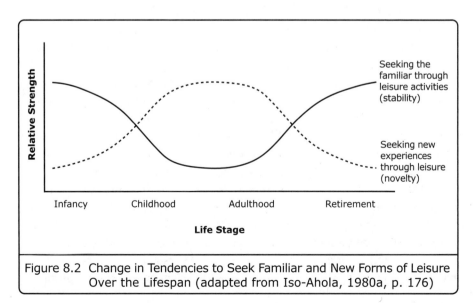

Figure 8.2 Change in Tendencies to Seek Familiar and New Forms of Leisure Over the Lifespan (adapted from Iso-Ahola, 1980a, p. 176)

for the future. If younger cohorts have grown up being more experimental, as has been suggested of Boomers and some of the cohorts following, there may be greater interest in change well into later life. Nimrod and Kleiber (2007) found a "readiness for innovation" in an in-depth study of a group of recent retirees.

While there are few studies that take in the entire lifespan, the Canadian study referred to earlier showed that, over the course of four stages of adulthood, those who chose to continue with the same activities increased in number while those who started new activities decreased. The authors (Iso-Ahola, Jackson, & Dunn, 1994) concluded that "the tendency to seek novelty through new leisure activities declines with advancing life stages, whereas the tendency to maintain stability through old and familiar activities increases with life stages" (p. 243). They hastened to point out, however, that this doesn't support an image of older people as disengaging entirely from activities but rather as being more selective and discriminating in what they do. Older people still have a need for stimulation and challenge for which leisure becomes, in many cases, ever more important. Indeed, as noted above, an interest in innovation is quite common in later life, even if it isn't the norm. Studies of achievement over the lifespan indicate that older adults look to particular leisure activities as a way to meet achievement needs when other avenues for achievement are less available (Veroff & Smith, 1985). Iso-Ahola and colleagues point out that in later life the "need for novelty may be satisfied within a narrower scope of activities" rather than by expanding the repertoire and replacing activities with new ones (Iso-Ahola, Jackson, & Dunn, 1994, p. 245). Nevertheless, in general, the decline in overt experimentalism is probably adaptive in the ways discussed earlier.

There are other indications of significant age differences that have relevance for leisure experience. Leah Carstenson and her colleagues (Carstensen, Fung, & Charles, 2003; Carstensen, Isaacowitz, & Charles, 1999) have established clear differences in emotional regulation patterns with age that suggest that because they have a more limited future, older people are more inclined to be present-centered (as opposed to the popular assumption of being past-oriented) and more likely to limit social interactions to those with whom they are more familiar, as was discussed in Chapter 7. Younger people, in contrast, are more likely to seek new social contacts because of their extended future and more likely to be future-oriented, having greater difficulty just being comfortable in the moment. Older people are less tolerant of negative emotions than younger people (the so called "positivity effect" in aging) while for younger folks it "goes with the territory" of becoming established and getting ahead. Of course, other personality factors would have an influence on such patterns, as would particular situations, but this work suggests that leisure orientations may in general be affected by age itself in these ways.

Such variations notwithstanding, leisure interests and activities remain relatively constant over time, and this may be less a matter of limited opportunities for change than preference for maintaining old and familiar patterns that, for those reasons mentioned, becomes more compelling with age. A favorite activity may be as important to hold onto as an old friend. Accordingly, a considerable amount of attention in leisure research has been devoted to the question of the predictability of adult leisure patterns from those of childhood. Depending on how similar the behavior (e.g., fishing in lakes in childhood versus ocean fishing in adulthood) 40% to 80% of adult leisure activities have been shown to have a close equivalent form in the person's childhood (McGuire, Dottavio, & O'Leary, 1987; Sofranko & Nolan, 1972; Yoesting & Christensen, 1978).

In a study using the 1982–1983 Nationwide Recreation Survey (NRS) of 6,600 individuals, researchers looked for evidence of *abandonment, continuity*, or *liberation* in outdoor recreation participation across the lifespan. They found that neither the abandonment pattern, where activities are consistently given up, nor the liberation pattern, where people regularly choose new activities, are accurate reflections of what generally happens with increasing age. Continuity is the more appropriate characterization of the activity-to-age relationship; other factors besides age were more important in determining the patterns of variation reflected in the data (McGuire & Dottavio, 1987; see also Searle, Mactavish, & Brayley, 1993).

These studies demonstrate that leisure behavior is influenced by individual differences (e.g., gender), role changes (e.g., retirement), and historical changes (e.g., changing work patterns of women). Relatively little of the change and variations in leisure behavior over the lifespan can be attributable to age alone, other than changes in play patterns in childhood and the decline in physical activity with the physical decrements of advanced age (e.g., Janke, Davey, & Kleiber, 2006). Perhaps the most significant thing about leisure and aging is, again, the degree of consistency to be found in people's interests and activities over time.

Of course, a picture of continuity of interest and activity may obscure rather different dynamics. Is continuity the result of the enduring influence of childhood experience or the relative lack of development in adult leisure? Does one continue with an activity because of a strong commitment to the activity, with too many "side bets" to comfortably discontinue, or because it is a source of personal identity and self-consistency, as Robert Atchley (1993) suggests? Or is an activity maintained primarily as a familiar pattern, a buffer against stress and a source of stability? Perhaps all of these apply to varying degrees in most cases. Alternatively, does change in activities reflect a response to other developmental changes, or is it a failure to find activities that are sufficiently meaningful to support a commitment and enduring involvement? In any case, studies of activity choice or consistency rarely do justice to the changes in meaning that occur across the lifespan. For a clearer picture, it is necessary to have a closer look at some of the dynamics of development of successive periods of the life course.

Childhood: The Emergence of Leisure

When and how does a child come to see that there is time to be used at his or her discretion? We would be amused if a 2-year-old responded to a request to talk to us with the words, "I don't have time." We might see it as a "cute" imitation, probably of some adult in her life. Time pressure seems somehow incongruous with the nature of childhood. Perhaps leisure has not been studied much in childhood because it is largely irrelevant to children's lives. Children are rarely heard to use the words leisure or recreation. Nevertheless, "recess," "after school," "weekend," and "vacation" come to have meaning for children once they have started school, and play is recognized well before that. The youngest of children tend to live in the infinite present, able to commit themselves to the moment as if nothing else mattered. Arguably, toddlers are the ultimate "leisure kind," to use de Grazia's (1962) expression, since they are more likely than older people to be led by their inclinations, wherever and whenever the spirit moves them. And this is not because they play—though that may be the quintessential leisure activity—it is that they are very likely to be relaxed in the present if their basic needs are met, unconcerned about the past or future. But let's turn to the subject of play, because it is in recognizable patterns of play that development is most clearly reflected. As behavior of choice, play reveals the intrinsic tendencies that motivate children of a given age.

Play

Some time ago, the 17-year-old son of one of the authors acquired a 2-month-old black Labrador retriever puppy who would respond to a water dish set in front of her by taking a few drinks, then putting her whole head in the water, then her paws, then knocking over the bowl, splashing in the puddle, carrying the bowl in her teeth, and knocking it all over the room. Initially, the annoyance of having to clean up the water was somewhat balanced by the amusement with the puppy's exuberant playfulness. Of course, this behavior got old rather quickly! It led to the question, though, of whether more mature dogs realize that the water is somehow to be treated more respectfully in the heat of a Georgia summer, or simply that spilling it is not in itself interesting anymore. Human babies play with their food on a regular basis, but, with the exception of the occasional cafeteria food fight among adolescents, such activities succumb to more "appropriate" behavior among adults.

Play is clearly an expression of freedom for children and occupies a great deal of the lives of children who are afforded such freedom. Play is not the same as exploration (Hutt, 1971; Piaget, 1962); it is not so specifically oriented to revealing the true nature of things. It is non-literal behavior, a transformation of reality (a doll represents a baby; a paper tube is a laser gun; a growl is mock anger). It is intrinsically motivated, freely entered into and actively engaging (Brown, 2009; Ellis, 1973; Hughes, 1991; Huizinga, 1955; Schwartzman, 1978). Given such characteristics, associating play with leisure may seem inappropriate. Leisure may or may not be taken up with active engagement, for example. But play shares the qualities of intrinsic motivation and perceived freedom with other forms of leisure, and, by being transformative, it represents the kind of action people seek in leisure to make it qualitatively different from what has been called the "paramount reality" of everyday life (Schutz, 1973).

As a free exercise of personal inclinations, play also provides a compelling manifestation, at least in childhood, of the essential motives and abilities that characterize a given age. Piaget pointed out that the play of infants and toddlers is generally practice play, reflecting the sensory-motor period of cognitive development. The child exercises whatever functions he or she can to create an effect and then to make it change, reflecting the basic need for competence discussed in Chapter 5. Typically, infants begin exploring and playing by putting objects into their mouths to experience them, and they repeat actions and sounds endlessly. The world of play at this time is limited primarily to the somatic (physical) self, the *autosphere* of the body, according to Erik Erikson (1963).

In the period lasting generally from the second to the fourth year, the child enters into the *microsphere*, where attention is directed into the near environment and where symbolic, pretend play emerges, reflecting the child's development of representative intelligence. It coincides with a tremendous growth in language development as well.

During the first two periods play is largely solitary, but as children become aware of others, their play expands from the *microsphere* to the *macrosphere*, the wider world of others beyond the family. Initially children relate to others by playing in parallel (i.e., next to each other) but they eventually learn to play together in what Mildred Parten (1932) referred to as "associative play." They share to some extent in this stage, imitate each other, and engage in what Piaget referred to as symbolic play, pretending and exploring with new physical and social skills. But children in this stage (4 to 7 years old) have not yet learned to decenter and fully take the perspective of others. It is in the next period, from about 7 to 12, that they engage in truly cooperative play and are able to play games with rules and organize themselves collectively for other play activities.

Table 8.1 provides a composite of the stages of play from the perspectives of Piaget, Erikson, and Mildred Parten, which highlight cognitive, psychological, and social aspects, respectively. While the ages are approximate, the functions described are thought to elicit the patterns of play indicated.

Early Developmental Tasks and Leisure Experience

Leisure in childhood involves more than play, however. We might well ask the question, when do children learn to relax? Certainly relaxation affords the emotional conditions for sleep and rest, but fatigue also does that. And what are the conditions of relaxed wakefulness? Erikson's stage model of

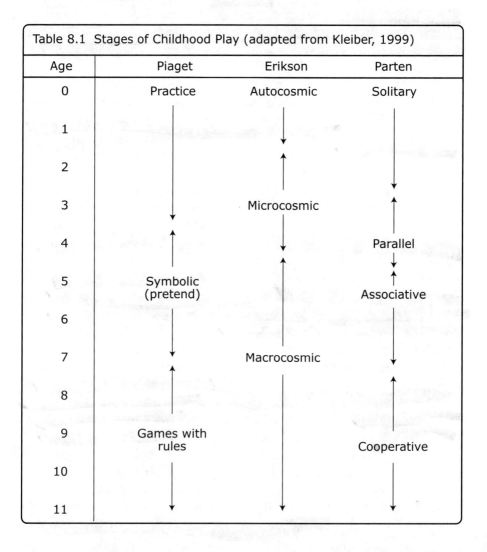

Table 8.1 Stages of Childhood Play (adapted from Kleiber, 1999)

Age	Piaget	Erikson	Parten
0	Practice	Autocosmic	Solitary
1			
2			
3		Microcosmic	
4			Parallel
5	Symbolic (pretend)		Associative
6			
7		Macrocosmic	
8			
9	Games with rules		Cooperative
10			
11			

development would suggest that this feeling is the best resolution of the first real issue in life, *trust versus mistrust* (1963). When babies become confident that their primary caregivers will return and tend to them in a predictable and continuous fashion, they show visible signs of relaxation. This condition in turn affords them the emotional security necessary for exploration, experimentation, and play. To call such a primitive emotional condition "leisure" may be a stretch; but the ability to cultivate a peacefulness about oneself throughout life may well depend on the earliest parent-child interactions, a point we will return to in the next chapter.

In the next of Erikson's stages, the 1-to-3-year-old child is faced with the task of establishing *autonomy*. Gaining control of vital functions, being able to say "no," and to move independently of parents provides children with an initial experience of freedom. As such it is a critically important antecedent to the realization of freedom in leisure later on. Failure to achieve autonomy results in a state of doubt and hesitancy that may undermine further development. Exploration and experimentation are likely to be attenuated as a result.

Typically by three or four years of age, according to Erikson, children who have successfully resolved the previous two issues begin to exercise a sense of *initiative*. Depending on the response received when venturing out and attempting some new activity, they are more or less likely to be predisposed to such risk-taking in the future. As we will see again in the next chapter, parents can stifle such initiative, and, according to Erikson, guilt is the prevailing response to the feeling of "overstepping one's bounds." The ability to optimize leisure, to create opportunities for enjoyment and to be one's own source of entertainment (Mannell, 1984b) would seem to rest on successfully traversing this period and overcoming such feelings (see also Larson, 2000).

When children have some freedom and independence and are not tethered to the television or computer, they are likely to involve siblings and peers in the creation of their own play worlds. Autonomy and a sense of initiative, by definition, both involve self-direction, and the organization of play activities gives form and action to such needs. The movement of children from the *autosphere* to the *microsphere* to the *macrosphere* in their play, in Erikson's view, is a reflection of a growing interest in being with others and shaping the world to one's own purposes. Venturing into the macrosphere requires: (1) sufficient cognitive maturity to interact effectively with others in planning social activities such as games; (2) the initiative to create one's own opportunities for enjoyment; and (3) the underlying intrinsic interest in relatedness. When adults organize and structure children's free time, such activities are preempted to a great extent (Bishop & Chace, 1971; Bjorklund, 2007; Elkind, 1981). And if children become accustomed to having the free time structured for them by parents and others, they are more likely to feel bored and helpless on those rare occasions when they do have free time.

The desire to be part of the wider world also moves most children beyond neighborhood friends. The latter years of childhood are devoted in large part to establishing relative competence, to achieving a sense that one has and can develop skills that are well regarded by others. Being able to "produce" in one way or another results in a sense of *industry*, according to Erikson (1963). Failure to do so is likely to result in a prevailing sense of inferiority. In this "age of instruction," children are attracted to group-learning activities where they can develop skills that compare favorably with those of others. They join Girl Scouts, Boy Scouts, girls' and boys' clubs, youth sport teams, and 4-H clubs among others. This is when they begin to take their expressive abilities seriously in a way that is likely to define future leisure interests as well. It is, in fact, the most likely starting place for the kind of "serious leisure" that was introduced in Chapter 1, though the cultivation of such interests at this point is still relatively rare and dependent upon particular child-rearing patterns.

Adolescence: Finding a Self to be Enjoyed

Many of the influences of childhood continue to direct the leisure of adolescents. Parents and peers, schools, and the world of popular culture continue to be important and become more so in some respects. In spite of the well-publicized "gap" that exists between adolescents and other generations, adolescents invest themselves in activities established and directed by adults. They are still typically very willing learners and continue to seek out instruction.

Adolescence is the beginning of the end of childhood; becoming a person in one's own right with a distinct identity is the principal task of the period. Failure to establish a sense of *identity,* according to Erikson, is reflected in a perpetuation of confusion about who one is and what one is to do. But resolution of this issue does not happen quickly, and much exploration is needed before commitments are made (Marcia, 1980). In fact, as Reed Larson points out, the self of childhood must first be deconstructed in early adolescence before new conceptions of self can be entertained (Larson, 1995). The clinging or petulant or impulsive child one views oneself to have been is rejected to some extent as new levels of self-possession and independence are sought. Creating some distance from parents and other adults—and even from peers at times—facilitates this process.

According to Piaget (1954), adolescents become preoccupied with themselves and who they are. The source of this preoccupation with the "self" coincides with the onset of the ability to engage in abstract reasoning, which brings with it the ability to consider hypothetical possibilities about themselves as well as such ideas as beauty, truth, and ultimately even leisure. The child's ability to be unself-consciously immersed in the present moment is limited by this change in self-awareness, which is a significant challenge to any emerging sense of leisure. Establishing a sense of identity comes about in the course of both *identification* with others and *individuation*. Individuation is the process of adolescents defining themselves as unique and different from others. Leisure plays a prominent role in reflecting, and even contributing to, the development of these apparently competing processes (Kleiber & Rickards, 1985), a topic that is taken up again in Chapter 11.

In the course of expressing their preferences in music, dress, and other indicators of style, including recreational activities, adolescents make a symbolic statement about who they are like, their peers and role models, and from whom they differ, often their parents. In many cases the experience of the moment is less important than the message conveyed to themselves and to others about who they are. Frequently, who adolescents are with is far more important than what they are doing (Bibby & Posterski, 1985; Hendry, Shucksmith, Love, & Glendinning, 1993). It is for this reason that Noe (1969) regarded most of adolescent leisure as "instrumental" in nature, rather than truly expressive and intrinsically motivated, as is true of leisure more generally. With the encouragement and support of parents to a great extent (see Shaw & Dawson, 2001) adolescents use leisure to develop skills and get ahead in some ways. Though somewhat dependent on the opportunities and resources available, the choices adolescents make frequently influence their efforts to deal with the developmental issue of identity and the stretch toward maturity (Silbereisen, Noack, & Eyferth, 1986). The leisure choices made during adolescence reflect the desire to become producers of their own life (cf. Lerner & Busch-Rossnagel, 1981), while the quality of the experience is often secondary.

Many activities are abandoned during adolescence. In the case of sports, for example, there is an enormous drop-off in participation, especially among girls. The reasons for the decline in participation have been the subject of a significant amount of research (e.g., Curtis & White, 1984; Gould & Petlikoff, 1988; Kirshnit, Ham, & Richards, 1989). An overemphasis on winning, a lack of fun, an unwillingness to endure "school-like" discipline, the perceived lack of ability to be competitive at a high level, the lack of social interaction with a broader range of friends outside of the sport and growing preferences for other activities are common reasons associated with giving up sport involvement; but the desire to move on and away from adult direction is part of it as well. With respect to girls, there is also the view of many that sport involvement is inconsistent with cultivating a feminine image.

While the conflict between generations tends to be exaggerated, the "fourth environment," as leisure is sometimes called (to distinguish it from work, school, and family) is often contested terrain. In one sense, the battle is over free time itself. Establishing emotional independence is a principal task of adolescence, and time away from home is a necessary but not sufficient condition for that. More than just the quantity of time away from home, it is the way that the time is spent that is critically important to both parents and adolescents. Adolescents embrace leisure, whether for the freedom to sleep until noon if they please or to become experts on the latest online happenings. Having control over one's time and one's choices within that time brings leisure, with its inherent freedom, front and center at this point in the life course.

Nevertheless, once again, it is generally not what an adolescent does, but with whom he or she does it that is important. "Being seen" is reinforcing, and being alone is especially painful in reminding an adolescent that she or he is not being seen. Reed Larson's (1990) experience sampling studies with adolescents have demonstrated that the experience of being alone is associated with depressed mood—hardly a state of fun and enjoyment. But his findings also indicated that older adolescents actually *choose* to be alone and that solitude is often used in personally expressive ways, writing or drawing, for example, or fantasizing about possible selves, images generated through reading, listening to music, and just daydreaming. In this regard, Larson contrasts music listening in one's room, where the music is created by and for young people and is stimulating to one's imagination, with television watching, which benefits from a familiar, if sometimes boring, adult format and is used apparently to escape stressful feelings and thoughts.

The value of solitude notwithstanding, the data indicate that adolescents feel happiest when they are with others (Larson, 1995). While taking a special interest in an activity and making it one's own is likely to reinforce a sense of independence and uniqueness, doing it with like-minded others, or just one significant other, contributes to a sense of relatedness and even intimacy, as we will consider again in Chapters 11 and 12.

The continuing development of competence in activities is itself a statement about moving into adulthood, where competencies are essential for the assumption of adult roles. Whether leisure-related competencies actually have any real preparation value is also addressed in later chapters. Even those who feel untalented and unaccomplished and prefer passive activities such as watching television to activities where competence is on display are still likely to see such demonstration of ability as a developmental task that must be addressed. The fourth environment of leisure offers a range of venues for the expression of abilities and interests, from the more visible arenas of organized sports to music and dance settings to more ambiguous situations such as restaurant conversations with friends.

High ability per se is not required to enjoy most activities, but those that are continued through adolescence and into adulthood are most likely to be complex enough to provide ever-increasing levels of challenge commensurate with growing skills, as well as a cohort of others with similar interests and similar circumstances. This describes many activities that people continue to take seriously throughout their lives, those that are likely to be the most intrinsically enjoyable and "flow-producing" (Csikszentmihalyi & Larson, 1984) as well as being relevant to changing life circumstances. Nevertheless, such activities remain far less common in adolescence than more casual activities such a television watching and socializing.

In fact, effort and perseverance are not generally associated with the concept of leisure as understood by adolescents. In one of the few studies of leisure meanings among adolescents, Mobily (1989) noted that, compared with the term "recreation," leisure was associated far more often with passivity, though both leisure and recreation were equally as likely to be associated with the word "fun." And in an experience sampling study of high school juniors and seniors in the southeastern U.S., Kleiber, Caldwell, and Shaw (1993) found that experiences designated as leisure most often involved social interaction, but usually in very low-challenge situations. In other words, when they were paged, if they regarded their experience as leisure, the adolescents studied were likely to be involved with others but not in activities they regarded as challenging. And when they were asked directly to indicate what leisure meant to them, "relaxation," "free choice," and "free time" were the most frequently used terms. Females in particular tended to place more emphasis on leisure as relaxation. In general, the findings indicated that leisure is not generally associated with self-development. In fact, for these adolescents, especially for the females, leisure seemed to be understood as a condition of easy, relaxed enjoyment, with little emphasis on action and challenge-seeking.

Adulthood: Is Leisure Only Role Determined?

In moving from adolescence to adulthood, it becomes clear that most behaviors are determined by the roles people assume and the situations they find themselves in rather than the unfolding of any developmental script. Nevertheless, there are some regularities and predictable changes.

With respect to leisure we can first start with what *doesn't* seem to change. What leisure orientations and interests do adolescents carry with them into adulthood? Some activities may be easier than others to continue and enjoy in some fashion throughout the life course. As noted earlier, there is considerable evidence of continuity of interests and activities from childhood through adolescence and into adulthood. Some activities taken seriously seem even to become leisure "careers" in some sense (Stebbins, 1992a). And perhaps these are helpful in buffering the transition into this new and challenging period. But for other leisure researchers, it is the vast discontinuity that is significant, with many adult leisure activities—over 50% by some estimates—having no childhood antecedents (Kelly, 1987b). New commitments to a significant other, to colleagues at work, or a job move to a new location often lead to involvement with new activities. In spite of the evidence for consistency of leisure interests and activities, the emergence of new leisure orientations following changing life circumstances is common throughout adulthood.

Movement from adolescence into adulthood usually corresponds with the achievement of emotional independence from the family and a fairly stable preliminary identity structure, but there is considerably more to this transition. Indeed, the idea of a separable period of "emerging adulthood" has come to be recognized, where individuals no longer feel like adolescents but do not quite feel like adults either (Arnett, 2000, 2004). Norma Haan (1981) suggested that young adults are typically more accommodative than they were when they were younger. This is generally necessary for joining the adult world. Even those who were somewhat unruly as adolescents in terms of drug and alcohol use and delinquent activities typically become relatively more conventional and achievement-oriented as they move into their twenties (Jessor, Donovan, & Costa, 1991; Raymore, Barber, Eccles, & Godbey, 1999). But this then speaks more to what is expected of young adults in most societies rather than to age per se, and it skips over some continued exploration in the early twenties. Indeed, experimentation is likely to continue and even increase, especially for college students. Thus, it is difficult at this point in the life course, and through adulthood more generally, to consider age as an individual difference influence, independent of situational/contextual factors. Clearly age is socially constructed and differs to some extent then by society, culture, and historical period; the changes that we can predict with any accuracy are dependent upon those forces. Starting full time work, starting a family, "launching" children in midlife, and retiring from work are significant role changes that have a very strong impact on leisure. We will consider them more thoroughly, then, in the next chapter when we turn to social influences. But what more can we say about age per se as a determinant of leisure activity, independent of such role changes?

We can return to the model of lifespan development of Erik Erikson and others to consider those possibilities. Are there "issues" of age that come up as they did in childhood and adolescence, regardless of the roles that individuals assume? Erikson and others (e.g., Arnett, 2000; Havighurst, 1972; Levinson, 1978; Vaillant, 2002) have made such a case. Erikson (1963) asserted a progression of the following issues that would confront every adult as part of a maturation process, even before being addressed with respect to the particularity of circumstances: *intimacy versus isolation* (in early adulthood), *generativity versus stagnation* (in the middle years), and *integrity versus despair* (in later life). But some have argued that Erikson's adult stages are overinclusive and therefore lose some of their powers of discrimination. Of his eight stages, five unfold before the age of 18, and the rest of life encompasses just three. Are adults so unchanging? As noted above, a case has been made for a period between adolescence and young adulthood called "emerging adulthood" (Arnett, 2000, 2004), while others have found differences between the recently retired "young-old" and the "old-old" (Antonovsky & Sagy, 1990; Vaillant, 2002), called the third and fourth ages, respectively. Levinson et al. (1978) also found in their interview studies that there were good reasons to differentiate a greater number of distinguishable periods in early and middle adulthood. We will say more about these periods shortly, but for us, the test is ultimately whether there are predictable differences in leisure behavior and interests that correspond with them.

Emerging and Early Adulthood

If you are a college student in your late teens or early twenties, you may not consider yourself an adolescent, but if you are like most North Americans that age (and age mates from many other countries), you are not done with dealing with identity issues; and if you do see yourself as an adult now, you don't see yourself as fully adult yet. While Erikson jumped from adolescence to young adult in his model, he also wrote of a "psychosocial moratorium" period (1968) in between, where people experimented with roles and ideas and, indeed, only resolved the business of identity formation—at least temporarily—at the end of that period in making commitments to initial work roles and relationships with significant others. But now we are talking about the mid to late twenties. Arnett (2000, 2004) argued that young adulthood only follows this period of emerging adulthood (EA), once preliminary commitments were made.

Following considerable research on the subject, Arnett noted that this emerging adulthood is significantly different for reasons related to demographics and subjective experience as well as identity formation. He noted that in industrialized countries, the age of marriage and childbirth has increased significantly, from the early twenties to the mid to later twenties, allowing a longer period for *exploration* of both partner relationships and work roles. One third of emerging adults are in college and most are just establishing residential independence from parents. In addition to not yet feeling like full-fledged adults, relatively few have established financial independence and most still have family significantly involved in decision making. With respect to identity, worldviews are only now coming into focus.

With respect to leisure, Arnett notes that Americans 19 to 29 spend more of their leisure time alone than any age group other than the elderly and spend more of their time in productive activities (school and work) than any age group under 40. He also notes that in this period of exploration, with growing independence from parents and yet short of commitments to work and family of their own, EAs are freer to pursue more intense experiences involving risk such as unprotected sex, substance abuse, and risky driving.

Binge drinking, which is often associated primarily with adolescence, is also more common in emerging adulthood (see also Bachman, Johnson, O'Malley, & Schulenberg, 1996).

According to Erikson, those people who have been able to resolve the identity crisis of adolescence are faced with the next challenge of having to establish intimacy with another person or other people, particularly once they have left their childhood home. But this brings up another criticism of Erikson— that in seeing identity formation as preceding the formation of enduring intimate attachments, he was representing more of a male pattern than a female pattern and that girls and women were as likely to resolve commitment issues right along with identity issues (Gilligan, 1982). The resolution of *both* identity and intimacy issues often takes the form of marriage and having children. Indeed, parenthood is the single event that most clearly defines a transition to early adulthood, according to Arnett (2000). But intimacy can also be characterized by the development of other types of strong, lasting relationships. Accordingly, it would be expected that leisure during this period is associated with the cultivation of intimate interpersonal relationships. And indeed, a priority for people in their twenties is to spend whatever free time is available to them with a significant other (Brehm, 1992). Often, the activity is irrelevant as long as "you are with the one you love." We will discuss the relevance of leisure for shaping interpersonal relationships in Chapter 11.

Establishing an intimate primary relationship with another is generally considered one of the principal tasks in the adolescent-to-adulthood transition, and being a committed partner often means tempering some values and interests to accommodate those of the other. The negotiation of discretionary patterns of activity for a couple can be a source of continued relationship development or a battleground for the preservation of self-interest and personal identity. A male acquaintance of one of the authors recently told him that in considering the question of marriage he had decided that it wouldn't be enough to just do things together, as bonding as that may be; more important, in his view, is the willingness to continue to explore possibilities for new experience together. Love is for many people a way of self-completion rather than self-sacrifice, of merging rather than matching. There is evidence, which will be reviewed in Chapter 12, that shared leisure contributes to marital success (Orthner, Barnett-Morris, & Mancini, 1992), but this research only more clearly establishes what most couples suspect when they commit to one another—that the stability of their relationship may depend somewhat on finding patterns of enjoyment and self-expression that are at least compatible. Such was the case of one couple who had been married for five years. Her dissatisfaction with his hunting trips (while she stayed at home) led to a threat of "finding something to do together or else." A search of local community education courses led to a Spanish language class. Three years of classes and numerous trips to Spain, Mexico, and South America later, their continuing interest in the language prompted them to establish a Spanish language club. The language learning has thus become a focal point of their shared leisure and a central life interest for both.

Middle Age

According to Erikson, the issue of intimacy that defines early adulthood gives way with some successful resolution to that of *generativity versus stagnation*. Erikson argues that generativity becomes an issue as a person approaches middle adulthood, and at this time productivity and contributions to society become priorities. For many, this productivity is not only a matter of having children and successfully raising them; becoming a productive member of society, successful at work, or being creative in some other demonstrable way also resolves the issue in favor of generativity rather than its opposite—stagnation. Stagnation is associated with self-absorption and psychological impoverishment. To some extent, a concern with the next generation and what contributions people are making to their future leads many to begin taking life "seriously" for the first time and relinquishing many forms of self-indulgence. Caring for others is not always compatible with leisure activities done only for personal satisfaction. Devotion to children or a work career often comes with a loss of free time (Witt & Goodale, 1981). But in the caregiving that characterizes family leisure or through volunteer leadership of youth activities, for example, generativity can be served in ways that enhance the enjoyment and self-expression normally associated with leisure (Freysinger, 1995; Kleiber, 1999; Kleiber & Ray, 1993; Shaw & Dawson, 2001). Still, it may be because of the imperative of generativity that many adults seem to defer the personal and immediate gratification of certain types of leisure activities, or to temper it significantly, during early and middle adulthood.

In a classic study of male adulthood, Daniel Levinson and his colleagues (1978) interviewed adult males of different ages and from various walks of life, and on the basis of the information gathered, they proposed more specific age periods, or *seasons of life*, during which certain developmental issues are predictably faced (see Figure 8.3, p. 252). Levinson et al. suggested that these "seasons" involved alternating periods of structure building and structure changing throughout the adult life course. These processes are similar to the ideas of stability and change discussed earlier and also to the dialectic of integration and differentiation discussed in Chapter 7. Midlife, in particular, drew the attention of Levinson et al. as a time of significant change. They found evidence of what they called "de-illusionment" where the goals of earlier adulthood were likely to be reconsidered and even relinquished in light of current realities.

In contrast to the emphasis on generativity that Erikson associated with middle adulthood, the research by Levinson et al. suggested that for many, midlife brings a growing unwillingness to keep up appearances and associate with people merely out of a sense of obligation and responsibility, a reaction driven by the need to establish a distinct identity. He referred to this process as "detribalization," or breaking with convention. Presumably, this response creates a sense of considerable freedom for experimentation, and leisure provides opportunities for this. But in an interview study of people who were in their midlives and who were presumably changing and building life structures, in Levinson and his colleagues' terms, Carpenter (1988) found that the builders perceived more freedom than the changers. Apparently, the loss of structure and the relinquishing of some commitments can also create a kind of confusion that requires a considerable amount of energy and attention.

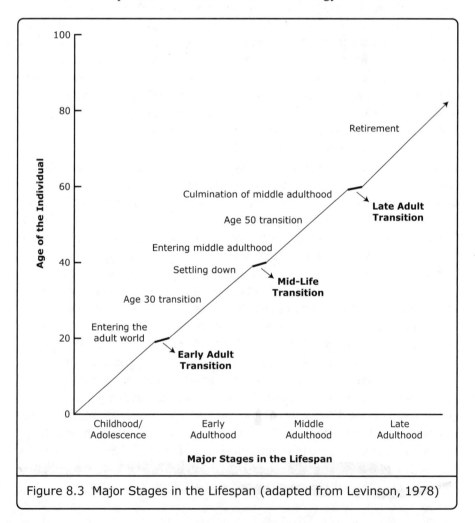

Figure 8.3 Major Stages in the Lifespan (adapted from Levinson, 1978)

Nevertheless, the "midlife crisis" that many people report—80% of the Levinson et al. middle-aged subjects demonstrated "tumultuous struggles within the self and with the external world" (p. 199)—is based on a growing awareness of their mortality that would naturally predispose them to make the most of the time left to live.

Midlife also typically brings a lot of changes for people. The work roles that people have been committed to often lose their importance and changes in the family structure similarly create significant new situations as children depart the family proper for their own adult activities. While there is still tremendous variation in the complexity of work and family life in this age group, more free time and greater financial security often provide ideal conditions for self-expression in leisure at this time. Also, though, the first signs of aging—loss of youthful appearance or health problems—are likely to lead to an awareness of one's mortality and create a sense of urgency about life. Indeed, many of the tensions around making the most of life left to live and turning in directions different from those served earlier in adulthood make leisure an idea context for exploration at this point in life (cf. Freysinger, 1995).

As an illustration, a very hard-working woman was diagnosed with conditions that were health-threatening. Among her responses were to go out and buy that grand piano she had been wanting and "to take every opportunity to hug the grandbabies." Even for those with the resources of more time and money than in their earlier years, time is likely to become a more precious commodity. As Bernice Neugarten (1977) and others have noted, time orientation changes from years-since-birth to years-left-to-live at this point in the life course. Furthermore, the emphasis on establishing oneself in the preceding years is likely to have shaped certain characteristics—competitiveness for some and nurturance for others, for example (Gutmann, 1975)—while other personal attributes have gone neglected. Leisure, then, is likely to be seen as an opportunity to explore those neglected aspects of oneself.

The experience of a 47-year-old private school teacher who was passed over for the position of principal offers another illustration of leisure-related consequences of changing life circumstances. The disillusionment he felt as a result caused him to reconsider how he spent his time and what brought him the most enjoyment and satisfaction. He turned to his home office to complete a photo display for the family and to a music collection that he had neglected. There are many such examples of people who come to an awareness that they have been chasing a dream or have been relatively locked into a job or a family situation and almost welcome some precipitating event that gives them a chance to make changes in lifestyle interests and patterns. Just how such changes contribute to continuing development is considered in Chapter 12.

Later life

As we noted earlier, research on later life has challenged the notion of just one period. With due appreciation to Erikson for his lifespan framework, several theorists (Antonovsky & Sagy, 1990; Vaillant, 2002) have nonetheless insisted that there is an early aging transition that differs in character from the issues of advanced age. And once again, as with emerging adulthood, the argument has been driven to some extent by demographic changes. People are not only living longer than when Erikson advanced his lifespan model; they are healthier as well (Agahi & Parker, 2005). Also, the attitudes of the cohort now reaching retirement—the Baby Boomers—having put a priority on growth and change, will also ensure differences in later life for years to come (Dychtwald & Flower, 1990; Freedman, 1999).

Although the age of retirement has shifted both forward and backward for social and economic reasons in recent decades, the transition itself has been marked by continuity of activities and interests rather than change as noted earlier. Still, there appear to be some important new tasks that face members of most industrialized societies around this time. According to Antonovsky and Sagy, the early period of later life asks that a person consider four questions: (1) What is to be *done*?—a question of engagement; (2) What is *personally* worth doing?—a matter of reevaluation of life satisfaction; (3) What do I still believe about my world?—a re-evaluation of world view with concern for coherence of purpose and approach to life; and (4) How can I stay healthy enough to do what I want?—which takes into account one's health vulnerability.

While he shares this view of the "young-old" period being one of activity, Vaillant (2002) puts more emphasis on play as a consequence of retirement, noting that retirement is only a problem when it is (1) involuntary or unplanned, (2) there is no other means of support besides salary, (3) when home life is unhappy, or (4) when it has been precipitated by preexisting bad health. When those don't apply, most people look for intrinsic satisfaction in their activities according to Vaillant, replacing workmates with other social networks, rediscovering how to play, exercising creativity, continuing to learn, and serving others in ways that are personally satisfying. While Vaillant's views are more the ideal for aging well than what is normally expected— especially among those with more limited resources and in poorer health— he does assert that a period of more passive contemplation around issues of integrity that Erikson raises would generally follow a period of activity, which is in the older-old period following that of the young-old.

With respect to later life for males, Levinson and his colleagues (1978) noted that a man who traverses the life event of retirement "has earned the right to be and do what is most important to himself. He is beyond distinctions between work and play. He can devote himself in a serious playful way to the interests that flow most directly from the depths of the self" (p. 36).

According to Erikson, the last period of life can be characterized by the issue of *integrity versus despair*. In later life, if a person does not come to terms with their past and present in a way that provides a sense of wholeness and continuity, despair is the likely result. Understanding and accepting ourselves is an important part of the process. Thus, one would expect a greater tendency in later life to reminisce about the past as time permits. Reminiscence can be done alone—as a kind of life review—or more casually with others, but in either case it can reinforce continuity and contribute to a sense of integrity (Parker, 1995). But the process of ego integration isn't only reflected in passive activities. Hobbies and expressive patterns of various kinds that connect one to the past and provide a sense of continuity are typically preferred over new activities, as was reflected in the research reported earlier (Lefrancois, Leclerc, Dube, Hamel, & Gaulin, 2001).

The work of Erikson and Levinson et al. has been criticized as being *androcentric*, that is, as applying only to males, and perhaps being *ethnocentric* as well, since little has been done to establish the validity of the theories in other cultures or in minority ethnic groups in North American societies. For example, girls and women are likely to be more consistently involved in issues and matters of intimacy and nurturing throughout their lives than simply in early and middle adulthood. As was noted before, intimacy and caregiving are also likely to be more directly related to identity formation in women (see Gilligan, 1982). Furthermore, a large number of people's jobs change very little during their working lives, while another sizable group goes from job to job without having anything resembling a "career." Thus there is good reason to see the Levinson et al. model as only a prototype of male life in middle-class, white, North American culture and perhaps an outdated one at that. The extent to which models such as these can be generalized and to which the psychological issues faced are characteristic of people in other life circumstances is still to be determined.

In fact, it is clear that the tremendous diversity in lifestyles that exists today is also accompanied by diversity in the developmental paths that people take over the lifespan. People who are single or divorced, single parents, partners in childless or same-sex couples, and people with different ethnic and cultural backgrounds likely follow different routes and face different issues as they age. For example, Zuzanek and Smale (1992) studied the amount of time a group of 25- to 44-year-old people devoted to leisure and work during a typical week. Even in this restricted age group, they were able to classify the people whom they studied into five major lifespan or life cycle groups on the basis of gender, marital status, presence of children, and employment status. The time devoted to leisure differed significantly among these groups.

Many of the changes that occur over the life course, then, are predictable but not inevitable (see also Adams, 2004; Agahi, & Parker, 2005; Gauthier & Smeeding, 2003; Lefrancois et al., 2001). There is considerable variance across cultures and among various segments of society. For example, there is evidence that in working-class communities, the experience of distinct stages and transitions is less common than in segments of the population with more education (Giele, 1980). The rates of participation in leisure activities discussed earlier are likely to have as much to do with the expectations of others as with the inevitable course of aging (Cutler & Hendricks, 1990; Lawton, 1993). Older people may be inclined to feel uncomfortable in certain recreational contexts, such as an outdoor concert, where everyone else is younger and where youth is the "target market." Miller (1965) once wrote of the "portent of embarrassment" in describing what keeps older people disengaged from active involvement. Trying new activities or even drawing on old skills often evokes the self-consciousness that comes with declining competence and the appearance of "being old." The prevailing evidence is that older people can learn new activities about as well (albeit perhaps more slowly) as younger people (Schaie & Geiwitz, 1982), but the expectation that "you can't teach an old dog new tricks" often keeps an older person from trying and may lead leisure service providers to prefer other clients. Nevertheless, times have changed and a fair bit of later life, albeit mostly the earlier periods of later life, is often given over to some degree of reinvention through new activities (e.g., Adams, 2004; Nimrod & Kleiber, 2007; Vaillant, 2002; Yarnal et al., 2008).

Summary

To see leisure activity and experience as the product of development is to recognize its prominence in demonstrating developmental changes. From childhood to old age, the ways in which people define and use their freedom speaks volumes about who they are and what is generally on their minds. Important distinctions exist between the ages, however: the biological maturation process of youth, while socially directed to a great extent, has the appearance of unfolding in play and self-expressive activities, while the tasks that confront adolescents and young adults prepare them for the world ahead and circumscribe leisure activities accordingly. Changes in the leisure activities and experiences of adults demonstrate the power of both assuming and departing from social roles, as well as the need to have such changes buffered in some ways. To see leisure only as a product of developmental change or as a kind of shock absorber, however, is to miss its full developmental significance, as later chapters will show.

Gender as a Source of Leisure Differences

We have considered gender in earlier chapters and will continue to do so in subsequent chapters, but we certainly should consider gender as an individual difference factor in this chapter and a relatively stable one at that. There is considerable debate as to how many, if any, gender differences in leisure behavior might be attributable to basic biological differences; even if gender differences were entirely a product of socialization and social construction, though, they do account for a lot of variance in leisure behavior across a wide variety of situations. In other words, gender differences, even as socially constructed, get internalized and become individual differences that are reinforced and maintained through social interaction and socialization influences. These differences are as visible in leisure as motivational, attitudinal, value, and personality-trait differences, and from our interactionist perspective they interact with factors in the social situation to influence leisure behavior.

Another important and related question, of course, is the extent to which the differences that can be observed are products of discrimination, prejudice, and limited opportunities. Indeed, much of the research on leisure and gender identifies the greater constraints that women feel with respect to participation in certain forms of leisure activity and the greater burdens they have that reduce the available time and freedom for leisure, especially among working mothers (Zuzanek & Smale, 1992; see also Henderson, 1990b, 1994; Henderson & Hickerson, 2007; and Shaw, 1999a, for reviews). There is also the case that in some respects women are objectified for the leisure of men—in prostitution, pornography and as ornamental accoutrements in leisure activities (Freysinger & Kelly, 2004; Shaw, 1999b). What we can focus on here, however, in addition to behavioral differences, is how leisure is experienced differently in various activities by males and females and what it means as a result.

Considerable research attention has been given to gender-related differences in children's play. Parents are often led to assume a biological basis for toy and play preferences that have girls playing with dolls and boys preferring trucks and more rough and tumble play from a very early age, and they tend to ignore their own influence—as well as the influence of peers, siblings, media, and the culture more generally—in reinforcing those choices. In the past, girls who preferred the latter were considered "tomboys" and boys who preferred the former "sissies," reflecting some of the prejudices born of such expressive patterns. Times have changed of course, but many of the stereotypes and prejudices remain (see Schmalz & Kerstetter, 2006). What is interesting, however, is how those who do "cross over" and resist conforming to standards for gender appropriateness in play and leisure often benefit in important ways, a point to which we will return shortly and again in Chapter 11.

As children begin to play games, other dynamics associated with gender have been noted. Janet Lever (1976) studied the tendency of boys and girls to engage in conflict resolution in games to keep those games going, arguing that boys' greater willingness to do that, in addition to having the games last longer, equipped them with skills that would ultimately translate into general organizational effectiveness as they matured. She regarded girls' lack of game-protecting efficacy as a liability derived from faulty and discriminatory socialization. But Carol Gilligan (1982) argued that girls are just more attentive to the relationships that are stressed by conflict over games and thus less willing to perpetuate games in which conflict arises.

In an experience sampling study of leisure in adolescence, different peer norms were reflected in what was regarded as leisure by males and females (Kleiber, Caldwell, & Shaw, 1993). Specifically, self-maintenance (e.g., grooming) and extracurricular activities were perceived as being leisure-like for females but not for males. The gender difference in the perception of maintenance activities as leisure may have been a function of the time and effort that the adolescent girls in the study devoted to clothes and cosmetics because of their concern with their appearance and the desire to present the "right image" (see Kotash, 1987). Much of this maintenance time was spent with friends, and so it had a strong social component as well.

With respect to sports, boys and men are clearly more involved than girls and women (Robinson & Godbey, 1993), but there is considerable overlap with some sports (e.g., basketball, swimming, and volleyball) while others are more clearly male-dominated (football) and others more female dominated (e.g., gymnastics). Various explanations for the differences have been offered (e.g., Metheny, 1967, 1976; Theberge, 1991), but the differences persist. Wiley, Shaw, and Havitz (2000) predicted that women would show different patterns of involvement and attachment to sport, particularly to the gender-inappropriate sports, but measurement problems clouded their findings and made a case for further research. They concluded nonetheless that experience in leisure activities is influenced by societal ideologies about the gender-appropriateness of activities, as well as by individual interests and preferences. And in a study of children's attitudes toward various sports, males had more stigma-consciousness and resistance to "crossing over" to sports and activities stereotyped as appropriate for females, but both genders had a clear awareness of the stereotypes (Schmalz & Kerstetter, 2006).

Even in the same sport, there may be significant differences in experience, however. Aronson (2008) points out that gender stereotyping hasn't changed as much as one might expect and that the effects on girls' attribution patterns are inherently limiting. Females are less likely to "own" success in both academic and athletic situations while being more likely than males to attribute responsibility for failure to their ability. He reviewed one study of tennis that demonstrated that female tennis players were more likely to attribute losses to their ability while male tennis players attributed losses to bad luck or a failure to try hard enough. As a result, the evidence shows that females who lose a first set are more likely to lose the second set while males who lose the first set are more likely to come back and win at least one set if not both. This is even true among professional tennis players!

In a study of the leisure needs of 438 members of 60 randomly selected teams in a university intramural basketball program (Iso-Ahola & Allen, 1982), researchers found that winning increased the need for affiliation and social interaction among women, whereas participation had little impact or slightly decreased this need among women who played on teams that lost their game. The opposite was found for men. Winning decreased the need for affiliation and social interaction among men and losing appeared to increase this need. These gender differences were likely due to social learning, and the meaning of winning and losing may have been quite different for the men and women in this study. For example, it has been argued that women are socialized to value positive interpersonal relationships above winning over others, whereas the opposite may be true for men (Gilligan, 1982). Consequently, by winning the women may have felt that they had created a distance from others that intensified their need for affiliation and positive social interaction. Because of their socialization experiences, the men in this study may have experienced competition as an appropriate and satisfactory way to affiliate with other men, and winning may actually have enhanced this type of interpersonal satisfaction, consequently decreasing the post-game need for it.

Gambling has also been a focus of gender difference research. Walker, Hinch, and Weighill (2005) tested the assertions from previous research that men gambled primarily out of preference for risk-taking, emotional excitement and mastery, and testing masculinity, while women gambled more to escape from everyday problems and connect with like-minded others. The investigators found some support for these generalities but found more subtle intra-gender differences as well, including a large percentage of men who sought the same communal experience that women did and that many women seemed to value gambling as a way of compensating for a degree of helplessness in everyday life.

Another way in which the genders seem to differ in their experience of the same activities is in their sense of freedom when participating in each, presumably a critical aspect of leisure experience. In the experience sampling study of working men and women discussed in Chapter 6, researchers (Csikszentmihalyi & Graef, 1980) found that males rated most activities as more voluntary, including cooking and childcare. The only activities for which this trend was reversed and women felt greater freedom of choice were in leisure settings outside the home (e.g., movies, restaurants) and during informal social gatherings. Idling, watching television, and reading were activities in which gender differences were least noticeable in terms of perceived freedom. Shaw had similar findings in her 1984 time-budget study.

In a later review of gender differences in leisure, Shaw (1999a) addressed three different areas: (1) activities, (2) activity constraints, and (3) outcomes. With respect to activities, in addition to those reviewed above, she noted that women's leisure in adulthood is more likely to be integrated with family roles, though family leisure may come then to be work as a result. Similarly, with respect to constraints, an ethic of care and responsibility for family outcomes often has the effect of making women feel less entitled to their own free time, and when they do participate in leisure activities, they are more likely than men to be constrained by fear, body image issues, or gender stereotyping. On the other hand, she pointed out that persevering in spite of such constraints may confer special advantages on those who resist gender stereotypes and engage in activities such as adventuring that are not generally regarded as "feminine."

Psychologists have also long recognized that there are distinct differences within males and females with respect to gender *orientation* (e.g., Bem 1974, 1993). The notion of *gender identity* is based on the idea that although people are born biologically male or female, they learn to become masculine or feminine through their socialization experiences. Consequently, people vary in how much they identify with and value the behaviors, attitudes, and motives that society labels masculine and feminine. From this perspective, masculinity and femininity can be seen as independent characteristics that are free to vary from high to low within the same individual (see Figure 8.4). A scale derived from the typology allows both the female and male participants to be classified as having an *androgynous orientation* (high on both gender identity characteristics), an *undifferentiated orientation* (low on both gender identity characteristics), or more distinctly *masculine* or *feminine orientations*.

These characteristics have been shown to be as predictive of leisure activity and differences in experience as gender itself. Hirschman (1984) administered the *Bem Gender Orientation Questionnaire* to 440 women and men. She also measured their leisure needs by having them rate how important it was for them to satisfy a variety of leisure needs in their three favorite leisure activities. Psychologically masculine people (women as well as men) were found to be most strongly motivated to seek out leisure activities that allowed for the satisfaction of the need for competitiveness whereas people who were classified as androgynous were most strongly motivated by needs for fun/pleasure, escape, adventure, and flow. Hirschman also found evidence to suggest that androgynous people were more likely to be looking for multiple and diverse satisfactions in their leisure behavior, and consequently, to be seeking satisfactions across a wide range of activities. Perhaps people who "are in touch" with both their feminine and masculine sides have a capacity to satisfy a wider range of needs in leisure.

In a study of barriers to leisure among 500 female college students, Henderson, Stalnaker, and Taylor (1988) discovered that those women with stereotypically masculine orientations were less likely to see "lack of awareness of leisure opportunities" and "difficulties in making decisions" as barriers to leisure involvement, while those women who were "feminine" in orientation were more likely to regard a lack of self-confidence, fitness, and physical skills as reasons for not participating. Women who were characterized as feminine were also more likely to be deterred from participation by a concern about their body image.

What is clear from other research, however, is that females are more inclined to depart from gender stereotypes in their leisure choices than are males (e.g., Dionigi, 2001; Henderson & Hickerson, 2007; Schmalz & Kerstetter, 2006) as reflected in studies of women motorcyclists (Auster, 2001), sea cadets (Raisborough, 2007), triathletes (Cronan & Scott, 2008), and aikido specialists (Noad & James, 2003), among others. It appears that many women use leisure activities to resist the burdens of social expectations of femininity and hegemonic masculinity (see also Henderson & Hickerson, 2007; Shaw, 1999a; Wearing, 1998; Yarnal, Chick, & Kerstetter, 2008).

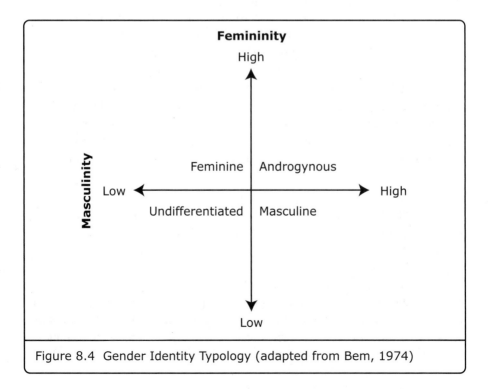

Figure 8.4 Gender Identity Typology (adapted from Bem, 1974)

Men and women may also use leisure differently in coping with difficult circumstances. In a focus group study of how professional managers cope with stress, males were more likely to use active physical play after feeling stressed, while females used exercise in a preventative way to reduce the impact of stress (Iwasaki, MacKay, & Mactavish, 2005). But there were more similarities than differences; both groups indicated using humor, travel, altruistic leisure, socializing with others, and escapist leisure to similar degrees. The *lack* of gender differences in adult leisure was also an unexpected theme of a New Zealand study of differences in the amount of, and satisfaction with, the free time that is available (Thompson, Grants, & Dharmalingam, 2002). Nevertheless, it is clear that women and men often have very different experiences with leisure and derive different things from those experiences.

The patterns of abandoning activities in later life described at the beginning of this chapter also appear to vary by gender. While involvement in sports and other physically demanding forms of recreation show decrements with successive age cohorts across genders (Gordon et al., 1976), the pattern applies most dramatically to men. Women in older cohorts today are somewhat more likely to begin new exercises than those of younger adult cohorts (Iso-Ahola, Jackson, & Dunn, 1994). But in another longitudinal study using more sophisticated growth curve modeling, it was women who declined more in formal and informal social activities with men staying relatively stable between 50 and 80 (Janke et al., 2006). And Iso-Ahola et al. (1984) also found that men in the last stages of life are more likely to begin a wider variety of other activities than women. Are men inherently more experimental in later life, then? A better explanation is that retirement typically affords men more new freedoms than women. The investigators suggested that there was no real retirement for many of the women studied; the role responsibilities they had assumed for meal preparation and house maintenance did not change significantly after 65, a subject we will turn to again in the next chapter.

Summary

As with age, gender appears to be a significant determinant of leisure behavior and experience, but also as with age, the influence does seem to vary considerably as a function of circumstance and history. Nevertheless, whether attributable to biologically based differences or social learning and conditioning, some differences seem enduring enough to apply across situations. Still, whether considering reactions to competitive success or failure, adventurousness in outdoor settings, the appeal of shopping, or the willingness to serve the community in volunteer roles, the overlap of experience of males and females raises questions about the practical importance of statistically significant differences. Where there is still importance, however, is first where the differences are a product of an inequitable opportunity structure based on stereotypes and discrimination, and second where resistance to those stereotypes in leisure actually confers some advantage or benefit to the individual or the community in the process, a subject to which we will return in Chapters 11 and 12.

Conclusion

We could have added other factors to our analysis of individual differences, such as race, ethnicity, disability, and sexual preference. We will focus on race, ethnicity, and culture when we address the influence of social context in the next unit and in Chapter 10 specifically. With respect to disability, we have clearly followed the lead of others (e.g., Burns & Graefe, 2003) in treating it more as a problem requiring adjustment and adaptation, seeing leisure as relevant to both what is lost with the disability and to how it might help in some kind of rehabilitation and adjustment process. But even there, because some disabling conditions are chronic and permanent, they constrain and delimit leisure accordingly. And for some, the disability may simply define a different kind of leisure. For example, many paraplegic basketball players want wheelchair basketball defined as a game that *anyone* could participate in (Brasile, 1990). There is also the view that for many with a disabling condition the leisure constraints imposed as a result become simply part of the challenge and thus also a part of the experience (See Carruthers & Hood, 2004; and Csikszentmihalyi, 1990, for more on this point.). A degree of resilience may be derived from coping with the disability that leaves one more, rather than less, inclined to adopt a learner's stance and to thrive on challenge. In that sense the disability becomes an asset (see also Kleiber et al., 2008). We will return to this perspective in Chapter 12 as well. Sexual preference differences might also have been considered, along with gender, as another individual leisure influence factor, but the limited amount of research available from that perspective has left us to consider them as they are affected by social circumstances, as we will in Chapter 9.

It is, of course, rather artificial to try to isolate individual differences such as those reviewed in this chapter, as well as personality factors reviewed in the last, as influences on leisure behavior when they mostly interact with situational factors in determining leisure behavior and experience in any case. But researchers often do just that to try to determine the degree of influence of such things in accounting for the variance in some leisure-related outcomes. Programmers and promoters also try to profile, graph, and type individuals for the purposes of marketing leisure services, as we will consider again in the last chapter. We turn now to the next unit on the other side of the equation in trying to isolate the influence of situational factors that have power—across all persons. But of course, as we have done in these last two chapters, we will be considering interactions as well, which comes closer to the way things operate in reality.

The Social Context of Leisure

9

Social Influence in the Creation of Leisure

Preview

Having focused more on individual differences as determinants of the activities and experiences of leisure in the last two chapters (the "P" in the **LB**=f{P x E} formula for **L**eisure **B**ehavior), this chapter and the next one deal more with the "E" side of the equation—in other words, the environment. This, of course, is not just the physical environment, though that is also relevant; it is the effect of any external influence on behavior. While leisure is largely a domain of free self-expression, it is clear that environmental/social influences on leisure are abundant and that leisure is affected (constrained or shaped) by these conditions. Thus, we will examine the influence of family, school, peers, media, work, and organized social services on leisure as well as the processes of influence that occur in those contexts. We will also examine the influence of leisure contexts like play and sports in creating further interest in leisure. And finally, we will consider resistance to social influence. We also recognize the uniqueness of play and leisure for allowing a degree of *self-socialization*; because they both often involve an intrinsic interest in interacting with others; they *invite* social influence. As we established in earlier chapters, the need for relatedness is generally regarded as one of the three most fundamental psychological needs, along with competence and autonomy (Deci & Ryan, 1991; Ryan & Deci, 2000; see also Fiske, 2004). But even the need for competence brings one in touch with others—to gain information and to learn about possibilities. So, in turning toward social influences on behavior we are not turning away from individual inclinations. On the contrary, social influences come about as much because of the intrinsic interests of individuals as from external social constraints, controls, and directives.

Consider your own leisure interests and activities. What or who has shaped them along the way? Are there any leisure activities that you engage in more to "go along with the crowd" than because you have a strong interest in the activity itself? If so, you are obviously not alone. In the course of childhood, there are many lessons to be learned about using time, wasting time, and alternating responsibility and effort with relaxation and diversion. This chapter will deal in part with how these lessons are taught and learned. It will also focus on how the natural, biologically directed tendencies of childhood change in some predictable ways with development and create changing interests that are also influenced by the responses of important "others" in a person's social environment. Most of the available research we will examine deals with factors that shape leisure interests and orientations.

We begin this chapter by examining basic social influence processes that would presumably influence leisure behavior and then turn to people and social forces that deliver those influences. There is considerably more research on the latter than the former, particularly as it relates to socialization of leisure attitudes and interests, but just as we would start with how to hold the racquet before teaching stroke techniques in tennis instruction, we must start with some of the basics to more fully understand social influence in the social psychology of leisure.

Some Basic Social Processes Influencing Leisure

When she was a young child, Kate was aware that her parents were often outside gardening on the weekends. Many of her friends spent time playing the latest video and computer games. Her older brother loved reading, and took every opportunity to grab a book or a magazine. Kate loved spending time with her maternal grandparents, who enthusiastically taught her a variety of card and board games. Upon reaching adolescence, Kate had a classmate who "tagged" walls and other surfaces with graffiti and occasionally "rolled" people's houses. She hung around with a few soccer players and admired them greatly, but she had given up playing a few years ago and was reluctant to pick it up again. In what directions do you think Kate will turn with her own leisure? Which of those past influences, if any, will shape those directions?

Imitation and Modeling

Imitation and modeling can have a significant influence on behavioral choices from infancy onward (Bandura, 1977b, 1986), including those related to leisure. The model that is being imitated may be setting the example to be imitated intentionally—as an act of instruction—or unintentionally. Models are usually those who are older (but not always much older), who are familiar, attractive in some way, and have status associated with a level of competence appreciated by the imitator. In the above vignette, Kate clearly had models: her parents as gardeners, her grandparents as game players, her siblings and her friends as readers, soccer players and somewhat delinquent adolescent peers. Shannon and Shaw (2008) specifically focused on mothers as agents of leisure socialization for daughters. They posited that "if mothers serve as an important model for their daughters, then their daughters' behavior may be influenced by what they observe in their mothers" (p. 4). This captures an important aspect of imitation and modeling. Leisure choice may be impacted or affected by those significant models found in individual lives in both positive and negative ways. To some extent, the girls in that study decided to do things *differently* from their mothers with respect to leisure, especially when they became mothers themselves, where they could see that their mothers didn't always take care of themselves. Mothers noted their belief in communicating the importance of leisure to their daughters, but many of the daughters revealed their conclusions that the role of leisure and leisure opportunities changed dramatically once they became mothers, and some accepted this as inevitable. As one participant said, "My mother definitely thought what you did with your leisure time was important...[but] I certainly grew up in an atmosphere where she never took time for herself, and I'm sure that has something to do with why I don't think it is an important thing" (p. 12). Imitation and modeling work on the principle that actions often communicate more loudly than words, and this applies to one's understanding of leisure and leisure choices as well. This was true in another study of parental influence on children's leisure, where children's playfulness and leisure interests were found to be strongly correlated with those of their parents (Barnett & Chick, 1986), suggesting that children do indeed "take after their parents."

So where else do models come from and how does the imitation process start? In Chapter 4, we considered how interests arise, and we contrasted those that seemed to emerge very organically from an individual versus those that were associated with the activities of admired others. Competence and physical appearance are well established as important factors in making models attractive (Aronson, 2008), but similarity to the imitator and the model's apparent enjoyment are also important, particularly in stimulating leisure interest. Besides parents, peers and siblings may also have all of those attractive qualities. Role models are found among high-status older children and adults, and certainly among those who seem to be enjoying what they are doing. Athletes and entertainers are the obvious choice as we not only enjoy watching them, we assume they are enjoying themselves (though they may in fact be laboring in strenuous and unappealing ways). But the ball game, the music, or the art becomes attractive as a result.

In many cases, it is the lack of role models that serves as a *constraint* to leisure or that role models are clearly different in some important ways, by gender, race, age, etc. As activities like swimming and kayaking have become more integrated with respect to race and gender, there is an inevitable boost in their appeal to and impact on others who can clearly model based on similarity. Diversity (heterogeneity) alone may also encourage cross category modeling—an African-American child feeling more comfortable joining an otherwise all-Caucasian group that includes a child of Asian heritage, for example—though there is insufficient research on this question.

With respect to models, especially media models, there is also the concern that the leisure activities chosen will not be healthy choices. Problems associated with alcohol and drug use as recreational activities, sexual activity to the point of promiscuity, and other risky behaviors often have their models in high-profile, older individuals and celebrities. The negative effects that play and leisure activity can have on people, both young and old, may also be a matter of modeling. We will take up this question when we turn the equation around and look at outcomes of leisure activity in Chapter 11, but it is clear that modeling of antisocial behaviors is often a public and parental concern. The modeling of aggressive and violent behavior occurring on TV (Huesmann, Moise-Titus, Podolski, & Eron, 2003) and in video games (e.g., Anderson & Bushman, 2001) is perhaps the most significant example.

Persuasion

Might Kate have been *persuaded* to join some of her more rowdy "expressive" friends? Have you ever been talked into something you didn't think you wanted to do at first, but then subsequently came to enjoy? Have you ever tried to persuade others to do something because you believed they would find the activity enjoyable or meaningful? This, of course, is the mission of people who are marketing leisure services, products, destinations, and events. Persuasion takes advantage of some of the same qualities that relate to modeling. Research shows that the attractiveness of the communicator as well as his/her credibility (competence and trustworthiness) are critical factors (Aronson, 2008). Family and friends may be more trustworthy in that regard, but so will those who have "been there" and can "do that." We are impressed by experts and those who clearly enjoy what they are doing.

But the message itself is also important. Attitudes may become as fixed, stable, and influential as individual differences ultimately, as we considered in Chapter 7, but their formation depends on a number of things. Does the message appeal to logic or emotion? (The "fun" communicated in the message or by the communicator clearly uses the latter.) Is it a direct (central) appeal ("Please come use our waterslide") or an indirect (peripheral) suggestion, as in simply showing people enjoying using a facility? Both work in what has been called the *elaboration likelihood model*, (ELM; Petty & Cacioppo, 1986). Counterarguments and "two-sided" appeals—where you hear both sides of an argument—have been utilized effectively for persuasion. (For example, "You might want to go to Disney World with all their wonderful attractions, but we are much closer and will offer many of the same opportunities and a lower price.") But that depends to a great extent on subject characteristics; those who are better educated or better informed about a subject are generally more susceptible to two-sided arguments (Aronson, 2008).

A worry with persuasion is that the recipient of the message might in fact feel manipulated or coerced. If his or her choices are effectively reduced or taken away in being "sold" on an idea, *psychological reactance* may set in, and resistance to the message and to the activity itself may take place. It is important—especially in leisure settings—that self-determination be protected and enhanced. Thus, in reconsidering the self-determination theory

(SDT; Ryan & Deci, 2000), introduced in Chapter 6, we might consider how persuasion is valuable in getting a person to participate in the activity. To sustain interest in an activity, though, that interest must be internalized. Intrinsic motivation is the best basis for this—where the activity is interesting and enjoyable based on its responsiveness to competence, autonomy, and relatedness needs. The cognitive evaluation theory (CET) component of SDT argues that "social-contextual events (e.g., feedback, communications, rewards) that conduce towards feelings of competence during action can enhance intrinsic motivation for that action" (p. 70). But extrinsic incentives—such as getting more fit through an exercise program—can also be internalized, if they make sense.

When we think of leisure as free time, responsible choices that are not inherently enjoyable may still make sense and feel leisurely in some basic ways. But what may require persuasion initially must become internalized. Another example of this is suggested by the principle and practice of "Leave No Trace" in outdoor recreation settings. Many fledgling outdoor enthusiasts give little attention to the principles inherent within this outdoor ethic, and yet subtle or explicit introduction to these principles may come from clothing and gear manufacturers, retailers, instructors, trip leaders, and peers. As individuals become more acquainted with this ethic, they may give greater consideration to the philosophy behind "leave no trace." As a result, they may gradually not only take on the practices of "leave no trace" (packing out what is packed in, digging cat holes a certain distance away from camp and water sources, minimizing impact by choosing not to build fire rings, etc.), they may have internalized the messages to the extent that they also become sources of motivation and information for others new to outdoor activities. One may have been persuaded about the value of the principle, but in practicing it without supervision, the position becomes "second nature." This is also referred to as "secondary gain" in the psychological literature (Aronson, 2008), when doing something that was resisted or has some cost, comes to be recognized for its inherent value after initial extrinsically motivated compliance.

Conformity

We mostly think of leisure activity as individualistic, with freedom for personal self-expression and limited external influence, but again, leisure activity is also the product of social influence. Perhaps no process speaks to such issues more clearly than *conformity*, or the change in a person's behavior resulting from real or imagined pressure from a person or a group of people (Aronson, 2008). Stop and think about your own leisure experiences. Have you ever just "followed the crowd" in some activities? Have you sensed that this was true of others? In your opinion, does such conformity have a positive or negative connotation?

According to social psychologists (e.g., Aronson, 2008; Fiske, 2004), we conform basically for two reasons: we want *to be liked* or we want *to be right*. Sometimes we conform to the behavior of others because we are unsure about what is called for in a situation, but we still want to be right. This might be the case when traveling in foreign country, and we see that people walk on one side of the street rather than the other. The old expression is "when in Rome, do as the Romans do." But another motive for conformity is *to belong*. In Fiske's (2004) view of social motives, belonging is the most prominent and "overarching" of the primary social motives (which also include understanding, controlling, trusting and self-enhancment). To fit in and be connected, or to build relationships, we tend to behave in accord with those we like and those we want to like us. Thus, to varying degrees, we all follow the crowd, going to the same events and the same places, wearing similar clothing and hairstyles, and doing some of the same things, maybe even dancing the same way. In Solomon Asch's famous 1950s experiment, six people viewed three uneven lines and were asked which was the longest. Five of the six were "confederates" of the experimenter and picked the second longest while the sixth, the subject, typically went along with the other five. Subjects "agreed" with the others presumably because they didn't want the others' disapproval. In a more recent study, Lincoln (2005) identified this sense of belonging or being unified with others (with subcultures, for example), as a tremendous force in teenager's choice of music.

What makes a difference in whether one follows the crowd or "dances to the beat of a different drummer?" Those with higher self-esteem are less likely to conform than those with lower self-esteem, and similarly, insecurity makes the pull of the group more powerful (Aronson, 2008). As for group characteristics, those with high status or high expertise are likely to command allegiance to a greater extent. Conformity can figuratively lead a person astray when the activity is destructive to self or others, but when it comes to learning new skills, following the lead of others who have the skills is part of the learning process. People are more inclined to follow that lead if they identify with the leader or see her or him as having the skills and expertise needed. The identification that takes place in serious leisure activities (Stebbins, 1992a, 2007) also reflects considerable conformity to the patterns of action displayed by more advanced, accomplished, or specialized members of a subgroup, both to approximate their competence but also to reflect some sense of unanimity of purpose. The notorious color bearing, chanting, and flag-waving behaviors of true fans also reflect a kind of passionate conformity associated with exclusive identification and attractiveness of the target of identification, the team. This has been called a kind of serious leisure as well (Gibson, Wilming, & Holdnak, 2002), but it reflects more of the motivation to be connected, that is, to be liked, than to be right.

Conformity may also be reflected in *not* acting. A study of what is called "the bystander effect" established that people will often fail to help a person in distress when everyone else is similarly unresponsive. Prompted by a well-publicized murder on the streets of New York City witnessed by many who failed to act in any helpful way, we are concerned about why people would be cowed into silence. Most of the evidence from the research that has been done on the phenomenon indicates that when responsibility is diffused among many onlookers, when there is no other connection to the victim or when people are in a position to "walk away" without helping, such neglect may be expected. When people find that they will continue to be in contact or feel some sense of community with the victim, they are inclined to offer help. Aronson (2008) found such circumstances while camping in a national park. A cry of alarm in the middle of the night brought just about everyone out of their tents to offer help for what turned out to be an exploding fuel canister. People chose to act here because they felt "we are all in this together," and there may be no one else to help. Littering in public parks may reflect similar inclinations if it appears that no one else is endeavoring to keep the place clean. Indications are that people are more likely to litter if there is already a good bit of litter in an area or to not litter if there is very little, suggesting that people will conform to one norm or its antithesis, depending on which appears to be prevailing.

Conformity in leisure is also driven to some extent by the need for validation. To have made the "right" decisions as to where to vacation, what to buy for the trip, and what to wear while making the trip and doing the appropriate activities is often less about the instrumental demands of the activity than about the messages being sent to others with respect to social status. In identifying in these ways with an activity, the personal meaning of the activity is conditioned to varying degrees by the meaning that is has for others and the need one has to be affiliated with those others. This may be particularly true when the other is a love interest one is trying to impress, but it would also apply to an entire subculture to which one wants to belong. The same dynamics can be seen with respect to music choice, clothing trends, and activities such as skateboarding, going to the mall, or participation in sporting activities. There is considerable "sign value" in being a member of an activity group, regardless of the activity, and in some cases again it is more important to be associated with "the band" than to be able to play the instrument very well (cf. Dimanche & Samdahl, 1994; Haggard & Williams, 1992).

Social Comparison

People look to others for information about themselves, especially when they are unsure how to behave. Conformity—whether driven by the need to be right or liked—involves social comparison processes. But we also use social comparison in achievement situations and to satisfy needs for self-enhancement. In doing "downward social comparison" we look at those who are worse off than we are in order to feel better about ourselves, while in "upward social comparison," we are measuring ourselves with the others at a level to which we aspire (Fiske, 2004). Consider behavior at a fitness club. Perhaps you are one of those who work out fairly regularly. Seeing others who look less fit, weaker, and slower than you may be gratifying at some level, but if you are still trying to improve, you are likely to pay attention to those who are slightly stronger and/or faster than you or appear to be in somewhat better shape. This is what Frederick, Havitz, and Shaw (1994) found in their study of aerobic exercise participants.

Sports and other competitive activities build social comparison right into the activity. In other words they are inherently comparative, since success or failure is a matter of relative difference from others in most cases. How we relate to others' success if we are not competing ourselves, though, is another matter. If we are fans of the winning participants, we identify with them and "bask in their reflected glory" (Cialdini et al., 1976) even if comparatively we are far inferior to them. But if a skill and performance is personally relevant to us, we may find another's success somewhat threatening, especially if he or she is a friend or a sibling. These are the conclusions of the *Self-evaluation Maintenance Model* designed by Abraham Tesser (1988). Testing out the assumptions that both comparison and reflection were influenced by the personal closeness of others, the quality of their performance, and the relevance of the performance areas to our own self-concept, he came to several conclusions: (1) the better the other's performance and closer the relationship, the greater the loss of self-esteem in the comparison process (i.e., when the activity is personally relevant); and (2) the better the other's performance and closer the relationship, the better for self-evaluation in the reflection process (i.e., when the activity is less personally relevant). Consider the successes and failures of your siblings and friends, the relevance of their endeavors to your interests, and how that makes you feel as a result. Have you ever moved away from participating in an activity because you 'paled in comparison?'

Discrimination and Exclusion

Discrimination and exclusion are the behavioral consequences of prejudice and stereotyping. Aronson (2008) defines prejudice as a "hostile or negative attitude toward a distinguishable group based on generalizations derived from faulty or incomplete information" (p. 243) and not just predisposition or bias. Stereotyping—assigning identical characteristics to any person in a group regardless of variation among members of that group—may be largely just convenient, lazy overgeneralization, but it too is hurtful and damaging to others, particularly when it stigmatizes them and deprives them of opportunities.

"Discrimination is the denial of equal treatment based on prejudice and ste-reotyping" (p. 24).

Race and ethnicity in particular have been used to exclude people from recreational opportunities, even when discrimination is legally prohibited (Floyd & Gramann, 1995; Gobster, 1998; Stodolska, 2005). Private clubs for golf and other activities can require that prospective members be "accepted" and thus may exclude individuals based on race and gender without being on record as doing so. And fees and charges are often too high for economically disadvantaged groups. But even where inclusion would be more readily pos-sible, the absence of members of a particular group will make the place or activity uninviting to that group, resulting in a kind of de facto discrimination. Scott (2000) notes in his provocative essay, "Tic, toc, the game is locked and nobody else can play," that such barriers can only be broken down where fees and charges are reduced or eliminated, protections for existing customer loyalty are relaxed, diversity is sought in both staffing and clientele, and ser-vices become need-driven rather than demand-driven.

If leisure experience is based on comfort to some extent, as we suggested in earlier chapters, the privilege of being unselfconscious falls to those who maintain primary occupation of a location to the exclusion of others. For example, in the post-"9/11" U.S., American Muslims have experienced subtle and not-so-subtle discrimination in leisure settings in the form of unfriendly stares and verbal abuse, as well as social isolation. This has resulted in restricting the range of available leisure options and co-participants, reducing their willingness to participate, and restricting their freedom of movement, travel, timing, and location of activities (Livengood & Stodolska, 2004). Philipp (2000) notes that services also need to break through the "comfort" levels of both the excluder and those excluded to create changes, and recreation facilities themselves must not be designed to accommodate exclusion. The next chapter will more fully consider cultural, ethnic, and racial issues related to leisure.

Disability is also a factor leading to stigmatization, discrimination, and exclusion. Although extensive steps have been taken to incorporate persons with disabilities into a variety of recreational and leisure opportunities, the impact of disabilities, differences, and perceived or actual limitations is still an area of concern. Dillenschneider (2007) recasts this issue in terms of accommodating the needs of *all* individuals instead of just focusing on inclu-sion for those with disabilities. Much of the shift that is proposed is to avoid considering participation solely in terms of the limited functions of the indi-vidual, and instead look at the total human experience as a continuum of abilities. By not focusing on a particular characteristic in including diverse populations, the effects of stigmatization can be reduced.

Still another source of potential discrimination and exclusion within leisure and recreation is gender. Girls are discouraged, by parents, peers, and active participants from activities such as sports and some outdoor adventure activities that have traditionally been male-dominated (McKenney, Budbill, & Roberts, 2008). At the same time, boys may be dissuaded by parents and peers from doing activities such as dance and other arts that may be more commonly seen as female sex-typed (e.g., Schmalz & Kerstetter, 2006). We reviewed this matter in Chapter 8 in trying to identify what gender differences were stable and consistent, but to a great extent those differences may have been the result of discouraging conditions and limited opportunities.

Exclusion on the basis of intentional discrimination may be the most painful, but even ability-based exclusion can have its costs. Where elite levels of performance are sought and limited resources are devoted to those activities, those not successfully making the teams may suffer in significant ways. Barnett (2007b) compared the reactions of high school girls who did not survive the competitive selection process in cheerleading and dance with those who were successful and found that the former had significantly higher levels of negative emotions, truancy, and lower self-esteem, feelings that endured for up to two months after the selection process.

Conclusion

There is ample evidence, then, of the dynamics of basic social processes in leisure settings. Persuasion, discrimination, conformity, social comparison, imitation, and modeling all find in leisure a fertile context for exercise. Understanding the research on these processes that constrain and determine behavior, both in and outside of leisure contexts, will enhance the prospects for interventions that can improve quality of life. Minimally, it will simply help us understand leisure better. An interesting counterpoint to the power of these forces, however, is that in leisure there is still usually a measure of freedom with which to respond to them and even resist them. In that spirit, we turn to the question of how children come to actually invite and engage with such processes.

Critical Influences on Leisure Orientations in Childhood

It has long been recognized that developing children are involved in some degree of *self-socialization* (Brewster-Smith, 1968). In other words, they intentionally seek to become a greater part of the world around them. They are, in fact, "producers of their own development" (Lerner & Busch-Rossnagel, 1981), though not yet in the self-conscious sense of adolescents whose thoughts and actions lead them progressively and constructively into their own imagined futures (see Chickering, 1969; Larson, 2000). In the earliest periods of life social integration is dictated largely by social interest and the desire to be more involved with others, even as it is also directed by aspirations and requirements of parents and society more generally. In the course of self-socialization, children initially seek out others in self-directed activities— such as "to come out to play" or "to sleep over"—and then join more formally organized activities either with friends, to create some shared involvement, or to actually make new friendships.

To a great extent then, a child moves himself or herself into a position to be influenced by others. As we described in earlier chapters, interests emerge at least partly out of biological predispositions and the forces of maturation, and some of the variability with which particular leisure orientations and interests take shape can be traced to inherent personality and gender differences. But probably more of the variability in leisure behavior is attributable to how such inclinations are responded to and reinforced by the society in which children live. This process, by which children acquire motives, attitudes, values, and skills that affect their leisure choices, behavior and experiences throughout their lives, is referred to in the literature as socialization *into* leisure (Kelly, 1974, 1975; Kleiber, 1999; Kleiber & Kelly, 1980). There are many agents of socialization that we will consider in more depth shortly. Parents, siblings, teachers, and coaches all have an impact, though to varying degrees. There is a "climate," beyond the weather, that is more or less favorable to the development and continuation of various activity patterns and interests. Included are the facilities at children's disposal, the programs in the community, the natural resources (e.g., lakes, mountains) that are accessible, the safety and security *afforded* in the near environment, and the prevailing norms of behavior that allow and encourage them to be playful, expressive, mischievous, restful, alone, or musical, for example.

So what was leisure socialization for you? Can you think of the various locations where your leisure interests came alive? Who was part of it? Your father? Mother? Siblings? Friends? Neighborhood leaders? Who created the space/place and why? What occurred in these spaces/places to encourage you? Did anything discourage your play and leisure activity? In the worst cases, play and leisure may be oppressed by such realities as poverty, hunger, homelessness, fear, and the threat of violence and external aggression (though the power and resilience of play is remarkable in that it still occurs in war-torn countries). Even in cases of relative peace and prosperity, the climate can still be discouraging of innovation, rest, unauthorized congregation, or socializing with peers. Leisure itself elicits a great deal of ambivalence in many contemporary societies and has done so for centuries. It is often regarded as the enemy of productivity. Relaxation and enjoyment are distrusted, whereas delay of gratification is seen as necessary for achievement, future success, and security (Fine, 1987). From this perspective, "leisure socialization" is an oxymoron. It is as if "leisure," in this case defined as idleness and self-indulgence, is the result of faulty or improper socialization.

Even where leisure is welcomed, it may be restricted to some forms rather than others. Organized and supervised activities are trusted by adults far more than those that are unstructured. And increasingly, children are discouraged from playing outside on their own. Part of that trend comes from the fear parents have that their children may be accosted or hurt in some way, however unwarranted such fears are (Furedi, 2002; Warner, 2005; Wilkinson, 2001). The book *Last Child in the Woods* (Louv, 2005) makes a case that such fears are contributing to what the author calls "nature deficit disorder," and there is clear evidence that children are less comfortable in outdoor environments than they used to be, even in relatively safe environments (see also Frost, 2006; James & Embrey, 2001; Skenazy, 2009).

Nevertheless, parents, and adults more generally, often see leisure as a vehicle for preparing children for their future social roles and responsibilities, as long as it involves so-called "healthy and wholesome" activities. Indeed, leisure is recognized by many as a valuable context and resource for cultural innovation, social solidarity, personal development, and other benefits (e.g., Driver, Brown, & Peterson, 1991). This is socialization *through* leisure. Parents and schools may arrange for sports and other kinds of physical activities with the idea of promoting a lifetime of healthy activity (Henderson, 2000; Henderson et al., 2001). Recently, there has been the advent of books for both young girls and boys that are a call to their participation in grand adventures through games, stories, sports, and leisure activities passed down through history. *The Daring Book for Girls* (Buchanan & Peskowitz, 2007) was written to "present stories and projects galore, drawn from the vastness of history, the wealth of girl knowledge, the breadth of sport, and the great outdoors" (p. viii). *The Dangerous Book For Boys* (Iggulden & Iggulden, 2007) begins similarly with the assertion that "when you are a boy . . . you want to learn coin tricks and how to play poker because you never know when the skills will come in handy. You want to be self-sufficient and find your way by the stars" (p. xi). These books represent a call to the influential power that these experiences have not only for current activity, but in encouraging growth and development throughout life.

Parents may use organized sports, music and dance, or other arts and activities to cultivate a breadth of interests that they see as advantageous for a child's future. They are well aware that noteworthy success in such activities can be "counted" when it comes to being selected for school awards and academic scholarships. That this may come too early or may undermine the "leisure" of such activities is a subject we have addressed before in this book and will again. But it is abundantly clear that leisure is used in an instrumental and purposeful way by adults in socializing children (Shaw & Dawson, 2001). In the creation of the Outward Bound School, now a popular alternative for personal development beyond traditional means, Kurt Hahn intentionally capitalized on experiences within nature that contained adventure, risk, and challenge to address development of moral character (James, 1980). Specifically, Hahn was concerned with what he called the "declines" or social diseases that he saw affecting youth: the decline of fitness, the decline of initiative and enterprise, the decline of memory and imagination, the decline of skill and care, the decline of self-discipline, and the decline of compassion. Hahn felt that outdoor recreation and education can be combined to resist these trends and also to encourage self-discovery, which William James (1890) regarded as critical to character development.

Thus, socialization *into* leisure occurs in large part because of an appreciation of the potential for socialization *through* leisure. In earlier work, these two approaches to leisure socialization have been treated somewhat independently (Kleiber & Kelly, 1980), but no one would support leisure socially if it was not perceived to have benefits for the child and society, a topic we will take up further in Chapter 11. Play is encouraged, for example, because it is viewed as a source of creativity (Bjorklund, 2007) and social and cognitive development (see Barnett, 1990, 2007; Bjorklund, 2007) which are highly valued. Sport is encouraged because it is thought to contribute to the ability to work with others in the achievement of shared goals and to be a source of character development. Structured leisure activities, such as music, sports, and creative activities have been hypothesized to provide an important developmental context for growth of the capacity to direct, control and focus attention. Larson (2000) pointed out that this ability is one of the most important achievements of child development. It allows individuals to formulate and act upon personal goals, and, in adulthood, it is associated with creative achievement and self-actualization (see also Larson, 1994; Larson & Kleiber, 1993a,b).

Such benefits may depend on how children learn to construe time itself. Children's experience of time and leisure is the result of many different factors. Being in a family of six or seven would probably promote a different feeling about control over one's time than being the only child of a single mother. Being in a culture where punctuality is stressed would be different from one in which everything happens "in due time." Institutional life at school teaches children that there is clearly time to be "on task" and time which is "free," as was reflected in a recent study of Norwegian school children (Øksnes, 2008). Consider your own sense of recess, for example. Most likely you felt far freer in that context that you did in the classroom or perhaps even at home.

Beyond the structure of a child's circumstances, society provides *agents* of influence. Parents, peers, teachers, television, and community programs are the usual sources of influence in childhood. But what is actually communicated to children by these various sources about what is appropriate use of time and leisure is extremely variable. So what was communicated to you about leisure during your childhood? What were the injunctions you were given? "Idleness is the devil's playground"? In other words, stay busy and avoid temptation. "If you are not helping yourself, you should be helping others." "Service to God and humankind should take preference over individual pleasures." Or perhaps it was recognized that, "All work and no play makes Jack a dull boy."

Some activities and patterns of enjoyment among adolescents, such as sexual activity, vandalism, and drug and alcohol use, are largely discouraged or prohibited by adults and society in general, while other activities may be seized upon and promoted to such an extent that the qualities of play and leisure are largely lost through everyone's overinvestment (Fine, 1987). The "fun" of a sport may come primarily in the joy of the activity itself, in being with friends, or in the prospect of being victorious. But this latter orientation can, in fact, be the undoing of leisure if the experience of playing ceases to be enjoyable in its own right. Early research on children's orientations toward game playing (Maloney & Petrie, 1972; Webb, 1969) found that children's reasons for participating in organized games and sports change with age and grade in school. In the Webb study, a group of children of different ages was asked the question, "What do you think is most important in a game?" and then asked to rank "to play as well as you are able," "to beat your opponent," and "to play fairly." Figure 9.1 (p. 282) shows the various combinations reflecting a continuum from a *play orientation* to a *professional orientation*. This research indicates that as children get older and become more involved in organized sports, they are more likely to value beating an opponent than playing well or fairly. In a sense, it is argued, children become "professionalized" in such games. The outcome becomes so important that the leisure involvement is more like work than play.

This process underlying "professionalization" can be applied to many areas of children's leisure and provides people who deal with children a useful lesson. An activity that has been intrinsically enjoyable, such as playing a musical instrument, can lose that quality if too many payoffs and other external contingencies, such as parental approval, are present. Indeed, the very idea of "overjustification" that was discussed in Chapter 6 was arrived at in a study of how play could be turned into work for kids by offering extrinsic rewards, "prizes," for doing something (drawing with magic markers) that they were already enjoying doing (Lepper & Greene, 1979). Parents, coaches, and camp directors should take heed when adding incentives to get children even more interested or invested in an activity. If the ultimate goal is for the activity to be intrinsically motivated (enjoyable in its own right), the practical challenge is facilitating the transition from extrinsically motivating factors to that of internalization and self-regulation. Ryan and Deci (2000) highlight specific actions that parents, coaches, teachers, and other supervisors must take to help encourage this change. These actions must reinforce competence, autonomy, relatedness and above all, self-determination. It's clear that with elite sport and other competitive activities, a level of commitment is required that may not be tolerable by everyone. Studies of collegiate athletes (e.g., Kimball & Freysinger, 2003) consistently demonstrate a high level of stress associated with performance; this stress seems to be occurring earlier and earlier in the lifespan (e.g., Fullinwider, 2006; Hyman, 2009). The practical implications for behavior management and preserving self-determination in play, sports, and leisure education more generally is taken up again in Chapter 13.

It is clear from studies of stress and dropping out of sports and other activities (e.g., Gould & Petlikoff, 1988; Kimball & Freysinger, 2003) that self-determination *in* leisure is important for making leisure attractive as well

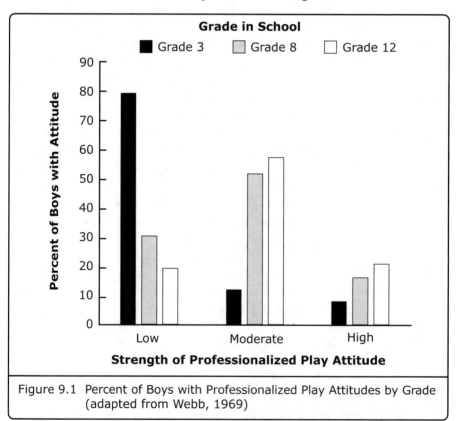

Figure 9.1 Percent of Boys with Professionalized Play Attitudes by Grade (adapted from Webb, 1969)

as useful. It may be easily compromised when activities are arranged for children and controlled by adults (see also Bjorklund, 2007, and Elkind, 1981). Children, adolescents, and adults alike may find themselves being pushed away from leisure, or at least certain leisure activities, under such circumstances. Finally, the assumption that leisure is intrinsically interesting may not always apply in some societies and subcultures. Free time may be dedicated intentionally to other purposes and activities such as devotion to God, service to others, or self-development. To call such activities "leisure" may be stretching its meaning somewhat, but these activities may be seen as the most appropriate for the use of discretionary time in some contexts. Again, as we discussed in Chapter 6, if the extrinsic regulations governing participation in these activities are integrated and internalized, continuing interest and involvement is likely to occur.

The Influence of the Family on Leisure

So, who were the leisure models in your family? In what kinds of leisure activities did you see those models participate when you were younger? If you had multiple models for leisure activities, were there any differences in the kinds of leisure, time available for leisure, or desire to participate in leisure activities among them? In this section, we consider not only who in the family is influential in shaping leisure activity, but also how they are influential. For example, while there is evidence that same-sex parents are typically more influential with children's leisure choices than opposite-sex parents (Kleiber & Kelly, 1980), what parents actually do may be more important than what they say. In the earlier discussion of modeling, we noted that mothers in the Shannon and Shaw (2008) study were not persuasive in their support of leisure for their daughters if they themselves were not finding or arranging time for leisure activities.

As noted in Chapter 8, play patterns generally seem to unfold for children in a predictable age progression corresponding to biological maturation. But parental attention and sibling influence also shape the direction of play and provide a basis for other leisure orientations. For example, a general orientation to leisure may be established very early in life in response to parental influence. This may happen simply in the form of the trust that comes with consistent care. According to some, a trusting attitude is necessary for the relaxed wakefulness and openness to experience that is central to the capacity to enjoy leisure (Neulinger, 1974). When do children learn to relax? And what are the conditions of relaxed wakefulness? Erikson's (1963) stage model of development suggests that this feeling is the best result of the first real developmental issue in life, that of *trust versus mistrust*. When babies become confident that their primary caregivers will return and tend to them in a predictable and continuous fashion, they show visible signs of relaxation.

This condition affords them the emotional security necessary for exploration, experimentation, and play. To call such a primitive emotional condition "leisure" may be a stretch, but the ability to cultivate a peacefulness about oneself throughout life may well depend on the earliest parent-child interactions.

When we considered Erikson's developmental model in Chapter 8, the point was to identify how play and leisure orientations change with age-related issues; but parenting and other sources of socialization are a critical part of that process. Thus, in the second and third stages, involving children from ages one to four, *autonomy* and *initiative* are orientations that may or may not be effectively cultivated by parents and caregivers. If children aren't reinforced for their initial efforts at independence and for their budding ideas and aspirations, they may be hesitant about taking chances in life, and, with respect to play and leisure, they may be inhibited as a result. Being willing to take some risks and respond positively to challenging play opportunities may affect both play and leisure orientations in the future. According to Erikson, not only doubt but also guilt may be reflected in that prevailing feeling of "overstepping one's bounds." Put more positively, being reinforced for initiating activity is likely to contribute to the ability to optimize leisure and to be one's own source of entertainment (Mannell, 1984b; see also Larson, 2000). Achieving a sense of autonomy and initiative, then, as with establishing trust, will depend on parental and family influences, with playfulness and exploratory behavior lying in the balance. Repressive, *authoritarian* parenting will clearly have a discouraging effect on autonomy and initiative. In early childhood, playfulness has been associated with parents having a flexible conceptual style, giving priority to enriching the play environment, and encouraging exploration and experimentation (Bishop & Chace, 1971; Lieberman, 1977).

A liberal approach to child rearing might seem then to be consistent with promoting autonomy and initiative and even facilitating leisure. As a result, play and self-expressiveness would be likely to flourish. But a *laissez-faire* approach to parenting, where adults simply leave children to their own devices, is often its own undoing. When children lack structure and predictability, trust and security are undermined, experimentation becomes less likely and concentration is made more difficult as a result. Parental limitations on behavior may constrain leisure, but they often do so in a way that enhances the experience. Somewhere in the middle of the parenting continuum are *democratic/authoritative* parents who include children in decision making but establish limits and guidelines and provide some direction. This combination encourages independence while providing children with the security necessary to build confidence (Baumrind, 1971). It may also be the best combination for realizing the full potential of leisure.

In early childhood, playfulness has been associated with flexibility in the cognitive style of parents. Parents with this style seem more likely to provide an enriched play environment (Bishop & Chace, 1971) and to encourage exploration and experimentation (Liebermann, 1977). In their widely cited study of a group of preschool children and their parents, Bishop and Chace (1971) examined the relationship between the cognitive style of the parents (how flexible and open-minded they were), their attitudes toward play, and how well the home environment promoted play (see Table 9.1). The researchers measured parents' cognitive style with a personality scale designed for this purpose and attitudes toward play with a specially developed questionnaire. They also visited the children's homes to observe how the parents interacted with their children, what rules they imposed and the availability of play space and materials. The more open, flexible, and less authoritarian parents' personalities, the more they valued fantasy and independence in the play of their children and the more the home environment seemed to foster play. In a separate phase of this study, the children were administered a creativity task

Table 9.1 Parenting style, Play, and Creativity Study Results (adapted from Bishop and Chace, 1971)

	Cognitive Style*	
	Concrete	Abstract
Cognitive Style and Play Attitude (percent of parents)		
Toys should be kept and used in separate places (No)	46.0	59.0
Few rules for watching television (Yes)	38.5	59.0
Children should be heard and not seen (No)	7.7	59.0
Allow or encourage play with opposite sex toys (Yes)	15.4	70.0
Play Environment and Cognitive Style (percent of homes)		
Child allowed to play anywhere in the home	7.7	29.5
Parent helped make toys	23.1	53.1
Child plays with noncommercial toys	53.9	88.5
Creative Productivity and Cognitive Style (higher scores indicate greater creativity)		
Sequential variation	7.3	13.2
Variation choice and color	0.9	1.3
Inflection points	6.7	8.2

* Abstract: Open and flexible, less authoritarian
  Concrete: Less open and flexible, more authoritarian

in a laboratory setting. Those children with parents having a more flexible cognitive style and who encouraged play were found to score higher on the creativity task (see Table 9.1).

Such flexibility may continue to be important as children move into adolescence, but *structure* is an additional ingredient that enables children to use leisure constructively and creatively. Rathunde (1988) found that the ability of adolescents to find optimal experience ("flow") in any situation was most common among those from homes where five conditions, what he called the "5 Cs," existed: (1) a feeling of *choice* and control, (2) *clarity* of rules and structures, (3) a recognition of the value of *centering* or focusing attention, (4) encouragement of *commitment* to tasks, and (5) the creation of meaningful *challenges*. According to Rathunde, taken all together, these conditions make up the *autotelic family context*, or in other words, a context where children learn to engage in activity for its own sake. Rathunde found that the resulting orientation to achieving optimal experience and enjoyment generalized from home to school settings as well.

Child-rearing emphases also differ by culture, again with resulting implications for patterns of self-expression. In a classic study of 56 different native cultures, Roberts and Sutton-Smith (1962) found that there was a relationship between a culture's particular emphasis in child rearing and the games that were preferred by the children in that culture. In cultures where there was a great emphasis on *obedience*, children were likely to prefer *games of strategy*. Where *achievement* was stressed, the *games of skill* were practiced. And where child rearing was *unpredictable*, that is, parents' rewards and punishments were somewhat arbitrary, *games of chance* were preferred. More complex societies combined these patterns in various ways. However, Roberts and Sutton-Smith proposed that two processes are involved in these differences in child rearing and children's game-play. First, it appears that the content of games has some value in helping children deal with the conflict and stresses created by the demands of the adults in their respective societies and their own natural inclinations for control and independence. If adults are highly controlling, stress is modulated in games related to strategy, and where high expectations for success create pressure, games of skill are preferred. If parents are relatively unpredictable in their dealings with their children, the stress of not knowing is relieved in games of chance. Second, game patterns may represent the workings of the larger culture and serve thereby to enculturate or socialize those who play them. Roberts and Sutton-Smith referred to both in the *conflict-enculturation hypothesis*: games and expressive activities both prepare children for their life in their culture and enable them to adjust and cope with the conflict and stress resulting from child-rearing practices that essentially attempt to control and shape their behavior.

Conscientious, authoritative child rearing also takes time and attention. The "time crunch" that contemporary parents feel as a result of trying to balance work and family roles may take its toll on active parenting (e.g., Higgins, Duxbury, & Lee, 1994; Kirchmeyer, 1993; Pittman, 1994). And while it has arguably gotten worse in recent years, it led David Elkind decades ago to the view that children are "hurried" to grow up and miss some of the ease and leisure of childhood (Elkind, 1981; see Bjorklund, 2007, for a more recent assessment of the problem). Too much is expected of them too soon. According to Elkind, such children experience responsibility overload, change overload, and emotional overload. He argued further that the hurrying of children results in large part because parents hurry themselves. The need to create a higher standard of living often takes precedence over leisure and relaxation and keeps even the most affluent families operating at a fever pitch. More recently, perhaps reflecting newer trends, Shaw and Hilbrecht (2008) spoke about the combination of such high expectations with increased fears about children's vulnerability as being part of a new "age of anxiety" for parents. Parents are led on one hand to restrict freedom in the interest of protecting children, while also expecting that leisure choices yield some physical, social, and psychological advantages. Arguably, the more relaxed leisure of childhood is compromised as a result, as is the leisure of parents.

The relatively high expectations for independence in children in contemporary society is also reflected in extensive television watching, with the TV readily adopted by absent parents as a kind of babysitter that is a safe alternative to outward-bound activities for "latchkey" children. The enormous amount of time spent watching television in childhood—from 25 to 30 hours per week by some accounts (Roberts, Foehr, & Rideout, 2005; Robinson, 1990; Tangney & Feshbach, 1988)—preempts more active involvement in play and other leisure activities, a subject we will address shortly in our consideration of the influence of media on leisure.[1]

Siblings may be at least as influential as parents in some cases. Older brothers and sisters often provide the closest models for fun, skill development, and activity involvement. Indeed they are likely playmates even before peers. Barnett and Kleiber (1984) found that later-born children are more playful than those born earlier. The process of socialization is clearly quite complex and there is a great deal that researchers don't know as yet. Parents' influence on children's leisure behavior and interests is not necessarily direct and unequivocal, and it may be complicated by socially acquired gender roles. For example, Barnett and Chick (1986) found that the social play of female and male children was related to their parents' satisfaction with their

---

[1] There are some indications that actual TV watching time may be decreasing as children spend more time online and with video games. But the amount of "screen time" then is at least as high.

own social leisure experiences. However, young boys' play styles appeared to be more affected by their parents' leisure than was true of young girls, and both girls' and boys' play was more strongly related to their mother's leisure participation than their father's.

Adolescents, of course, draw different attention, concerns, responses and directions from parents than younger children and rely on them less for leisure influence (relative to peers) than do younger children (e.g., Zeijl, te Poel, du Bois-Reymond, Ravesloot, & Meulman, 2000). But to a great extent adolescents are still learning about leisure, both directly and indirectly, from their parents, as evidenced in the study of mothers and daughters referred to earlier (Shannon & Shaw, 2008). Shannon (2006) also found in a study of Canadian teenagers that parents were important sources of information in the shaping of leisure values, attitudes, and behaviors. The study indicated that adolescents learned that leisure can be restorative, that some leisure pursuits are more valuable than others, that leisure is a means to various ends that can benefit individuals personally, and that the role of leisure changes with one's stage of life. But her findings did suggest that the emphasis was usually on the functional, instrumental values of leisure activities rather than in promoting unstructured activities as an opportunity for pleasure and enjoyment (see also Shaw & Dawson, 2001).

Control is also a theme in the messages that adolescents receive from parents. In another study of teenagers, groups of both Canadian and U.S. adolescents, Hutchinson, Baldwin, and Caldwell (2003) found parents varied in terms of the following: (a) beliefs about and expectations of the free-time context, (b) ways of communicating and enforcing these beliefs and expectations, (c) actions to direct their adolescents' activity engagement, (d) strategies they used to monitor their adolescents' activities, (e) their provision of resources to support preferred activity engagement, and (f) their efforts to support autonomous behavior in the free-time context.

An interview study of adolescents who were involved in using leisure for delinquent purposes (Robertson, 1999) demonstrated a general lack of parental involvement in leisure with adolescents beyond age 10 and a perceived lack of parental interest in their activities. And yet study participants expressed a desire for more shared leisure experiences with parents, fathers in particular.

Finally, it is important to reiterate and expound on what was suggested earlier with respect to differences between mothers' and fathers' influence. Clearly, mothers have more responsibility for leisure in childhood, though this is less true in adolescence and is changing in some important ways throughout both childhood and adolescence. Fathers are taking increasingly more responsibility both in sharing the burdens of child rearing (a subject we will return to shortly in discussing family influences on adult leisure) and also in terms of their interest in directing the purposes of leisure for their children (Shaw & Dawson, 2001). Furthermore, in traditional families, fathers generally have more of a playful relationship with children while mothers are more the arrangers and controllers of leisure activity (Larson & Richards, 1994). Still, a considerable difference remains, with fathers being far more likely to be absent from the scene and mothers assuming the bulk of child rearing, including leisure socialization, but often with a lack of time to get more effectively involved with children's leisure as a result. This is especially true in relatively poor, inner-city areas (Outley & Floyd, 2002) and in rural areas (Trussell & Shaw, 2007).

Leisure socialization in poorer urban areas may in fact extend the boundaries of family influence. Parents in the immediate community often accept the responsibility for children who are not their own. Outley and Floyd (2002) found that inner-city Houston parents combated the constraints associated with poverty and physical danger by utilizing kinship networks and "chaperonage" of neighbors to allow children to participate in mainstream leisure activities. Nevertheless, parental restrictions on children's social interactions with peers and others perceived to be undesirable curtailed the range of leisure for many children in that study.

The Influence of Peers on Leisure

Thinking back again, who were your playmates, your pals, your running buddies, and your confidants in years past? If you are like most people, your peers were very influential, at least in your later childhood and adolescence. As noted earlier, the play of very young children is essentially solitary— though it may be encouraged by others like parents and siblings. With respect to age mates, play typically doesn't move beyond a kind of parallel participation with others until the third or fourth year. But association with others ultimately becomes a very powerful motivation for shared play and may even be biologically directed. In a classic study of Rhesus monkeys, Harlow and Harlow (1962) found that infant monkeys who were deprived of peer play were more retarded in social and sexual development than those who were not. As we discussed in earlier chapters, the recognition that human beings seem to have similar needs led Deci and Ryan (1991) to revise their view of intrinsic motivation to recognize *relatedness* as an intrinsic need comparable to competence and autonomy, while others (Fiske, 2004) see it as an overarching social motive.

Parents and siblings are the significant others for children in early childhood, but children come to seek outside-of-family friendships as soon as they are of school age. The relationships with these new friends and peers increasingly shape play and leisure interests and experiences. In a study of influences on involvement in physical activity at different levels, parents were most influential for younger children, but peers are more important than parents to children in junior high school (Thompson, Rehman, & Humbert, 2005). Peers are role models for one another, and their play patterns offer examples of competence—physical, social, and emotional (Caldwell, 2005). This may be particularly important in situations where general social norms are not encouraging. In a study of young girls participating in outdoor recreation activities (Culp, 1998), the most influential factor in encouraging participation was having other girls the same age participating. The author suggested that connecting with other girls of the same age may be an even more powerful influence for girls than for boys in such situations. In another study, those with similar levels of disability were the peers who were most influential in the histories of members of the USA National Wheelchair Basketball Team (Ruddell & Shinew, 2006).

Although adults often direct the form and content of play and leisure activities in later childhood, age mates consistently provide the social context for the experience. This becomes increasingly true as children grow older. Research on sport suggests that peers are more influential for boys' interest in sports while the family is more influential in getting girls started (McPherson, 1983). But sustained interest for girls seems to be dependent on an actively participating cohort of friends. Investigators in the Dutch study referred to earlier (Zeijl et al., 2000) examined the relative influence of peers and parents on leisure activity across several phases of childhood and adolescence, taking gender and social class into account as well. They found that 10- to 12-year-old children from higher social classes were more influenced by parents and siblings. While 14- and 15-year-old boys, especially those from higher social classes, focused more on peer groups, girls of the same age had a salient preference for dyadic friendships. Teenage girls from lower socioeconomic circles encountered the most parental attention concerning peer contacts.

Intensity of experience is also an important part of adolescence. Loud music, bright lights, and other extreme forms of stimulation are more characteristic of adolescence than of any other age group. To a large extent, this is a function of group identification, affiliation, and conformity. Exhibiting extremes in behavior with others confers a sense of belonging. This leads to what Csikszentmihalyi and Larson (1984) refer to as the *deviation amplifying* effects of adolescents on each other. Behavior and activities that are departures from the norms of society by adolescents' closest friends are less likely to be reproached than they are encouraged, especially when done in the interest of enjoyment. Experimentation with alcohol and other drugs is consistent with this tendency, although many other factors are involved. Alcohol use combined with aggressive and boisterous acts is part of masculine socialization in many societies (Burns, 1980), while the use of psychoactive drugs is attractive as a means to enhance awareness and alter perceptions in other societies (Bachman et al., 1996). Whatever the particular experience, sharing it with friends and peers, apart from others (especially adults), is often part of the process of establishing identity since identification with others is as big a part of identity formation as individuation, as discussed in Chapter 7. But equally clear is that much of adolescent leisure is driven by the need to belong and thus is influenced by processes of conformity.

Certain leisure activities and expressive patterns are important for defining distinct groups, largely because of the status they confer. In Eckert's (1989) ethnographic study, the labels used by high school students to identify groups of their peers differing in status were based on the extent of their involvement in extracurricular school activities. Those students who were involved in extracurricular activities, not necessarily just sports, were called "jocks"; those who were uninvolved or unidentified with any extracurricular activities were called "burnouts." The stereotyping of groups has undoubtedly changed, but leisure activities inevitably define them. In Coleman's classic study of adolescent life (1961), being involved in sports was the most important factor contributing to the social status of high school boys. Popularity for girls was less dependent on extracurricular activities at that time. Perhaps this has changed (Holland & Andre, 1994), as girls and women have become more involved and more prominent in physically active leisure pursuits (Archer & McDonald, 1990), but a 1993 survey in the U.S. revealed that the participation gap for physically active leisure and exercise between men and women in general, particularly younger women, had actually increased (Robinson & Godbey, 1993).

Peers may also be influential in promoting forms of recreation that are health-compromising, exercising various degrees of coercion to induce others to participate in drug and alcohol use, vandalism, or sexually promiscuous activity (Caldwell, 2005). With respect to drug and alcohol use per se, peer influence may be particularly strong, but it is mitigated by parental involvement. In a study of nearly 8,000 adolescents (Caldwell & Darling, 1999), the investigators found that if adolescents perceived low levels of parental monitoring and associated with peers who used substances, they were more likely to use substances themselves. The results also suggested that spending time in unstructured social contexts, hanging out, and partying also predicted substance use, but this process was mediated by openness to peer influence. In the Swedish study of 14-year-old teen-center users referred to in Chapter 7, peer influence was a critical predictor of whether those attending the center were involved in norm-breaking activity (Person, Kerr, & Stattin, 2004). Nevertheless, *resistance* to peer influence was also identified in the Caldwell study as quite common and quite influential. The subject of resistance to social influence will be taken up later in this chapter.

Newer communications technologies, principally cellular telephones, have expanded contact between peers astronomically in recent years. One may be walking or riding in the car and still "converse" in various ways with peers around the community, country, or even the globe. The very act of conversation is often leisure, in being about sociability and casual interaction as often as it is for more instrumental purposes. And the plans for future shared activity are often arranged through those media as well. Cybercultures are also created through online gaming and other social networking (Palfrey & Gasser, 2008; Tapscott, 2009). Online relationships often lead to face-to-face relationships.

Finally, there is more to say about the influence of romantic relationships in general. Romantic partners may be the strongest peer influence of all. In a qualitative study of young women's leisure within heterosexual romantic relationships (Herridge, Shaw, & Mannell, 2003), it was clear that their leisure activities were very much influenced by their partner, in both sharing many of the partner's interests and preferred activities and in moving into new areas; but their relationships also constrained leisure in forcing participants into activities in which they were less interested and in restricting involvement in other non-romantic relationships. Study participants were more or less effective in resisting this latter influence.

Leisure Education

You may not have regarded your parents as teachers, but chances are they or your siblings—or perhaps some coaches or activity leaders—"showed you the ropes" of the activities that first captured your interest. School authorities may have discouraged your playing in various ways, so that you would have been a better student, but there too, leisure interests and activities were cultivated—in physical education, art, music, literature courses, and even in recess. All of these sources of instruction are agents of *leisure education* and some are influential very early in life.

An awareness of the value of play has led to an integration of play in the preschool curriculum and sometimes beyond. *Play training* has even been employed to develop children's ability to play (Smilansky, 1968). In these activities, often targeted at disadvantaged children, teachers and play leaders teach children to engage in sociodramatic play (especially role-playing) in the interest of cultivating cognitive abilities, social skills, and creativity. Some of the results have been encouraging (e.g., Curry, 1988; Dinwiddie, 1993; Galda & Pellegrini, 1982), but whether the structure imposed in such training situations is truly conducive to real play is an issue. As noted earlier, children have a way of socializing themselves. In fact, in spite of all the criticism of daycare settings where children are largely on their own, there is evidence that children who have been in daycare longer typically play at a more sophisticated level (Howes, 1988).

Seeing play and leisure activity as being worthy of intentional and systematic cultivation—as many people do—has contributed to the development of leisure education (Albrechtsen, 2001; Dattilo, 2008). This subfield of recreation and leisure studies has been used mostly to influence the understanding of leisure and development of leisure skills in children and adults with special needs, such as mental retardation. Arguably, though, all that is done inside and outside of schools to build leisure knowledge and lifelong leisure skills fits the category, for any person at any age. Nevertheless, there are special "teachable moments," such as in later childhood (Erikson, 1963), when children are eager for instruction, or when older adults retire and open their eyes to new non-work possibilities (considered later in this chapter).

The latter years of childhood are devoted in large part to establishing competence, to achieving a sense that one has and can develop skills that are well regarded by others. Being able to "produce," in one way or another, results in a sense of *industry* (Erikson, 1963, p. 252). Failure to do so is likely to result in a prevailing sense of inferiority. It should come as no surprise, then, that in this "age of instruction" children are most likely to take on group-learning activities where they can develop skills that compare favorably with those of others. During this time children join Girl Scouts, Boy Scouts, and youth sport teams. And as expressive and creative abilities are taken more seriously, they may even serve as the basis for adult and lifelong leisure pursuits. It is the most likely starting place for the "serious leisure" discussed in previous chapters.

Children typically rely on parents and their family contexts for guidance throughout childhood and adolescence. Nevertheless, most cultures have established practices and opportunity structures for moving children out of a dependence on families and into preparation for becoming a productive member of society. This is the essence of socialization. Ages vary as do cultural and subcultural contexts, but as children step into school and other adult-controlled settings, they begin the task of separation from families that will be continued into and through adolescence. The socializing systems of school and community are established in some respects to coincide with a child's natural inclination for both establishing competence and for connecting more effectively with others. Leisure activities move accordingly away from purely child-directed play and games to activities that have some connection with the wider world. These are to be found in both school and community contexts, though the impacts of these transitional settings are quite varied and complex (cf. Henderson, 2000; Larson, 2000).

The influence of schools on the development of leisure interests and orientations is inherently problematic. The knowledge base developed in schools, as well as the cognitive skills associated with learning to read and write, provides a strong foundation for learning activities outside of the school, but children all too often leave such capabilities at the schoolroom door. Most schools use an elaborate system of extrinsic motivation, primarily in the form of grades, to ensure that the knowledge and skills necessary for continuing on in school, for participation in the work force, and for contributing to society are developed. In so doing, however, the intrinsic interest that children bring to learning is often undermined in the same way that prizes, money, and emphasis on winning sometimes take the fun out of children's games and sports (Boggiano & Pittman, 1992; Lepper & Greene, 1979). On the other hand, many schools provide exposure to a wide variety of activities in the context of art, music, and physical education classes, as well as in recess and in after school extracurricular activity programs.

Summer camps and adventure education programs must also be regarded as mechanisms of leisure education and leisure socialization. All such activities are structured efforts to expose children to leisure opportunities and develop leisure skills. The fact that they have other socialization goals and other effects—building social skills and self-esteem, for example—beyond promoting leisure per se, will be addressed again in Chapter 11.

Other Opportunity Structures for Leisure

Do you intend to become a "leisure socializer" yourself, then? Perhaps you see that in your role as a parent in the future. Or maybe your professional aspirations would have you working in a leisure service agency. Such agencies are among the many settings and opportunities—beyond home and school—that shape leisure interests and development more generally (see, for example, Witt & Caldwell, 2005).

Municipal recreation departments, youth sport agencies, community theatre, scouts, and other youth-serving agencies also provide opportunities for an enormous number of young people in the U.S. and Canada. As with school sports, much of the initial attraction is to join with friends in learning activities, an inclination that is true for all ages. It is also the case, as noted earlier, that children in later childhood seek opportunities to develop respected skills that can be tested against and compared with those of their age mates. Instruction in sport is, at least initially, readily accepted in most cases. From the perspective of public agencies, the assumption of responsibility for the health and welfare of citizens in the community has also provided a strong rationale for creating structured opportunities for children. Lately, this responsibility has been reflected mostly in programs to enhance physical activity for the purpose of combating sedentary lifestyles and reducing childhood obesity (e.g., Henderson et al., 2001). Evidence indicates that structured opportunities for physical activity are particularly influential with junior and senior high school students, although parents are still more influential with younger children (Thompson et al., 2005).

The belief that structured activities such as organized sports might meet both physical and developmental needs in ways that school does not has made them very popular with parents for some time; if a child shows talent, he or she is often pushed along into more advanced training. But as was noted before, while this can have a positive influence on skill-building, it may also be a kind of "premature structuring" that makes a child a performer before he or she may be ready (Elkind, 1981). Rather than encouraging continued interest in the activity, this position may make it more work-like, as we have noted, and discourage future involvement as a result. One important factor in determining the impact of the program is if the participants are still having fun. It takes a skilled instructor—and one who is truly enjoying the activity and the teaching of it—to successfully carry it off. One study of instructors in leisure service agencies (Collishaw, Dyer, & Boies, 2008) demonstrated that "faking it" (enjoyment and enthusiasm) was clearly detected by participants and affected their interest.

Of course, opportunities for such structured experiences are not distributed evenly across all segments of society, either. For whatever problems over-structuring and bad instruction might create, there are many children who have relatively little access to structured programs of any kind. In a California study, Elliott Medrich and his associates found that children from lower socioeconomic conditions, especially urban children, rarely had the provision of community services in terms of people, places, and physical resources that middle and upper socioeconomic status children do (Medrich et al., 1982), and this appears to have continued over time at least to some degree (see, for example, Outley & Floyd, 2002). Opportunities in sports for girls and for children with disabilities also still lag far behind despite significant gains in recent years. A study of wheelchair sport involvement indicated that even with an available program it was necessary for prospective participants to have strong social support to enable them to participate (Anderson, Wozencroft & Bedini, 2008). In fact the combination of being female and having a physical disability can serve as a "double whammy" to discourage participation in activities (e.g., Devine, 2004).

Influences of Media and Technology

Think of commercials or advertisements in which recreation and leisure activities are portrayed. What is being sold? What relationships do these activities have with other aspects of life? with romantic relationships? friendships? family relationships? What about the use of games and physical activities in reality television shows such as "Survivor"? Sports are available to watch on television at any hour. Which, if any, of these programs do you watch, and how do they affect your own activity beyond spending time?

It is certainly true that children get an enormous number of ideas about leisure opportunities and possibilities—including the idea that it is good to enjoy oneself—from watching television. Nevertheless, the amount of time given to watching television and using other media in childhood—estimated to be more than 53 hours per week among 8–18 year olds in the U.S. according to a recent report by the Kaiser Family Foundation (2010)—can preempt more active involvement in play and other leisure activities, even if the TV is just on in the background (Schmidt et al., 2008). In a study of 1,000 children six years of age and younger, investigators found that in two out of three homes the TV is left on at least half the time, even without viewers present, and that in one third of the homes the TV is on "almost all" or "most" of the time (Rideout, Vandewater, & Wartella, 2003). They also found that children in the latter group (where TV is almost always on) appear to read less than other children and to be slower to learn to read. Higher levels of television watching have also been found to be associated with play styles that are less imaginative (Singer, 1973), though television can, under some conditions, stimulate the child's imagination (Singer & Singer, 1986). In an older study (Barnes, 1970), the play behavior of a group of preschool children was found to be significantly less social than that of children 40 years earlier, and greater exposure to television was considered as the most likely explanation. More recent research demonstrates that the negative correlation between television watching and social play continues (Bickham & Rich, 2006).

Of course, involvement with the media need not be passive. Video-game play is more physically involving and newer "Wii" games can involve a full range of simulated exercise and activity. More important, they may expand rather than reduce interactive social play, especially with online interactive games. Some researchers and many parents have been concerned that video games promote gender stereotypes and aggressive behavior and even discourage prosocial behavior (see Anderson & Bushman, 2001; Braun & Giroux, 1989; Provenzo, 1991; Sneed & Runco, 1992); but a more recent review that distinguishes interactive social computer use from more passive television watching and impersonal computer use, suggests clear differences. Valkenburg and Peter (2009) looked back at a decade of research and the original predictions that the Internet and online communication would have a negative or detrimental effect on youth, and they instead found improved social relationships among regular online communication participants. The authors attributed these positive effects to enhanced self-disclosure afforded through this medium. More will be said about the effects of television and Internet involvement in Chapter 11.

Social Influences on Leisure in Adulthood

Even though social scientists associate socialization with childhood, it is a lifelong process. As social animals, we continue to be influenced by others in a variety of ways, even with the purpose of improving our relationships with others. We never quite "grow up," and, maybe more important for our interests in leisure, we may find "it is never too late to have a happy childhood." In any case, it is clear that the basic social processes outlined earlier in this chapter—such as persuasion, conformity, and affiliation—continue to determine much of the leisure behavior of adulthood and later life. Once children and adolescents make the transition to adulthood, the number of available roles increase. In addition to worker, spouse, and parent, one may be a volunteer, community leader, politician, deacon in the church, association president, etc., all involving what roles do—define expectations of others, norms, and opportunities for action. In the previous chapter, we looked at age as an individual difference variable affecting leisure choices, but as one gets older, age is more likely to be simply the arranger of different social influences.

Family- and work-role changes are also likely to dictate changes in behavior and experience, including those related to leisure. Graduation and the transition from school leave young adults with a newfound independence but also typically with a somewhat narrower set of recreational activities and opportunities (Kelly & Masar, 1970). This pattern of constriction continues with work, marriage, and especially with having children, for those who find themselves in those circumstances (Rapoport & Rapoport, 1975; Witt & Goodale, 1981), finding some change in the other direction when children leave home, job security is enhanced and then work responsibilities are reduced with retirement.

The assumption of the roles of worker, spouse, and parent, for those moving out of adolescence into adulthood in most cultures, brings dramatic changes in behavior and experience, changes that are reflected in leisure choices as well. As has been well established, leisure experience does not emerge in a vacuum; as relatively free as it is, leisure is contextualized by the various roles and activities of everyday life, including those of family, work, and community life. To the extent that performance of the roles becomes part of a socially constructed self, leisure activities that are consistent with those roles will be preferred. Leisure provides free space for role interpretation beyond that which is essentially required, whether it be in parenthood, employment, or religious observance (Kelly, 1987b). While a person may put in long hours to demonstrate commitment to the job, time spent preparing a meal for people or organizing a social event for coworkers not only solidifies his or her place in the organization, it provides alternate roles for being a member of that organization.

So what about for you? Will things change dramatically for you when you graduate? Has the role of college student defined leisure for you in ways that will likely be abandoned when you leave it? Are you married, committed to another, perhaps even a parent already? Do you anticipate these changes? What do you think they will mean for your leisure? And how about your parents and other adults you have known? What have the role changes in their lives meant for them? How much of their leisure is determined by family and work responsibilities? Think of them as we continue here, but also project yourself—your "possible self" as some have discussed it (Markus & Nurius, 1986)—into the future.

The Influence of Work on Leisure

If you are like many college students, you may be astounded by how consuming your first full-time job is. In the previous chapter we noted Arnett's assessment that time is more at a premium in the emerging adulthood period than at any other (Arnett, 2000). New workers, new parents, or continuing students eventually adjust to the hours and establish a rhythm that allows them to anticipate "time off for good behavior." In some cases leisure is little more than a time for rest and recovery, but it is often influenced by work in more significant ways. A job brings a person into a community of coworkers or colleagues, and friendships and relationships are often extended into the context of leisure. If work itself is important enough, discussion of it may continue over dinner, at a local pub, at a hair salon, or on the golf course. Conversely, being familiar with the status of local sports teams or talk show personalities often facilitates interaction with coworkers on the job. Competence in a leisure activity, or the ability to converse intelligently about it, may enhance one's status among coworkers just as volunteer work may contribute to feeling a part of the community. An entry-level job typically offers limited opportunities for self-expression, and leisure can be used to address needs and explore interests not addressed in the workplace. Even if work is fulfilling, the intensity of it may necessitate retreat and escape in the interest of recuperation. In any case, as Daniel Levinson and colleagues (1978) pointed out years ago, the transition from adolescence into the adult world must be negotiated with awareness of gaining entry to adult society, however diverse and varied that may be. The conventionality this implies is not singular; the approaches to becoming established are as varied as there are cultures and subcultures. Becoming a laborer for a construction company would necessitate a responsiveness to others and attentiveness to norms of conduct that could be compared to that required of someone joining a religious order. Coming to terms with such demands and expectations contributes still more to the formation of identity (Arnett, 2000).

Changes in work roles are significant in dictating leisure activities and interests. To the extent that young adults find themselves heavily involved in establishing work careers, they may not want to stray too far from those tasks that will ensure progression toward getting established and are thus likely to choose recreation and leisure activities that complement work roles or compensate in some useful way. By middle age, there may be some reduction in the pressures to become established, but the desire to contribute to the well-being of others may be equally as demanding on time and energy. Furthermore, midlife is often a time when women return to the work force after completing child rearing, thus reintroducing all the pressures of becoming established. Retirement from paid work, of course, brings an end to most work-related role constraints, but dramatic increases in free time are often offset by dwindling resources and a decline in physical health.

The relationship between work and leisure goes in both directions. In Chapter 12, we take up the question of how leisure activities—such as vacations—may contribute to (or detract from) work productivity and satisfaction. Our interest in this chapter on social influences on leisure is in how work roles and experiences shape leisure activities and interests. There is now a considerable literature on how work influences people's leisure activity preferences (e.g., Bacon, 1975; Banner, 1985; Spreitzer & Snyder, 1987) and how the job affects leisure satisfaction (e.g., Chambers, 1986). The rationale for this research focus is rooted in the assumption that the job dictates activity selection, participation times, and the people with whom an individual has frequent contact. On the other hand, leisure that occurs during free time is relatively unconstrained, and consequently, it is free to vary in response to paid work demands and arrangements (Iso-Ahola & Mannell, 1985).

Two theories have dominated thinking regarding the nature of work's influence on leisure (Kando & Summers, 1971; Parker, 1971; Wilensky, 1960). The *spillover* and *compensation* theories suggest that the nature of people's work directly influences their choice of leisure activities. Based on the former theory, workers are thought to participate in leisure activities that have characteristics similar to their job-related activities and tasks. Conversely, compensation theory, which we briefly mentioned in the previous chapter, suggests that deprivations experienced at work are made up for during leisure, or that people participate in activities that satisfy needs that they cannot satisfy at work. Research testing these theories has provided findings that are generally contradictory and inconclusive, though there has been more support for spillover than compensation (see Iso-Ahola & Mannell, 1985; Kabanoff, 1980; Staines, 1980; Zuzanek & Mannell, 1983).

The Influence of Family on Leisure

Many writers and researchers have spoken of the compromises in lifestyle that having a family brings. In a slightly overdramatized way, Gutmann (1975) referred to it as the "chronic emergency of parenthood." In the life course study of leisure referred to in the previous chapter, Gordon, Gaitz, and Scott (1976) noted, "Nothing changes life like the marriage-parenthood package." There is often precious little time left after children are satisfied and/or asleep, and when it comes to leisure, children influence the leisure of parents and caregivers as much as they are influenced by parents, though this is more typically true of women than men (Horna, 1989a; Shaw, 1992). Nevertheless, there are important changes that occur even in the course of the family life cycle. When children are young and "portable," or teenagers are off on their own, it is possible for parents to choose activities that are of special interest to themselves, but in the middle years of childhood, children's interests typically dictate much of what parents do. Research on the constraints to leisure experienced by parents indicates that these years are accompanied by an increasing scarcity of time (Crawford & Godbey, 1987; Witt & Goodale, 1985). When children have grown up and are off on their own, adults often have the experience of not knowing how to get back to their own interests. But the leisure of parenting has a special quality of its own and is thus part of the elaboration of leisure interests and abilities and, as we noted before, can contribute to a sense of *generativity*. Indeed, the view that adult leisure is defined largely as when children are cared for by others is decidedly androcentric, as Leslie Bella (1989) has pointed out. For women, and maybe mothers especially, leisure is more "relational" in that it includes caregiving roles and is less defined by segmentation of free time away from other roles. Increasingly, though, fathers share this point of view (Kay, 2007; Shaw & Dawson, 2001). Modeling, teaching, and providing opportunities are all part of family-oriented leisure.

It is also true, however, that relationships may suffer to the extent that attention to children prevents couples from relating to each other. In one study (Orthner, 1976), it was found that only in the first and last phases of the family life cycle did shared leisure enhance marital satisfaction, and those are the phases when children are the least demanding. Certainly childcare responsibilities, however much they are welcomed, constrain involvement in other activities. Evidence suggests that women who are mothers of young children have lower levels of physical activity than women of similar age who do not have children (Brown, Lee, Mishra, & Bauman, 2000). Studies of recreation specialization also indicate that the ability to progress deeper into an activity in more complex and engaging ways is also negatively associated with having a family (Kuentzel & Heberlein, 2008).

Becoming a parent often entails participation in activities of the child's liking, albeit generally on the parent's terms. Relaxing and being available to children may have special advantages for developing a child's self-confidence, trust, and imagination, as we will explore in Chapter 11, but tending to their play patterns and leisure needs in one way or another, often at the expense of one's own personal interests, seems to come with the advent of parenthood in any case. Having vacations and weekends in which to enact the role of parent gives leisure special significance in family relations (Kelly, 1987b). Family cohesiveness seems to be linked to shared leisure activities that facilitate emotional bonding, relational identification, stress management, the development of communication skills, and the feeling of support (Orthner, Barnett-Morris, & Mancini, 1992). And as indicated earlier, much of what children learn to enjoy with their parents will stay with them as options throughout their lives. Parents often have some awareness of this and take it on as their parental responsibility (Shaw & Dawson, 2001).

As child-rearing values have changed over the years, shared play and leisure have become a more predictable part of family experience. A decline in the division of household labor and an increase in emphasis on individual expression and equity of interaction have replaced the institutional family, where roles are instrumental and specialized, with the "companionate" family, where pleasurable family interaction is a priority (Orthner et al., 1992)

Children are also very determining of leisure; they can bring to family leisure both joys and frustrations and commonly both. Leisure for child-centered parents becomes defined very much by activities that children enjoy. In many cases, the decisions about what to do with family leisure come as much from children as adults; children are often the "lobbyists" for particular leisure activities (Howard & Madrigal, 1990).

Men are increasingly a part of the family-leisure picture, but gender differences are still apparent. Mothers are still more likely to create the conditions for family leisure activity, and according to available evidence, they are somewhat less likely to enjoy it (Larson & Richards, 1994) or even to recognize it as leisure (Shaw, 1992). Single mothers, who greatly outnumber single fathers, and women working outside the home typically have far less freedom to exercise their own interests and preferences and to escape the child-rearing context, even if there is a male partner available to assist (Larson & Richards, 1994). Others have shown that there is precious little free time in such circumstances (Shaw, 1992). Even with husbands available, working women frequently have a "second shift" after work, tending to the family and house (Hochschild, 1989). While the picture is changing somewhat—nuclear families are only one of a variety of family patterns any more—leisure is still distributed unequally in the domestic context.

As was noted earlier, women's leisure is different from that of men in some respects, less segmented and more integrated with their other roles (Bella, 1989). But the reality for mothers of adolescent children, according to experience sampling data from middle- and working-class families (Larson & Richards, 1994), is that while they may be fundamentally fulfilled in parental roles, women experience little of the sense of freedom and enjoyment at home that is normally associated with leisure. The women participating in this study had a general "leisure-lack," with little time for themselves and few indications in their mood reports of the freedom, relaxation, or positive affect generally associated with leisure. Instead, their greatest enjoyment was found outside the home in conversational relationships with friends and colleagues. By contrast, men experienced their most positive, relaxed, enjoyable circumstances at home, even if this involved some degree of housework and child care, because, the authors argue, these things are experienced by them as voluntary. Perhaps, though, with other social changes these patterns have changed as well. A similar experience sampling study of parents and families today is certainly needed.

Grandparenthood

Becoming a grandparent has a very different impact on leisure experience than becoming a parent. This is particularly true in situations where grandparents are not expected or required to provide primary child care (as they often are in low-income families) and can instead define the role of taking care of grandchildren differently, and more expressively, than was the case in parenting their own children. But the grandparents' own aging processes are also implicated; they often have (or take) the prerogative of being the bearers of the message that, given adequate resources, life should be enjoyed. In approaching the end of the road, they are regularly reminded that the journey is the important thing and that the present should not be wholly sacrificed for the future. These are also the circumstances for demonstrating a degree of wisdom and a variety of ways of caring (Carstenson, Fung, & Charles, 2003; Robinson, 1993).

Widowhood

The expanded role of grandparent can be contrasted with the role constriction associated with the loss of a spouse or other significant friends. A loss of leisure experience typically accompanies such changes. The loss of shared leisure may mean the loss of companionship all together. Married people have been found to have a narrower range of activities than single people (Holman & Epperson, 1984), and thus the loss of a spouse may be particularly consequential for those who have done things mostly together (e.g., Janke, Nimrod, & Kleiber, 2008a,b). A study from Australia suggested that widows in older adulthood reduce the number of activities that they engage in after the death of a spouse and that their leisure shifts from community-based activities to home-centered activities (Patterson, 1996). However, a study in the United States by Utz and colleagues (2002) comparing older adults who were continuously married with those who became widowed found that social participation in formal settings during widowhood did not change significantly, while participation in informal activities was maintained or actually increased slightly. Specifically this study found that participation in formal social leisure activities did not differ by marital status but that continuously married adults reported a significant decline in informal social participation compared with widowed adults whose social involvement was relatively constant over time. The differences in these findings may be reflective of the different locations of data collection as well as the use of different methodological approaches—one used mixed methods (Patterson, 1996) while the other used a sub-sample of a larger quantitative study (Utz et al., 2002). In any case, it is clear that the loss can also have a liberating effect, especially in the case where the spouse was overbearing and determining. In such cases, a kind of "blossoming" of self-expression often follows, with leisure taking on special new meaning (Lopata, 1993).

Other Constraints and Facilitators of Leisure in Adulthood

Changes in work and family roles are probably the most significant factors that both constrain and facilitate leisure activity in adulthood and modify leisure experience (cf. Raymore, 2002). But there are other factors that have been studied as well. Companionship with friends, or the lack thereof, has been shown to be a significant interpersonal factor in determining involvement in leisure activities. Being preoccupied with work or family roles may limit the development of leisure-supportive friendships, while the termination of those roles would open up opportunities. Also, work and family are clearly generators of relationships themselves, and children from different families connect their respective parents in relationships around the children's activities or play locations.

Launching children and retirement from work don't always result in expanded opportunity. In some sense, family and work responsibilities are isolating from other leisure experience and knowledge, leaving people unprepared when they come to an end. Lack of information is one of the larger constraints that adults feel when they suddenly have time but are ill equipped with the knowledge of what to do (Witt & Goodale, 1981). And while effective communication, persuasion, and marketing may facilitate leisure involvement, the flip side is that the lack of information often explains the lack of participation (e.g., Pennington-Gray, Thapa, & Holland, 2002). Although there are clearly other populations of adults who need it, leisure education in adulthood has primarily been focused on the elderly and those with disabilities (e.g., Dattilo, 2008; Searle & Mahon, 1991; Searle, Mahon, Iso-Ahola, Sdrolias, & van Dyck, 1998).

Spaces and places may be more or less inviting for leisure experience as well. Environmental/ecological psychologists use the word *affordance* to describe what the environment "speaks of" in terms of the possibilities for immediate experience (Gibson, 1979; Greeno, 1994; Kleiber, Wade, & Loucks-Atkinson, 2005; Pierskalla & Lee, 1998). For example, in the physical environment, it might be an overlook that will afford a beautiful view when approached or a warning of the risk of a fall. But to see all that is there, one must be *attuned* effectively to the environment. And previous experience with the particular environment will sharpen the awareness of what is to be experienced there again. The "built" environment may be regarded in the same way. Some places (e.g., a park bench) are more inviting than others (e.g., a crowded bus stop). People who have favorite leisure settings have a "sense of place" about the location, be it a city, a wilderness area or a particular beach (e.g., Altman & Low, 1992; Kyle & Chick, 2007). As was noted in Chapter 7, they may even define themselves in relation to that place (e.g., Brooks, Wallace, & Williams, 2006; Williams, 2002). Familiar places often evoke a feeling of comfort. But perhaps by association, the apprehension of new places may also influence emotions in variety of ways. For some, fear may even be evoked in places that are otherwise associated with leisure and recreation, as in the fears of some women in wilderness settings and at night (e.g., Bialeschki, 2005; Coble, Selin, & Erickson, 2003; James & Embry, 2001), and the self-consciousness and threat generated when girls and women are viewed as sexual objects at the pool, beach or gym by boys and men (e.g., James, 2000).

Whatever the space alone suggests to someone, how the space is inhabited by others will typically have far more significance and impact. Regular events such as festivals may be in the same place every year, but it is the familiar arrangements of objects and people that define the event and thus the space (see, for example, Kyle & Chick, 2007). One may also be encouraged or discouraged from activity based simply on observations of other participants. As noted in our earlier discussion on discrimination, even where there is no sense of ownership, the level of attractiveness of a location, an event, or an activity goes up dramatically if one sees similar or familiar others in that context. There are other reasons for ethnic and racial differences in participation in various venues and activities (see Shinew, Floyd, & Parry, 2004), but anticipated comfort in that context depends to some extent on its use by similar others. It may also be the explanation for why immigrants often choose to organize leisure among themselves rather than participate in the activities of the host country (e.g., Tcha & Lobo, 2003). These themes will be examined further in the next chapter.

Social norms may also be constraining or facilitating. This is noticeable in a wide variety of activities and venues, but perhaps the most determining factor is gender. The fact that boys and men are expected to participate in and enjoy watching sports is an encouragement to them (though that may be oppressive in its own way), but girls who participate in sports, particularly those sports that have a more male-exclusive history, such as football, combat sports, and more high-adventure activities, tend to do so at their social peril. They may be ostracized or may have their femininity and sexual orientation questioned. Of course, this is changing and gender norms are no longer as strong as they once were, but their influence persists, especially among younger girls (Warren, Mitten, & Loeffler, 2008). That these and other norms may be resisted in leisure settings is a subject we turn to at the end of this chapter.

Physical illness and disability are also constraining in significant ways, even beyond the obvious physical limitations. When considered in the constraints literature, they are generally discussed as *intrapersonal constraints*, that is, as internal individual factors such as discussed in Chapter 8. But the losses that are experienced in such circumstances usually involve others. Leisure companions who may have been there for an able-bodied and well person are suddenly no longer there. Furthermore, people with illness and disabilities are often stigmatized and even blamed for their conditions (Aronson, 2008; Lerner, 1980; Montada & Lerner, 1996). Social isolation is often the result. Thus, while leisure may be important in transcending the event (see Chapter 12), the *loss* of leisure experience is often prominent in defining the event. The "illness" experience of a disability frequently includes the loss of relationships and abilities as sources of pleasure, enjoyment, and self-expression (Kleiber et al., 1995). One grieves for those things as part of the self that must be relinquished. However, with such events also come two competing tendencies: (1) the readiness for experimentation/differentiation—the events themselves are turning points, and (2) the need for continuity/familiarity to stabilize oneself. Continuity of interests should not be taken as a lack of development, however, as the change created by the event itself requires integration and assimilation, a kind of "restorying" in its own right. In such cases, it is clear that life has changed dramatically. The choices available will determine how well one can reinterpret the change into a meaningful life story. Disability and illness can thus be facilitators of leisure. They lead to new activities and new relationships that are selected and formed to redeem life in some meaningful way around new pleasures and more meaningful experiences (Kleiber et al., 2008).

The *size* of a group of fellow participants can also be both a facilitator and a constraint. Indeed, *social facilitation theory* (Zajonc, 1965) is based on the premise of "the more the merrier" when the task/activity to be performed or engaged in is familiar and well-learned; on the other hand, the more of a crowd there is to witness the learning or performance of an unfamiliar task or skill, the more disruptive and self-consciousness-inducing it is. This is also related to the principle of crowding, which has attracted a lot of attention in resource-management research (e.g., Manning, 1999; Vaske & Donnelly, 2002). While the "carrying capacity" of a place may be judged with respect to risks to the physical environment, among other things, it is also a subjective matter influenced by the experience of crowding. Crowding in turn is oppressive when it is associated with extreme temperatures (i.e., when people are uncomfortable), with people doing activities that have inconsistent values (e.g., the noise made by snowmobilers when quiet and solitude are sought by cross-country skiers), or when the subject or activity at hand is neither interesting nor absorbing (Worchel & Brown, 1984). Conflict among users may result in such cases. And generally, high density will exacerbate whatever emotion (positive or negative) that people are experiencing. Thus, passionate concertgoers will embrace a crowd while the sight of masses of people at the entrance to a large city will often be unnerving.

Finally, in returning to the idea of self-socialization, we need to recognize that there are "social affordances" in the environment itself that signal one to either approach or avoid. As noted earlier, affordance indicates what one might derive as the result of an encounter with a particular context. And most research on affordance addresses the physical environment, but there is research on social affordance as well. In a social situation, as was suggested earlier, the potential to be relaxed and unselfconscious may be judged in that way. So an older man entering a bar that is primarily populated by younger people who regard him skeptically may see little affordance for sociability. Indeed, eye contact, posture, and other nonverbal cues will often communicate the level of comfort to be expected in a situation (Kleiber, Wade, & Loucks-Atkinson, 2005; McArthur & Baron, 1983). Social support also suggests more than just encouragement and companionship in doing activities; there is a kind of scaffolding afforded by others in the leisure environment or others behind the scenes (Larson, 2000). A study of older participants in lifetime physical activity demonstrated how important a supportive peer group was to initiating and continuing participation (Orsega-Smith, Payne, Mowen, Ho, & Godbey, 2007).

Resistance to Social Influence

In this chapter, we have reviewed a wide variety of ways in which leisure behavior and experience are influenced by other people, either directly or indirectly. Certainly roles we play in school, at home, and at work have been defined by others before us and are quite determining. And we are subject to the same principles of human nature—modeling and social learning, conformity, and persuasion, among others—that influence all forms of social behavior including leisure activity and experience. But is it inevitable that we will respond to such influences? Are we self-determining? Can we resist? And how about you? Have you found yourself saying "No, I don't want to do that," in spite of some strong push to go in a particular direction? As it turns out, leisure with all its freedom is a perfect context in which to resist the forces that seem burdensome and limiting and that may be destructive.

Of course, some resistance may be largely about rebelliousness, defiance, or even just self-indulgence as when authoritarian parents, teachers, or law enforcement officials limit expressive activities. There is certainly some wicked fun and even some beneficial self-assertion in doing so, but there is rarely a broader agenda in such actions, whether it be in taking on the establishment or asserting one's individuality. In fact, resistance in adolescence may come in treating the *peer culture* as the source of coercion. With respect to drug and alcohol use, the large population study of Caldwell and Darling (1999) referred to earlier may be instructive. Being in unstructured situations, partying and hanging out, and having peers who were users was strongly associated with drug and alcohol use; but there were a large number who apparently resisted peer influence under those conditions. Recalling the self-determination model of Ryan and Deci (2000) that we reviewed in Chapter 5, the fact that parental involvement was a mitigating factor in reducing the influence of the other variables in that study may have suggested compliance to parental wishes. But it is at least as likely that the values that enabled some to resist peer influence were introjected and internalized.

As noted earlier, stereotypical gender-typed leisure involvement can constrain women and men's behavior in a variety of life domains, if they reinforce traditional views of "femininity" and "masculinity" (Shaw, 1994) and thereby discourage self-expression. But, leisure involvement can also be a form of resistance against such role constraints (Auster, 2001; Freysinger & Flannery, 1992; Shaw, 2001, 2006; Wearing, 1998), as when older women join social groups like the "Red Hat Society," where they can dress and be expressive in a manner that is atypically playful and even outrageous (Yarnal, et al., 2008), or when older women and men engage in competitive sports (Dionigi, 2006). Presumably, when women engage in certain types of physical recreation (Bialeschki, 1990) and highly competitive sports (Dionigi,

2006; Griffiths, 1988; Kleiber & Kane, 1984), for example, the dominant views in society about what women can and should do are challenged. Whether society is effectively changed by such resistance, and how individuals who resist are themselves changed, is a subject we take up in Chapter 12, when we examine the impact of such defiant activities.

10

Race, Ethnicity, Culture, and Leisure

Preview

As with the previous chapter, and in contrast to the preceding section on individual differences, we continue to seek to understand the power of the situation in determining behavior. Race, ethnicity, and culture may come to have an enduring influence on the behavior of individuals, but we first need to recognize that these concepts are social constructions that assert their influence as collective conditions. Of course, the same can be said about age and gender, being defined as they are by social and cultural norms and movements. But age and gender are also commonly construed as individual difference factors, and we have chosen to view them as such in this book. Race, ethnicity, and culture, on the other hand, operate more clearly in socio-historical context, and although they may come to be integrated at an individual psychological level, we treat them here as contextual/situational determinants of leisure behavior.

We begin this chapter by defining and differentiating among race, ethnicity, culture, and other related terms before discussing why those of us who employ a social psychological approach to leisure need to understand these concepts. We then outline research that has examined the effects of race, ethnicity, and culture on objective leisure (e.g., activity participation, park visitation) and subjective leisure (e.g., needs, motivations, constraints, and experiences) phenomena, and the explanations that have been put forth for why differences were found. We conclude by describing how research on race, ethnicity, culture, and leisure might inform and direct recreation practice, but we also caution that past research in this area, by overemphasizing difference and underemphasizing similarity, may have actually restricted our understanding of leisure and leisure behavior.

Introduction

Race, Ethnicity, Culture, and Other Related Terms

Race and ethnicity are not identical concepts. *Race* is concerned with shared physical features (e.g., skin color, eye shape) whereas *ethnicity* is concerned with shared socio-cultural qualities (e.g., language, religion, values, traditions, ancestral origin, food preferences, family patterns). Although use of race to classify people has a long history (Painter, 2010) it became prevalent around the same time White (or Caucasian) colonial leaders "deliberately selected Africans to be permanent slaves" (Smedley & Smedley, 2005, p. 19). Because this classification system was not only categorical but hierarchical, it was critical for Whites to differentiate themselves from Blacks, which they did by defining the latter as individuals who had *any* known African ancestors (the so-called "one drop rule"). Over time Whites slotted other racial groups between themselves and Blacks, including Asians, Native Americans, and even Irish immigrants, who, upon their arrival in North America, were considered non-White in part because of their Roman Catholic faith (Ignatiev, 1995). The one-drop rule, and the capacity for some groups to be classified as non-White for non-physical reasons and then to "become" White at a later date makes obvious the arbitrariness of the racial classification system (Lee & Bean, 2004). But while race clearly was and is a socially constructed concept, it does not mean that it did not and does not have at least two important social consequences. First, racial discrimination in school, at work, and during leisure continued after slavery was abolished and continues today. Second, even though a person may have "inherited" his or her racial category, he or she may now freely and actively self-identify with this racial identity. On the other hand, as interracial marriage has become more common, the same person could now self-identify as being biracial or even multiracial, an option not available to her or his ancestors.

In hindsight, we now know that the Irish who came to North America—with their shared language (Irish Gaelic), religion (Catholicism), ancestral origin (Ireland), food and drink preferences (Irish stew, Guinness beer), traditional arts (jigs, reels, step dancing), et cetera—are an example of an ethnic rather than a racial group. But much in the same way a person may self-identify with one (or more) racial category, so too may she or he self-identify with one (or more) ethnic category. For instance, many of the people who emigrated from Ireland to the United States in the nineteenth century likely continued to see themselves as solely "Irish," with only their children, grandchildren, or even great grandchildren recognizing the effect America's socio-cultural qualities—with its shared language (English), food and drink preferences (turkey, bourbon whisky), arts (Mark Twain's stories, square dancing), and values (individualism)—had on them. Only after this recognition occurred would these later generations likely begin to self-identify as "Irish-Americans," and it might be a few more generations (if at all) before only "American" remained. This example of *acculturation* is, of course, somewhat simplistic, and so we will examine this process more fully in a future section.

There are a few other concepts that require clarification. First, in the previous paragraph we described how a person's self-identity could change when she or he moved from one place (Ireland) to another (the United States). But what if a man stayed in Ireland? Or what if a woman's great-great-great-grandfather came from Ireland, but she has always lived in the U.S., speaks only English, eats turkey on Thanksgiving, watches *American Idol*, loves the NFL, and self-identifies solely as American? In both of these cases, we are describing *culture* rather than ethnicity. Although there are many different definitions of culture, Chick (2009) argues that Goodenough's is the best for explaining leisure behavior. According to Goodenough (1996), culture is both phenomenal (i.e., group characteristics that allow distinct cultures to be distinguished from one another) and ideational (i.e., what members of a group have to know in order to be accepted). Typically, researchers use the phenomenal approach to inform the ideational approach (Chick & Dong, 2005), and so focus on how persons self-identify to explain their behavior. Second, some researchers believe race and ethnicity occasionally overlap and therefore they use the phrase *racialized ethnicity* (Omi & Winant, 1994). African Americans could, potentially, fall into this category, given their classification as Black during and after slavery, in conjunction with certain shared socio-cultural characteristics (musically, for example, the development of blues, jazz, and more recently rap and hip-hop comes to mind). Third, in the U.S., reference is sometimes made to *people of color*, which suggests everyone who is non-White, whereas in Canada the federal government uses the phrase *visible minority group* to describe people who are non-White and who are not Aboriginal (i.e., Indian, Metis, or Inuit; Statistics Canada, 2003).

Although leisure researchers (Gramann & Allison, 1999; Stodolska & Walker, 2007) are often concerned with the tendency to lump together or "homogenize" different groups (e.g., Chinese, Japanese, and Korean study participants), members of these groups may occasionally self-identify as such (e.g., as East Asians) because they feel they share certain *pan-ethnic* characteristics. Besides history and geography, these shared qualities could also include religion and values, with, for example, Buddhism and Confucianism being prevalent among East Asians, and Islam and *Sharia* (or Islamic Law) being predominant among Arabs. Shared language and culture as an outcome of colonialization could also lead to pan-ethnicity, as illustrated by Spain's rule over people in North, Central, and South America, the Caribbean, and even parts of Africa and Asia, all of whom may self-identify as Hispanic or Latino.

Relevance for the Social Psychology of Leisure

When a leisure researcher writes a journal article, typically in the first page or two she or he will address the question, "So why does this topic matter?" In terms of race, ethnicity, culture, ancestry, et cetera, there are at least three reasons why it is important for those of us who use a social psychological approach to leisure to understand these concepts and to employ this understanding in our daily research or practice: (1) leisure is a basic human right, and the social psychology of leisure can help ensure this right is experienced equally (though not necessarily similarly); (2) the United States and Canada are both undergoing major socio-demographic change, and this change will affect how leisure is conceived, experienced, and delivered in the future; and (3) the Chinese, Japanese, Korean, and Indian economies have grown rapidly over recent decades, with two outcomes of this growth being increased leisure availability and increased interest in studying leisure from a social psychological perspective. Each of these three points is discussed more fully below.

In 1948 the United Nations General Assembly adopted the Universal Declaration of Human Rights. According to the Declaration, everyone is entitled to all the rights and freedoms set forth within it, "without distinction of any kind, such as race, color, sex, language, religion, political or other opinion, national or social origin, property, birth or other status" (United Nations, n.d.). Twenty-seven fundamental human rights are identified, including the right to equality before the law (Article 7); free movement within one's country and to other countries (Article 13); freedom of thought, conscience, and religion (Article 18); free choice of employment and equal pay for equal work (Article 23); and, most importantly for us, "the right to rest and leisure, including reasonable limitation of working hours and periodic holidays with pay" (Article 24).

Article 24 specifically and the Universal Declaration generally are important, from a social psychology of leisure perspective, for four reasons: first, the Article's wording suggests that leisure is both an objective phenomenon (because leisure is seen as free or spare time) and a subjective phenomenon (because "including" means leisure is not limited to only free or spare time). Second, because social psychology of leisure researchers are concerned with the objective aspect of leisure, they may be best able to determine if the right to free time is enjoyed equally, regardless of a person's race, ethnicity, culture, ancestry, or religion. Third, because social psychology of leisure researchers are concerned with the subjective aspect of leisure, they may be best able to determine if people's perception of and experiences during leisure are similar or different across racial, ethnic, cultural, ancestral, and religious groups. Finally, because social psychology of leisure research informs leisure practice, it is important that current and future recreation practitioners understand that leisure is a basic human right *and* that it may, for various reasons to be elaborated shortly, be similar and different, objectively and subjectively, depending on a person's race, ethnicity, culture, ancestry, or religion.

There is little doubt the world is changing—economically, politically, and socio-demographically. The last is a product of: (1) increased or decreased *life expectancy* rates in some countries or among certain groups in some countries, (2) increased or decreased *fertility* (birth) and *mortality* (death) rates in some countries or among certain groups in some countries, (3) increased or decreased *immigration* (arrival) and *emigration* (departure) rates in some countries or among certain groups in some countries, or (4) a combination of all three. Among the nations experiencing the greatest increases and decreases are the United States and Canada. Given this information, we believe it is crucial for those of us who study and employ social psychology of leisure concepts and theories to understand the socio-demographic changes taking place if we want to fully understand the increasingly diverse popula-tions—whose leisure behavior may not always be the same as our own—we will be a part of in the future.

In 2007, there were slightly less than 300 million people in the United States, with 76% reporting being only White, 12% being only Black or African American, 4% being only Asian, 2% being two or more races (Black and White, for example), less than 1% being American Indian or Native Alaskan or Hawaiian, and the remainder being "some other race" (U.S. Census Bureau, n.d.). As we learned earlier, however, race is a socially constructed concept. This point is apparent in two ways: first, by the Census' decision to include "one or more races" as a category, an option not available in the 1990 census. This inclusion could be called the "Tiger Woods effect," as the celebrated golfer describes himself as being "Cablinasian," a combination of Caucasian, Black, Indian, and Asian (Wu, 2002). Second, 15% of census respondents also self-identified as being ethnically (or, more accurately, pan-ethnically) Hispanic or Latino, with over 40% of this number having self-identified earlier as being "some other race." Although this outcome reflects many Hispanics' view that other racial groups exist besides those included in the census, it also caused considerable consternation in many federal agencies that were not prepared for reporting this category (Swarns, 2004). As a result, there have been ongoing discussions about deleting the "some other race" classification from future U.S. censuses.

The "some other race" category has, in fact, become such an issue that the U.S. Census has not incorporated it in some of its recent reports, includ-ing its population projections by race and Hispanic self-identification. Still, there is great value in looking at these projections for selected years (see Table 10.1). Some of the key socio-demographic changes that are projected in Table 10.1 include: (1) while the majority of people will likely still report being a single race, the percent who report two or more races will double by 2050; (2) the percent of people reporting only White will decrease by 5%, while the percent of people reporting only Asian will nearly double, by 2050; (3) those who self-identify as non-Hispanic White alone will no longer be the majority by 2050; and (4) the percent of people who self-identify as Hispanic will nearly double by 2050 (U.S. Census Bureau, 2008).

Canada, too, will undergo significant socio-demographic change in the future. For example, according to the 2006 census (Statistics Canada, 2010) 16% of Canadians were visible minority group members (meaning non-White but not Aboriginal), with this percentage being even higher in major urban centers such as Toronto and Vancouver. Although this national figure is much greater than the 5% reported in 1981, it is much lower than that projected for 2031, when it is estimated that around 31% of Canada's population will be visible minority group members (Statistics Canada, 2010). Interestingly, the number of people reporting their ancestry as being only Canadian also grew from 1% in 1981 to 23% in 2001, with a slightly smaller percentage stating that their ancestry was Canadian and from one or more other ethnic groups (Thomas, 2005). According to Thomas this "ethnic realignment" may be the result of a variety of factors, including Canada's particular democratic institutions and collective achievements (e.g., multiculturalism, universal health care), a desire to differentiate themselves from both Americans and recent immigrants (most of whom are visible minority group members), as well as changes in how the census is conducted (as late as 1990, for instance, census interviewers were told to dissuade people from responding "Canadian"). Thus, it appears there are three major trends transforming Canadian society: (1) the growing number of visible minority group members, with Chinese and South Asians (who are generally from India or Pakistan) being the two largest ethnic and pan-ethnic groups; (2) the rising number of people who say they are either solely or partly Canadian; and (3) the increasing number of people who self-identify as Aboriginal.

The world is changing economically as well as socio-demographically. According to the World Bank (2009), China's Gross Domestic Product (or GDP, meaning the total value of all the goods and services produced in a country in a year) is now larger than that of Germany, France, and the United Kingdom, and trails only that of Japan and the United States. Similarly, India's GDP is ranked just below Canada's (12th), while South Korea's GDP is ranked

Table 10.1 U.S. Population Projections

Category	2010		2020		2050	
One race	304,734	(98%)	333,913	(98%)	422,828	(96%)
White	246,630	(79%)	266,275	(78%)	324,800	(74%)
Black	39,909	(13%)	44,389	(13%)	56,944	(13%)
Asian	13,415	(5%)	18,756	(5%)	34,399	(8%)
American Indian or Alaskan Native	3,188	(1%)	3,759	(1%)	5,462	(1%)
Native Hawaiian or Pacific Islander	592	(<1%)	734	(<1%)	1,222	(<1%)
Two or more races	5,499	(2%)	7,474	(2%)	16,183	(4%)
Non-Hispanic White alone	200,853	(65%)	205,255	(60%)	203,347	(46%)
Hispanic	49,726	(16%)	66,365	(19%)	132,792	(30%)
Total Population	310,233	(100%)	341,387	(100%)	439,010	(100%)

Note: Numbers in thousands. Percentages may not add up to 100% because of rounding.

just below Australia's (14th). The phenomenal growth in these countries' economies has led to increased leisure time and leisure consumption for many. (However, in China's case, the reverse could also be argued, as the government there doubled the number of major holidays in 1999 in an attempt to stimulate domestic consumption and so avoid an economic downturn; China-Window, 2004.) Readers may wonder why they should care about leisure and leisure studies in Asia, but there are at least three compelling reasons for doing so. First, as we have already learned, an increasing number of immigrants to the United States and Canada come from China, India, and to a lesser degree, other Asian countries such as Korea. Understanding these people's leisure behavior *before* they leave their native countries could help us better understand their leisure behavior *after* they arrive in their chosen countries; and this knowledge in turn could help recreation practitioners develop programs and services that could make the immigration experience less stressful. Second, China will be the fourth largest outbound-tourism market by 2020, with nearly 100 million Chinese visiting other countries (World Tourism Organization, 2000). Being able to identify and satisfy these Chinese travelers' needs and motivations could be crucial if a company or community wants to attract others from that country. Third, undertaking cross-cultural comparative research (between, for example, Americans and South Koreans) could prove beneficial for the leisure studies field. A discussion of how exactly these benefits might accrue will have to wait, however, until after we have examined existing research on race, ethnicity, culture, and leisure.

Overview of Research on Race, Ethnicity, Culture, and Leisure

Though research on race, ethnicity, and culture has increased greatly since the first edition of *A Social Psychology of Leisure* was published in 1997, Floyd, Bocarro, and Thompson (2008) believe "we still have far to go." Floyd and colleagues base this assertion on a systematic review of all of the articles published in five major leisure studies journals: *Journal of Leisure Research*, *Journal of Park and Recreation Administration*, *Leisure et Societe*, *Leisure Sciences*, and *Leisure Studies*. According to their calculations, from their inception to 2005, these 5 journals published 3,369 articles, with slightly less than 5% of this total being identified as having race, ethnicity, or culture as a major focus. These 313 articles fall into 19 "thematic categories," with the top 5 being "commentaries/theoretical discussions" (13%), "activity participation/preferences" (12%), "outdoor recreation" (9%), "race relations" (8%), and "leisure constraints" (7%).

That the largest category indicated by Floyd et al. (2008) is concerned with essays and theories is not surprising given that, while a number of leisure scholars argue that this area is under-researched, many of the same scholars also hold that research in this area could lead to the development of new and improved leisure concepts, theories, and frameworks. With regard to their next largest categories (activity participation/preferences and outdoor recreation), we see these two and a third smaller category (race/ethnicity, travel, and tourism) being quite similar as all three focus on variation in participation or visitation levels. In social psychological terms, we would call this "super theme," representing 22% of all of the research conducted in this area, *leisure as an objective phenomenon*. In contrast, we would combine Floyd and associates' fifth largest category (leisure constraints) with one of their smaller categories (perceived benefits, motivation, and leisure meanings) and call this social psychological super theme, representing 12% of all of the research conducted in this area, *leisure as a subjective phenomenon*. Given the importance of leisure as objective and subjective phenomena in the social psychology of leisure generally (see Chapters 2 and 3), in conjunction with these super themes accounting for over one third of all research conducted on race, ethnicity, culture, and leisure, the remainder of this chapter will focus on these two dimensions.

The Effect of Race, Ethnicity, and Culture on Leisure as an Objective Phenomenon

As we learned above, nearly a quarter of all of the racial, ethnic, and cultural research published in our journals has focused on leisure participation and park and tourist site visitation differences. Arguably, the earliest evidence on racial differences in recreation is found in a United States Outdoor Recreation Resources Review Commission (1962) report that indicated that urban Blacks were "underrepresented" in outdoor recreation activities. Another early racial study (Jung, 1967) found that "Caucasian," "Negro," and "Oriental" elementary school children watched television equally, but that Negro children rode their bikes more than the other two groups, while the Oriental children read more than the other two groups. Jung provided few explanations for his findings (beyond that, the Oriental children had less leisure time because they were often attending language school), but he did caution that most of the comparisons he made were not, in fact, significant. Crandall and Thompson (1978) conducted one of the first cross-cultural studies, comparing the leisure preferences of college students in the U.S. and Uganda. Americans preferred 10 of 21 activities (e.g., sports, outdoor activities) more than Ugandans, while Ugandans preferred four activities (e.g., reading, watching television) more than Americans. In Canada, research on race, ethnicity, and culture began much later than in the U.S., with Hall and Rhyne's (1989) study of 17 ethnic groups in Ontario being among the earliest studies. They found that Chinese residents were more likely to participate in passive activities (e.g., watching television, visiting libraries) compared with those in other ethnic groups.

Most of the early leisure research on racial, ethnic, and cultural differences was largely descriptive, and when explanations were proposed they were usually tentative and seldom theory-based. This began to change in the late 1970s and today the opposite is largely true (Stodolska & Walker, 2007). At least five explanations for why variations in leisure participation and park and tourism visitation have been put forth. Two of these explanations—marginality and subcultural hypotheses (Washburne, 1978) and perceived discrimination—are well-known in leisure studies. A third, lesser-known, explanation—acculturation—has also been employed in leisure studies (Stodolska, 2000; Stodolska & Alexandris, 2004), but seldom from a social psychological perspective. A fourth explanation—ideal affect (Tsai, Knutson, & Fung, 2006; Tsai, Miao, & Seppala, 2007)—originates in mainstream social psychology and, while it has been referred to in our field (Walker & Wang, 2009), how it could result in participation and visitation differences has not been described in detail before. The final explanation—Gomez's (2002, 2006) ethnicity and public recreation participation model—integrates the first three reasons in conjunction with psychosocial benefits (Driver & Bruns, 1999).

Marginality and Subcultural Hypotheses

According to Washburne (1978), "underparticipation" in a leisure activity occurs when members of a racial or ethnic group are either not encouraged or allowed to be part of the larger society because of "poverty and the various consequences of socioeconomic discrimination [e.g., inadequate transportation, lack of nearby facilities]" (p. 177), or when group members' norms, values, and leisure-socialization patterns do not match up with that activity. Washburne called his first proposition or hypothesis *marginality* and his second proposition the *subcultural* (or, even more confusingly, the "ethnicity") hypothesis. Testing these alternatives usually involved "controlling" for poverty and socioeconomic discrimination (by comparing members of different ethnic or racial groups who had similar income levels) and then examining if the groups still participated in an activity at different levels. If not, the marginality hypothesis was supported; if so, the subcultural hypothesis was supported. These two hypotheses guided most of the research on racial and ethnic leisure differences during the late-1970s and early- to mid-1980s, with the subcultural hypothesis generally garnering more support (Gramann & Allison, 1999). However, researchers also found that neither hypothesis explained racial and ethnic leisure differences very well, which led a number of scholars to call for new concepts and theories to be developed and tested (Floyd, 1998; Gramann & Allison, 1999; West, 1989). Thus, a third explanation—perceived discrimination—was proposed.

Perceived Discrimination

In contrast with the discrimination Washburne (1978) described, perceived discrimination is concerned with a person either feeling unsafe or uncomfortable participating in a leisure activity because of other people (i.e., *perceived personal discrimination*) or being less able or unable to participate in a leisure activity because of the barriers an agency or organization, often unintentionally, has erected (i.e., *institutional discrimination*; see Feagin & Eckbert, 1980). Lee (1972) was among the first to describe the effect of perceived personal discrimination on leisure visitation, and while he did not use this precise term, his report of a Chinese person stating that he did not go to a certain natural area because "It's a White man's park" is certainly consistent with this concept. West (1989), in part because of his belief that the marginality and subcultural hypotheses were deficient, was among the first to systematically examine how perceptions of prejudice could influence leisure engagement. Specifically, when he asked Detroiters about their negative experiences when using local parks, he found that while just 17% of White users reported interracial issues, 37% of Black users did so. In a similar study (Gobster & Delgado, 1992), 14% of African Americans who visited a Chicago park reported feeling discriminated against, followed by 9% of Asian Americans, and 7% of Hispanics. Finally, in a study of visitors to two National Forest areas in Southern California, Chavez (1993) found that while only 3% of Anglo-American visitors felt victimized by an act of discrimination, 32% of all Hispanic and Mexican Americans did so. When asked who the most common perpetrators were, Hispanics and Mexican Americans pointed to law enforcement officials, even though the majority of these officials were other Hispanics.

For comparative purposes, a Canadian study (Statistics Canada, 2003b) found that 35% of visible minority group members felt discriminated against during the past five years (15% rarely, 17% sometimes, and 3% often). Although this study did not ask when, where, or by whom the discrimination transpired, Tirone (1999) discovered that South Asian Canadian teenagers reported experiencing numerous discriminatory acts during community recreation programs, in competitive sport activities, and at YMCAs and summer camps. In contrast, Stodolska and Jackson (1998) found that Polish immigrants in Canada perceived markedly *less* personal discrimination in leisure settings than in other settings (e.g., schools, the workplace, government offices)—a result the researchers believe may have been because Poles, being racially

White, were less easily identifiable and therefore less often targeted than visible minority group members.

The second type of perceived discrimination, institutional discrimination, occurs when "organizational or community-prescribed practices motivated by neither prejudice nor intent to harm nevertheless have a negative and differential impact on members of a subordinate group" (Feagin & Eckbert, 1980, p. 12). Unfortunately, "little research has been done to identify how [leisure] agencies, either implicitly or explicitly, erect institutional barriers that inhibit access to programs" (Gramann & Allison, 1999, p. 291). Scott (2005), however, has developed a brief list of four ways he believes public parks and recreation agencies could commit institutional discrimination, including: (1) taking a too "entrepreneurial" approach, by focusing on fees, marketing, and privatization, thereby neglecting social equity; (2) overemphasizing customer loyalty and therefore overlooking inclusion; (3) having a lack of staff diversity and little diversity training; and (4) having too narrow a conception of need and assuming that it is equally easy for everyone to "just do it."

Acculturation

Because much of the socio-cultural change mentioned earlier is driven by immigration, leisure scholars have begun to examine how *acculturation* affects activity participation. Acculturation refers to the changes an individual or cultural group experiences as a result of contact with another cultural group (Berry, Poortinga, Segall, & Dasen, 2002). Stodolska (2000), for example, looked at how Polish immigrants' leisure activities changed after they arrived in Canada. Although immigrants' starting and ceasing behavior was similar to that of a non-immigrant sample conducted in the same province (Jackson & Dunn, 1988), Stodolska identified three unique themes: (1) *latent demand*, where "after having settled in Canada, immigrants found themselves released from constraints that had blocked their participation in desired outdoor and exercise-oriented activities" in Poland (p. 57); (2) the *forbidden fruit effect*, where new activities were engaged in not because of intrinsic interest (as with latent demand) but because of their novelty; and (3) the *demonstration effect*, where new activities were participated in because of their perceived popularity among either "mainstream" Canadians or other Polish immigrants.

A follow-up study (Stodolska & Alexandris, 2004) examined the role recreational sports played in Polish and Korean immigrants' adaptation to living in the United States. Low levels of participation were generally found, which was not surprising given that "sport and physical recreation are typically quite low on the priority list of immigrants who struggle to adjust to the new environment, who often hold several low-wage but physically demanding jobs and who have hardly any free time available" (p. 393). Still, variations in the level, and more importantly the type, of sport engaged in were uncovered, with three distinct themes being evident: (1) sport, either as a participant or as the parent of a participant, helped immigrants learn more about life in America and establish social contacts with "mainstream" Americans; (2) sport participation helped preserve traditional ethnic values; and, (3) sport participation was a manifestation of the demonstration effect.

According to Berry (1970; see also 2009), besides *assimilation* (where an immigrant prefers to become absorbed into the "mainstream" culture and so shed her or his heritage culture) and *separation* (where an immigrant prefers to hold on to his or her heritage culture and tries to keep the mainstream culture largely at bay), two other acculturative "strategies" are possible: *integration* (where an immigrant prefers to maintain his or her heritage culture and to be involved in mainstream culture) and *marginalization* (where an immigrant is not only unable or unwilling to maintain her or his heritage culture but also, often for reasons of exclusion or discrimination, unable or unwilling to be involved in mainstream culture). Unfortunately, while Berry's model has been widely used in social psychology, it has seldom been employed in the social psychology of leisure.

Ideal and Actual Affect

Affect is one of the properties researchers often measure when they study the experiences accompanying leisure participation (see Chapter 4). But while measuring how people really feel (or what Tsai, Knutson, and Fung, 2006, call "actual affect") is valuable, measuring how people want to feel (or what they call "ideal affect") could prove equally so. The rationale for this statement is twofold. First, individuals may try to reduce the discrepancy between their actual and ideal affect by participating in specific mood-producing behaviors, including leisure activities (Tsai, Miao, & Seppala, 2007). Second, cultural factors can influence which type of affect an individual considers ideal (Tsai et al., 2006), and this in turn could influence which kind of recreational activities she or he participates in (Tsai et al., 2007). For example, Tsai et al. (2006) found that European Americans preferred high-arousal positive affect (or HAP, including elated, excited, and enthusiastic) more than Hong Kong Chinese, while Hong Kong Chinese preferred low-arousal positive affect (or LAP, including calm, relaxed, and peaceful) more than European Americans. Based on these preferences, we would predict Westerners would be more inclined to engage in HAP-producing leisure activities while Asians would be more inclined to engage in LAP-producing leisure activities—and these predictions seem consistent with Jackson and Walker's (2006) finding that Canadian university students participated in more "active" activities (e.g., exercise, team sports) while Chinese students participated in more "passive" activities (e.g., reading, computer games).

Ethnicity and Public Recreation Participation Model

As is clear from the aforementioned, most of the research on ethnic, racial, and cultural variation in leisure participation and park and tourist site visitation has been relatively limited in its scope. As a result, Floyd (1998) recommended leisure researchers move beyond Washburne's (1978) hypotheses and begin, among other things, to develop more sophisticated frameworks. In response, Gomez (2002, 2006) developed the Ethnicity and Public Recreation Participation (EPRP) model, composed of five factors he felt affected leisure participation, either directly or indirectly: socioeconomic status (which he said reflects Washburne's marginality hypothesis), subcultural identity (which he said reflects Washburne's subcultural hypothesis), perceived (personal) discrimination, acculturation, and perceived benefits of recreation (e.g., it allows you to escape, or to socialize, or to exercise). Using a sophisticated statistical technique with data collected from Puerto Ricans living in the United States, Gomez (2006) was able to test whether the relationships among his six variables (the sixth being recreation participation) were consistent with his expectations. Overall they were, with his final results suggesting that: (1) recreation participation is positively affected by acculturation, perceived benefits, and subcultural identity; (2) perceived benefits, in turn, are negatively affected by acculturation, perceived discrimination, and socioeconomic status; and (3) acculturation not only influences recreation participation, it also positively affects socioeconomic status and negatively affects subcultural identity. Although further testing is necessary to determine if these relationships are consistent across racial, ethnic, and cultural groups, Gomez's model does show promise in explaining variation in leisure participation and park and tourist site visitation in a more systematic manner.

The Effect of Race, Ethnicity, and Culture on Leisure as a Subjective Phenomenon

As noted earlier, two of Floyd and associates' (2008) race, ethnicity, culture, and leisure categories (leisure constraints, and perceived benefits, motivation and leisure meanings) can be combined into a social psychological "super theme" called *leisure as a subjective phenomenon*. This new, more comprehensive category accounted for 38 of the 313 leisure journal articles published on race, ethnicity, culture, and leisure, or about half of those written on leisure as an objective phenomenon. A number of these articles were likely published after Floyd (1998) recommended that researchers not only move beyond Washburne's (1978) hypotheses but that they also give more attention to how race, ethnicity, and culture affect leisure motivations and constraints. In this section, we will examine these and many other research articles to learn more about how certain subjective aspects of leisure are, and sometimes are not, influenced by race, ethnicity, and culture.

General Psychosocial Needs and Leisure Needs

As mentioned in Chapter 5, some research psychologists have sought to identify a complete list of psychological needs while others have tried to identify the most important psychological needs, and still others have sought not only to identify these "core" psychological needs but also to arrange them into a framework. The last is exemplified by Maslow's (1968) needs hierarchy, where physiological needs are positioned at the bottom level, followed by safety and security needs, belongingness and love needs, ego and esteem needs, and, at the top level, self-actualization. Schutte and Ciarlante (1998) argue, however, that while physiological and safety and security needs are shared by everyone, Maslow's other needs are more relevant for Westerners (i.e., people in Europe, Canada, the United States, Australia, and New Zealand) than for East Asians (i.e., people in China, Japan, and Korea). Instead, these researchers believe Asians' top three needs are, from third to most highest: affiliation, admiration, and status (Figure 10.1). Status, Schutte and Ciarlante contend, replaces self-actualization because it is socially directed, whereas self-actualization is personally directed. This difference is consistent with some social psychologists' (Markus & Kitayama, 1991; Triandis, 1995) proposition that while the individual is primary in Western cultures, the group or collective is primary in Asian cultures, an important point and one we will discuss more fully in the upcoming section on self-construal.

Unfortunately, as with Maslow's (1968) hierarchy, leisure research using Schutte and Ciarlante's (1998) framework is relatively rare. A recent study of

Highest	Self-Actualization		Status
	Ego & Esteem		Admiration
	Belongingness & Love		Affiliation
	Safety & Security		Safety & Security
Lowest	Physiological		Physiological
	Maslow (1968)		**Schutte and Ciarlante (1998)**

Figure 10.1 Comparison of Two Needs Hierarchies

spa-goers in Hong Kong is one exception, with Mak, Wong, and Chang (2009) identifying five underlying reasons Asian travelers visited these leisure facilities. Most important was "relaxation and relief," which the researchers interpreted in terms of satisfying Maslow's physiological need; a necessary condition they added before higher level needs could be satisfied. The second and third most important reasons were "escape" and "self-reward and indulgence," neither of which Mak and colleagues explained with reference to either of the needs hierarchies. They did, however, explicate their participants' fourth most important reason—"health and beauty"—in terms of satisfying both Maslow's physiological and Schutte and Ciarlante's admiration needs. In contrast, they did not mention either hierarchy when explaining their participants' fifth most important reason—"friendship and kinship"—which is somewhat surprising, given this explanation appears consistent with both Maslow's belonging and Schutte and Ciarlante's affiliation needs.

Although Mak, Wong, and Chang (2009) did not examine "escape" in terms of either needs hierarchy, they did discuss it with respect to Iso-Ahola's (1982, 1989) seeking and escaping dimensions which were reviewed in Chapter 5. Iso-Ahola held that seeking is a powerful leisure need because people seek satisfaction, including personal satisfactions involving autonomy and competence. He also held that escaping is a powerful leisure need because of the constraining nature of a person's life, particularly her or his work. Escape is also based on the need for optimal arousal; individuals are constantly trying to escape from under- and over-arousing conditions. Mak and colleagues propose that travelers can deal with Hong Kong's extremely fast-paced lifestyle and excessive overstimulation by escaping to a more serene, healthy environment, such as by visiting a spa. The importance of escape for Chinese people is also supported by another study. Wang (2009) had Chinese and Canadian student travelers rate Recreation Experience Preference (REP; Manfredo, Driver, & Tarrant, 1996) items and then she developed separate escaping and seeking scales based on their responses. Chinese university students indicated that escape was a more important reason for traveling compared with Canadian students, whereas Canadian students indicated that seeking was a more important reason for traveling compared with Chinese students.

Potentially, Iso-Ahola's (1982, 1989) seeking and escaping dimensions could also help explain some of the cultural differences Sheldon et al. (2001) found in their comparison of 10 psychological needs. As described in Chapter 5, the U.S. university students in their study rated self-esteem highest, followed by relatedness, autonomy, and competence (with these three not being significantly different). Although self-esteem's top ranking initially appears to conflict with Deci and Ryan's (1985, 2000) proposition that autonomy, competence, and relatedness are the core psychological needs, Sheldon and colleagues noted that self-esteem is sometimes considered to be a component of competence. Notably, however, self-esteem was not the most important need for South Korean university students who also rated the same 10 psychological needs. Instead, for these students, relatedness was rated highest, followed by self-esteem, then autonomy, pleasure-stimulation, and competence (with these three not being significantly different). Given Schutte and Ciarlante's (1998) contention that Asians are more socially directed than Westerners, the discovery that South Korean students rated relatedness as their most important need is not too surprising. On the other hand, given the emphasis placed on autonomy in both social psychology and the social psychology of leisure, its tertiary ranking is surprising. Why this result was found will be discussed in detail in the upcoming section on self-construal.

Motivations for Leisure

Deci and Ryan (1985) held that motivations could be arranged along a continuum depending on how much a motive was either externally or internally regulated (i.e., self-determination theory, or SDT), as was noted in Chapter 6. *External* is the most other-determined motivation. To review further, this motivation is performed to obtain external rewards (so others will feel good about you or privilege you in some way) or avoid external punishments (so others won't feel ashamed of you or deprive you in some way). Next to it and somewhat external is *introjected*. This motive is performed to obtain internal rewards (so you will feel good about yourself) or avoid internal punishments (so you won't feel bad about yourself). *Identified* is somewhat internal and involves valuing a goal as being personally important. *Integrated* is internal and involves assimilating an activity or behavior into the self. Because integration is still instrumental, however, *intrinsic* motivation, which involves interest, enjoyment, and engagement in activities for their own sake, is considered the most internally regulated (or self-determined) motivation. The opposite of intrinsic motivation is *amotivation*, where you either don't know why you are doing an activity or you are doing it only because there is nothing else to do. It should be noted that some researchers (Walker & Wang, 2008) sub-divide SDT's external and introjected motivations into "reward" and "punishment" sub-dimensions.

To date, few studies have examined how race, ethnicity, or culture could affect motivations for leisure. Caldwell and Li (2006), for example, examined the leisure motivations of adolescents in seven cultural and regional groups (Colombia, Germany, Ireland, Nigeria, South Africa, and rural and urban America) using SDT. They found that Nigerian and South African youth reported the highest levels of extrinsic motivation, whereas German, Irish, and rural U.S. youth reported the highest levels of intrinsic motivation. Caldwell and Li added that further research was necessary to determine why these differences existed. Walker and Wang (2008) asked Canadian and Chinese university students to report their motivations for leisure using a modified version of SDT. They hypothesized that Canadian and Chinese students would *not* rate the intrinsic, integrated, external reward, and external punishment motivations differently for several reasons. First, interest and enjoyment, integral aspects of intrinsic motivation (Deci & Ryan, 1985), are basic emotions (Izard, 1977) that are beneficial across all cultures (Sheldon et al., 2004). Second, although the external reward and punishment motivations are concerned with how people think, feel, and behave toward others, participants were told to respond as individuals with respect to their leisure-time activities. As a result, Chinese students were likely less concerned with other people's thoughts, feelings, and behaviors than usual. At the same time, Chinese students were likely less motivated by external promises of rewards and threats of punishment than usual as well. And third, as serious leisure (Stebbins, 1992a) is congruent with integrated motivation, and research suggests that some Asian students engage in serious leisure (Heo & Lee, 2007), it seemed unlikely that Chinese and Canadian students would differ in terms of this motive. Statistical analyses supported all four hypotheses, with the average for each motivation, by cultural group, shown in Figure 10.2. As is evident in this figure, intrinsic motivation was the most important leisure motivation for both Chinese and Canadian students.

Walker and Wang (2008) also hypothesized that Canadian university students would rate the identified, introjected reward, and introjected punishment motivations higher than the Chinese students because: (1) identification involves "conscious valuing of a behavioral goal" (Ryan & Deci, 2000, p. 72),

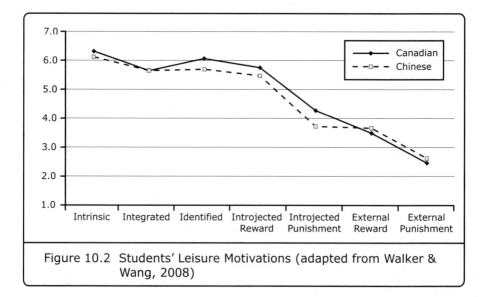

Figure 10.2 Students' Leisure Motivations (adapted from Walker & Wang, 2008)

and research has found that Chinese people generally view leisure less positively than Westerners (Walker, Deng, & Chapman, 2007); and (2) the introjected reward and punishment motivations are concerned with how people think and feel about themselves, and because participants were told to respond as individuals and in regard to their leisure activities, Canadian students were likely more aware of their own thoughts and feelings than usual. At the same time, Canadian students were likely more motivated by internal promises of rewards (pride) and threats of punishment (guilt) than usual. Statistical analyses supported all three hypotheses, with the average for each motivation, by cultural group, shown in Figure 10.2. As is evident from this figure, although identified, introjected reward, and introjected punishment motivations did significantly differ between Canadian and Chinese students the magnitude of these three differences was relatively small. Finally, Walker and Wang proposed that a third concept—self-construal (Markus & Kitayama, 1991; Triandis, 1995)—located between culture and leisure motivations could potentially help explain the similarities and differences they found. What is meant by self-construal, and how this concept could improve our understanding of leisure behavior, will be discussed immediately after the section on race, ethnicity, culture, and constraints to leisure.

Constraints to Leisure

If research on the effects of race, ethnicity, and culture on leisure motivations is relatively rare, research on the effects of race and ethnicity on leisure constraints is comparatively common. As discussed in earlier chapters, three types of constraints are generally discussed in the literature (Crawford & Godbey, 1987): (1) *intrapersonal*, which are individual psychological qualities that affect the formation of leisure preferences (e.g., ability); (2) *interpersonal* constraints, which are social factors that affect the formation of leisure preferences (e.g., friends who prefer other activities); and (3) *structural* constraints, which occur after leisure preferences are formed but before actual leisure participation takes place (e.g., lack of time and money).

As Stodolska and Yi-Kook (2005) recognized, many of the reasons used to explain ethnic and racial groups' "under-participation" in certain leisure activities (e.g., the marginality hypothesis, the sub-cultural hypothesis, perceived personal discrimination) are consistent with leisure constraint theory. What these researchers' comprehensive review of this literature does, however, is to expand these often-cited explanations beyond their usual conceptual boundaries. Stodolska and Yi-Kook, for example, described marginality not only in terms of low income, but also in terms of having less leisure time (because you have to work longer as a result of your low wage) and residential segregation (because you have to live in a low-income neighborhood, you may not have access to the same quality and quantity of leisure programs, services, and facilities as those in higher-income neighborhoods). Similarly, Stodolska and Yi-Kook described the subcultural hypothesis not only in terms of variation in norms, values, and leisure socialization patterns but also in terms of the resource implications that are often associated with these differences. For example, the extended family is an integral part of Hispanic culture, but in the parks and campgrounds at which Hispanic families gather, the facilities—such as a typical six-person, bolted-down picnic table surrounded by trees and bushes—are much more suitable for smaller, more privacy-focused, mainstream American families (Irwin, Gartner, & Phelps, 1990). Finally, these researchers extend our understanding of the barriers commonly faced by immigrants beyond time and money (although they do note these are the most important constraints for immigrants) to include other structural (e.g., lack of English skills) as well as interpersonal (e.g., post-arrival social isolation) constraints.

If, as Stodolska and Yi-Kook (2005) stated, the volume of race, ethnicity, and leisure constraint research is "modest," the volume of culture and leisure constraint research can be described as "minimal." In fact, Chick and Dong (2005) contended that "the disregard of culture as an independent variable in the study of leisure constraints is itself highly constraining" (p. 179). In one of the few leisure studies of any kind conducted in the Middle East, Arab-Moghaddam, Henderson, and Sheikholeslami (2007) found that the five most important constraints for Iranian women were: (1) community structure (which included not only typical structural barriers such as unsuitable equipment but also more institutional barriers such as lack of government concern about leisure, especially leisure for women); (2) home expectations (e.g., family and housework responsibilities, an intrapersonal constraint); (3) economic concerns (a structural constraint); (4) social security (e.g., lack of safety and fear of violence, both intrapersonal constraints that women in the West have also reported experiencing; Bialeschki, 2005); and (5) culture-leisure significance (e.g., lack of information and leisure not being personally important, also both intrapersonal constraints). Cultural traditions, a constraint composed of items such as "restrictions for women in public" and "permission needed to participate," was the sixth most important barrier, slightly below lack of personal time and available companions. In regard to the most important constraint mentioned by study participants, the researchers concluded that the Iranian government's "lack of concern for and subsequent facilitation of activities was likely exacerbated by the cultural issues associated with the role of women in public places" (p. 122).

Most of the other culture and leisure constraint studies have involved Chinese people. For example, Tsai and Coleman (2007) compared Hong Kong Chinese and Australian university students' constraints to regular "active recreation" (i.e., team sports, non-team sports, and physical activities) participation. The two groups did not differ in their perceptions of the importance of time and access constraints, but the Chinese students did perceive financial constraints lower, and interpersonal, competence, and physiological (e.g., feeling tired) constraints higher, than the Australian students. Of these differences, the most dramatic involved financial constraints, with the Chinese students ranking this barrier the lowest overall while the Australian students ranked it the highest overall. Tsai and Coleman believe this may have been because of the importance of "collectivism" in Chinese culture, where economic support for younger family members is expected and highly valued, in contrast with the importance of "individualism" in Australian culture, where younger family members' independence, including their economic independence, is expected and highly valued. Chick and Dong (2005), after conducting interviews with six Chinese and six Japanese couples, found support for the existence of intrapersonal, interpersonal, and structural constraints, but they also proposed that a fourth type of leisure constraint might exist: cultural constraint. Two of their interview fragments illustrate their rationale for this proposition: in one, a Chinese man stated, "Chinese parents cannot accept that their children don't visit them and traditional culture also doesn't allow me to do my leisure activities instead of visiting my parents"; in the other, a Japanese woman stated, "I have to visit my husband's parents during the New Year holiday because my culture doesn't allow me to do leisure activities instead" (p. 342).

Walker, Jackson, and Deng (2007) countered, however, that rather than culture being a new kind of barrier, it should be conceived as an antecedent factor that affects all three current types of constraint. This was the approach Walker and colleagues took in a study of how various intrapersonal, interpersonal, and structural constraints influenced whether Chinese and Canadian university students started a new leisure activity. In summarizing their findings, these researchers stated: (1) all but one of the ten intrapersonal constraints examined differed between the two groups, with Chinese students being more intrapersonally constrained in every instance but one. Of these differences, the two most pronounced involved lack of social support ("The people who are important to me would not support me starting a new leisure activity") and role requirements ("I am less likely to start a new leisure activity if it would hurt me in my role as a friend, student, or son/daughter"). (2) Although the Chinese students were more interpersonally constrained than the Canadian students, Canadians were more structurally constrained than Chinese. Walker et al. believed that some of the cross-cultural differences exhibited in their study may have been a function of their participants having different types of "self-construal" (Markus & Kitayama, 1991; Triandis, 1995).

Self-Construal and Leisure Needs, Motivations, and Constraints

Research on self-construal has grown tremendously during the past 20 years, with the PsycINFO database identifying over 500 published articles on this topic. Self-construal refers to how a person thinks about her or himself in relation to others. According to Markus and Kitayama (1991), the majority of people in the United States, Canada, Western Europe, and Australia and New Zealand, have *independent (or individualistic) self-construals* and so they endorse being unique, asserting oneself, expressing one's inner attributes, and promoting one's own goals. In contrast, the majority of people in Asia, Africa, and Southern Europe have *interdependent (or collectivistic) self-construals* and so they endorse belonging, fitting in, maintaining harmony, restraining oneself, and promoting others' goals. Markus and Kitayama hold that these two types of self-construal "are among the most general and over-arching schemata of the individual's self-system" (p. 230).

Triandis (1995) expanded Markus and Kitayama's (1991) framework by developing a self-construal model that included equality and hierarchy as well as individualism and collectivism. Equality stresses that people should be similar on most attributes, especially status, whereas hierarchy stresses inequality and accepts that rank has its privileges. A two-by-two matrix (Figure 10.3) results, composed of: (a) vertical collectivism (i.e., hierarchy and interdependence); (b) horizontal collectivism (i.e., equality and interdependence); (c) horizontal individualism (i.e., equality and independence); and (d) vertical individualism (i.e., hierarchy and independence). One method Triandis used to measure self-construal was scenarios, and the following example may help readers better understand similarities and differences

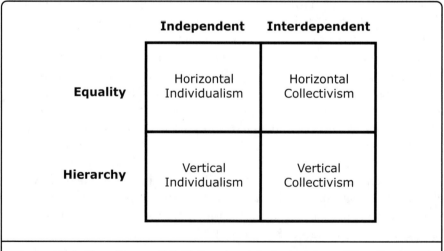

Figure 10.3 Four Types of Self-Construal (adapted from Triandis, 1995)

amongst the four types: *If you had to describe yourself to another person, which of the following descriptions would you choose (1) dutiful, (2) cooperative, (3) unique, or (4) achievement oriented?* (p. 47). "Dutiful" exemplifies vertical collectivism because social cohesion is primary, and cohesion occurs when people (e.g., family members, employees) fulfill their rank's roles and related tasks. "Cooperative" typifies horizontal collectivism because social cohesion is primary, and cohesion occurs when people are equal. "Unique" exemplifies horizontal individualism because it suggests that personal, but not status, differences exist. "Achievement oriented" typifies vertical individualism because it reflects personal and status differences, with competitive success leading to the moving "up the ranks."

In spite of these conceptual differences, Markus and Kitayama (1991) and Triandis (1995) agreed on two important points concerning self-construal. First, individuals, and the cultures that encompass them, are multidimensional but some dimensions predominate over others (see also Chick, 2006, 2009; Li et al., 2007). Thus, Triandis believed that "a vertical individualistic culture, such as the United States, may be composed as follows: horizontal individualism, 40%; vertical individualism, 30%; horizontal collectivism, 20%; and vertical collectivism, 10%" (p. 47). Canadians, Triandis felt, are less individualistic than Americans, but he did not indicate whether they are the same, more, or less vertical and horizontal. In contrast, Triandis (1994) held that Chinese are approximately 70% collectivist (30%–40% horizontal, 30%–40% vertical) and 30% individualist (15% horizontal, 15% vertical). The second point Markus and Kitayama and Triandis agreed upon was that the type of self-construal a person has affects her or his needs, motivations, emotions, and cognitions. This proposition is important for the social psychology of leisure because: (1) needs, which are often satisfied through leisure (see Chapter 5), could differ by self-construal; (2) motivations, which help predict leisure participation (see Chapter 6), could vary by self-construal; (3) need satisfaction facilitates motivation (Deci & Ryan, 2000), and self-construal could affect this process; (4) leisure motivations interact with leisure constraints (Jackson, 2005), and if self-construal influences leisure motives, then it likely influences leisure constraints too (Walker & Virden, 2005); and (5) if self-construal affects emotion and cognition, and we know that certain emotions and cognitions are associated with leisure experiences (see Chapter 4), then self-construal could shape the kind of leisure experience a person has or even whether she or he defines that experience as leisure.

Walker, Deng, and Dieser (2001) examined the effect self-construal had on the expressed leisure needs of Chinese-Canadian and Euro-North American outdoor recreationists. Because these researchers believed the commonly used Recreation Experience Preference scales (REP; Manfredo, Driver, & Tarrant, 1996) did not fully reflect the expressed needs of people with interdependent self-construals, they first developed five new scales (i.e., humility/modesty, group autonomy, group membership, attention to others, and respect for/sensitivity to others) to use alongside four REP-based scales (i.e., introspection, social security, nature/tranquility, and personal autonomy/independence). Findings indicated that, as expected, Euro-North Americans had more independent and Chinese Canadians more interdependent, self-construals. In addition, rather than ethnicity *directly* affecting the perceived importance of expressed needs, it generally did so *indirectly*, in one of three ways: either ethnicity affected independence which in turn influenced a need's importance; or ethnicity affected interdependence, which in turn influenced a need's importance; or ethnicity affected both types of self-construal and both in turn influenced a need's importance. Those with more interdependent selves, for example, rated social security, group autonomy, group membership, humility/ modesty, attention to others, and respect for/sensitivity to others as being more important than those with less interdependent selves. Both more independent and more interdependent people rated nature/tranquility as more important than, respectively, those with less independent and less interdependent selves, however. Based on Markus and Kitayama's (1991) contention that, while "on the surface, such actions could look remarkably similar . . . the exact source, or etiology . . . may be powerfully different" (p. 231), it seems possible that natural environments may be valued by outdoor recreationists with independent self-construals because they facilitate personal expression and self-realization, whereas these environments are valued by outdoor recreationists with interdependent self-construals because they facilitate social cohesion and group realization.

If the importance of expressed leisure needs varies by self-construal, so too could the importance of core psychological needs. Earlier, we described a study (Sheldon et al., 2001) where American and South Korean university students rated the same 10 psychological needs. The U.S. students (who presumably had more independent self-construals) rated self-esteem the highest, followed by relatedness, autonomy, and competence (with these three not being significantly different), whereas the South Korean students (who presumably had more interdependent self-construals) rated relatedness the highest, followed by self-esteem, then autonomy, pleasure-stimulation, and competence (with these three not being significantly different). Assuming once again that self-esteem is an aspect of competence, then it appears that, for independent selves, autonomy, competence, and interpersonal relatedness are all equally important core needs, whereas for interdependent selves interpersonal relatedness is the primary core need, with autonomy and competence being secondary core needs. The former is largely consistent with Deci and Ryan's (2000) basic needs theory (with the exception that autonomy is usually considered predominant), while the latter is plainly at odds with it, although it must be added that these theorists have stated that "in a collectivist culture, people may resonate to group norms so acting in accord with them might lead to them to experience relatedness and autonomy insofar as they fully internalize the collectivist values of their culture" (p. 246).

Markus and Kitayama (1991) and Triandis (1995) also held that self-construal shapes motivations, and this could hold true for leisure motives as well. Building on earlier work (Walker & Wang, 2008), Walker (2009) examined Canadian and Chinese university students' self-construals and motivations for leisure. Results showed that, while some SDT-based (Deci & Ryan, 2000) leisure motives did differ by culture, culture's overall effect was relatively small compared with that of self-construal. Moreover, while neither vertical individualism nor vertical collectivism predicted any of the most self-determined motivations, horizontal individualism predicted three (integrated, identified, and introjected reward), and horizontal collectivism predicted all four (intrinsic, integrated, identified, and introjected reward) of these motives. This suggests that people who are predominantly "horizontal" (i.e., those who emphasize equality over hierarchy) may enjoy, value, and benefit from leisure more than people who are predominantly "vertical" (i.e., those who emphasize hierarchy over equality) By extension, it also suggests that racial, ethnic, and cultural groups that emphasize "horizontalism" may enjoy, value, and benefit from leisure more than racial, ethnic, and cultural groups that emphasize "verticalism."

Although Walker (2009) did not measure whether his participants' core needs were satisfied during leisure, he did refer to this occurrence when explaining why different types of selves might be motivated differently during leisure. As outlined in Chapter 5, organismic integration theory proposes that people attempt to transform socially prescribed norms or standards into personally endorsed values or "self-regulations" (Deci & Ryan, 2000). This internalization process is variable in degree; how well we internalize something depends on how well our needs for autonomy, competence, and interpersonal relatedness are satisfied. Satisfying our need for autonomy, Deci and Ryan (2000) hold, is particularly important, and how much an activity involves "a full sense of volition and choice" (p. 237) largely determines how autonomous or "self-determined" we feel. Additionally, Deci and Ryan (2000) hold that the "gold standard" for self-determined activity is intrinsic motivation. Given the importance of this need and this motive in the social psychology of leisure (see Chapters 4 and 6), we can see how self-construal could affect whether satisfaction of the need for autonomy facilitates, inhibits, or has no effect on intrinsic motivation. We also recognize how self-construal could affect whether satisfaction of the other core needs (i.e., competence, interpersonal relatedness) influences intrinsic motivation.

Iyengar and Lepper (1999), for example, found that while Anglo-American children were most intrinsically motivated when they personally chose aspects of a puzzle experiment, Asian-American children were most intrinsically motivated when they were told that an in-group member (their mothers) had chosen for them. These findings led them to conclude that "the provision of individual choice seems to be more crucial to [Anglo] American independent selves, for whom the act of making a personal choice offers not only an opportunity to express and receive one's personal preference, but also a chance to establish one's unique self-identity" (p. 363).

Other social psychologists have come to same conclusion, but they often use everyday leisure events to illustrate it. Fiske et al. (1998), for example, describe visiting a coffee house in Western countries:

> . . . will you have caf or decaf? Swiss water process or chemical decaffeination? large, medium, or small? Columbian, Ethiopian, hazelnut, vanilla, chocolate raspberry, or house blend? organic or regular? espresso, French roast, or light? cinnamon, chocolate, or nutmeg on top? cream, milk, or non-dairy whitener? brown sugar, refined sugar, aspartame, or saccharin? for here or to go? plastic or paper bag? cash, debit card, or charge? Choosing involves knowing, communicating, and realizing one's own preferences or attitudes; consequently, choice allows people to manifest their individuality, to express themselves, and to be active agents who control their own destinies. (p. 921)

Markus and Kitayama (1991) depict a similar leisure event, but they compare and contrast how it would look for independent and interdependent selves. For example: imagine that one has a friend over for lunch and has decided to make a sandwich for him. If both people have independent selves the conversation might be: "Hey, Tom, what do you want in your sandwich? I have turkey, salami, and cheese." Tom responds, "Oh, I like turkey." Note that the friend is given a choice because the host assumes that the friend has a right, if not a duty, to make a choice reflecting his inner attributes, such as preferences or desires. And the friend makes his choice exactly because of the belief in the same assumption. (p. 229). Here, as with the Anglo-American children in Iyengar and Lepper's study (1991), the core need is autonomy, and it is satisfied through being able to make personal choices. However, if both people have interdependent selves, the conversation might be "Hey, Tomio, I made you a turkey sandwich because I remember that last week you said you like turkey more than beef." And Tomio will respond, "Oh, thank you, I really like turkey." (p. 229). In this case, it is the responsibility of the host to be able to "read" the mind of the friend and offer what the host perceives to be the best for the friend. And the duty of the guest, on the other hand, is to receive the favor with grace and to be prepared to return the favor in the near future, if not right at the next moment (Markus & Kitayama, p. 229). Here, as with the Asian-American children in Iyengar and Lepper's study, the core need is interpersonal relatedness, and it is satisfied through fulfilling one's responsibilities and "taking the role of the other" (Mead, 1934).

Culture and self-construal may affect not only the need for relatedness but also the need for competence. For example, Heine, Kitayama, Lehman, Takata, and Ide (as cited in Heine, Lehman, Markus, & Kitayama, 1999) found that, while Canadians (considered as independent selves) persisted significantly longer on a second creativity test after having been told that they had successfully completed an earlier test, Japanese (considered as interdependent selves) persisted significantly longer on the second test after they had been told that they had *failed* the first test. In interpreting these results, Heine and associates state that in interdependent cultures such as Japan, "the individual has neither the liberty nor the inclination to inflate his or her perceptions of competence . . . . [because] doing so likely would only serve to alienate the individual from others" (p. 771). Thus, for interdependent selves, it is less "being" good that is important than the process of "becoming" better (Heine et al.), because it is the latter that is most likely to satisfy the need for relatedness (see also Triandis, 1995).

In summary, while Fiske et al. (1998) and Markus and Kitayama (1991) provide leisure examples of how self-construal could affect intrinsic motivation through the satisfaction of core needs, most of the research (Heine et al., 1999; Iyengar & Lepper, 1999) on this topic has been conducted in classrooms or laboratories. Though some social scientists argue that still more lab-based research should be performed, others believe a more naturalistic approach is preferable. Waterman et al. (2003), for example, state that "the trade-off for being able to control relevant variables has been the use of activities of limited personal importance or salience in the lives of research participants" (p. 1447). As it happens, only one study of ethnicity, self-construal, need satisfaction, and intrinsic motivation has been conducted in the leisure studies field to date, and it used the experience sampling method.

Walker (2010) asked 31 Chinese Canadians to complete a questionnaire that measured their self-construals and then to respond to watch alarms programmed to ring randomly once every 2 hours, 7 times a day, for 12 days. Each time an alarm rang, participants reported what activity they were doing; their motivation for, competence in, and autonomy during, the activity; and whether they considered the context to be leisure or non-leisure. Results indicated that none of the four types of self-construal interacted with competence and subsequently affected intrinsic motivation. However, Chinese Canadians who were more horizontal-individualistic and who experienced high levels of autonomy reported *higher* levels of intrinsic motivation overall. On the other hand, Chinese Canadians who were more vertical-collectivistic and who experienced high levels of autonomy reported *lower* levels of intrinsic motivation overall, as did Chinese Canadians who were more vertical-individualistic. These results suggest that while it is important to understand how the interactions between individualism and collectivism and autonomy affect intrinsic motivation, equally important is how the interactions between horizontalism, verticalism, and autonomy influence this process. For instance, for horizontal-individualists, it appears that equality and independence may have an additive effect such that autonomy strongly fosters intrinsic motivation. In contrast, for vertical-individualists, it appears that independence may regulate hierarchy slightly such that autonomy inhibits intrinsic motivation, whereas for vertical-collectivists it seems that hierarchy and interdependence may have an additive effect such that autonomy inhibits intrinsic motivation. One potential reason for the last finding is that people who are vertical are more likely to have an external locus of control (Chen, Fok, Bond, & Matsumoto, 2006). This discovery, in conjunction with Chinese people's penchant for less active leisure activities, seems congruent with Mannell and Bradley's (1986) finding that "externals" in a low-structure setting who had more free choice were also less psychologically involved (that is, intrinsically motivated) in a puzzle game.

Finally, leisure motivations, according to constraints theory (Jackson, 2005), interact with leisure constraints, and Walker and Virden (2005) proposed that if self-construal influences motives for leisure then it likely influences constraints to leisure too. Building on their earlier work in 2007, Walker, Jackson, and Deng (2008) examined Chinese and Canadian university students' self-construals and constraints to starting a new leisure activity. Using cluster analysis they identified two distinct Chinese groups: primarily horizontal-collectivist, and a combination of vertical- and horizontal-collectivist. They also identified two distinct Canadian groups: primarily horizontal-collectivist, and primarily horizontal-individualist. Study findings indicated that the two Chinese groups varied in terms of leisure constraints, as did the two Canadian groups, which suggests that self-construal can increase our understanding of leisure constraints and that it is important to test for intra-ethnic as well as inter-ethnic group differences.

Optimal Experiences and the Meaning of Leisure

Of all the different types of leisure experience (see Chapter 4), Csikszentmihalyi's (1975) concept of flow is the most researched. Unfortunately, however, research on how race, ethnicity, and culture might affect flow conditions and characteristics is lacking. In one of the few flow studies conducted with non-Westerners, Han (1988) looked at the experiences of elderly Koreans who had recently immigrated to the United States. Using items from Csikszentmihalyi's research, Han found that "although all respondents agreed that there could be such an experience as flow, only 12 (33%, 6 men and 6 women) recognized at least one quotation as being similar to an experience they had had" (p. 141). According to Han, his findings may have been a result of the measurement technique he used, the age of his participants, or, potentially, cross-cultural differences in the incidence of flow experiences. Another possibility however is that, for Asians, a balance of high skill and high challenge is only one way—and perhaps even a less common way—to experience flow's characteristics of intrinsic motivation, perceived competence, and a changed perception of time. A study of Chinese Canadians' *rumi* (literally, "to enter into" and "to become lost in") experiences supports this proposition. Walker and Deng (2003/2004) found that while all three of these characteristics occurred during *rumi*, high challenge was reported during some (e.g., playing a computer game) but not all (e.g., reading a book) activities. This led the researchers to conclude that *rumi* might be a broader phenomenon, one that includes both flow (Csikszentmihalyi) and absorbing (Quarrick, 1989; Tellegen & Atkinson, 1974) experiences. That flow could vary across cultures is also supported by an experience sampling method study of American and Hong Kong university students. Moneta (2004) found that, while his U.S. participants reported experiencing the highest level of intrinsic motivation when, as Csikszentmihalyi proposed, they perceived *maximum* challenges and skills, his Chinese participants reported experiencing the highest level of intrinsic motivation when they perceived *minimum* challenges and *maximum* skills. Moneta proposed his findings reflected the role Taoism plays in Chinese culture, especially its emphasis on prudence, interconnectedness, and emotional moderation. This proposition is consistent with that of Wang and Stringer (2000), who also put forth that Taoism influenced Chinese leisure through its principles of yielding, softness, slowness, and balance. (See also Liu et al., 2008.)

Potentially, race, ethnicity, and culture could affect not only the nature of a person's experience but also how she or he defines that experience. In Shaw's (1984) Canadian study that we have frequently referred to in earlier chapters, of the six subjective factors that were found to be most closely associated with participants' self-defined leisure experiences, enjoyment and freedom of choice correctly differentiated between leisure and non-leisure the best, with the addition of lack of self-evaluation increasing predictive ability slightly. In contrast, an experience sampling study conducted with Chinese Canadians (Walker & Wang, 2009) discovered that participants differentiated between leisure and non-leisure primarily in terms of high intrinsic motivation followed by low effort and low introjected reward motivation (i.e., pride) when they were alone, and high intrinsic motivation and low introjected reward motivation followed by high closeness and low effort when they were with other people. Surprisingly, perceived freedom contributed very little to predicting leisure in either case.

These findings led Walker and Wang (2009) to conclude that Shaw's (1984) Canadian participants and their own Chinese-Canadian participants' leisure meanings were both similar (i.e., in terms of intrinsic motivation's relevance) and different (i.e., in terms of perceived freedom's relevance, and irrelevance, respectively). Based on this conclusion, Walker and Wang stated that: "Unger and Kernan's (1983) contention that intrinsic motivation is leisure's quintessential quality garners additional support whereas Iso-Ahola's (1999) and other's (Neulinger, 1974) claim that 'a sense of freedom—autonomy—is the central defining characteristic of leisure' (Iso-Ahola, p. 36) is called into question" (p. 11). Other ethnic and cultural research also suggests that perceived freedom may not be leisure's defining attribute. A study of Italian-Australians' leisure meanings (Pereira & Stagnitti, 2008), for instance, found that most of the subjective experiences described by participants could be categorized as intrinsic motivation, while "choice," "freedom," and "autonomy" were not mentioned anywhere in this article's results. On the other hand, a study of Japanese youths' leisure meanings (Nishino & Chinen, 1998) found freedom of choice and freedom from obligation did help define leisure, but so too did intrinsic motivation, and all three of these attributes were much less successful at doing so than positive mood. In conclusion, if perceived freedom's status as the defining characteristic of leisure is in fact questionable, "also questionable, therefore, are the numerous leisure paradigms that have privileged perceived freedom (e.g., Iso-Ahola, Neulinger)—at least in regard to their cross-cultural applicability" (Walker & Wang, p. 12).

Implications for the Social Psychology of Leisure

In this chapter, we have tried to clarify various conflicting and often contentious terms; describe the tremendous socio-demographic and economic changes taking place in North America and East Asia, respectively; and provide an overview of what social psychologists currently know about how race, ethnicity, and culture affect leisure as objective and subjective phenomenon. From a practical perspective, we believe there is great value in understanding the above, as social psychological concepts often inform and direct sport, recreation, and tourism planning, marketing, and programming. But leisure service providers must not only understand these concepts, changes, and findings, they must also consider what the findings mean and how they should behave in response. From a leisure constraints standpoint, for example, how will you as a practitioner respond to a racial, ethnic, or immigrant group member who lacks the funds to attend your classes or the English skills necessary to succeed in them? Or how will you deal with the safety issues this person may face before or after the class, or the personal discrimination she or he may perceive from other participants or even members of your staff? And, more broadly speaking, how will you decide whether the right course of action is to be *informative* (e.g., by translating a brochure on the health benefits of physical activity into Mandarin), *encouraging* (e.g., by having a Mandarin-speaking staff member talk to Chinese groups about the physical activity classes offered at your facility), *facilitative* (e.g., by subsidizing some of the physical activity classes offered at your facility), or *prescriptive* (e.g., by replacing a culturally accepted but passive activity, such as Chinese dominoes, with a new physical activity class because exercising is more "worthwhile")? Based on what we have learned about internalization and psychological reactance alone, the last would seldom be the best choice.

We also believe there is great value in understanding the concepts, changes, and findings described in this chapter from a research perspective. By doing cross-cultural research, we can lessen leisure studies' disciplinary ethnocentrism. Berry, Poortinga, Segall, and Dasen (2002) assert, albeit in regard to mainstream psychology, that "by recognizing the limits of our current knowledge . . . and by seeking to extend our data and theory through the inclusion of other cultures . . . we can reduce the culture-bound nature of the discipline" (p. 9; see also Walker and Wang, 2009). From a promotional perspective, Valentine, Allison, and Schneider (1999) hold that there are many benefits that can accrue from cross-cultural and cross-national studies, including the "opportunity to test and validate the generalizability of leisure phenomena and constructs" (p. 242). Similarly, Stodolska (2000) states that "studying minority groups provides a rare opportunity for expanding theory applicable to human leisure experience in general" (p. 158). Thus, there are sound conceptual and theoretical reasons for conducting more racial, ethnic, and cultural leisure research in the future.

But a third perspective exists, that of leisure researchers who are also members of these "need to be studied more" groups. Iwasaki, Nishino, Onda, and Bowling (2007) support more non-Western leisure research, but they add that Western terminologies and assumptions should not be unduly imposed because cultural concepts are sometimes incongruous—for example, there is no equivalent word in Japanese for the English word "leisure." Liu, Yeh, Chick, and Zinn (2008) also support more non-Western leisure research, but they suggest that "the field of leisure studies often fails to acknowledge that non-Western cultures may have concepts *similar* to the Western idea of 'leisure'" (p. 488) and, further, that "different shades of meaning of the Chinese word *Xiu xian* (in both mainland China and Taiwan) are similar to the different shades of meaning of the English word *leisure*" (p. 485). Thus, while similarities (i.e., the need for more non-Western leisure research) and differences (i.e., whether the Western concept of leisure "makes sense" in non-Western cultures) in these scholars' views are evident, it is also apparent that future racial, ethnic, and cultural leisure research must be done carefully, respectfully, and, ideally, with the active involvement of researchers who are members of the groups being studied.

Although this is the logical time to recommend *what* data on race, ethnicity, and culture leisure researchers should consider collecting, instead we want to advocate *how* researchers (and those who read their research) should consider interpreting their results. Mannell (2005), in response to an article on culture, self-construal, and leisure theory and practice (Walker, Deng, & Dieser, 2005), cited Hoshino-Browne, Zanna, Spencer, and Zanna's (2004) three-generation model of cross-cultural psychological research. In their model: the *first generation* of research was intent on identifying cross-cultural similarities in order to demonstrate the prevalence of psychological constructs; the *second generation* of research was intent on identifying culture-specific phenomena in order to demonstrate differences in psychological constructs; and the *third generation* of research synthesized the two in order to develop a more comprehensive and more realistic view of the effect culture has, and does not have, on psychological functioning. Mannell maintained that leisure studies had become stuck at the second-generation level and Walker, Deng, and Dieser (2005) agreed, suggesting two reasons why this may have happened: first, some leisure scholars are *unintentionally* over-attentive to differences, perhaps because they subconsciously believe this is what editors and reviewers prefer; and second, some leisure scholars are *intentionally* over-attentive to differences. Eagleton (2003), for example, proposed that many postmodern theorists not only would "like a world made entirely out of differences" they "think the world *is* made entirely out of differences" (p. 14). Unfortunately, according to Eagleton, this viewpoint eventually led to the belief that "whatever linked us—whatever was the *same*—was noxious" (p. 45), and a "fetish of difference" (p. 46) subsequently developed.

The result has been slow progress toward a third generation of cross-cultural (and, for that matter, cross-racial and cross-ethnic) leisure research. There have been a few exceptions, however. Walker and Wang (2008), for example, held that their finding that both Chinese and Canadian students reported that their leisure was highly intrinsically motivated supported Chick's (1998) proposition that leisure is universal. According to Berry et al. (2002), *universalism* "adopts the working assumptions that basic psychological processes are likely to be common features of human life everywhere, but that their manifestations are likely to be influenced by culture" (p. 326). In contrast, Berry et al. state that *relativists* assume a general egalitarian stance (e.g., "all people are equal") and explain any differences as being due to cultural contexts that influence people's development. Berry et al. add that *absolutists* place little if any value on culture. From a universalist perspective, therefore, Walker and Wang expected there to be some similarities, but also some culturally influenced differences, in motivations for leisure, and this is what they found.

Three frameworks commonly used in leisure studies have also exhibited a universalistic orientation: self-determination theory (SDT; Deci & Ryan, 1985, 2000), the hierarchical leisure constraints model (Crawford, Jackson, & Godbey, 1991), and the theory of planned behavior (TPB; Ajzen, 1991). Specifically, Walker and Wang (2008) hypothesized that SDT would be cross-culturally applicable (i.e., motivations would be ordered from external to introjected to identified to integrated to intrinsic) but that while Canadian students would be more identified and introjected reward-and-punishment-motivated than Chinese students, the two groups would not differ in their intrinsic, integrated, and external reward and punishment motivations. Results supported SDT's applicability for both cultural groups and cross-cultural similarities and differences were consistent with expectations. Similarly, Walker, Jackson, and Deng (2007) hypothesized that the hierarchical leisure constraints model would be cross-culturally applicable (i.e., constraints would be ordered from intrapersonal to interpersonal to structural), but that Chinese students would be more intrapersonally and less structurally constrained than Canadian students. Findings supported the hierarchical leisure constraints model's applicability for both cultural groups, and cross-cultural similarities and differences were in line with study hypotheses. Finally, Walker, Courneya, and Deng (2006) hypothesized that the TPB would be cross-ethnically applicable (i.e., attitudes, norms, and perceived behavioral control would predict intentions, and intentions would predict behavior), but that injunctive norms would predict lottery play only for Chinese/Canadian males, whereas descriptive norms would predict lottery play only for British/Canadian males. Results supported the TPB's applicability for both ethnic groups and cross-ethnic similarities and differences were consistent with expectations.

In conclusion, while some scholars (Chick & Dong, 2005) have suggested that leisure studies' strong paradigmatic basis in social psychology is partly responsible for the gap in cross-cultural research, we would counter that what is required is not less social psychology but more—albeit of a certain kind. This new, improved social psychology of leisure must be cross-cultural as well as cross-racial and cross-ethnic. By incorporating culture, race, and ethnicity more fully into social psychology of leisure research, we can learn more about how leisure is similar and different across *and* within these groups. This in turn will improve existing leisure concepts, theories, and frameworks, and will lead to the development of new ones, resulting in better practices by those who employ them. There is little doubt that considerable progress has been made since the first edition of *A Social Psychology of Leisure* concluded that there was no comprehensive social psychology of cultural differences; but as the Chinese adage maintains, *lu chang er dao yuan* ("there is a long way to go;" Gao, Ting-Toomey, & Gudykunst, 1996, p. 293).

Section Five

Identifying and Cultivating the Best of Leisure

Impacts of Leisure Experience on Childhood and Adolescence

Preview

Two Players

When Chelsea was just a toddler, her parents were struck by how much more adventurous and imaginative she was than her older siblings had been. Not only did she show a flair for drama in her play with animal puppets and dolls, but she also was frequently found experimenting with utilitarian objects like boxes for their alternative uses or exploring the near environment—first the backyard and then the neighborhood—in an apparently joyful way. How responsible such patterns may have been for her subsequent success in school cannot be asserted with any certainty, but she clearly came to excel in the sciences and creative writing in ways that evoked some of the same curiosity and adventurousness that characterized her early play.

Mario was always a very physical child, engaging readily in "rough and tumble" play with his younger brother and the children who lived in the apartment next door. And despite a broken arm sustained from falling out of a tree in a nearby park at one point, he also seemed to be a "natural" when introduced to the youth sports of basketball, football, and soccer, especially where he could use his energy to "push the envelope." But in spite of the skills he developed in his early involvement with sports, he soon found the structure to be too limiting and instead came to delight in the attentions of others who found his disruptive activities in the classroom amusing. School eventually proved too confining for Mario and some of his "entourage", and they sought other venues for their excitement, eventually turning to illegal activities including drug use.

These are just two cases in a wide-ranging collection of possibilities for the influence of leisure activity and experience in childhood and adolescence. We offer contrasting scenarios here of good and bad effects, but in the pages that follow it will become clear that even the same activity can have multiple effects, good and bad, and that the question of impact depends on the circumstances.

Play as Formative and Therapeutic

The Formative Capacity of Play, Games, and Sport

There is more to the leisure of childhood than play, but we begin with play because it has its greatest impact in early childhood and because, as we saw in Chapter 8, it has distinctive properties that have been the subjects of a great deal of writing and research. While leisure can be directed by extrinsic motivation to some extent (e.g., exercising to lose weight), play is always intrinsically motivated, governed by positive affect and enjoyment and characterized by a degree of divergent thinking, make-believe, or pretense. This latter characteristic gives play much of its alleged value as a breeding ground for inventiveness and creativity. And because it often involves large-muscle physical activity, people often look to play for its physical as well as cognitive benefits. But in this volume our concern has been primarily with social psychological influences on play (in Chapter 9, especially); now we turn our attention to social psychological impacts of that play experience.

The influences of play on patterns of growth derive in large part from the survival values that accrue to species engaging in play and exploration, primarily by promoting behavioral flexibility, or *plasticity* (see Bjorklund, 2007; Brown, 2009; Elkind 2007; Ellis, 1973). By bringing about novel encounters with the environment, learning and adaptation are facilitated (see also Barnett, 1990; Bruner, Jolly, & Sylva, 1976; Christie & Johnson, 1983). A child who playfully and experimentally drops a ball down an embankment and follows cautiously learns about the embankment, the properties of the ball, and her or his own abilities. As discussed in Chapter 4, the sense of growing competence and mastery that such activities create is associated with positive affect. Enjoyment is increasingly recognized as the optimal experience of psychological absorption resulting from a good fit between one's exerted skills and the demands of the environment (Csikszentmihalyi, 1990) rather than simply as pleasure. Because skills improve through repeated encounters with the environment, there is a steadily increasing need for greater complexity in the environment. Thus, enjoyment becomes the psychic energy that fuels much of the process of development.

Play activities allow children to express themselves in enjoyable ways, and *enjoyment*, as noted in Chapter 8, is inherently developmental when it is associated with engagement. Expressive activities are "ontogenetically" prior to instrumental ones (Csikszentmihalyi, 1981). In other words, enjoyment can motivate children to try challenging activities in which they must "work hard" at acquiring new skills and achieving emergent goals, such as wanting to be a chess champion. Both Chelsea and Mario showed these patterns in their early experience. These types of activities can be socially integrative to the extent that they require the young person to speak the language of a wider world (cf. Kleiber, Larson, & Csikszentmihalyi, 1986). For example, the 16-year-old son of a friend of one of the authors developed a collection of baseball cards that he was able to bring as trading material to baseball card and hobby fairs. By carefully researching the value of the cards ahead of time, he was able to successfully engage with other collectors, mostly adults, in the activity of trading. While having fun, he learned some useful lessons: negotiation and other communication skills, long-term planning, and even some financial management. But as was illustrated in Mario's case, whether continuing engagement is constructive or not generally depends on the particular nurturing and facilitating aspects of the environment.

Even in the games children organize themselves, they are exercising certain skills that will continue to be useful. In fact, Elkind (1981), Piaget (1962) and others (e.g., Devereux, 1976; Lever, 1976) have suggested that games and sports are the primary context for children to learn organizational skills, such as the ability to manage and cope with a diversity of perspectives, adjudicate disputes, work for collective goals, and even develop a more sophisticated level of moral reasoning based on reciprocity, learning to take the perspective of others and abiding by rules out of a sense of mutuality rather than just compliance. Elkind (1981) in particular, spoke of the importance of children's self-directed games for the development of social and moral competence:

> I believe that children learn the other side of contracts with other children and with siblings. Here the relationship is one of mutuality; it is not unilateral. In playing and working with other children, young people can begin to expect such behaviors in return for certain favors. In childhood, the rewards for obeying contracts are most often personal acceptance. For example, a child that shows he or she is willing to abide by the rules of the game is permitted to play. It is with peers that children learn the reciprocal nature of contracts and how to be on the giving as well as the receiving end." (p. 133).

Janet Lever (1976) noted that such experiences with game management are far more common to boys during this period of later childhood. Their games show greater role differentiation, interdependence, group size, explicitness of goals, number of rules, and coordination processes than do those of girls, thus conferring on boys an advantage in this kind of "training." But Carol Gilligan (1982) asserted that the style with which girls enter into game playing, protecting relationships rather than the game itself, shows different kinds of social competence. By abandoning games if they became difficult and strain relationships, Gilligan argued, girls show greater sensitivity to each other and an unwillingness to put friendship at risk to preserve a game, thus reinforcing the greater sensitivity girls typically have to protecting relationships. To what extent such tendencies are biologically based (sex-typed) or socially and culturally construed is a matter of some controversy, as we considered in Chapter 8, but clearly play forms and activities can influence and magnify existing differences. As evidence for gender differences, for example, Frydenberg and Lewis (1993) found that in coping with stress, boys tend to get involved in physical recreation and girls typically turn to others for social support. But a case has been made that the interpreters of gender differences in children's games have not looked deep enough—focusing only on the form and structure of the games themselves rather than on the interactional dynamics of even the "simplest" of girls' games. In a study of Hopscotch, Goodwin (1995, 2006) established that while the rules and roles are relatively simple, observers exercise a sophisticated pattern of discrimination in "refereeing" the course of action, often quite competitively and critically, interpreting the rules and execution rhetorically along the way.

In spite of some participation style differences, the fact that many structured and challenging leisure activities are found enjoyable and intrinsically interesting by both boys and girls clearly motivates them to participate; consequently, they have the opportunity to receive the benefits the activities have to offer. For example, in a study of 483 fifth- through ninth-graders, using the experience sampling method, Larson and Kleiber (1993b) examined how children "paid attention" in a wide variety of contexts. They found that "paying attention" was more frequently experienced in self-controlled leisure contexts than other contexts, including schoolwork. These contexts provide opportunities for the development of voluntary control of attention that, while clearly demanding and formative with respect to cognitive capacity, also attune individuals to the wider world. Can play, games, and sports be used then to promote social understanding and improve cooperation and interpersonal understanding?

On one hand, competition can be destructive to understanding, cooperation, and other forms of prosocial (helping) behavior, as has been shown in numerous social psychological investigations (e.g., Aronson, 2008; Fiske 2004), and the realm of games and sports is clearly no exception (see Shields & Bredemeier, 1995, 2001, for reviews). Certainly we are well-aware of the fighting, cheating, and other kinds of destructive behavior that occur in and around sports, at all levels. Participants and spectators (particularly parents) become so intensely emotional and angry that they have to be reminded that "it is only a game." In a field experiment conducted with fifth-graders some years back, the investigators created a 3-week "kick soccer world series" during the recess of an experimental group while a matched control group was engaged in a noncompetitive alternative form of play (Kleiber & Roberts, 1981). When, after the soccer game series, participants were given a *Social Behavior Scale*, a procedure which established the readiness to be generous and altruistic, experimental group participants—those who had played in the series of games—were less inclined to be generous than the control group participants.

On the other hand, sports and games at least require some degree of cooperativeness within teams to be effective as a team, and individuals often learn to subordinate their self-interest ("me") to that of the group ("TEAM"). This is the principle of the *superordinate goal* (in this case, winning) that was established as important to cooperation in the classic Robbers Cave Experiment (Sherif et al., 1961) where campers who had been competing against each other for various resources—generating considerable animosity in the process—found that shared purposes (restoring water to the whole camp) required their collective, cooperative attention. Attitudes between the groups improved as a result. In its application to games and sports, the super-ordinate goal of winning may facilitate in-group (team) cooperation while the competition between teams offers little to enhance their relationships and can even turn ugly. On the other hand, if teams share some responsibility for the creation and management of the game itself, as is true in self-directed games and as was established in Lever's studies, then the preservation of the game can become the superordinate goal.

Applying such principles to the context of public recreation and community sports programs, Jamieson and Ross (2007) reported on the value of such activities for "peace building" and improving relations between ethnically diverse populations in the community. Obviously, the more participants can all take responsibility for the actual management and execution of the events, the greater the likelihood that intergroup relations will be enhanced. The organization "Play for Peace" also attempts to capture the socializing power of leisure and play. The mission of Play for Peace is "to bring together children, youth, and organizations from communities in conflict, using cooperative play to create laughter, compassion, and play." Play is thus intentionally selected in this case for both community development outcomes and its impact on learning.

The Impact of Play on Social Adjustment

The connection of play with cognitive and social development is evident in the earliest stages, but emotional development and adjustment are affected as well. For example, toward the end of the first year, children develop what is called *object permanence* (Piaget, 1954). This is the understanding that people and things continue to exist somewhere even when they are out of the child's presence. (Prior to this change, the egocentrism of infants does not account for a world beyond themselves.) The difficulty with this development is that it also brings an awareness that parents actually leave and go somewhere else and, as a result, separation anxiety can emerge. Most infants and toddlers find "peek-a-boo" a delightful game—a game that would be impossible if a child had not achieved object permanence. Arousal is raised when a big sister hides behind the chair (disappears), and the tension is dissipated with great relief and laughter when she reappears with a resounding "peek-a-boo." Knocking things off their high chairs, much to the chagrin of parents, they learn to look over the edge of the chair tray to see the result. These play patterns speak to the emotional value of play that gives it importance as a resource for children throughout childhood.

Play has a long history of being used to help children deal with emotional problems (Axline, 1947; Erikson, 1963; Landreth, 2002), primarily with the assumption that if anxiety can be at least temporarily reduced enough so that they are able to play, children will use whatever is available in their environment to act out and work through some of their traumas and fears imaginatively. Lynn Barnett (1984) looked at this problem through the somewhat fearful eyes of children waiting for the dentist, seeing that "relevant" toys (those with a medical theme, such as a toy stethoscope) were preferred over irrelevant toys (trucks, dolls, board games, etc.) in the doctor's waiting room. What is closer to our concern here, though, is where play and games can be used to reduce *social* anxieties.

The research on this topic is limited, but early anthropological work suggests that children use play forms to assuage their general anxieties related to child rearing and socialization (Roberts & Sutton-Smith, 1962). The research on the *conflict enculturation model* was reviewed in Chapter 9 when considering how parents and families influenced game playing and leisure preferences. We return to it here as a model of *coping* through play. If you recall those hypotheses, in cultures and subcultures where obedience is stressed in child rearing, children would be more interested in games of strategy, while in societies where success and security was less predictable, games of chance would likely be preferred. In these ways, games serve to *assuage* childhood anxieties. By examining the practices and expressive patterns of well over 56 societies with the Yale Human Relations Area Files, the investigators found support for their hypotheses.

Specific Impacts of Leisure Activities and Experiences in Childhood and Adolescence

LaKeisha almost lost her life in a car accident when she was 12, leaving her partially paralyzed with a head injury and impaired speech. After much rehabilitation, and a period of withdrawal and social isolation, this once very popular girl found that she could both renew acquaintances and establish new ones with people like herself all over the world through the internet, particularly through Facebook. She finally returned to school and used this new venue for expansion of her social self.

Thomas had always been somewhat of an introvert and, unlike many of his classmates, was quite happy in his room, spending his time reading and listening to music when not studying. His father worried about him, but Thomas assured him that he was better able to function subsequently—both in school and socially—if he could "get lost" in his own favorite music for a time.

What these two cases suggest is that leisure in childhood and adolescence is about considerably more than play, games, and sport, and that other activities offer a variety of opportunities and challenges that can have an impact on one's life. Play and sport activities do continue to be popular and influential throughout life, but the realm of leisure seems to open up widely during adolescence. We thus turn to some of the functions of leisure activities, why they are attractive, what children and adolescents derive from them, and in some cases, what the risks are.

Pleasure, Relaxation, and Coping

A principal objective of leisure involvement is the experience of *pleasure*, *relaxation*, or *fun* it can provide. In fact, as we mentioned in our earlier discussions of leisure meanings and experiences, pleasure, relaxation, and fun are the elements most associated with moments and activities people regard as leisure (e.g., Shaw, 1985a). An experience sampling study conducted with adolescents (Kleiber, Caldwell, & Shaw, 1993) revealed that when the respondents were asked directly to indicate what leisure meant to them, "relaxation" was one of the most frequently used terms. Females, in particular, tended to place more emphasis on leisure as relaxation. Pleasure and relaxation also represent the outcomes actually *sought* with the activities that are chosen.

The theory of *hedonism* holds that people act in such a way as to bring about pleasure and avoid pain (Chaplin, 1985). Many psychological theories are in part based on the idea that pleasure seeking and its kin are important elements in understanding people's behavior. For example, psychoanalytic theory proposes that the "pleasure principle" is a primary process in mental functioning (Freud, 1933). And it is the principal assumption of psychological need theories that it is the pleasure experienced when needs are fulfilled or satisfied that gives them their power (see Murray, 1938, and Chapter 5).

Pleasure-relaxation-fun theories suggest that people seek fun or pleasurable experiences in their leisure and that these relatively brief and transient experiences not only enhance the quality of the present moment but that, cumulatively, they can "spice up" and enhance long-term psychological well-being. In fact, Larsen, Diener, and Cropanzano (1987) proposed that to maintain well-being, people gain more from many small moments of enjoyment than they do from less frequent great peaks of pleasure. Consequently, leisure activities may influence health and well-being by promoting positive moods (Caldwell, 2005a; Carruthers & Hood, 2004; Hull, 1991). A great deal of the leisure that people engage in during their daily lives is, in fact, characterized by fun and pleasure seeking. People spend substantial amounts of time, energy, and money to be entertained, to be amused, and to have fun. There are television sitcoms, amusement parks, stand-up comedy, and so forth. The entertainment (Chapman & Foot, 1976; Fry & Allen, 1975; Zillmann & Vorderer, 2000) and tourism (Pearce, 1982) industries know how important it is to make people laugh and provide opportunities for fun and pleasure.

The notions of fun and pleasure have been recognized by some writers as being an important leisure construct (Smith, 1990b). Even authors who have advocated the importance of *serious leisure* for well-being (e.g., Stebbins, 1992a, 2001) have recognized that entertainment and diversionary activities are also important to subjective well-being.

The fact that people tell researchers that feelings of pleasure, relaxation, and fun are an important part of their leisure is consistent with growing evidence that a greater number of pleasurable moments experienced in daily life leads to higher levels of psychological well-being (e.g., Folkman, 2008; Fredrickson, 2001). Positive emotional states contribute to global and integrative thinking, according to Fredrickson's review of the medical literature, leading her to a "Broaden and Build" view of the connection between positive emotions and adaptation. Mannell and McMahon (1982) had a group of students keep diaries of all the humorous and pleasurable events they encountered in the course of a day. They also assessed their mood states in these diaries. These humorous events occurred primarily during their unstructured interactions with other people; only a small percentage was triggered by watching television or listening to music. Those respondents who reported more of these pleasurable events felt more relaxed and happy, and less anxious and hostile at the end of the day. Tarrant (1996) found that when the students he studied in a laboratory experiment simply *recalled* past outdoor recreation experiences, they reported greater positive moods and fewer physical health problems.

When used to cope with stress, pleasurable experiences may be particularly important. Most of the research on this subject has been conducted with adults who are ill, injured, or experiencing other losses of various kinds, and we will turn to that research in Chapter 12; but stress is common in childhood and adolescence too, as in the case of LaKeisha above and also in those situations that have lent themselves to the application of play therapy in the past. A study of playfulness in nearly 300 Canadian adolescents established that those who were more playful were better able to cope with stress (Staempfli, 2007).

Some adolescents are more intentional than others in using leisure to cope. In a qualitative study of about 150 12- to 14-year-olds in a rural middle school in the northeastern United States (Hutchinson, Baldwin, & Sae-Sok 2006), the investigators found that those with an active/accommodation coping style used both structured and family-based leisure activities and informal activities far more often in coping with stress than those with a more avoidant style, the latter preferring to watch television and listen to music as a way of coping. Both styles, however, appeared to be therapeutic in their own ways. Structured leisure was also found to be useful in managing stress in another study of adolescents (King, Valerius, & Collins, 1998), this one with youth judged to be "at-risk." The program was specifically designed to help with coping skills in the context of recreation, something we will turn to again in Chapter 13.

Distraction

One explanation of how leisure may be beneficial to people is what we will call the *keeping idle hands busy* theory. It is probably the most basic explanation of all. People are thought to be happiest, or at least mentally healthy, when they are busy. From this perspective, leisure activities are important because they keep people with too much free time on their hands (idle hands) occupied. Having unoccupied time available is assumed to be psychologically and behaviorally risky for some people, resulting in a state of boredom and/ or participation in destructive activities. This view of idleness has a long history, with strong roots in Christian thinking—most notably the Protestant work ethic. "Idleness was considered an enemy of the soul" (Goodale & Godbey, 1988, p. 34) and work a religious obligation because it prevented idleness. From this perspective, play, recreation, and leisure only become acceptable when they are constructive and more work-like and thus prevent the evils of idleness.

Whether such assertions are true or not, adolescents are commonly identified as being susceptible to the perils of idleness. Juvenile delinquency is often seen to be a result of adolescents having too much free time available with few socially acceptable leisure alternatives; this leads to boredom and, consequently, to engagement in harmful activities such as drug use (see Crompton, 1993; Iso-Ahola & Crowley, 1991; Wegner et al., 2006). There is also some evidence that the experience of boredom during free time is associated with other health-compromising behaviors (Caldwell & Smith, 1994; Smith & Caldwell, 1989). In a study of 2,756 high school students in the Southeastern United States, Caldwell and Smith (1995) found that adolescents who were bored in their leisure or whose leisure was chosen to reject adult values and structure were more likely to engage in risky health behaviors (e.g., smoking, alcohol abuse, bulimia, attempting suicide). And in a study of over 8,000 adolescents, Caldwell and Darling (1999) found that just hanging out with peers in unstructured activities was one of the significant predictors of substance use.

Leisure activities and programs to keep people busy are considered to be constructive behavioral alternatives (e.g., Grubb, 1975; McKay, 1993; Munson, 1991). However, little or no research has been carried out to actually test this theory. It is also doubtful that simply keeping people busy without fostering other changes (e.g., leisure skill development, positive leisure attitudes, intrinsic leisure interest) would do anything more than temporarily delay the occurrence of whatever problems are of concern. As we will explain, other theories do suggest that activities with certain types of characteristics may be necessary to produce substantial benefits.

Personal Growth

As we noted in Chapter 9 in addressing the matter of the external conditions responsible for socialization *for,* or into, leisure, it would not be a subject for study if there wasn't also a case for socialization *through* leisure. Parents, we recognized, even arrange for leisure in a purposeful way with their children, seeing the benefits it presents for personal and social growth (Shaw & Dawson, 2001). And in spite of the more general tendency for people to associate leisure with simple relaxation, many, including children and adolescents, do use leisure as a context for challenge-seeking and self-expansion, as we have noted.

Leisure pursuits that become personally meaningful and important to people and that provide psychological benefits are inevitably structured or organized in ways that nevertheless bring enjoyment as part of the ongoing experience (Fine, 1989; Podilchak, 1991a, 1991b; Wankel, 1985, 1993). The ability to experience enjoyment (beyond fun and pleasure only) in leisure, particularly in serious leisure activities, is important to acquire during adolescence (Hamilton, 1983a, 1983b; Kleiber, Larson, & Csikszentmihalyi, 1986; Kleiber & Rickards, 1985; Larson, 2000). In distinguishing enjoyment from pleasure, Csikszentmihalyi (1990) argues that the former involves experiences that are not only pleasurable but are accompanied by feelings of increased competence and growth—by a sense of "forward movement . . . . a sense of novelty, of accomplishment" (Csikszentmihalyi, 1990, p. 46).

The idea that leisure may afford opportunities for personal growth invites a closer examination of *personal growth theories* as they relate to leisure. From this perspective, leisure provides an opportunity for people to develop a clear idea of their strengths and weaknesses, continually develop their skills and abilities, become the kind of people they would like to be and feel good about who they are. Terms used to describe these types of personal growth outcomes include "self-esteem" and "self-actualization."

Maslow (1968) described self-actualization as the process of developing one's true potential as an individual to the fullest extent, and expressing one's skills, talents, and emotions in a personally fulfilling manner. His view was that people possess an innate set of potentials that serves as a blueprint to describe what they are uniquely capable of becoming; and while they are more or less continually in the process of moving toward the goal of self-actualization, it may or may not be realized. For one individual, the process of self-actualization might take the form of becoming an ideal parent, while others could express this same need athletically, musically, artistically, or vocationally. According to Maslow, self-actualization does not demand that individuals be the best in the world, only the best they can be. For example, people expressing their self-actualization through music do not have to be world-class musicians to develop and enjoy their musical talents. Fulfillment can be derived from achieving personal best performances.

Tinsley and Tinsley (1986) proposed a similar theory based in part on the *flow* principle. According to this theory, leisure experiences that are challenging, intense, and to which people are committed are likely to satisfy a variety of needs not met in other areas of life. The satisfaction of these needs can contribute to physical and mental health and consequently, life satisfaction. Similar to Maslow, Tinsley and Tinsley argue that people must meet most of their needs and be reasonably satisfied with their lives before they can experience personal growth. People who are relatively dissatisfied with their lives must attend to the satisfaction of their physiological, safety, and belongingness needs. Consequently, they have little energy available to direct toward personal growth. However, if these needs are met, psychological resources are freed up, allowing people the time to focus on those aspects of themselves that they would like to change and develop through their leisure.

This line of thinking has found new variations recently, recognizing more dimensionality in human potentials that can be actualized in different ways (e.g., Gardner, 1999). One of the most prominent models that operationalizes some of the processes of self-actualization is the self-determination theory discussed in earlier chapters (Deci & Ryan, 1991, 2000, 2008; Ryan & Deci, 2000, 2002). Whatever individual capacities exist, the realization of growth in those areas is driven by the basic needs for competence, autonomy, and relatedness. Competence, in particular, becomes defined around individual capacities, and one's trajectory of self-realization is then affected by circumstances that facilitate or discourage self-determination. This in turn will determine whether potentials are realized and a sense of growth and well-being are achieved.

Leisure, because it is based on freedom of choice, allows people to structure social settings and participate in activities that foster the development of these feelings, even in childhood and adolescence. Feelings of competence and autonomy are viewed as the basis of a positive self-concept, which, in turn, has been described as an essential component of self-actualization and personal growth. From this perspective, then, if leisure is to provide growth benefits, it must be challenging and require some effort.

More recently, this view of growth from challenge has been reinforced in the research and writing in the general area of "positive psychology" (e.g., Keyes & Haidt, 2003; Lopez, 2008; Peterson, 2006; Seligman & Csikszentmihalyi, 2000). Positive psychology focuses to a great extent on the cultivation of strengths and capacities that lead to happiness and well-being and those that build resilience for overcoming the forces in life that would undermine mental health. Positive psychology thus concerns itself with imagination, creativity, humor, flow, playfulness, authenticity, courage, savoring, spirituality, and other experiences that are often the focus of leisure studies and leisure services (see also Carruthers & Hood, 2004).

One important idea to come out of this tradition, particularly with respect to positive development in adolescence, is the idea of *initiative*, which is a critical component of success in adulthood (Larson, 2000). Larson speaks of three important components of initiative—intrinsic motivation, concerted engagement in the environment, and a temporal arc—that are, unfortunately, too rarely evident among adolescents. Instead, adolescents, at least those in North America, are more likely to be bored at any given moment, as indicated in experience sampling data (e.g., Larson & Kleiber, 1993a, 1993b; Larson & Verma, 1999). This occurs whether they are in school or in more casual leisure settings. School is associated with high concerted effort but low intrinsic motivation ("other-controlled attention"), while casual leisure activities (including television watching and socializing) are associated with high intrinsic motivation but low concerted effort ("spontaneous attention"). Only structured and organized leisure activities—sports, music, arts, and organizations ("voluntary attention")—seem to fit the bill and have both characteristics (see Figures 11.1a and 11.1b, pp. 358–359). And many such activities also have the "temporal arc" of a season, summer, or preparation for an event that makes them project-like and therefore supportive of initiative. Because such activities typically involve self-directed planning, practice, preparation, and assessment with respect to goals (and the language for such things), as well as "collaborative agency" in bringing activities to fruition, they are particularly important developmental experiences (see also Darling, Caldwell, & Smith, 2005; Heath, 1999; Heath & McLaughlin, 1993).

Larson (2000) referred to a study of Girl Scouts involved in a cookie sale (Rogoff et al., 1995) and the sense of "collaborative agency" that comes from working effectively as a team. In another study of nearly 400 adolescents from Massachusetts high schools, Watts and Caldwell (2008) sought to assess Larson's idea of initiative as a product of leisure involvement, by seeing if it could be predicted by measures of activity participation and motivation. The investigators found support for Larson's ideas by determining that intrinsic motivation (sample item "I do what I do in my leisure time because I want to") and the amount of time spent participating in structured activities were positively associated with initiative (e.g., "When I start something, I stick with it").

Larson's view is consistent with the earlier work on the constructs of *commitment* (Haworth, 1986), *serious leisure* (Stebbins, 1982, 1992a), *flow* (Csikszentmihalyi, 1975), *high-investment activities* (Kelly, Steinkamp, & Kelly, 1987; Mannell, 1993) and *high-yield activities* (Caldwell, 2005b) that have been at the forefront of leisure research. Collectively, these ideas have

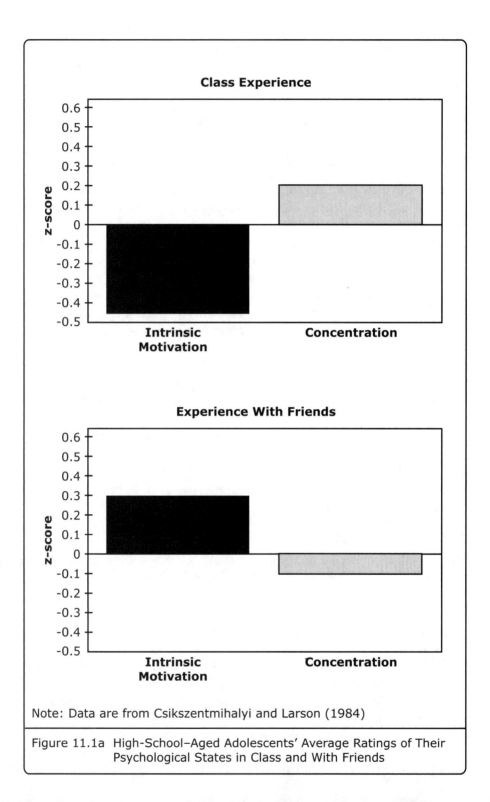

Note: Data are from Csikszentmihalyi and Larson (1984)

Figure 11.1a High-School–Aged Adolescents' Average Ratings of Their
Psychological States in Class and With Friends

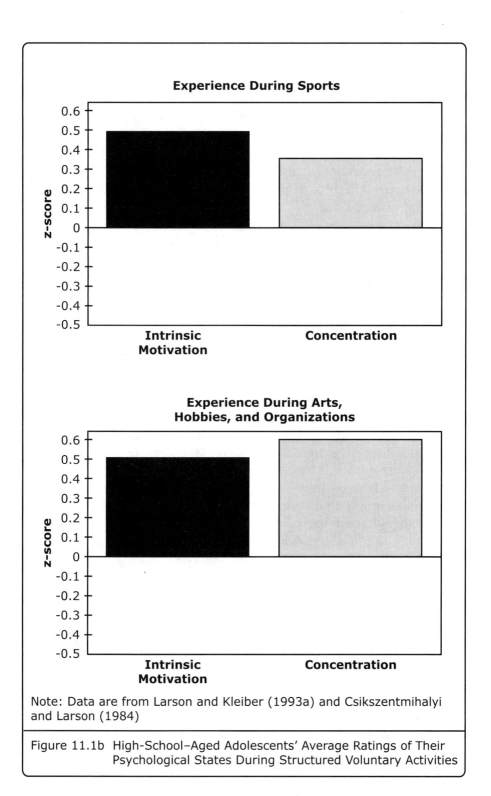

Note: Data are from Larson and Kleiber (1993a) and Csikszentmihalyi and Larson (1984)

Figure 11.1b High-School–Aged Adolescents' Average Ratings of Their Psychological States During Structured Voluntary Activities

led to the growing belief among researchers and practitioners that leisure must be more than simply a pleasant, diversionary, escape-oriented experience if it is to contribute substantially to psychological well-being. (See also Witt & Caldwell, 2005, for applications in recreation settings.) The idea is that people who experience higher levels of well-being and life satisfaction are more involved in freely chosen activities that challenge their knowledge and skills and require an investment of effort. Such high-investment/high-yield activities have been learned over time, require a great deal of effort and acquisition of skill, and are most likely to yield an enhanced sense of competence and worth (Kelly, Steinkamp, & Kelly, 1987; Kelly & Ross, 1989; Mannell, 1993). To put it simply, it could be said that *the more a person invests in the activities in which they choose to participate, the more they get out of these activities.* Of course, this is not a new idea. It is an adage that many people have frequently heard from parents, teachers, and coaches.

In a cross-sectional sequence study of over 4,000 California adolescents (i.e., examining multiple age groups over time), Darling, Caldwell, and Smith (2005) found that involvement in extracurricular activities (ECAs) was predictive of positive academic attitudes, achievement, and expectations, with demographic and prior measures of those things held constant. The method used in the study helped to rule out the alternative explanation for such associations that more positive adjustment makes extracurricular activity involvement more likely. Nevertheless, does it make sense that all ECA involvement would be equally supportive of such activities and equally generative of initiative? Perhaps the association would have been even stronger if some distinction would have been made between those activities where participants had the responsibility for planning and decision making and those, such as many sports, where that kind of work rests entirely in the hands of others, such as teachers and coaches.

Another area of leisure activity commonly associated with personal development is outdoor adventure recreation, which involves "activities utilizing an interaction with the natural environment, that contain elements of real or apparent danger, in which the outcome, while uncertain, can be influenced by the participant and circumstance" (Ewert, 1989, p. 7). From ropes course training to winter camping to wilderness survival, it is intended to build competence, self-confidence, and self-esteem, particularly in those who lack such confidence or who are at risk for trouble in other aspects of society. Research has thus established that experiences with risk and challenge in the outdoors can build resiliency (Green, Kleiber, & Tarrant, 2000), self-efficacy (Sibthorp, 2003), self-esteem (Iso-Ahola, Graefe, & LaVerde, 1989), and feelings of community (Sharpe, 2005). However, it is not clear just what aspects of the experience, especially when they are organized and led by others, are most influential. There is also the risk that experiences that are too demanding may have a negative effect on fear and self-confidence. And the other common problem when such experiences are programmed is that any effects that are achieved are short-lived, with the everyday environment causing participants to revert to their earlier levels (see Creyer, Ross, & Evers, 2003; Ewert & McAvoy, 2000; Turner, 2009).

Nevertheless, whatever the circumstances, finding continuing challenge in activities seems important to personal growth. And this is often a matter of commitment. Commitment is at the core of Stebbins' (1982, 1992, 2007) theory of *serious leisure*, which was developed from his studies of amateurs, hobbyists, and volunteers (and discussed briefly in Chapter 4). In fact, the construct of serious leisure provides a clear picture of what being committed to a leisure activity entails: perseverance, personal effort in the development of specially acquired knowledge and skill, the development of a career in the activity, and strong attachment to or identification with the activity and those who practice it. Stebbins' formulations have also suggested that serious leisure can make a significant contribution to the quality of life of the individual. In the short-term, this type of leisure may be no fun. However, the hard work and perseverance by amateurs, hobbyists, and volunteers to meet the challenges of their leisure is predicted to engender feelings of accomplishment and provide psychological benefits that include self-enrichment, self-gratification, self-actualization, self-expression, positive social identity, escape from personal problems, social belonging, and a feeling of contributing to a group (Stebbins, 1992a, p. 17).

Although most of Stebbins' research participants have been adults, the seeds of commitment and serious leisure are sown earlier in life. Certainly there are cases of adolescents and even children who become committed to activities like music and sports at an early age, and their personal growth may be influenced accordingly. In fact, a concern of parents and others is that they may be *overcommitted*, at some cost to developing other aspects of themselves, a point to which we will return shortly. What seems also to be an important ingredient of growth-producing involvement, however, is the manner in which initiative is shaped in childhood and adolescence.

Summarizing then, while casual activities that are fun and distracting can improve one's mood, enhance subjective well-being, and even set the stage for more growth, the activities that contribute most to personal growth appear to be those that are structured in some way and demand attention, effort, and perseverance. But we would reiterate the point that some structured activities may have mixed effects and also that the opportunities for self-direction, organization, and execution of extracurricular activity would be critical to some aspects of personal development.

Identity Formation

In Chapter 7, we discussed identity as an aspect of personality that derives from self-awareness. As such, it is shaped in personal and social directions by pressures for differentiation and integration, individuation and identification, exploration and commitment, and coherence and authenticity. The emergence of leisure interests, the expression of personal inclinations, and the identification with the leisure activities of others *reflect* those dynamics and some of the essence of one's identity. But indications are that they also *contribute to* identity formation. For example, based on the successes and failures of an individual's efforts and the feedback she or he receives from others, that person may come to see herself or himself as good at fixing things, a lousy golfer, concerned about the environment, fun-loving, etc. To the extent these images form a somewhat consistent and stable picture, they contribute to an identity but one which is always "under construction," particularly in adolescence. Though this identity can, and indeed must, change to allow for growth and development, its stability, however temporary, derives from the consistency of the messages received about oneself. Taking action, expressing ourselves, and assuming social roles provide that information.

For the most part, research and writing on the factors that influence identity formation have emphasized work, religion, sex roles, and political ideology. It is around these matters that important values and beliefs are typically developed. Yet the process of identity formation is an active one, requiring self-expression and interaction with other people, and leisure is considered significant for its capacity to afford opportunities and be a context for the expression of individual interests, as was established in Chapter 7. One of the leading writers on the psychology of self and identity, Roy Baumeister, pointed out (1995) that many traditional sources of identity have been trivialized, destabilized, or altogether lost. Religion, marriage, vocation, gender, geographical home, and ancestral family, among other sources, no longer have the defining effect on individuals they once did. They have been replaced, he argued, by individual personality, personal accomplishment, personal style and interest, and *leisure* as contemporary sources of identity. About leisure he says in an earlier volume (Baumeister, 1986):

> The spread of leisure time to all levels of society has enabled people to take part in a wide variety of activities, and these hobbies and memberships help define the self. One is not just a clerk; one is a jogger and a guitarist as well as a clerk. Although most of the activities are done by many others, they provide a kind of local differentiation because there are so many possible combinations that one's own combination seems unique among one's acquaintances. With the

other joggers, one is the guitar player; among musicians, one is the clerk (with the daytime job); at work, one is known as the jogger or the guitarist (pp. 137–138).

It is in the liberal context of leisure that identity alternatives are often initially considered through the expression of interests. In leisure, people "feel free" not only to be themselves but also to try out new possibilities (see Kelly, 1983; Kleiber, 1999), as was reflected with older women in the Red Hat Society groups referred to earlier (Yarnal, 2006). For all ages, leisure can provide an opportunity to play and experiment with the kind of person one might want to be. As just a general test of the proposition that identity formation is influenced by leisure involvement, Campbell and Smale (2008) found that although measures of social identity formation could not be predicted by the amount of leisure activities, the meaningfulness of leisure activities did show some association with social identity formation.

Identity theorists have long recognized the significance of expressive (i.e., leisure-based) activities for identity formation. Erik Erikson (1959) examined the common paths of family and work roles for identity formation, but he also noted that "favored capacities" play a role in the evolving configuration of identity as well (p. 116). Sports, music, and other arts are often embraced as play, shaped into competencies through instruction and self-discipline, and emerge as clearly defined identity alternatives, even leading to vocations in some cases. Choices can be digressive or even regressive, but, to the extent that they reflect on the continuity of the self from one time to the next, they are important in the course of identity formation. And as was argued about commitment in relation to personal growth in the previous section, a critical factor that determines whether this expressive individuation is influential in the identity-formation process is whether such activities are taken seriously. The investment of time and effort in such activities to the point that there is perseverance, a sense of future possibilities (a "career" in the activity), a recognition of effort, knowledge and training required, and an identification with others makes them "serious" (Kleiber & Kirshnit, 1991; Stebbins, 1992a).

When activities are entered into seriously—but still for their intrinsic value—they contribute to self-development and individuation (becoming more distinctly oneself). The natural course of enjoyment of any moderately complex activity, from playing a musical instrument to raising golden retrievers, leads to the refinement of judgments and the development of skills that are constitutive of the self (Csikszentmihalyi, 1990, 1993); this, in turn, helps to clarify one's uniqueness, which can either distinguish oneself in important ways related to individuation or can unite and identify one with others of similar interests and competencies.

For adolescents, the same characteristics of perseverance and focused attention are sometimes found in part-time jobs. Indeed, most discussions of adolescent identity-formation place great importance on developing a work ethic or ideology. But most of the work opportunities adolescents have are not very demanding of their abilities or very significant for them psychologically (Greenberger & Steinberg, 1986), whereas many serious leisure activities are. Additionally, serious leisure activities can present a more optimistic view of the future, for they suggest that activities requiring "hard work" can be enjoyed and self-directed. As noted earlier, this feature is what led Csikszentmihalyi and Larson (1984) to discuss such leisure activities as "transitional." Involvement in them can make adolescents aware that the patterns of enjoyment and intrinsic interest experienced in childhood play can be found in the structured and required activities of adult society.

The development of skills, then, is important in identity formation. Learning to ride a bicycle extends one's range of competence and makes other bike riders part of an accessible reference group (Kleiber & Kirshnit, 1991). Iso-Ahola, Graefe, and LaVerde (1989) studied participants in risk recreation and sports. Increases in self-esteem as a consequence of participation were found to be linked to increases in perceived competence in these activities. In other words, it is not enough just to do an activity to feel good about yourself; some expression of skill is necessary to create that effect. A study of girls' participation in female adolescents' jazz bands in Scotland demonstrated that such an experience could contribute to identity formation and be socially integrative. It provided a sense of friendship and identification and an opportunity to practice self-discipline and develop a sense of pride and commitment (Grieves, 1989).

The idea that leisure participation can *affirm* one's identity is also important. It is based on the view that people choose to participate in leisure activities partially on the basis of the identity images associated with them. Schlenker (1984) proposed that people are motivated to develop and maintain a consistent and positive self-concept or identity, and consequently, they engage in behavior that allows them to affirm or validate "desired identity images," that is, images they have or would like to have of themselves. Participation in certain types of leisure activities may provide a way of doing this (Haggard & Williams, 1991; Neulinger, 1981). First, different leisure activities embody distinct and measurable *identity images*; people in a particular society share beliefs or stereotypes about the characteristics of people (e.g., physical appearance, personality, attitudes, skills, and abilities) who participate in different activities. For example, people may perceive those who rock climb to be competent, strong, and adventurous. Second, people may want to be "competent, strong, and adventurous" themselves. By participating in activities that embody this set of identity images (e.g. by climbing rocks), people are able to *validate* or *affirm* that they are (or aspire to be) this kind of person. Wearing certain types of clothing and using the "right" equipment can also signify and reinforce one's identification with a particular leisure activity (Kelly, 1983; Mitchell, 1983). This view of identity images is similar to the concept of "sign value" found in the consumer behavior literature (Dimanche, Havitz, & Howard, 1991; Dimanche & Samdahl, 1994). People often purchase leisure products and services for their symbolic value, that is, to identify with a social group, to express something about themselves to others, or to affirm something meaningful about their personal identity.

Most of the evidence for identity affirmation through leisure participation is indirect and addresses the first component of the theory—that certain activities have identity images associated with them. In a survey study, Paluba and Neulinger (1976) asked their respondents to rate golfers, bowlers, and tennis players on a variety of personality traits. A distinct personality profile was found to characterize people who participated in each of these activities. Golfers, for example, were perceived to be higher in extroversion than bowlers and tennis players. Spreitzer and Snyder (1983) found that the runners, racquetball players, and nonparticipants they studied also systematically differed according to the identity images they associated with these activities. Interestingly, highly-involved runners and racquetball players felt that their preferred leisure activities said more about what kind of person they were than did the type of job they had.

Haggard and Williams (1992) conducted two studies to test this identity affirmation theory. In the first study, they mailed a survey to students registered in eight different university recreation classes (volleyball, weight training, racquetball, backpacking, kayaking, outdoor cooking, folk guitar, and chess) and asked them to define the characteristics of people who participate in "their" activity. Distinct images or stereotypes were found for different types of leisure activities (see Table 11.1, p. 366, for examples), confirming the earlier studies of Paluba and Neulinger (1976) and Sprietzer and Snyder (1983).

In the second study, Haggard and Williams (1992) attempted to test the idea that people "desire the identity images associated with their respective leisure activity" and "the leisure activities they select should symbolize identity images that are highly desirable to that individual, representing greater identity affirmation potential" (p. 10). Using different students but ones who regularly participated in one of the four leisure activities examined in Study 1 (those activities shown in Table 11.1), the researchers administered a questionnaire to measure their desire to acquire the different identity images that had been found to be associated with these activities (also in Study 1). They were asked to rate on 7-point Likert scales how important these identity images were to them, that is, to indicate which of the characteristics they most wanted to acquire. No reference was made during the study to the leisure activities in which they were presently active participants. The findings indicated that the students rated as most important those identity images associated with the leisure activities in which they were currently heavily involved. These findings provide some support for the identity affirmation theory of leisure behavior. The greater freedom afforded by leisure likely allows people the flexibility to choose activities with identity images that are consistent with the kind of person they are or would like to be.

Of course, what we may ask about such inclinations is how much they represent the "true self" or just the need for social status, approval, recognition, or maybe even love from others. Certainly there is a question of *authenticity* in the leisure choices people make, particularly young people who want to impress others. And identity formation may in fact be confused in the process. There are so many ways in which consumer culture offers attractive identity images in leisure activities it is easy to see the appeal. Such is the case with personal appearance and even smoking, as we will see shortly. Activities that are embraced only in response to social expectations end up contributing very little to identity formation. This may have been the reason that Shaw, Kleiber, and Caldwell (1995) found that sport involvement was more influential to identity formation for females than for males—because it is less expected of them.

But even if participation begins in imitation with the desire to be like attractive others, it can actually contribute to the development of the desired identity, if skills are developed and interests refined. Involvement in appealing activities may challenge an individual and over time lead to the development

---

Table 11.1 Leisure Identity Images of Participants in Four Leisure Activities (adapted from Haggard and Williams, 1992)

Volleyball Player	**Kayaker**
Athletic	Adventurous
Energetic	Fun loving
Health conscious	Likes scenic beauty
Physically fit	Loves fresh air
Sports minded	Naturalist
Team player	Outdoorsy
Guitarist	**Chess Player**
At peace with themselves	Analytical
Creative	Good problem solver
Introspective	Logical
Intelligent	Math minded
Patient	Quiet
Quiet	Strategic

of psychological resources that enable one to "live up" to that new identity. Of course, some leisure pursuits may have identity images that are negative from society's perspective. The identity affirmation that participation in illegal or antisocial activities might encourage, as in the case of Mario described at the beginning of this section, is not likely to be seen as a positive outcome or benefit of leisure.

Identifying with others who display desired characteristics is the more *social* side of identity formation, that of a self who belongs, a self that is a member of a group with similar characteristics, interests, or attitudes. But the other, more *personal*, side of identity has to do with who one knows oneself to be in private, one's values, attitudes, interests, and behaviors that may seem quite idiosyncratic and maybe even "weird" to others. These aspects may be celebrated parts of one's individuation, as noted above, or they may be sources of anxiety when tested socially. In a study of a group of gay and lesbian adolescents, Kivel and Kleiber (2000) found that leisure was seen as a site for private and personal self-expression and identity development but not public and social identity formation. Reading, media consumption, and music appreciation were all prominent sources of personal identity development, but the need to conceal their sexual identity made individuals avoid more social leisure contexts for fear of exclusion and mistreatment, a subject we will consider again shortly. Stigmas associated with race, gender, disability, ethnicity, and social class limit the opportunities for full social identity formation in some leisure contexts.

Finally, we can see evidence of the contribution of leisure to identity formation in the "breach," where a personally meaningful leisure activity is suddenly no longer available. Studies of injured athletes—who can no longer continue their activities as they did—demonstrate a level of disruption to a sense of self that is experienced as traumatic and requires significant self-reorganization and "identity work" (Brock & Kleiber, 1994; Collison & Hockey, 2007) to recover and find modified leisure identity alternatives or entirely new directions.

Formation of Primary Relationships

Identification with others is also driven by the intrinsic need for relatedness discussed in earlier chapters. Sharing free time and enjoyable activity with others serves this need extremely well. As with play activities discussed earlier, shared leisure activities in adolescence builds friendships, intimate relationships between pairs of individuals in some cases, and often a sense of community with larger groups.

Positive psychology recognizes both that relatedness and love are compatible with personal growth and that responsibility to others is part of the realization of human potential (Seligman & Csikszentmihalyi, 2000).

Earlier humanistic theories of self-actualization were often criticized for emphasizing individual self-gratification to the neglect of social connectedness. But research has established that such purposes need not be incompatible (e.g., Josselson, 1994). The social activities of adolescents may appear in some ways to detract from self-development, but connectedness also plants the seeds of community-building and collectivism. And as a context of relative freedom, leisure offers room for the exploration of the interface of individual self-expression and social interest and possibility. The early interest in community-building that children show when they form "clubs" around adventuring or game playing can evolve into more refined forms of social grouping necessary to sustain a rock band, a rock-climbing club, or a sorority service group. Of course, the potential for excess conformity or for hurtful discrimination and exclusion that may accompany such activities also needs to be recognized— and will be reconsidered shortly—but the identification with others for serious collective purposes can create personal growth that is both individually self-actualizing and socially constructive.

Formation of a sense of community may even be an objective of recreation programs. An international camp was studied for the impact of its activities— which were directed toward cooperation and effective communication—on the development of social capital and sense of community in a group of 32 11-year-old campers (Yuen, Pedlar, & Mannell, 2005). Examining and discussing campers' drawings with them, the investigators concluded that leisure provided a common ground for the children's relationship building and the development of shared meanings. Sharpe (2005) studied the attempts of a private leisure service provider, *Wilderness Inquiry*, to bring about a sense of community in an outdoor recreation context. She found some tensions with the expectation of the freedom of leisure and the imposition of structure, but recognized the capacity of shared adventure to create a bonding experience in any case. And as was noted earlier, Jamieson and Ross (2007) even sought to use sports and recreation to build a sense of community between ethnic groups that were otherwise estranged.

Such structured programs as camps and guided wilderness trips are only the tip of the iceberg, however, when it comes to the ways that social leisure affects relationships. Indeed, it may be argued that most friendships are formed around sources of shared enjoyment. And the same may be said for intimate relationships as well. Much of the flirting and cavorting of adolescence is directed ultimately to finding mates whose interests are compatible with one's own. Cliques are formed around expressive patterns and interests that are shared. These, of course, can be limiting and destructive in other respects—when they lead to antagonism toward out-group members, for example. It is important to recognize that the social outcomes of play, sport, and recreation are not always positive, as demonstrated in some of the research on sport and moral development (Shields & Bredemeier, 1995, 2001). We turn now to one particular problematic subject for understanding the impacts of leisure in childhood and adolescence.

Conformity and Exclusion

Among the more *negative* consequences of affiliation and association in adolescent leisure, especially where there is strong identification, are stifling conformity, out-group discrimination and exclusion, and outright hostility. Even without the negative effects of exclusion, conformity alone can lead to destructive patterns. Certainly peer-group pressure is associated with the use of alcohol and illegal drugs in adolescence—as was established in Chapter 9—and with broader forms of delinquency as well (Ennett et al., 2008). Looking only at the patterns of activities that are fun and leisure-like still leaves one with a wide array of dysfunctional and hazardous activities that are embraced in the name of affiliation and identification (Osgood et al., 1996).

As noted in the case of Mario, the fun in leisure can be expressed in a wide variety of ways, including those that are illegal, illicit, or simply deviate from normal practice. Throwing stones to break windows in an old abandoned building may seem pretty innocuous, but the throwers would not likely be doing it if an adult authority figure was watching. The thrill of getting away with stealing items of clothing may have less to do with being better attired than in having the outrageous behavior entertain and impress one's girlfriends. As the old song goes, "girls [and boys] just want to have fun," and fun for adolescents can be about stretching the bounds of convention. There is something to be said about the rebelliousness of adolescence in asserting one's independence from parents and authority figures (cf. Silbereisen & Todt, 1994) but, as was noted in the previous section, much of the activity is simply stimulated by being among peers.

An even greater risk of leisure-based association and conformity, however, is that those who are seen as different may be directly or indirectly excluded. Certainly there is discrimination related to ability in, and understanding of, activities from sports to wine tasting. Elitism may be a source of satisfaction for those who are accomplished and privileged while discouraging interest among those who lack such skills. But even where ability and interest are comparable, exclusion may occur. Sports have long asserted the leveling power of athletic ability with respect to differences of race, ethnicity, and even gender, but exclusion in sport can nevertheless be found. In a study of little league baseball, Glover (2007) found that the presumed "color-blindness" of the organization was belied by policies and practices related to player selection, travel/transportation to games, isolation of minority players, spectator behavior, and coaching/role modeling that clearly favored white children while disadvantaging children of color, even causing African-American parents to form "a league of their own."

Peers are often co-conspirators in adolescent capers, what Csikszentmihalyi and Larson (1984) referred to as the "deviation amplifying" circumstances of peer cultures in adolescence. Larson has even identified the intrinsic (play and leisure-like) enjoyment of school crime as a large part of the motivation. And the combination of boredom and socializing with a relatively undirected group of peers is predictive of drug and alcohol use and other kinds of delinquent activities (Osgood et al., 1996). An important distinction to make in this chapter, though, is that we are speaking here about the *outcomes* of leisure. There are many factors that lead to turning free time and leisure activities in a deviant direction, some of which were reviewed in Chapter 9. But the point here is to look at the free time of leisure as the *source* of boredom that then leads to delinquent and deviant leisure activities. It is also saying that time alone without both personal resources and appropriate opportunities can be used in just the way people have been worried about for centuries: that is, "idle hands are the devil's workshop." Even where television is available, leisure boredom may still be a consequence. Indeed, most television watching is associated with low activation and boredom (Csikszentmihalyi & Larson, 1984; Kubey & Csikszentmihalyi, 1990; Larson, 2000). One implication of this then is to see some kind of leisure education as a way to enable one to make more of the free-time and personal resources available, even in conditions of relative external deprivation (Caldwell et al., 2004; Larson, 2000). We take up this topic again in Chapter 13.

The Influence of Television and Internet Experience

David Jansen, his sister Alicia, and two friends from their neighborhood, all between the ages of 13 and 16, have spent most of the summer watching movies and playing video games in the Jansen game room while their parents are at work. They have a preference for horror movies where violent acts and murder are common, and the video games that most appeal to them are the very popular "first-person shooter" games. All four of the children have scored well on the games and feel somewhat accomplished with them as a result. The two older boys have also joined the multiplayer online game *World of Warcraft*, finding themselves drawn into a worldwide community of players and feeling some sense of connection and self-expansion as a result. Sometime in August, the four of them are walking in the neighborhood and noticed a group of older boys—about their age—pushing around two younger kids near a skateboard park, but after a brief glance at the scuffle, the walkers just shrugged and headed on to the movie theatre in town.

TV, Video Game, and Internet Violence as Causes of Aggression

Should we hold the Jansens and their friends responsible for not intervening when they saw the bullying going on? Might we have expected that they would have at least shown a little more interest in what was going on, if not empathy and concern for the younger children? Perhaps there are a wide variety of factors that could have explained their indifference. But research on the effects of television and video game violence on aggressive and violent behavior in other settings suggests that indifference to violence is one of the effects of sustained viewing of aggressive and violent activity on television and in video games (e.g., Anderson & Bushman, 2001; Bushman & Huesmann, 2001; Huesmann & Miller, 1994; Johnson et al., 2002; see also Aronson, 2008). However, while Internet involvement shares the feature of a monitor as hardware for viewing, there are significant differences between watching television and playing video games, and still other differences from online gaming. So let's look a little more closely at the evidence.

As with much of the research that is reported, we should be skeptical of simple correlational data that show a relationship between watching televised violence and aggressive behavior. After all, if and where there is an association, maybe aggressive and violent children and adolescents are simply more drawn to those programs. In fact, it may be good for them to have such an "outlet," if only to keep them from being aggressive and violent with others (though the evidence does not support such a "catharsis effect"). But how then shall we consider the relationship more carefully? We need to look for *experimental* evidence. When exposed to programming that shows people being hurt or killed, are people more prone to do similar things themselves? Random assignment of subjects to such programming while others are assigned to non-violent program might tell us if there is any affect on the willingness to hurt someone else, to condone the hurting of someone else, or even to ignore the hurting of someone else, as was true with the Jansens and their friends.

And what about with video games? One might argue that with games children are learning the right and wrong times to be aggressive and even violent—against the "bad guys" and the criminals only—and might be therefore learning behavioral controls in the process. Such has been the argument in the case of sports aggression when athletes have been shown to be no more aggressive off the field than non-athletes. But what, then, is the evidence? In a large meta-analysis of much of the research on the effects of violent video games on aggressive behavior, aggressive cognition, aggressive affect, physiological arousal, and pro-social behavior, Anderson and Bushman (2001) found that both experimental and non-experimental, and laboratory and field, investigations all generally support the case that involvement with violent video games increases aggressive thoughts, behavior, and physiological arousal and reduces the tendencies to be helpful to others. However, another more recent meta-analysis (Ferguson, 2007) has once again raised questions with this set of conclusions. Clearly more research is needed.

Other Effects of Television and Internet Involvement

The tremendous increase in internet use and online gaming in recent years has raised a number of concerns. While it may have the advantage of keeping children and adolescents occupied in an apparently harmless activity, it also keeps them away from other beneficial activities. The biggest concern in this regard is that viewers will become sedentary computer chair potatoes if not couch potatoes. In an experience sampling study of electronic media activities (Mannell, Kaczynski, & Aronson, 2005), adolescents who were more involved with television watching, video game playing and Internet use were far less likely to be engaged in physically active forms of leisure activity than those with less involvement, and they were less likely to enjoy physical activity when they were involved.

It would be a mistake, however, to see involvement with all media forms as passive (or even inactive) and antisocial. Online gaming, for example, is both extremely interactive and often very social, sometimes engaging individuals with an entire world community of players. In fact, such activities have been known to lead to "off-screen" relationships and even marriages. The mental capacity required for such involvement is often considerable and likely conveys some useful cognitive skills. Research on the subject is limited, but Ferguson's meta-analysis (2007) of the studies that have been conducted suggests some support for such effects. Indeed, most serious gamers can get so intensely involved it can become almost addictive. While it may lack some of the physiological concomitants of drug and alcohol addiction, it can have the same pathological features of addictive gambling (Chou & Ting, 2003; Holt & Kleiber, 2009).

Another very noteworthy technological development has been the spread of social networking, with variations such as Facebook and MySpace, among others. This is the "space" to present oneself and to reach out and share with others to find online "friends." It offers most of the aspects of sociability found in face-to-face encounters and may even afford some safety for those who find themselves stigmatized and alienated because of physical appearance. But it can also be used in destructive ways, where even intimidation and bullying may result; "cyberbullying"—which is also prevalent through the use of email, instant messages, chat rooms, and other digital messaging systems—has become so oppressive at times that victims have resorted to suicide (Kowalski, Limber, & Agatston, 2008).

It may be important to distinguish the impacts of social networking from those of Internet gaming and other interactive forms of Internet use, but the inclusive analyses that have been conducted to date have raised concerns about the impact of such activities on in-person relationships and on psychological well-being in general, in spite of such activities being more interactive than television and general video game play (Kiesler & Kraut, 1999; Seepersad, 2004; Subrahmanyam et al., 2001). Nevertheless, in an expansive review of the social consequences of Internet use, Valkenburg and Peter (2009) note first that adolescents are the defining users of the Internet, spending more time online than adults and exercising considerable autonomy in doing so. And while they recognize the potential excesses of Internet use, they also read the results of research as indicating that by enhancing opportunities for self-disclosure, Internet use has a largely benign effect on adolescent social connectedness. Again, though, more research is needed.

Conclusion

As people come to understand the impacts of play and leisure behavior, it becomes immediately clear that socialization and personal and social development do not rely exclusively on the influence of family and other adult agents of socialization, such as churches and schools. Given the freedom of leisure, children and adolescents will use play, games, sports and other activities to socialize themselves. Furthermore, there is a unique contribution of active engagement to development when it is shaped around enjoyment and intrinsic motivation. But structure appears to matter, as does some degree of self-direction, for the benefits to occur, especially those that would help shape a young person's identity. Unstructured play and social interaction may bring some benefits, on the other hand: relaxation may bring perspective and self-control; experimentation is a source of creativity and individuation; and casual sociability may lead to new relationships and even preliminary forms of community. But left on their own in the absence of structure and purpose, children and adolescents are vulnerable to the temptations of risky activities. Indeed, undirected leisure peers are even provocative of such deviant behavior. It is, after all, one way to assert independence from adults (while still reflecting some conformity to the norms of peers). Finally, though, the evidence of the impact of new forms of technologically based leisure challenges some previously held assumptions. Similarities to television watching—ingesting content that is provocative in its own right—leave online gaming and Internet use open to the same criticisms with respect to impacts on aggressive and violent behavior, as well as perpetuating gender stereotypes and sedentary lifestyles. But the apparently isolating effects of such "unnatural" activities are belied by the social interaction that is generated with them. Furthermore, the cognitive operations employed to participate are quite similar to those touted for structured activities. Indeed, technology can facilitate the investment, commitment, and overall engagement associated so clearly with personal development. Nevertheless, are the gains offered by such experiences the province of childhood and adolescence alone? To address that question we turn now to the impacts of leisure activities in adulthood.

Impacts of Leisure Experience on Adulthood and Later Life

Preview

In the previous chapter, we considered the question of impacts of leisure in the earlier periods of life. Now we turn our attention to the lives of people once they have grown up, as they become established, and in the years in which they negotiate many life changes. We have also established that play and leisure activities can have both positive and negative effects in childhood and adolescence. Is the same true of adulthood? Some of the same issues may apply, such as excessive conformity, exciting activities that may be destructive to self and others, or challenging activities that contribute to self-esteem. Most of the impacts of leisure in childhood and adolescence—relaxation, distraction, personal growth, and relationship formation—continue on into adulthood, albeit in different ways. But there are differences as well. Leaving home at the end of adolescence, for one example—whether to continue on independently in college or making one's way in the world of work—often affords new freedoms and indeed a new kind of leisure as a result. At the same time, adulthood is a context for assuming roles—worker, parent—that are constraining and determining in a variety of ways that may redefine leisure while recasting its value and purpose. We begin here with some illustrations of the possibilities.

Leisure as a Life Force and a Life Resource

Given the changes that occur in moving out of adolescence into the adult world and on through the life course, can the things that people do during their leisure help them enjoy life and deal with the challenges and demands that they often face along the way? And can leisure lead people to be something more—to themselves and others—than what might have been the case without it? Can leisure contribute to how positively or negatively people feel about their lives as a whole?

Take the case of Maria, for example. She has recently graduated from a nearby university and has taken a job in a large city where she has very few acquaintances. She is eager to find friends and, having recently suffered a painful breakup with a love interest, is interested in the prospects for a more permanent relationship with someone. But she also sees the opportunity to indulge her passion for dance and to cultivate her emerging interest in urban landscapes. Is there reason to expect that her leisure interests would play a prominent role in her transition?

Or consider Sally and Lebron, a couple who have had the good fortune to find work together at the same hospital for 30 years, Sally as an administrator and Lebron as a nurse. With an attractive early-retirement-package offer, both have decided to give up their jobs. Sally has a large number of leisure interests and was very active in her free time prior to retirement. Lebron had few leisure interests and most of his friends and acquaintances were associates from work. How will they adjust? What will they do to make life livable and enjoyable?

These scenarios are not uncommon, and they suggest some of the variety of ways that leisure may be influential over the span of adulthood. In the second scenario, one might expect that Sally would be able to make the best of somewhat unplanned early retirement, *if* her identity is based not only on her work activities but on meaningful leisure interests as well. In Maria's case, we can wonder if her leisure interests will help her reconstitute a social life that has been dealt a severe blow. And even without new friends, is there a prospect for her interests to help her get past the pain of the breakup? Such questions suggest at least the hunch that leisure may be influential in smoothing the way in other areas of life.

Nevertheless, researchers studying the relationship between the leisure and non-leisure domains of life have mostly treated leisure behavior as the *dependent variable*, that is, as the area of life that, while *relatively* unconstrained, is influenced by the demands of the other domains such as work, school, home, family, and interpersonal relationships and obligations. In other words, researchers often assume that leisure is more likely to be influenced by experiences in other areas of life than it is to have an influence on what goes on in those other domains. For example, in Chapter 9, we noted that the social role of parent, particularly that of a working mother, substantially reduces the amount of leisure time available (see, for example, Shaw, 1985b; Zuzanek & Smale, 1992). The demands and obligations in the work and family domains combined to strongly influence behavior in the leisure domain. Family, work, and gender roles have a powerful effect on leisure (e.g., Bella, 1989; Currie, 2004; Horna, 1989a; Horna & Lupri, 1987; Larson & Richards, 1994; Shaw, 1988). However, it is also important to consider the ways in which leisure participation might positively and negatively influence experiences of work, family, and community and adjustment to illness, loss, and aging. In the pages that follow, we look more closely at the issues raised in these cases and the evidence that bears on them. First, though, we will consider the more general evidence about the relationship between leisure participation, leisure experience, and leisure satisfaction as they relate to life satisfaction and other indicators of subjective well-being. Then we will look at the mechanisms of influence—such as enhancing mood, managing stress, compensating for imbalances, and creating social support—found in leisure activity. After that, we will turn more specifically to the contexts of work, family, and community to see what influence, if any, leisure experience has in each of these domains. And finally, we will examine still more specific circumstances of adult life where leisure experience has been shown to be influential, sometimes in negative as well as positive ways.

The Contribution of Leisure Activity to Subjective Well-Being

When researchers have examined the impact of leisure on well-being, they have often focused on satisfaction with the whole of life—that is, what is called *life satisfaction*. Life satisfaction is a popular measure of quality of life. People are typically asked to rate their satisfaction with life as a whole or some aspect of it. Satisfaction is seen to have a past-orientation, and life-satisfaction scales measure relatively enduring and stable beliefs or cognitions about what has transpired. Various measures differ in terms of whether they assess global satisfaction or satisfaction with specific domains of life (e.g., work, family, leisure, and neighborhood). By examining satisfaction with each of these domains, some researchers believe that a more accurate picture of overall quality of life can be obtained (see Mannell & Dupuis, 2007).

Numerous studies have attempted to establish that a positive relationship exists between what people do during their leisure time and their general feelings of well-being and life satisfaction. In this research, rarely have specific hypotheses about the nature of the links been examined. A general assumption has been that the more leisure activity in which people are involved and/or the higher their satisfaction with what they do in their leisure, the higher the level of satisfaction with life as a whole (see Haworth, 2003, and other articles, in that journal issue).

Generally, small but significant relationships have been found between the amount of leisure participation and life satisfaction. Positive relationships have been found for a number of different age groups including adults over the age of 18 years (Herzog & Rodgers, 1981), individuals 55 years and older (Romsa, Bondy, & Blenman, 1985), and those aged 65 and over (e.g., Fernandez-Ballesteros, Zamarron, & Ruiz, 2001; Kelly, Steinkamp, & Kelly, 1987; Menec, 2003). Though a few studies have found that social and psychologically involving pursuits, such as hobbies, sports, and outdoor recreation, may be more strongly related to life satisfaction than participation in passive pursuits (e.g., Butrica & Schaner, 2005; Kelly, Steinkamp, & Kelly, 1987; Ragheb, 1993), these relationships appear to differ according to gender, age, and stage in the life course (e.g., Brown, Frankel, & Fennell, 1991). Some of the strongest support for the link between leisure participation and life satisfaction comes from research on successful aging and life satisfaction, even suggesting that leisure activity levels may be better predictors of life satisfaction in later life than health and income (see Mannell & Dupuis, 2007).

Additionally, there is growing evidence that the strength of the influence of leisure participation on well-being varies substantially depending not only on age and gender, but on socioeconomic status, ethnicity, and race (Brown & Frankel, 1993; Brown, Frankel, & Fennell, 1991; Cutler Riddick & Gonder Stewart, 1994; Evans & Haworth, 1991). It is too early to identify any clear patterns. More research is needed to improve our understanding of the meaning of the differences that have been found. This understanding would be aided if researchers would design their studies to examine and test the various social psychological links that have been suggested to exist between leisure and well-being outcomes, and we will return shortly to some of those possibilities.

Measures of *leisure satisfaction* have been found to be better predictors of life satisfaction than have leisure participation measures—the higher the leisure satisfaction, the higher the life satisfaction (e.g., Brown, Frankel, & Fennell, 1991; Pearson, 1998; Ragheb, 1993; Ragheb & Griffith, 1982; Russell, 1987). However, the relationship between leisure satisfaction and life satisfaction appears to be moderated by occupation (Trafton & Tinsley, 1980; Willmott, 1971), gender (Allison & Duncan, 1987; Brown & Frankel, 1993), age and ethnicity (Allison, 1991; Allison & Smith, 1990), and marital and employment status (Haavio-Mannila, 1971). In a relatively early study on the subject, London, Crandall, and Seals (1977) found that job satisfaction and leisure satisfaction contributed independently to the quality of life, and that leisure satisfaction was the better predictor. However, they found the pattern to be more pronounced for some people than others. For example, neither leisure nor work satisfaction was important to the quality of life of relatively disadvantaged groups; and leisure satisfaction was more important for individuals with lifestyles not dominated by work activity. This latter finding was supported by Guinn (1980), who reported that, among retired recreational vehicle (RV) tourists, leisure satisfaction was strongly associated with life satisfaction. This latter finding points out an important issue: regardless of how satisfying people find their leisure to be or how frequently they participate in activities, their leisure may not strongly influence life satisfaction if they are at a place in their lives where leisure is overshadowed in importance by other concerns. On the other hand, there are likely times in people's lives when leisure participation and satisfaction are highly salient and important to them. We will look at such situations shortly, but first let's turn to just *how* leisure activity and experience is likely to be influential in people's lives.

How is Leisure Influential in Adulthood?

The general evidence of a relationship between leisure activity and life satisfaction, even when mediated by leisure satisfaction and other factors, doesn't tell how the activity or experience contributes or under what circumstances it contributes. In fact, because most of the evidence is correlational, we're not sure what influences what. Does satisfaction with leisure lead people to be more satisfied with other aspects of their lives, or does satisfaction in those contexts lead people to expand their involvement in more satisfying leisure activities? It is necessary then to look more closely at the ways in which leisure activities are influential when they are. Research suggests a number of possibilities: mood enhancement, compensation, self-preservation, self-protection, self-expansion, relationship formation, and aid to others. We will look at each of these in turn.

Leisure Activity Can Enhance Mood and Happiness

Perhaps the most obvious way that leisure activity impacts well-being and life in other domains is in the essence of leisure experience itself, as discussed in Chapters 3 and 4. Leisure choices are directed mostly at enhancing mood, principally by following interests to raise arousal to an optimal level, reducing arousal to an optimal level through relaxation, and relishing the affection and support of others. As was discussed in the previous chapter, simple pleasures and relaxation are important to well-being throughout the life course, whether it be through travel, watching television, or swinging in a hammock with a grandchild. Modulating emotions in these ways through leisure activities and experience not only affords temporary adjustment but can improve functioning in other aspects of life and subjective well-being in general. We'll have more to say about modulating negative emotions and coping with stress in the section on self-protection below.

Research on emotion indicates that positive emotions lead to a variety of effects that strengthen general psychological capacity (Folkman, 2008; Fredrickson, 2001, 2002, 2003; see also Carruthers & Hood, 2004). Joy, especially, seems to endure, to spill over in some ways, and to make one more resilient. This effect is true throughout life, as was suggested in Chapter 11, but studies of aging in particular have been revealing. For example interviews with a group of members of a "Red Hat Society" demonstrated that the joy, contentment, and love that is experienced in playful interactions with others—with the intention of having fun and being "outrageous"—empowered the older participants and made them feel happier and stronger in the other aspects of their lives (Mitas, Qian, & Yarnal, 2008; Yarnal, Chick, & Kerstetter, 2008). Subjective well-being, and happiness in particular, may be attributable to a variety of causes, some of which will be addressed shortly, but clearly the generation of positive emotions and the reduction of negative emotions contribute. Some of it, no doubt, derives from competent role performance at work, home, and in family and community contexts; to be happy, it helps to bring in the buoyancy of positive experiences from other circumstances. Thus, it may go in multiple directions, working from one context to another as situations change; but it is worth noting that good feelings are frequently generated in leisure first, whatever the subsequent effects may be.

So what leisure activity or setting works best? Any activity might afford some of the emotional uplift that we have been considering. But some activities in particular have been singled out for their reputed effects. For many people, just being in outdoor settings for extended periods of time has a salubrious effect. A review of the therapeutic effects of parks and protected areas revealed several ways in which the experience of walking, hiking, wandering, or just looking enhance mood and a sense of well-being: the contrast from everyday life is novel and stimulating; the activity demands some initiative and action from the individual; and interaction with the environment provides immediate feedback (Ewert, Hollenhorst, McAvoy, & Russell, 2003; see also Schwartz & Campagna, 2008).

Gardening, as another example, seems to invoke for some people a sense of connectedness with the physical world that may be missing in other contexts. The smells themselves may stimulate sensory associations that are thought to stimulate the limbic system and the memory in pleasant ways (Driedger, 1996). Despite only limited scientific evidence in support of such observations, confidence in this perspective has contributed to rapid growth of wilderness therapy and horticulture therapy in the U.S. and Canada. Target populations typically are those with special mental health needs, but the effects are likely experienced by the average person walking in the woods or pushing a spade into the ground to plant flowers, fruit trees, or vegetables. Gardening has even been shown to have a spiritual aspect, by providing a sense of connectedness with nature as a life force, a sense of the future, an expression of inner being, a spiritual journey, and feelings of stewardship (Unruh & Hutchinson, 2008).

Leisure Can Be a Resource for Balance and Compensation

Another way in which leisure contributes to psychological well-being is suggested by the *need-compensation* theory. As we saw in our discussion of leisure needs in Chapter 5, human beings are thought to have a variety of physiological and psychological needs that they must regularly satisfy if they are to lead happy and fulfilled lives. These needs can be met through a wide range of activities and experiences. However, due to the particular lifestyle circumstances in which people find themselves, they are often unable to satisfy specific needs as fully as they would like. Given that leisure is typically the least constrained domain of people's lives and provides greater freedom of choice, leisure activities can be selected to "compensate" or satisfy these unmet needs.

This need-compensation idea has its roots in theories about the relationship between work and leisure, particularly the impact of work on leisure (see Iso-Ahola & Mannell, 1985; Kabanoff, 1980). One of these theories suggests that people can compensate for the negative aspects of their jobs in their leisure. For example, if their jobs are constraining and socially isolating, they will participate in leisure activities that allow them to exercise control over their lives and socialize. Most of the research on work-leisure relationships has focused on determining if the activities or tasks that comprise people's work influence the activities in which they engage during their leisure. At the behavioral level, only limited support has been found for the compensation notion. Little research has been reported that examines whether needs that go unmet on the job actually influence people to choose leisure activities on the basis of their need-satisfying properties and ability to compensate. Nevertheless, several studies have suggested that working people do feel that their leisure compensates for needs that go unmet in other areas of their lives (e.g., Hildebrand & Mannell, 1996; Kelly, 1975), a subject we will take up again shortly when we look at work per se. Lounsbury and Hoopes (1985) found that one of the main reasons the workers they studied gave for taking vacations was to escape the routines of work. In a study of vacation preferences, Wahlers and Etzel (1985) determined that if work was stressful, relaxing leisure activities were preferred, and if work was not stimulating, people would look for stimulation and excitement in their leisure. It has also been suggested that leisure can compensate for needs that go unmet due to loss of a job because of unemployment or retirement (e.g., Haworth, 1984; Shamir, 1988; Stebbins, 1992a, 2007). We will examine this issue of leisure, unemployment, and retirement in a later section of this chapter.

Compensation in leisure would seem particularly important when work is narrowing, alienating, degrading, or exhausting. Social psychologists write about such effects as being "ego-depleting" (Baumeister, 1998), and it is reasonable to assume that whatever depletion results from tending to one's job requirements, leisure activities might have the effect of restoring a sense of balance and well-being. For this to happen, though, the activities would probably need to draw on one's competence, perhaps enhancing a sense of competence in the process. Clearly skill-based leisure activities have this potential, particularly "serious" leisure activities (Stebbins, 2007). On the other hand, even casual, relaxing leisure may compensate for the excesses of work, especially where work is stressful and tiring, particularly physically so. Over the last 60 years or so, television watching has assumed the lion's share of our free time activities, and most people use it as a form of relaxation. The experience-sampling research that has been done on the quality of experience watching television suggests that while it comes up well short of other activities in terms of optimal experience, it does seem to be relaxing (Kubey & Csikszentmihalyi, 1990). Whether it actually has the effect of restoring energy, however, has not been very well-established.

Other ways in which leisure activities may compensate or even correct for some of the negative effects of work include: providing togetherness where work is isolating, creativity and self-expression in response to repetitive and tedious work patterns, physical activity in response to sedentary work, and a focus on the present in response to an emphasis on planning and preparation.

This is not to suggest that compensation will occur automatically. If it did, all workers should have high levels of psychological well-being and job satisfaction. Constraints, such as a lack of skill, time, or opportunity may prevent people from engaging in the appropriate leisure activities to achieve compensation for alienating, unfulfilling, or depleting work.

Work at home, much of it unpaid, may also be a cause of imbalance and create a need for compensation. Child rearing and other kinds of caregiving can be exhaustingly demanding and leave a person in a condition of deficit of one kind or another. Caring for children, or aging parents, offers a wide variety of rewards—including those afforded by shared leisure—but the needs for self-expression, solitude, and more age-specific companionship often need to be redressed. This may be especially true in more demanding caregiving situations. For example, a study of work, family, and leisure balance among women teleworkers (Shaw, Andrey, & Johnson, 2003) demonstrated that even with some of the advantages of flexibility as to when to work at home, the problem of balance can be exacerbated by ambiguities of purpose and undermine the compensatory potential of leisure. It may be difficult to finish that report when one's 3-year-old wants to play ball.

It should be recognized, of course, that work may be satisfying in and of itself. It may be intrinsically *and* extrinsically rewarding (cf. Wrzesniewski, Rozin, & Bennett, 2003). "Good work" has both properties, as well as a sense of meaning and purpose (Gardner, Csikszentmihalyi, & Damon, 2001). In this case leisure may not be critically important. We worry about workaholics, because we think they are neither having any fun nor relaxing, but if their work brings them the same optimal experience as do some leisure activities, then compensation through leisure isn't necessary. Indeed, studies of the experiences of work and leisure overall find that work is even more likely to yield the optimal experiences of flow than leisure (Csikszentmihalyi & Lefevre, 1989; though, again, that also follows from the fact that the bulk of leisure activity for most people is television watching). So, should we be concerned about those apparently "addicted" to work? They may well be in flow for much of the time and their extended hours may simply reflect the desire to continue to experience such "leisure-like" experience. But the answer to the question is, yes, we should be concerned, because while psychological experience may be optimal in such circumstances, role relationships often suffer and such intense involvement may be narrowing and limiting in other respects. Workaholics' relationships with families and friends routinely suffer from such excesses (Machlowicz, 1980). But, interestingly, the same may be said of serious leisure activities (e.g., Stenseng, 2008). Our primary source on the subject, Robert Stebbins, who has studied musicians, collectors, and many others who have passionate attachments to their activities, acknowledges that such individuals may be subject to some of the same negative consequences as the workaholic (1992b, 2007). In this case, rather than redressing an imbalance through compensation, leisure activities *create* an imbalance; as was the case with adolescent electronic media use, they may act to *displace* activities and relationships in life that may be at least as important.

Leisure Can Be a Source of Self-Preservation and Continuity

Similar to the idea of compensation for needs unmet in other domains of life is the idea that leisure may be the place where a sense of self is maintained regardless of the difficulties and losses that beset one in other aspects of life. We are often forced to abandon activities—to compromise to meet the domains of circumstances such as leaving one's job or moving to a new location—that are disruptive to a sense of self, especially when favored leisure activities may be lost in the process. The ability to draw on other activities in a repertoire or to substitute activities for those that are lost can preserve a sense of self and a sense of personal continuity. Indeed, to the extent that activity involvement is associated with personal identity, then maintaining that activity in some ways is crucially important to emotional stability, as was suggested in Chapter 7.

This function of leisure is perhaps best represented in theories of successful aging that emphasize persistent activity in the face of loss of work and other roles. The idea of staying active compensates for some of the activity losses associated with ending work roles through retirement, and we will deal with this replacement/substitution function shortly, but the theory that most accurately describes the patterned activities of later life is the continuity theory (Atchley, 1989, 1993, 1999) in which people maintain their favorite activities, and associated companionships, as a familiar convoy for enduring the losses associated with later life. Atchley hastens to point out that the activities need not be exactly the same to provide a sense of continuity; indeed new activities may be substituted for older activities—and for lost work tasks and roles—while being familiar enough to preserve a sense of self. Atchley refers to this as maintaining *inner continuity,* where external activities may be changed in some respects but the underlying meaning is preserved, while others have talked about this as preservation of self (Kleiber, Hutchinson, & Williams, 2002; Nimrod & Kleiber, 2007).

This brings up the more general issue of *substitution* as it relates to continuity and self-preservation. Can one activity substitute for another that is no longer available? Can trail biking substitute for cross-country skiing for someone who moves from Minnesota to Alabama for the summer? Can Maria, who has recently graduated from college and left her college friends, use her passion for dance to bring her together with others in her new city? Can those activities at work that were satisfying—skills that afforded a specific sense of competence, for example— find adequate substitutes in leisure when the job has been lost or given up? It obviously depends to some extent on how close the new activity is in form and experience to the replaced activity as to how well the substitution will be received. Substitutability has long been a special problem for leisure researchers (e.g., Iso-Ahola, 1986), because there is considerable complexity in judging comparability of activities.

Activity theory (Havighurst, 1963) suggests that as people age they should maintain active lifestyles by replacing or substituting lost roles and social activities with new ones, in order to maintain their self-concept and a sense of well-being or life satisfaction. Leisure is seen as crucial in allowing the maintenance of this active lifestyle. As with the research on leisure activity and life satisfaction referred to earlier, reviews of the activity theory of aging conclude that there is substantial support for the hypothesis that the more active people are in their later years, the greater will be their subjective well-being (Chiriboga & Pierce, 1993; Dupuis, 2008; Kelly, 1987a; Kelly & Ross, 1989; Kelly, Steinkamp, & Kelly, 1987; Lawton, 1994; Menec, 2003; Nimrod, 2007a,b; Steinkamp & Kelly, 1986). But as with much of the research on leisure and well-being, the process by which leisure activities contribute to life satisfaction and successful aging has been left unspecified and unfortunately has had insufficient empirical examination (Dupuis, 2008; Dupuis & Smale, 1995; Kelly & Ross, 1989; Mannell & Dupuis, 2007). However, if older adults are able to remain active by continuing to engage in life-long leisure involvements or by substituting new activities to replace those they have lost, then it is reasonable to believe that the psychological mechanisms that link leisure participation and successful adaptation and aging have at least as much to do with self-preservation as does the activity per se. In fact, just doing activity for activity's sake, where activities are not meaningfully associated with a person's past or goals, is not a recommended strategy for successful aging or adaptation to change in general (cf. Kleiber, 1985; Kleiber et al., 2008).

Enduring personal meaning is also often reflected in one's attachment to leisure places (Kyle, Graefe, & Manning, 2004; Williams, 2002). Personal identity is reinforced and restored simply by being in a preferred place at times, whether in the woods and mountains of a particular state or in one's hometown library. There is even a spirituality associated with special places for some that adds to one's personal connection (Heintzman & Mannell, 2003). And, of course, this sense of place may apply particularly to places of worship as well, where time is voluntarily spent for purposes of self-renewal and spiritual transcendence.

Finally, the function of self-preservation and continuity in leisure activities is important to group solidarity and cultural preservation (e.g., Kim, Kleiber, & Kropf, 2001; Stodoska, 1998). Regular events such as festivals, holidays, and parades not only contribute to social and community connectedness (as we will consider again shortly), but may also be personally reassuring and stabilizing (Kyle & Chick, 2002).

Self-Protection and Coping Can Be Facilitated with Leisure Activity

Leisure as a Source of Protection

Sometimes leisure experience and activity may have the greatest impact in the *protection* of feelings of well-being rather than in the production of them. As noted earlier and in Chapter 11, people turn to leisure to reduce stress related to frustration and fatigue. Activities, whether physical or mental, that lead to relaxation and the refreshment of capacities are important antidotes to the pressures of everyday life (see Norling & Sibthorp, 2006, for a review related to recreation). Moving to a more tranquil setting or even *viewing* one can also bring relief and restoration (Kaplan, 1995).

A few studies have found evidence that when people in stressful conditions are actively involved in leisure, the negative impact of the stress on health and well-being is reduced. In an early experimental study, Heywood (1978) demonstrated that the stress of performing a challenging task was relieved to a greater extent by passive activities such as music, reading, and television viewing, when they were perceived as leisure. Physically active leisure has been found to help patients reduce hypertension resulting from stress (Pierce, Madden, Siegel, & Blumenthal, 1993) and help older adults decrease anxiety and the symptoms of depression (King, Barr Taylor, & Haskell, 1993). Caltabiano (1995) found that people who participated more frequently in passive cultural and hobby activities also reported fewer illness symptoms when they were under greater stress. And in a study of gender differences in coping with stress in professional management settings, Iwasaki and colleagues (2005) found that male managers were more inclined to use physically active forms of recreation than females, but that both groups recognized the value of activities for "deflecting stressful thoughts." In occupations where stress is commonplace —as with emergency workers (Iwasaki et al., 2002)—low-demand leisure activities have been shown to be better than high-demand activities for being distracting. The likely effect with high demand activities is that while they may have a better prospect of being flow-producing, performance demands may increase levels of stress.

But is leisure still a resource when the stress is severe, where an assaulting event results in more significant harm or loss? Evidence indicates that it can be, in both direct and indirect ways (e.g., Carpenter, 1989; Coleman, 1993; Coleman & Iso-Ahola, 1993; Hutchinson et al., 2003b; Iso-Ahola & Park, 1996; Iwasaki, 2003; Iwasaki & Mannell, 2000a,b; Kleiber, Hutchinson, & Williams, 2002). We will have more to say about how leisure is actually *used* in the face of threat, injury, and loss a bit later, but in a more general and perhaps less direct sense, leisure activities, experiences, and associations with others can serve to "buffer" such effects in life. To some extent, people differ in relatively stable ways with respect to the leisure-generated psychological resources or assets that may have the effect of reducing the impact of the stressors (i.e., resources that people *carry over* into a stressful situation).

Coleman and Iso-Ahola (1993) first elaborated this theory based on the findings of social psychological research on coping with stressful life events, noting that various life events, especially negative events such as losing a job or acquiring financial debt, have been shown to lead to a higher incidence of mental and physical illness. They argued that leisure participation facilitates coping with such stressful life events in two ways (see Figure 12.1). First, it has been found that an effective source of relief from life stress is the perception that *social support* is available, if needed. Therefore, leisure that is highly social in nature can facilitate the development of companionship and friendship, and consequently, social support. Second, enduring beliefs of *self-determination* have been found to contribute to people's coping capacity and health. When people feel that they generally have some ability to control the good and bad things that happen to them, they experience less mental and physical illness or ill health. The central characteristics of leisure, perceptions of freedom and control, allow the development and maintenance of stable self-determination dispositions, that is, feelings of being in control of one's life. These perceptions of social support and self-determination are described as *buffers* against life stress, and when life stress is high, leisure's contribution

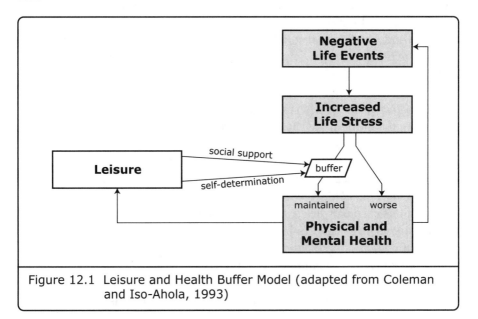

Figure 12.1 Leisure and Health Buffer Model (adapted from Coleman and Iso-Ahola, 1993)

to health is expected to be greater. The leisure buffer and coping theory postulates that:

> . . . leisure impacts health by providing buffering mechanisms that come into play when life presents significant problems. On the other hand, when life stress is relatively low leisure's contribution to health is expected to be less substantial on the short-term basis. In the long run, however, leisure is hypothesized to contribute to health by building health-promoting dispositions, such as self-determination. (Coleman & Iso-Ahola, 1993, p. 113)

This theory has been supported in a number of studies (see Dupuis, 2008; Iwasaki & Mannell, 2000a,b; and Iwasaki & Schneider, 2003, for reviews). Earlier research from clinical and counseling psychology is also consistent. Reich and Zautra (1981), in an experimental study, failed to find any benefit to mental health for students who faced lower levels of life stress, but those students under higher levels of stress did benefit from having engaged in leisure activities. Wheeler and Frank (1988) found that people whose leisure participation was high or who were satisfied with their leisure were less vulnerable to the adverse effects of life stress than those who were less active and satisfied with their leisure. A similar buffering effect was found by Brown (1991) for exercise and stress, and the buffering effect did not appear to be due solely to the increased physical fitness benefits of physical recreation. Brown speculated that the increased feelings of competency that the exercise provided might have contributed to its buffering effects. Caltabiano (1995) examined the buffering effects of participation in several types of leisure activities and found partial support for the leisure buffer and coping theory, though she did not directly examine whether participation fostered feelings of social support and self-determination. In 1993, Coleman attempted to more directly test the linking mechanisms. He found that among people who experienced higher levels of life stress, those who perceived a high degree of freedom and control in their leisure reported significantly lower levels of illness than those people who perceived low levels of freedom and control (see Figure 12.2). However, he found no evidence that leisure-based social support acted as a buffer. Clearly more research is needed on these and other possible buffering mechanisms. We will turn again to the matter of coping in a later section of this chapter, when we examine specific circumstances where research has shown leisure to have an impact.

When it comes to protection of a sense of well-being, leisure experience can be protective in both direct and indirect ways. The indirect ways were reflected in how prior leisure experience and leisure associations contribute to a sense of self-determination and social support, enabling one to be resilient and resourceful in the face of significant stressors (Coleman & Iso-Ahola, 1993; Iso-Ahola & Park, 1996; Iwasaki & Mannell, 2000b). In the next two sections, however, we look more specifically at how leisure experience works *directly* in coping with stressful events and situations and with loss as actions taken in response to the occurrence. Self-protection in direct coping takes two essential forms, one that minimizes the impact of the threat or stressor, what is sometimes called a *palliative* effect, and one that uses more of an interpretation to allow for a *reappraisal* of the situation and somewhat more control over it as a result. As adjustment to events continues, leisure may be used still further to restore a sense of self, as we have just considered in the previous section, and even to grow from the experience in a kind of self-transformation, as we will turn to shortly, but here we will just address the two essential self-protection functions of coping.

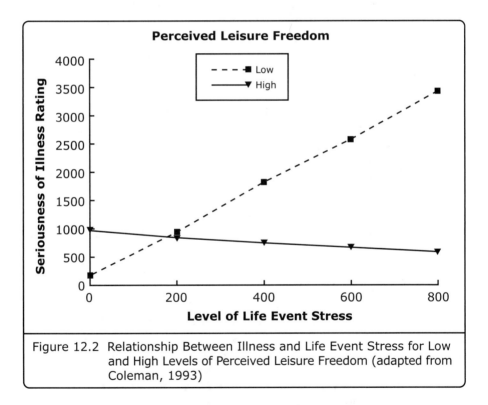

Figure 12.2 Relationship Between Illness and Life Event Stress for Low and High Levels of Perceived Leisure Freedom (adapted from Coleman, 1993)

Minimizing the Impact of Stressors through Distraction

In Chapter 11, we considered diversion and distraction in leisure activity to be a valuable alternative in childhood and adolescence to risky and health-compromising behavior. But preoccupying activities also have the virtue of keeping one's mind diverted from distressing thoughts that may be triggered by stressful life events, such as the death of a spouse or the excessive demands of a job. By keeping the mind busy, people may temporarily avoid or escape the stress of these events. Television programs, exercise, and other activities that distract are among a wide range of diversionary actions that have the value of substituting positive feelings for negative ones and breaking into the negative ruminations ("Why did it happen to me?" "What did I do to deserve it?" etc.) that follow most unexpected and unwanted disruptive events (Folkman, 1997, 2008; Folkman & Moskowitz, 2000). Such activities, sometime called "breathers," (Folkman, 1997), allow those who are so stressed to psychologically "regroup," and when they "return" they may be better able to deal with their problems (e.g., Folkman, 2008; Harvey & Bahr, 1980; Lazarus & Folkman, 1984; Lopata, 1967; Parkes, 1972). This kind of coping is referred to as "emotion focused" or palliative coping. In the past, there was speculation in the leisure literature about the role of leisure participation in dealing with stress that is consistent with the notion of palliative coping (Hogan & Santomier, 1982; Kleiber, 1985). This hypothesis is based upon the assumption that while people are involved in a leisure activity, their attention shifts away from the source of their stress. Even if involvement in an activity is not very deep, focusing on it distracts one from a focus on self and the stressors. Leisure participation may thus serve as an adaptive form of palliative coping.

Loss of a spouse is usually a very negative and stressful life event. In a test of the "keeping busy" or palliative leisure coping hypothesis, Sharp and Mannell (1996) studied 62 recently widowed older women and a comparison group of 19 married women. They found that those widowed women who were more active in their leisure experienced less guilt and sadness and greater happiness during their daily lives. Also, the higher their overall leisure participation and level of enjoyment of their three most frequent leisure activities, the lower the emotional distress (e.g., depression) reported (see Figure 12.3). The widowed women reported that they attempted to keep busy with leisure activities to temporarily escape or distract themselves from emotional distress (palliative coping). Among the married women in the study, only a small proportion kept busy for these types of reasons. A much higher proportion of the married women kept busy to enjoy themselves and used leisure for personal development than did the widowed women (see Figure 12.4).

Restoring a Sense of Optimism through Pleasant Experience
Using leisure to keep busy is then a very common palliative strategy in coping with stress and loss. But if such actions are primarily escapist, they may only have short-term value, without enabling a person to adjust more completely to the problem. More complete adjustment requires some reappraisal of the situation, "reframing" of a sort that leaves a person with a new view. Such reframing may be made more likely with relaxing leisure that allows

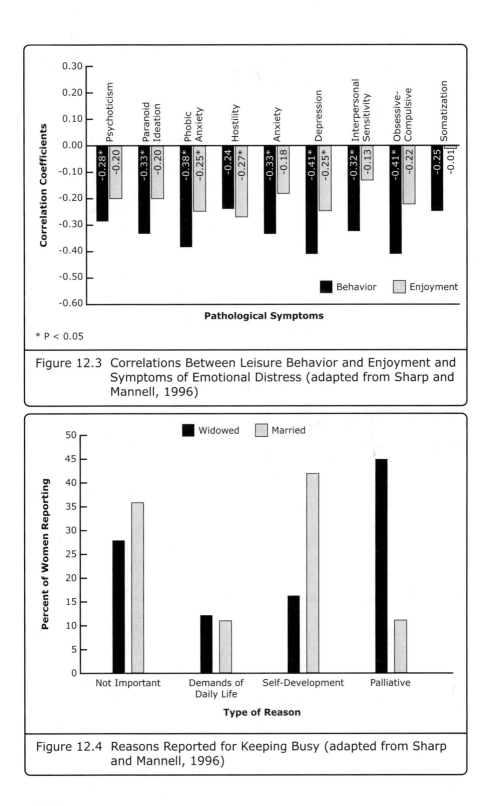

Figure 12.3 Correlations Between Leisure Behavior and Enjoyment and Symptoms of Emotional Distress (adapted from Sharp and Mannell, 1996)

Figure 12.4 Reasons Reported for Keeping Busy (adapted from Sharp and Mannell, 1996)

one to "breathe deeply" and get perspective, and it may use the enjoyment created through the activities to restore an element of faith and hopefulness about life after the troubling events (Kleiber et al., 2002). And while serious leisure and flow may offer the preoccupying activity that keeps a person's mind off the trouble, the humor-generating aspects of casual, relaxing, and social leisure situations can be "relativizing" in a way that puts the problem into some manageable perspective. In a recent study, comparing humor (watching a video of stand-up comedy) with a bout of exercise, the former was found to be more effective in reducing anxiety (Szabo, 2003).

Sometimes having others around when stressed and depressed has value for mood elevation, but the impact of having friendly co-participants involved in an activity is not always consistently positive. Their presence may also be a source of anxiety, especially where the activity requires some skill and social comparison is likely (e.g., Caltabiano, 1994; Glover & Parry, 2008; Iwasaki et al., 2002; Iwasaki & Mannell, 2000b).

Leisure Experiences Influence Relationship Formation and Stability

Research on the subjects of attraction and love demonstrates that friendship and attachment are constructed around shared experience, shared enjoyment and understanding in particular, and familiarity (Aron & Aron, 1986). To some extent, the leisure interests and activities of others are a first source of attraction, indicators that shared meaning may be created and preferred experience might be shared. Novelty and familiarity both play a role in such patterns, and these sources of meaning even change in relative importance with age, as we will see. But it is inevitable that both friendship and romantic attachments are solidified with common experience and understanding.

"Opposites attract" so we are told, and this may be true initially to some extent; the same curiosity and intrinsic interest that shapes the arousal-seeking behavior so common to leisure experience is also reflected in our interest in other people. But there is in fact very little evidence to support contrast and even complementarity as the basis for a continuing or enduring relationship (Aronson, 2008; Fiske, 2004). Shared interests and attitudes play a much bigger role, even when gender is different. But the basic need for relatedness also draws us to others more essentially. Others are a source of information and potential growth, but they offer human connection first and foremost. We go from being intrigued by the differences in others to an appreciation for "what we have in common." What people actually do for enjoyment may intrigue us initially for the change and growth it suggests and this becomes important again in the enrichment and growth of an established relationship, but the sharing of interests and passions has the greatest impact in drawing people closer together in the first place, be they friends or lovers.

Dance is not only a leisure activity that can be a precious means of relationship formation; it also offers a metaphor for what happens with a lot of shared activity. Interacting in some reactive way to one another, whether in sport, written correspondence, or coordination of travel plans, creates a connection that has some enduring impact. The guru of "flow," Mihaly Csikszentmihalyi, has even written about romantic love as being shaped around "shared flow" (1980). Certainly we can see physical intimacy and sexuality as having that quality at their best, but running together, decorating a room together, or even listening to music together can produce some of the same effects.

Is it different for friendship? Is it just a matter of degree? Perhaps. There are other differences as well, no doubt, but friendships are formed and strengthened in much the same ways; we find friends among those with similar characteristics and similar interests and with differences as well. We are attracted to those who are competent and who like us (Aronson, 2008).

And what about the internal dynamics of groups larger than two? Certainly social groups and cliques gain their strength of cohesion in part from what they share and this may be in what they experience together as fun or enjoy as interests in common. Still larger groups gain a sense of solidarity around shared activities and rituals as well. A study of "social synchrony" and cooperation in marching bands demonstrated that the participants were equally as likely to be generous toward each other outside of the context of performing as in that context (Wiltermuth & Heath, 2009).

Generally, then, we can argue along with others (e.g., Kelly, 1983, 1993) that leisure is a major social space for the development and maintenance of relationships, and that the need and desire for social interaction is a powerful motive for a great deal of leisure behavior (Aron & Aron, 1986; Aron et al., 2000; Herridge, Shaw, & Mannell, 2003; Iso-Ahola, 1980a). There is some evidence that certain kinds of leisure can "spice up" or enhance both friendships and marital relationships by making the social interaction more exciting and enjoyable (Larson, Mannell, & Zuzanek, 1986), as well as by contributing to the participants' personal growth through the enhancement of those relationships (Berg, Trost, Schneider, & Allison, 2001; Reissman, Aron, & Bergen, 1993). We will turn again to leisure in marriage relationships when we focus on families later in this chapter, but the impact on relationships more generally warrants closer scrutiny here.

In a study using the experience sampling method, Larson, Mannell, and Zuzanek (1986) examined the influence of leisure on the quality of interpersonal relationships with friends and family members in leisure and non-leisure settings. When the quality of the respondents' experiences in these relationships was examined, it was found that interactions with a spouse were experienced as the least positive and exciting; interactions with friends were experienced as much more positive and exciting. However, before one gets too cynical about long-term committed relationships, it should be noted that the researchers found that the most positive and exciting experiences occurred when individuals were interacting with friends *along with* their spouse (see Figure 12.5. Further analysis suggested that the power of friends to generate positive feelings and excitement was tied to the more frequent participation in active leisure pursuits that typically occurred when with them. Most interaction with family members, particularly spouses, was done in the context of maintenance and passive leisure activities—housework and watching television. In contrast, when the people in the study were with friends, or friends and spouses, socializing was engaged in more than a third of the time, and active pursuits, such as religious and cultural activities, hobbies and sport, were more frequent. Watching television and doing housework were well down the list in frequency.

In their initial stages, romantic relationships may be threatened by activities that are individualistically self-expanding, especially for traditional males and females. An interview study with 13 Canadian women between the ages of 19 and 24 revealed real tensions between accommodating the

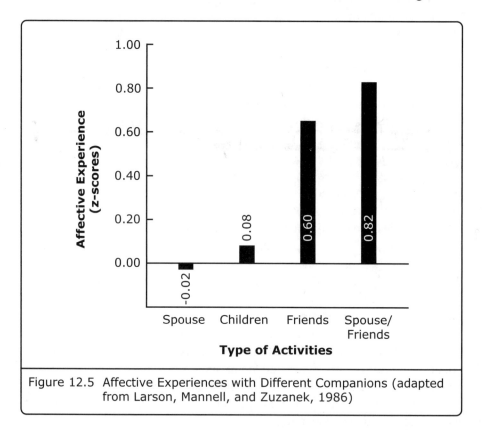

Figure 12.5 Affective Experiences with Different Companions (adapted from Larson, Mannell, and Zuzanek, 1986)

leisure interests of one's romantic partner and resisting them in the interest of one's own (non-couple) leisure preferences (Herridge et al., 2003). Non-romantic relationships as well are often fraught with similar tensions over leisure. Establishing similarity of interests and preferences is a primary response to attraction to others and the desire to develop and maintain relationships. While the more celebrated examples of conformity in leisure have already been discussed with respect to adolescents in the previous chapter, the pull of social relatedness as a basic need, and accommodation and conformity in expressive behavior as a strategic response, applies well into adulthood. Thus, people bowl or play golf primarily for the opportunity it affords to be in close proximity to another, whether that be a prospective sexual partner or influential work associate, sometimes without enjoying the "leisure activity" at all. Of course, there are great individual differences in who will conform under such circumstances and how far that conformity will take them, but such accommodation is, again, often strategic in early adulthood. Only after one has ceased to need to be persuasive or to accommodate others to "get along" does the need to associate in this way diminish. From midlife on, such social needs change and more emphasis is typically placed on doing activities for their own sake, their own intrinsic merits and for the more meaningful personal and pleasant relationships that they afford (e.g., Carstensen, Isaacowitz, & Charles, 1999; Nimrod, 2008b). Here again, though, we can find exceptions in later life as well.

Other, perhaps greater, risks associated with conforming in leisure to the behaviors of others have also been reviewed (with respect to adolescence in particular in Chapter 11), but some of these patterns continue through emerging adulthood (Arnett, 2000, 2004) into early adulthood. Behavior that affords entry into a desirable subgroup may be illegal or personally destructive (e.g., drug and alcohol use) or demeaning to others (e.g., hostile humor or pornography; cf. Shaw, 1999b). But maintaining attachments may be the draw and shared leisure—however much it is actually enjoyed for its own sake—the means for creating and maintaining the relationships. Even styles of dress or smoking cigarettes may be embraced in leisure primarily for their social cache, rather than their intrinsic value (Wearing & Wearing, 2000).

In fact, conformity to the group can lead to extremes in negative behavior, including aggression and violence. The best examples are associated with soccer "hooliganism"—common and often studied in Great Britain and Europe (e.g., Wakefield & Wann, 2006)—where crowds of ecstatic fans become riotous and unruly, often causing damage to property and person alike. A social psychological phenomenon associated with such behavior is *deindividuation* (Aronson, 2008), whereby one's own sense of self as separate from the group is relaxed to the point where one literally follows the crowd and abandons the usual conventional codes of moral and ethical behavior. Under such a spell, a person is disinhibited and behaves in uncharacteristic ways. Intoxication from alcohol and other drugs, leisure experiences in their own right, commonly provoke and exacerbate such effects.

Leisure Activities May Promote Self-Expansion and Personal Growth

Since leisure is readily appropriated to serve the basic needs for competence and autonomy, it is reasonable to consider that the various components of subjective well-being, such as self-esteem and life satisfaction, may be enhanced when activities raise levels of perceived competence and self-determination. The flow model that we have considered earlier is predicated on the idea that improved skills in an activity may make an activity that was too difficult and challenging (consider rock climbing for beginners) manageable and flow-producing, and that once mastery occurs, flow is only recovered when challenges are increased and skills are improved yet further. This is felt as enhanced competence and, indeed, the "complexification" and expansion of self (see especially Csikszentmihalyi, 1993). Similarly, activities taken seriously to the extent that one perseveres and develops a sense of being one of "those who are good at" something (knitting, playing the mandolin, raising show dogs, etc.) will provide "enduring benefits" to self-esteem (Stebbins, 1992, 2007). Leisure activities that seem associated with enhanced self-esteem probably have that impact by building self-efficacy (essentially self-confidence) and the powers of self-regulation (Iso-Ahola et al., 1989; Loucks-Atkinson & Mannell, 2007; Mannell & Loucks-Atkinson, 2005; Pohl, Borrie, & Patterson, 2000).

Again though, one should be careful not to assume that these benefits are simply a matter of mastering leisure skills. Being a top performer may indeed have some social value, enhancing one's status with others, as we noted in the preceding section and in Chapter 11. But it is the prospect that such skill mastery will be sufficiently impactful to be transformative, generating a new version of self that is at least slightly different from earlier versions, that gives the activity its power. That is the meaning of self-expansion and self-complexification. Such changes may also have social value and indeed may even enhance primary relationships, but that is beside the point.

Skill development is not entirely necessary, however, for change and transformation to occur in the context of leisure. In some cases, exposure to nature alone may have the power to bring about such changes (Ewert et al., 2003; Johnson & Hood, 2008). Exposure to aspects of life not previously considered—through travel, through exploration, through experimentation—can also be revealing of aspects of self that may not have previously been there or recognized as being there (Nimrod, 2008c; Roberson, 2001). The experience can also have the impact of enhancing a sense of self-determination.

Even drug use may be self expansive in a limited way. In studying cannabis usage of tourists, researchers found several motivations to consume marijuana while traveling—including experimentation, pleasure, and diversion-seeking, and quest for authenticity—that they attributed to loosening of social control and the normalization of drug use (Belhassen, Santos, & Uriely, 2007). Of course, taking part in such illegal activities can be destabilizing and disintegrative to the individual in some respects and also to his or her relationships. This is especially true when the activity involves some distancing from others or some violation of social norms. Deviant and illegal activities may be fun, interesting, and self-expressive in some respects—serving the goal of individuation for some as we have noted—and embraced as a means to enhance sociability or escape social convention (e.g., Carruthers, 1993; Shinew & Parry, 2005); but the social costs of such deviance may make any internalization of the changes to self more difficult if not impossible or may lead to some acceptance of undesirable self-perceptions.

Some of the more positive ways in which leisure experience can lead to self-expansion, however, may occur where least expected. People faced with difficult life circumstances and stressful life events—rather than giving into helplessness and relying on leisure only for escape—may take their conditions and circumstances as catalysts for change. Research on the role of leisure in coping with negative life events suggests that not only are leisure activities sources of distraction, renewed optimism, and self-restoration as we've discussed above, they are also sometimes reflected in the ways people respond to those events in making a new life (Kleiber et al., 2002). For example, a young man whose auto accident has deprived him of the sports that he had loved so much turns to writing and finds that he has a gift for narrative and the short story. Researchers studying response to traumatic events have judged such changes as "post-traumatic growth." They have observed that among the changes made by people who have experienced injuries, lost a child, suffered life-threatening illness like cancer or heart attacks, been sexually assaulted, or undergone other traumatic events—are changes in perspective about living in and enjoying the present and turning to new expressive activities (Tedeschi & Calhoun, 2004). Self-renewal is an important part of life, and although not everyone responds to challenges in a way that sees them as opportunities or even takes advantage of what is afforded for personal change, many do.

Personal change may seem more the purpose of early adulthood than later adulthood. There are clear differences in preferences for novel leisure among younger people and for more familiar pleasures and interests in later life as we noted in Chapter 8, but using leisure for self-renewal occurs throughout the life course (e.g., Carpenter, 2003; Grafanaki et al., 2005), and even peo-ple in their later years are often inclined to try new things (Nimrod, 2008a; Nimrod & Kleiber, 2007; Vaillant, 2002). It is tempting to draw a connection to activity theories of aging that we referred to above in the sections on com-pensation and continuity, but new activities that are somehow consistent with the old, that are meaningful in making connections with future generations, are generally preferred over those that offer entirely new directions (Carstenson et al., 1999, 2003). And yet, the spark of possibility continues to be considered in the selection of activities of the healthiest older people, even as they have had to give up many of the activities that have interested them previously. Indeed, healthy aging and adaptation may be best reflected in the ongoing evaluation of optional activities (Baltes & Carstensen, 1996; Burnett-Wolle & Godbey, 2007; Nimrod & Kleiber, 2007; Vaillant, 2002).

When looking at the value of leisure for compensation, as we did earlier, we look first to whether it will offer some contrast for the limitations of work or other aspects of life. But we also look to leisure for the expansion of a repertoire of possibilities that also keeps individuals engaged with significant others and the community. Even from a purely psychological perspective, a repertoire of competencies is protective when one or more are lost due to ill-ness, accident, relocation, or the debilitating aspects of aging (Linville, 1987). Evidence supports the value of a breadth of activities for identity develop-ment, self-actualization, and adaptation, whether it is in the context of work or leisure (e.g., Dupuis & Smale, 1995). In a study of leisure-activity predic-tors of well-being in later life, Dupuis and Smale found that having a breadth of interests, whether they be active or passive, was associated with lower levels of depression. But let us turn now to other contexts of adult life, where the effects of leisure experience just reviewed may be most influential.

Where and *When* is Leisure Influential in Adulthood?

Given the number of ways in which leisure activity and experience can affect well-being, we can ask more specifically where and under what circumstances such effects typically occur and to what advantage. Consider Carlos and Sean, who hold similar positions in the design department of a successful company that is downsizing its work force to remain competitive. Fear of further job cuts and the increased workloads for those remaining have cre-ated a stressful work environment. Of the two, Carlos seems to have better maintained his enthusiasm for his work. He appears to be less anxious, has maintained his sense of humor, and has taken fewer sick days during the pre-vious year than Sean. He has also created several new product designs that show some commercial promise. It would be interesting to know if some of his leisure involvements have contributed directly to his work performance and job satisfaction, maybe even stimulating creative design ideas.

Or consider Susan, a single mother who has taken her two children, now aged 13 and 15, on a 2-week vacation to Disney World and Florida beaches in each of the previous 5 years. At home they don't get to spend much time together because of involvements with friends, school, and work. Although they seem to have some fun on the vacations, it is becoming more difficult to convince the children to leave their friends. Also, the three of them seem to argue more during the trip than when they are at home. Susan is concerned now that the type of leisure she has planned is having a negative effect on the relationships among her children and herself, as well as on their sense of being a family—exactly the opposite outcome from the one she has intended.

These scenarios are not so unusual. There is certainly good reason to believe that people's leisure can contribute to their satisfaction with the "rest of life," but under what circumstances?. Sometimes it may even cause more harm than good. As we discussed above, leisure can enhance psychological well-being in a variety if ways. But how does it actually work in the contexts of everyday life, when it does work? Let's look at some of the evidence.

At Work

In an effort to improve worker productivity and reduce absenteeism and labor turnover, social and organizational psychologists have devoted considerable attention to understanding the factors that affect job satisfaction (e.g., Argyle, 1990; Steers & Porter, 1991). Unfortunately, although workers' leisure is sometimes assumed to contribute to satisfaction with the job, research has primarily concentrated on how job-related variables affect job satisfaction. In fact, as noted earlier, when the relationship between work and leisure has been studied, the leisure domain is typically seen to be dominated by the "long arm of the job" (Meissner, 1970), rather than vice versa. In studies of job satisfaction, the influence of job-related factors such as working conditions, pay and promotions, and adequacy of workplace resources have typically been examined (Argyle, 1990; Steers & Porter, 1991). Little attention has been paid to leisure variables. However, a social psychological understanding of job satisfaction could profit from a broader perspective and there have been suggestions for some time that workers' involvement in a variety of activities external to the job can influence satisfaction with paid work (e.g., Kirchmeyer, 1993; Near, Rice, & Hunt, 1978).

Leisure may be one such non-work variable that can contribute to job satisfaction. Though few tests of this proposition have been reported, the belief that leisure has some effect on work has been with us since the beginning of the Industrial Revolution. Early classical theories of play and recreation (e.g., Patrick, 1916) suggest that leisure is an important element in determining satisfaction at work. The recreation and relaxation theories of play were based on the belief that most work was boring and monotonous and that engagement in play and sports had restorative qualities (see Ellis, 1973), serving perhaps two of the functions referred to above, compensation and self-preservation. Play and leisure, in this respect, were seen to enhance the quality of work by revitalizing people, so that they would be able to return to the job to work hard day after day.

There is some evidence that enhanced job satisfaction may, in fact, be a benefit of leisure. In one study, (Lounsbury, Gordon, Bergermaier, & Francesco, 1982) the more satisfied workers were with the amount of leisure time they had available, the less likely they were to leave their jobs and search for another one. In another, Kirchmeyer (1993) studied a sample of 221 experienced managers and assessed their perceptions of the impact of their nonwork involvements on their work. Both the men and women in her study perceived nonwork involvements, including what they did during their leisure, as supporting and enhancing the quality of their work experiences. Hildebrand and Mannell (1996) found that the 103 school teachers they studied generally perceived that their leisure contributed to their job satisfaction in a variety of ways—by providing for relaxation, relieving stress, "recharging batteries," creating a positive frame of mind, maintaining self-esteem, and influencing teaching ideas. They also found that a greater frequency of participation in leisure activities by the teachers was associated with higher levels of need satisfaction in leisure, and higher levels of leisure satisfaction contributed to higher levels of job satisfaction. Of course, certain forms of leisure activity may be more influential in some respects than other activities. In a national population health study of over 17,000 Canadians, physical leisure activities were found to be more helpful in managing work-related stress than other activities (Iwasaki, Zuzanek, & Mannell, 2001).

In two Israeli studies, one of female elementary school teachers (Meir & Melamed, 1986) and the other of engineers, physicians, and lawyers (Melamed, Meir, & Samson, 1995), researchers looked at the degree of correspondence between the workers' personality-based needs and the opportunities available to satisfy these needs in both their work and their leisure. They found that the opportunity to meet important needs in both work and leisure contributed to job satisfaction. In fact, when participants were unable to meet their needs at work, engaging in leisure appeared to compensate for these unmet needs and contribute to job satisfaction.

The question of the impact of vacations on satisfaction with work has also attracted the attention of researchers (e.g. Lounsbury & Hoopes, 1986). Paid vacations are the subject of organization policies and are considered to be very important benefits by workers and unions. Generally, vacations are viewed as a time for such positive outcomes as escape, tension release, personal improvements, and an expanded opportunity to engage in satisfying activities which should increase life satisfaction and have carryover effects into the job setting (Klausner, 1968; Rubenstein, 1980a, 1980b). Klausner (1968) surveyed 361 steel workers and found that 25% of the respondents felt that their "work efficiency" had increased and 16% felt that their jobs were "more interesting" after their vacations.

In a study that directly examined the impact of taking a vacation on job satisfaction, Lounsbury and Hoopes (1986) measured the job satisfaction of 128 working men and women in a number of occupations from a variety of work organizations. The researchers measured job satisfaction 1 week before and 1 week after a vacation. The influence of taking the vacation on job satisfaction differed depending on how satisfying the vacation was judged to be by the individual worker. For those workers who experienced their vacations as highly satisfying, their level of job satisfaction was higher after their vacations than before (see Figure 12.6). Job satisfaction actually decreased for those workers who experienced their vacations as less satisfactory. Job stress

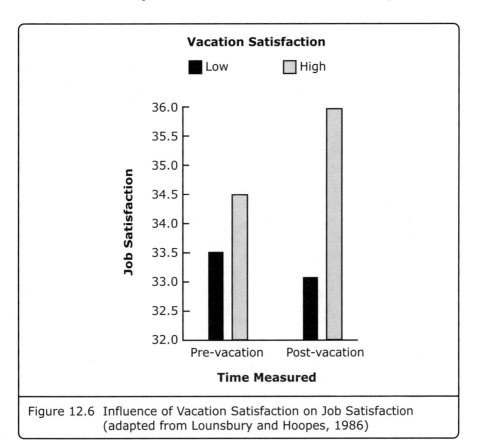

Figure 12.6 Influence of Vacation Satisfaction on Job Satisfaction (adapted from Lounsbury and Hoopes, 1986)

may also be reduced by vacations. A study examining stress and burnout before and after a vacation found a measureable decrease in both indicators, while a comparison group of non-vacationers didn't change (Etzion, 2003). Stress levels for the vacationers returned to comparable levels after 3 weeks, but burnout levels stayed lower for longer. The ameliorative effects of the vacations were the same for long vacations (more than 10 days) or shorter vacations (7–10 days). A related study showed a return of burnout and absenteeism to pre-vacation levels after 4 weeks following an initial decline (Westman & Etzion, 2001). In still another study, physical stress-related symptoms were reduced by restful vacations but only where vacations were regarded as recuperative and post-vacation workloads were not increased (Strauss-Blasche, Ekmekcioglu, & Marktl, 2002).

It appears from some of this research that there often is a "contrast" effect, where a respite from the demands of work brings down stress but returning to work after a satisfying break may actually have the effect of *reducing* a sense of well-being on the job, especially where the workload is high (Strauss-Blasche et al., 2004; Westman & Eden, 1997). Once again, these studies reinforce the need for researchers to study the social psychological links between leisure involvements and outcomes to better understand the conditions under which leisure can produce benefits.

Theory and research such as the aforementioned—suggesting both positive and negative effects of off-the-job leisure on work performance and satisfaction—also provide a rationale for work organizations to support their own recreation programs for employees, attempting, of course, to create positive effects. In partial response to the demands of the labor movement and concern about poor working conditions for employees at the turn of the previous century, work organizations began to provide leisure activities to promote employee loyalty, fellowship, and physical and intellectual development, all in an attempt to make the employee work harder for the company (e.g., Toleman, 1909). The emerging recognition that employee health and well-being are important for company success led to the beginning of the wellness movement in the 1970s, with the implementation of leisure and wellness programs to help deal with employee psychological and physical health on the job. Unfortunately, research into the effectiveness of organizational recreation programs, despite some inroads (e.g., Ellis & Richardson, 1991), has lagged behind.

In the Family

Leisure has been described as "the central social space for the development and expression of primary relationships" (Kelly, 1993, p. 6), and the family is a focal point for many of these important interpersonal relationships. Some types of leisure are generally assumed to have positive outcomes for families. Studies by Kelly (1983) and others (Horna 1989b; Shaw & Dawson, 2001;

Shaw, 2001b; Zabriskie & McCormick 2001, 2003) suggest that parents see family leisure activities as important to family satisfaction and even as more important than their own individual activities. In a review of the literature, Orthner and Mancini (1991) found that research studies have been relatively consistent in demonstrating the positive impact of shared leisure experiences on the quality of family relationships. However, this positive view of family leisure can be challenged (Shaw, 1992); family leisure may lead to conflict and some family members may feel obligated to participate (Orthner, 1985; Shaw, 1992).

The benefits for families claimed for leisure can be divided into three major types: family stability, family interaction, and family satisfaction (Orthner & Mancini, 1991, p. 290). The idea of *family stability* is reflected in the common phrase used to promote family recreation, "The family that plays together stays together." Stability implies a continuity of interpersonal relationships in the family and a reduction in the probabilities of marital separation and divorce. Few studies have directly examined the leisure and family stability hypothesis. However, using the United States 1975–1981 Time Use Longitudinal Panel Study, Hill (1988) found that the more shared leisure reported by married couples at the beginning of the study, the greater their marital satisfaction and stability over the next 5 years, even when controlling for the presence and age of children in the household.

Family interaction refers to communication, conflict, and the distribution of household tasks and roles among family members (Orthner & Mancini, 1991). A few studies have supported the hypothesis that family leisure can enhance communication, reduce conflict, and lead to greater equity in the distribution of household tasks and roles (e.g., Orthner, 1976). Several studies have found that leisure participation can increase conflict between family members (e.g., Strauss, Gelles, & Steinmetz, 1980; see Orthner & Mancini, 1991). The more frequently couples did things together, the more likely they were to communicate and, as part of that communication, to argue. On the other hand, verbal disagreements have been viewed as indicators of strategies being used for reducing family tension and disagreements (Orthner & Mancini, 1980). Where there was clear evidence of cooperation, the effects appear to be even stronger. A study of shared service activities in particular, where family members took a variety of roles and responsibilities related to volunteer work, was shown to have the effect of deepening a sense of family for parents and children (Palmer, Freeman, & Zabriskie, 2007). Such effects may be even stronger in families of children with special needs (Mactavish & Schleien, 2004).

Most of the research that has focused on family leisure behavior has examined its consequences for *family satisfaction*, and most often, *marital satisfaction.* The consistent finding is that husbands and wives who share leisure time together in joint activities tend to be much more satisfied with their marriages than those who do not (see Orthner & Mancini, 1980, 1991; Holman & Epperson, 1984). Another consistent finding is the negative impact on marital satisfaction of frequent independent, individual activities by family members. If there are too many "girls'" or "boys' nights out," marital satisfaction appears to be lower. This pattern seems to be stronger for women than men, suggesting that women may be more likely to interpret the time spent in individual activities without their spouse as a lack of concern about the relationship by their marital partner. Parallel leisure activity (Orthner, 1975), which involves sharing time but without substantial amounts of interaction (e.g., watching television, going to the movies), was found to have a moderately positive impact on the marital satisfaction of husbands and wives. But Holman and Jacquart (1988) found that such parallel activities were actually negatively associated with marital satisfaction for both husbands and wives. They concluded that leisure activities that involve little or no communication provide little benefit to families and may actually harm relationships.

The same may be said of activities done together. There is some research that joint wife-husband leisure activities lead to greater marital stability (e.g., Hill, 1988; Orthner, 1975); and surveys of married couples suggest that spending time together is considered to be an important relationship-maintenance strategy by couples themselves (Baxter & Dindia, 1990; Dindia & Baxter, 1987). Consequently, some marital therapists have encouraged couples experiencing marital problems to spend more time together as an intervention strategy (e.g., Stuart, 1980). However, it is not likely that simply spending more time with a spouse or partner will enhance satisfaction with the relationship; the activities must be enjoyable for both partners. As with the impact of leisure activity on job satisfaction, satisfaction with shared leisure activity is more important than activity alone in contributing to relationship satisfaction (Berg et al., 2001). It is not how much you do together but how much you like what you do together that matters.

Aron and Aron (1986) proposed that if leisure time spent together is to enhance marital satisfaction, the partners need to engage in joint activities which are "expanding," that is, activities which are exciting and stimulating because they provide new experiences. This notion of "expansion" assumes that people are motivated to expand and grow, as we described in the discussion of personal growth theories. The theory further suggests that one way in which people seek to expand or grow is through social relationships, since interacting with other people can open up new perspectives and opportunities for people to learn about themselves. The authors (1986) go on to argue that this opportunity is enhanced with participation in new and exciting activities (see also Aron et al., 2000).

Conversely, some shared activities with a long-term partner might even intensify boredom with the partner, by forcing the individual to spend time with her or him in ways that do not expand the self. Reissman, Aron, and Bergen (1993) carried out a field experiment to determine if spending time with one's partner was a good strategy for maintaining a marital relationship, and if leisure activities that provided opportunities for "expansion" were critical to this process. Fifty-three married couples were randomly assigned to one of three study groups and each couple was asked to engage in leisure activities together for 1.5 hours each week for 10 weeks. One group was asked to choose what they thought were "exciting" activities. The second group was asked to choose "pleasant" activities and the control group was given no special instructions, other than to make sure that they spent an additional 1.5 hours together each week. The couples recorded the activities in which they chose to participate together. Marital satisfaction was measured before and after the 10-week period. Only the group that engaged in "exciting" activities demonstrated a significant increase in marital satisfaction over the 10-week period, supporting self-expansion theory that sharing stimulating leisure activities will enhance marital satisfaction.

Of course, when it comes to family satisfaction, family constellation and gender-role orientations may also play a significant role. There is a lack of research on the outcomes of family leisure when children are also involved (Shaw, 1992). While shared family leisure—especially when satisfying to all or most family members—contributes to overall family satisfaction (Zabriskie & McCormick 2001, 2003), marital satisfaction may depend to some extent on time together in the absence of children. As with work satisfaction, some amount of time away from caregiving may have the effect of preserving marital relationships while also enhancing family satisfaction overall. Though there are clearly advantages to be gained in shared leisure activities with children and other family care recipients (as with Susan in our opening illustration), vacations may also be considered as "respite" opportunities where relief from caregiving has a protective function (see also Currie, 2004). This may be especially true where family members needing care are very young, ill or disabled, or very old (Mannell, 1994).

The influence of gender relations on family leisure is still in need of research. The greater responsibility of mothers for family leisure identified by some authors (e.g., Bella, 1992; Hunter & Whitson, 1991) may interfere with the ability of family leisure to foster more positive experiences of family life (Shaw, 1992). Freysinger (1994) found that satisfaction with being a parent was predicted by frequency of leisure with children for men but not for women, again suggesting that the mother's involvement with children's leisure may be experienced more often as an obligation, a burden, or even a source of stress. Mannell and Zuzanek (1995) found that family leisure was experienced as the most satisfying type of activity during the course of daily life by both the female and male parents in their study. However, joint participation by family members in social and active leisure activities was related to satisfaction with family life only for the men in the study. Active leisure activities such as sports, games, and hobbies were more positively impactful than other less overtly active patterns, and men participated in twice as many of these types of family activities as women.

These different leisure meanings for men and women are mostly a reflection of role differentiation in families. The greater responsibilities for planning and managing family leisure experienced by women may prohibit them from experiencing some of the benefits. For men, family leisure may be the primary context for establishing and maintaining family relationships. This may be changing, however, to the extent that gender-based role differentiation in family settings has declined; if the burdens of child rearing are more evenly shared, the gender differences should disappear, and to some extent this is occurring. On the other hand, it is clear that women still assume the greater burden of child rearing, and indeed, those who have full time jobs in addition to child rearing more frequently come home to a "second shift" of work (Hochshild, 1989).

In the Community

The impact of leisure activities on community life is more difficult to pin down than is the case with work and family satisfaction and functioning. As a result there is limited research on the subject. Nevertheless, there is a long history of neighbors and community residents coming together to celebrate their shared circumstances and build togetherness and a sense of community through shared enjoyment. Fairs and festivals have that purpose essentially, as do Independence Day parades, other holiday celebrations, and neighborhood picnics. Even sporting events, if competition is put in perspective, have the potential to build a sense of community (Lyons & Dionigi, 2007). Indeed, the ancient Greeks saw shared experience in community settings, the "polis," as the essence of leisure (*schole*) and the most important function of the community (Hemingway, 1988). But if this has been common in almost all cultures and societies over the centuries, Western postmodern society may be losing the benefit from such patterns. In his book, *Bowling Alone*, Robert Putnam (2000) pointed out that we are far less inclined to engage in collective activities than we were in the past. The result, according to Putnam, is a loss in *social capital*. People instead "cocoon" to a greater extent in their own homes, venturing out only by necessity. Putnam attributes this pattern in part to the rise of television watching, the most common leisure activity in North American households. So here is a case where one leisure activity may have a negative influence on social well-being by pre-empting those activities that might have a more positive effect.

Nevertheless, although the trends in enjoyable civic engagement may be down, there are still many examples of positive effects. Participation in regular festivals contributes to one's sense of place in a community (Kyle & Chick, 2002). And even just providing opportunities and space for community members to have their own gardens has also been shown to build social capital, as long as sociability is an intentional part of the endeavor (Glover, Perry, & Shinew, 2005). Public leisure events that are inclusive may also go a long way toward reducing prejudice and discrimination. There have even been cases where ethnic tensions have been eased through organized sports and games (Jamieson & Ross, 2007). On the other hand, the *communitas* created for some groups may also lead to expressions of prejudice and hostility against those who are clearly outside the group. Indeed, a study of collective social activity in the summer holidays of Irish Protestant Unionists has identified both its benefits and costs (see Table 12.1) in terms of destructive and hostile behavior toward Nationalists who resist and defy the others' collective expressions (Murphy, 2003).

Perhaps the most obvious place where leisure benefits the community is where it is used for volunteerism. As we have established before, volunteerism is most often a mixture of work and leisure in that its productive outcomes define its purpose while the fact that it is voluntary and intrinsically motivated to a great extent brings it into the realm of leisure as well. In fact, as noted before, it is one of the three forms of "serious leisure," according to Stebbins (1992), the other two being amateurism and hobbies. Although not all occasions of volunteer work are associated with the continuing commitment associated

---

Table 12.1   Consequences of Social Activities of Summer Holiday among Irish Protestant Unionists (adapted from Murphy, 2002)

Potential Psychological Benefits	Actual Social Costs
• "Serious Leisure" • "Flow" • Maintenance of in-group beliefs and values • Strengthening of in-group beliefs and values • Positive in-group interaction during a leisure space • Contact with (or re-establishment of) family and friendship groups • Strengthening of ties with community church • Experience of continuity and affirmation through traditional activities • Sense of religious security	• 632 petro bombs thrown (2250 recovered) • 615 attacks on security forces • 25 shooting incidents targeting police and army • 178 vehicle jackings • 476 vehicles damaged • 165 buildings damaged • 144 homes damaged • 107 families driven from homes • 837 baton rounds fired by the RUC • 284 people arrested (from Royal Ulster Constabulary figures, July 1998)

with serious leisure, it is often true that identification with social causes and local purposes can take on career-like characteristics. There are of course many kinds of volunteer activities that have people working freely on behalf of "communities" and associations that are national and even international in scope; but most volunteerism is directed toward one's local community. Working for the local soup kitchen or food bank, doing neighborhood cleanup and landscape development, or stuffing envelopes in a political campaign are common examples.

In such cases, the benefit to the organizations served is obvious. But what is sometimes missed in these outcome assessments is the benefit to the individuals involved. Volunteering is associated with life satisfaction (Aquino et al., 1996), self-efficacy, happiness and contentment, lower negative affect, and lower depression (Menec, 2003; Morrow-Howell et al., 2003; Musick & Wilson, 2003), and sense of community (Okun & Michel, 2006), including when the volunteers have functional limitations (Morrow-Howell et al., 2003). Community initiatives may even be *created* to elicit community participation. Arai and Pedlar (1997) reported on the organization in Kitchener, Ontario, called "Healthy Communities," an initiative intended to involve people in various voluntary service activities. The initiative led to five positive outcomes for participants: (a) learning and developing new skills, (b) becoming more vocal, (c) balance and renewal, (d) group accomplishment and ability to influence change, and (e) development of community.

Reducing Marginalization

In Chapter 10, we considered how race, ethnicity, and culture influence leisure both objectively and subjectively, but we can turn that around somewhat and ask if leisure can influence the well-being of racial, ethnic, or other groups who may find themselves to be "outsiders" in the dominant society as a result of their differences. To be on the outside looking in or to be driven outside of what seems like the mainstream is a condition of deprivation, isolation, loneliness, and alienation, often created through overt prejudice and discrimination. Many people in North America and elsewhere in the world find themselves in just such a predicament. To take ethnic minorities first, consider the case of just arriving in a foreign land and what it would take to make you feel comfortable. We are not talking about being tourists here, the commitment is to make this strange place your new home. Differences of language, custom, and tradition are immediately daunting and the attitudes and behavior of those in the "host" country may perpetuate the alienation. Leisure patterns, since they relate more to expressive behavior than to that which is functional for survival, may perpetuate the distance.

To some extent those of the host, majority, or dominant society look to the newcomers to fit in and become like themselves. This is the metaphor of the "melting pot." Adopting leisure patterns of the host country or region may facilitate that in some ways, embracing some of the same festivals and traditions, taking an interest in and even participating in local sport and recreation opportunities, watching and discussing the television programs common in their new home environment, and generally abandoning those leisure patterns that have been associated with the home or region that has been left behind. To a great extent this is the pressure that immigrants face; and if they want to *assimilate* in this way leisure is often the "context of entry" into their new world (Kim, Kleiber, & Kropf, 2001; Stodolska, 1998; Stodolska & Yi, 2003). In many cases, their inability or unwillingness to respond to this pressure has a negative impact on their leisure (e.g., Stodolska, 2002).

But holding onto leisure of the past is also critical to maintaining cultural identity, and it serves the functions of self-preservation and continuity discussed earlier. Maintaining familiar patterns of self-expression is often critical to well-being in the face of disruptive circumstances. This is what Berry (1970, 2009) refers to as *separation*, where the immigrant keeps the mainstream culture largely at bay for purposes of self and cultural preservation. Preserving expressive patterns, in others words those exercised in and through leisure, is often the most effective way of serving this purpose (Kim et al., 2001; Stodolska, 1998; Stodolska & Yi, 2003). But Berry also points to the acculturative strategy of *integration*, where an immigrant maintains his or her heritage culture and yet seeks to be involved in mainstream culture. A number of the Korean immigrants interviewed by Kim et al. (2001) showed this attempt to have the "best of both worlds" through their leisure choices.

Ultimately, to the extent that multiculturalism is embraced by a society, tolerance is expanded to the appreciation of difference in much the same way novelty drives other leisure interests. Parades and festivals may celebrate diversity and expose all participants to the richness of experiences from other countries and other lands. These events can lead to the kind of cultural integration that does not sacrifice cultural identity and instead suggests a tapestry of difference and variety.

Such appreciation of diversity is an *ideal* of leisure and community, of course; the reality is that there is considerable struggle around issues of inclusion and exclusion, issues that we discussed in Chapters 9, 10, and 11. We consider it here again because of the evidence that leisure can moderate "immigrant experience" in good and bad ways. But if immigrants are marginalized by coming to a country or society that is new to them and to which they want and hope to belong, other minorities are marginalized in spite of the fact that the country or region may have always been "home" (see, for example, Floyd & Gramann, 1995; Gobster & Delgado, 1992; Iwasaki & Bartlett, 2006; and for a review, Freysinger, 2006). Other individual differences such as religion, sexual preference, and political ideology may also evoke strong feelings in a community (Iwasaki, Mackay, Mactavish, Ristock, & Bartlett, 2006). Differing sexual preferences, for example, may be an alienating and marginalizing feature of adult life. Awareness of them may lead to discrimination and ostracism in the community at large or may be accepted and even embraced as other sources of diversity (e.g., Iwasaki & Ristock, 2004). Leisure activities and events are often the catalysts for both feeling alienated and feeling welcome in communities and, indeed, for making meaning in "strange lands" (Iwasaki, 2008).

Extending the Bounds of Community

Finally, we would be remiss in not considering other definitions of community, particularly those that are "virtual" in nature. Cyber-communities have been shown to be particularly important to people who are stigmatized and marginalized in some way or who have physical limitations that make face-to-face congregation unlikely or unappealing. Social networking online can be especially valuable for such individuals, but Internet technology offers possibilities for developing feelings of community for anyone. Older adults in particular—in spite of the alleged "digital divide"—are finding opportunities to connect with others in ways previously impossible (Carpenter & Buday, 2007; Furlong, 1989; Henke, 1999; Pew Internet in American Life, 2004).

In Coping with Illness and Loss

In the previous section on how leisure influences well-being, we considered ways in which leisure helps in adjusting to negative life events and circumstances: in providing a distraction, serving to restore optimism, and as way to reconnect with a former self, among other possibilities, including having it offer some new alternative selves. We also considered ways in which leisure activity and experience improved mood and enhanced relationships and individual self-perceptions. In this section, we offer examples of illness and loss that are common enough to have been studied systematically, and we thus provide a context for examining further some of the propositions already discussed.

Leisure in the Management of Injury and Illness

Illnesses have a variety of forms. Some are slow in coming and long enduring, while others are sudden, shocking, and immediately debilitating. They may be chronic or acute. Serious injuries fit more commonly into the latter, though injuries also produce chronic illness effects sometimes. As was noted earlier, the loss of leisure may be among the most immediate casualties of such events and may be part of the illness itself. Studies of negative life events such as spinal cord injury, the sudden onset of illness, or the loss of a loved one suggest that a loss of leisure abilities, leisure opportunities, and leisure companions are regularly part of the "illness experience" that people endure

(Kleiber et al., 1995). And yet leisure activities and experiences do appear to play a prominent role in adjusting and adapting to those circumstances in many cases as well (Kleiber et al., 2002; Patterson, 2000).

In studies of *spinal cord injury* (e.g., Loy, Dattilo, & Kleiber, 2003) many of the patterns referred to earlier have been found. As devastating as the loss of mobility is, finding alternative skills and interests and even recovering one's old skills appear to have therapeutic effects (Chun, Lee, & Heo, 2008). Diversity, frequency, and intensity of leisure engagement are all associated with adjustment. Leisure engagement also contributes indirectly through building social support (see also Lee & McCormick, 2006). But initially, as with other trauma, the more attractive activities are more often those that take one's mind off the pain. The fact that these injuries are acute and dramatic in their impact on physical activity, however, does seem to make the recovery of old physical functions and the identification of new physical activities an urgent priority in most cases. On the other hand, the possibilities for change and self-expansion may also open up. In the case of those who were more body-oriented in their interests and activities, the life of the mind may be the new focus. Studies of people with traumatic brain injury show similar patterns and outcomes (cf. Hutchinson, Loy, Kleiber, & Dattilo, 2003); leisure has been found to be a source of self-preservation and continuity (recovering valued aspects of past self), escape, hope and optimism, structure and a sense of purpose, sense of belonging and acceptance, and competence.

On the more chronic side, middle age may bring on the occurrence of seriously debilitating and chronic diseases like *arthritis*. These illnesses lack the dramatic blows that a spinal cord or traumatic brain injury inflicts, but they require adjustment and adaptation nonetheless. In a study of a group of older adults with arthritis, leisure-based social interaction was found to be a significant hedge against declines in mental health (Payne, Mowen, & Montoro-Rodriguez, 2006). *Cancer* also becomes chronic over time, but the initial awareness of it—life-threatening as it can be—often has much the same effect as more acutely dramatic and debilitating injuries. It may even be transformative, as how best to use the life left to be lived becomes the critical, existential question. And some of the answers show themselves to be intimately associated with leisure (e.g., Glover & Perry, 2008; Hutchinson, Unruh, King, & Wood, 2008; Parry, 2007).

Finally, we must recognize *depression* as amenable to the influence of leisure. Unlike other chronic conditions, however, it is not always obvious nor does it have the social "respectability" that cancer and other more clearly identifiable illnesses do. Men in particular tend to conceal or deny depression since there is a stigma of weakness associated with it. But it is certainly reasonable to expect that activities that change mood, even to the point of changing brain chemistry, would be important. Although there hasn't been a great deal of research on the subject, an interview study with 48 women with depression in Australia revealed the use of leisure practices in their experience of coping and recovery, building on friendships to overcome feelings of lack of entitlement (to just lay and rest on the couch, for example), and developing feelings of vitality through exercise and gardening (Fullagar, 2008).

Loss of Employment

The loss of a job, whether through retirement or unemployment, can involve problems similar to those generated by illness and injury—loss of income, social isolation (e.g., loss of contact with friends and coworkers), and psychological losses (e.g., feelings of no longer being able to contribute to society; no opportunity to develop and exercise skills and abilities). Of course, loss of a job and the resulting unemployment before the age of retirement is likely to be a more traumatic change due to the lack of a "retirement" income, lack of opportunity to plan for the change, and the social stigma associated with it. Retirement is socially accepted today and is usually seen as a reward after many years of work. It has, in effect, been "earned." Many factors have been proposed to affect successful coping with both retirement and unemployment. Leisure is one of these factors, and its impact on psychological well-being when people are dealing with job loss has been of interest to researchers.

Considerable attention has been given to the role that leisure can play in helping people contend with unplanned and unwanted job loss and unemployment (e.g., Havitz, Morden, & Samdahl, 2004; Haworth, 1986; Haworth & Drucker, 1991; Lobo, 1996, 2002; Pesavento Raymond, 1984; Pesavento Raymond & Kelly, 1991; Reid & Smit, 1986; Spigner & Havitz, 1992, 1993). Based on a review of the research, Warr (1983) identified nine potentially negative features of unemployment from financial anxiety to reduced social status (see Table 12.2). However, in spite of all these potentially negative consequences of unemployment, not all unemployed people report being worse off in terms of psychological health. In a study of nearly 1,000 unemployed

---

Table 12.2 Potential Costs of Unemployment (adapted from Warr, 1983)

- Financial anxiety
- Less variety in life due to reduced income
- Fewer goals or aims in life
- Reduced opportunity for making important decisions
- Reduced opportunities to exercise skills or expertise
- Increase in psychologically threatening activities
- Insecurity about the future
- Fewer social contacts
- Reduced social status

men, Warr and Jackson (1984) found that although 20% reported a decline in health, 8% actually reported an improvement. Consequently, researchers have been interested in discovering the possible moderating factors that may explain the considerable individual variation in response to unemployment. In a review of the literature, Winefield, Tiggemann, Winefield, & Goldney (1993) found important factors that made people more or less vulnerable to the negative consequences of unemployment, including: attitudes toward paid employment (the more positive, the more psychological distress experienced); age (middle-aged men compared to younger and older men experienced more stress because of greater family responsibilities); length of unemployment (decline in psychological health, particularly in middle-aged men during the first few months before it stabilizes), availability of social support (more support, less stress); local unemployment levels (less stress at higher levels because people are more likely to see their unemployment as due to economic and social conditions beyond their control rather than as a failing on their part); and *access to constructive and stimulating leisure activity.* Indeed, job loss may be one of the clearer situations where leisure activity can be both compensatory and self-protective.

Researchers have found that although leisure participation and satisfaction often decrease with unemployment (e.g., Havitz et al., 2004; Pesavento Raymond, 1984; Pesavento Raymond & Kelly, 1991; Reid & Smit, 1986), the way in which unemployed people use their free time and leisure can reduce the negative effects to some extent. In a study of unemployed university graduates, Feather and Bond (1983) found that the structured and purposeful use of free time was positively correlated with self-esteem and negatively correlated with depressive symptoms. Other studies have also shown that unemployed people who cope best are engaged in purposeful activity and maintain regular contact with people outside the nuclear family (McKenna & Fryer, 1984; Warr & Jackson, 1985). At least some of this "purposeful" activity takes the form of serious leisure (Stebbins, 1992, 2007).

Haworth and Ducker (1991) found that young unemployed adults who were engaged in more work-like and active leisure pursuits also had higher levels of psychological well-being. In a study of 228 unemployed African-American and Hispanic youth in the United States, Pesavento Raymond and Kelly (1991) concluded that leisure activity appeared to help reduce the negative effects of unemployment. Kilpatrick and Trew (1985) showed that mental health in a group of 121 unemployed men was affected by how they spent their "free" time. They identified four groups among the people they studied. The *passive* group spent most of their time watching television or doing nothing. They showed the poorest psychological well-being. The *domestic* group also spent most of their time at home, but unlike the first, assisted with household tasks. They showed only slightly better mental health than the first group.

A third, *social* group spent much of their time with people outside their immediate family. They exhibited superior mental health to the first two groups. Finally, a fourth group, the *active* group, not only spent more time on work-related activities, but also engaged more frequently in active leisure pursuits outside the home. They were the least psychologically affected by unemployment (see Table 12.3).

Another group of researchers (Winefield et al., 1993) reported the results of a longitudinal study of employment among a group of young people in Australia. Not only did they study people who were unemployed, but they also followed employed individuals who differed in how satisfying they found their jobs. They assessed the study participants' psychological well-being by measuring their self-esteem, level of depression, moods and leisure activity levels at various points in time—for the unemployed young adults this meant early in the period of their unemployment and approximately 4 years later. The main factors that were found to moderate the affects of unemployment were age, length of unemployment, financial security, social support, and *leisure*. Interestingly, the dissatisfied employed group was more similar to the unemployed group than they were to the satisfied employed group. With respect to leisure, unemployed people whose leisure was characterized as "doing nothing" and "watching television" developed lower self-esteem during the period of unemployment. Those who were engaged in more challenging activities, both social (e.g., sport, dancing) and solitary (e.g., hobbies, reading, cooking) had higher levels of self-esteem. These relationships became much stronger as time went on and were also found among those people who were employed but unhappy with their jobs.

Losing a Spouse
Losing one's spouse has a variety of effects according to the research, but it can be the most significant event in one's life, especially for relationships that have endured for a long time. As with many other negative life events,

Table 12.3 Unemployment, Leisure, and Mental Health (adapted from Kilpatrick & Trew, 1985)

Group	Primary Activity	Mental Health
Passive	Watching TV; doing nothing	Worst
Domestic	Watching TV; household tasks	Better
Social	With people outside family	Still Better
Active	Work-related; active leisure	Best

leisure is often immediately implicated in the "illness" experience of widow-hood; a spouse is often a companion for leisure activities and that loss changes the opportunity to participate and the experience itself in many cases. Certainly home-based leisure is different as well. But according to research, widows often increase involvement in activities for two reasons: (1) they feel the need to "keep busy" (Sharp & Mannell, 1996), in other words to use activities for their distraction value to reduce the grieving and distress; and (2) they take the opportunity to do new things that their previous marital status—often as a caregiver—did not afford them. In the latter case, usually occurring some-what after an initial adjustment period, there is sometimes a "blossoming" effect, where widows discover new aspects of themselves (Lopata, 1993), often in expressive leisure activities such as joining a "Red Hat Society" society, as was described earlier in the chapter. There is considerable evidence now that widows who stay engaged or increase engagement in satisfying lei-sure activities, particularly social activities, exercise, and religious activities, have higher life satisfaction and less depression than those who reduce such activities (e.g., Janke, Nimrod, & Kleiber, 2008a,b,c). On the other hand, the importance of being selective about leisure activities was also born out in the Janke et al. studies; some activities (maintaining member-ship in clubs for one) was not associated with subjective well-being in this national sample.

In Aging Successfully

Leisure and Retirement

The study of reactions to retirement has generated a large body of literature (see, for example, Calasanti, 1993; Gee & Baillie, 1999; McPherson, 1983, 1991; Nimrod, 2007a; Nuttman-Shwartz, 2004; Theriault, 1994; Weiss, 2005). Much of this work has been based on the assumption that being retired is a troublesome if not traumatic event, and that many elderly people, particularly men, do not adjust well. But clearly, to the extent that it is predictable and planned, it has far less of an immediate negative impact than losing one's job earlier in life. And indeed, most research indicates that retirement is generally a positive experience, though it depends largely on circumstances: the kind of job one has had, the leisure lifestyle one has maintained, the roles one has played in family and community life, and how prepared the individual is for retirement (e.g., Hyde et al., 2004). Gender differences have attracted the attention of retirement researchers as well (e.g., Dorfman, Heckert, & Hill, 1988; Szinovacz & Washo, 1992), as have the problems of the synchroniza-tion of retirement for couples (e.g., Henretta, Orand, & Chan, 1993). The retirement literature has been further expanded by the long-standing interest of researchers, as we have noted, in accounting for the life satisfaction and well-being of older adults (Dupuis, 2008; Larson, 1978; Higginbottom, Barling, & Kelloway, 1993; Mannell & Dupuis, 2007; Reis & Gold, 1993).

A longitudinal study of 44 older men who had retired at least 5 years before (Chiriboga & Pierce, 1993) demonstrated how leisure behavior may play a role in successful retirement and psychological well-being. The respondents' participation in solitary activities, sports, social activities, and contemplative activities was measured early in retirement and about 5 years later. Measures of the stressful life events they had experienced during the previous year, psychological distress symptoms, happiness, and self-reported health were also collected. Participation levels in the various leisure activities were not related to self-concept at or soon after retirement. After 5 years, however, the situation had changed. Activity involvement was significantly related to self-concept. Specifically, those retired individuals who were more positive about themselves were also more likely to be engaged in outdoor and social activities, and tended to participate less in contemplative activities which were characterized as solitary and passive.

The onset of retirement does represent a major transition point that has the potential to alter lifestyle, but again, the accumulated evidence shows that most have few problems in adjusting to retirement, though there is still substantial variation in the degree of adjustment and the subsequent quality of life experienced (see, for example, McPherson, 1983; Jensenscott, 1993; Vaillant, 2002). Research suggests that the retirement transition is less traumatic and more satisfying among people with higher perceived levels of health and economic status and those who have harmonious marriages and social support from their spouses and families. Consistent with activity and continuity theories, research has also shown that those people who use their free time to continue to participate in similar types of social activity at about the same level as they did prior to retirement, and who have positive attitudes toward leisure, adjust better and are more satisfied with their lives (e.g., Goudy & Myers, 1985; Long, 1987; Nimrod, 2007a,b; Nimrod & Adoni, 2006; Nimrod, Janke, & Kleiber, 2008; Russell, 1987). And as noted earlier, there are also indications that those who begin new leisure activities after retirement benefit substantially from the adventure (Nimrod, 2008b; Nimrod & Kleiber, 2007; Vaillant, 2002). However, as with adjustment to widowhood, there is also evidence that being selective is important, that activities must be meaningful to contribute to life satisfaction, and that giving up some less meaningful activities is generally warranted (Kleiber et al., 2008; Kleiber & Nimrod, 2009).

Aging in General

Although we can locate issues and crises in the life course as more common during one age period than others, aging is experienced by everyone who has the good fortune to survive into later life. And one of the most notable things about aging is that it is associated with loss—loss of capacity, loss of companions, loss of role centrality, etc.—and with a growing awareness of one's mortality and finiteness. There are many prescriptions for aging well, of course, some supported by research. One feature that seems to contribute is engagement. We have noted that both activity and continuity theory emphasize the idea of being and staying actively engaged, mentally as well as physically. In part this is a matter of keeping one's capacities sharp—the old adage is 'use it or lose it'—but it is also about finding meaning in activities that are personally expressive and in those that contribute to the well-being of others (see also Kleiber, 1999). Maintaining or adopting physical activities in later life appears to be particularly important, by virtue not only of the health benefits but also the companionship that such activities usually bring (e.g., Dergance et al., 2003; Dionigi, 2006; Mobily et al., 1993; Yau & Packer, 2002). Learning activities also seem to have a high potential to be meaningful, valuable, and impactful in maintaining later life well-being (e.g., Nimrod, 2008; Roberson, 2005).

But aging well also comes with some acceptance of loss and of the value in relinquishing lower-priority activities in favor of giving optimal attention to those activities that are most important. The *Selective Optimization with Compensation* theory referred to earlier suggests that to age well, it is important to optimize involvement in some activities by being selective, discriminating in what one chooses to do, and by taking advantage of available sources of assistance to maintain involvement wherever desirable (see also Burnett-Wolle & Godbey, 2007). Learning to be peaceful, even meditative, and appreciative of the world around seems to be associated with wisdom and derives also from learning to be truly leisurely (cf. Kleiber et al., 2008).

When the Effects of Leisure are *Not* So Positive

There is also the prospect that leisure activity may have *negative* effects on subjective well-being and overall quality of life. This may happen in at least two ways. First, activities that were expected to be enjoyable may prove to be disappointing in some respects; and second, some activities are seriously engaging, at the expense of other aspects of one's life. In the first instance, the disappointment of expectations sometimes arises when they are unrealistic or when unforeseen circumstances make their realization impossible. Consider bad weather over the whole week of a much anticipated beach vacation, for example. Also, the research on *carrying capacity* suggests that most facilities and resources have their limits, and too many people, or too many people with different purposes (snowmobiling versus cross-country skiing, for example, or novice dilettantes in an activity versus those who are specialized and committed), creates the experience of *crowding*, which is fundamentally frustrating and destructive to most of the more preferred forms of leisure experience (relaxation, flow, quiet and solitude, etc.; Vaske & Shelby, 2008; see also Kyle, Graefe, Manning, & Bacon, 2004). When we share leisure activities with friends and family we are inclined to say "the more the merrier," but even those contexts have their limits.

Crowding can create stress, but stress can be generated through leisure activities in other ways as well. In reviewing the "hassles" that sometimes arise in outdoor settings, Schuster, Hammitt, and Moore (2006) found that litter and damage to the resource were common circumstances that actually raised the stress level of participants in addition to the effect of crowding. Also, in considering the idea of optimal experience and flow, when the challenges of an activity exceed one's capacities, anxiety may result, or when challenges are insufficient to maintain interest and involvement, boredom can be the result. When individuals have control over the activity themselves, they can find the level that is most enjoyable (flow producing) and may even endure some amount of anxiety and discomfort for the prospects of developing greater competence and enriching the experience. When leisure activities are organized by others, though, skill levels often vary greatly and the sociability afforded may not compensate for the anxiety or boredom that is produced for some.

Taking an activity seriously, in the way Stebbins and others have discussed it, may also have some costs (cf. Stebbins, 2007). Specialization requires commitment, commitment brings obligation, and a sense of freedom may thus be diminished. If someone has been playing saxophone with a group for years, he may reach a point where this commitment leaves him with a more limited sense of freedom of choice and self-determination. The commitment associated with involvement in specialized serious leisure activities may also undermine other relationships. Show dog owners, for example, have spoken honestly about the stress it sometimes puts on their marriages (Gillespie, Leffler, & Lerner, 2002). And, of course, in competitive activities like dog shows and sports, the more serious one is, the greater the disappointment and frustration (indeed, anger and despair in many cases) when one loses (e.g., Muir, 1991). There is also the cost of having to abandon those activities for which one has developed a passionate attachment (Stebbins, 2008). A sense of loss may be palpable in such cases. Finally, it is important to recognize that the leisure of some people may diminish the subjective well-being of others. Identification with an activity and the particular participants who enjoy it may lead to or perpetuate out-group prejudice and discrimination, as noted earlier (Stodolska, 2005).

Scenarios for Social Change

There is also the prospect that leisure involvement may precipitate constructive social change, intentionally or unintentionally, particularly around issues
of social justice. This subject has been addressed primarily through the sociology of leisure and sociological social psychology (see especially Freysinger
& Flannery, 1992; Green, 1998; Shaw, 2001a, 2006; and Wearing, 1990, 1998),
but it also reflects a psychological and developmental imperative toward
autonomy and individuation and away from accommodation. Stereotypical
gender-typed leisure involvement can constrain women's and men's behavior
in a variety of life domains if they reinforce traditional views of "femininity"
and "masculinity" (Shaw, 1999a) and thereby discourage self-expression.
But, leisure involvement can also be a form of *resistance* against role constraints that may lead to changes in other areas of life, for example when older
women create groups such as "The Red Hat Society" (Yarnal et al., 2008)
where they can be expressive in manner and dress in ways more commonly
associated with youth, when mothers insist on their own workout times (Currie,
2004), or when women engage in traditionally male sports (Shaw, 2001a). In
fact, this idea of leisure as resistance has been applied primarily to understanding the role that leisure can play in helping women resist and challenge
gender stereotypes that limit what is seen as appropriate behavior (Freysinger
& Flannery, 1992; Wearing, 1990). Presumably, when women engage in certain
types of physical recreation (Bialeschki, 1990) such as motorcycling (Auster,
2001) and highly competitive sports (Griffiths, 1988; Kleiber & Kane, 1984),
including sports for older adults (Dionigi, 2006), then the dominant views in
society about what women can and should do are challenged.

Nor is resistance only about women. Children, people with disabilities,
and other marginalized groups are often forced into conformity and compliance, and their preferences and interests are silenced in various ways. For
example, in a study of elderly persons in a long-term-care facility, it became
clear that they acted as "institutionalized bodies" as recreation was prescribed,
and only when they were able to assert their alternative preferences did they
feel a sense of freedom (Wiersma & Dupuis, 2008). Even older people in
early stages of dementia have shown the capacity to resist stereotypic treatment (Genoe, 2009).

Summary

Leisure experience and activities contribute substantially to quality of life, to
functioning in the various domains of adulthood, and to coping with the
challenges and threats that arise over the life course. In the preceding pages
we have explored not only when and where those effects occur but also how:

in enhancing mood and happiness; in providing balance, compensation, and continuity with the past; in being a distraction and source of optimism when negative events occur; in affording a context for personal growth, strengthened relationships and even transformation of self and society. Leisure may be a context for more negative effects as well, however. At times, leisure activities may undermine functioning in other domains or may perpetuate patterns of avoidance in coping. Collective enjoyment of some activities may also take the form of hurtful exclusion of others, for example, or even target out-groups with hostility. Again, research is needed that examines and tests theories about the nature of the links between leisure and well-being. The next and final chapter addresses the practical side of the social psychology of leisure and how policy makers and providers of services might make the most of enhancing the positive outcomes while reducing the negative, in an applied social psychology of leisure.

Optimizing Leisure Outcomes

Preview

Clearly, from the previous two chapters, there are good indications that what people do in leisure and as leisure can bring about a wide range of psychological outcomes, some quite positive. However, the operative word is "can"; that is, it is possible, but it is not inevitable. Leisure is not automatically beneficial, whether it is considered free time, preferred experience, or certain activities. The nature of people's leisure behavior and experience, the skills, attitudes, and needs people possess, and the social circumstances of their lives, all interact to affect whether their leisure is a benefit, a cost, or a mixture of the two. Researchers have found evidence that various kinds of leisure experience can make people feel better temporarily during the present moment, facilitate long-term personal growth, affirm their identities, provide a buffer against stress, enhance their satisfaction with their work and personal relationships, and support their efforts to deal with transitions in their lives, among other beneficial outcomes. However, researchers have also seen that leisure may, at times, have no effect, or in some cases negative effects, on a person's well-being and satisfaction with different domains of his or her life.

If previous chapters have created the impression that the psychological outcomes of leisure are thoroughly studied and well-documented, it should be noted that in all but a few of the areas we examined, research is still very limited. The alleged links between leisure and well-being need to be more fully developed and tested. The research examined, however, does suggest that it is possible to explore and study leisure and psychological well-being. Many interesting research questions were encountered in our review, and there are many opportunities for researchers to improve existing theories and develop new ones. But perhaps we have learned enough to be a bit prescriptive about what we think would be best—for our friends and their children and, of course, our own families, as well as ourselves. This would possibly translate into what we would want provided for our community or, perhaps, for those who seem to need help in terms of leisure services. Practically speaking, we might have learned enough to be persuasive in changing attitudes toward experiences, activities, or environments about which we care. We may also have learned a few things about how to bring leisure more clearly into focus and benefit for ourselves as well.

This chapter, then, is about utilizing social psychology and what we have learned about leisure to offer concrete ideas for making the most of opportunities to enhance our leisure experience and make it more valuable and to facilitate the leisure experiences of others. These ideas are strongly influenced by what we have considered in previous sections of the book about the social and psychological factors that influence people's engagement in and experience of leisure. We will use theory that attempts to answer the question of how to best recognize the leisure opportunities available, reconsidering the concept of *affordance* as that which is there in the environment but perhaps undetected. We also deal again with the concept of *constraint* and the ways conditions constraining leisure can be overcome. Finally, we will address all the ways in which leisure experience can be cultivated to good effect for ourselves and others, utilizing ideas about facilitation, education, instruction, persuasion, and management.

Recognizing Leisure Opportunities

Affordance

Let us begin with the practical problem that opportunities for leisure may not even be recognized. Earlier we introduced the concept of *affordance* which comes from perceptual and environmental psychology (Gibson, 1986 [1979]; Greeno, 1994). An affordance is a property of the environment that signals certain opportunities for action. Just as there are personality characteristics and psychological dispositions that facilitate leisure behavior and experience, so there are social and physical environmental conditions that are conducive to leisure behavior and experience. The abundance of natural resources in North America, for example, affords a wide variety of leisure opportunities (see also Pierskalla & Lee, 1998).

Perceptual psychologist J. J. Gibson suggested an environmental model of behavior that identifies characteristics in the environment which, once perceived, afford certain behaviors (Greeno, 1994). As a couple of simple examples, a mailbox affords delivery of mail and a fishing rod affords catching fish. Technology creates a wealth of affordances, as do forests and rivers. Even a crowd can be an affordance; a concert might lose its appeal if a person were one of only a few people in attendance. Creating leisure opportunities is often a matter of helping people to see the possibilities, the affordances, that are available to them, or in fact arranging such possibilities. Recognizing and creating leisure affordance is almost always a partner to managing and negotiating leisure constraints, to which we turn in the next section.

Affordance is not the opposite of constraint on some continuum of appraisal of the situation, however, a mistake we made in the first edition of this book. Indeed, affordance is defined *by* the constraints as well as the possibilities for action that are present in a particular situation (Greeno, 1994). For example, the affordances of a public library's reading material include the constraints associated with access and loan regulations and the defining limits of the collection itself. And the boundaries of a field of play circumscribe and thus constrain the action, as do other rules but, in so doing, afford the behavioral options assumed for both participating and spectating.

Shogan (2002) points out that rules of games have the effect of *prescribing*, *proscribing*, and *describing* action, thereby enabling and facilitating action in addition to constraining it. Prescriptive rules, of course, tell you what to do (the tennis ball must be served into the opposite front court box on the opponent's side), and proscriptive rules say what is disallowed (the ball cannot be hit twice in normal tennis play, or three times in wheelchair tennis play), while descriptive boundaries delimit conditions in the field of play, making the game possible. Knowing the rules of games, how the actions are constrained, allows one to see the affordance for enjoyment in the actions. Games are, of course, a special case of constraint, but the actions proscribed in a given situation—for example, "please turn off all cell phones"—will often raise the level of expectation for other kinds of experience.

An affordance telegraphs to the perceiver/actor what is possible in that environmental context. A baseball bat has a shape that affords an adequate grip (narrow handle) with some width at the other end to increase the probability of striking the ball when swung. A trail marker is located and presented at a specific height and angle, and with limited verbal information, so as to be clearly instructive to a literate human being with some prospect of getting lost and some interest in avoiding such an outcome. The environment affords an individual such opportunities for action, though, again, *detection* of the affordances in a setting will depend on needs and interests. An affordance is more likely to be perceived if it has importance for an individual's needs and interests. For example, an interest in climbing draws attention to the "climb-ability" of features of a landscape. Thus, a cliff may be perceived as a place to avoid, presenting primarily danger and possible injury to one who merely wants to descend or ascend safely and comfortably while, for another, it affords an opportunity for climbing.

Leisure Affordance in Outdoor Environments

Pierskalla and Lee's (1998) ecological analysis of leisure affordance in the context of outdoor recreation demonstrated that the environment possesses information that reveals an individual's opportunities for action and potential for experience. Information is perceived in relation to the mode of activity and the skill level and interests of the perceiver. Further, they argued that the environment, mode of activity, and skill level of the actor are elements that influence the process of perceiving affordances that offer opportunities for leisure. What constitutes a leisure affordance, however, is not entirely clear in Pierskalla and Lee's analysis. Leisure qualities are not fully described. We submit that those qualities include "preferred experience" (Kleiber, Wade, & Loucks-Atkinson, 2005), particularly enjoyment, relaxation, and a feeling of comfortable present-centeredness, as discussed in Chapter 4. For example, the juxtaposition of a rock next to a waterfall affords experiences of both sensory stimulation and relaxed tranquility, commonly recognized manifestations of leisure.

A change in the actor's needs or motives does not change an affordance, as affordances are the properties and events present in the environment (Pierskalla & Lee, 1998). However, a change in the actor's needs or motives may change what the actor *perceives* among existing affordances. An affordance can be many things to many people. For example, a lake affords swimming for an individual who possesses this skill but may only afford splashing for a child who cannot swim. For another individual it affords boating and for another, bathing. Therefore, the lake affords certain actions and behaviors depending on the skills, needs, interests, and perceptions of an individual. By manipulating the environment (as Disneyworld managers, Montessori teachers, adaptive equipment designers, and park engineers do), leisure providers may be able to create an even greater range of opportunities, but they will only be realized if potential actors are sensitized to the possibilities. That is, we cannot create an affordance to be acted upon without knowing the potential actors/perceivers.

Using the example of the individual who cannot swim, we can consider how constraint and affordance perspectives create different orientations. From the perspective of constraints, we would be inclined to see individuals as constrained from using the lake to the extent that they lack swimming skills or boating resources. From the affordance perspective, on the other hand, we would examine the environment for what it does offer them in the way of splashing, bathing, and socializing. Or we might manipulate the environment to expand leisure affordances by designing a water slide that does not drop them off into deep water. Helping them become "attuned" to the possibilities, however, is a critical aspect of the affordance perspective.

Attunement is an important concept for understanding how affordances are perceived. We are all sensitive to opportunities in the environment, but self-tuning, or directed attention, enables the individual to detect the features of the environment that are most relevant and meaningful in relation to his or her abilities and interests. Individuals tune out certain information and attune themselves to other information in the environment. The process of attunement allows individuals to perceive certain environmental properties or events as *leisure* affordances to the extent that they suggest the experiences noted above and in Chapter 4. Pierskalla and Lee (1998) point out that "experience is the education of attention" (p. 73), implying that, as leisure is experienced, the associated affordances are brought into sharper relief.

The utility of leisure affordance as a concept is in what it specifies to people about the leisure opportunities available to them. The notion of creating leisure affordance may be misleading, however; affordances are not a consequence of education, persuasion, or even attunement alone. While these are all important processes that may be addressed in the context of programming and intervention, it is important to reiterate that affordances are present in the perceived environment. Any actual creation of affordance might occur either through environmental design and/or re-engineering. We will elaborate on this notion in the final section of this chapter.

Leisure Affordance in Social Contexts

As is true with Pierskalla and Lee (1998), ecological psychology as a whole has concerned itself mostly with the perception of and interaction with the physical environment and how attunement to its affordances facilitates effective action, but the environment is social as well as physical. Social affordances that individuals perceive come in a variety of forms, including facial expressions, gestures, and kinematic specification, or what is more commonly called "body language" (Runeson & Frykholm, 1983), as well as verbal communication. These are perceived both before and in response to their own actions. The social occasion of a party may be perceived as an enjoyable leisure event for one individual but as an uncomfortable social context by another.

An ecological analysis of a social interaction emphasizes perception rather than cognition (seeing directly what is actually being done by others rather than needing an interpretation of what is seen) in describing an individual's response to the social world (McArthur & Baron, 1983). Individuals (actors) develop understanding directly from information available (Gibson, 1986 [1979]) in the social environment as they interact with it, rather than requiring internal representation and subsequent interpretation of that environment.

This social ecological perspective has been used to describe encounters with the environment that discourage or encourage play in individuals with developmental disabilities (e.g., McArthur & Baron, 1983; Van Acker & Valenti, 1989) or physical disabilities (Goodwin & Watkinson, 2000). By extension, then, the social ecological perspective should also specify conditions of social affordance that are conducive to self-expression more generally. As with other kinds of affordance, sensitivity to social affordances changes as a result of a person's characteristics, actions and interactions. As a person enters a novel social situation, the reactions of others (e.g., turning of the eyes, smiling, scowling, or a lack of attention from others) further define the affordances of the context. This makes social affordance more difficult to specify, and yet recognition of this complexity promises a more complete explanation and understanding of behavior in context. Specifying leisure affordance in social situations can provide a more complete description of leisure behavior and experience than has been the case in leisure research to date, and it also offers possibilities for intervention and instruction.

The *absence* of others is its own affordance, of course; privacy and solitude may not be desired by everyone, but they are afforded, as leisure conditions, out in the woods or even in one's bedroom (cf. James, 2001; Larson, 1995). Still, it may take some reconsideration of the value of being out of contact with others, where a sense of isolation and loneliness is often expected. Being freed of the self-consciousness that accompanies social situations is one such benefit that may be recognized.

Attunement through Leisure Education

An ecological perspective on leisure experience, utilizing the concept of affordance, also has much to offer in the realm of professional recreation and the management of leisure services and resources. How does one come to detect affordance in the environment? This is essentially a matter of attunement. If a given setting is intended to elicit recreation and leisure experience, but a prospective participant detects only the conditions that constrain or inhibit voluntary participation because the experiences anticipated lack the qualities of leisure, then leisure is not being realized. Ameliorating some of the inhibiting factors (e.g., providing elbow pads for a prospective rollerblader) might bring about a different view of this situation, but it will be necessary for the perception of the experience to change. In some cases, this may be accomplished not by altering the environment or providing the resources to overcome constraints but, rather, through a process of refined projection as to the possibilities. Attunement suggests a merging of action and awareness (cf. flow) that allows a person to interact effectively with the environment in actually experiencing affordance. But there are a wide variety of factors—many of them falling in the various constraints categories—that keep a person from attending adequately and accurately to the possibilities in the environment for desirable experience, whether related to the construction of leisure or other, more instrumental, behaviors.

Leisure education is largely about *facilitation*, a subject that has drawn some attention in the literature on constraints (see, especially, Raymore, 2002). Hubbard and Mannell (2001) identify "facilitory" characteristics in the resources and strategies used to "negotiate," or overcome, constraints. The facilitating *resources* (available playmates, agreeable weather, a library of reading materials) are, essentially, affordances. And attuning individuals to those resources may be facilitated by educational intervention processes.

It may be the case, however, that a lack of attunement to the possibilities comes through the acceptance of norms that are discriminating based on others' characteristics, such as race or gender. We considered multiple explanations for nonparticipation in Chapters 9 and 10, but if providers accept such differences as a matter of course—for example, the view that Black people simply do not like wilderness rather than finding it uninviting—then they may fail to see the opportunities for cultivating interest in underrepresented groups. In a study of women participating in the statistically and traditionally male-dominated and stereotypically masculine activity of motorcycle riding, Auster (2001) found that participants needed to see other women involved to begin to see the "enrichment" possibilities offered by the activity. Facilitating attunement to the possibilities afforded, even when they may be unconventional, is thus a function of leisure education. We will look at other aspects of leisure education after we consider the research on constraint negotiation.

Interpreting and Managing Leisure Constraints

Let's begin with the case of Bill, an active, adventurous type who has been rendered paraplegic as a result of a diving accident at the age of 25. He advances from feeling his life is virtually over to considering just what he has lost, what he cannot do, and what he still can. His physical limitations clearly constrain the range of sporting opportunities available to him, but the change in his social life—as a result of being removed from friends who do such things—has also been daunting. He suffers from depression and a loss of self-confidence as well. As a leisure service provider, how would you help?

While constraints may define affordances to some extent, they also serve as barriers to participation in many cases. As noted in previous chapters, barriers and constraints to leisure come in a variety of forms. There are intrapersonal constraints, such as low self-esteem and shyness (see Chapter 7); there are interpersonal constraints, such as competing role responsibilities or a lack of activity companions (see Chapter 9); there are structural constraints, such as poverty, laws and regulations, and cultural taboos (see Chapter 10); and there are the interactions of these, such as when prejudice or the prospect of encountering wild animals makes a person fearful. Nevertheless, individuals often do manage to stay active in their leisure in spite of encountering constraints; they continue to participate in and enjoy favorite activities (Jackson, Crawford, & Godbey, 1992; Jackson & Rucks, 1995; Shaw, Bonen, & McCabe, 1991), and they even begin new pursuits (McGuire & Norman, 2005). Indeed, constraints may even indirectly lead to increased participation or operate in more complex ways depending on a person's motivation, age, and interests (cf. Hubbard & Mannell, 2001; Son, Mowen, & Kerstetter, 2008).

How people manage to mitigate the effects of constraints has been of interest to researchers and leisure providers, as well. An understanding of the strategies used by individuals to overcome and cope with constraints, as well as the psychological and social factors that influence their success at using these strategies, would be very useful in efforts to help people engage in beneficial leisure. Two leisure-related mechanisms that have been proposed are "constraint negotiation" and "recreation substitution," both of which have been introduced earlier in the text. *Constraint negotiation* refers to the strategies people use to avoid or reduce the impact of the constraints and barriers to leisure participation and enjoyment that were discussed earlier (Jackson, Crawford, & Godbey, 1992). The *theory of recreation substitutability* explains a narrower range of constraint coping behavior. It deals with how people stay active and continue to meet their leisure needs by choosing a new leisure activity or setting when a preferred leisure activity is no longer available (Iso-Ahola, 1986). We also consider a third mechanism for adaptation to constraint, the *selective optimization with compensation* (SOC) process that considers both substitution and negotiation within a broader lifespan perspective.

Negotiating Constraint

Constraints on leisure vary in intensity and impact, according to Jackson, Crawford, and Godbey (1992). Many constraints can be overcome rather easily (e.g., finding someone with whom to go to the movies when alone), though others, such as a spinal cord injury, can be permanent and severe in their negative impact on leisure behavior and experience. But, even in the most extreme cases, people often find ways to manage constraining conditions and to find or create circumstances that afford new possibilities (see, for example, Coble, Selin, & Erickson, 2003; Henderson, Bedini, & Schuler, 1995; Hubbard & Mannell, 2001; Son, Mowen, & Kerstetter, 2008; Whyte & Shaw, 1994).

People engage in constraint negotiation when they are interested in participating and have difficulty doing so because of intervening interpersonal and/or structural constraints. In some cases an activity is abandoned in the face of constraints; in other circumstances the constraints result in less participation and/or enjoyment than desired; and in still others, people find ways to work through or around constraints. Jackson, Crawford, and Godbey (1992) have discussed a variety of strategies for negotiating constraints. Though there is certainly thought and action associated with all of them, they distinguish between "cognitive" and "behavioral" strategies.

Cognitive strategies include such processes as *cognitive dissonance* reduction, where unchosen or constrained activity alternatives are devalued and no longer seen as interesting. Not having the money to attend a concert, for example, might lead to less interest in the music or performer featured. Emphasizing the benefits of the activity that was chosen and the costs of an activity not chosen or constrained reduces cognitive dissonance (cf. Aronson, 2008). This type of cognitive strategy can be both positive and negative. On the plus side, it allows people to enjoy and feel good about the leisure choices they make and experience a reduction in interest for activities that may be unavailable to them. On the negative side, people can be so adaptable that they "lose interest" in potentially worthwhile and satisfying activities when, in fact, there are other strategies that might allow them to become involved. If Bill was to devalue and lose interest in physically active leisure because of his injury, he would be unlikely to be motivated to expend the effort to get involved and become successful at wheelchair basketball.

Another cognitive strategy is just to resist the power of a constraint such as the judgmental gazes of observers. Some of the adolescent girl swimmers in an Australian study (James, 2000) who were initially self-conscious and inhibited about showing more of their bodies in public decided to just "get over it" and were gradually desensitized. Others used more behavioral strategies to make themselves less visible, including covering up their bodies, staying in groups, and swimming at remote venues.

Behavioral strategies also include modifying other aspects of leisure (e.g., giving up "happy hour" with coworkers to go ice skating with a niece), making an effort to learn about other leisure opportunities, altering the timing and frequency of participation, learning new recreation skills, and changing other aspects of lifestyle (e.g., spending less time at work). In a study of 425 junior-high and high-school students, Jackson and Rucks (1995) asked the students if they participated "even though [they] have problems in doing so." The 23% who indicated that they often did so reported encountering a variety of constraints in their daily lives: other commitments (e.g., school, family); inaccessible activity; ill health; and lack of necessary skills, partners, self-confidence, transportation, and/or approval of parents. Of the strategies used to overcome these problems, the students most frequently mentioned better time management and the acquisition of necessary skills. But the strategies used varied according to activity; for example, skill-related constraints were more common with competitive activities and were addressed by lowering aspirations (a cognitive strategy) as well as raising competence levels (a behavioral strategy).

Even the intrapersonal constraints of fear can be negotiated to allow participation. In a study of solo hikers (Coble, Selin, & Erickson, 2003), fears associated with the prospects of being attacked by dogs or other hikers, particularly strong among women hikers, were managed with various behavioral strategies such as hiking with a staff, carrying protective devices, avoiding certain areas, or hiking only at certain times. The structural constraint of discrimination created the intrapersonal/interpersonal constraint of self-consciousness in the leisure activities of Muslims in the post-9/11 United States (Livengood & Stodolska, 2001), but those who still wanted to participate adopted strategies to "blend in," such as wearing more Western-style clothing and participating only with other family members or friends.

Time management is a major behavioral negotiation strategy that is common throughout adulthood. Contrary to the popular opinion that older people have an abundance of time, Mannell and Zuzanak (1991) found that a lack of time was even a significant leisure constraint experienced by a group of older retired adults, just as it often is with adolescents and younger adults. In interviews with 88 adults ages 30 to 65, Samdahl and Jekubovitch (1993) identified several common time-management strategies for dealing with constraints. First, daily routines were controlled to guarantee that opportunities for desired activities were available, despite being very busy in other respects. Second, with family helpmates, chores were effectively divided up to accommodate leisure interests. Third, alternative activities were chosen that were less time intensive. Finally, many of the adult respondents simply accepted that life changes make continuing participation in the same activities unappealing in some cases.

To the extent that time continues to be in limited supply, some people cope by simply recognizing that they cannot do everything and indeed must make some sacrifices and set priorities. Goodale and Witt (1989) point out that "increased participation in various activities may not be a panacea, or even an improvement, in a culture where pace, stress, and overload seem already to have exceeded the limits of well-being for many" (p. 444). Success in negotiating a constraint, especially when that constraint is a shortage of time, often lies in people recognizing their priorities and resisting the temptation to do more than is possible, prudent, or in keeping with personal and social commitments and values.

With attention, then, to priorities and values, more recent research on leisure constraints and constraint negotiation has integrated the concept of motivation and, particularly, that reflected in the self-determination theory (Alexandris, Tsorbatzoudis, & Grouios, 2002; Hubbard & Mannell, 2001; Son, Mowen, & Kerstetter, 2008). Being more intrinsically interested in an activity leads potential participants to find ways to overcome constraints and participate in an activity more readily than would be the case for someone with only moderate intrinsic interest, a proposition that has been born out by research on motivation and constraints to participation in an employee wellness program for adult workers (Hubbard & Mannell, 2001). And in an

Australian study of women involved in adventure recreation (Little, 2002), recommitment to the priority of adventure recreation and to resistance more generally led to persistence in spite of constraining social influences.

Recreation Substitutability

Recalling our opening scenario in this section on constraints: Bill has to negotiate the constraints created by his permanent physical injury to be able to stay active in his leisure. One way he can do this is by substituting entirely new or adapted pre-injury activities for the old activities in which he can no longer participate. What approach is he likely to take? What type of activity substitution is likely to be most successful and lead to the greatest amount of satisfaction? Recreation substitutability theory attempts to answer these types of questions.

Introduced in the mid-1970s (Hendee & Burdge, 1974), the theory has primarily been of interest to researchers concerned with understanding what happens to outdoor recreation users when they are displaced from an activity that they are committed to and enjoy because of changes in social, environmental, or managerial conditions (Brunson & Shelby, 1993). For example, what would you do if the friend with whom you annually took a canoe trip moved and could no longer participate? What if pollution barred you from swimming at a favorite beach, or you could not get a permit for the river you had fished on most of your life due to the implementation of new wildlife conservation policies? Recreation substitutability theory suggests that people will choose as substitutes those activities that provide similar psychological experiences, satisfactions, and benefits as the original activity. For example, if risk and challenge were the primary motives for participation, activities that meet these needs would be chosen and substituted.

The theory has also been applied to leisure behavior in general whenever an "originally intended activity is no longer possible and therefore must be replaced by another behavior if leisure involvement is to be initiated or continued" (Iso-Ahola, 1986, p. 369). Iso-Ahola (1986) has proposed that *psychological reactance* (Brehm, 1972; see Chapter 6 in this book) is a key process underlying people's willingness to substitute. Essentially, he has argued that the greater a person's feeling of choice or freedom in selecting a new activity, the greater his or her willingness to substitute. In other words, if people perceive that there is a great deal of external pressure for them to substitute, if the reasons for substitution are perceived to be unjustified or unfair, if the number of substitute alternatives is small, or if the need for substitution is unexpected, then psychological reactance will set in and the willingness to substitute will be lower. Iso-Ahola also contends that the more similar the substitute activity is perceived to be to the original, the greater the willingness to substitute will be. This similarity consists of the motives, rewards available, attractiveness, and costs of participation. To return to the scenario, because Bill's injury forces him to make changes in his leisure life-style, he is unlikely to feel a great deal of choice. Initially, he may even feel that the need for substitution is unfair, that his injury restricts his options, and that those assisting him in becoming independent again are pressuring him to participate (of course, for his own good). However, the greater the number of options he has, the more willing he will be to substitute and become involved during his leisure again. Also, the less adaptation required for him to continue to participate in activities that he enjoyed before his accident, the more likely he is to successfully substitute. For example, rather than substi-tuting a completely new activity for nature photography, he might begin to pursue portrait photography which he may perceive as more similar.

The task of identifying the ways in which original and new substitute activities are similar remains a major challenge for recreation substitutability theory. As Brunson and Shelby (1993) note, some people may require sub-stitutes that provide the same set of motives, needs, and preferences as the original activity. Some may require only that a substitute promises to be as enjoyable an experience as the original, even if an entirely different set of motives, needs, or preferences is associated with the substitute activity. And still others may not require that the substitute be enjoyable at all, as long as other recreation benefits (e.g., physical fitness) can be derived. Brunson and Shelby defined recreation substitutability somewhat more broadly than previ-ous writers on the subject: "The term recreation substitutability refers to the interchangeability of recreation experiences such that acceptably equivalent outcomes can be achieved by varying one or more of the following: the time of the experience, the means of gaining access, the setting, and the activity" (p. 68). This view of substitution is based on Shelby and Vaske's (1991) identification of substitution strategies other than the "replacement of one activity with another." These other forms of substitution include temporal (i.e., participating in the original activity at a different time), resource (i.e., finding a new setting to participate in the original activity), and strategic (i.e., finding a different way to participate in the original activity in the same set-ting at the same time) (see also Kyle et al., 2005).

In later life, when some loss of physical capacity makes involvement in favorite activities more difficult, there are often suitable alternatives that offer many of the same rewards. In a qualitative study of 20 recent retirees (Kleiber & Nimrod, 2009), nearly all could point to having made such adjustments, for example turning to cross-country skiing when downhill skiing became too treacherous, playing doubles tennis instead of singles, or reading only larger print books. These substitutions are a way of compensating for losses in function while maintaining aspects of activities that are most enjoyable and satisfying.

Selective Optimization with Compensation

Negotiating constraints and substituting activities or settings for one another are essentially mechanisms of adaptation. Adaptation is important throughout life, but it becomes particularly important in managing the challenges and losses of later life. In fact, of all the many ideas about "aging successfully," the *Selective Optimization with Compensation* model (Baltes & Baltes, 1990) has received the most attention among gerontologists in recent years. It differs from other ideas about successful aging in not assuming high levels of functioning; older people can be very happy and "successful" in spite of hearing loss, relative social isolation, etc. (see also Baltes & Baltes, 1998; Baltes & Carstenson, 1996; Lang, Rieckmann, & Baltes, 2002). And it really applies *throughout* the lifespan in making the most of whatever life has presented as challenges, including those related to leisure.

Essentially, the SOC model argues that it is adaptive and healthy to respond to the limiting factors in the environment, especially as they mount with the losses accompanying aging, by being *selective* about activities of choice, abandoning those that are less personally meaningful, and *compensating* in whatever way necessary to *optimize* a more restricted number of alternatives. Baltes and Carstensen (1996) point out that "in their orchestration" these three processes "generate and regulate development and aging" (p. 218). Selection is the process of *reducing* the number of activity domains to those that are most important. Abandoning activities that have been practiced for some time is often accompanied by some regret, but it allows for a reprioritization of other activities, usually along a continuum of what is most personally meaningful. As a process that has been found to be important to adaptation in later life, it gives new meaning and value to the concept of *disengagement*. If and when disengagement is voluntary, it may be adaptive in preserving integrity and well-being and in enhancing the prospect for optimizing other higher priority activities. But even when it is involuntary—as with a physically disabling illness—the cognitive reappraisal that takes place may be ultimately liberating. For example, as Bill comes to accept his inability to run and race his bike competitively as he had in the past, he finds more time available for further development of his interest in photography.

Compensation is a process that has the effect of *preserving* involvement in a preferred activity, *in spite of* emerging constraints. Lang, Rieckmann, and Baltes (2002) use the example of a preference for tennis that, in the face of the constraining effects of declining mobility and strength, would result in the elimination of other strenuous physical activities to make playing tennis both more likely and more satisfying. Turning to a larger racquet face and learning shot placement strategies less reliant on physical strength and power would be mechanisms of compensation that preserve the opportunity for effective engagement. As another example, consider the impact of failing eyesight on driving for pleasure. Rather than abandoning car touring all together, finding companions (with good eyesight!) with whom to share such experience preserves the opportunity for car travel—even enhancing the prospects for visual exposure given freedom of attention from driving itself—while also affording a new dimension of companionship. As with the tennis example above, compensation in this way serves to actually optimize the experience. In summarizing their analysis of the SOC model, Baltes and Baltes (1998) note that "by careful selection, optimization, and compensation we are able to minimize the negative consequences from losses that occur with aging and to work on aspects of growth and new peaks of success, albeit in a more restricted range" (p. 17). They added, "making smaller territories of life larger and more beautiful is at the core of *savoir vivre* in old age" (p. 19).

Optimization, at any age, is about making the most of any activity, by giving it sufficient time and attention, and using the resources that are available, including those that allow one to compensate for limitations of various kinds. Lowering the basket from 10 to 8 feet for an 8-year-old who has expressed an interest in basketball, compensates for her limitations and enables her to optimize her performance in that activity. If she likes the sport and wants to continue, she will eventually outgrow the need for such an accommodation. But if she does want to continue and wants to improve her skills and her experience with the game, she may want to give it more time and attention and let go of some other activities. This is the selection process.

Persistence with an activity in the face of constraints can foster a generalized attitude to dealing with constraints in this manner, increasing motivation and enhancing "negotiation self-efficacy" (Hubbard & Mannell, 2001; Little, 2002; Loucks-Atkinson & Mannell, 2007). But responding to constraints reflectively, questioning the value of the activity, and maybe even abandoning it when it becomes frustrating, unrewarding, or uninteresting makes us more discriminating and allows us to make more of the activities we can do. We are inclined in Western society to try to do as much as we can sometimes, but this is often at the expense of optimizing experience in some activities, as well as adding to, rather than reducing, the level of stress in our lives. Learning to be discriminating in the face of constraints and abandoning those activities that have become too difficult in favor of alternatives, including substitutes that are more promising, draw on different skills, or offer a different set of rewards, may be critical to maintaining or creating a good quality of life. Indeed, constraints may even be *beneficial* in forcing such careful consideration and leading one to more satisfying alternatives (see Kleiber et al., 2008).

Cultivating Leisure Experience

The potential for increasing leisure participation and enhancing leisure experience lies in understanding both affordances and constraints and how people typically take advantage of the former and adjust to the latter. This is largely a matter of *facilitation*. Raymore (2002) examined the constraints and constraints-negotiation literature and concluded that there was not enough attention to enhancing opportunities and experiences, irrespective of constraints. She pointed out that just as the presence of constraints does not mean the end of participation, nor does the absence of constraints inevitably result in participation. Using an ecological framework, she addressed intrapersonal, interpersonal, and structural factors that enhance participation and experience. Thus, with respect to the intrapersonal, she identified personality and self-concept conditions that enhance leisure experience and participation. And the same interpersonal factors that constrain leisure behavior—peers, family expectations, and authority figures—may also work to facilitate leisure activity and experience. She used the example of a child—who finds age mates in the neighborhood—being a facilitator to parents' participation in social activities in that community. Similarly, structural factors such as income, recreation facilities, ethnic customs, and institutional regulations that constrain leisure may also have the effect of enhancing opportunities. All of these factors may have the potential to facilitate leisure experience, but to put them to use—for ourselves as well as others—we need to reconsider what we have learned about them. Thus, in this final section we offer some guidelines for enhancing leisure participation and experience—both for yourself and for those you may be in a position to influence.

Learning to Optimize Leisure Personally

Because leisure is based largely on the perception of freedom, it is often assumed that if we have discretionary time, we have leisure, but most people want more out of leisure than just the free time. They seek ideal, "optimal," experience. We will consider how to promote such things with others shortly, but let us start here with some "self-help" ideas. The ideas of selection, optimization, and compensation reviewed above are certainly relevant to this task. The selection of alternative courses of action means discriminating among available options, investing in those that are most important (optimizing), and compensating for limiting conditions along the way as necessary. Again, while the framework was created for positive aging, it is relevant for the entire lifespan, at least for anyone who can read this book. Starting with ourselves will help us know better how to facilitate leisure experience with others.

First of all, then, what are *you* looking for in leisure? This is a *value clarification* question. What you most want takes some careful self-examination and perhaps some resistance to that which comes along most easily; watching television and following the crowd may be relaxing and stimulating, but they may not be very intentional courses of action and may feel like wasted time in retrospect. Of course, relaxation and relatedness are themselves among preferred leisure experiences, so it's a question of what you most truly want at a given moment (for example, when you finish this reading assignment!). What do you want for a given moment, a weekend, a vacation, a trip, or an adventure? To use some of the experiences referred to in Chapter 4, do you want excitement, relaxation, sociability, love, deep flow-like engagement, or something else? There are self-help books for most of these things, but let us take just a couple of them here, finding flow and finding relaxation.

Finding Flow

If the experience of flow appeals to you, as it does to most people, your first task at creating it, or more of it, is to consider the action patterns that you have enjoyed in the past and ask yourself, "Is there a growth edge here? Can I get still better at this? Can I find even greater challenge in the activity and thereby greater fulfillment?" Almost any activity will offer possibilities for growth and what Csikszentmihalyi (1990, 1997) refers to as "complexifixation." If the activity you have enjoyed, and really gotten into, in the past is no longer appealing to you, ask yourself, "Why?" Perhaps other things have intervened since you last participated, in which case you may have to retreat a few steps to a more basic level of the activity to find a more appropriate level of challenge than where you left it. Or, do you feel there are no new (or old) challenges for you in it (a passion for a particular table game that has run its course, for example)? Or, perhaps you just haven't considered how to make it more challenging. Take rock climbing, for example. Mitchell (1983) describes how rock climbers can intentionally make a particular climb more or less difficult by their choice of equipment, how much they party the night before a climb, and the route they take up the mountain.

Of course, you just might not see the new opportunities in that activity; turning to something entirely new, then, may be the best option. But you will have to accommodate, perhaps, to the position of being a "novice" and feeling awkward and incompetent for a time until you pick up some skill. This is usually characteristic of those activities that offer the most complexity and the greatest chances for sustained involvement over time, offering a "career," in fact (Stebbins, 1992, 2007), with increasing degrees of specialization (Bryan, 1977, 2000; Scott & Shafer, 2001). And, again, selection and compensation may both be necessary to find flow. You may need to let some things go to focus on an activity and invest in it sufficiently to get more deeply involved in a satisfying way. You may also have to deal with what stands in the way of deeper involvement. Compensation is largely a matter of negotiating constraints. What is standing in the way, physical changes? Role changes? Other interests? (If it's the last, then go deeper into one of those!) Remember there are both behavioral and cognitive strategies to use to deal with the constraint.

Finally, do not underestimate the power of structured activities—such as organized sports, voluntary associations, clubs, and online communities— that are led by others, to some extent, but responsive to your initiative. Not only are there prospects for optimization of experience in responding to a pre-existing structure, but there is the value of the relatedness created in doing it with others. These activities are a critical part of adolescent development (Larson, 2000), as was established in Chapter 11, but they can work their magic at any age, depending on how the activity is structured and how much self-direction an individual has. Research (see Caldwell, 2005; Larson, 2000; Witt & Caldwell, 2005) tells us that to optimize the potential of such structured activities—for you and others—such activities should: (1) allow participants the opportunity to be planful and self-directed; (2) be intrinsically motivated; (3) require concerted attention (toward creating some kind of order); and (4) have an enduring quality for a substantial period of time (cf. Larson, 2000).

Such activities also have the capacity for enhancing social integration, building social capital, and contributing to a sense of community (Eccles & Barber, 1999; Lyons & Dionigi, 2007). Of course, the challenge for any such activities in the context of leisure is to try to maintain those structural elements and benefits while not undermining the sense of freedom and the prospects for enjoyment.

Finding Relaxation

Because we North Americans typically have a strong activity orientation, we may be more challenged to find relaxation than those in other societies and thus may need more help. Saying, "Just relax!" when you are either energetically engaged or somewhat stressed by circumstances may be downright annoying, but the state of true relaxation may require some disengagement from well-accepted patterns. For one thing, you don't need to be doing everything. There is no prize for those who can do the most at any one time. "Use it or lose it" makes some sense for maintaining function, particularly in later life, but indiscriminant activity, even repeated exercise of some function, is counter-productive. Pausing and taking an "open stance" to life, "kicking back" or "throttling back," as have been common expressions, allows one to better see what is most worth doing, what can be done, and what the challenges are for doing it. This is the selection process again. But selecting doing nothing is also a reasonable option—letting the mind wander, being open to appreciating the present moment and what life genuinely affords, even before action is taken. Taking action may benefit from such a period of disengagement, of course, not only for the recovery of energy and for value clarification and discrimination but also to improve on the concentration necessary for effective allocation of attention. Research and theory on creativity, for example, emphasizes the value of an "incubation" period—where the mind is actually distracted or relaxed from the demands of concerted action for awhile—for an improved and more creative product (cf. Amabile, 1996; Boden, 2004).

Again, though, the value of relaxation isn't only in what it provides for subsequent productivity. Learning to relax effectively cultivates a general level of mindfulness and well-being that has health benefits. People who have had a close brush with death or other traumatic life events, as we discussed in earlier chapters, may become more effective at "just being"—sitting in a chair alone or with friends, taking in appreciatively what life affords. But it may take some training—in meditation, for example—to enable hard-charging Westerners to find that condition. If you are one of those, and you come to see the value of true relaxation, consider the prescription to start with a *discipline* of meditation to get there, counterintuitive as that may sound.

As was the case in finding flow, or any other experience for that matter, selection and compensation will very likely be necessary. To be able to relax, you may well have to give some things up. Remember, you don't have to be busy every minute. Just say no to some things and give yourself the time to really let go and just be in the moment. This may be challenged by a variety of circumstances. You may need to overcome the constraint of "noise" or distracting others by finding a quiet place to just sit for awhile—getting away from those roommates, for example.

Relaxation can also complement engagement and flow, especially as it allows for the *savoring* of that experience, as we noted in Chapter 4. Savoring is the process by which people bring about, appreciate, and enhance positive experiences in life (Bryant & Veroff, 2007). It is about sharing with others, memory building, self-congratulation, comparing (e.g., "it doesn't get any better than this"), sensory and perceptual sharpening, absorption, behavioral expressiveness, temporal awareness, and counting blessings. It can be past-, present-, or future-oriented, anticipating, experiencing, and recollecting pleasure and enjoyment. Bryant and Veroff see it as the antithesis of coping, which is about dealing with negative events; savoring dwells on the positive experiences in life. In seeing it as a form of self-regulation, like coping, they note that marveling regulates awe, thanksgiving regulates gratitude, basking regulates pride, and luxuriating regulates physical pleasure (compare these to mourning in response to grief and adjustment in response to disabling loss). They note further that people can *choose* to bring savoring into their lives to a greater extent. Savoring can be invoked through reminiscence, storytelling, mindfulness, and speculation about future events. But it does require a willingness to shed performance pressures and others' evaluations and discard expectations for achievement and social well-being, though emotional well-being has been shown to be enhanced by such experiences.

Attitudes toward idleness may still be the biggest constraint, however. The Protestant work ethic still has a hold in most industrialized societies. If this is your accepted cultural condition, you may not see any need to change it. But if you see the value in relaxation and yet still feel guilty when you do, it may be important to first see the reason and then find some way of addressing it. Even if it is your responsibility to others—who may indeed need you—that both drives you and constrains you, consider the possibility that you may be of better service to them if you are relaxed and in better spirits. And speaking of others, let's now see how to enhance *their* leisure experience.

Fostering Leisure Experience in Others

Assume an interest for starters. (We'll return to the "lack of interest" problem shortly.) How do we bring about flow, relaxation, and other leisure experiences for others who we know want such experiences? This returns us to the subject of leisure education and intervention more generally, where activities are designed and arranged to create some kind of experience and perhaps achieve some number of the outcomes that were reviewed in Chapters 11 and 12. You may be involved in designing programs for the explicit purpose of raising self-esteem, building a sense of community, reducing obesity, or improving cognitive functioning in later life; and the assumption is that such things can be accomplished with attention to the experience that is generated and the social context in which it is generated.

Leisure education has a rich history within the field of recreation and leisure studies and beyond, as we noted when we introduced it as a situational influence in Chapter 9 (see also Albrechtsen, 2001). It has been used mostly in a compensatory way for those with constraints related to disability, illness, or poverty, but the principles may be more generally applied. These principles rely extensively on basic understandings from social psychology, particularly those related to self-awareness, self-determination, and self-efficacy. A variety of components have been implemented and tested (see Dattilo, 2008, for a review of this research), resulting in a now-recognizable set including: leisure awareness and appreciation (benefits of participation, place of leisure in society, entitlement to leisure); self-awareness and value clarification (leisure preferences past, present and future; leisure skills); identification of leisure resources (human and environmental); development of social interaction skills (communication and emotional control); nurturance of self-determination (identification of constraints and shaping of personal autonomy and responsibility); shaping of decision-making skills (making choices); and activity skill development. Some of these components—the development of social interaction skills, in particular—are necessary precursors for participation for many children and youth with disabilities, but the other components are regarded as generic enough to be generally applicable.

Leisure awareness and identification of leisure resources were introduced to some extent above in the section about recognizing opportunities; part of the task of leisure education is *exposure* to what is available and what participation might lead to in terms of enjoyment and other benefits. But leisure education takes facilitation further in promoting skill development for enhancing leisure experience and making more of it. This may involve helping someone get more deeply involved in an activity, developing a leisure repertoire that offers a wider range of activity options, or finding alternatives to activities that may be undesirable or no longer available due to emergent constraints. And, of course, program development, instruction, and leadership must be conducted with great sensitivity to the readiness of the learners and the impact of group processes and to the variety of experiences preferred and sought (e.g., Johnson, Hodges, & Keller, 2007). Even without considering a professional role of leisure educator or leisure service provider, however—a subject to which we will return shortly—nearly all of you will find yourselves in the roles of parent, instructor, coach, or mentor at some point, roles which include the task of teaching leisure skills and facilitating leisure experiences. We can start with what we have reviewed for finding flow and enjoyment for ourselves.

Promoting Flow and Serious Leisure

Flow can be generated for others if situations can be arranged wherein the challenges are reasonably well-matched with participants' skills. If the challenges are too low for a person, boredom is the result; if they are too great, anxiety can be expected (Csikszentmihalyi, 1975, 1990, 1997). This matching is made much more difficult, of course, when there are multiple participants at different levels of ability. But to the extent that ability levels can be matched through pairing or grouping and instruction otherwise individualized, flow becomes more likely. In any case, the match for all participants should be considered carefully (Voelkl, 1990). Allowing as much self-direction as possible is also conducive to flow. As we have discussed previously, some activities, such as video games, are almost self-managing when it comes to automatically adjusting challenges to the skill level of the participant. As people become more proficient at an activity, they develop the ability to optimize challenge themselves.

Providing appropriate feedback is another important aspect of setting and activity management. The setting can afford involvement and enjoyment if it allows feedback about learning and mastery, whether that feedback is offered by instructors, co-participants, or comes from interaction with objects, playthings, or other materials. Generally speaking, anything that takes a person away from his or her focus on the task at hand can be regarded as disruptive and potentially undermining to intrinsic motivation and enjoyment. With respect to children, Ellis, Witt, and Aguilar (1983) point out that parents, coaches, and teachers can be disruptive to leisure experience when they are so invested in their children's activities that they praise or correct them to the point that the children lose their focus.

Helping an individual find flow-type enjoyment may depend on negotiating intrapersonal constraints to some extent, such as overcoming issues of self-confidence. Full participation in and enjoyment of leisure activities are often constrained by a perception of oneself as incompetent or inadequate with respect to a particular activity. As was noted in research reviewed in Chapter 6 (Sarrazin et al., 2002), initial intrinsic interest based on excitement alone is likely to fade if skills aren't developed; improvement in competence appears necessary to maintain continued interest. The goal in such cases, then, is to create enough challenge to allow the individual to experience some success as a function of effort and learning and thereby to gain a sense of self-efficacy in that activity. There is also the potential that this sense of efficacy (i.e., sense of competence or self-confidence) will generalize to other activities, thus encouraging increased participation.

Although the evidence for self-efficacy as it relates to changing health behavior (see Strecher et al., 1986) and exercise behavior (e.g., Brawley & Rodgers, 1993; Loucks-Atkinson & Mannell, 2007; McAuley & Rowney, 1990) is fairly well-established, the importance of self-efficacy in leisure behavior has not been adequately considered. A couple of studies were suggestive, however: Ellis and his colleagues (Ellis, Maughan-Pritchett, & Ruddell, 1993; Maughan & Ellis, 1991) demonstrated that adolescent psychiatric patients playing video games come to see themselves as more effective players if they have appropriate role models who are successful at the game, are given some control over the leisure setting, and are given feedback that focuses on their performance. In general, it appears that individuals who are confident in their abilities to engage in a particular leisure behavior will tend to participate more actively. They will persist with or initiate the activity even in the face of obstacles to do so. Less leisure-efficacious individuals would not be likely to initiate activity or to maintain their activity patterns. Dropping out or participating more irregularly would be more characteristic of their behavior.

The critical challenge in trying to promote flow, self-efficacy, and continued interest in others is that the structure, goals, and rewards arranged by adults and program leaders are used effectively and don't undermine the sense of autonomy and self-determination that is so central to the experience of leisure, where freedom and enjoyment are paramount. In providing structured instruction, there is always the prospect for undermining intrinsic motivation. Larson (2000) compares the high adult "scaffolding" in Cub Scouts with low scaffolding in publishing a school newspaper, seeing the former as more appropriate for younger children and the latter requiring some maturity, while recognizing that "Leaders face the fundamental problem of allowing participants' actions to be self directed, voluntary and intrinsically motivated yet also structured and challenging enough that participants are stretched into new domains of complexity" (p. 179). Recall the discussion at the end of Chapter 6 about how to use praise carefully to preserve and enhance an autonomy supportive environment.

The research on coaching effectiveness in youth sports (Roberts et al., 1997; Smith & Smoll, 1990) demonstrates that emphasizing task mastery (with high levels of positive reinforcement for desirable performance, effort, and improvement) rather than the performance-/ego-oriented goal of winning is far more likely to sustain interest in the sport (or nearly any other activity). Larson (2000) concludes with the suggestions that instructors, coaches, and program supervisors should (1) place kids in appropriately structured settings, (2) provide "process mentoring" to keep them "in the envelope," and (3) design programs that maximize individual and group growth. While Larson's suggestions apply to youth, they might apply to instruction with any age group. Indeed, leisure education that focuses on promoting self-determination and skill development has been shown to be effective in improving the quality of life of older people as well (Searle et al., 1995, 1998).

Finally, flow, involvement, and commitment in activities can be reinforced by making it a collective matter. Helping to connect people with others who have an interest and some history with an activity raises the prospect that it will be taken seriously and may introduce the participant to a social world surrounding participation. Such identification with others in serious leisure activities may contribute to the quality of experience and to the likelihood it will be continued.

Overcoming Lack of Interest

But what if there is no apparent interest in what we might want to teach or maybe in anything leisure related? Although affordance refers to setting and activity opportunities, enabling someone to take advantage of these alternatives requires more than just managing the environment. It means "getting into the heads" of prospective participants to understand their needs, the constraints they feel, and how their leisure orientations differ. As we have shown earlier in the section on attunement, there are a variety of psychological dispositions (e.g., needs, motives, interests, attitudes, personality traits, self-esteem, competence, self-efficacy, identity) that influence how people construe the social situation and setting and, consequently, leisure behavior and experience.

The most difficult intrapersonal "constraint" or psychological disposition to deal with when helping people with their leisure is lack of interest in participating. Knowing what is causing the lack of interest in a particular activity and whether it is due to a constraint can be tricky (see Mannell & Zuzanek, 1991). Sometimes what is expressed as a lack of interest is a reflection of a different intrapersonal constraint, for example, a lack of confidence in one's ability to successfully engage in an activity or a negative attitude toward the activity. Interventions that lead to skill improvements, the development of feelings of self-efficacy for an activity, or the promotion of positive attitudes toward it may be required.

Lack of interest may also result from continued lack of success in overcoming interpersonal constraints (e.g., finding other people with whom to participate) or structural constraints (e.g., lack of facilities); people finally give up and "lose interest." In some cases a lack of interest in an activity is the result of the successful negotiation of constraints to other activities. For example, by finding the time and money to commit to regularly going to live theater, one may have little time and money and, consequently, little interest in attending professional sport events. It cannot be assumed, therefore, that lack of interest necessarily reflects a constraint. Nonparticipation in a particular activity may be largely a matter of having previously established priorities and choosing those leisure involvements that are the most important. Here lack of interest may reflect a low priority.

However, where lack of interest is more a matter of intrapersonal constraints—the lack of confidence, especially—it is possible to intervene and "remedy" it in a variety of ways. Our earlier review of the principles of self-determination theory provide some guidance (cf. Ryan & Deci, 2000). First, avoid the use or overuse of rewards as incentives or bribes for participation. This runs the risk of "overjustifying" the activity and undermining what little intrinsic interest may be emerging. Second, use rewards only as informational feedback contingent on the participant's progress or success in learning the activity or for effort produced, and avoid doing so if it appears to undermine the participant's sense of self-determination or control in any way. And third, be sure that participation leads to feelings of competence, autonomy, and relatedness with others for the participant, as these are the basic needs underlying intrinsic motivation. More generally, take the person's perspective and show care for her or him as an individual and not just for the behavior or performance exhibited. Involving the participant in the decision-making process is a good way to do this.

Girls, in particular, largely because of gender role stereotyping, may need assistance and opportunities for overcoming self-doubt. McKenney, Budbill, and Roberts (2008) found that experience with single-sex, adventure-based activities and programs acted as a significant counterforce to prevailing social messages, empowering the girls and providing them a significant source of personal growth. The five key concepts focused on in these programs were: (1) strengths-based program philosophy that respected girls' experiences; (2) guidelines that required instructors to be competent and understanding of adolescent girls and their experiences; (3) respect for the value of choice, specifically, so that girls can make choices about and within their experiences; (4) a wealth of opportunities for both action and reflection that allow for technical skill development; and (5) opportunities for self-expression and relationship building.

But considering the messages from Chapters 5 and 6 further, we recognize that direction and control of participants' activities does raise an ethical dilemma (Goodale, 1990; Sylvester, 1985). On one hand, caregivers and practitioners intuitively understand that by forcefully promoting them they run the risk of making potentially enjoyable activities grim and unappealing (as well as unleisurely). On the other hand, they may feel the responsibility to promote "healthy" leisure activities and to use structured activities in all the ways that have been shown to be impactful (e.g., Shaw & Dawson, 2001). Promoting interest in such activities—without being coercive and manipulative or undermining intrinsic motivation—may thus require attention to some principles of persuasion and attitude change.

Persuasion and Attitude Change

Typically, leisure service providers have attempted to create positive attitudes toward activities by exposing people to activities in recreation programs where skills and knowledge in the activity are taught. Leisure counseling and education programs are also used to change attitudes towards leisure activities (e.g., Aguilar, 1987; Backman & Mannell, 1986; Dattilo, 2008; Searle & Mahon, 1991). Backman and Mannell (1986) found that just the opportunity to think about and discuss their attitudes and values toward leisure with other people, and to have it affirmed that leisure is appropriate behavior, was sufficient to change leisure attitudes and encourage greater participation among a group of institutionalized older adults. However, they also found that those participants who were involved in both a leisure-counseling program and a recreation activity program designed to expose them to new activities showed the greatest increase in leisure behavior—an increase that was maintained after the program was over.

Influencing attitudes held toward a specific leisure activity can also create an interest and motivation to participate. Attitudes may be a type of intrapersonal constraint, and negative attitudes toward leisure may reduce or completely suppress interest in participation. For example, a middle-aged man who might enjoy attending an exhibit on aerial photography does not even consider it because he regards museum- and gallery-going as too "highbrow." Practitioners in a variety of fields have given considerable attention to attitude change as a way to promote behavior that is viewed as beneficial by people in their fields. Leisure researchers and service providers have only recently begun to formally explore and assess attitude change as a way to overcome constraints and create affordance.

One approach to changing attitudes is to engage in persuasive communication. Personal, face-to-face communication, signs and billboards, brochures and pamphlets, and television and radio advertisements can be used. Petty and Cacioppo (1986) have proposed a dual-process model of persuasion and attitude change, the *Elaboration-Likelihood Model (ELM)*. This model is based on the assumption that individuals do not always process communications the same way. The term "elaboration likelihood" refers to the probability that people will either think about and analyze the information contained in a communication or attend instead to peripheral cues accompanying the message's delivery (e.g., use of an attractive or celebrity spokesperson to deliver the message). Elaboration differences determine both the extent to which a message affects attitude change and the persistence of the change. When people think carefully about the contents of a message, they take a *central* route in responding to persuasion and are influenced by the strength and quality of the arguments. When people do not think carefully about the contents of a message but focus instead on other cues (e.g., the handsome face or athletic prowess of the spokesperson), they take a *peripheral* route in responding to persuasion. Thus, people may be persuaded to try new activities because of the appeal of those promoting it—a peripheral approach—or by projection of themselves into an activity that they could learn and enjoy in personal ways—the central route. The peripheral route may be just as persuasive in the beginning, but it is the central route that is more likely to have an enduring effect over time.

The ELM social-persuasion approach has been applied to overcoming resistance to health and exercise behavior (see Brawley & Rodgers, 1993; Kaplin, Sallis, & Patterson, 1993) and it has also been used in addressing other leisure-related issues. The nature and effectiveness of messages intended to be persuasive have been assessed with respect to the purchase of recreation services from public or commercial providers (Havitz & Crompton, 1990), the willingness to pay fees for recreational services (Kerr & Manfredo, 1991;

McCarville, Driver, & Crompton, 1992), and attitudes toward management decisions in parks (Bright, Fishbein, Manfredo, & Bath, 1993). Finally, consider again the phenomenon of reactance (discussed earlier in this chapter and in earlier chapters) in any efforts to persuade and market. If people feel that they are being manipulated, they are likely to resist the attempts to move them in that particular direction. To avoid such reactions, it is always important to keep the clients' needs and interests in mind and to be sure, especially with respect to leisure activities, that they feel a sense of control and self-determination. Ideally, though, if educational exposure and persuasion have been effective, interest has been piqued, and reactance has been overcome, there is readiness to engage. The challenge, then, is often to find effective leadership and supervision.

Setting and Activity Management for Participation and Leisure Satisfaction

One of the major tools available to enable someone to become more involved in leisure is an intimate familiarity with leisure activities and settings. Recreation practitioners are traditionally very knowledgeable in this area of leisure services. Whether trying to get a child involved in painting, running a summer arts festival sponsored by the local community, or operating a commercial white-water rafting business on a stretch of wild river, leisure service providers must be able to manage the setting and activity in such a way as to optimize interest and the experience and benefits participants are seeking. Consider the following scenario involving a service provided by a commercial recreation company:

> Christine took a 3-hour trip in an inflatable raft down a section of a wild river, that has a series of huge rapids and churning falls. During this rough trip, she got wet, cold, and bounced around in the raft. After she returned home, she told friends that she had had so much fun that the substantial travel time to the site and the cost was very worthwhile. Her "fun" experience included fear, extreme excitement, a sense of adventure, relief at surviving, a sense of accomplishment, and wonder at the power of nature.

The leisure behavior described in this scenario requires an extremely high level of setting and activity management to produce the successful rafting experience. It is somewhat like a theatrical production whereby the company carefully "orchestrates" the sequence of events to ensure that their customers get down the river safely, but in such a way that the event is experienced as exciting and risky and not *too* safe! This balance between safety and risk is the most critical management task for the company. First, there is arrival at the site, hearing, and then seeing the roaring river. Next, Christine puts on the protective clothing and equipment with the other apprehensive, yet excited, adventurers. Then she receives directions on how to behave while in the raft, followed by boarding the heaving raft itself. All this activity is designed to set the "stage" and create the appropriate expectations. Once on the river, the comments of the company guides who steer the raft down the river are calculated to raise tension and excitement levels. At the completion of the trip, opportunities are provided to share stories of the experience with fellow adventurers over a meal; and, finally, there are photographs of the participants, in their rafting gear, to remind them of the experience after returning home.

Of course, not all leisure opportunities and services are this "scripted," and most people seem to desire a variety of leisure involvements that range from the completely spontaneous to the well-orchestrated. Also, successfully managing leisure settings and activities would be impossible without a good knowledge of the psychological state of the participants. For example, this raft trip would likely only work well with whitewater rafting novices who come to the event with certain kinds of needs and expectations. As we noted in Chapters 5 and 6, researchers have devoted a great deal of attention to understanding both the needs and motives that shape leisure interests and preferences and the characteristics of settings and activities that can allow people to meet these.

During our discussion of leisure and personality in Chapter 7, we referred to evidence that high-quality leisure experiences are more likely to occur when personality-environment congruency is created (Meir & Melemud, 1986). In the study of aerobic participants referred to earlier (Frederick, Havitz, & Shaw, 1994), there were substantial differences in participant responses to the social environment of the aerobics class. There were those whose experience would not be positive if they worked out with people with greater skills (preferring downward social comparison), and those for whom participation with slightly superior co-participants would actually enhance the experience (upwards social comparison). On the other hand, it might be a mistake to assume such individual differences are consistent and stable; in some cases the same individual may change and develop and modify orientations to leisure experiences accordingly. The experiences themselves may be formative in that regard, thus requiring that individuals not be "pigeon-holed" (stereotyped) with respect to individual dispositions. Or, said more simply, providers and managers should always keep in mind that "people change."

Optimization of a setting for leisure also involves attending to how it is socially defined and who is seen to "belong" there. People may feel uncomfortable or uninterested in leisure participation in certain settings and activities.

For example, as we noted in Chapters 9 and 10, some ethnic, cultural, and racial groups have been traditionally underrepresented among park users (Floyd & Gramann, 1995; Karlis, 1990). Promoting inclusiveness is a setting management strategy that involves making it clear that activities are open to everyone regardless of race, age, gender, social status, sexual preference, or level of ability. An expressed lack of interest may well mask a sense of being unwelcome there, as we noted above, and it behooves providers then to use some of the principles of persuasion and leadership referred to above to bring outsiders into the fold. Nevertheless, participant diversity in programs, particularly with respect to the level of experience and knowledge, may not facilitate the interests of those committed to a certain level of involvement, activity specialization, or style of performance. And it may even undermine a level of comfort and relaxation among participants. Competing values and competing purposes need to be examined reflexively by practitioners with respect to program goals and participant desires.

Creating Leisure Affordance through Environmental Design

Affordances that suggest the likelihood of leisure experience currently exist in a wide variety of settings in both the natural physical environment and in social leisure contexts. Achieving leisure experience in these settings is largely a matter of attunement to the conditions that would interact effectively with individual abilities and interests. Creating *additional* affordances, on the other hand, involves the manipulation of the environment or the construction or arrangement of new environments. Designing environments that promote leisure experience—whether in the construction of theme parks, playgrounds, and new trails; in the organization of special events; or in the design of online games and social networking opportunities—would benefit from an ecological perspective that recognizes the nature of affordances. Such a perspective would also recognize the value of creating spaces and opportunities for interaction that have psychological significance, that is, that have leisure meanings and values for particular individuals.

While the application of affordance principles to the design of environments for adult leisure is largely nonexistent (though there are certainly many suggestions of such in the work of recreation resource planning and design), when affordance has been studied in relation to children's environments, the subject of play affordances is prominent. As with adult leisure experience, play is a preferred experience (i.e., it is intrinsically motivated) and takes advantage of opportunities for enjoyment that revolve around experimentation and diversion. In an interesting analysis using Gibson's affordance principles, Heft (1988) presents a functional approach to describing environmental resources for children and provides a taxonomy based on psychologically meaningful features of the play environment rather than on form-based classifications (trees, walls, slopes, etc.).

Heft notes that affordances are psychologically meaningful when adequately detected and are specified relationally in ways such as the following: climb-on-able surfaces, throw-able objects, mold-able materials, walk-on-able surfaces, and hide-behind-able, jump-over-able and swing-on-able features. As Heft notes, affordances are determined simultaneously by attributes of the environment (physical and social) and attributes of particular individuals or species. Age also differentiates as adults and children will overlap only partially. For example, the affordance a child sees in a group of bushes for hiding may not be seen by adults because of both their size and their lack of interest in being concealed. More generally, Heft's analysis suggests that, while children are oriented in their play to certain environmental affordances, any environment might be designed, à la Maria Montessori (1964) and others (cf. Moore & Anderson, 1969), to be "autotelic," having features that afford and invite action; create interest that leads to activity, exploration, and enjoyment; and/or elicit relaxation.

Technology can also be both facilitative and daunting. With respect to leisure, the development of assistive devices for people with disabilities has had an extremely positive impact on participation. People without the use of their legs, for example, are able to swim, ski, and do auto mechanics, while people with sensory impairments and communication disorders have devices to enhance nearly all of the senses. Nevertheless, though technology is intended to make life easier, if not more leisurely, it may have quite the opposite effect at times. Being able to converse while operating multiple sources of media and still driving or working contributes to the kind of time deepening that leads people to feel rushed and overburdened. This observation is not entirely new. Linder spoke of the problem about four decades ago in *The Harried Leisure Class* (1971). In fact, communication technology has made it difficult for many people to get away from their work. Computers and cell phones that have multiple applications can easily be taken on holidays and seem to have fostered the expectation that people are always on call. The fusion or interpenetration of work and leisure seems to be benefiting work but not leisure.

The "toys" of leisure represent an endless list of possibilities for capturing people's attention, distracting them or enhancing their leisure experience. The linkage of the mundane telephone with computers to enable access to the Internet allowed this technology to achieve a distinction that was once claimed by in-car citizen band radios as "the world's fastest growing communication sport." Technology is not always or inevitably leisure affordant, but it has great potential.

Building Community Leisure

Whether it is for yourself or because you believe in leisure as a fundamentally social experience, you are in a position to build community through leisure.

Something as simple as shared laughter is a bonding experience, and shared flow, even outside the bedroom, can be a truly powerful source of intimate connection and relatedness. But shared experience also can break down barriers and bring an entire community together. Sociable, communal experience is a way of building *social capital* (Putnam, 2000), even where the purpose is enjoyable self-expression. Leisure has an ancient history of being a context used intentionally for building community (Hemingway, 1988), and such purposes have been given new form and interpretation lately (cf. Arai & Pedler, 1997; Maynard & Kleiber, 2005) especially around such things as community gardens and neighborhood centers (cf. Glover, 2007). As was noted in previous chapters, it has also long been a hope that play, sport competitions, and even Olympic sports could reduce hostilities between peoples and build a degree of trust and mutual responsibility (e.g., Jamieson & Ross, 2007; PlayforPeace.org). And classic social psychological experiments have used game-type settings to build cooperation and interdependence (Aronson, 2008; Sherif et al., 1961). Play, sport, and leisure activities can be used apparently to build community if done strategically and conscientiously.

But are we putting too much faith in shared leisure, then? Some have suggested that even when taking activities seriously, amateur enthusiasts and devotees such as those studied by Stebbins, build community in only a limited way (Bellah et al., 1985). Because of the exclusive commitment required, they may even isolate participants from other collective and worthwhile purposes. But shared enjoyment is found in other kinds of collective activities as well—talking politics in a neighborhood coffee shop, for example, or gardening with others in a community plot—such that the power of collective association is established. It is important to recognize that such activities can be both enjoyable and socially integrative.

Cultivating communal leisure interests where community loyalty and responsibility are nurtured seems a worthy goal of leisure education and public leisure services, but it may take a greater openness to accommodating to and even surrendering to the interests of others than is characteristic of those merely seeking activity expertise and fun. The well-being of the state is an ancient leisure interest, perhaps the first subject of social intercourse of those ancient Greek philosophers, such as Plato and Aristotle, who are generally regarded as the source points of Western leisure ideals (cf. de Grazia, 1964; Hemingway, 1988). To engage in conversation about ideas and ideals, tempering that with enjoyable self-expression and appreciation of cultural art forms and traditions, may still be among the better ways to build a sense of community.

Conclusion

There are many more social psychological ideas that we have discussed throughout the pages of this book that could be applied to the development of effective interventions to enable people to get more out of their leisure. When researchers theorize and study these ideas, they tend to isolate and treat them as distinct, to more easily understand the social psychological processes they represent. However, one should keep in mind that any effective intervention to assist people with their leisure usually involves a number of these social psychological processes. Being aware of them and sensitive to their operation can help us better design methods of assistance and intervention as well as learn to make life better for ourselves and others.

A Final Note

In this book, we have tried to convey our enthusiasm for studying leisure. Simply put, it is fascinating to examine why people do what they do in their free time. We have also attempted to demonstrate that the social psychological perspective, with its focus on both the person and the social situation, provides an ideal framework to study people at leisure and satisfy this curiosity. On the practical side, hopefully this social psychological analysis of leisure will prove useful by sensitizing you to the cues to look for and the issues to be aware of when managing your own leisure as well as assisting others. Goodale and Witt (1989) have pointed out that "among the tasks of education and other social- ization processes is teaching each generation how to find contentment and happiness in a world of constraints and barriers" (p. 444). As we presented in Chapter 9, people acquire most of their leisure orientations and attitudes through the informal processes of socialization. This involves the spontaneous experi- mentation facilitated by childhood leisure, influences by various socialization agents (e.g., parents, peers, coaches, and the media), and involvement in for- mal leisure activity programs in the community and at school. Most people find leisure and make of it what they will based on their own personal and social resources. In fact, to the extent that others arrange activities and experiences for people, there is a real potential that the perceived freedom and intrinsic motivation that are the preconditions or foundations of leisure will be under- mined. Where independence is desired, people find ways to negotiate the constraints that they face to enable continuing participation at some level. However, it is sometimes necessary to intervene directly and "educate" for leisure, and for some people, leadership, therapy, counseling, and environmental management will be necessary to make the most of leisure. Given that the most common leisure activity is television watching and that it offers so little in terms of satisfying experience, finding ways to move people into satisfying leisure action patterns would seem to be a reasonable goal for intervention and the application of the social psychology of leisure.

References

Abramson, L., Garber, J., & Seligman, M. E. P. (1980). Learned helplessness in humans: An attributional analysis. In J. Garber & M. Seligman (Eds.), *Human helplessness: Theory and applications* (pp. 3–57). New York, NY: Academic Press.

Adams, K. B. (2004). Changing investment in activities and interests in elders' lives: Theory and measurement. *International Journal of Aging and Human Development, 58,* 87–108.

Agahi, N., Ahacic, K., & Parker, M. (2006). Continuity of participation from middle age to old age. *Journal of Gerontology, 61,* 340–346.

Agahi, N., & Parker, M. G. (2005). Are today's older people more active than their predecessors? Participation in leisure-time activities in Sweden in 1992 and 2002. *Aging and Society, 25,* 925–941.

Aguilar, T. E. (1987). Effects of a leisure education program on expressed attitudes of delinquent adolescents. *Therapeutic Recreation Journal, 21,* 43–51.

Aguilar, T. E. & Petrakis, E. (1989). Development and initial validation of perceived competence and satisfaction measures for racquet sports. *Journal of Leisure Research, 21,* 77–91.

Ajzen, I. (1991a). Benefits of leisure: A social psychological perspective. In B. L. Driver, P. J. Brown & G. L. Peterson (Eds.), *Benefits of leisure* (pp. 411–417). State College, PA: Venture Publishing, Inc.

Ajzen, I. (1991b). The theory of planned action. *Organizational Behavior and Human Decision Processes, 50,* 179–211.

Ajzen, I., & Driver, B. L. (1991). Prediction of leisure participation from behavioral, normative, and control beliefs: An application of the theory of planned behavior. *Leisure Sciences, 13,* 185–204.

Ajzen, I., & Driver, B. L. (1992). Application of the theory of planned behavior to leisure choice. *Journal of Leisure Research, 24,* 207–224.

Ajzen, I. & Madden, T. J. (1986). Prediction of goal directed behavior: Attitudes, intentions, and perceived behavioral control. *Journal of Experimental Social Psychology, 22,* 453–474.

Albrechtsen, S. J. (2001). Technology and lifestyles: Challenges for leisure education in the new millennium. *World Leisure, 43,* 11–19.

Alexandris, K., & Carroll, B. (1997). An analysis of leisure constraints based on different recreational sport participation levels: Results from a study in Greece. *Leisure Sciences, 19,* 1–15.

Alexandris, K., Tsorbatzoudis, C., & Grouios, G. (2002). Perceived constraints on recreational sport participation: Investigating their relationship with intrinsic motivation, extrinsic motivation and amotivation. *Journal of Leisure Research, 34,* 233–252.

Allen, L. R. (1982). The relationship between Murray's personality needs and leisure interests. *Journal of Leisure Research, 14,* 63–76.

Allen, L. R. (1988). Management and evaluation of leisure programs and services: Past, present, and future research. In L. A. Barnett (Ed.), *Research about leisure: Past, present, and future* (pp. 95–107).Champaign, IL: Sagamore Publishing.

Allen, L. R. (1991). Benefits of leisure services to community satisfaction. In B. L. Driver, P. J. Brown & G. L. Peterson (Eds.), *Benefits of leisure* (pp. 331–350). State College, PA: Venture Publishing, Inc.

Allison, M. T. (1988). Breaking boundaries and barriers: Future directions in cross-cultural research. *Leisure Sciences, 10,* 247–259.

Allison, M. T. (1991). Leisure, sport and quality of life: Those on the fringes. In *Sport for all* (pp. 45–55). New York, NY: Elsevier Science Publishers.

Allison, M. T. & Duncan, M. C. (1987). Women, work and leisure: The days of our lives. *Leisure Sciences, 9,* 143–161

Allison, M. T. & Smith, S. (1990). Leisure and the quality of life: Issues facing racial and ethnic minority elderly. *Therapeutic Recreation Journal, 24,* 50–63.

Allport, F. H. (1924). *Social psychology.* Boston, MA: Houghton Mifflin.

Allport, G. W. (1954). *The nature of prejudice.* Reading, MA: Addison-Wesley.

Allport, G. W. (1955). *Becoming.* New Haven, CT: Yale University Press.

Allport, G. W. (1968). *Social psychology.* Boston, MA: Houghton Mifflin.

Allport, G. W. (1985). The historical background of social psychology. In G. Lindzey & E. Aronson (Eds.), *Handbook of social psychology* (3rd ed., Vol. 1, pp. 1–46). New York, NY: Random House.

Altergott, K. (Ed.) (1988). *Daily life in later life.* Newbury Park, CA: Sage Publications.

Altman, I., & Low, S. (Eds.) (1992). *Place attachment.* New York, NY: Plenum Press.

Amabile, T. M. (1996). *Creativity in context.* Boulder, CO: Westview Press.

Amabile, T. M., & Hennessey, B. A. (1992). The motivation for creativity in children. In A. K. Boggiano & T. S. Pittman (Eds.), *Achievement and motivation* (pp. 54–74). New York, NY: Cambridge University Press.

Ammassari, E. K.-W. (1991). A framework for the quantitative study of leisure styles. *Loisir et Société/Society and Leisure, 14,* 411–432.

Anderson, C. A., & Bushman, B. J. (2001). Effects of violent crime on aggressive behavior, aggressive cognition, aggressive affect, physiological arousal, and pro-social behavior. *Psychological Science, 12,* 353–360.

Anderson, D. M, Wozencroft, A., & Bedini, L. (2008). Adolescent girls' involvement in disability sport: A comparison of social support mechanisms. *Journal of Leisure Research, 40,* 183–207.

Antonovsky, A., & Sagy, S. (1990). Confronting developmental tasks in the retirement transition. *The Gerontologist, 30*, 362–368.

Aquino, J. A., Russell, D. W., Cutrona, C. E., & Altaier, E. M. (1996). Employment status, social support, and life satisfaction among the elderly. *Journal of Counseling Psychology, 43*, 480–489.

Arab-Moghaddam, N., Henderson, K., & Sheikholeslami, R. (2007). Women's leisure and constraints to participation: Iranian perspectives. *Journal of Leisure Research, 39*, 109–126.

Arai, S. M., & Pedlar, A. M. (1997). Building communities through leisure: Citizen participation in a healthy communities initiative. *Journal of Leisure Research, 29*, 167–182.

Archer, J. & McDonald, M. (1990). Gender roles and sports in adolescent girls. *Leisure Studies, 9*, 225–240.

Argyle, M. (1990). *The social psychology of work*. London, UK: Penguin Books.

Argyle, M. (1996). *The social psychology of leisure*. London, UK: Penguin Books.

Arnett, J. J. (2000). Emerging adulthood: A theory of development for the late teens through the twenties. *American Psychologist, 55*, 469–480.

Arnett, J. J. (2004). *Emerging adulthood: The winding road through the late teens and the twenties*. New York, NY: Oxford University Press.

Aron, A., and Aron, E. N. (1986). *Love and the expansion of self: Understanding attraction and satisfaction*. New York, NY: Hemisphere.

Aron, A., Norman, C., Aron, E., McKenna, C., & Heyman, R. (2000). Couple's shared participation on novel and arousing activities and experiences enhances relationship quality. *Journal of Personality and Social Psychology, 78*, 273–284.

Aronson, E. (2008). *The social animal* (10th ed.). New York, NY: Worth.

Asch, S. (1956). Studies of independence and conformity: A minority of one against a unanimous majority. *Psychological Monographs, 70*(9), (Whole No. 416).

Atchley, R. (1989). The continuity theory of normal aging. *The Gerontologist, 29*, 183–190.

Atchley, R. (1993). Continuity theory and the evolution of activity in later adulthood. In J. R. Kelly (Ed.), *Activity and aging: Staying involved in later life* (pp. 5–16). Newbury Park, CA: Sage Publications.

Atchley, R. (1999). *Continuity and adaptation in aging*. Baltimore, MD: The Johns Hopkins University Press.

Augustinos, M., Walker, I., & Donaghue, N. (2006). *Social cognition: An integrated introduction*. London, UK: Sage Publications.

Auster, C. J. (2001). Transcending potential antecedent leisure constraints: The case of women motorcycle operators. *Journal of Leisure Research, 33*, 272–298.

Avni, A., Kipper, D., & Fox, S. (1987). Personality and leisure activities: An illustration with chess players. *Personality and Individual Differences, 8*, 715–719.

Axline, V. (1947). *Play therapy*. New York, NY: Ballantine Books.

Babbie, E. (1992). *The practice of social research* (6th ed.). Belmont, CA: Wadsworth Publishing Company.

Bachman, J., Johnson, L., O'Malley, P., & Schulenberg, J. (1996). Transitions in drug use during late adolescence and young adulthood. In J. Graber, J. Brooks-Gunn, & A. Peterson (Eds.), *Transition through adolescence: Interpersonal domains and context* (pp. 111–140). Mahwah, NJ: Erlbaum.

Backman, S. J. & Crompton, J. L. (1991). The usefulness of selected variables for predicting activity loyalty. *Leisure Sciences, 13*, 205–220.

Backman, S. J. & Mannell, R. C. (1986). Removing attitudinal barriers to leisure behavior and satisfaction A field experiment among the institutionalized elderly. *Therapeutic Recreation Journal, 20*, 46–53.

Bacon, A. W. (1975). Leisure and the alienated worker: A critical reassessment of three radical theories of work and leisure. *Journal of Leisure Research, 7*, 179–190.

Baldwin, C. A., & Caldwell, L. L. (2003). Development of the free time motivation scale for adolescents. *Journal of Leisure Research, 35*, 129–151.

Baldwin, C. A., & Norris, P. A. (1999). Exploring the dimensions of serious leisure: "Love me—Love my dog!" *Journal of Leisure Research, 31*, 1–17.

Baltes, M. M., & Carstensen, L. L. (1996). The process of successful aging. *Aging and Society, 16*, 398–404.

Baltes, P. B., Cornelius, S. W., & Nesselroade, J. R. (1980). Cohort effects in developmental psychology. In J. R. Nesselroade & P. B. Baltes (Eds.), *Longitudinal research in the study of behavior and development* (pp. 61–87). New York, NY: Academic Press.

Baltes, P. B., & Baltes, M. M. (1990). Psychological perspectives on successful aging: The model of selective optimization with compensation. In P. Baltes & M. Baltes (Eds.), *Successful aging: Perspectives from the behavioral sciences* (pp. 1–34). New York, NY: Cambridge University Press.

Baltes, P. B., & Baltes, M. M. (1998). Savior vivre in old age: How to master the shifting balance between gains and losses. *National Forum, 78*(2), 13–18.

Bandura, A. (1973). *Aggression: A social learning analysis.* Englewood Cliffs, NJ: Prentice-Hall.

Bandura, A. (1974). Behavior theory and the models of man. *American Psychologist, 29*, 859–869.

Bandura, A. (1977). *Social learning theory.* Englewood Cliffs, NJ: Prentice Hall.

Bandura, A. (1986). *Social foundations of thought and action: A social cognitive theory.* Englewood Cliffs, NJ: Prentice-Hall.

Banner, D. K. (1985). Towards a theoretical clarification of the 'spillover' and 'compensatory' work/leisure hypotheses. *OMEGA: The International Journal of Management Science, 13*, 13–18.

Barnes, K. (1970). Preschool play norms: A replication. *Developmental Psychology, 1*, 99–103.

Barnett, L. A. (1980). The social psychology of children's play: Effects of extrinsic rewards on free play and intrinsic motivation. In S. E. Iso-Ahola (Ed.), *Social psychological perspectives on leisure and recreation* (pp. 138–170). Springfield, IL: Charles C. Thomas.

Barnett, L. A. (1984). Young children's resolution of distress through play. *Journal of Child Psychology and Psychiatry, 25*, 477–483.

Barnett, L. A. (1988). *Research about leisure: Past, present, and future*. Champaign, IL: Sagamore Publishing.

Barnett, L. A. (1990). Developmental benefits of play for children. *Journal of Leisure Research, 22*, 138–153.

Barnett, L. A. (1991). Developmental benefits of play for children. In B. L. Driver, P. J. Brown, & G. L. Peterson (Eds.), *Benefits of leisure* (pp. 215–247). State College, PA: Venture Publishing, Inc.

Barnett, L. A. (1995). *Research about leisure: Past, present, and future* (2nd ed.). Champaign, IL: Sagamore Publishing.

Barnett, L. A. (2005). Measuring the ABCs of leisure experience: Awareness, boredom, challenge, distress. *Leisure Sciences, 27*, 131–155.

Barnett, L. A. (2006). Accounting for leisure preferences from within: Contributions of gender, race, or ethnicity, personality, affective style and motivational orientation. *Journal of Leisure Research, 38*, 445–474.

Barnett, L. A. (2007a). The nature of playfulness in young adults. *Personality & Individual Differences, 43*, 949–958.

Barnett, L. A. (2007b). "Winners" and "losers": The effects of being allowed or denied entry into competitive extracurricular activities. *Journal of Leisure Research, 39*, 316–344.

Barnett, L. A., & Chick, G. C. (1986). Chips off the ol' block: Parents leisure and their children's play. *Journal of Leisure Research, 18*, 266–283.

Barnett, L. A. & Kane, M. J. (1985). Individual constraints on children's play. In M. G. Wade (Ed.), *Constraints on leisure* (pp. 43–82). Springfield, IL: Charles C. Thomas.

Barnett, L. A. & Kleiber, D. A. (1982). Concomitants of playfulness in early childhood: Cognitive abilities and gender. *The Journal of Genetic Psychology, 141*, 115–127.

Barnett, L. A. & Kleiber, D. A. (1984). Playfulness and the early play environment. *The Journal of Genetic Psychology, 144*, 153–164.

Barnett, L. A., & Klitzing, S. (2006). Boredom in free time: Relationships with personality, affect, and motivation for different gender, racial and ethnic student groups. *Leisure Sciences, 28*, 223.

Barnett, L. A. & Wade, M. G. (1988). In celebration of leisure research: A reflective look back. In L. A. Barnett (Ed.), *Research about leisure: Past, present, and future* (pp. 1–16). Champaign, IL: Sagamore Publishing.

Barone, D. F., Maddux, J. E., & Snyder, C. R. (1997). *Social cognitive psychology: History and current domains*. New York, NY: Plenum Press.

Baumeister, R. F. (1986). *Identity: Cultural change and the struggle for self*. New York, NY: Oxford University Press.

Baumeister, R. F. (1991). *Escaping the self: Alcoholism, spirituality, masochism, and other flights from the burden of selfhood*. New York, NY: Basic Books.

Baumeister, R. F. (1995). Self and identity: An introduction. In A. Tesser (Ed.), *Advanced Social Psychology* (pp. 51–97). New York, NY: McGraw-Hill.

Baumeister, R. F. (1998). The self. In D. T. Gilbert, S. T Fiske, & G. Lindzey (Eds.), *Handbook of social psychology* (4th Ed., pp. 680–740). New York, NY: McGraw-Hill.

Baumrind, D. (1971). Current patterns of parental authority. *Developmental Psychology Monographs, 4*, No. 1, Pt. 2.

Baumrind, D. (1985). Research using intentional deception: Ethical issues revisited. *American Psychologist, 40*, 165–174.

Baxter, L. A., & Dindia, K. (1990). 'Marital partners' perceptions of marital maintenance strategies. *Journal of Social and Personal Relationships, 7*, 187–208.

Beard, J. G., & Ragheb, M. G. (1983). Measuring leisure motivation. *Journal of Leisure Research, 15*, 219–228.

Becker, H. (1960). Notes on the concept of commitment. *American Journal of Sociology, 66*, 32–40.

Becker, M. A., & Byrne, D. (1984). Type-A behavior and daily activities of young married couples. *Journal of Applied Social Psychology, 14*, 82–88.

Belanger, L., & Delisle, M. (1979). Relationships between compulsory activities, leisure, life satisfaction and boredom in a group of aged people. *Loisir et Société/Society and Leisure, 2*, 427–447.

Belhassen, Y., Santos, C., & Uriely, N. (2007). Cannabis usage in tourism: A sociological perspective. *Leisure Studies, 26*, 303–319.

Bella, L. (1989 Women and leisure: Beyond androcentrism. In E. L. Jackson & T. L. Burton (Eds.), *Understanding leisure and recreation: Mapping the past, charting the future* (pp. 151–179). State College, PA: Venture Publishing, Inc.

Bella, L. (1992). *The Christmas imperative*. Halifax, NS: Fernwood Publishing.

Bellah, R., Madsen, R., Sullivan, W., Swidler, A., & Tipton, S. (1985). *Habits of the heart*. New York, NY: Harper Row.

Bem, S. L. (1974). The measurement of psychological androgyny. *Journal of Consulting and Clinical Psychology, 42*, 155–162.

Bem, S. (1993). *The lenses of gender*. New Haven, CT: Yale University Press.

Bendle, L. J., & Patterson, I. (2009). Mixed serious leisure and grassroots organizational capacity: A study of amateur artist groups in a regional Australian city. *Leisure Sciences, 31*, 272–286.

Bengtson, V. (1969 Cultural and occupational differences in level of present role activity in retirement. In R. Havighurst, J. Munnichs, & H. Thomae (Eds.), *Adjustment to retirement: A cross-national study* (pp. 35–53). Assen, The Netherlands: Van Gorcum.

Benjamin, L. T., Jr. (1986). Why don't they understand us? A history of psychology's public image. *American Psychologist, 41*, 941–946.

Berg, E. C., Trost, M., Schneider, I., & Allison, M. (2001). Dyadic exploration of the relationship of leisure satisfaction, leisure time, and gender to relationship satisfaction. *Leisure Sciences, 23*, 35–41.

Berkowitz, L., & Devine, P. G. (1989). Research traditions, analysis, and synthesis in social psychological theories: The case of dissonance theory. *Personality and Social Psychology Bulletin, 15*, 493–507.

Berlyne, D. E. (1960). *Conflict, arousal and curiosity.* New York, NY: McGraw Hill.

Berlyne, D. E. (1971). *Aesthetics and psychobiology.* New York, NY: Appleton-Century-Crofts.

Bernier, Y., & McCarville, R. E. (2005). Service guarantees and opportunistic behavior in a leisure setting: The influence of selected personal and situational variables. *Journal of Park and Recreation Administration, 23*, 39–57.

Berry, J. (1970). Marginality, stress and identification in an acculturating Aboriginal community. *Journal of Cross-Cultural Psychology, 1*, 239–252.

Berry, J. (2009). A critique of critical acculturation. *International Journal of Intercultural Relations, 33*, 361–371.

Berry, J., Poortinga, Y., Segall, M., & Dasen, P. (2002). *Cross-cultural psychology: Research and applications* (2nd ed.). Cambridge, UK: Cambridge University Press.

Berscheid, E. (1992). A glance back at a 1/4 century of social psychology. *Journal of Personality and Social Psychology, 63*, 525–533.

Berscheid, E., & Walster, E. (1974). Physical attractiveness. In L. Berkowitz (Ed.), *Advances in experimental social psychology* (Vol. 7, pp. 157–215). New York, NY: Academic Press.

Best, F. (1988). *Reducing work weeks to prevent layoffs: The economic and social impacts of unemployment insurance.* Philadelphia, PA: Temple University Press.

Bialeschki, M. D. (1990). The feminist movement and women's participation in physical recreation. *Journal of Physical Education, Recreation and Dance, 61*, 44–47.

Bialeschki, M. D. (2005). Fear of violence: Contested constraints by women in outdoor recreation activities. In E. L. Jackson (Ed.), *Constraints to leisure* (pp. 103–114). State College, PA: Venture Publishing, Inc.

Bibby, R. W., & Posterski, D. C. (1985). *The emerging generation: An inside look at Canada's teenagers.* Toronto, ON: Irwin.

Bickham, D. S., & Rich, M. (2006). Is television viewing associated with social isolation? Roles of exposure time, viewing context, and violent content. *Archives of Pediatric Adolescent Medicine, 160*, 387–392.

Bishop, D. W. (1970). Stability of the factor structure of leisure behavior: Analyses of four communities. *Journal of Leisure Research, 2*, 160–170.

Bishop, D. W., & Chace, C. A. (1971). Parental conceptual systems, home play environments, and potential creativity in children. *Journal of Experimental Child Psychology, 12*, 318–338.

Bishop, D. W., Jeanrenaud, C., and Lawson, K. (1975). Comparison of a time diary and recall questionnaire for surveying leisure activities. *Journal of Leisure Research, 7*, 73–80.

Bishop, D. W., & Witt, P. A. (1970). Sources of behavioral variance during leisure time. *Journal of Personality and Social Psychology, 16*, 352–360.

Bittman, M. (1999). The land of the lost weekend? Trends in free time among working age Australians, 1974–1992. *Loisir et Société/Society and Leisure, 21*, 353–378.

Bjorklund, D. (2007). *Why youth is not wasted on the young: Immaturity in human development.* Malden, MA: Blackwell.

Blanke, K., & Corneliben, W. (2005). German adolescents' time use from 1991–2001: Is gender symmetry in sight? *Loisir et Société/Society and Leisure, 28,* 511–530.

Boden, M. A. (2004). *The creative mind: Myths and mechanisms.* New York, NY: Routledge.

Boggiano, A. K., & Pittman, T. S. (1992). *Achievement and motivation.* New York, NY: Cambridge University Press.

Borrie, W. T., & Roggenbuck, J. W. (2001). The dynamic, emergent, and multi-phasic nature of on-site wilderness experiences. *Journal of Leisure Research, 33,* 202–228.

Bowers, K. S. (1973). Situationalism in psychology: An analysis and critique. *Psychological Review, 80,* 307–336.

Bradburn, N. M. (1969). *The structure of psychological well-being.* Chicago, IL: Aldine Publishing.

Bradley, W., & Mannell, R. C. (1984). Sensitivity of intrinsic motivation to reward procedure instructions. *Personality and Social Psychology Bulletin, 10,* 426–431.

Bradshaw, R., & Jackson, J. (1979). Socialization for leisure. In H. Ibrahim & R. Crandall (Eds.), *Leisure: A psychological approach* (pp. 93–121). Los Alamitos, CA: Hwong.

Brandmeyer, G. A., & Alexander, L. K. (1986). "I caught the dream": The adult baseball camp as fantasy leisure. *Journal of Leisure Research, 18,* 26–39.

Brandstätter, H. (1994). Pleasure of leisure-pleasure of work: Personality makes the difference. *Personality and Individual Differences, 16,* 931–946.

Brasile, F. (1990). Wheelchair sports: A new perspective on integration. *Adaptive Physical Activity Quarterly, 7,* 3–11.

Brasile, F. M., Kleiber, D. A., & Harnisch, D. (1991). Analysis of participation incentives among athletes with and without disabilities. *Therapeutic Recreation Journal, 25,* 18–33.

Braun, C. M. J., & Giroux, J. (1989). Arcade video games: Proxemic, cognitive and content analyses. *Journal of Leisure Research, 21,* 92–105.

Brawley, L. R. and Rodgers, W. M. (1993). Social-psychological aspects of fitness promotion. In P. Seraganian (Ed.), *Exercise psychology: The influence of physical exercise on psychological processes* (pp. 254–298). New York, NY: John Wiley & Sons.

Bregha, F. J. (1980). Leisure and freedom re-examined. In T. L. Goodale & P. A. Witt (Eds.), *Recreation and leisure: Issues in an era of change* (pp. 30–37). State College, PA: Venture Publishing, Inc.

Brehm, J. W. (1966). *A theory of psychological reactance.* New York, NY: Academic Press.

Brehm, J. W. (1972). *Responses to loss of freedom: A theory of psychological reactance.* Morristown, NJ: General Learning Press.

Brehm, S. S. (1992). *Intimate relationships.* New York, NY: McGraw-Hill.

Brehm, S. S., & Brehm, J. W. (1981). *Psychological reactance: A theory of freedom and control.* New York, NY: Academic Press.

Brent, S. (1978). Individual specialization, collective adaptation, and rate of environmental change. *Human Development, 21,* 21–33.

Brewer, M. B. (1991). The social self: On being the same and different at the same time. *Personality and Social Psychology Bulletin, 17*, 475–482.

Brewster-Smith, M. (1968). Competence and socialization. In J. A. Clausen (Ed.), *Socialization and society*. Boston, MA: Little, Brown & Co.

Bricker, K., & Kerstetter, D. (2000). Level of specialization and place attachment: An exploratory study of whitewater recreationists. *Leisure Sciences, 22*, 233–257.

Bright, A. D., Fishbein, M., Manfredo, M. J., & Bath, A. (1993). Application of the theory of reasoned action to the National Park Service's controlled burn. *Journal of Leisure Research, 25*, 263–280.

Brock, S., & Kleiber, D. (1994). Narrative in medicine: The stories of elite college athletes' career-ending injuries. *Qualitative Health Research, 4*, 411–430.

Brooks, J. J., Wallace, G. N., & Williams, D. R. (2006). Place as relationship partner: An alternative metaphor for understanding the quality of visitor experience in a backcountry setting. *Leisure Sciences, 28*, 331–349.

Brown, B. B. (1990). Peer groups and peer cultures. In S. S. Feldman & G. R. Elliott (Eds.), *At the threshold: The developing adolescent*. Cambridge, MA: Harvard University Press.

Brown, B. A., & Frankel, B. G. (1993). Activity through the years: Leisure, leisure satisfaction, and life satisfaction. *Sociology of Sport Journal, 10*, 1–17.

Brown, B. A., Frankel, B. G., & Fennell, M. (1991). Happiness through leisure: The impact of type of leisure activity, age, gender, and leisure satisfaction on psychological well-being. *Journal of Applied Recreation Research, 16*, 368–392.

Brown, C. A. (2007). The Carolina shaggers: Dance as serious leisure. *Journal of Leisure Research, 39*, 623–647.

Brown, J. D. (1991). Staying fit and staying well: Physical fitness as a moderator of life stress. *Journal of Personality and Social Psychology, 60*, 555–561.

Brown, P. J. (1970). Sentiment changes and recreation participation. *Journal of Leisure Research, 2*, 264–268.

Brown, S. (2009). *Play*. New York, NY: Avery/Penguin.

Brown, W., Lee, C., Mishra, G., & Bauman, A. (2000). Leisure time physical activity in Australian women: Relationship with well-being and symptoms. *Research Quarterly for Exercise and Sport, 7*(3), 206–216.

Browne, M. A., & Mahoney, M. J. (1984). Sport psychology. *Annual Review of Psychology, 35*, 605–625.

Bruner, J. S., Jolly, H., & Sylva, K. (1976). *Play: Its role in development and evolution*. New York, NY: Basic Books.

Brunson, M. W., & Shelby, B. (1993). Recreation substitutability: A research agenda. *Leisure Sciences, 15*, 67–74.

Bryan, H. (1977). Leisure value systems and recreational specialization: The case of trout fisherman. *Journal of Leisure Research, 9*, 174–187.

Bryan, H. (2000). Recreation specialization revisited. *Journal of Leisure Research, 32*, 18–21.

Bryant, F., & Veroff, J. (2007). *Savoring: A new model of positive experience*. Mahwah, NJ: Erlbaum.

Bryce, J., & Haworth, J. (2002). Well being and flow in sample of male and female office workers. *Leisure Studies. 21*, 249–263.

Buchanan, A. J., & Peskowitz, M. (2007). *The daring book for girls.* New York, NY: HarperCollins.

Buchanan, T. (1985). Commitment and leisure behavior: A theoretical perspective. *Leisure Sciences, 7*, 401–420.

Buchanan, T., Christensen, J. E., & Burdge, R. J. (1981). Social groups and the meanings of outdoor recreation activities. *Journal of Leisure Research, 13*, 254–266.

Bull, N. C. (1971). One measure for defining a leisure activity. *Journal of Leisure Research, 3*, 120–126.

Bull, N. C. (1982). Leisure activities. In D. J. Mangen & W. A. Peterson (Eds.), *Research instruments in social gerontology: Vol. 2, Social roles and social participation*. Minneapolis, MN: University of Minnesota Press.

Bultena, G. L., & Klessig, L. L. (1969). Satisfaction in camping: A conceptualization and guide to social research. *Journal of Leisure Research, 1*, 348–364.

Bultena, G. L., & Taves, M. J. (1961). Changing wilderness images and forest policy. *Journal of Forestry, 51*, 167–171.

Burch, W. R. (1965). The play world of camping: Research into the social meaning of outdoor recreation. *American Journal of Sociology, 69*, 604–612.

Burch, W. R. (1969). The social circles of leisure: Competing explanations. *Journal of Leisure Research, 1*, 125–148.

Burch, W. R., & Hamilton-Smith, E. (1991). Mapping a new frontier: Identifying, measuring, and valuing social cohesion benefits related to nonwork opportunities and activities. In B. L. Driver, P. J. Brown, & G. L. Peterson (Eds.), *Benefits of leisure* (pp. 369–382). State College, PA: Venture Publishing, Inc.

Burger, J. M. (1992). *Desire for control: Personality, social, and clinical perspectives*. New York, NY: Plenum Press.

Burnett-Wolle, S., & Godbey, G. (2007). Refining research on older adults' leisure: implications of selection, optimization and compensation, and socioemotional selectivity theories. *Journal of Leisure Research, 39*, 498–513.

Burns, R. C., & Graefe, A. R. (2007). Constraints to outdoor recreation: Exploring the effects of disabilities on perceptions and participation. *Journal of Leisure Research, 39*, 156–181.

Burns, T. (1980). Getting rowdy with the boys. *Journal of Drug Issues*, 273–285.

Bushman, B. J., & Huesmann, L. R. (2001). Effects of televised violence on aggression. In D. G. Singer, & J. L. Singer (Eds.), *Handbook of children and the media* (pp. 223–225). Thousand Oaks, CA: Sage Publications.

Buss, A. H. (1989). Personality as traits. *American Psychologist, 44*, 1378–1388.

Buss, A. H., & Plomin, R. (1984). *Temperament: Early developing personality traits*. Hillsdale, NJ: Erlbaum.

Buss, A. R. (1979). *A dialectical psychology*. New York, NY: John Wiley & Sons.

Butrica, B. A., & Schaner, S. G. (2005). Satisfaction and engagement in retirement. *Perspectives on Productive Aging (No. 2)*. Washington, DC: The Urban Institute.

Bynner, J., & Ashford, S. (1992). Teenage careers and leisure lives: An analysis of lifestyles. *Loisir et Société/Society and Leisure, 15*, 499–520.

Cacioppo, J. T., & Petty, R. E. (1982). The need for cognition. *Journal of Personality and Social Psychology, 42*, 116–131.

Calasanti, T. M (1993). Bringing in diversity: Toward an inclusive theory of retirement. *Journal of Aging Studies, 7,* 133–150.

Caldwell, L. L. (2005a). Leisure and health: Why is leisure therapeutic? *British Journal of Guidance & Counseling, 33*, 7–26.

Caldwell, L. L.(2005b). Recreation and youth development. In P. A. Witt & L. L. Caldwell (Eds.), *Recreation and youth development.* State College, PA: Venture Publishing, Inc.

Caldwell, L. L., Adolph, S., & Gilbert, A. (1989). Caution! Leisure counselors at work: Long-term effects of leisure counseling. *Therapeutic Recreation Journal, 23*, 41–49.

Caldwell, L. L., & Andereck K. L. (1994). Motives for initiating and continuing membership in a recreation related voluntary association. *Leisure Sciences, 16*, 33–44.

Caldwell, L. L., & Darling, N. (1999). Leisure context, parental control, and resistance to peer pressure as predictors of adolescent partying and substance use: An ecological perspective. *Journal of Leisure Research, 31*, 57–68.

Caldwell, L. L., Darling, N., Payne, L. L., & Dowdy, B. (1999). "Why are you bored?": An examination of psychological and social control causes of boredom among adolescents. *Journal of Leisure Research,* 31, 103–121.

Caldwell, L. L., & Li, H. (2006). A cross-national comparison of leisure motivation among adolescents. In W. Hendricks & I. Schneider, (Compilers), *Abstracts from the 2006 Symposium on Leisure Research* [p. 37; CD]. Ashburn, VA: National Recreation and Parks Association.

Caldwell, L. L., & Smith, E. A. (1988). Leisure: An overlooked component of health promotion. *Canadian Journal of Public Health, 79*, 44–48.

Caldwell, L. L., & Smith, E. A. (1994). Leisure and mental health of high-risk adolescents. In D. M. Compton & S. E. Iso-Ahola (Eds.), *Leisure and mental health* (pp. 330–345). Park City, UT: Family Development Resources.

Caldwell, L. L., & Smith, E. A. (1995). Health behaviors of leisure alienated youth. *Loisir et Société/Society and Leisure, 18*, 143–156.

Caldwell, L. L., Smith, E. A., Wegner, L., Vergnani, T., Mpofu, E., Flisher, A., & Matthews, C. (2004). HealthWise South Africa: Developing a life skills curriculum for young adults. *World Leisure Journal, 46*(3), 4–17.

Call, J. (1970). Games babies play. *Psychology Today, 3*, 34–37.

Caltabiano, M. L. (1994). Measuring the similarity among leisure activities based on a perceived stress-reduction benefit. *Leisure Studies, 13*, 17–31.

Caltabiano, M. L. (1995). Main and stress-moderating health benefits of leisure. *Loisir et Société/Society and Leisure, 18*, 33–52.

Cameron, J. M., & Bordessa, R. (1981). *Wonderland: Through the looking glass*. Maple, ON: Belsten.

Campbell, A. (1980). *The sense of well-being in America*. New York, NY: McGraw-Hill.

Campbell, A., Converse, P. and Rodgers, W. (1976). *The quality of American life.* New York, NY: Russel Sage.

Campbell, J., & Smale, B. (2008). Leisure lifestyle and identity in late adolescence. In P. A. Morden, S. Hebblethwaite, & R. Hopp (Eds.), *Proceedings of the Twelfth Canadian Congress on Leisure Research* (pp. 43–47). Montréal, QC: Concordia University.

Caplow, T., Bahr, H. M., Chadwick, B. A., Hill, R., & Williamson, M. H. (1982). *Middletown families.* Minneapolis, MN: University of Minnesota Press.

Caprara, G. V., & Cervone, D. (2000). *Personality: Determinants, dynamics, and potentials.* New York, NY: Cambridge University Press.

Carnegie, D. (1964). *How to win friends and influence people.* New York, NY: Simon & Schuster.

Carpenter, B. D., & Buday, S. (2007). Computer use among older adults in a naturally occurring retirement community. *Computers in Human Behavior, 23,* 3012–3024.

Carpenter, G. (1988, October). *Perceived freedom in leisure in middle adulthood.* Paper presented to the Leisure Research Symposium, Indianapolis, IN.

Carpenter, G. (1989). Life change during middle adulthood and valuing leisure. *World Leisure and Recreation, 31,* 29–31

Carpenter, G. (2003). Leisure and life perceptions of a mid-life woman experiencing epiphany associated with leisure and family. *World Leisure Journal, 45,* 44–54.

Carruthers, C. P. (1993). Leisure and alcohol expectancies. *Journal of Leisure Research, 25,* 229–244.

Carruthers, C. P., & Busser, J. A. (1995). Alcohol consumption and leisure participation. *Loisir et Société/Society and Leisure, 18,* 125–142.

Carruthers, C. P., & Hood, C. D. (2004). The power of the positive: Leisure and well-being. *Therapeutic Recreation Journal, 38,* 225–245.

Carstensen, L. L., Fung, H. H., & Charles, S. T. (2003). Socioemotional selectivity theory and the regulation of emotion in the second half of life. *Motivation and Emotion, 27,* 103–123.

Carstensen, L. L., Isaacowitz, D. M., & Charles, S. T. (1999). Taking time seriously: A theory of socioemotional selectivity. *American Psychologist, 54,* 165–181.

Ceci, S. J., Peters, D., & Plotkin, J. (1985). Human subjects review, personal values, and the regulation of social science research. *American Psychologist, 40,* 994–1002.

Chalip, L., Csikszentmihalyi, M., Kleiber, D. A., & Larson, R. W. (1984). Variations of experience in formal and informal sport. *Research Quarterly For Exercise and Sport, 55,* 109–116.

Chambers, D. A. (1986). The constraints of work and domestic schedules on women's leisure. *Leisure Studies, 5,* 309–325.

Chaplin, J. P. (1985). *Dictionary of psychology.* New York, NY: Dell Publishing.

Chapman, A. J., & Foot, H. C. (1976). *Humour and laughter: Theory, research and applications.* New York, NY: John Wiley & Sons.

Chase, D. R., & Godbey, G. C. (1983). The accuracy of self-reported participation rates. *Leisure Studies, 2,* 231–235.

Chavez, D. J. (1993). *Visitor perceptions of crowding and discrimination at two national forests in southern California* (Research paper PSW-RP-216). Albany, CA: Pacific Southwest Research Station, USDA Forest Service.

Chen, S., Fok, H., Bond, M., & Matsumoto, D. (2006). Personality and beliefs about the world revisited: Expanding the nomological network of social axioms. *Personality and Individual Differences, 41*, 201–211.

Cherrington, D. J. (1989). *Organizational behavior*. Needham Heights, MA: Allyn & Bacon.

Chick, G. E. (1987). Anthropology and leisure: Research and practical issues. In S. Parker & A. Graefe (Eds.), *Recreation and leisure: An introductory handbook* (pp. 5–9). State College, PA: Venture Publishing, Inc.

Chick, G. E. (1995). The anthropology of leisure: Past, present, and future. In L. A. Barnett (Ed.), *Research about leisure: Past, present, and future* (2nd ed.) pp. 43–64. Champaign, IL: Sagamore Publishing.

Chick, G. E. (1998). Leisure and culture: Issues for an anthropology of leisure. *Leisure Sciences, 20*, 111–133.

Chick, G. E. (2006). Leisure and cultural identity. In Edgar L. Jackson (Ed.), *Leisure and the quality of life: Impacts on social, economic, and cultural development: Hangzhou Consensus* (pp. 164–178). Zhejiang, China: Zhejiang University Press.

Chick, G. E. (2009). Culture as a variable in the study of leisure. *Leisure Sciences, 31*, 305–310.

Chick, G. E., & Dong, E. (2005). Cultural constraints on leisure. In E. L. Jackson (Ed.), *Constraints to leisure* (pp. 169–183). State College, PA: Venture Publishing, Inc.

Chickering, A. W. (1969). *Education and identity*. San Francisco, CA: Jossey-Bass.

China-Window. (2004). *Policies and regulations*. Retrieved November 23, 2004, from http://www.china-window.com/china_travel/china_tourism/policies-and-regulations.html

Chiriboga, D. A., & Pierce, R. C. (1993). Changing contexts of activity. In J. R. Kelly (Ed.), *Activity and aging: Staying involved in later life* (pp. 42–59). Newbury Park, CA: Sage Publications.

Chou, T. J., & Ting, C. C. (2003). The role of flow experience in cyber-game addiction. *CyberPsychology Behavior, 6*, 663–675.

Christiansen, C. H., & Matuska, K. M. (2006). Lifestyle balance: A review of concepts and research. *Journal of Occupational Science, 13*, 49–61.

Christie, J. F., & Johnson, E. P. (1983). The role of play in social-intellectual development. *Review of Educational Research, 53*, 93–115.

Chubb, M., & Chubb, H. (1981). *One-third of our time?* New York, NY: John Wiley & Sons.

Chun, S., Lee, Y., & Heo, J. (2008, October). *The benefits of serious leisure following traumatic spinal cord injury*. Paper presented at the 12th Canadian Conference on Leisure Research. Montreal.

Cialdini, R. B., Borden, R. J., Thorne, A., Walker, M. R., Freeman, S., & Sloan, L. R. (1976). Basking in reflected glory. Three (football) field studies. *Journal of Personality and Social Psychology, 34*, 366–375.

Clawson, M., & Knetsch, J. L. (1966). *Economics of outdoor recreation*. Baltimore, MD: The Johns Hopkins University Press.

Clough, P., Shepherd, J., & Maughan, R. (1989). Motives for participation in recreational running. *Journal of Leisure Research, 21*, 297–309.

Coble, T. G., Selin, S. W., & Erickson, B. B. (2003). Hiking alone: Understanding fear, negotiation strategies and leisure experiences. *Journal of Leisure Research, 35*, 1–22.

Cohen, D. (1993). *The development of play*. London, UK: Routledge.

Cohen, E. (1979a). A phenomenology of tourist experiences. *Sociology, 13*, 179–201.

Cohen, E. (1979b). Rethinking the sociology of tourism. *Annals of Tourism Research, 6*, 18–35.

Cohen, E. (1988). Authenticity and commoditization in tourism. *Annals of Tourism Research, 15*, 371–386.

Cohen, E. (1991). Leisure—The last resort: A comment. In B. L. Driver, P. J. Brown, & G. L. Peterson (Eds.), *Benefits of leisure* (pp. 439–444). State College, PA: Venture Publishing, Inc.

Coleman, D. (1993). Leisure based social support, leisure dispositions and health. *Journal of Leisure Research, 25*, 350–361.

Coleman, D., & Iso-Ahola, S. E. (1993). Leisure and health: The role of social support and self-determination. *Journal of Leisure Research, 25*, 111–128.

Coleman, J. S. (1961). *The adolescent society*. New York, NY: Free Press.

Collinson, J. A., & Hickey, J. (2007). 'Working Out' identity: Distance runners and the management of disrupted identity. *Leisure Studies, 26*, 381–398.

Colenutt, C. E., & McCarville, R. E. (1994). The client as problem solver: A new look at service recovery. *Journal of Hospitality and Leisure Marketing, 2*, 23–35.

Collishaw, M. A., Dyer, L., & Boies, K. (2008). The authenticity of positive emotional displays: Client responses to leisure service employees. *Journal of Leisure Research, 40*, 23–46.

Cook, K. S. (2000). Advances in the microfoundations of sociology: Recent developments and new challenges for social psychology. *Contemporary Sociology, 29*, 685–692.

Cook, M., Young, A., Taylor, D., & Bedford, A. P. (1998). Personality correlates of alcohol consumption. *Personality and Individual Differences, 24*, 641–647.

Cook, S. W. (1976). Ethical issues in the conduct of research in social relations. In C. Selltiz, L. S. Wrightsman & W. Cook (Eds.), *Research methods in social relations* (3rd ed., pp. 199–249). New York, NY: Holt, Rinehart and Winston.

Costa, P. T., & McCrae, R. R. (1985). *The NEO personality inventory*. Odessa, FL: Psychological Assessment Resources.

Costa, P. T., & McCrae, R. R. (1988). From catalog to classification: Murray's needs and the 5-factor model. *Journal of Personality and Social Psychology, 55*, 258–265.

Costa, P. T., McCrae, R. R., & Dye, D. A. (1991). Facet scale for agreeableness and conscientiousness: A revision of the NEO Personality Inventory. *Personality and Individual Differences, 12*, 887–898.

Courneya, K. S., & Hellsten, L. (1998). Personality correlates of exercise behavior, motive, barriers and preferences: An application of the five-factor model. *Personality and Individual Differences, 24*, 625–633.

Coyle, C. P., & Kinney, W. B. (1990). A comparison of leisure and gambling motives of compulsive gamblers. *Therapeutic Recreation Journal, 24*, 32–39.

Crandall, R., Nolan, M., & Morgan, L. (1980). Leisure and social interaction. In S. E. Iso-Ahola (Ed.), *Social psychological perspectives on leisure and recreation* (pp. 285–306). Springfield, IL: Charles C. Thomas.

Crandall, R., & Slivken, K. (1980). Leisure attitudes and their measurement. In S. E. Iso-Ahola (Ed.), *Social psychological perspectives on leisure and recreation* (pp. 261–284). Springfield, IL: Charles C. Thomas.

Crandall, R., & Thompson, R. (1978). The social meaning of leisure in Uganda and America. *Journal of Cross-Cultural Psychology, 9*, 469–481.

Crawford, D. W., & Godbey, G. (1987). Reconceptualizing barriers to family leisure. *Leisure Sciences, 9*, 119–127.

Crawford, D., & Jackson, E. L. (2005). Leisure constraints theory: Dimensions, directions, and dilemmas. In E. L. Jackson (Ed.), *Constraints to leisure* (pp. 153–167). State College, PA: Venture Publishing, Inc.

Crawford, D., Jackson, E. L., & Godbey, G. (1991). A hierarchical model of leisure constraints. *Leisure Sciences, 13*, 309–320.

Creasey, G. L., & Meyers, B. J. (1986). Video games and children: Effects on leisure activities, schoolwork, and peer involvement. *Merrill-Palmer Quarterly, 32*, 251–262.

Creswell, J. W. (1994). *Research design: Qualitative and quantitative approaches.* London, UK: Sage Publications.

Creswell, J. W. (2009). *Research design: Qualitative, quantitative, and mixed methods approaches* (3rd ed.). Thousand Oaks, CA: Sage Publications.

Creyer, E. H., Ross Jr., W. T., & Evers, D. (2003). Risky recreation: An exploration of factors influencing the likelihood of participation and the effects of experience. *Leisure Studies, 22*, 239–253.

Crompton, J. L. (1979). Motivations for pleasure vacations. *Annals of Tourism Research, 6*, 408–424.

Crompton, J. L. (1993). Rescuing young offenders with recreation programs. *Trends, 30*, 23–26.

Crompton, J. L., & Mackay, K. J. (1989). Users' perceptions of the relative importance of service quality dimensions in selected public recreation programs. *Leisure Sciences, 11*, 367–375.

Cronan, M. K., & Scott, D. (2008). Triathlon and women's narratives of bodies and sport. *Leisure Sciences, 30*, 17–34.

Cropley, M., & Millward, L. J. (2009). How do individuals "switch off" from work during leisure? A qualitative description of the unwinding process in high and low ruminators. *Leisure Studies, 28*, 333–348.

Crosby, F. J. (1991). *Juggling: The unexpected advantages of balancing career and home for women and their families.* New York, NY: Free Press.

Crozier, W. R. (2001). Understanding shyness: Psychological perspectives. Basingstoke, UK: Palgrave.

Csikszentmihalyi, M. (1975). *Beyond boredom and anxiety: The experience of play in work and games.* San Francisco, CA: Jossey-Bass.

Csikszentmihalyi, M. (1980). Love and the dynamics of personal growth. In K. S. Pope (Ed.), *On love and loving* (pp. 306–326). San Francisco, CA: Jossey-Bass.

Csikszentmihalyi, M. (1981). Leisure and socialization. *Social Forces: An International Journal of Social Research, 60*, 332–340.

Csikszentmihalyi, M. (1990). *Flow: The psychology of optimal experience.* New York, NY: Harper Perennial.

Csikszentmihalyi, M. (1993). *The evolving self: A psychology for the third millennium.* New York, NY: HarperCollins.

Csikszentmihalyi, M. (1997). *Finding flow: The psychology of engagement with everyday life.* New York, NY: Basic Books.

Csikszentmihalyi, M., & Csikszentmihalyi, I. (Eds.). (1988). *Optimal experience: Psychological studies of flow in consciousness.* New York, NY: Cambridge University Press.

Csikszentmihalyi, M., & Graef, R. (1980). The experience of freedom in daily life. *American Journal of Community Psychology, 8*, 401–414.

Csikszentmihalyi, M., & Kleiber, D. A. (1991). Leisure and self-actualization. In B. L. Driver, P. J. Brown, & G. L. Peterson (Eds.), *Benefits of leisure* (pp. 91–102). State College, PA: Venture Publishing, Inc.

Csikszentmihalyi, M., & Larson, R. W. (1984). *Being adolescent: Conflict and growth in the teenage years.* New York, NY: Basic Books.

Csikszentmihalyi, M., & Larson, R. W. (1985). *The experience sampling method: Towards a systematic phenomenology.* Unpublished manuscript: University of Chicago.

Csikszentmihalyi, M., & LeFevre, J. (1989). Optimal experience in work and leisure. *Journal of Personality and Social Psychology, 56*, 815–822.

Csikszentmihalyi, M., & Rathunde, K. (1998). The development of the person: An experiential perspective on the ontogenesis of psychological complexity. In W. Damon (Series Ed.) & R. M. Lerner (Vol. Ed.), *Handbook of child psychology: Vol. 1. Theoretical models of human development* (5th ed., pp. 635–684). New York, NY: Wiley.

Culp, R. H. (1998). Adolescent girls and outdoor recreation: A case study examining constraints and effective programming. *Journal of Leisure Research, 30*, 356–379.

Cumming, E., and Henry, W. (1961). *Growing old.* New York, NY: Basic Books.

Cunningham, P. H., & Bartuska, T. (1989). The relationship between stress and leisure satisfaction among therapeutic recreation personnel. *Therapeutic Recreation Journal, 23*, 65–70.

Currie, J. (2004). Motherhood, stress and the exercise experience: freedom or constraint? *Leisure Studies, 23*, 225–243.

Curry, N. (1988). Enhancing dramatic play potential in hospitalized children. *Children's Health Care, 16*.

Curtis, J. E., & White, P. T. (1984). Age and sport participation: Decline in participation or increased specialization with age? In N. Theberge and J. Donelly (Eds.), *Sport and the sociological imagination* (pp. 273–293). Fort Worth, TX: TCU Press.

Cutler, S. J. (1977). Aging and voluntary association participation. *Journal of Gerontology, 32*, 470–479.

Cutler, S. J., & Hendricks, J. (1990). Leisure and time use across the life course. In R. H. Binstock and L. K. George (Eds.), *Handbook of aging and the social sciences* (pp. 169–185). New York, NY: Academic Press.

Cutler Riddick, C. (1985). Life satisfaction determinants of older males and females. *Leisure Sciences, 7*, 47–63.

Cutler Riddick, C., Drogin, E. B., & Spector, S. G. (1987). The impact of videogame play on the emotional well-being of senior center participants. *The Gerontologist, 27*, 425–427.

Cutler Riddick, C., & Gonder Stewart, D. (1994). An examination of the life satisfaction and importance of leisure in the lives of older female retirees: A comparison of blacks to whites. *Journal of Leisure Research, 26*, 75–87.

Dargitz, R. E. (1988). Angling activity of urban youth: Factors associated with fishing in a metropolitan context. *Journal of Leisure Research, 20*, 192–207.

Darling, N., Caldwell, L. L., & Smith, R. (2005). Participation in school-based extracurricular activities and adolescent. *Journal of Leisure Research, 37*, 51–76.

Dattilo, J. (2008). *Leisure education program planning: A systematic approach* (3rd ed.). State College PA: Venture Publishing, Inc.

Dattilo, J., & Kleiber, D. A. (1993). Psychological perspectives for therapeutic recreation research: The psychology of enjoyment. In M. J. Malkin & C. Z. Howe (Eds.), *Research in therapeutic recreation: Concepts and methods* (pp. 57–76). State College, PA: Venture Publishing, Inc.

Dattilo, J., & Kleiber, D. (2002). Self-determination and enjoyment in therapeutic recreation. In D. Austin, J. Dattilo, & B. McCormick (Eds.), *Conceptual foundations of therapeutic recreation*. State College, PA: Venture Publishing, Inc.

Davidson, R. J., Goleman, D. J., & Schwartz, G. E. (1976). Attentional and affective concomitants of meditation. *Journal of Abnormal Psychology, 85*, 235–238.

Davidson, R. J., Schwartz, G. E., & Rothman, L. P. (1976). Attentional style and self-regulation of mode-specific attention: An electroencephalographic study. *Journal of Abnormal Psychology, 85*, 611–621.

Davis, C., Fox, J., Brewer, H., & Ratusny, D. (1995). Motivations to exercise as a function of personality characteristics, age, and gender. *Personality and Individual Differences, 19*, 165–174.

Dawson, D. (1986). Unemployment, leisure, and liberal-democratic ideology. *Loisir et Société/ Society and Leisure, 9*, 165–179.

deCharms, R. (1968). *Personal causation: The internal affective determinants of behavior*. New York, NY: Academic Press.

Deci, E. L. (1971). Effects of externally mediated rewards on intrinsic motivation. *Journal of Personality and Social Psychology, 18*, 105–115.

Deci, E. L. (1975). *Intrinsic motivation*. New York, NY: Plenum Press.

Deci, E. L. (1992). The relation of interest to the motivation of behavior. In K. Renniger, S. Hidi, & A. Krapp (Eds.), *The role of interest in learning and development* (pp. 43–69). Hillsdale, NJ.

Deci, E. L., & Ryan, R. M. (1985). *Intrinsic motivation and self-determination in human behavior*. New York, NY: Plenum Press.

Deci, E. L., & Ryan, R. M. (1991). A motivational approach to self: Integration in personality. In R. Dienstbier (Ed.), *Nebraska Symposium on Motivation: Vol. 38. Perspectives on motivation* (pp. 237–288). Lincoln, NE: University of Nebraska Press.

Deci, E. L., & Ryan, R. M. (2000). The "What" and "Why" of goal pursuits: Human needs and the self-determination of behavior. *Psychological Inquiry, 11*, 227–268.

Deci, E. L., & Ryan, R. M. (2008). Facilitating optimal motivation and psychological well-being across life's domains. *Canadian Psychology, 49*, 14–23.

Decker, J. M., & Crompton, J. L. (1990). Business location decisions: The relative importance of quality of life and recreation, park, and cultural opportunities. *Journal of Park and Recreation Administration, 8*, 26–27.

Deem, R. (1986). *All work and no play? The sociology of women and leisure.* Philadelphia, PA: Open University Press.

Degman, J. M. (1990). Personality structure: Emergence of the Five-Factor Model. *Annual Review of Psychology, 41*, 417–440.

de Grazia, S. (1962). *Of time, work, and leisure.* New York, NY: Anchor Books, Doubleday.

Delespaul, P., Reis, H., & DeVries, M. (2004). Ecological and motivational determinants of activation: Studying compared to sports and watching TV. *Social Indicators Research, 67*, 129–143.

Delle Fave, A., & Massimini, F. (2003). Optimal experience in work and leisure among teachers and physicians: Individual and bio-cultural implications. *Leisure Studies, 22*, 323–342.

Demitrakis, K. M. (1997). Social psychology: Different perspectives and presentations. *Contemporary Psychology, 42*, 896–897.

Denzin, N. K. (1970). Symbolic interactionism and ethnomethodology. In J. D. Douglas (Ed.), *Understanding everyday life: Toward the reconstruction of sociological knowledge.* Chicago, IL: Aldine Publishing Co.

Dergance, J. M., Calmbach, W. L., Dhanda, R., Miles, T. P., Hazuda, H. P., & Mouton, C. P. (2003). Barriers and benefits of leisure time physical activity in the elderly: Differences across cultures. *Journal of the American Geriatrics Society, 51*, 863–868.

Devereux, E. (1976). Backyard versus Little League baseball: The impoverishment of children's games. In D. Landers (Ed.), *Social problems in sport* (pp. 37–56). Urbana, IL: University of Illinois Press.

Devine, M. (2004). "Being a 'doer' instead of a 'viewer'": The role of inclusive leisure contexts in determining social acceptance for people with disabilities. *Journal of Leisure Research, 36*, 137–159.

Devine, P. G., Hamilton, D. L., & Ostrom, T. M. (1994). *Social cognition: Impact on social psychology.* New York, NY: Academic Press.

Diener, E., & Crandall, R. (1978). *Ethics in social and behavioral research.* Chicago, IL: University of Chicago Press.

Diener, E., Emmons, R. A., Larsen, R. J., & Griffin, S. (1985). The satisfaction with life scale. *Journal of Personality Assessment, 49*, 71–76.

Diener, E., Larsen, R. J., & Emmons, R. A. (1984). Person x situation interactions: Choice of situations and congruence response models. *Journal of Personality and Social Psychology, 47*, 580–592.

Dillenschneider, C. (2007). Integrating persons with impairments and disabilities into standard outdoor adventure education programs. *Journal of Experiential Education, 30*, 70–83.

Dimanche, F., Havitz, M. E., & Howard, D. R. (1991). Testing the involvement profile (IP) scale in the context of selected recreational and touristic activities. *Journal of Leisure Research, 23*, 51–66.

Dimanche, F., & Samdahl, D. (1994). Leisure as symbolic consumption: A conceptualization and prospectus for future research. *Leisure Sciences, 16*, 119–129.

Dindia, K., & Baxter, L. A. (1987). Strategies for maintaining and repairing marital relationships. *Journal of Social and Personal Relationships, 4*, 143–158.

Dinwiddie, S. A. (1993). Playing in the gutters: Enhancing children's cognitive and social play. *Young Children, 48*, 70–75.

Dionigi, R. (2006). Competitive sport as leisure in later life: Negotiations, discourse and aging. *Leisure Sciences, 28*, 181–196.

Dishman, R. K. (1988). Determinants of physical activity and exercise for persons 65 years of age and older. *American Academy of Physical Education Papers, 22*, 140–162.

Dishman, R. K. (Ed.). (1994). *Advances in exercise adherence.* Champaign, IL: Human Kinetics.

Dorfman, L. T., Heckert, D. A., & Hill, E. A. (1988). Retirement satisfaction in rural husbands and wives. *Rural Sociology, 53*, 25–39.

Douse, N. A., & McManus, I. C. (1983). The personality of fantasy game players. *British Journal of Psychology, 84*, 505–510.

Driedger, S. D. (1996). Soothing souls. *Maclean's, 109*(17), 63–67.

Driscoll, R., Davis, K. W., & Lipetz, M. E. (1972). Parental interference and romantic love. *Journal of Personality and Social Psychology, 24*, 1–10.

Driver, B. L. (1972). Potential contributions of psychology to recreation resources management. In J. F. Wohlwell & D. H. Carson (Eds.), *Environment and the social sciences: Perspectives and applications* (pp. 233–248). Washington, DC: American Psychological Association.

Driver, B. L. (1976). Quantification of outdoor recreationists' preferences. In B. Van Der Smissen (Ed.), *Research, camping, and environmental education* (pp. 165–187). University Park, PA: The Pennsylvania State University Department of Health, Physical Education and Recreation.

Driver, B. L., & Brown, P. J. (1975). A socio-psychological definition of recreation demand, with implications for recreation resource planning. In *Assessing demand for outdoor recreation* (pp. 62–88). Washington, DC: National Academy of Sciences.

Driver, B. L., & Brown, P. J. (1984). Contributions of behavioral scientists to recreation resource management. In I. Altman & J. F. Wohlwill (Eds.), *Behavior and the national environment* (pp. 307–339). New York, NY: Plenum Press.

Driver, B. L., Brown, P. J., & Peterson, G. L. (Eds.). (1991a). *Benefits of leisure.* State College, PA: Venture Publishing, Inc.

Driver, B. L., Brown, P. J., & Peterson, G. L. (1991b). Research on leisure benefits: An introduction to this volume. In B. L. Driver, P. J. Brown, & G. L. Peterson (Eds.), *Benefits of leisure* (pp. 3–11). State College, PA: Venture Publishing, Inc.

Driver, B. L., Brown, P. J., Stankey, G. H., & Gregoire, T. G. (1987). The ROS planning system: Evolution, basic concepts, and research needed. *Leisure Sciences, 9*, 201–212

Driver, B. L., & Bruns, D. H. (1999). Concepts and uses of the benefits approach to leisure. In E. L. Jackson & T. L. Burton (Eds.), *Leisure studies: Prospects for the twenty-first century* (pp. 349–369). State College, PA: Venture Publishing, Inc.

Driver, B. L., & Knopf, R. C. (1977). Personality, outdoor recreation, and expected consequences. *Environment and Behavior, 9*, 169–193.

Driver, B. L., Tinsley, H. E. A., & Manfredo, M. J. (1991). The Paragraphs About Leisure and Recreation Experience Preference scales: Results from two inventories designed to assess the breadth of the perceived psychological benefits of leisure. In B. L. Driver, P. J. Brown, & G. L. Peterson (Eds.), *Benefits of leisure* (pp. 263–286). State College, PA: Venture Publishing, Inc.

Driver, B. L., & Tocher, S. R. (1970). Toward a behavioral interpretation of recreational engagements, with implications for planning. In B. L. Driver (Ed.), *Elements of outdoor recreation planning* (pp. 9–31). Ann Arbor, MI: University of Michigan Press.

Duda, J. (1989). Relationship between task and ego orientation and the perceived purpose of sport among high school athletes. *Journal of Sport & Exercise Psychology, 11*, 318–335.

Dumas, A., & Laforest, S. (2009). Skateparks as a health-resource: Are they as dangerous as they look? *Leisure Studies, 28*, 19–34.

Dunn, J., Causgrove Dunn, J., & Syrotuik, D. (2002). Relationship between multidimensional perfectionism and goal orientations in sport. *Journal of Sport & Exercise Psychology, 24*, 376–395.

Dunn Ross, E. L., & Iso-Ahola, S. E. (1991). Sightseeing tourists' motivation and satisfaction. *Annals of Tourism Research, 18*, 226–237.

Dupuis, S. L. (2000). Institution-based caregiving as a container for leisure. *Leisure Sciences, 22*, 259–280.

Dupuis, S. L. (2008). Leisure and aging well. *World Leisure, 50*, 91–107.

Dupuis, S. L., & Smale, B. J. A. (1995). An examination of relationship between psychological well-being and depression and leisure activity participation among older adults. *Loisir et Société/Society and Leisure, 18*, 67–92.

Dupuis, S. L., & Smale, B. J. A. (2000). Bittersweet journeys: Meanings of leisure in the institutional-based caregiving context. *Journal of Leisure Research, 32*(3), 303–340.

Dweck, C. (1999). *Self theories: The role of motivation, personality, and development.* Philadelphia, PA: Psychology Press.

Dweck, C., & Elliott, S. (1983). Achievement motivation. In P. Mussen (Ed.), *Handbook of Child Psychology: Socialization, personality, and social development* (Vol. 4, pp. 643–691). New York, NY: John Wiley & Sons.

Dychtwald, K., & Flower, J. (1990). *Age wave: How the most important trend of our time will change your future.* New York, NY: Bantam Books.

Eagleton, T. (2003). *After theory*. London, UK: Penguin Books.

Eagly, A. H., & Chaiken, S. (1993). *The psychology of attitudes*. Forth Worth, TX: Harcourt, Brace & Co.

Eccles, J. & Barber, B. L. (1999). Student council, volunteering, basketball, or marching band: What kind of extracurricular participation matters? *Journal of Adolescent Research, 14*(1), 10–43.

Eckert, P. (1989). *Jocks and burnouts: Social categories and identity in the high school*. New York, NY: Teachers College Press.

Egan, S., & Stelmack, R. M. (2003). A personality profile of Mount Everest climbers. *Personality and Individual Differences, 34*, 1491–1494.

Egli, E., & Meyers, L. (1984). The role of video game playing in adolescent life: Is there reason to be concerned? *Bulletin of the Psychonomic Society, 22*, 309–312.

Egloff, B., & Gruhn, A. J. (1996). Personality and endurance sports. *Personality and Individual Differences, 21*, 223–229.

Eisenman, L. (2007). Self-detemination interventions: Building a foundation for school completion. *Remedial and Special Education, 28*, 2–8.

Ekerdt, D. J. (1986). The busy ethic: Moral continuity between work and retirement. *The Gerontologist, 26*, 239–244.

Ekman, P., & Friesen, W. V. (2003). *Unmasking the face: a guide to recognizing emotions from facial clues*. Cambridge, MA: Malor Books.

Elder, G. (1974). *Children of the great depression*. Chicago, IL: University of Chicago Press.

Elkind, D. (1981). *The hurried child*. Boston, MA: Addison-Wesley.

Elkind, D. (2007). *The power of play: Learning what comes naturally*. Cambridge, MA: Da Capo Press.

Ellis, D. (1984). Video arcades, youth, and trouble. *Youth and Society, 16*, 47–65.

Ellis, G. D., Maughan-Pritchett, M., & Ruddell, E. (1993). Effects of attribution-based verbal persuasion and imagery on self-efficacy of adolescents diagnosed with major depression. *Therapeutic Recreation Journal, 27*, 83–97.

Ellis, G. D., Voelkl, J., & Morris, C. (1994). Measurement and analysis issues with the explanation of variance in daily experience using the flow model. *Journal of Leisure Research, 26*, 337–356.

Ellis, G. D., & Witt, P. A. (1984). The measurement of perceived freedom in leisure. *Journal of Leisure Research, 16*, 110–123.

Ellis, G. D., & Witt, P. A. (1991). Conceptualization and measurement of leisure: Making the abstract concrete. In T. L. Goodale & P. A. Witt (Eds.), *Recreation and leisure: Issues in an era of change* (3rd ed., pp. 377–395). State College, PA: Venture Publishing, Inc.

Ellis, G. D., Witt, P. A., & Aguilar, T. E. (1983). Facilitating flow through therapeutic recreation services. *Therapeutic Recreation Journal, 17*, 6–15.

Ellis, G. D., & Yessick, J. T. (1989). Toward person by situation research in therapeutic recreation. *Therapeutic Recreation Journal, 23*, 24–35.

Ellis, M. J. (1973). *Why people play*. Englewood Cliffs, NJ: Prentice Hall.

Ellis, T., & Richardson, G. (1991). Organizational wellness. In B. L. Driver, P. J. Brown, & G. L. Peterson (Eds.), *Benefits of leisure* (pp. 303–329). State College, PA: Venture Publishing, Inc.

Elms, A. C. (1975). The crisis of confidence in social psychology. *American Psychologist, 30*, 967–976.

Emmons, R. A., Diener, E., & Larsen, R. J. (1986). Choice and avoidance of everyday situations and affect congruence: Two models of reciprocal interactionism. *Journal of Personality and Social Psychology, 51*, 815–826.

Endler, N. S. (1983). Interactionism: A personality model, but not yet a theory. In M. M. Page (Ed.), *Nebraska Symposium on Motivation* (pp. 155–200). Lincoln, NB: University of Nebraska Press.

Ennett. C. K., Foshee, V. A., Bauman, K. E., Hussong, A., Cai, L., Reyes, H., Luz, M., Faris, R., Hipp, J., DuRant, R. (2008). The social ecology of adolescent alcohol misuse. *Child Development, 79*, 1777–1791.

Epstein, L., Raja, S., Gold, S., Paluch, R., Pak, Y., & Roemmich, J. (2006). Reducing sedentary behavior: The relationship between park area and physical activity of youth. *Psychological Science, 17*, 654–659.

Erikson, E. (1959). Identity and the life cycle: Selected papers. *Psychological Issues, 1*, 5–165.

Erikson, E. (1980 [1959]). *Identity and the life cycle*. New York, NY: Norton.

Erikson, E. (1963). *Childhood and society*. New York, NY: Norton.

Erikson, E. (1968). *Identity: Youth and Crisis*. New York, NY: Norton.

Etzion, D. (2003). Annual vacation: Duration of relief from job stressors and burnout. *Anxiety, Stress, & Coping: An International Journal, 16*, 213–226.

Evans, J. (1989). *Children at play: Life in the school playground*. Geelong, Australia: Deakin University Press.

Evans, S. T., & Haworth, J. T. (1991). Variations in personal activity, access to "categories of experience," and psychological well-being in young adults. *Leisure Studies, 10*, 249–264.

Ewert, A.W. (1989). *Outdoor adventure pursuits: Foundations, models, and theories*. Worthington, OH: Publishing Horizons.

Ewert, A. W. (1993). Differences in the level of motive importance based on trip outcome, experience level and group type. *Journal of Leisure Research, 25*, 335–349.

Ewert, A. W. (1994). Playing the edge: Motivation and risk taking in a high-altitude wilderness-like environment. *Environment and Behavior, 26*, 3–24.

Ewert, A. W., & Hollenhorst, S. J. (1989). Testing the adventure model: Empirical support for a model of risk recreation participation. *Journal of Leisure Research, 21*, 124–139.

Ewert, A. W., Hollenhorst, S. J., McAvoy, L., & Russell, K. C. (2003). Therapeutic values of parks and protected areas. In D. Harmon & A. D. Putney (Eds.), *The full value of parks*. New York, NY: Bowman & Littlefield Publishers.

Ewert, A.W., & McAvoy, L. (2000). The effects of wilderness settings on organized groups: A state-of-knowledge paper. In S. McCool, D. Cole, W. Borrie, & J. O'Loughlin (Compilers), *Wilderness science in a time of change conference–Volume 3: Wilderness as a place for scientific inquiry* (pp. 13–26). Proceedings RMRS-P-15-VOL-3. Ogden, UT: U.S. Department of Agriculture, Forest Service, Rocky Mountain Research Station.

Eysenck, H. J. (1967). *The biological basis of personality*. Springfield, IL: Thomas Frewd.

Falk, J. H. (1995). Factors influencing African American leisure time utilization of museums. *Journal of Leisure Research, 27*, 41–60.

Farr, R. M. (1991). The long past and the short history of social psychology. *European Journal of Social Psychology, 21*, 371–380.

Feagin, J. R., & Eckbert, D. L. (1980). Discrimination: Motivation, action, effects, and context. *Annual Review of Sociology, 6*, 1–20.

Feather, N. T., & Bond, M. J. (1983). Time structure and purposeful activity among employed and unemployed university graduates. *Journal of Occupational Psychology, 56*, 241–254.

Ferguson, C. J. (2007). The good, the bad and the ugly: A meta-analytic review of positive and negative effects of violent video games. *Psychiatric Quarterly, 78*, 309–316.

Fernandez-Ballesteros, R., Zamarron, M., & Ruiz, M. (2001). The contribution of socio-demographic and psycho-social factors to life satisfaction. *Ageing and Society, 21*(1), 25–43.

Festinger, L. A. (1954). A theory of social comparison processes. *Human Relations, 7*, 117–140.

Festinger, L. A. (1957). *A theory of cognitive dissonance*. Stanford, CA: Stanford University Press.

Field, D. R., & O'Leary, J. T. (1973). Social groups as a basis for assessing participation in selected water activities. *Journal of Leisure Research, 5*, 16–25.

Fincham, R., & Rhodes, P. S. (1988). *The individual, work, and organization*. London, UK: Weidenfeld and Nicolson.

Fine, G. A. (1983). *Shared fantasy*. Chicago, IL: The University of Chicago Press.

Fine, G. A. (1987). *With the boys: Little league baseball and preadolescent culture*. Chicago, IL: The University of Chicago Press.

Fine, G. A. (1989). Mobilizing fun: Provisioning resources in leisure worlds. *Sociology of Sport Journal, 6*, 319–334.

Fine, G. A. (1993). The sad demise, mysterious disappearance, and glorious triumph of symbolic interactionism. *Annual Review of Sociology, 19*, 61.

Fishbein, M. (1980). A theory of reasoned action: Some applications and implications. In H. E. Howe & M. M. Page (Eds.), *Nebraska Symposium on Motivation* (Vol. 27, pp. 65–116). Lincoln, NE: University of Nebraska Press.

Fiske, A., Kitayama, S., Markus, H., & Nisbett, R. (1998). The cultural matrix of social psychology. In D. Gilbert, S. Fiske, & G. Lindzey (Eds.), *The handbook of social psychology* (Vol. 2, 4th ed., pp. 915–981). New York, NY: Oxford University Press, Inc.

Fiske, S. T. (2003). Five core social motives, plus or minus five. In S. Spencer, S. Fein, M. Zanna, & S. Olson (Eds.), *Motivated social perception* (pp. 233–256). Mahwah, NJ: Lawrence Erlbaum.

Fiske, S. T. (2004). *Social beings: A core motives approach to social psychology*. New York, NY: Wiley.

Fiske, S. T., & Depret, E. (1996). Control, interdependence, and power: Understanding social cognition in its social context. In W. Stroebe & M. Hewstone (Eds.), *European Review of Social Psychology* (Vol. 5, pp. 31–61). New York, NY: Wiley.

Floyd, M. F. (1998). Getting beyond marginality and ethnicity: The challenge for race and ethnic studies in leisure research. *Journal of Leisure Research, 30*, 3–22.

Floyd, M. F. (1999). Race, ethnicity and use of the national park system. *Social Science Research Review, 1*(2, Spring/Summer), 24.

Floyd, M. F., Bocarro, J., & Thompson, T. (2008). Research on race and ethnicity in leisure studies: A review of five major journals. *Journal of Leisure Research, 40*, 1–22.

Floyd, M. F., & Gramann, J. H. (1995). Perceptions of discrimination in a recreational context. *Journal of Leisure Research, 27*, 192–199.

Fodness, D. (1994). Measuring tourist motivation. *Annals of Tourism Research, 21*, 555–581.

Folkman, S. (1997). Positive psychological states and coping with severe stress. *Social Science and Medicine, 45*, 1207–1221.

Folkman, S. (2008). The case for positive emotions in the stress process. *Anxiety, Stress, & Coping, 21*, 3–14.

Folkman, S., & Moskowitz, J. T. (2000). Stress, positive emotion and coping. *Current Directions in Psychological Science, 9*, 115–118.

Foote White, W. (1943). *Street Corner Society*. Chicago, IL: University of Chicago Press.

Foster, R. J., & Jackson, E. L. (1979). Factors associated with camping satisfaction in Alberta Provincial Park campgrounds. *Journal of Leisure Research, 11*, 292–306.

Francken, D. A., & van Raaij, W. F. (1981). Satisfaction with leisure time activities. *Journal of Leisure Research, 13*, 337–352.

Franken, R. E. (1982). *Human motivation*. Monterey, CA: Brooks-Cole.

Franklin, A. (2006). Tourism. In C. Rojek, S. Shaw, & A. Veal (Eds.), *A handbook of leisure studies* (pp. 386–403). London, UK: Palgrave.

Frederick, C. J., Havitz, M., & Shaw, S. M. (1994). Social comparison in aerobic exercise classes: Propositions for analysing motives and participation. *Leisure Sciences, 16*, 161–176.

Frederick, C. J., & Shaw, S. M. (1995). Body image as a leisure constraint: Examining the experience of aerobic exercise classes for young women. *Leisure Sciences, 17*, 57–73.

Fredrickson, B. (2001). The role of positive emotions in positive psychology: The broaden-and-build theory of positive emotions. *American Psychologist, 56*, 218–226.

Fredrickson, B. (2002). Positive emotions. In C. R. Snyder & S. Lopez, (eds.), *Handbook of positive psychology* (pp. 120–134). New York, NY: Oxford University Press.

Fredrickson, B. (2003). The value of positive emotions. *American Scientist, 91*, 330–335.

Freedman, M. (1999). *Prime time: How Baby Boomers will revolutionize retirement and transform America*. Cambridge, MA: Perseus.

Freud, S. (1933). *Introductory lectures on psychoanalysis*. New York, NY: Norton.

Freysinger, V. J. (1990). A life span perspective on women and physical recreation. *Journal of Physical Education, Recreation and Dance, 61*, 48–51.

Freysinger, V. J. (1994). Leisure with children and parental satisfaction: Further evidence of a sex difference in the experience of adult roles and leisure. *Journal of Leisure Research, 26*, 212–226.

Freysinger, V. J. (1995). The dialectics of leisure and development of women and men in mid-life: An interpretive study. *Journal of Leisure Research, 27*, 61–84.

Freysinger, V. J. (2005). Leisure and aging. In E. Jackson & T. Burton (Eds.), *Leisure studies: Prospects for the twenty-first century*. State College, PA: Venture Publishing, Inc.

Freysinger, V. J. (2006). Race and leisure. In C. Rojek, S. Shaw, & T. Veal (Eds.), *Handbook of leisure studies* (pp. 250–270). London, UK: Palgrave.

Freysinger, V. J., & Flannery, D. (1992). Women's leisure: Affiliation, self-determination, empowerment and resistance? *Loisir et Société/Society and Leisure, 15*, 303–322.

Freysinger, V. J., & Kelly, J. (2004). *21st century leisure: Current issues* (2nd ed.). State College, PA: Venture Publishing, Inc.

Freysinger, V. J. and Ray, R. O. (1994). The activity involvement of women and men in young and middle adulthood: A panel study. *Leisure Sciences, 16*, 193–217.

Friedman, M., & Rosenman, R. H. (1974). *Type-A behavior and your heart*. New York, NY: Fawcett.

Friedman, M., & Ulmer, D. (1984). *Treating Type-A behavior and your heart*. New York, NY: Alfred A. Knopf.

Froelicher, V. F., & Froelicher, E. S. (1991). Cardiovascular benefits of physical activity. In B. L. Driver, P. J. Brown, & G. L. Peterson (Eds.), *Benefits of leisure* (pp. 59–72). State College, PA: Venture Publishing, Inc.

Frost, J. L. (2006). *The dissolution of children's outdoor play: Causes and consequences*. Conference paper delivered at The Value of Play: A forum on risk, recreation and children's health. Washington, DC, May 31, 2006. Available at http://cgood.org/assets/attachments/Frost_ .

Fry, S. K., & Heubeck, B. G. (1998). The effects of personality and situational variables on mood states during outward bound wilderness courses: An exploration. *Personality and individual differences, 24*, 649–659.

Fry, W. F., & Allen, M. (1975). *Make 'em laugh: Life studies of comedy writers*. Palo Alto, CA: Science and Behavior Books, Inc.

Frydenberg, E., & Lewis, R. (1993). Boys play sport and girls turn to others: Age, gender, and ethnicity as determinants of coping. *Journal of Adolescence, 16*, 253–266.

Fryer, D., & Payne, R. (1984). Proactive behavior in unemployment: Findings and implications. *Leisure Studies, 3*, 273–295.

Fullagar, S. (2008). Leisure practices as counter-depressants: Emotion-work and emotion-play within women's recovery from depression. *Leisure Sciences, 30*, 35–52.

Fullinwider, R. K. (2006). *Sports, youth, and character*. The Center for Research on Civic Learning and Engagement. (CIRCLE Working Papers, #44). Available at http://www.civicyouth.org.

Furedi, F. (2002). *Paranoid parenting*. Chicago: Chicago Review Press.

Furlong, M. (1989). An electronic community for older adults: The Seniornet network. *Journal of Communication, 39*, 145–153.

Galda, L., & Pellegrini, A. D. (1982). The effects of thematic-fantasy play training on the development of children's story comprehension. *American Education Research Journal, 19*, 443–452.

Gao, G., Ting-Toomey, S., & Gudykunst, W. B. (1996). Chinese communication processes. In M. H. Bond (Ed.), *The handbook of Chinese psychology* (pp. 280–293). Hong Kong: Oxford University Press.

Gardner, H. (1999). *Intelligence reframed: Multiple intelligences for the 21st century*. New York, NY: Basic Books.

Gardner, H., Csikszentmihalyi, M., & Damon, W. (2001). *Good work: When excellence and ethics meet*. New York, NY: Basic Books.

Gauthier, A. H., & Smeeding, T. M. (2003). Time use at older ages: Cross national differences. *Research on Aging, 25*, 247–274.

Gee, S., & Baillie, J. (1999). Happily ever after? An exploration of retirement expectations. *Educational Gerontology, 25*, 109–128.

Genoe, M. R. (2008). *Leisure as resistance in the context of dementia*. Proceedings of the 12th Canadian Conference on Leisure Research, Montreal, QC.

Genoe, M. R. (2009). *Living with hope in the midst of change: The meaning of leisure within the context of dementia*. Unpublished doctoral dissertation, University of Waterloo.

Gergen, K. (1973). Social psychology as history. *Journal of Personality and Social Psychology, 26*, 309–320.

Gergen, K. (1999). *An invitation to social construction*. London, UK: Sage Publications.

Gergen, K. (2001). Psychological science in a postmodern context. *American Psychologist, 56*, 803–813.

Geva, A., & Goldman, A. (1991). Satisfaction measurements in guided tours. *Annals of Tourism Research, 18*, 177–185.

Gibson, H., Willming, C., & Holdnak, A. (2002). "We're Gators . . . not just Gator fans": Serious leisure and University of Florida football. *Journal of Leisure Research, 34*, 397–425.

Gibson, J. J. (1979). *The Ecological approach to visual perception*. Boston, MA: Houghton Mifflin.

Giele, J. (1980). Adulthood as a transcendence of age and sex. In T. Sinclair, & E. Erikson (Eds.), *Themes of work and love in adulthood* (pp. 151–173). Cambridge, MA: Harvard University Press.

Gillard, A., Watts, C., & Witt, P. (2007). The effect of perceptions of support for autonomy, relatedness, and competence on interest in camp for adolescent girls. In C. LeBlanc & C. Vogt (Compilers), *Proceedings of the 2007 Northeastern Recreation Research Symposium* (pp. 152–159). Newtown Square, PA: USDA Forest Service.

Gillespie, D. L., Lefler, A., & Lerner, E. (2002). If it weren't for my hobby, I'd have a life: dog sports, serious leisure, and boundary negotiations. *Leisure Studies, 21*, 285–304.

Gilligan, C. (1982). *In a different voice: Psychological theory and women's development.* Cambridge, MA: Harvard University Press.

Glancy, M. (1988). The play-world setting of the auction. *Journal of Leisure Research, 20,* 135–153.

Glass, D. C., & Singer, J. E. (1972). *Urban stress.* New York, NY: Academic Press.

Gleich, J. (1999*). Faster: The acceleration of just about everything.* New York, NY: Pantheon Books.

Glover, T. D. (2004). The 'community' center and the social construction of citizenship. *Leisure Sciences, 26*(1), 63–83.

Glover, T. D. (2004). Social capital in the lived experiences of community gardeners. *Leisure Sciences, 26*(1), 143–162.

Glover, T. D. (2007). Ugly on the diamonds: An examination of white privilege in youth baseball. *Leisure Sciences, 29,* 195–208.

Glover, T. D., & Parry, D. C. (2008, May). *Gilda's club as a third place in the everyday lives of people living with cancer.* Paper presented at the 12th Canadian Conference on Leisure Research, Montreal, QC.

Glover, T. D., & Parry, D. C. (2008). Friendship developed subsequent to a stressful life event: The interplay of leisure social capital and health. *Journal of Leisure Research, 40,* 208–230.

Glover, T. D., Parry, D. C., & Shinew, K. J. (2005). Building relationships, accessing resources: Mobilizing social capital in community garden contexts. *Journal of Leisure Research, 37,* 450–474.

Glynn, M. A., & Webster, J. (1993). Refining the nomological net of the adult playfulness scale: Personality, motivational, and attitudinal correlates for highly intelligent adults. *Psychological Reports, 72,* 1023–1026.

Gobster, P. H. (1998). Explanations for minority "underparticipation" in outdoor recreation: A look at golf. *Journal of Park and Recreation Administration, 16,* 46–64.

Gobster, P. H., & Delgado, A. (1992). Ethnicity and recreation use in Chicago's Lincoln Park: In-park user survey findings. In P. Gobster (Ed.), *Managing urban parks and high-use recreation settings* (General Technical Report NC-163, pp. 75–81). St. Paul, MN: USDA Forest Service Northcentral Forest Experiment Station.

Godbey, G. (1988). The sociology of leisure: Past, present, and future research. In L. A. Barnett (Ed.), *Research about leisure: Past, present, and future* (pp. 35–44). Champaign, IL: Sagamore Publishing.

Godbey, G. (1994). *Leisure in your life* (4th ed.). State College, PA: Venture Publishing, Inc.

Goldberg, L. R. (1981). Language and individual differences: The search for universals in personality lexicons. In L. Wheeler (Ed.), *Review of personality and social psychology,* Vol. 2, (pp. 145–165). Newbury Park, CA: Sage Publications.

Gomez, E. (2002). The ethnicity and public recreation participation model. *Leisure Sciences, 24,* 123–142.

Gomez, E. (2006). The ethnicity and public recreation participation (EPRP) model: An assessment of unidimensionality and overall fit. *Leisure Sciences, 28,* 245–265.

Goodale, T. L. (1990). Perceived freedom as leisure's antithesis. *Journal of Leisure Research, 22,* 296–302.

Goodale, T. L., & Godbey, G. (1988). *The evolution of leisure.* State College, PA: Venture Publishing, Inc.

Goodale, T. L., & Witt, P. A. (1989). Recreation non-participation and barriers to leisure. In E. L. Jackson & T. L. Burton (Eds.), *Understanding leisure and recreation: Mapping the past, charting the future* (pp. 421–449). State College, PA: Venture Publishing, Inc.

Goodenough, W. H. (1996). Culture. In D. Levinson & M. Ember (Eds.), *Encyclopedia of cultural anthropology* (Vol 1, pp. 291–299). New York, NY: Henry Holt and Company.

Goodwin, D. L., & Watkinson, E. J. (2000). Inclusive physical education for the perspective of students with physical disabilities. *Adapted Physical Education Quarterly, 17,* 144–160.

Goodwin, M. H. (1995). Co-construction in Girls' Hop Scotch. *Research on Language and Social Interaction 28*(3), 261–81.

Goodwin, M. H. (2006). *The Hidden Life of Girls: Games of Stance, Status, and Exclusion.* Oxford, UK: Blackwell.

Gordon, C., Gaitz, C. M., & Scott, J. (1976). Leisure and lives: Personal expressivity across the life span. In R. Binstock & E. Shanas (Eds.), *Handbook of aging and the social sciences* (pp. 310–341). New York, NY: Van Nostrand Reinhold Company.

Goudy, W. J., & Myers, P. M. G. (1985). Retirement and leisure: A review of five books. *Leisure Sciences, 7,* 479–486.

Gould, D., & Petlikoff, L. (1988). Participant motivation and attrition in young athletes. In F. L. Smoll et al. (Eds.), *Children in sport.* (3rd ed., pp. 161–162). Champaign, IL: Human Kinetics.

Gould, J., Moore, D., McGuire, F., & Stebbins, R. (2008). Development of the serious leisure inventory and measure. *Journal of Leisure Research, 40,* 47–68.

Graef, R., Csikszentmihalyi, M., & Gianinno, S. M. (1983). Measuring intrinsic motivation in everyday life. *Leisure Studies, 2,* 155–168.

Graefe, A. R., & Fedler, A. J. (1986). Situational and subjective determinants of satisfaction in marine recreational fishing. *Leisure Sciences, 8,* 275–295.

Grafanaki, S., Pearson, D., Cini, F., Godula, D., McKenzie, S., Nason, S., & Anderegg, M. (2005). Sources of renewal: A qualitative study on the experience and role of leisure in the life of counselors and psychologists. *Counseling Psychology Report, 18,* 31–40.

Graham, D. F., Graham, I., & MacLean, M. J. (1991). Going to the mall: A leisure activity of urban elderly people. *Canadian Journal on Aging, 12,* 345–358.

Graham, R., Nilsen, P., & Payne, R. J. (1988). Visitor management in Canadian National Parks. *Tourism Management, 44–62.*

Gramann, J. H. (1995). Ethnicity, race, and outdoor recreation: A review of trends, policy, and research. Vicksburg, MS: U.S. Army Corps of Engineers, Waterways Experiment Station, Environmental Laboratory, Natural Resources Division.

Gramann, J. H., & Allison, M. T. (1999). Ethnicity, race, and leisure. In E. Jackson & T. Burton (Eds.), *Leisure studies: Prospects for the twenty-first century* (pp. 283–297). State College, PA: Venture Publishing, Inc.

Gramann, J. H., & Bonifield, R. L. (1995). Effect of personality and situational factors on intentions to obey rules in outdoor recreation areas. *Journal of Leisure Research, 27*, 326–343.

Green, F. (1998). "Women doing friendship": An analysis of women's leisure as a site of identity construction, empowerment, and resistance. *Leisure Studies, 17*, 171–185

Green, G., Kleiber, D., & Tarrant, M. (2000). The effect of an adventure-based recreation program on the development of resiliency in low income, minority youth. *Journal of Park and Recreation Administration, 18*, 76–97.

Greenberg, J., & Folger, R. (1988). *Controversial issues in social research methods*. New York, NY: Springer-Verlag.

Greenberg, J., Pyszczynski, T., & Solomon, S. (1986). The causes and consequences of the need for self-esteem: A terror management theory. In R. F. Baumeister (Ed.), *Public self and private self* (pp. 189–212). New York, NY: Springer-Verlag.

Greenberger, E., & Steinberg, L. (1986). *When teenagers work*. Englewood Cliffs, NJ: Prentice-Hall.

Greeno, J. G. (1994). Gibson's affordances. *Psychological Review, 101*, 336–342.

Grieves, J. (1989). Acquiring a leisure identity: Juvenile jazz bands and the moral universe of "healthy" leisure time. *Leisure Studies, 8*, 1–9.

Griffiths, V. (1988). From playing out to dossing out: Young women and leisure. In E. Wimbush & M. Talbot (Eds.), *Relative freedoms: Women and leisure* (pp. 48–59). Milton Keynes, UK: Open University Press.

Grolnick, W. S., & Ryan, R. M. (1989). Parent styles associated with children's self-regulation and competence in school. *Journal of Educational Psychology, 81*, 143–154.

Gronlund, G. (1992). Coping with ninja-turtle play in my kindergarten classroom. *Young Children, 48*, 21–25.

Grossman, J., & Bulle, M. (2006). Review of what youth programs do to increase connectedness of youth with adults. *Journal of Adolescent Health, 39*, 788–799.

Grubb, E. A. (1975). Assembly line boredom and individual differences in recreation participation. *Journal of Leisure Research, 7*, 256–269.

Gueguen, N., Fischer-Lokou, J., Lefebvre, L., & Lamy, L. (2008). Women's eye contact and men's later interest: Two field experiments. *Perceptual & Motor Skills, 106*, 63.

Guinn, R. (1980). Elderly recreational vehicle tourists: Life satisfaction correlates of leisure satisfaction. *Journal of Leisure Research, 12*, 198–204.

Gunter, B. G. (1987). The leisure experience: Selected properties. *Journal of Leisure Research, 19*, 115–130.

Gunter, B. G., & Gunter, N. C. (1980). Leisure styles: A conceptual framework for modern leisure. *The Sociological Quarterly, 21*, 361–374.

Gurin, G., Veroff, J., & Feld, S. (1960). *Americans view their mental health*. New York, NY: Basic Books.

Gutmann, D. (1975). Parenthood: A key to the comparative study of the life cycle. In N. Datan & L. Ginsburg (Eds.), *Life-span developmental psychology: Normative life crises* (pp. 167–184). New York, NY: Academic Press.

Gutmann, D. (1977). The cross-cultural perspective: Notes toward a comparative psychology of aging. In J. Birren & K. W. Schaie (Eds.), *Handbook of the psychology of aging* (pp. 302–326). New York, NY: Van Nostrand Reinhold.

Haan, N. (1981) Adolescents and young adults as producers of their own development. In R. Lerner & N. Busch-Rossnagel (Eds.), *Individuals as producers of their own development.* New York, NY: Academic Press.

Haavio-Mannila, E. (1971). Satisfaction with family, work, leisure, and life among men and women. *Human Relations, 24,* 585–601.

Haggar, M., Chatzisarantis, N., & Harris, J. (2006). From psychological need satisfaction to intentional behavior: Testing a motivational sequence in two behavioral contexts. *Personality and Social Psychology Bulletin, 32,* 131–148.

Haggard, L. M., & Williams, D. R. (1991). Self-identity benefits of leisure activities. In B. L. Driver, P. J. Brown, & G. L. Peterson (Eds.), *Benefits of leisure* (pp. 103–119). State College, PA: Venture Publishing, Inc.

Haggard, L. M., & Williams, D. R. (1992). Identity affirmation through leisure activities: Leisure symbols of the self. *Journal of Leisure Research, 24,* 1–18.

Hall, M., & Rhyne, D. (1989). *Leisure behaviour and recreation needs of Ontario's ethnocultural populations.* Toronto, ON: Ministry of Tourism and Recreation.

Hamilton, J. A. (1981). Attention, personality, and the self-regulation of mood: Absorbing interest and boredom. *Progress in Experimental Personality Research, 10,* 281–315.

Hamilton, J. A. (1983a). Development of interest and enjoyment in adolescence. Part I: Attentional capacities. *Journal of Youth and Adolescence, 5,* 355–362.

Hamilton, J. A. (1983b). Development of interest and enjoyment in adolescence. Part II: Boredom and psychopathology. *Journal of Youth and Adolescence, 5,* 363–372.

Hammitt, W. E. (1980). Outdoor recreation: Is it a multi-phase experience? *Journal of Leisure Research, 12,* 107–115.

Han, S. (1988). The relationship between life satisfaction and flow in elderly Korean immigrants. In M. Csikszentmihalyi & I. Csikszentmihalyi (Eds.), *Optimal experience: Psychological studies of flow in consciousness* (pp. 138–149). New York, NY: Cambridge University Press.

Harackiewicz, J. (1979). The effects of reward contingency and performance feedback on intrinsic motivation. *Journal of Personality and Social Psychology, 37,* 1352–1363.

Harlan, J. E., & Hawkins, B. A. (1992). Terminal illness, aging, and developmental disability: A therapeutic art intervention. *Therapeutic Recreation Journal, 26,* 49–52.

Harlow, H. F. (1950). Learning and satiation of a response in intrinsically motivated complex puzzle performance by monkeys. *Journal of Comparative Physiological Psychology, 43,* 289–294.

Harlow, H. F. and Harlow, M. (1962). Social depreciation in monkeys. *Scientific American, 207,* 137–146.

Harper, W. (1981). The experience of leisure. *Leisure Sciences, 4,* 113–126.

Harper, W. (1986). Freedom in the experience of leisure. *Leisure Sciences, 8,* 115–130.

Harter, S. (1990). Self and identity development. In S. S. Feldman & G. R. Elliot (Eds.), *At the threshold: The developing adolescent* (pp. 352–387). Cambridge, MA: Harvard University Press.

Harvey, C. D. H., & Bahr, H. M. (1980). *The sunshine widows: Adapting to sudden bereavement.* Lexington, MA: Lexington Books.

Hastorf, A., & Cantril, H. (1954). They saw a game: A case study. *Journal of Abnormal and Social Psychology, 49*, 129–134.

Hatcher, M. (1988). What happens to the early retiree. *Career Development Quarterly, 37*, 184–190.

Havighurst, R. J. (1953). *Older people.* New York, NY: Longmans and Green.

Havighurst, R. J. (1963). Successful aging. In R. Williams, C. Tibbitts, & W. Donahue (Eds.), *Process of aging* (pp. 299–320). New York, NY: Atherton.

Havighurst, R. J. (1972). *Developmental tasks and education.* New York, NY: David McKay.

Havighurst, R. J., & Albrecht, R. (1953). *Older people.* New York, NY: Longman, Green.

Havitz, M. E., & Crompton, J. L. (1990 The influence of persuasive messages on propensity to purchase selected recreational services from public or from commercial suppliers. *Journal of Leisure Research, 22*, 71–88.

Havitz, M. E., & Dimanche, F. (1997). Leisure involvement revisited: Conceptual conundrums and measurement advances. *Journal of Leisure Research*, 29, 245–278.

Havitz, M. E., & Dimanche, F. (1999). Leisure involvement revisited: Drive properties and paradoxes. *Journal of Leisure Research, 31*, 122–149.

Havitz, M. E. & Mannell, R. C. (2005). Enduring involvement, situational involvement, and flow in leisure and non-leisure activities. *Journal of Leisure Research, 37*, 152–177.

Havitz, M. E., Morden, P., & Samdahl, D. (2004). *The diverse worlds of unemployed adults: Consequences for leisure, lifestyle, and health.* Waterloo, ON: Wilfred Laurier Press.

Hawkins, B., Foose, A. K., & Binkley, A. L. (2004). Contributions of leisure to the life satisfaction of older adults in Australia and the United States. *World Leisure Journal, 46*(2), 4–12.

Haworth, J. T. (1984). The perceived nature of meaningful pursuits and the social psychology of commitment. *Loisir et Société/Society and Leisure, 7*, 197–216.

Haworth, J. T. (1986). Meaningful activity and psychological models of non-employment. *Leisure Studies, 5*, 281–297.

Haworth, J. T. (2003). Editorial: Leisure and wellbeing. *Leisure Studies, 22*, 317–322.

Haworth, J. T. (2004). *The future of work and leisure.* New York, NY: Routledge.

Haworth, J. T. and Ducker, J. (1991). Psychological well-being and access to categories of experience in unemployed young adults. *Leisure Studies, 10*, 265–274.

Haworth, J. T., & Millar, T. (1986). Research note: Time diary sampling of daily activity and intrinsic motivation in unemployed young adults. *Leisure Studies, 5*, 353–359.

Hazel, K. L., Langenau, E. E. Jr., & Levine, R. L. (1990 Dimensions of hunting satisfaction: Multiple-satisfactions of wild turkey hunting. *Leisure Sciences, 12*, 383–393.

Heath, S. B. (1999). Dimensions of language development: Lessons from older children. In A. S. Masten (Ed.), *Cultural processes in child development: The Minnesota symposium on child psychology* (Vol. 29, pp. 59–75). Mahwah, NJ: Erlbaum.

Heath, S. B., & McLaughlin, M. W. (Eds.). (1993). *Identity and Inner City Youth.* New York, NY: Teachers College Press.

Heberlein, T. A. (1973). Social psychological assumptions of user attitude surveys: The case of the wildernism scale. *Journal of Leisure Research, 5, 18–33.*

Heckhausen, H., & Kuhl, J. (1985). From wishes to action: The dead ends and short cuts on the long way to action. In M. Frese & J. Sabini (Eds.), *Goal-directed behavior: Psychological theory and research on action.* Hillsdale, NJ: Erlbaum.

Heckhausen, J. (1999). *Developmental regulation in adulthood: Age-normative and socio-structural constraints as adaptive challenges.* New York, NY: Cambridge University Press.

Heft, H. (1988) Affordances of children's environments: A functional approach to environmental description. *Children's Environments Quarterly, 5, 29–37.*

Heider, F. (1958). *The psychology of interpersonal relations.* New York, NY: John Wiley & Sons.

Heine, S., Lehman, D., Markus, H., & Kitayama, S. (1999). Is there a universal need for positive self-regard? *Psychological Review, 106, 766–794.*

Heintzman, P., & Mannell, R. C. (2003). Spiritual functions of leisure and spiritual well-being: Coping with time pressure. *Leisure Sciences, 25, 207–230.*

Hektner, J. M., Schmidt, J. A., & Csikszentmihalyi, M. (2007). Experience sampling method: Measuring the quality of everyday life. Thousand Oaks, CA: Sage.

Hemingway, J. L. (1988). Leisure and civility: Reflections of a Greek ideal. *Leisure Sciences, 10,* 179–191.

Hendee, J. C., & Burdge, R. J. (1974). The substitutability concept: Implications for recreation research and management. *Journal of Leisure Research, 6,* 157–162.

Henderlong, J., & Lepper, M. (2002). The effects of praise on children's intrinsic motivation: A review and synthesis. Psychological Bulletin, 128, 774–795.

Henderson, K. A. (2000). New terms, broader approaches, recreation, and the new social ecology of physical activity. *Parks and Recreation,* December, 28–35.

Henderson, K. A. (1990a). An oral life history perspective on the containers in which American farm women experienced leisure. *Leisure Studies, 9,* 121–133.

Henderson, K. A. (1990b). The meaning of leisure for women: An integrative review of the research. *Journal of Leisure Research, 22,* 228–243.

Henderson, K. A. (1991a). *Dimensions of choice: A qualitative approach to recreation, parks, and leisure research.* State College, PA: Venture Publishing, Inc.

Henderson, K. A. (1991b). The contribution of feminism to an understanding of leisure constraints. *Journal of Leisure Research, 23,* 363–377.

Henderson, K. A. (1994). Broadening an understanding of women, gender, and leisure. *Journal of Leisure Research, 26,* 1–7.

Henderson, K. A., Bedini, L. A., & Schuler, R. (1995). Women with physical disabilities and the negotiation of leisure constraints. *Leisure Studies, 14*, 17–31.

Henderson, K. A., & Bialeschki, M. D. (1993). Negotiating constraints to women's physical recreation. *Loisir et Société/Society and Leisure, 16*, 389–412.

Henderson, K. A., & Hickerson, B. (2007). Women and leisure: Premises and performances uncovered in an integrative review. *Journal of Leisure Research, 39*, 591–610.

Henderson, K. A., Hodges, S., Kivel, B. D. (2002). Context and dialogue in research on women and leisure. *Journal of Leisure Research, 34*, 253–271.

Henderson, K. A., Neff, L., Sharpe, P., Gfreanet, M., Royce, S., & Ainsworth, B. (2001). "It takes a village" to promote physical activity: The potential of public park and recreation departments. *Journal of Park and Recreation Administration, 19*, 23–41.

Henderson, K. A., & Rannells, J. S. (1988). Farm women and the meaning of work and leisure: An oral history perspective. *Leisure Sciences, 10*, 41–50.

Henderson, K. A., Stalnaker, D., & Taylor, G. (1988). The relationship between barriers to recreation and gender-role personality traits for women. *Journal of Leisure Research, 20*, 69–80.

Hendry, L. B., Shucksmith, J., Love, J. G., & Glendinning, A. (1993). *Young people's leisure and lifestyles*. London, UK: Routledge.

Henke, M. (1999). Promoting independence in older adults through the internet. *CyberPsychology & Behavior, 2*, 521–562.

Henning, B., & Vorderer, P. (2001). Psychological escapism: Predicting the amount of television viewing by need for cognition. *Journal of Communication, 51*, 100–120.

Henretta, J. C., Orand, A. M., & Chan, C. G. (1993). Joint role investments and synchronization of retirement: A sequential approach to couples' retirement timing. *Social Forces, 71*, 981–1000.

Heo, J., & Lee, Y. (2007). "I don't want to feel like a stranger": Korean students who play basketball seriously. *Leisure/Loisir, 31*, 133–154.

Herridge, K. L., Shaw, S. M., & Mannell, R. C. (2003). An exploration of women's leisure within heterosexual romantic relationships. *Journal of Leisure Research, 35*, 274–291.

Herzog, A. R. and Rodgers, W. L. (1981). The structure of subjective well-being in different age groups. *Journal of Gerontology, 36*, 472–479.

Heywood, L. A. (1978). Perceived recreative experience and the relief of tension. *Journal of Leisure Research, 10*, 86–97.

Higginbottom, S. F., Barling, J., & Kelloway, E. K. (1993). Linking retirement experiences and marital satisfaction: A mediational model. *Psychology and Aging, 8*, 508–516.

Higgins, C., Duxbury, L. and Lee, C. (1994). Impact of life-cycle stage and gender on ability to balance work and family responsibilities. *Family Relations, 43*, 144–150.

Hilbrecht, M. (2007). Changing perspectives on the work-leisure relationship. *Annals of Leisure Research, 10*, 368–390.

Hilbrecht, M., Shaw, S. M., Johnson, L. C., & Andrey, J. (2008). 'I'm home for the kids': Contradictory implications for work-life balance of teleworking mothers. *Gender, Work and Organization, 15*, 454–476.

Hilbrecht, M., Zuzanek, J., & Mannell, R. C. (2008). Time use, time pressure and gendered behavior in early and late adolescence. *Sex Roles, 58*, 342–357.

Hildebrand, M., & Mannell, R. C. (1996). Leisure and the job satisfaction of teachers. In P. Stokowsk & J. Hultsman (Eds.), *Abstracts of presentations: 1996 Leisure Research Symposium.* Arlington, VA: National Recreation and Parks Association.

Hilgard, E. R. (1962). *Introduction to psychology.* New York, NY: Harcourt, Brace and World, Inc.

Hill, M. S. (1988). Marital stability and spouses' shared time. *Journal of Family Issues, 9*, 427–451.

Hills, P., & Argyle, M. (2003). Uses of the Internet and their relationships with individual differences in personality. *Computers in human behavior, 19*, 59–70.

Hiroto, D. (1974). Locus of control and learned helplessness. *Journal of Experimental Psychology, 102*, 187–193.

Hirschman, E. C. (1984). Leisure motives and sex roles. *Journal of Leisure Research, 16*, 209–223.

Hochschild, A. (1989). The second shift: Working parents and the revolution at home. New York, NY: Viking.

Hogan, P. I., & Santomier, J. P. (1982). Stress and leisure activities. *Leisure Information Newsletter, 8*, 7–8.

Hogan, R. (1987). Personality psychology: Back to basics. In J. Aronoff, A. I. Rabin, & R. A. Zucker (Eds.), *The emergence of personality.* New York, NY: Springer.

Holland, A., & Andre, T. (1994). Athletic participation and the social status of adolescent males and females. *Youth and Society, 25*, 388–407.

Holman, T. B., & Epperson, A. (1984). Family and leisure: A review of the literature with research recommendations. *Journal of Leisure Research, 16*, 277–294.

Holman, T. B., & Jacquart, M. (1988). Leisure activity patterns and marital satisfaction: A further test. *Journal of Marriage and the Family, 50*, 69–78.

Holt, N., & Kleiber, D. A. (2009). The siren's song of multiplayer online games. *Children, Youth and the Environment, 19*, 223–244.

Honore, K. (2004). *In praise of slowness.* New York, NY: HarperCollins.

Hooyman, N. and Kiyak, H. (1996). *Social gerontology* (4th ed.). Boston, MA: Allyn & Bacon.

Hormuth, S. (1984). Transitions in commitments to roles and self-concept change: Relocation as a paradigm. In V. Allen & E. Van de Vliert (Eds.), *Role transitions* (pp. 109–124). New York, NY: Plenum Press.

Horna, J. L. A. (1989a). The dual asymmetry in the married couples' life: The gender-differentiated work, family, and leisure domains. *International Journal of Sociology of the Family, 19*, 113–130.

Horna, J. L. A. (1989b). The leisure component of the parental role. *Journal of Leisure Research, 21*, 228–241.

Horna, J. L. A., & Lupri, E. (1987). Fathers' participation in work, family life and leisure: A Canadian experience. In C. Lewis & M. O'Brien (Eds.), *Reassessing fatherhood: New observations on fathers and the modern family* (pp. 54–73). London, UK: Sage Publications.

Hoshino-Browne, E., Zanna, A. S., Spencer, S. J., & Zanna, M. P. (2004). Investigating attitudes cross-culturally: A case of cognitive dissonance among East Asians and North Americans. In G. Haddock & G. R. Maio (Eds.), *Contemporary perspectives on the psychology of attitudes* (pp. 375–397). New York, NY: Psychology Press.

Houts, A. C., Cook, T. D., & Shadish, Jr., W. R. (1986). The person-situation debate: A critical multiplist perspective. *Journal of Personality, 54*, 52–105.

Hovland, C. I., Janis, I. L., & Kelley, H. H. (1953). *Communication and persuasion: Psychological studies of opinion change.* New Haven, CT: Yale University Press.

Howard, D., & Madrigal, R. (1990). Who makes the decision: The parent or the child? The perceived influence of parents and children on the purchase of recreation services. *Journal of Leisure Research, 22*, 244–258.

Howe, C. Z., & Qui, Y. (1988). The programming process revisited: Assumptions underlying the needs-based models. *Journal of Park and Recreation Administration, 6*, 14–27.

Howe, N., & Strauss, W. (1997). *The fourth turning: An American prophecy.* New York, NY: Broadway Books.

Howes, C. (1988). Peer interaction of young children. *Monographs of the Society for Research in Child Development, 53*(1).

Hrubes, D., Ajzen, I., & Daigle, J. (2001). Predicting hunting intentions and behavior: An application of the theory of planned behavior. *Leisure Sciences, 23*, 165–178.

Hubbard, J., & Mannell, R. (2001). Testing competing models of the leisure constraint negotiation process in a corporate employee recreation setting. *Leisure Sciences, 23*, 145–163.

Huesmann, L. R., & Miller, L. (1994). Long term effects of repeated exposure to media violence in childhood. In L. R. Huesmann (Ed.), *Aggressive behavior: Current perspectives* (pp. 53–86). New York, NY: Plenum.

Huesmann, L. R., Moise-Titus, J., Podolski, C. L., & Eron, L. D. (2003). Longitudinal relations between children's exposure to TV violence and their aggressive and violent behavior in young adulthood: 1977–1992. *Developmental Psychology, 39*, 201–221.

Hughes, F. P. (1991). *Children, play and development.* Needham Heights, MA: Allyn & Bacon.

Hughes, S., Case, H., Stuempfle, K., & Evans, D. (2003). Personality profiles of Iditasport ultra-marathon participants. *Journal of Applied Sport Psychology, 15*, 256–261.

Huizinga, J. (1955). *Homo ludens: A study of the play element in culture.* Boston, MA: Beacon Press.

Hull, R. B., IV. (1991). Mood as a product of leisure: Causes and consequences. In B. L. Driver, P. J. Brown, & G. L. Peterson (Eds.), *Benefits of leisure* (pp. 249–262). State College, PA: Venture Publishing, Inc.

Hull, R. B., IV., & Michael, S. E. (1995). Nature-based recreation, mood change, and stress restoration. *Leisure Sciences, 17*, 1–14.

Hull, R. B., IV., Michael, S., Walker, G. J., & Roggenbuck, J. (1996). Ebb and flow of brief leisure experiences. *Leisure Sciences, 18*, 299–314.

Hull, R.B., IV., Stewart, W. B., & Yi, R. K. (1992). Experience patterns: Capturing the dynamic nature of recreation experience. *Journal of Leisure Research, 24*, 240–252.

Hull, R. B., IV., William, P. S., & Young, K. Y. (1992). Experience patterns: Capturing the dynamic nature of a recreation experience. *Journal of Leisure Research, 24*, 240–252.

Hultsman, J. T., & Russell, R. V. (1988). Assessing the reliability of the measurement component of Neulinger's paradigm. *Journal of Leisure Research, 20*, 1–9.

Hultsman, W. Z. (1998). The multi-day, competitive leisure event: Examining satisfaction over time. *Journal of Leisure Research, 30*, 472–497.

Hunt, S. (2004). Acting the part: 'living history' as a serious leisure pursuit. *Leisure Studies, 23*, 387–403.

Hunter, P. L., & Whitson, D. J. (1991). Women, leisure and familism: Relationships and isolation in small town Canada. *Leisure Studies, 10*, 219–233.

Hutchinson, S. L., Baldwin, C. K., & Caldwell, L. L. (2003). Differentiating parent practices related to adolescent behavior in the free time context. *Journal of Leisure Research, 35*, 396–422.

Hutchinson, S., L., Baldwin, C., K., & Sae-Sok, O. (2006). Adolescent coping: Exploring adolescents' leisure-based responses to stress. *Leisure Sciences, 28*, 115–131.

Hutchinson, S. L., Loy, D. P., Kleiber, D. A., & Dattilo, J. (2003). Leisure as a coping resource: Variations in coping with traumatic injury and illness. *Leisure Sciences, 25*, 143–161.

Hutchinson, S. L., Unruh, A., King, A., & Wood, S. (2008, May). *Spiritual dimensions of leisure in the context of coping with cancer*. Paper presented at the 12th Canadian Conference on Leisure Research, Montreal, QC (proceedings).

Hutchison, P., & McGill, J. (1992). *Leisure, integration and community*. Concord, ON: Leisurability Publications, Inc.

Hutt, C. (1971). Exploration and play in children. In R. Herron & B. Sutton-Smith (Eds.), *Children's play* (pp. 231–251). New York, NY: John Wiley & Sons.

Hyde, M., Ferrie, J., Higgs, P., Mein, G., & Nazroo, J. (2004). The effects of pre-retirement factors and retirement route on circumstances in retirement: Findings from the Whitehall II study. *Aging & Society, 24*, 279–296.

Hyman, M. (2009). *Until it hurts: America's obsession with youth sports and how it harms our kids*. Boston, MA: Beacon Press.

Ibrahim, H., & Crandall R. (1980). *Leisure: A psychological approach*. Los Angeles, CA: Hwong Publishing.

Iggulden, C., & Iggulden, H. (2007). *The dangerous book for boys*. New York, NY: HarperCollins.

Ignatiev, N. (1995). *How the Irish became White*. New York, NY: Routledge.

Ingham, R. (1986). Psychological contributions to the study of leisure—Part one. *Leisure Studies, 5*, 255–279.

Ingham, R. (1987). Psychological contributions to the study of leisure—Part two. *Leisure Studies, 6*, 1–14.

Irwin, P. N., Gartner, W. C., & Phelps, C. C. (1990). Mexican-American/Anglo cultural differences as recreation style determinants. *Leisure Sciences, 12*, 335–348.

Iso-Ahola, S. E. (1976). On the theoretical link between personality and leisure. *Psychological Reports, 39*, 3–10.

Iso-Ahola, S. E. (1977). Effects of team outcome on children's self-perception: Little League Baseball. *Scandinavian Journal of Psychology, 18*, 38–42.

Iso-Ahola, S. E. (1979a). Basic dimensions of definitions of leisure. *Journal of Leisure Research, 22*, 38–39.

Iso-Ahola, S. E. (1979b). Some social psychological determinants of perceptions of leisure: Preliminary evidence. *Leisure Sciences, 2*, 305–314.

Iso-Ahola, S. E. (1980a). *The social psychology of leisure and recreation.* Dubuque, IA: Wm. C. Brown Company.

Iso-Ahola, S. E. (Ed.) (1980b). *Social psychological perspectives on leisure and recreation.* Springfield, IL: Charles C. Thomas.

Iso-Ahola, S. E. (1980c). A social psychological analysis of Little League Baseball. In S. E. Iso-Ahola (Ed.), *Social psychological perspectives on leisure and recreation* (pp. 171–218). Springfield, IL: Charles C. Thomas.

Iso-Ahola, S. E. (1982). Toward a social psychological theory of tourism motivation: A rejoinder. *Annals of Tourism Research, 12*, 256–262.

Iso-Ahola, S. E. (1983). Towards a social psychology of recreational travel. *Leisure Studies, 2*, 45–56.

Iso-Ahola, S. E. (1986). A theory of substitutability of leisure behavior. *Leisure Sciences, 8*, 367–389.

Iso-Ahola, S. E. (1988). The social psychology of leisure: Past, present, and future research. In L. A. Barnett (Ed.), *Research about leisure: Past, present, and future* (pp. 75–93). Champaign, IL: Sagamore Publishing.

Iso-Ahola, S. E. (1989). Motivation for leisure. In E. L. Jackson & T. L. Burton (Eds.), *Understanding leisure and recreation: Mapping the past, charting the future* (pp. 247–279). State College, PA: Venture Publishing, Inc.

Iso-Ahola, S. E. (1995). The social psychology of leisure: Past, present, and future research. In L. A. Barnett (Ed.), *Research about leisure: Past, present, and future research*, 2nd ed. (pp. 65–96). Champaign, IL: Sagamore Publishing.

Iso-Ahola, S. E. (1999). Motivational foundations of leisure. In E. L. Jackson & T. L. Burton (Eds.), *Leisure studies: Prospects for the twenty-first century* (pp. 35–51). State College, PA: Venture Publishing, Inc.

Iso-Ahola, S. E., & Allen, J. R. (1982). The dynamics of leisure motivation: The effects of outcome on leisure needs. *Research Quarterly For Exercise and Sport, 53*, 141–149.

Iso-Ahola, S. E., & Crowley, E. D. (1991). Adolescent substance abuse and leisure boredom. *Journal of Leisure Research, 23*, 260–271.

Iso-Ahola, S. E., Graefe, A. R., & LaVerde, D. (1989). Perceived competence as a mediator of the relationship between high risk sports participation and self-esteem. *Journal of Leisure Research, 21*, 32–39.

Iso-Ahola, S. E., Jackson, E., & Dunn, E. (1994). Starting, ceasing, and replacing leisure activities over the life-span. *Journal of Leisure Research, 26*, 227–249.

Iso-Ahola, S. E., & Mannell, R. C. (1985). Social and psychological constraints on leisure. In M. G. Wade (Ed.), *Constraints on leisure* (pp. 111–151). Springfield, IL: Charles C. Thomas.

Iso-Ahola, S. E., & Park, C. J. (1996). Leisure-related social support and self-determination as buffers in the stress-illness relationship. *Journal of Leisure Research, 28,* 163–181.

Iso-Ahola, S. E., & Weissinger, E. (1987). Leisure and boredom. *Journal of Social and Clinical Psychology, 5,* 356–364.

Iso-Ahola, S. E., & Weissinger, E. (1990). Perceptions of boredom in leisure: Conceptualization, reliability and validity of the Leisure Boredom Scale. *Journal of Leisure Research, 22,* 1–17.

Iwasaki, Y. (2003). The impact of leisure coping beliefs and strategies on adaptive outcomes. *Leisure Studies, 22,* 93–108.

Iwasaki, Y. (2008). Pathways to meaning-making through leisure in global contexts. *Journal of Leisure Research, 40,* 231–249.

Iwasaki, Y., & Bartlett, J. (2006). Culturally meaningful leisure as a way of coping with stress among Aboriginal individuals with diabetes. *Journal of Leisure Research, 38,* 321–338.

Iwasaki, Y., & Havitz, M. E. (2004). Examining relationships between leisure involvement, psychological commitment, and loyalty to a recreation agency. *Journal of Leisure Research, 36,* 45–72.

Iwasaki, Y., Hitoshi, N., Onda, T., & Bowling, C. (2007). Leisure research in a global world: Time to reverse the Western domination of leisure? *Leisure Sciences, 29,* 113–117.

Iwasaki, Y., MacKay, K., & Mactavish, J. (2005). Gender-based analyses of coping with stress among professional managers: Leisure coping and non-leisure coping. *Journal of Leisure Research, 37,* 1–28.

Iwasaki, Y., MacKay, K., Mactavish, J., Ristock, J., & Bartlett, J. (2006). Voices from the margins: Stress, active living, and leisure as a contributor to coping with stress. *Leisure Sciences. 28,* 163–180.

Iwasaki, Y., & Mannell, R. C. (1999). Situational and personality influences on intrinsically motivated leisure behavior: Interaction effects and cognitive processes. *Leisure Sciences, 21,* 287–306.

Iwasaki, Y., & Mannell, R. C. (2000a). Hierarchical dimensions of leisure stress coping. *Leisure Sciences, 22,* 163–181.

Iwasaki, Y., & Mannell, R. C. (2000b). The effects of leisure beliefs and coping strategies on stress-health relationships: A field study. *Leisure/Loisir, 24*(1–2), 3–57.

Iwasaki, Y., Mannell, R. C., Smale, B. J. A., & Butcher, J. (2002). Short-term longitudinal analysis of leisure coping used by police and emergency response service workers. *Journal of Leisure Research, 34,* 311–339.

Iwasaki, Y., Nishino, H., Onda, T., & Bowling, C. (2007). Leisure research in a global world: Time to reverse the Western domination of leisure? *Leisure Sciences, 29,* 113–117.

Iwasaki, Y., & Ristock, J. (2004). Coping with stress among gays and lesbians: Implications for human development over the lifespan. *World Leisure Journal, 46,* 26–37.

Iwasaki, Y., & Schneider, I. E. (2003). Leisure stress and coping: An evolving area of inquiry. *Leisure Sciences, 25,* 107–113.

Iwasaki, Y., & Smale, B. J. A. (1998). Longitudinal analyses of the relationships among life transitions, chronic health problems, leisure and psychological well-being. *Leisure Science, 20*, 25–52.

Iwasaki, Y., Zuzanek, J., & Mannell, R. (2001). The effects of physically active leisure on stress-health relationships. *Canadian Journal of Public Health, 92*, 214–218.

Iyengar, S., & Lepper, M. (1999). Rethinking the value of choice: A cultural perspective on intrinsic motivation. *Journal of Personality and Social Psychology, 76*, 349–366.

Izard, C. E. (1977). *Human emotions*. New York, NY: Plenum Press.

Jackson, D. N. (1974). *Personality research form manual*. Goshen, NY: Research Psychologists Press.

Jackson, E. L. (1988). Leisure constraints: A survey of past research. *Leisure Sciences, 10*, 203–215.

Jackson, E. L. (1990). Variations in desire to begin a leisure activity: Evidence of antecedent constraints? *Journal of Leisure Research, 22*, 55–70.

Jackson, E. L. (1993). Recognizing patterns of leisure constraints. *Journal of Leisure Research, 25*, 129–149.

Jackson, E. L. (2005). Leisure constraints research: Overview of a developing theme in leisure studies. In E. L. Jackson (Ed.), *Constraints to leisure* (pp. 3–19). State College, PA: Venture Publishing, Inc.

Jackson, E. L., & Burton, T. L. (Eds.). (1989). *Understanding leisure and recreation: Mapping the past, charting the future*. State College, PA: Venture Publishing, Inc.

Jackson, E. L., Crawford, D. W., & Godbey, G. (1992). Negotiation of leisure constraints. *Leisure Sciences, 15*, 1–12.

Jackson, E. L., & Dunn, E. (1988). Integrating ceasing participation with other aspects of leisure behavior. *Journal of Leisure Research, 20*, 31–45.

Jackson, E. L., & Henderson, K. A. (1995). Gender-based analysis of leisure constraints. *Leisure Sciences, 17*, 31–51.

Jackson, E. L., & Rucks, V. C. (1995). Negotiation of leisure constraints by junior-high and high-school students: An exploratory study. *Journal of Leisure Research, 27*, 85–105.

Jackson, E. L., & Walker, G. J. (2006). A cross-cultural comparison of leisure styles and constraints experienced by Chinese and Canadian university students. *Ninth World Leisure Congress Abstracts: Oral and Poster Presentations* (p. 28). Hangzhou, China: World Leisure.

Jackson, S. A. (1992). Athletes in flow: A qualitative investigation of flow states in elite figure skaters. *Journal of Applied Sport Psychology, 4*, 161–180.

Jacob, G. & Schreyer, R. (1980). Conflict in outdoor recreation: A theoretical explanation. *Journal of Leisure Research, 12*, 368–380.

James, K. (2000). 'You can feel them looking at you': The experiences of adolescent girls at swimming. *Journal of Leisure Research, 32*, 262–280.

James, K. (2001). "I just gotta have my own space!": The bedroom as a leisure site for adolescent girls. *Journal of Leisure Research, 33*, 71–91.

James, K., & Embrey, L. (2001). "Anyone could be lurking around!": Constraints on adolescent girls' recreational activities after dark. *World Leisure Journal, 44*, 44–52.

James, T. (1980). Sketch of a moving spirit: Kurt Hahn. *Journal of Experiential Education, 3*, 17–22.

James, W. (1890). The principles of psychology. New York, NY: Henry Holt.

Jamieson, L. M., & Ross, C. M. (2007). Using recreation to curb extremism. *Parks & Recreation,* January, 26–29.

Janke, M., Davey, A., & Kleiber, D. (2006). Modeling change in older adults' leisure activities. *Leisure Sciences, 28*, 285–303.

Janke, M., Nimrod, G., & Kleiber, D. A. (2008a). Leisure patterns and health among recently widowed adults. *Activities, Adaptation and Aging, 32*, 19–39.

Janke, M., Nimrod, G., & Kleiber, D. A. (2008b). Leisure activity and depressive symptoms of widowed and married women in later life. *Journal of Leisure Research, 40*, 250–266.

Janke, M., Nimrod, G., & Kleiber, D. A. (2008c). Reduction in leisure activity and well-being during the transition to widowhood. *Women and Aging, 20*(1/2), 83–98.

Jenkins, C. D., Zyzanski, S., & Rosenman, R. H. (1979). *Jenkins activity survey manual*. New York, NY: The Psychological Corporation.

Jensenscott, R. L. (1993). Counseling to promote retirement adjustment. *Career Development Quarterly, 41*, 246–256.

Jessor, R., Donovan, J. E., & Costa, F. M. (1991). *Beyond adolescence: Problem behaviour and young adult development*. New York, NY: Cambridge University Press.

Johnson, E. & Hood, C. (2008, May). *The essence of a tacit intersection: A heuristic inquiry into nature-based leisure and personal transformation*. Paper presented at the 12th Canadian Conference on Leisure Research, Montreal, QC.

Johnson, J. G., Cohen, P., Smailes, E., Karen, S., & Brook, J. (2002). Television viewing and aggressive behavior during adolescence and adulthood. *Science, 295*, 2468–2471.

Johnson, N. L., Hodges, J. S., & Keller, M. J. (2007). Get moving and keep moving: Motivating older people for participation in LTPA. *Activities, Adaptation, & Aging, 31*(2), 57–71.

Johnson, R. C. A. (1978). Attitudes toward the use of designated versus non-designated urban recreation space. *Leisure Sciences, 1*, 259–269.

Johnston, E., & Johnson, A. (2008). Searching for the second generation of American women psychologists. *History of Psychology, 11*, 40–72.

Jones, C. (2008). Examining interactions between adventure seeking and states of the four channel flow model. *Leisure/Loisir, 32*, 139–162.

Jones, C., Hollenhorst, S., & Perna, F. (2003). An empirical comparison of the four channel flow model and adventure experience paradigm. *Leisure Sciences, 25*, 17.

Jones, C., Hollenhorst, S., Perna, F., & Selin, S. (2000). Validation of the flow theory in an on-site whitewater kayaking setting. *Journal of Leisure Research, 32*, 247–262.

Josselson, R. (1994). Identity and relatedness in the life cycle. In H. A. Bosma, T. L. Graafsma, H. D. Grotevant, & D. J. de Levita (Eds.), *Identity and development*. Thousand Oaks, CA: Sage Publications.

Jung, R. (1967). Leisure in three cultures. *The Elementary School Journal, 67*, 285–295.

Kabanoff, B. (1980). Work and nonwork: A review of models, methods and findings. *Psychological Bulletin, 88*, 60–77.

Kabanoff, B., & O'Brien, G. E. (1986). Stress and the leisure needs and activities of different occupations. *Human Relations, 39*, 903–916.

Kaczynski, A. T., & Henderson, K. A. (2008). Parks and recreation settings and active living: A review of associations with physical activity function and intensity. *Journal of Physical Activity & Health, 5*, 619–632.

Kaiser Family Foundation (2010). *Generation M2: Media in the Lives of 8- to 18-Year-Olds* (http://www.kff.org/entmedia/mh012010pkg.cfm).

Kando, T. M., & Summers, W. C. (1971). The impact of work on leisure: Toward a paradigm and research strategy. *Pacific Sociological Review, July*, 310–327.

Kane, J. E. (1972). *Psychological aspects of physical education and sport*. London, UK: Routledge and Kegan Paul.

Kaplan, S. (1995). The restorative benefits of nature: Towards an integrative framework. *Journal of Environmental Psychology, 15*, 169–182.

Kaplin, R. M., Sallis Jr., J. F., & Patterson, T. L. (1993). *Health and human behavior*. New York, NY: McGraw-Hill.

Karlis, G. (1990). Ethnic maintenance and recreation: A case study. *Journal of Applied Recreation Research, 15*, 85–99.

Kaufman, J. E., McBride, L. G., Hultsman, J. T., & Black, D. R. (1988). Perceptions of leisure and an eating disorder: An exploratory study of bulimia. *Therapeutic Recreation Journal, 22*, 55–63.

Kay, T. (2000). Leisure, gender and family: The influence of social policy. *Journal Leisure Studies, 19*, 247–265.

Kay, T. (2003). Leisure, gender and self in the analysis of family. *World Leisure Journal, 45*, 4–14.

Kay, T. (2007). Fathering through sport. *World Leisure, 49*(2), 69–82.

Keele, S. W., & Hawkins, H. L. (1982). Explorations of individual differences relevant to high level skill. *Journal of Motor Behavior, 14*, 3–23.

Keen, R. (2007). *Time orientation and subjective well-being: A developmental analysis*. Unpublished doctoral dissertation, University of Georgia, Athens, GA.

Kelley, H. H. (1967). Attribution theory in social psychology. In D. Levine (Ed.), *Nebraska Symposium on Motivation* (Vol. 15, pp. 192–241). Lincoln, NE: University of Nebraska Press.

Kelly, J. R. (1972). Work and leisure: A simplified paradigm. *Journal of Leisure Research, 4*, 50–62.

Kelly, J. R. (1973). Three measures of leisure activity: A note on the continued incommensurability of oranges, apples and artichokes. *Journal of Leisure Research, 5*, 56–65.

Kelly, J. R. (1974). Socialization toward leisure: A developmental approach. *Journal of Leisure Research, 6*, 181–193.

Kelly, J. R. (1975). Life styles and leisure choices. *The Family Coordinator, Apr*, 185–190.

Kelly, J. R. (1977). Leisure socialization: Replication and extension. *Journal of Leisure Research, 9*, 121–132.

Kelly, J. R. (1978). A revised paradigm of leisure choices. *Leisure Sciences, 1*, 345–363.

Kelly, J. R. (1983). *Leisure identities and interactions*. London, UK: Allen and Unwin.

Kelly, J. R. (1987a). *Peoria winter: Styles and resources in later life*. Lexington, MA: Heath.

Kelly, J. R. (1987b). *Freedom to be: Toward a new sociology of leisure*. New York, NY: Macmillan.

Kelly, J. R. (1988). History and philosophy of leisure: Past, present, and future directions. In L. A. Barnett (Ed.), *Research about leisure: Past, present, and future* (pp. 19–33). Champaign, IL: Sagamore Publishing.

Kelly, J. R. (1993). Leisure-family research: Old and new issues. *World Leisure and Recreation, 35*, 5–9.

Kelly, J. R. (1996). *Leisure* (3rd ed.). Boston, MA: Allyn & Bacon.

Kelly, J. R. (2009). Work and leisure: A simplified paradigm. *Journal of Leisure Research, 41*, 439–451.

Kelly, J. R., & Masar, S. (1970). *Leisure identities through a life course transition*. Unpublished Paper, University of Illinois at Urbana-Champaign.

Kelly, J. R., & Ross, J. E. (1989). Later-life leisure: Beginning a new agenda. *Leisure Sciences, 11*, 47–59.

Kelly, J. R., Steinkamp, M. W., & Kelly, J. R. (1987). Later-life satisfaction: Does leisure contribute? *Leisure Sciences, 9*, 189–200.

Kelman, H. C. (1967). Human use of human subjects: The problem of deception in social psychology experiments. *Psychological Bulletin, 67*, 1–11.

Kerr, G. N., & Manfredo, M. J. (1991). An attitudinal based model of pricing for recreation services. *Journal of Leisure Research, 23*, 37–50.

Keyes, C. L., & Haidt, J. (2003). *Flourishing: Positive psychology and the life well-lived*. Washington, DC: American Psychological Association.

Kiesler, C., & Kraut, R. (1999). Internet use and the ties that bind. *American Psychologist, 54*, 783–784.

Killinger, B. (1991). *Workaholics: The respectable addicts*. Toronto, ON: Key Porter Books.

Kilpatrick, R., & Trew, K. (1985). Lifestyles and psychological well-being among unemployed men in Northern Ireland. *Journal of Occupational Psychology, 58*, 207–216.

Kim, E., Kleiber, D., & Kropf, N. (2001). Social integration and ethnic preservation in the leisure activities of older Korean immigrants. *Journal of Gerontological Social Work, 36*, 107–109.

Kimball, A. & Freysinger, V. J. (2003). Leisure, stress, and coping: The sport participation of collegiate student-athletes. *Leisure Sciences, 25*, 115–142.

King, A. C., Barr Taylor, C., & Haskell, W. L. (1993). Effects of differing intensities and formats of 12 months of exercise training on psychological outcomes in older adults. *Health Psychology, 12*, 292–300.

King, T. C., Valerius, L., & Collins, J. R. (1998). Ground Zero: A collaborative substance abuse and prevention and intervention program for at risk adolescents. *Journal of Park and Recreation Administration, 16*, 81–94.

Kirchmeyer, C. (1993). Nonwork-to-work spillover: A more balanced view of the experiences and coping of professional women and men. *Sex Roles, 28*, 531–552.

Kirkcaldy, B. D. (1989). Gender and personality determinants of recreational interests. *Studia Psychologica, 30*, 115–127.

Kirkcaldy, B. D., & Cooper, C. L. (1992). Work attitiudes and leisure pursuits: Sex differences. *Personality and individual differences, 12*, 737–745.

Kirkcaldy, B. D., & Furnham, A. (1991). Extraversion, neuroticism, psychoticism and recreational choices. *Personality and Individual Differences, 12*, 737–745.

Kirkcaldy, B. D., Shephard, R. J., & Cooper, C. L. (1993). Relationships between Type-A behaviour, work, and leisure. *Personality and Individual Differences, 15*, 69–74.

Kirshnit, C. E., Ham, M., & Richards, M. H. (1989). The sporting life: Athletic activities during early adolescence. *Journal of Youth and Adolescence, 18*, 601–616.

Kivel, B. (2000). Leisure experience and identity: What difference does difference make? *Journal of Leisure Research, 32*, 79.

Kivel, B., & Kleiber, D. (2000). Leisure in the identity formation of lesbian/gay youth: Personal, but not social. *Leisure Sciences, 22*, 215.

Klausner, W. J. (1968). An experiment in leisure. *Science Journal, 4*, 81–85.

Kleiber, D. A. (1979). Fate control and leisure attitudes. *Leisure Sciences, 2*, 238–248.

Kleiber, D. A. (1985). Motivational reorientation in adulthood and the resource of leisure. *Advances in Motivation and Achievement, 4*, 217–250.

Kleiber, D. A. (1999). *Leisure experience and human development.* New York, NY: Basic Books.

Kleiber,D. A. (2000). The neglect of relaxation. *Journal of Leisure Research, 32*, 82–86.

Kleiber, D. A. (2004). Reflections on the etiology of enduring interest. *Boletin ADOZ: Revista de Estudio de Ocio (Journal of Leisure Studies), 28*, 39–46.

Kleiber, D. A., Brock, S.C., Dattilo, J., Lee, Y., & Caldwell, L. L. (1995). The relevance of leisure in an illness experience: Realities of spinal cord injury. *Journal of Leisure Research, 27*, 283–299.

Kleiber, D. A., Caldwell, L. L., & Shaw, S. M. (1993). Leisure meanings in adolescence. *Loisir et Société/Society and Leisure, 16*, 99–114.

Kleiber, D. A., & Crandall, R. (1981). Leisure and work ethics and locus of control. *Leisure Sciences, 4*, 477–485.

Kleiber, D. A., & Dirkin, G. R. (1985). Intrapersonal constraints to leisure. In M. G. Wade (Ed.), *Constraints on leisure* (pp. 17–42). Springfield, IL: Charles C. Thomas.

Kleiber, D. A., & Hemmer, J. D. (1981). Sex differences in the relationship of locus of control and recreational sport participation. *Sex Roles, 7*, 801–810.

Kleiber, D. A., Hutchinson, S., & Williams, R. (2002). Leisure as a resource in transcending negative life events: Self-protection, self restoration and personal transformation. *Leisure Sciences, 24*, 219–235.

Kleiber, D. A., & Kane, M. J. (1984). Sex differences and the use of leisure as adaptive potentiation. *Loisir et Société/Society and Leisure, 7*, 165–173.

Kleiber, D. A., & Kelly, J. R. (1980). Leisure, socialization, and the life cycle. In S. E. Iso-Ahola (Ed.), *Social psychological perspectives on leisure and recreation* (pp. 91–137). Springfield, IL: Charles C. Thomas.

Kleiber, D. A., & Kirshnit, C. (1991). Sport involvement and identity formation. In L. Diamant (Ed.), *Mind-body maturity: Psychological approaches to sport, exercise and fitness.* New York, NY: Hemisphere.

Kleiber, D. A., Larson, R. W., & Csikszentmihalyi, M. (1986). The experience of leisure in adolescence. *Journal of Leisure Research, 18*, 169–176.

Kleiber, D. A., McGuire, F., Aybar-Damali, B., & Norman, W. (2008). Having more by doing less: The paradox of leisure constraints in later life. *Journal of Leisure Research, 40*, 343–359.

Kleiber, D. A., & Nimrod, G. (2009). "I can't be very sad": Constraints and adaptations in the leisure of a 'learning in retirement' group. *Leisure Studies, 28*, 67–83.

Kleiber, D. A., & Ray, R. O. (1993). Leisure and generativity. In J. Kelley (Ed.), *Activity and aging* (pp. 106–177). Newbury Park, CA: Sage Publications.

Kleiber, D. A., & Rickards, W. H. (1985). Leisure and recreation in adolescence: Limitation and potential. In M. G. Wade (Ed.), *Constraints on leisure* (pp. 289–317). Springfield, IL: Charles C. Thomas.

Kleiber, D. A., & Roberts, G. (1981). The effects of sport experience in the development of social character. *Journal of Sport Psychology, 3,* 114–122.

Kleiber, D. A., Wade, M., & Loucks-Atkinson, A. (2005). The utility of the concept of affordance for leisure research. In E. Jackson (Ed.) *Constraints to leisure.* State College, PA: Venture Publishing, Inc.

Knapp, R., & Hartsoe, C. (1979). *Play for America The National Recreation Association, 1906–1965.* Arlington, VA: National Recreation and Park Association.

Knopf, R. C. (1983). Recreational needs and behavior in natural settings. In I. Altman & J. F. Wohlwill (Eds.), *Behavior and the natural environment* (pp. 205–240). New York, NY: Plenum Press.

Knopp, T. B. (1972). Environmental determinants of recreation behavior. *Journal of Leisure Research, 4*, 129–138.

Kotash, M. (1987). *No kidding: Inside the world of teenage girls.* Toronto, ON: McClelland and Stewart.

Kowalski, R. M., Limber, S. P., & Agatston, P. W. (2008) *Cyber bullying: Bullying in the digital age.* New York, NY: Wiley-Blackwell.

Kubey, R., & Csikszentmihalyi, M. (1990). *Television and the quality of life.* Hilldale, NJ: Lawrence Erlbaum.

Kuentzel, W. F., & Heberlein, T. A. (2008). Life course changes and competing leisure interests as obstacles to boating specialization. *Leisure Sciences, 30*, 143–157.

Kulka, R. A. (1979). Interaction as person-environment fit. In L. R. Kahle (Ed.), *New directions for methodology of behavioral science* (pp. 55–72). San Francisco, CA: Jossey-Bass.

Kyle, G., Absher, J., & Chancellor, C. (2005). Segmenting forest recreationists using their commitment profiles. *Journal of Park and Recreation Administration, 23*, 64–86.

Kyle, G., Absher, J., Norman, W., Hammitt, W., & Jodice, L. (2007). A modified leisure involvement scale. *Leisure Studies, 26*, 399–427.

Kyle, G., & Chick, G. (2002). The social nature of leisure involvement. *Journal of Leisure Research, 34*, 426.

Kyle, G., & Chick, G. (2007). The social construction of a sense of place. *Leisure Sciences, 29*, 209–225.

Kyle, G., Graefe, A., & Manning, R. (2004). Satisfaction derived through leisure involvement and setting attachment. *Leisure/Loisir, 28*(3–4), 277–306.

Kyle, G., Graefe, A., Manning, R., & Bacon, J. (2004). Effect of activity involvement and place attachment on recreationists' perceptions of setting density. *Journal of Leisure Research. 36*, 209–231.

Landreth, G. L. (2002). *Play therapy: The art of the relationship.* (2nd ed.). New York, NY: Brunner-Routledge.

Lang, F. R., Rieckmann, N., & Baltes, M. M. (2002). Adapting to aging losses: Do resources facilitate strategies of selection, compensation, and optimization in everyday functioning. *Journal of Gerontology: Psychological Sciences, 57B*, 501–509.

Langer, E. J. (1975). The illusion of control. *Journal of Personality and Social Psychology, 32*, 311–328.

Langer, E. J. (1983). *The psychology of control.* London, UK: Sage Publications.

LaPage, W. F. (1974). Family camping trends: An eight-year panel study. *Journal of Leisure Research, 6*, 101–112.

Larsen, R. J., Diener, E., & Cropanzano, R. S. (1987). Cognitive operations associated with individual differences in affect intensity. *Journal of Personality and Social Psychology, 53*, 767–774.

Larson, R. W. (1978). Thirty years of research on the subjective well-being of older Americans. *Journal of Gerontology, 33*, 109–125.

Larson, R. W. (1990). The solitary side of life: An examination of the time people spend alone from childhood to old age. *Developmental Review, 10*, 155–183.

Larson, R. W. (1994). Youth organizations, hobbies, and sports as developmental contexts. In R. K. Silbereisen & E. Todt (Eds.), *Adolescence in context: The interplay of family, school, peers, and work in adjustment* (pp. 46–65). New York, NY: Spinger-Verlag.

Larson, R. W. (1995). Secrets in the bedroom: Adolescents' private use of media. *Journal of Youth and Adolescence, 16*, 535–550.

Larson, R. W. (2000). Toward a psychology of positive youth development. *American Psychologist, 55*, 170–183.

Larson, R. W., & Csikszentmihalyi, M. (1983). The experience sampling method. In H. T. Reis (Ed.), *Naturalistic approaches to studying social interaction* (pp. 41–56). San Fransisco, CA: Jossey-Bass.

Larson, R. W., Gillman, S. A., & Richards, M. H. (1997). Divergent experiences of family leisure: Fathers, mothers, and young adolescents. *Journal of Leisure Research, 29*, 78–97.

Larson, R. W., & Kleiber, D. A. (1993a). Structured leisure as a context for the development of attention during adolescence. *Loisir et Société/Society and Leisure, 16*, 77–98.

Larson, R. W., & Kleiber, D. A. (1993b). Daily experience of adolescents. In P. Tolan & B. Cohler (Eds.), *Handbook of clinical research and practice with adolescents* (pp. 125–145). New York, NY: Wiley.

Larson, R. W., Mannell, R. C., & Zuzanek, J. (1986). Daily well-being of older adults with friends and family. *Journal of Psychology and Aging, 1*, 117–126.

Larson, R. W., & Richards, M. W. (1994). *Divergent realities: The emotional lives of mothers, fathers and adolescents.* New York, NY: Basic Books.

Larson, R. W., & Verma, S. (1999). How children and adolescents spend time across the world: Work, play and developmental opportunities. *Psychological Bulletin, 125*, 701–736.

Latane, B., & Darley, J. M. (1970). *The unresponsive bystander: Why doesn't he help?* New York, NY: Appleton-Century-Crofts.

Lawton, M. P. (1975). The Philadelphia Geriatric Center Moral Scale: A revision. *Journal of Gerontology, 30*, 85–89.

Lawton, M. P. (1993). Meanings of activity. In J. Kelly (Ed.), *Activity and aging* (pp. 125–144). Newbury Park, CA: Sage Publications.

Lawton, M. P. (1994). Personality and affective correlates of leisure activity participation by older people. *Journal of Leisure Research, 26*, 138–157.

Lazarus, R. S., & Folkman, S. (1984). *Stress, appraisal, and coping.* New York, NY: Springer.

Leary, M. R. and Atherton, S. C. (1986). Self-efficacy, anxiety, and inhibition in interpersonal encounters. *Journal of Social and Clinical Psychology, 4*, 256–67.

Leckey, P., & Mannell, R. C. (2000). Confidence in personality impressions of others in leisure and work contexts: The role of implicit theories of leisure as expressive behavior. *Leisure/Loisir, 24*, 279–298.

Lee, B., & Shafer, C. S. (2002). The dynamic nature of leisure experience: An application of affect control theory. *Journal of Leisure Research, 34*, 290–310.

Lee, B., Shafer, C. S., & Kang, I. (2005). Examining relationships among perceptions of self, episodic-specific evaluations, and overall satisfaction with a leisure activity. *Leisure Sciences, 27*, 93–109.

Lee, J., & Bean, F. (2004). America's changing color lines: Immigration, race/ethnicity, and multicultural identification. *Annual Review of Sociology, 30*, 221–242.

Lee, R. E. (1972). The social definition of outdoor recreation places. In W. R. Burch, Jr., N. Cheek, & L. Taylor (Eds.), *Social behavior, natural resources, and environment* (pp. 68–84). New York, NY: Harper and Row.

Lee, R. E., & King, A. C. (2003). Discretionary time among older adults: How do physical activity promotion interventions affect sedentary and active behaviors? *Annals of Behavioral Medicine, 25*, 112–119.

Lee, Y., Dattilo, J., & Howard, D. (1994). The complex and dynamic nature of leisure experience. *Journal of Leisure Research, 26*, 195–211.

Lee, Y., & Halberg, K. J. (1989). An exploratory study of college students' perception of freedom in leisure and shyness. *Leisure Sciences, 11*, 217–228.

Lee, Y., & McCormick, B. (2006). Examining the role of self-monitoring and social leisure in the life quality of individuals with spinal cord injury. *Journal of Leisure Research, 38,* 1–19.

Lefcourt, H. M. (1973). The function of the illusions of control and freedom. *American Psychologist, 28,* 417–425.

Lefcourt, H. M. (1976). *Locus of control.* New York, NY: Wiley.

Lefcourt, H. M. (1982). *Locus of control: Critical trends in theory and research* (2nd ed.). Hillsdale, NJ: Erlbaum.

Lefrancois, R., Leclerc, G., Dube, M., Hamel, S., & Gaulin, P. (2001). Valued activities of everyday life among the very old: a one-year trend. *Activities, Adaptation, and Aging, 25*(3&4), 19–34.

Lepper, M. R., & Greene, D. (1979). *The hidden costs of rewards.* New York, NY: Wiley.

Lepper, M. R., Greene, D., & Nisbett, R. E. (1973). Undermining children's intrinsic interest with extrinsic reward: A test of the "overjustification" hypothesis. *Journal of Personality and Social Psychology, 28,* 129–137.

Lerner, M. (1980). *The justice motive.* New York, NY: Plenum Press.

Lerner, R., & Busch-Rossnagel, N. (1981). *Individuals as producers of their own development.* New York, NY: Academic Press.

Lever, J. (1976). Sex differences in the games children play. *Social Problems, 23,* 478–487.

Levinson, D., Darrow, C., Klein, F., Levinson, M., & McKee, B. (1978). *The seasons of a man's life.* New York, NY: Alfred A. Knopf.

Lewin, K. (1935). *Dynamic theory of personality.* New York, NY: McGraw-Hill.

Lewin, K. (1947). Group decision and social change. In T. M. Newcomb & E. L. Hartley (Eds.), *Readings in social psychology* (pp. 330–344). New York, NY: Henry Holt & Co.

Lewinsohn, P. M., & Graf, M. (1973). Pleasant activities and depression. *Journal of Consulting and Clinical Psychology, 41,* 261–268.

Lewis, S. (2003).The integration of paid work and the rest of life: Is post-industrial work the new leisure? *Leisure Studies, 22,* 343–355.

Li, C., Chick, G., Zinn, H., Absher, J., & Graefe, A. (2007). Ethnicity as a variable in leisure research. *Journal of Leisure Research, 39,* 514–545.

Lieberman, J. N. (1977). *Playfulness: Its relationship to imagination and creativity.* New York, NY: Academic Press.

Likert, R. (1932). A technique for the measurement of attitudes. *Archives of Psychology, 140,* 1–55.

Lincoln, S. (2005). Feeling the noise: Teenagers, bedrooms, and music. *Leisure Studies, 24,* 399–414.

Linder, S. (1971). *The harried leisure class.* New York, NY: Academic Press.

Lindlof, T. R., & Taylor, B. C. (2002). *Qualitative communication research methods* (2nd ed.). Thousand Oaks, CA: Sage Publications.

Linville, P. W. (1987). Self-complexity as a cognitive buffer against stress-related illness and depression. *Journal of Personality and Social Psychology, 52,* 663–676.

Little, D. E. (2002). Women and adventure recreation: Reconstructing leisure constraints and adventure experiences to negotiate continuing participation. *Journal of Leisure Research, 34*, 157–178.

Liu, H., Yeh, C-K., Chick, G.E., & Zinn, H. (2008). An exploration of meanings of leisure: A Chinese perspective. *Leisure Sciences, 30*, 482–488.

Livengood, J. S., & Stodolska, M. (2004). The effects of discrimination and constraints negotiation on leisure behavior of American Muslims in the Post-September 11 America. *Journal of Leisure Research, 36*, 183–208.

Lobo, F. (1996). Coping with bulk unobligated time: The case of unemployment. *Society and Leisure, 19*, 377–413.

Lobo, F. (2002). *Leisure, family and lifestyle: Unemployed young people.* Jaipur, India: Rawat Publications.

Loflin, & Musig (2005). *Juggling elephants: Balancing roles and responsibilities in your daily life.* New York, NY: Penguin Group.

London, M., Crandall, R., & Fitzgibbons, D. (1977). The psychological structure of leisure: Activities, needs, people. *Journal of Leisure Research, 9*, 252–263.

London, M., Crandall, R., & Seals, G. W. (1977). The contribution of job and leisure satisfaction to quality of life. *Journal of Applied Psychology, 62*, 328–334.

Long, J. (1987). Continuity as a basis for change: Leisure and male retirement. *Leisure Studies, 6*, 55–70.

Lopata, H. J. (1967). *Widowhood in an American city.* Cambridge, MA: Schenkman Publishing.

Lopata, H. J. (1993). Widows: Social integration and activity. In J. R. Kelly (Ed.), *Activity and aging* (pp. 99–105). Newbury Park, CA: Sage Publications.

Lopez, S. J. (Ed.). (2008). *Encyclopedia of positive psychology.* New York, NY: Wiley.

Loucks-Atkinson, A., & Mannell, R. C. (2007). The role of self-efficacy in the constraints negotiation process: The case of individuals with Fibromyalgia Syndrome. *Leisure Sciences, 29*, 19–36.

Lounsbury, J. W., Gordon, S. R., Bergermaier, R. L., & Francesco, A. M. (1982). Work and nonwork sources of satisfaction in relation to employee intention to turnover. *Journal of Leisure Research, 14*, 285–294.

Lounsbury, J. W., & Hoopes, L. L. (1986). A vacation from work: Changes in work and nonwork outcomes. *Journal of Applied Psychology, 71*, 392–401.

Lounsbury, J. W., & Hoopes, L. L. (1985). An investigation of factors associated with vacation satisfaction. *Journal of Leisure Research, 17*, 1–13.

Lounsbury, J. W., & Hoopes, L. L. (1988). Five-year stability of leisure activity and motivation factors. *Journal of Leisure Research, 20*, 118–134.

Lounsbury, J. W., & Polik, J. R. (1992). Leisure needs and vacation satisfaction. *Leisure Sciences, 14*, 105–119.

Louv, R. (2005). *Last child in the woods: Saving our children from nature-deficit disorder.* Chapel Hill, NC: Algonquin Books.

Loy, D. P., Dattilo, J., & Kleiber, D. A. (2003). Exploring the influence of leisure on adjustment: development of the leisure and spinal cord injury adjustment model. *Leisure Sciences, 25*, 231–255.

Lundberg, G., Komarovsky, M., & McInerny, M. A. (1934). *Leisure: A suburban study*. New York, NY: Columbia University Press.

Lynd, R. S., & Lynd, H. M. (1929). *Middletown: A study in American culture*. New York, NY: Harcourt, Brace, and World.

Lynd, R. S., & Lynd, H. M. (1937). *Middletown in transition*. New York, NY: Harcourt, Brace, and World.

Lyons, K., & Dionigi, R. (2007). Transcending emotional community: A qualitative examination of older adults and masters' sports participation. *Leisure Sciences, 29*, 375–389.

MacCannell, D. (1973). Staged authenticity: Arrangements of social space in tourist settings. *The American Journal of Sociology, 79*, 589–603.

MacCannell, D. (1976). *The tourist: A new theory of the leisure class*. New York, NY: Schocken.

MacCannell, D. (1992). *Empty meeting grounds: The tourist papers*. London, UK: Routledge.

MacCannell, D. (2001). Tourist agency. *Tourist Studies, 1*, 23–38.

Machlowitz, M. (1980). *Workaholics: Living with them, working with them*. Reading, MA: Addison-Wesley.

MacNeil, R. D. (1995). Leisure programs and services for older adults. In L. A. Barnett (Ed.), *Research about leisure: Past, present, and future* (2nd ed., pp. 149–176). Champaign, IL: Sagamore Publishing.

MacNeil, R. D., & Teague, M. (1987). *Aging and leisure: Vitality in later life*. Englewood Cliffs, NJ: Prentice-Hall.

Mactavish, J. B., & Schleien, S. (2004). Re-injecting spontaneity and balance in family life: Parents' perspective on recreation in families that include children with developmental disabilities. *Journal of Intellectual Disability Research, 48*, 123–141.

Madden, T. J., Ellen, P. S., & Ajzen, I. (1992). A comparison of the theory of planned behavior and the theory of reasoned action. *Personality and Social Psychology Bulletin, 18*, 3–9.

Madrigal, R. (2006). Measuring the multidimensional nature of sporting event performance consumption. *Journal of Leisure Research, 38*, 267–292.

Maier, S. F., & Seligman, M. E. P. (1976). Learned helplessness: Theory and evidence. *Journal of Experimental Psychology: General, 105*, 3–46.

Major, W. F. (1994). *Serious running: An interpretive analysis*. Unpublished doctoral dissertation, University of Georgia, Athens, GA.

Major, W. F. (2001). The benefits and costs or serious running. *World Leisure Journal, 43*(2), 12–25.

Mak, A., Wong, K., & Chang, R. (2009). Health or self-indulgence? The motivations and characteristics of spa-goers. *International Journal of Tourism Research, 11*, 185–199.

Mallett, C., Kawabata, M., Newcombe, P., Otero-Forero, A., & Jackson, S. (2007). Sport motivation scale-6 (SMS-6): A revised six-factor sport motivation scale. *Psychology of Sport and Exercise, 8*, 600–614.

Maloney, T. L., & Petrie, B. M. (1972). Professionalization of attitude toward play among Canadian school pupils as a function of sex, grade, and athletic participation. *Journal of Leisure Research, 4*, 184–195.

Malouff, J., Thorsteinsson, E., Rooke, S., & Schutte, N. (2007). Alcohol involvement and the five factor model of personality: A meta-analysis. *Journal of Drug Education, 37*, 277–294.

Malouff, J., Thorsteinsson, E., & Schutte, N. (2006). Smoking and the five-factor model of personality: A meta-analysis. *Journal of Drug Education, 36,* 47–58. meta-analytic update. *Personality and Individual Differences, 18*, 491–502.

Manfredo, M. J. (1992). *Influencing human behavior: Theory and applications in recreation, tourism, and natural resources management.* Champaign, IL: Sagamore Press.

Manfredo, M. J., Driver, B., & Tarrant, M. (1996). Measuring leisure motivation: A meta-analysis of the Recreation Experience Preference scales. *Journal of Leisure Research, 28*, 188–213.

Mannell, R. C. (1979). A conceptual and experimental basis for research in the psychology of leisure. *Loisir et Société/Society and Leisure, 2*, 179–194.

Mannell, R. C. (1980). Social psychological techniques and strategies for studying leisure experiences. In S. E. Iso-Ahola (Ed.), *Social psychological perspectives on leisure and recreation* (pp. 62–88). Springfield, IL: Charles C. Thomas.

Mannell, R. C. (1984a). A psychology for leisure research. *Loisir et Société/Society and Leisure, 7*, 13–21.

Mannell, R. C. (1984b). Personality in leisure theory: The self-as-entertainment construct. *Loisir et Société/Society and Leisure, 7*, 229–242.

Mannell, R. C. (1985). Reliability and validity of a leisure-specific personality measure: The self-as-entertainment construct. In *Abstracts from the 1985 Symposium on Leisure Research.* Alexandria, VA: National Recreation and Parks Association.

Mannell, R. C. (1986). Problems, progress and usefulness of theory and research on leisure. In *Abstracts from the 1986 Symposium on Leisure Research.* Alexandria, VA: National Recreation and Park Association.

Mannell, R. C. (1989). Leisure satisfaction. In E. L. Jackson & T. L. Burton (Eds.), *Understanding leisure and recreation: Mapping the past, charting the future* (pp. 281–301). State College, PA: Venture Publishing, Inc.

Mannell, R. C. (1990). On the joys of research. In D. Dustin (Ed.), *Beyond promotion and tenure: On being a professor* (pp. 47–61). San Diego, CA: San Diego State University Institute for Leisure Behavior.

Mannell, R. C. (1991). The "psychologization" of leisure services. In T. L. Goodale & P. A. Witt (Eds.), *Recreation and leisure: Issues in an era of change* (3rd ed., pp. 429–439). State College, PA: Venture Publishing, Inc.

Mannell, R. C. (1993). High investment activity and life satisfaction among older adults: Committed, serious leisure and flow activities. In J. R. Kelly (Ed.), *Activity and aging* (pp. 125–145). Newbury Park, CA: Sage Publications.

Mannell, R. C. (1994). Constraints, leisure participation, and well-being among older adults. In D. M. Compton & S. E. Iso-Ahola (Eds.), *Leisure and mental health* (Vol. 1, pp. 79–97). Salt Lake City, UT: Family Development Resources, Inc.

Mannell, R. C. (1996). Approaches in the social and behavioral sciences to the systematic study of hard-to-define human values and experiences. In B. L. Driver, D. Dustin, T. Baltic, G. Elsner, & G. Peterson (Eds.), *Nature and the human spirit: Toward an expanded land management ethic.* State College, PA: Venture Publishing, Inc.

Mannell, R. C. (1999). Leisure experience and satisfaction. In E. L. Jackson, & T. L. Burton (Eds.), *Leisure studies: Prospects for the twenty-first century* (pp. 235–251). State College, PA: Venture Publishing, Inc.

Mannell, R. C. (2003). Free time. In J. M. Jenkins, & J. J. Pigram (Eds.), *Encyclopedia of leisure and outdoor recreation* (pp. 189–191). London, UK: Routledge.

Mannell, R. C. (2005). Evolution of cross-cultural analysis in the study of leisure: Commentary on "Culture, self-construal, and leisure theory and practice." *Journal of Leisure Research, 37,* 100–105.

Mannell, R. C. (2007). Health, well-being and leisure. *World Leisure Journal, 49,* 114–128.

Mannell, R. C., & Backman, S. J. (1979). The effects of perceived freedom of choice and locus of control on transient "leisure" experiences. In E. M. Avedon, M. Lelevre, & T. Stewart (Eds.), *Contemporary leisure research.* Waterloo, ON: Ontario Research Council on Leisure.

Mannell, R. C., & Bradley, W. (1986). Does greater freedom always lead to greater leisure? Testing a person x environment model of freedom and leisure. *Journal of Leisure Research, 18,* 215–230.

Mannell, R. C., & Dupuis, S. (1994). Leisure and productive activity. In M. P. Lawton, and J. Teresi (Eds.), *Annual review of gerontology and geriatrics* (Vol. 14, pp. 125–141). New York, NY: Springer.

Mannell, R. C., & Dupuis, S. (1996). Life satisfaction. In J. E. Birren (Ed.), *Encyclopedia of gerontology:* (Vol. 1, pp. L6:1–6). New York, NY: Academic Press.

Mannell, R. C., & Dupuis, S. (2007). Life satisfaction. In J. E. Birren (Ed.), *Encyclopedia of gerontology* (Vol. 2, 2nd ed., pp. 73–79). Oxford, UK: Academic Press.

Mannell, R. C., & Iso-Ahola, S. E. (1987). Psychological nature of leisure and tourism experience. *Annals of Tourism Research, 14,* 314–331.

Mannell, R. C., & Iwasaki, Y. (2005). Advancing quantitative research on social cognitive theories of the constraint-negotiation process. In E. Jackson (Ed.), *Constraints to leisure* (pp. 261–275). State College, PA: Venture Publishing, Inc.

Mannell, R. C., Kaczynski, A. T., & Aronson, R. M. (2005). Adolescent participation and flow experience in physically active leisure and electronic media activities: Testing the displacement hypothesis. *Loisir et Société/Society and Leisure, 28,* 653–675.

Mannell, R. C. & Kleiber, D. A. (1997). *A social psychology of leisure.* State College, PA: Venture Publishing, Inc.

Mannell, R. C., Kleiber, D. A., & Staempfli, M. (2006), Psychology and social psychology and the study of leisure. In C. Rojek, S. Shaw, & T. Veal (Eds.), *Handbook of leisure studies.* (pp. 109–124) London, UK: Palgrave Macmillan.

Mannell, R.C., & Loucks-Atkinson, A. (2005). Why don't people do what's "good" for them? Comparing the psychologies of non-participation in leisure, health and exercise behaviors. In E. Jackson (Ed.), *Constraints to leisure* (pp. 221–232). State College, PA: Venture Publishing, Inc.

Mannell, R. C., & McMahon, L. (1982). Humor as play: Its relationship to psychological well-being during the course of a day. *Leisure Sciences, 5*, 143–155.

Mannell, R. C., & Reid, D. (1996). *The impact of changes in the workplace on employed and unemployed workers: Phase three of the "Changing Patterns of Work and Leisure Study."* Waterloo, ON: University of Waterloo.

Mannell, R. C., & Reid, D. G. (1999). Work and leisure. In E. L. Jackson, & T. L. Burton (Eds.), *Leisure studies: Prospects for the twenty-first century* (pp. 151–165). State College, PA: Venture Publishing, Inc.

Mannell, R. C., & Stynes, D. J. (1991). A retrospective: The benefits of leisure. In B. L. Driver, P. J. Brown, & G. L. Peterson (Eds.), *Benefits of leisure* (pp. 461–473). State College, PA: Venture Publishing, Inc.

Mannell, R. C., & Zuzanek, J. (1991). The nature and variability of leisure constraints in daily life: The case of the physically active leisure of older adults. *Leisure Sciences, 13*, 337–351.

Mannell, R. C., & Zuzanek, J. (1995). Married with children: Family leisure in daily life and satisfaction with family life. In *Symposium on Leisure Research* (p. 16). Arlington, VA: National Recreation and Park Association.

Mannell, R. C., Zuzanek, J., & Larson, R. W. (1988). Leisure states and "flow" experiences: Testing perceived freedom and intrinsic motivation hypotheses. *Journal of Leisure Research, 20*, 289–304.

Manning, R. E. (1999). *Studies in outdoor recreation: A review and synthesis of the social science literature in outdoor recreation.* Covallis, OR: Oregon State University Press.

Mansfeld, Y. (1992). From motivation to actual travel. *Annals of Tourism Research, 19*, 399–419.

Marcia, J. E. (1980). Identity in adolescence. In J. Adelson (Ed.), *Handbook of adolescent psychology.* New York, NY: Wiley

Marcuse, H. (1964). *One-dimensional man.* Boston, MA: Beacon Press.

Markus, H. R., & Kitayama, S. (1991). Culture and the self: Implications for cognition, emotion, and motivation. *Psychological Review, 98*, 224–253.

Markus, H. R., & Nurius, P. (1986). Possible selves. *American Psychologist, 41*, 954–969.

Martin, W. S., & Myrick, F. L. (1976). Personality and leisure time activities. *Research Quarterly, 47*, 246–253.

Martin, L., & Tesser, A. (1996). Some ruminative thoughts. In R. S. Wyer (Ed.), *Advances in social cognition* (Vol. 9, pp. 1–47). Hillsdale, NJ: Erlbaum.

Marx, K. (1970). *The economic and philosophical manuscripts of 1844.* London, UK: Lawrence and Wishart.

Maslow, A. H. (1954). *Motivation and personality* (2nd ed.). New York, NY: Harper and Row.

Maslow, A. H. (1968). *Toward a psychology of being* (2nd ed.). Toronto, ON: Van Nos Reinhold.

Maslow, A. H. (1970). *Motivation and personality* (2nd ed.). New York, NY: Harper & Row.

Matalon, B. (1999). The individual and the social: Some reflections on the range and limits of social psychology. *Psychologie Francaise, 44*, 221–226.

Matute, H., Vadillo, M., Vegas, S., & Blanco, F. (2007). Illusion of control in internet users and college students. *CyberPsychology & Behavior, 10*, 176–181.

Maughan, M., & Ellis, G. D. (1991). Effects of efficacy information during recreation participation on efficacy judgments of depressed adolescents. *Therapeutic Recreation Journal, 25*, 51–59.

May, R. (1981). *Freedom and destiny*. New York, NY: W. W. Norton.

Maynard, S. S., & Kleiber, D. A. (2005). Using leisure services to build social capital in later life: Classical traditions, contemporary realities, and emerging possibilities. *Journal of Leisure Research, 37*(4), 475–493.

McAdams, D. P. (1997). The case for unity in the (post)modern self: A modest proposal. In R. D. Ashmore & L. Jussim (Eds.), *Self and identity: Fundamental issues*. New York, NY: Oxford University Press.

McArthur, L. Z., & Baron, R. M. (1983). Toward an ecological theory of social perception. *Psychological Review, 90*, 215–238.

McAuley, E., & Rowney, T. (1990). Exercise behavior and intentions: The mediating role of self-efficacy cognitions. In L. VanderVelden & J. H. Humphrey (Eds.), *Psychology and sociology of sport* (Vol. 2, pp. 3–15). New York, NY: AMS Press.

McCarville, R. E., Driver, B. L., & Crompton, J. L. (1992). Persuasive communication and the pricing of public leisure services. In M. J. Manfredo (Ed.), *Influencing human behavior: Theory and applications in recreation, tourism, and natural resources management* (pp. 263–291). Champaign, IL: Sagamore Publishing.

McCormick, B. (1991). Self-experience as leisure constraint: The case of Alcoholics Anonymous. *Journal of Leisure Research, 23*, 345–362.

McCrae, R. R., & Costa, P. T. (1987). Validation of the five-factor model of personality across instruments and observers. *Journal of Personality and Social Psychology, 52*, 81–90.

McCrae, R. R., & Costa, P. T. (1999). A five-factor theory of personality. In L. A. Pervin & O. P. John (Eds.), *Handbook of personality: Theory and research*. (2nd ed., pp. 139–153). New York, NY: Academic Press.

McCrae, R. R., & John, O. P. (1992). An introduction to the five-factor model and its application. *Journal of Personality, 60*, 175–215.

McCullough, L. S. (1993). Leisure themes in international advertising: A content analysis. *Journal of Leisure Research, 25*, 380–388.

McDaniels, C. (1990). *The changing workplace: Career counseling strategies for the 1990s and beyond*. San Francisco, CA: Jossey-Bass.

McDougall, W. (1908). *An introduction to social psychology*. London, UK: Methuen.

McFarlane, B. L. (1994). Specialization and motivations of birdwatchers. *Wildlife Society Bulletin, 22*, 361–370.

McFarlane, B. L. (2001). Comments on recreational specialization: A critical look at the construct. *Journal of Leisure Research, 33*, 348–350.

McGuire, F. A. (1985). Constraints in later life. In M. G. Wade (Ed.), *Constraints on leisure* (pp. 335–353). Springfield, IL: Charles C. Thomas.

McGuire, F. A., & Dottavio, F. (1987). Outdoor recreation participation across the lifespan: Abandonment, continuity, or liberation. *International Journal of Aging and Human Development, 24*, 87–99.

McGuire, F. A., Dottavio, F. D., & O'Leary, J. T. (1987). The relationship of early life experiences to later life leisure involvement. *Leisure Sciences, 9*, 251–257.

McGuire, F. A., & Norman, W. (2005). The role of constraints in successful aging: Inhibiting or enabling? In E. L. Jackson (Ed.), *Constraints to leisure* (pp. 89–101). State College, PA: Venture Publishing, Inc.

McGuire, F. A., O'Leary, J. T., Yeh, C. K., & Dottavio, F. D. (1989). Integrating ceasing participation with other aspects of leisure behavior: A replication and extension. *Journal of Leisure Research, 21,* 316–326.

McIntosh, R. W., & Goeldner, C. R. (1990) *Tourism: Principles, practices, philosophies* (6th ed.). New York, NY: Wiley.

McIntyre, N. (1989). The personal meaning of participation: Enduring involvement. *Journal of Leisure Research,* 21, 167–179.

McIntyre, N., & Pigram, J. J. (1992). Recreation specialization reexamined: The case of vehicle-based campers. *Leisure Sciences, 14*, 3–15.

McIntyre, N., & Roggenbuck, J. (1998). Nature/person transactions during an outdoor adventure experience: A multiphasic analysis. *Journal of Leisure Research, 30*, 401–422.

McKay, S. (1993). Research findings related to the potential of recreation in delinquency intervention. *Trends, 30*, 27–30.

McKenna, J., & Thew, M. (2008). Getting the balance right: Managing work-home conflict. In M. Thew, & J. McKenna (Eds.), *Lifestyle management in health and social care* (pp. 57–83). Malden, MA: Blackwell Publishing.

McKenna, S. P., & Fryer, D. M. (1984). Perceived health during lay-off and early unemployment. *Occupational Health, 36*, 201–206.

McKenney, P., Budbill, N. W., & Roberts, N. S. (2008). Girls' outdoor adventure programs: History, theory, & practice. In K. Warren, D. Mitten, & D. A. Loeffler. (Eds.), *Theory and Practice of Experiential Education.* Boulder, CO: Association for Experiential Education.

McLeod, D. I. (1983). *Building character in the American boy: The Boy Scouts, YMCA, and their forerunners, 1870–1920.* Madison, WI: University of Wisconsin Press.

McPherson, B. D. (1983). Socialization into and through sport involvement. In W. W. Widemeyer (Ed.), *Physical activity and the social sciences* (pp. 190–213). Ithaca, NY: Mouvement Publications.

McPherson, B. D. (1990). *Aging as a social process.* Toronto, ON: Butterworth.

McPherson, B. D. (1991). Aging and leisure benefits: A life cycle perspective. In B. L. Driver, P. J. Brown, & G. L. Peterson (Eds.), *Benefits of leisure* (pp. 423–430). State College, PA: Venture Publishing, Inc.

Mead, G. H. (1934). *Mind, self, and society.* Chicago, IL: University of Chicago Press.

Medrich, E., Roizen, J., Rubin, V., & Buckley, S. (1982). *The serious business of growing up: A study of children's lives outside of school.* Berkeley, CA: University of California Press.

Mehrabian, A. (1976). *Public places and private spaces: The psychology of work, play, and living environments*. New York, NY: Basic Books.

Meir, E. I., & Melamed, S. (1986). The accumulation of person-environment congruences and well-being. *Journal of Occupational Behavior, 7,* 315–323.

Meir, E. I., Melamed, S., & Abu-Freha, A. (1990). Vocational, avocational, and skill utilization congruences and their relationship with well-being in two cultures. *Journal of Vocational Behavior, 36,* 153–165.

Meissner, M. (1970). The long arm of the job: A study of work and leisure. *Industrial Relations, 10,* 239–260.

Melamed, S., & Meir, E. I. (1981). The relationship between interests-job incongruity and selection of avocational activity. *Journal of Vocational Behavior, 18,* 310–325.

Melamed, S., Meir, E. I., & Samson, A. (1995). The benefits of personality-leisure congruence: Evidence and implications. *Journal of Leisure Research, 27,* 25–40.

Menec, V. H. (2003). The relation between everyday activities and successful aging: A 6-year longitudinal study. *Journal of Gerontology, 58,* 74–82.

Mercer, D. (1973). The concept of recreational need. *Journal of Leisure Research, 5,* 37–50.

Metheny, E. (1967). *Connotations of movement in sport and dance.* Dubuque, IA: William C. Brown.

Metheny, E. (1976) Symbolic forms of movement: The feminine image in sport. In M. Hart (Ed.), *Sport in the sociocultural process* (pp. 227–290). Dubuque, IA: William C. Brown.

Meyersohn, R. (1981). *Tourism as a socio-cultural phenomenon: Research perspectives.* Waterloo, ON: OTIUM Publications, Research Group on Leisure and Cultural Development, University of Waterloo.

Michelson, W. (1999). Time pressure and human agency in home-based employment. *Loisir et Société/Society and Leisure, 21,* 455–472.

Milgram, S. (1963). Behavioral study of obedience. *Journal of Abnormal and Social Psychology, 67,* 371–378.

Milgram, S. (1965). Some conditions of obedience and disobedience to authority. *Human Relations, 18,* 57–76.

Miller, C., & Graefe, A. (2000). Degree and range of specialization across related hunting activities. *Leisure Sciences, 22,* 195–207.

Miller, S. J. (1965). The social dilemma of the aging leisure participant. In A. M. Rose & W. Peterson (Eds.), *Older people and their social worlds* (pp. 77–92). Philadelphia, PA: F. A. Davis Company.

Mischel, W. (1977). On the future of personality measurement. *American Psychologist, 32,* 246–254.

Mitas, O., Qian, X., & Yarnal, C. (2008). *"I've got my joy back:" Positive emotions in older women's leisure.* Paper presented at the 12th Canadian Conference on Leisure Research, Montreal.

Mitchell, G. J., Jonas-Simpson, C., & Dupuis, S. L. (2006). *I'm Still Here* (DVD) *and a teaching-learning guide to understanding living with dementia through the medium of the arts.* Waterloo, ON: Murray Alzheimer Research and Education Program.

Mitchell, R. G. (1983). *Mountain experience: The psychology and sociology of adventure.* Chicago, IL: The University of Chicago Press.

Mobily, K. E. (1989). Meanings of recreation and leisure among adolescents. *Leisure Studies, 8*, 11–23.

Mobily, K. E., Lemke, J. H., Ostiguy, L. J., Woodard, R. J., Griffee, T. J., & Pickens, C. C. (1993). Leisure repertoire in the sample of mid-western elderly: The case for exercise. *Journal of Leisure Research, 25*, 84–99.

Moghaddam, F. M. (1987). Psychology in the three worlds: As reflected by the crisis in social psychology and the move toward indigenous third-world psychology. *American Psychologist, 42*, 912–920.

Monat, A., & Lazarus, R. (1977). Stress and coping: Some current issues and controversies. In A. Monat & R. Lazarus (Eds.), *Stress and coping: An anthology* (pp. 1–11). New York, NY: Columbia University Press.

Moneta, G. (2004). The flow model of intrinsic motivation in Chinese: Cultural and personal moderators. *Journal of Happiness Studies, 5*, 181–217.

Monson, T. C., Hesley, J. W., & Chernick, L. (1982). Specifying when personality can and cannot predict behavior: An alternative to abandoning the attempt to predict single-act criteria. *Journal of Personality and Social Psychology, 43*, 385–399.

Montada, L., & Lerner, M. (1996). *Current societal concerns about justice.* New York, NY: Plenum Press.

Montessorri, M. (1964). *The Montessori method.* New York, NY: Shocken Books.

Montgomery, K. C. (1954). The role of exploratory drive in learning. *Journal of Comparative and Physiological Psychology, 47*, 60–64.

Moore, O., & Anderson, A. (1969). Some principles for the design of clarifying educational environments. In D. Goslin (Ed.), *Handbook of socialization theory and research.* New York, NY: Rand McNally.

More, T. A., & Payne, B. R. (1978). Affective responses to natural areas near cities. *Journal of Leisure Research, 10*, 7–12.

Moriarity, T. (1975). Crime, commitment, and the responsive bystander: Two field experiments. *Journal of Personality and Social Psychology, 31*, 370–376.

Morrow-Howell, N., Hinterlong, J., Rosario, P. A., & Tang, F. (2003). Effects of volunteering on the well-being of older adults. *Journal of Gerontology, Social Sciences, 58B*, S137–S145.

Moscardo, G. M., & Pearce, P. L. (1986). Historic theme parks: An Australian experience in authenticity. *Annals of Tourism Research, 13*, 467–479.

Moscovici, S., & Zavalloni, M. (1969). The group as a polarizer of attitudes. *Journal of Personality and Social Psychology, 12*, 125–135.

Moss, M. S., & Lawton, M. P. (1982). Time budgets of older people: A window on four life-styles. *Journal of Gerontology, 37*, 115–123.

Moss, W. T., & Lamphear, S. C. (1970). Substitutability of recreational activities in meeting stated needs and drives of the visitor. *Environmental Education, 1*, 129–131.

Muir, D. E. (1991). Club tennis: A case study in taking leisure very seriously. *Sociology of Sport Journal, 8*, 70–78.

Munson, W. W. (1991). Juvenile delinquency as a societal problem and social disability: The therapeutic recreator's role as ecological change agent. *Therapeutic Recreation Journal, 25*, 19–30.

Munson, W. W. (1993). Perceived freedom in leisure and career salience in adolescence. *Journal of Leisure Research, 25*, 305–314.

Murphy, H. (2003) Exploring leisure and psychological health and wellbeing: Some problematic issues in the case of Northern Ireland. *Leisure Studies, 22*, 17–36.

Murray, C., & Nakajima, I. (1999). The leisure motivation of Japanese managers: A research note on scale development. *Leisure Studies, 18*, 57–65.

Murray, H. A. (1938). *Explorations and personality.* New York, NY: Oxford University Press.

Musick, M. A., & Wilson, J. (2003). Volunteering and depression: The role of psychological and social resources in different age groups. *Social Science and Medicine, 56*, 259–269.

Myrtek, M. (1995). Type A behavior pattern, personality factors, disease, and physiological reactivity: A meta-analytic update. *Personality and Individual Differences, 18*, 491–502.

Near, J., Rice, R., & Hunt, R. (1978). Work and extra-work correlates of life and job satisfaction. *Academy of Management Journal, 21*, 248–264.

Neugarten, B. L. (1977). Personality and aging. In J. Birren & K. W. Schaie (Eds.), *Handbook of the psychology of aging* (pp. 626–649). New York, NY: Van Nostrand Reinhold.

Neugarten, B. L., Havighurst, R. J., & Tobin, S. S. (1961). The measurement of life satisfaction. *Journal of Gerontology, 16*, 134–143.

Neugarten, B. L., Moore, J. W., & Lowe, J. C. (1968). Age norms, age constraints, and adult socialization. In B. L. Neugarten (Ed.), *Middle age and aging* (pp. 22–28). Chicago, IL: University of Chicago Press.

Neulinger, J. (1974). *The psychology of leisure: Research approaches to the study of leisure.* Springfield, IL: Charles C. Thomas.

Neulinger, J. (1981). *The psychology of leisure* (2nd ed.). Springfield, IL: Charles C. Thomas.

Neulinger, J. (1986). *What am I doing? The WAID: An introductory guide designed to help you measure and improve the quality of your life.* Dolgeville, NY: The Leisure Institute.

Neulinger, J., & Breit, M. (1969). Attitude dimensions of leisure. *Journal of Leisure Research, 1*, 255–261.

Nias, D. K. B. (1977). The structuring of recreational interests. *Social Behavior and Personality, 5*, 383–388.

Nicholls, J. (1984). Conceptions of ability and achievement motivation. In R. Ames & C. Ames (Eds.), *Research on motivation in education: Student motivation* (Vol. 1, pp. 39–73). New York, NY: Academic Press.

Nickerson, N. P., & Ellis, G. D. (1991). Traveler types and activation theory: A comparison of two models. *Journal of Travel Research, 29*, 26–31.

Nimrod, G. (2007a). Retirees' leisure: Activities, benefits, and their contribution to life satisfaction. *Leisure Studies, 26*, 65–80.

Nimrod, G. (2007b). Expanding, reducing, concentrating and diffusing: Post retirement leisure behavior and life satisfaction. *Leisure Sciences, 29*, 91–111.

Nimrod, G. (2008a). In support of innovation theory: Innovation in activity patterns and life satisfaction among recently retired individuals. *Aging & Society, 28*, 831–846.

Nimrod, G. (2008b). Time for old friends and grandchildren? Post retirement get-togethers and life satisfaction. *Leisure/Loisir, 32*, 21–46.

Nimrod, G. (2008c). Retirement and tourism: themes in retirees' narratives. *Annals of Tourism Research, 35*(4), 859–878.

Nimrod, G. (2009). The Internet as a resource in older adults' leisure. *International Journal on Disability and Human Development, 8, 207–214.*

Nimrod G. & Adoni, H. (2006). Leisure styles and life satisfaction among recent retirees in Israel. *Aging and Society, 26*, 607–630.

Nimrod, G., Janke, M., & Kleiber, D. A. (2007). Retirement, activity, and subjective well-being in Israel and the Unites States. *World Leisure Journal, 49*(4). 18–32.

Nimrod, G., Janke, M. C., & Kleiber, D. A. (2009). Expanding, reducing, concentrating and diffusing: Activity patterns of recent retirees in the U.S. *Leisure Sciences, 31*, 37–52.

Nimrod, G., & Kleiber, D. A. (2007). Reconsidering change and continuity in later life: Toward an innovation theory of successful aging. *International Journal of Aging and Human Development, 65*, 1–22.

Nishino, H., & Chinen, Y. (1998). A pilot study on the daily activities of Japanese youth using ESM: Part III: Perceived leisure experiences and variables. *Tokai University, 27*, 1–12.

Noad, K., & James, K. (2003). Samurai of gentle power: An exploration of aikido in the lives of women aikidora. *Annals of Leisure Research, 6*, 134–152.

Noe, F. P. (1969). An instrumental conception of leisure for the adolescent. *Adolescence, 4*, 385–400.

Norling, J. C., & Sibthorp, J. (2006). Mental restoration and recreation. *Parks & Recreation*, March, 30–38.

Norman, D. A. (2004). *Emotional design: Why we love (or hate) everyday things.* New York, NY: Basic Books.

Nuttman-Shwartz, O. (2004). Like a high wave: Adjustment to retirement. *Gerontologist, 44*, 229–236.

O'Brien, G. E. (1986). *Psychology of work and unemployment.* Toronto, ON: Wiley.

OECD. (2009). *Society at a Glance 2009: OECD Social Indicators.* Paris, France: OECD Publishing.

Ogilvie, B. C. (1968). Psychological consistencies within the personality of high level competitors. *Journal of the American Medical Association, 205*, 780–786.

Ogilvie, B. C., & Tutko, T. (1985). Sport: If you want to build character, try something else. In D. Chu, J. Seagraves, & B. Becker (Eds.), *Sport and higher education* (pp. 267–273). Champaign, IL: Human Kinetics.

Ohler, P., & Nieding, G. (2006). An evolutionary perspective on entertainment. In J. Bryant & P. Vorderer (Eds.), *Psychology of entertainment* (pp. 423–434). New York, NY: Routledge.

Øksnes, M. (2008) The carnival goes on and on! Children's perceptions of their leisure time and play in SFO. *Leisure Studies, 27*, 149–164.

Okun, M. A., & Michel, J. (2006). Sense of community and being a volunteer among the young-old. *Journal of Applied Gerontology, 25*, 173–188.

Omi, M., & Winant, H. (1994). *Racial formation in the United States*. New York, NY: Routledge.

Orne, M. T. (1962). On the social psychology of the psychological experiment: With particular reference to demand characteristics and their implications. *American Psychologist, 17*, 776–783.

Orsega-Smith, E. M., Payne, L. L., Mowen, A. J., Ho, C., & Godbey, G. (2007). The role of social support and self-efficacy in shaping the leisure time physical activity of older adults. *Journal of Leisure Research, 39*, 705–727.

Orthner, D. K. (1975). Leisure activity patterns and marital satisfaction over the marital career. *Journal of Marriage and the Family, 37*, 91–102.

Orthner, D. K. (1976). Patterns of leisure and marital interaction. *Journal of Leisure Research, 8*, 98–111.

Orthner, D. K. (1985). Leisure and conflict in families. In B. G. Gunter, J. Stanley, & R. St. Clair (Eds.), *Transitions to leisure: Conceptual and Human Issues*. Lanham, MD: University Press of America.

Orthner, D. K., Barnett-Morris, L., & Mancini, J. A. (1992). Leisure and the family over the life cycle. In L. L'Abate (Ed.), *Handbook of Developmental Family Psychology and Psychopathology*. New York, NY: Wiley.

Orthner, D. K., & Mancini, J. A. (1980). Leisure behavior and group dynamics: The case of the family. In S. E. Iso-Ahola (Ed.), *Social psychological perspectives on leisure and recreation* (pp. 307–328). Springfield, IL: Charles C. Thomas.

Orthner, D. K., & Mancini, J. A. (1991). Benefits of leisure for family bonding. In B. L. Driver, P. J. Brown, & G. L. Peterson (Eds.), *Benefits of leisure* (pp. 289–301). State College, PA: Venture Publishing, Inc.

Osgood, N., & Howe, C. Z. (1984). Psychological aspects of leisure: A life cycle developmental perspective. *Loisir et Société/Society and Leisure, 7*, 175–195.

Osgood, D. W., Wilson, J. K., O'Malley, P. M., Bachman, J. G., & Johnston, L. D. (1996). Routine activities and individual deviant behavior. *American Sociological Review, 61*, 635–655.

Ouellet, G. (Ed.) (1984). *Society and leisure* (Vol. 7). Sillery, QC: University of Quebec Press.

Outley, C. W., & Floyd, M. F. (2002). The home they live in: Inner city children's views on the influence of parenting strategies on their leisure behavior. *Leisure Sciences, 24*, 161–179.

Paffenbarger, R. S., Hyde, R. T., & Dow, A. (1991). Health benefits of physical activity. In B. L. Driver, P. J. Brown, & G. L. Peterson (Eds.), *Benefits of leisure* (pp. 49–57). State College, PA: Venture Publishing, Inc.

Painter, N. I. (2010). *The history of White people*. New York, NY: W. W. Norton.

Palfrey, J., & Gasser, U. (2008). *Born digital*. New York, NY: Basic Books.

Palmer, P., Freeman, P. A., & Zabriskie, R. B. (2007). Family deepening: A qualitative inquiry into the experience of families who participate in service expeditions. *Journal of Leisure Research, 39,* 438–458.

Palmore, E. (1981). *Social patterns in normal aging*. Durham, NC: Duke University Press.

Paluba, G. V., & Neulinger, J. (1976). Stereotypes based on free time activities. *Loisir et Société/Society and Leisure, 3*, 89–95.

Parker, R. G. (1995). Reminiscence: A continuity theory framework. *The Gerontologist, 35*, 515–525.

Parker, S. R. (1971). *The future of work and leisure*. New York, NY: Praeger.

Parkes, C. M. (1972). *Bereavement: Studies of grief in adult life*. London, UK: The Tavistock Institute of Human Relations.

Parks and Recreation Federation of Ontario. (1992). *The benefits of parks and recreation: A catalogue*. Toronto, ON: Ontario Ministry of Tourism and Recreation.

Parry, D. C. (2007). "There is life after breast cancer": Nine vignettes exploring dragon boat racing for breast cancer survivors. *Leisure Sciences, 29*, 53–69.

Parry, D. C. (2009). Dragon boat racing for breast cancer survivors: Leisure as a context for spiritual outcomes. *Leisure/Loisir: Journal of the Canadian Association for Leisure Studies, 33*, 317–350.

Parry, D. C., & Johnson, C. W. (2007). Contextualizing leisure research to encompass complexity in lived leisure experience: The need for creative analytic practice. *Leisure Sciences, 29*, 119–130.

Parry, D. C., & Shinew, K. J. (2004). The constraining impact of infertility on women's leisure lifestyles. *Leisure Sciences, 26*, 295–308.

Parten, M. (1932). Social play among preschool children. *Journal of Abnormal and Social Psychology, 28*, 136–147.

Patrick, G. T. W. (1916). *The psychology of relaxation*. Boston, MA: Houghton Mifflin Co.

Patterson, I. (1996). Participation in leisure activities by older adults after a stressful life event: The loss of a spouse. *International Journal of Aging and Human Development, 42*, 123–142.

Patterson, I. (2000). Developing a meaningful identity for people with disabilities through serious leisure activities. *World Leisure Journal, 42*, 41–51.

Patterson, I., & Carpenter, G. (1994). Participation in leisure activities after the death of a spouse. *Leisure Sciences, 16*, 105–117.

Patterson, M. E., Watson, A. E., Williams, D. R., & Roggenbuck, J. R. (1998). An hermeneutic approach to studying the nature of wilderness experiences. *Journal of Leisure Research, 30*, 423–452.

Payne, L., Mowen, A., & Montoro-Rodriguez, J. (2006). The role of leisure style in maintaining the health of older adults with arthritis. *Journal of Leisure Research, 38*, 20–45.

Pearce, P. L. (1982). *The social psychology of tourist behavior*. Oxford, UK: Pergamon.

Pearson, Q. M. (1998). Job satisfaction, leisure satisfaction and psychological health. *Career Development Quarterly, 46*, 418–426.

Pellegrini, A. D. (1995). *School recess and playground behavior: Educational and developmental roles*. Ithaca, NY: State University of New York Press.

Pellegrini, A. D., & Bohn, C. M. (2005). The role of recess in children's cognitive performance and school adjustment. *Educational Researcher, 34*, 13–19.

Pellegrini, A. D., & Smith, P. K. (1993). School recess: Implications for education and development. *Review of Educational Research, 63*, 51–67.

Pennington-Gray, L., Thapa, B., & Holland, S. (2002). Florida residents' constraints to parks and public lands visitation: An assessment of the validity of an intrapersonal, interpersonal, and structural model. *World Leisure Journal, 44*, 51–60.

Pereira, R., & Stagnitti, K. (2008). The meaning of leisure for well-elderly Italians in an Australian community: Implcations for occupational therapy. *Australian Occupational Therapy Journal, 55*, 39–48.

Person, A., Kerr, M., & Stattin, H. (2004). Why a leisure context is linked to norm-breaking for some girls and not others: personality characteristics and parent-child relations as explanations. *Journal of Adolescence, 27*, 583–598.

Pervin, L. A. (1968). Performance and satisfaction as a function of individual-environment fit. *Psychological Bulletin, 69*, 56–68.

Pervin, L. A. (1985). Personality: Current controversies, issues, and directions. *Annual Reviews of Psychology, 36*, 83–114.

Pervin, L. A. (1990). A brief history of modern personality theory. In L. A. Pervin (Ed.), *Handbook of personality: Theory and research* (pp. 3–18). New York, NY: The Guilford Press.

Pesavento Raymond, L. C. (1984). The effects of unemployment on the leisure behavior of unemployed steelworkers. *World Leisure and Recreation, 26*, 61–64.

Pesavento Raymond, L. C., & Kelly, J. R. (1991). Leisure and life satisfaction of unemployed North American urban minority youth. *Loisir et Société/Society and Leisure, 14*, 497–511.

Peterson, C. (2006). *A primer in positive psychology.* New York, NY: Oxford University Press.

Peterson, G. L., Driver, B. L., & Gregory, R. (1988). *Amenity resource valuation: Integrating economics with other disciplines.* State College, PA: Venture Publishing, Inc.

Petty, R. E., & Cacioppo, J. T. (1986). The elaboration likelihood model of persuasion. In L. Berkowitz (Ed.), *Advances in experimental social psychology*: Vol. 19 (pp. 123–205). New York, NY: Academic Press.

Petty, R. E., McMichael, S., & Brannon, L. A. (1992). The Elaboration Likelihood Model of persuasion: Applications in recreation and tourism. In M. J. Manfredo (Ed.), *Influencing human behavior: Theory and applications in recreation, tourism, and natural resources management* (pp. 77–101). Champaign, IL: Sagamore Publishing.

Pew Internet and American Life (2004). Older Americans and the Internet 2004. Retrieved January 3, 2005 from http://www.pewinternet.org/pdfs/PIP_Seniors_On-line_2004.pdf.

Philipp, S. (2000). Race and the pursuit of happiness. *Journal of Leisure Research, 32*, 121–124.

Piaget, J. (1954). *The construction of reality in the child.* New York, NY: Basic Books.

Piaget, J. (1962). *Play, dreams and imitation in childhood.* Boston, MA: Beacon.

Pieper, J. (1952). *Leisure: The basis of culture.* New York, NY: Pantheon Books.

Pierce, R. C. (1980). Dimensions of leisure I: Satisfactions. *Journal of Leisure Research, 12*, 5–19.

Pierce, T. W., Madden, D. J., Siegel, W. C., & Blumenthal, J. A. (1993). Effects of aerobic exercise on cognitive and psychological functioning in patients with mild hypertension. *Health Psychology, 12*, 286–291.

Pierro, A., Mannetti, L., & Livi, S. (2003). Self-identity and the theory of planned behavior in the prediction of health behavior and leisure activity. *Self & Identity, 2*, 47–60.

Pierskalla, C. D., & Lee, M. E. (1998). An ecological perception model of leisure affordances. *Leisure Sciences, 20*, 67–79.

Pietropinto, A. (1986). The workaholic spouse. *Medical Aspects of Human Sexuality, 20*, 89–96.

Pine, B. J., & Gilmore, J. H. (1999). *The experience economy.* Boston, MA: Harvard Business School Press.

Pittman, J. F. (1994). Work/family fit as a mediator of work factors on marital tension: Evidence from the interface of greedy institutions. *Human Relations, 47*, 183–210.

Pizam, A., Neumann, Y., & Reichel, A. (1978). Dimensions of tourist satisfaction with a destination area. *Annals of Tourism Research, 5*, 314–322.

Play for peace. Retrieved March 31st, 2009 from http://www.playforpeace.org.

Plog, S. C. (1972). *Why destination areas rise and fall in popularity.* Paper presented to the Travel Research Association Southern California Chapter, Los Angeles.

Podilchak, W. (1991a). Distinctions of fun, enjoyment and leisure. *Leisure Studies, 10*, 133–148.

Podilchak, W. (1991b). Establishing the fun in leisure. *Leisure Sciences, 13*, 123–136.

Pohl, S. L., Borrie, W. T., & Patterson, M. E. (2000). Women, wilderness, and everyday life: A documentation of the connection between wilderness recreation and women's everyday lives. *Journal of Leisure Research, 32*(4), 415–434.

Pope, K. S. and Singer, J. L. (1978). *The stream of consciousness: Scientific investigations into the flow of human experience.* New York, NY: Plenum Press.

Power, M., & Dalgleish, T. (2007). *Cognition and emotion* (2nd ed.). New York, NY: Psychology Press.

Presson, P., & Benassi, V. (1996). Illusion of control: A meta-analytic review. *Journal of Social Behavior and Personality, 11*, 493–510.

Price, C. (1999). Australian population: Ethnic origins. *People and Place, 7*(4), 12.

Price, R. H., & Bouffard, D. L. (1974). Behavioral appropriateness and situational constraint as dimensions of social behavior. *Journal of Personality and Social Psychology, 30*, 579–586.

Priest, S. (1992). Factor exploration and confirmation for the dimensions of an adventure experience. *Journal of Leisure Research, 24*, 127–139.

Provenzo, E. F. (1991). *Video kids: Making sense of Nintendo.* Cambridge, MA: Harvard University Press.

Przeclawski, K. (1985). The role of tourism in contemporary culture. *The Tourist Review, 40*, 2–6.

Putnam, R. (2000). *Bowling alone: The collapse and revival of American community.* New York, NY: Simon & Schuster.

Quarrick, G. (1989). *Our sweetest hours*. Jefferson, NC: McFarland & Co.

Quiñones-Vidal, E., Lozpez-García, J., Peñarañda-Ortega, M., & Tortosa-Gil, F. (2004). The nature of social and personality psychology as reflected in JPSP, 1965–2000. *Journal of Personality and Social Psychology, 86*, 435–452.

Ragheb, M. G. (1980). Interrelationships among leisure participation, leisure satisfaction, and leisure attitudes. *Journal of Leisure Research, 12*, 138–149.

Ragheb, M. G. (1988). Leisure and recreation needs or motivations as a basis for program planning. *Journal of Park and Recreation Administration, 6*, 28–40.

Ragheb, M. G. (1993). Leisure and perceived wellness: A field investigation. *Leisure Sciences, 15*, 13–24.

Ragheb, M. G., & Beard, J. G. (1982). Measuring leisure attitude. *Journal of Leisure Research, 14*, 155–167.

Ragheb, M. G., & Griffith, C. A. (1982). The contribution of leisure participation and leisure satisfaction to life satisfaction of older persons. *Journal of Leisure Research, 14*, 295–306.

Ragheb, M. G., & Tate, R. L. (1993). A behavioural model of leisure participation, based on leisure attitude, motivation and satisfaction. *Leisure Studies, 12*, 61–70.

Raisborough, J. (2007). Gender and serious leisure careers: A case study of women sea cadets. *Journal of Leisure Research, 39*, 686–704.

Ramos, C. I., & Folkers, E. (1994). The relationship of perception of time and attributes of leisure in daily experiences. *Leisure Studies, 13*, 140–147.

Rapoport, R., & Rapoport, R. N. (1975). *Leisure and the family life cycle*. London, UK: Routledge & Kegan Paul.

Rathunde, K. (1988). Optimal experience and the family context. In M. Csikszentmihalyi and I. Csikszentmihalyi (Eds.), *Optimal experience* (pp. 342–363). New York, NY: Cambridge University Press.

Raymore, L. A. (2002). Facilitators to leisure. *Journal of Leisure Research, 34*, 37–52.

Raymore, L.A., Barber, B.L., Eccles, J.S., & Godbey, G.C. (1999). Leisure behavior pattern stability in the transition from adolescence to young adulthood. *Journal of Youth and Adolescence, 28*, 79–103.

Reich, J. W., & Zautra, A. (1981). Life events and personal causation: Some relationships with satisfaction and distress. *Journal of Personality and Social Psychology, 41*, 1002–1012.

Reid, D. G. (1995). *Work and leisure in the 21st century*. Toronto, ON: Wall and Emerson, Inc.

Reid, D. G., & Mannell, R. C. (1993). Future possibilities: The changing patterns of work and leisure. In A. J. Veal, P. Jonson, & G. Cushman (Eds.), *Leisure and tourism: Social and environmental change* (pp. 373–378). Sydney, Australia: University of Technology Sydney Press.

Reid, D. G., and Smit, P. (1986). Recreation participation patterns of the unemployed: A preliminary perspective. *Recreation Research Review, 1*, 43–49.

Reis, M., and Gold, D. P. (1993). Retirement, personality, and life satisfaction: A review of two models. *Journal of Applied Gerontology, 12*, 261–282.

Reissman, C., Aron, A., & Bergen, M. R. (1993). Shared activities and marital satisfaction: Causal direction and self-expansion versus boredom. *Journal of Social and Personal Relationships, 10*, 243–254.

Rentfrow, P. J., & Gosling, S. D. (2003). The do-re-mi's of everyday life: The structure and personality correlates of music preferences. *Journal of Personality and Social Psychology, 84*, 1236–1256.

Ricci, P. R., & Holland, S. M. (1992). Incentive travel: Recreation as a motivational medium. *Tourism Management, 13*, 288–296

Rideout, V. J., Vandewater, E. A., & Wartella, E. A. (2003). *Zero to six: Electronic media in the lives of infants, toddlers and preschoolers*. Menlo Park, CA: Henry J. Kaiser Family Foundation.

Riesman, D. (1950). *The lonely crowd*. New Haven, CT: Yale University Press.

Rigby, C. S., Deci, E. L., Patrick, B. C., & Ryan, R. M. (1992). Beyond the intrinsic-extrinsic dichotomy: Self-determination in motivation and learning. *Motivation and Emotion, 16*, 165–185.

Ringelmann, M. (1913). Recherches sur les moteurs animes: Travail de l'homme. *Annales de l'Institut National Agronomique, 12*, 1–40.

Ritzer, G., & Gindoff, P. (1992). Methodological relationalism: Lessons for and from social psychology. *Social Psychology Quarterly, 55*, 128–140.

Roadburg, A. (1983). Freedom and enjoyment: Disentangling perceived leisure. *Journal of Leisure Research, 15*, 15–26.

Robbins, B. D. (2008). What is the good life? Positive psychology and the renaissance of humanistic psychology. *The Humanistic Psychologist, 36*, 96–112.

Robbins, S. P., Bergman, R., Stagg, L, & Coulter, M. (2003). *Management* (3rd Edition). Sydney, Australia: Prentice.

Roberson, D. N. (2001). The impact of travel on older adults: An exploratory investigation. *Tourism, 49*, 99–108.

Roberson, D. N., Jr. (2005). Leisure and learning: An investigation of older adults and self-directed learning. *Leisure/Loisir, 29*, 203–237.

Roberts, D. F., Foehr, U. G., & Rideout, V. (2005). *Generation M: Media in the lives of 8-18 year-olds*. Kaiser Family Foundation.

Roberts, G. C., Treasure, D. C., & Kavussanu, M. (1997). Motivation in physical activity contexts: An achievement goal perspective. *Advances in Motivation and Achievement, 10*, 413–447.

Roberts, J., & Sutton-Smith, B. (1962). Child training and game involvement. *Ethnology, 1*, 166–185.

Roberts, K., Lamb, K. L., Dench, S., & Brodie, D. A. (1989). Leisure patterns, health status, and employment status. *Leisure Studies, 8*, 229–235.

Robertson, B. J. (1999). Leisure and family: Perspectives of male adolescents who engage in delinquent activity as leisure. *Journal of Leisure Research, 31*, 335–359.

Robertson, R. A., & Regula, J. A. (1994). Recreational displacement and overall satisfaction: A study of central Iowa's licensed boaters. *Journal of Leisure Research, 26*, 174–181.

Robinson, D. W. (1992). A descriptive model of enduring risk recreation involvement. *Journal of Leisure Research, 24*, 52–63.

Robinson, J. C. (1993). *Death of a hero, birth of the soul: Answering the call of midlife.* Tulsa, OK: Council Oaks Books.

Robinson, J. P. (1977). *How Americans use time: A social-psychological analysis of everyday behavior.* New York, NY: Praeger.

Robinson, J. P. (1990). I love my TV (TV Viewing). *American Demographics, 12*, 24–28.

Robinson, J. P., & Godbey, G. (1993). Sport, fitness, and the gender gap. *Leisure Sciences, 15*, 291–307.

Robinson, J. P., & Godbey, G. (1997). *Time for life: The surprising ways Americans use their time.* University Park, PA: Pennsylvania State University Press.

Robrecht, L. C. (1995). Grounded theory: Evolving methods. *Qualitative Health Research, 5*, 169–177.

Roche, S. M., & McConkey, K. M. (1990). Absorption: Nature, assessment, and correlates. *Journal of Personality & Social Psychology, 59*, 91–101.

Rogers, C. (1961). *On becoming a person.* Boston, MA: Houghton-Mifflin.

Roggenbuck, J., & Driver, B. (2000). Benefits of nonfacilitated uses of wilderness. In S. McCool, D. Cole, W. Borrie, & J. O'Loughlin (Compilers), *Wilderness science in a time of change conference* (Vol. 3). Denver, CO: USDA Forest Service.

Rogoff, B., Baker-Sennett, J., Lacasa, P., & Goldsmith, D. (1995). Development through participation in sociocultural activity. Cultural practices as contexts for development: *New Directions for Child Development, 67*, 45–65.

Rolston, H., III (1991). Creation and recreation: Environmental benefits and human leisure. In B. L. Driver, P. J. Brown, & G. L. Peterson (Eds.), *Benefits of leisure* (pp. 393–403). State College, PA: Venture Publishing, Inc.

Romsa, G., Bondy, P., & Blenman, M. (1985). Modeling retirees' life satisfaction levels: The role of recreational, life cycle, and socio-environmental elements. *Journal of Leisure Research, 17*, 29–39.

Rosenberg, S., & Gara, M. A. (1985). The multiplicity of personal identity. In P. Shaver (Ed.), *Self, situations, and social behavior: Review of personality and social psychology* (Vol. 6). Beverly Hills, CA: Sage.

Rosenthal, D. H., Waldman, D. A., & Driver, B. L. (1982). Construct validity of instruments measuring recreationists' preferences. *Leisure Sciences, 5*, 89–108.

Rosenthal, R. (1966). *Experimenter effects in behavioral research.* New York, NY: Appleton-Century-Crofts.

Ross, E. A. (1908). *Social psychology: An outline and source book.* New York, NY: Macmillan.

Ross, L., & Nisbett, R. (1991). *The person and the situation: Perspectives of social psychology.* New York, NY: McGraw-Hill Publishing Co.

Rotter, J. B. (1966). Generalized expectancies for internal versus external control of reinforcement. *Psychological Monographs: General and Applied, 80*, 1–28.

Rowley, J., Landers, D., Kyllo, L. B., & Etnier, J. (1995). Does the iceberg profile discriminate between successful and less successful athletes? A meta-analysis. *Journal of Sport & Exercise Psychology, 17*, 185–199.

Rubenstein, C. (1980a). Survey report: How Americans view vacations. *Psychology Today, 13*, 62–76.

Rubenstein, C. (1980b). Vacations: Expectations, satisfactions, frustrations, fantasies. *Psychology Today, 14*, 62–66, 71–76.

Rubin, K. H., Watson, K. S., & Jambor, T. W. (1978). Free-play behaviors in preschool and kindergarten children. *Child Development, 49*, 534–536.

Ruddell, J. L., & Shinew, K. J. (2006). The socialization process for women with physical disabilities: The impact of agents and agencies in the introduction to an elite sport. *Journal of Leisure Research, 38*, 421–444.

Runeson, S., & Frykholm, G. (1983). Kinematic specification of dynamics as an informational basis for person-and-action perception. *Journal of Experimental Psychology: General, 116*, 585–615.

Russell, R. V. (1987). The importance of recreation satisfaction and activity participation to the life satisfaction of age-segregated retirees. *Journal of Leisure Research, 19*, 273–283.

Rutter, D. R., & Quine, L. (1994). *Social psychology and health: European perspectives.* Aldershot, UK: Avebury.

Ryan, R., Bernstein, J., & Brown, K. (2010). Weekends, work, and well-being: Psychological need satisfactions and day of the week effects on mood, vitality, and physical symptoms. *Journal of Social and Clinical Psychology, 29*, 95–122.

Ryan, R., & Connell, J. (1989). Perceived locus of causality and internalization: Examining reasons for acting in two dimensions. *Journal of Personality and Social Psychology, 57*, 749–761.

Ryan, R., & Deci, E. (2000). Self-determination theory and the facilitation of intrinsic motivation, social development, and well-being. *American Psychologist, 55*, 68–78.

Ryan, R., & Deci, E. (2002). An overview of self-determination theory: An organismic-dialectic perspective. In E. L. Deci & R. M. Ryan (Eds.), *Handbook of self-determination* (pp. 3–37). Rochester, NY: University of Rochester Press.

Ryan, R. M., Mims, V., & Koestner, R. (1983). Relation of reward contingency and interpersonal context to intrinsic motivation: A review and test using cognitive evaluation theory. *Journal of Personality and Social Psychology, 45*, 735–750.

Ryder, A., Alden, L., & Paulhaus, D. (2000). Is acculturation unidimensional or bidimensional? A head-to-head comparison in the prediction of personality, self-identity, and adjustment. *Journal of Personality and Social Psychology, 79*, 49–65.

Sakamoto, A. (1994). Video game use and the development of sociocognitive abilities in children: Three surveys of elementary school students. *Journal of Applied Social Psychology, 24*, 21–42.

Samdahl, D. M. (1988). A symbolic interactionist model of leisure: Theory and empirical support. *Leisure Sciences, 10*, 27–39.

Samdahl, D. M. (1991). Issues in the measurement of leisure: A comparison of theoretical and connotative meanings. *Leisure Sciences, 13*, 33–49.

Samdahl, D. M. (1992). Leisure in our lives: Exploring the common leisure occasion. *Journal of Leisure Research, 24*, 19–32.

Samdahl, D. M., & Jekubovich, N. J. (1993). Patterns and characteristics of adult daily leisure. *Loisir et Société/Society and Leisure, 16*, 129–149.

Samdahl, D. M., & Kleiber, D. A. (1989). Self-awareness and leisure experience. *Leisure Sciences, 11*, 1–10.

Sandholtz, K., Derr, B., Buckner, K., & Carlson, D. S. (2002). *Beyond juggling: rebalancing your busy life.* San Francisco, CA: Berrett-Koehler.

Santos, L. R, Ribeira, J. P., & Guimarães, L. (2003). Study of a scale for children and strategies of coping through leisure activity/Estudo de uma escala de crenças e de estrategias de coping através do lazer. *Analise Psicologica, 21*, 441–451.

Sarrazin, P., Vallerand, R., Guillet, E., Pelletier, L., & Cury, F. (2002). Motivation and dropout in female handballers: A 21-month study. *European Journal of Social Psychology, 32*, 395–418.

Schachter, S. (1964). The interaction of cognitive and physiological determinants of emotional state. In L. Berkowitz (Ed.), *Advances in experimental social psychology* (Vol. 1, pp. 49–80). New York, NY: Academic Press.

Schachter, S., & Singer, J. (1962). Cognitive, social and physiological determinants of emotional state. *Psychological Review, 69*, 379–399.

Schaie, K. W., & Geiwitz, J. (1982). *Adult development and aging.* Boston, MA: Little, Brown and Co.

Scherl, L. (1989). Self in wilderness: Understanding the psychological benefits of individual-wilderness interaction through self-control. *Leisure Sciences, 11*, 123–135.

Schill, T., Beyler, J., & Sharp, M. (1993). Pleasure from activities and self-defeating personality. *Psychological Reports, 72*, 627–630.

Schlenker, B. R. (1984). Identities, identifications, and relationships. In V. Derlaga (Ed.), *Communication, intimacy and close relationships* (pp. 71–104). New York, NY: Academic Press.

Schmalz, D. L., & Kerstetter, D. L. (2006). Girlie girls and manly men: Children's stigma consciousness of gender in sports and physical activities. *Journal of Leisure Research, 38*, 536–557.

Schmidt, M. E., Pempek, T. A., Kirkoria, H. L., Lund, A. F., & Anderson, D. R. (2008). The effects of background television on the toy play behavior of very young children. *Child Development, 79*, 1137–1151.

Schmitz-Scherzer, R. (1976). Longitudinal change in leisure behavior of the elderly. *Contributions to Human Development, 3*, 127–136.

Schneider, I. E. (2000). Revisiting and revising recreation conflict research. *Journal of Leisure Research, 32*, 129–133.

Schor, J. B. (1991). *The overworked American: The unexpected decline of leisure.* New York, NY: Basic Books.

Schor, J. B. (1998). *The overspent American: Upscaling, downshifting, and the new consumer.* New York, NY: Basic Books.

Schor, J. B. (2005) Sustainable consumption and worktime reduction. *Journal of Industrial Ecology, 9*(1–2), 37–50.

Schrader, M. P., & Wann, D. L. (1999). High risk recreation: The relationship between participant characteristics and the degree of involvement. *Journal of Sport Behavior, 22,* 426–441.

Schurr, K. T., Ashley, M. A., & Joy, K. L. (1977). A multivariate analysis of male athlete characteristics. *Multivariate Experimental Clinical Research, 3,* 53–68.

Schuster, R., Hammitt, W. E., & Moore, D. (2006). Stress appraisal and coping response to hassles experienced in outdoor recreation settings. *Leisure Sciences, 28,* 97–113.

Schutz, A. (1973). *Collected papers.* (M. Natanson, Ed.) The Hague: Martinus-Nijhoff.

Schutte, H., & Ciarlante, D. (1998*). An alternative consumer behaviour model for Asia.* London, UK: Creative Print & Design.

Schwartz, B. (2000). Self-determination: The tyranny of freedom. *American Psychologist, 55,* 79–88.

Schwartz, B., Ward, A., Monterosso, J., Lyubomirsky, S., White, K., & Lehman, D. (2002). Maximizing versus satisficing: Happiness is a matter of choice. *Journal of Personality and Social Psychology, 83,* 1178–1197.

Schwartz, G. M. & Campagna, J. (2008). New meaning for the emotional state of the elderly, from a leisure standpoint. *Leisure Studies, 27,* 207–211.

Schwartzman, H. (1978). *Transformations: The anthropology of children's play.* New York, NY: Plenum Press.

Scott, D. (2000). Tic, toc, the game is locked and nobody else can play! *Journal of Leisure Research, 32,* 133–137.

Scott, D. (2005). The relevance of constraints research to leisure service delivery. In E. L. Jackson (Ed.), *Constraints to leisure* (pp. 279–293). State College, PA: Venture Publishing, Inc.

Scott, D., & Shafer, C. S. (2001b). Recreational specialization: A critical look at the construct. *Journal of Leisure Research, 33,* 319–343.

Scott, D., & Thigpen, J. (2003). Understanding the birder as tourist: Segmenting visitors to the Texas Hummer/Bird Celebration. *Human Dimensions of Wildlife, 8,* 199–218.

Scott, D., & Willits, F. K. (1989). Adolescent and adult leisure patterns: A 37-year follow-up study. *Leisure Sciences, 11,* 323–335.

Searle, M. S., & Brayley, R. E. (1993). *Leisure services in Canada.* State College, PA: Venture Publishing, Inc.

Searle, M. S., Mactavish, J., & Brayley, R. E. (1993). Integrating ceasing participation with other aspects of leisure behavior: A replication and extension. *Journal of Leisure Research, 25,* 389–404.

Searle, M. S., & Mahon, M. J. (1991). Leisure education in a day hospital: The effects on selected social-psychological variables among older adults. *Canadian Journal of Community Mental Health, 10,* 95–109.

Searle, M. S., Mahon, M. J., Iso-Ahola, S., Adam Sdrolias, H., & van Dyck, J. (1995). Enhancing a sense of independence and psychological well-being amongst the elderly: A field experiment. *Journal of Leisure Research, 30*, 107–124.

Searle, M. S., Mahon, M. J., Iso-Ahola, S., Adam Sdrolias, H., & van Dyck, J. (1998). Examining the long-term effects of leisure education on a sense of independence and psychological well-being among the elderly. *Journal of Leisure Research, 30*, 331–340.

Seepersad, S. (2004). Coping with loneliness: Adolescent online and offline behavior. *CyberPsychology Behavior, 7*, 35–39.

Seib, H. M., & Vodanovich, S. J. (1998). Cognitive correlates of boredom proneness: The role of private self-consciousness and absorption. *Journal of Psychology, 132*, 642–652.

Seligman, M. E. P. (1975). *Helplessness: On depression, development, and death*. San Francisco, CA: Freeman.

Seligman, M. E. P. (1991). *Learned optimism*. New York, NY: Pocket Books.

Seligman, M. E. P., & Csikszentmihalyi, M. (2000). Positive psychology. *American Psychologist, 55*, 5–14.

Sessoms, H. D. (1986). "Of time, work, and leisure" revisited. *Leisure Sciences, 8*, 107–113.

Shafer, S. C., & Hammitt, W. E. (1995). Purism revisited: Specifying recreational conditions of concern according to resource intent. *Leisure Sciences, 17*, 15–30.

Shamir, B. (1988). Commitment and leisure. *Sociological Perspective, 31*, 238–258.

Shamir, B. (1992). Some correlates of leisure identity salience: Three exploratory studies. *Journal of Leisure Research, 24*, 301–323.

Shannon, C. S. (2006). Parents' messages about the role of extracurricular and unstructured leisure activities: Adolescents' perceptions. *Journal of Leisure Research, 38*, 398–420.

Shannon, C. S., & Shaw, S. M. (2008). Mothers and daughters: teaching and learning about leisure. *Leisure Sciences, 30*, 1–16.

Sharp, A., & Mannell, R. C. (1996). Participation in leisure as a coping strategy among bereaved women. In *Proceedings of the Eight Canadian Congress on Leisure Research* (pp. 241–244). Ottawa, ON: University of Ottawa.

Sharp, E., Caldwell, L. L., Graham, J., & Ridenour, T. (2006). Individual motivation and parental influence on adolescents' experiences of interest in free time: A longitudinal examination. *Journal of Youth and Adolescence, 35*, 359–372.

Sharpe, E. (2005). Delivering communitas: Wilderness adventure and the making of community. *Journal of Leisure Research, 37*, 255–280.

Shary, J. M., & Iso-Ahola, S. E. (1989). Effects of a control-relevant intervention on nursing home residents' perceived competence and self-esteem. *Therapeutic Recreation Journal, 23*, 7–16.

Shaw, S. M. (1984). The measurement of leisure: A quality of life issue. *Loisir et Société/ Society and Leisure, 7*, 91–107.

Shaw, S. M. (1985a). The meaning of leisure in everyday life. *Leisure Sciences, 7*, 1–24.

Shaw, S. M. (1985b). Gender and leisure: Inequality in the distribution of leisure time. *Journal of Leisure Research, 17*, 266–282.

Shaw, S. M. (1988). Gender in the definition and perception of household labor. *Family Relations, 37*, 333–337.

Shaw, S. M. (1992) Dereifying family leisure: An examination of women's and men's everyday experiences and perceptions of family time. *Leisure Sciences, 14*, 271–286.

Shaw, S. M. (1994). Gender, leisure, and constraint: Toward a framework for the analysis of women's leisure. *Journal of Leisure Research, 26*, 8–22.

Shaw, S. M. (1999a). Gender and leisure. In E. Jackson & T. Burton (Eds.), *Leisure studies: Prospects for the twenty-first century*. State College, PA: Venture Publishing, Inc.

Shaw, S. M. (1999b). Men's leisure and women's lives: The impact of pornography on women. *Leisure Studies, 18*, 197–212.

Shaw, S. M. (2001a). Conceptualizing resistance: Women's leisure as political practice. *Journal of Leisure Research, 33*, 186–201.

Shaw, S. M. (2001b). The family leisure dilemma: Insights from research with Canadian families. *World Leisure Journal, 44*, 53–62.

Shaw, S. M. (2006). Resistance. In C. Rojek, S. Shaw, & A. Veal (Eds.), *Handbook of leisure studies*. (pp. 533–545). New York, NY: Palgrave Macmillan.

Shaw, S. M., Andrey, J., & Johnson, L. (2003). The struggle for life balance: Work, family, and leisure in the lives of women teleworkers. *World Leisure Journal, 45*, 15–29.

Shaw, S. M., Bonen, A., & McCabe, J. F. (1991). Do more constraints mean less leisure? Examining the relationship between constraints and participation. *Journal of Leisure Research, 23*, 286–300.

Shaw, S. M., & Dawson, D. (2001). Purposive leisure: Examining parental discourses on family activities. *Leisure Sciences, 23*, 217–232.

Shaw, S. M., & Hibrecht, M. (2008). "It could be your fault": Parental responsibility for children's health and children's leisure in the age of anxiety. *Abstracts of the Twelfth Canadian Conference on Leisure Research, Montreal*, 412–415.

Shaw, S. M., Kleiber, D., & Caldwell, L. L. (1995). Leisure and adolescent development: An examination of the relationship between leisure and identity formation for male and female adolescents. *Journal of Leisure Research, 27*, 245–263.

Shelby, B., & Vaske, J. J. (1991). Resource and activity substitutes for recreational salmon fishing in New Zealand. *Leisure Sciences, 13*, 21–32.

Sheldon, K., Elliot, A., Kim, Y., & Kasser, T. (2001). What is satisfying about satisfying events? Testing 10 candidate psychological needs. *Journal of Personality and Social Psychology, 80*, 325–339.

Sheldon, K., Elliot, A., Ryan, R., Chirkov, V., Kim, Y., Wu, C., Demir, M., & Sun, Z. (2004). Self-concordance and subjective well-being in four cultures. *Journal of Cross-Cultural Psychology, 35*, 209–223.

Shen, X. S., Chick, G., & Zinn, H. (2009). *Playfulness in adulthood as a personality trait: A new measurement*. Paper presented at the annual NRPA Leisure Research Symposium, Salt Lake City.

Sheppard, B. H., Hartwick, J., & Warshaw, P. R. (1988). The theory of reasoned action: A meta-analysis of past research with recommendations for modifications and future research. *Journal of Consumer Research, 15*, 325–343.

Sherif, M. (1936). *The psychology of social norms*. New York, NY: Harper.

Sherif, M., Harvey, O. J., White, B. J., Hood, W. R., & Sherif, C. W. (1961). *Intergroup conflict and cooperation: The Robbers Cave Experiment*. Norman, OK: Institute of Groups Relations, University of Oklahoma.

Shields, D. L., & Bredemeier, B. J. L. (1995). *Character development and physical activity*. Champaign, IL: Human Kinetics.

Shields, D. L., & Bredemeier, B. J. L. (2001). Moral development and behavior in sport. In R. N. Singer et al. (Eds.), *Handbook of sports psychology* (2nd ed.). New York, NY: Wiley.

Shin, W. S. (1993). Self-actualization and wilderness attitudes: A replication. *Journal of Social Behavior and Personality, 8*, 221–240.

Shinew, K. J., Floyd, M. F., & Parry, D. (2004). Understanding the relationship between race and leisure activities and constraints: Exploring an alternative framework. *Leisure Sciences, 26*, 181–199.

Shinew, K. J., & Parry, D. C. (2005). Examining college students' participation in the leisure pursuits of drinking and illegal drug use. *Journal of Leisure Research, 37*, 364–386.

Shogan, D. (2002). Characterizing constraints of leisure: A Foucaultian analysis of leisure constraints. *Leisure Studies, 21*, 27–38.

Shores, K., & Scott, D. (2007). The association of individual time perspective and recreation experience preferences. *Journal of Leisure Research, 39*, 28–59.

Short, S. (2005). Adolescents' health and well-being in the United Kingdom. *Loisir et Société/ Society and Leisure, 28*, 591–609.

Sibthorp, J. (2003). An empirical look at Walsh and Golins' adventure education process model: Relationships between antecedent factors, perceptions of characteristics of an adventure education experience, and changes in self-efficacy. *Journal of Leisure Research, 35*, 80–106.

Silbereisen, R. K., Noack, P., & Eyferth, K. (1986). Place for development: Adolescents, leisure settings, and developmental tasks. In R. K. Silbereisen, K. Eyferth, & G. Rudinger (Eds.), *Development as action in context* (pp. 87–107). New York, NY: Springer-Verlag.

Silbereisen, R. K., & Todt, E. (Eds.). 1994. *Adolescence in context: The interplay of family, school, peers, and work in adjustment*. New York, NY: Free Press.

Silvia, P. J. (2008). Interest—The curious emotion. *Current Directions in Psychological Science, 17*, 57–60.

Singer, D. G. (1993). *Playing for their lives*. New York, NY: Free Press.

Singer, J. L. (1973). *The child's world of make believe*. New York, NY: Academic Press.

Singer, J. L., & Singer, D. G. (1986). Family experiences and television viewing as predictors of children's imagination, restlessness, and aggression. *Journal of Social Issues, 42*, 107–124.

Singleton, J. F., Forbes, W. F., & Agwani, N. (1993). Stability of activity across the lifespan. *Activities, Adaptation, & Aging, 19*, 19–27.

Sinha, J. B. P. (2003). Trends toward indigenization of psychology in India. In K. Yang, K. Hwang, P. B. Pedersen, & I. Daibo (Eds.), *Progress in Asian social psychology: Conceptual and empirical contributions.* (pp. 11–27). Westport, CT: Praeger Publishers.

Skeels, H. M. (1973). Adult status of children with contrasting early life experiences: A follow-up study. *Monographs for Social Research on Child Development, 31*(3, Serial No. 105).

Skenazy, L. (2009). *Free range kids: Giving our children the freedom we had without going nuts with worry.* San Francisco, CA: Jossey-Bass.

Skinner, B. F. (1971). *Beyond Freedom and Dignity.* New York, NY: Knopf.

Skinner, K., & Louw, J. (2009). The *feminization* of *psychology*: Data from South Africa. International *Journal of Psychology, 44*, 81–92.

Smedley, A., & Smedley, B. (2005). Race as biology is fiction, racism as a social problem is real. *American Psychologist, 60*, 16–26.

Smigal, E. (1963). *Work and leisure.* New Haven, CT: College and University Press.

Smilansky, S. (1968). *The effect of sociodramatic play in disadvantaged children.* New York, NY: Wiley.

Smith, E. A., & Caldwell, L. L. (1989). The perceived quality of leisure experiences among smoking and nonsmoking adolescents. *Journal of Early Adolescence, 9*, 153–162.

Smith, R. E., & Smoll, F. L. (1990). Self-esteem and children's reactions to youth sport coaching behaviors: A field study of self-enhancement processes. *Developmental Psychology, 26*, 987–993.

Smith, S. L. J. (1990a). A test of Plog's allocentric/psychocentric model: Evidence from seven nations. *Journal of Travel Research, 28*, 40–43.

Smith, S. L. J. (1990b). *Dictionary of concepts in recreation and leisure studies.* New York, NY: Greenwood Press.

Sneed, C., & Runco, M. A. (1992). The beliefs adults and children hold about television and video games. *Journal of Psychology, 126*, 273–284.

Snepenger, D., King, J., Marshall, E., & Uysal, M. (2006). Modeling Iso-Ahola's motivation theory in the tourism context. *Journal of Travel Research, 45*, 140–149.

Snibbe, A., & Markus, H. (2005). You can't always get what you want: Educational attainment, agency, and choice. *Journal of Personality and Social Psychology, 88*, 703–720.

Sofranko, A. J., & Nolan, M. F. (1972). Early life experiences and adult sports participation. *Journal of Leisure Research, 4*, 6–18.

Son, J., Mowen, A., & Kerstetter, D. (2008). Testing alternative leisure constraint negotiation models: An extension of Hubbard and Mannell's study. *Leisure Sciences, 30*, 198–216.

Spigner, C., & Havitz, M. E. (1992–1993). Health, recreation, and the unemployed: An interactive model. *International Quarterly of Community Health Education, 13*, 31–45.

Spreitzer, E. A., & Snyder, E. E. (1976). Socialization into sport: An exploratory path analysis. *The Research Quarterly, 47*, 239–245.

Spreitzer, E. A., & Snyder, E. E. (1983). Correlates of participation in adult recreational sports. *Journal of Leisure Research, 15*, 27–38.

Spreitzer, E. A., & Snyder, E. E. (1987). Educational-occupational fit and leisure orientation as related to life satisfaction. *Journal of Leisure Research, 19*, 149–158.

Staempfli, M. B. (2007). Adolescent playfulness, stress perception, coping and well-being. *Journal of Leisure Research, 39*, 393–412.

Staines, G. L. (1980). Spillover vs. compensation: A review of the literature on relationship between work and nonwork. *Human Relations, 33*, 111–130.

Stalp, M. C. (2006). Negotiating time and space for serious leisure: Quilting in the modern U.S. home. *Journal of Leisure Research, 38*, 104–132

Stanley, D., & Freysinger, V. (1995). The impact of age, health, and sex on the frequency of older adults' leisure activity participation: A longitudinal study. *Activities, Adaptation, and Aging, 19*, 31–42.

Statistics Canada. (2003a). Canada's ethnocultural portrait: The changing mosaic. Retrieved February 21, 2003, from http://www12.statcan.ca/english/census01/Products/Analytic/companion/etoimm/canada.cfm

Statistics Canada. (2003b). Ethnic diversity survey. Retrieved September 29, 2003 from http://www.statcan.ca/Daily/English/030929/d030929a.htm

Statistics Canada. (2005). *Canada's visible minority population in 2017*. Retrieved March 22, 2005 from http://www/statcan.ca?Daily/English/050322/d050332b.htm

Statistics Canada. (2010). *Projections of the diversity of the Canadian population*. Retrieved March 12, 2010 from http://www.statcan.gc.ca/pub/91-551-x/91-551-x2010001-eng.pdf

Stebbins, R. A. (1981). Science amators? Rewards and costs in amateur astronomy and archaeology. *Journal of Leisure Research, 13*, 289–304.

Stebbins, R. A. (1982). Serious leisure: A conceptual statement. *Pacific Sociological Review, 25*, 25–72.

Stebbins, R. A. (1983). *The magician: Career, culture, and social psychology in a variety art.* Toronto, ON: Clarke Irwin.

Stebbins, R. A. (1992a). *Amateurs, professionals, and serious leisure*. Montreal, QC: McGill-Queen's University Press.

Stebbins, R. A. (1992b). Costs and rewards in barbershop singing. *Leisure Studies, 11*, 123–134.

Stebbins, R. A. (1992c). Hobbies as marginal leisure: The case of barbershop singers. *Loisir et Société/Society and Leisure, 15*, 375–386.

Stebbins, R. A. (1993). *Career, culture and social psychology in a variety art: The magician* (reprinted ed.). Malabar, FL: Krieger.

Stebbins, R. A. (1997). Casual leisure: A conceptual statement. *Leisure Studies, 16*, 17–25.

Stebbins, R. A. (2000). Obligation as an aspect of leisure experience. *Journal of Leisure Research, 32*, 152–155.

Stebbins, R. A. (2001a). *New directions in the theory and research of serious leisure*. Lewiston, NY: Edwin Mellen Press.

Stebbins, R. A. (2001b). The costs and benefits of hedonism: Some consequences of taking casual leisure seriously. *Leisure Studies, 20*, 305–309.

Stebbins, R. A. (2005). Challenging *mountain nature: Risk, motive, and lifestyle in three hobbyist sports.* Calgary, AB: Detselig Enterprises.

Stebbins, R. A. (2007). *Serious leisure: A perspective for our time.* New Brunswick, NJ: Transaction Press.

Stebbins, R. A. (2008). Leisure Reflections No. 81: Leisure abandonment: Quitting free-time activity that we love. *Leisure Studies Association Newsletter* (November).

Steers, R. M., & Porter, L. W. (1991). *Motivation and work behavior.* New York, NY: McGraw-Hill.

Stein, G. L., Kimiecik, J. C., Daniels, J., & Jackson, S. A. (1995). Psychological antecedents of flow in recreational sport. *Personality and Social Psychology Bulletin, 21*, 125–135.

Steiner, I. D. (1970). Perceived freedom. In L. Berkowitz (Ed.), *Advances in experimental social psychology,* (Vol. 5, pp. 187–248). New York, NY: Academic Press.

Steinkamp, M. W., & Kelly, J. R. (1986). Relationships among motivation orientation, level of leisure activity and life satisfaction in older men and women. *The Journal of Psychology, 119*, 509–520.

Steinkamp, M. W., & Kelly, J. R. (1987). Social integration, leisure activity, and life satisfaction in older adults: Activity theory revisited. *International Journal of Aging and Human Development, 25*, 293–307.

Stenseng, F. (2008). The two faces of leisure activity engagement: Harmonious and obsessive passion in relation to intrapersonal conflict and life domain outcomes. *Leisure Sciences, 30*, 465–481.

Stephan, C. W., Stephan, W. G., & Pettigrew, T. F. (Eds.). (1991). *The future of social psychology: Defining the relationship between sociology and psychology.* New York, NY: Springer-Verlag.

Stephens, N., Markus, H., & Townsend, S. (2007). Choice as an act of meaning: The case of social class. *Journal of Personality and Social Psychology, 93*, 814–830.

Stevenson, C. L. (1975). Socialization effects of participation in sport: A critical review of the literature. *Research Quarterly, 46*, 287–301.

Stewart, W. P. (1992). Influence of the onsite experience on recreation experience preference judgments. *Journal of Leisure Research, 24*, 185–198.

Stewart, W. P., & Floyd, M. F. (2004). Visualizing leisure. *Journal of Leisure Research, 36*, 445–460.

Stodolska, M. (1998). Assimilation and leisure constraint: Dynamics of constraints on leisure in immigrant populations. *Journal of Leisure Research, 30*, 521–551.

Stodolska, M. (2000). Looking beyond the invisible: Can research on leisure of ethnic and racial minorities contribute to leisure theory? *Journal of Leisure Research, 32*, 156–160.

Stodolska, M. (2002). Ceasing participation in leisure activities after immigrations: Eastern Europeans. *Society & Leisure, 25*, 79–117.

Stodolska, M. (2005). A conditioned attitude model of individual discriminatory behavior. *Leisure Sciences, 27*, 1–20.

Stodolska, M., & Alexandris, K. (2004). The role of recreational sport in the adaptation of first generation immigrants in the United States. *Journal of Leisure Research, 3*, 379–413.

Stodolska, M., & Jackson, E. L. (1998). Discrimination in leisure and work experienced by a white ethnic minority group. *Journal of Leisure Research, 30*, 521–551.

Stodolska, M., & Walker, G. J. (2007). Ethnicity and leisure: Historical development, current status, and future directions. *Leisure/Loisir, 31*, 3–26.

Stodolska, M., & Yi, J. (2003). Impacts of immigration on ethnic identity and leisure behavior of adolescent immigrants from Korea, Mexico, and Poland. *Journal of Leisure Research, 35*, 49–79.

Stodolska, M., & Yi-Kook, J. (2005). Ethnicity, immigration, and constraints. In E. L. Jackson (Ed.), *Constraints to leisure* (pp. 53–73). State College, PA: Venture Publishing, Inc.

Stoep, G. A. V., & Gramann, J. H. (1987). The effect of verbal appeals and incentives on depreciative behavior among youthful park visitors. *Journal of Leisure Research, 19*, 69–83.

Strauss-Blasche, G., Ekmekcioglu, C., & Marktl, W. (2002). Moderating effects of vacation on reactions to work and domestic stress. *Leisure Sciences, 24*, 237–249.

Strauss-Blasche, G., Muhry, F., Lehofer, M., Moser, M., & Marktl, W. (2004). Time course of well-being after a three-week resort-based respite from occupational and domestic demands: Carry-over, contrast and situation effects. *Journal of Leisure Research, 36*, 293–300.

Strauss, M., Gelles, R., & Steinmetz, S. (1980). *Behind closed doors.* New York, NY: Doubleday.

Strecher, V. J., DeVills, B. M., Becker, M. H., & Rosenstock, I. M. (1986). The role of self-efficacy in achieving health behavior change. *Health Education Quarterly, 13*, 73–81.

Stringer, P. F. (Ed.). (1984). *Annals of Tourism Research* (Vol. 11). New York, NY: Pergamon Press.

Strube, M. J., Turner, C. W., Patrick, S., & Perrillo, R. (1983). Type-A and Type-B attentional responses to aesthetic stimuli. *Journal of Personality and Social Psychology, 45*, 1369–1379.

Stryker, S. (1987). Identity theory: Development and extensions. In L. Yardley & T. Honess (Eds.), *Self and identity* (pp. 89–103). Chichester, UK: Wiley.

Stryker, S. (1997). "In the beginning there is society": Lessons from a sociological social psychology. In C. McGarty & S. A. Haslam (Eds.), *The message of social psychology: Perspectives on mind in society* (pp. 315–327). Malden, MA: Blackwell Publishers.

Stryker, S. (2000). Identity theory. In E. F. Borgatta & R. J. V. Montgomery (Eds.), *Encyclopedia of Sociology* (2nd ed., pp. 1253–1258). New York, NY: Macmillan.

Stuart, R. B. (1980). *Helping couples change.* New York, NY: Guilford.

Subrahmanyam, K., Greenfield, M. P., Kraut, R., & Gross, E. (2001). The impact of computer use on children's and adolescents' development. *Journal of Applied Developmental Psychology, 22*, 7–30.

Sullivan, H. S. (1953). *The interpersonal theory of psychiatry.* New York, NY: Norton.

Suman, V., Deepali, S., & Larson, R. (2002). School stress in India: Effects on time and daily emotions. *International Journal of Behavioral Development, 26*, 500–508.

Surgeon General, Office of the (2006). The Surgeon General's call to action to prevent and decrease overweight and obesity: Overweight in children and adolescents. Retrieved on February 12, 2007 from http://www.surgeongeneral.gov/topics/obesity/calltoaction/fact_adolescents.htm

Sutton, S., & Ditton, R. (2005). The substitutability of one type of fishing for another. *North American Journal of Fisheries Management, 25,* 536–546.

Swanson, G. E. (1978). Travels through inner space: Family structure and openness to absorbing experiences. *American Journal of Sociology, 83,* 890–919.

Swarns, R. (2004, October 24). Hispanics resist racial grouping by Census. *New York Times,* pp. A1, A18.

Sylvester, C. D. (1985). Freedom, leisure and therapeutic recreation: A philosophical view. *Therapeutic Recreation Journal, 19*(1), 6–13.

Szabo, A. (2003). The acute effects of humor and exercise on mood and anxiety. *Journal of Leisure Research, 35,* 152–162.

Szalai, A. (1972). *The use of time.* The Hague: Mouton.

Szinovacz, M., & Washo, C. (1992). Gender differences in exposure to life events and adaptation to retirement. *Journal of Gerontology, 47,* S191–S196.

Tang, T. L. (1986). Effects of Type-A personality and task labels (work vs. leisure) on task preference. *Journal of Leisure Research, 18,* 1–11.

Tang, T. L. (1988). Effects of Type-A personality and leisure ethic on Chinese college students' leisure activities and academic performance. *Journal of Social Psychology, 128,* 153–164.

Tangney, J. P., & Feshbach, S. (1988). Children's television viewing frequency. *Personality and Social Psychology Bulletin, 14,* 145–158.

Tapscott, D. (2009). *Grown up digital.* New York, NY: McGraw-Hill.

Taris, T. W., Geurts, S. A. E., Schaufeli, W. B., Blonk, R. W. B., & Lagerveld, S. E. (2008). All day and all of the night: The relative contribution of two dimensions of workaholism to well-being in self-employed workers. *Work and stress, 22,* 153–165.

Tarrant, M. A. (1996). Attending to past outdoor recreation experiences: Symptom reporting and changes in affect. *Journal of Leisure Research, 28,* 1–17.

Tcha, S. S., & Lobo, F. (2003). Analysis of constraints to sport and leisure participation—the case of Korean immigrants in Western Australia. *World Leisure Journal, 45,* 13–23.

Tedeschi, R. G., & Calhoun, C. G. (2004) Posttraumatic growth: Conceptual foundations and empirical evidence. *Psychological Inquiry, 15,* 1–18.

Tellegen, A., & Atkinson, G. (1974). Openness to absorbing and self-altering experience ("absorption"), a trait related to hypnotic susceptibility. *Journal of Abnormal Psychology, 83,* 268–277.

Tellegen, A., Lykken, D. T., Bourchard, T. J., Jr., Wilcox, K. J., Segal, N. L., & Rich, S. (1988). Personality similarity in twins reared apart and together. *Journal of Personality and Social Psychology, 54*(6), 1031–1039.

Tesser, A. (1988). Toward a self-evaluation maintenance model of social behavior. *Advances in Experimental Social Psychology, 21,* 181–227. New York, NY: Academic Press.

Thackeray, R. I., Jones, K. N., & Touchstone, R. M. (1974). Personality and physiological correlates of performance decrement on a monotonous task requiring sustained attention. *British Journal of Psychology, 65,* 351–358.

Theberge, N. (1991). Reflections on the body in the sociology of sport. *Quest, 43*(2), 123–134.

Theriault, J. (1994). Retirement as a psychological transition: Process of adaptation to change. *International Journal of Aging and Human Development, 38*, 153–170.

Thibaut, J. W., & Kelley, H. H. (1959). *The social psychology of groups.* New York, NY: Wiley.

Thirlaway, K., & Upton, D. (2009). *The psychology of lifestyle: Promoting healthy behavior.* New York, NY: Routledge/Taylor and Francis Group.

Thoits, P. A. (1995). Social psychology: The interplay between sociology and psychology. *Social Forces, 73*, 1231–1243.

Thomas, D. (2005). "I am Canadian." *Canadian Social Trends, Spring*, 2–7.

Thompson, A., Rehman, L., & Humbert, M. R. (2005). Factors influencing the physically active leisure of children and youth: A qualitative study. *Leisure Sciences, 27*, 421–438.

Thompson, S. M., Grant, B. C., & Dharmalingam, A. (2002). Leisure time in midlife: What are the odds? *Leisure Studies, 21*, 125–143.

Tinsley, H. E. A. (1984). The psychological benefits of leisure counseling. *Loisir et Société/ Society and Leisure, 7*, 125–140.

Tinsley, H. E. A., & Kass, R. A. (1980). The construct validity of the Leisure Activities Questionnaire and of the Paragraphs About Leisure. *Educational and Psychological Measurement, 40*, 219–226.

Tinsley, H. E. A., & Tinsley, D. J. (1986). A theory of the attributes, benefits, and causes of leisure experience. *Leisure Sciences, 8*, 1–45.

Tinsley, H. E. A., Tinsley, D. J., & Croskeys, E. (2002). Park usage, social milieu, and psychosocial benefits of park use reported by older urban park users from four ethnic groups. *Leisure Sciences, 24*, 199–218.

Tirone, S. (1999). Racism, indifference and the leisure experience of South Asian Canadian teens. *Leisure/Loisir 24*, 89–114.

Toffler, A. (1970). *Future shock.* New York, NY: Random House, Inc.

Toleman, W. (1909). *Social engineering.* New York, NY: McGraw-Hill Publishing.

Trafton, R. S., & Tinsley, H. E. A. (1980). An investigation of the construct validity of measures of job, leisure, dyadic, and general life satisfaction. *Journal of Leisure Research, 12*, 34–44.

Triandis, H. (1995). *Individualism & collectivism.* Boulder, CO: Westview Press.

Triplett, N. (1897/1898). The dynamogenic factors in pacemaking and competition. *American Journal of Psychology, 9*, 507–533.

Trussell, D. E., & Shaw, S. M. (2007). Daddy's gone and he'll be back in October: Farm women's experiences of family leisure. *Journal of Leisure Research, 39*, 366–387.

Tsai, E., & Coleman, D. (2007). Preferences for active recreation and perceived constraints to regular active recreation participation: A cross-cultural study of Hong Kong and Australian university students. *Leisure/Loisir, 31*, 155–189.

Tsai, J. L., Knutson, B., & Fung, H. H., (2006). Cultural variation in affect valuation. *Journal of Personality and Social Psychology, 90*, 288–307.

Tsai, J. L., Miao, F., & Seppala, E. (2007). Good feelings in Christianity and Buddhism: Religious differences in ideal affect. *Personality and Social Psychology Bulletin, 33*, 409–421.

Tubesing, D. A., & Loving-Tubesing, N. (1991). *Seeking your healthy balance.* Duluth, MN: Whole Person Associates.

Tucker, L. A. (1993). Television viewing and exercise habits of 8,885 adults. *Perceptual and Motor Skills, 77*, 938–939.

Turner, J. S. (2009). Social interaction in adventure recreation programs. Unpublished doctoral dissertation. University of Georgia, Athens, GA.

Turner, R. H. (1978). The role and the person. *American Journal of Sociology, 84*, 1–23.

Turner, R. H. (1987). Articulating self and social structure. In K. Yardley, & T. Honess (Eds.), *Self and Identity* (pp. 128–144). New York, NY: Wiley.

Unger, L. S., & Kernan, J. B. (1983). On the meaning of leisure: An investigation of some determinants of the subjective experience. *Journal of Consumer Research, 9*, 381–392.

United Nations. (n.d.). *The universal declaration of human rights.* Retrieved August 6, 2009 from http://www.un.org/en/documents/udhr/

United Nations World Tourism Organization News. (Thursday, October 8, 2009). Retrieved from http://www.unwto.org

United States Census Bureau. (n.d.). 2005–2007 American Community Survey 3-year estimates— What's this? Data profile highlights. Retrieved July 30, 2009 from http://www.census.gov/Press-Release/www/releases/archives/population/001720.html

United States Census Bureau. (2008). Projection of the population by race and Hispanic origin for the United States: 2008 to 2050. Retrieved July 30, 2009 from http://factfinder.census.gov/servlet/ACSSAFFFacts?_event=&geo_id=01000US&_geoCo

United States Outdoor Recreation Resources Review Commission. (1962). *National recreation survey.* ORRRC Study Report 19, Berkeley, CA: University of California, Wildland Research Center.

Unkel, M. B. (1981). Physical recreation participation of females and males during the adult life cycle. *Leisure Sciences, 4*, 1–27.

Unruh, A. M. & Hutchinson, S. L. (2008). *Gardening as spiritual leisure activity.* Paper presented at the 12th Canadian Conference on Leisure Research, Montreal.

Unruh, D. R. (1980). The nature of social worlds. *Pacific Sociological Review, 23*, 271–296.

Urry, J. (2002) *The tourist gaze* (2nd ed.). London, UK: Sage Publications.

Utz, R. L., Carr, D., Nesse, R., & Wortman, C. B. (2002). The effect of widowhood on older adults' social participation: An evaluation of activity, disengagement, and continuity theories. *Gerontologist, 42*, 522–533.

Vaillant, G. (2002). *Aging well.* New York, NY: Little Brown.

Valentine, K., Allison, M., & Schneider, I. (1999). The one-way mirror of leisure research: A need for cross-national social scientific perspectives. *Leisure Sciences, 21*, 241–246.

Valkenburg, P. M., & Peter, J. (2009). Social consequences of the internet for adolescents: A decade of research. *Current Directions in Psychological Science, 18*, 2–5.

Vallerand, R. J., & Losier, G. (1999). An integrative analysis of intrinsic and extrinsic motivation in sport. *Journal of Applied Sport Psychology, 11*, 142–169.

Vallerand, R. J., Salvy, S. J., Mageau, G. A., Elliot, A. J., Denis, P. L., Grouzet, F. M., & Blanchard, C. (2007). On the role of passion in performance. *Journal of Personality, 75*, 505–533.

Van Acker, R. & Valenti, S. S. (1989). Perception of social affordance with mild handicapping conditions: Implications for social skills training. *Ecological Psychology, 1*, 383–405.

Van Egeren, L., Sniderman, L., & Ruggelin, M. (1982). Competitive two person interactions of Type-A and Type-B individuals. *Journal of Behaviorial Medicine, 5*, 55–66.

Van Evra, J. (1990). *Television and child development*. Hillsdale, NJ: Erlbaum.

Van Strien, P. J. (1997). The American "colonization" of northwest European social psychology after World War II. *Journal of the History of the Behavioral Sciences, 33*, 349–363.

Vaske, J. J., & Donnelly, M. (2002). Generalizing the encounter-norm-crowding relationship. *Leisure Sciences, 24*, 255–269.

Vaske, J. J. , Needham, M. D., & Cline, R. C. (2007). Clarifying interpersonal and social values conflict among recreationists. *Journal of Leisure Research, 39*, 182–195.

Vaske, J. J., & Shelby, L. B. (2008). Crowding as a descriptive indicator and an evaluative standard: Results from 30 years of research. *Leisure Sciences, 30*, 111–126.

Vaughan, G. M., & Hogg, M. A. (1995). *Introduction to social psychology*. Upper Saddle River, NJ: Prentice-Hall.

Veal, A. J. (1989). Leisure, lifestyle, and status: A pluralist framework for analysis. *Leisure Studies, 8*, 141–153.

Veal, A. J. (1993). The concept of lifestyle: A review. *Leisure Studies, 12*, 233–252.

Veblen, T. (1899). *The theory of the leisure class*. New York, NY: Viking Press.

Veroff, J., & Smith, D. A. (1985). Motives and values over the adult years. In D. A. Kleiber & M. L. Maehr (Eds.), *Motivation and adulthood* (p. 1–53). Greenwich, CT: JAI Press.

Vitterso, J., Chipeniuk, R., Skar, M., & Vistad, O. I. (2004). Recreational conflict is affective: the case of cross-country skiers and snowmobiles. *Leisure Sciences, 26*, 227–243.

Voelkl, J. E. (1990). The challenge skill ratio of daily experiences among older adults residing in nursing homes. *Therapeutic Recreation Journal, 24*, 7–17.

Vogt, C. A., & Stewart, S. I. (1998). Affective and cognitive effects of information use over the course of a vacation. *Journal of Leisure Research, 30*, 498–520.

Vooijs, M. W., & vanderVoort, T. H. A. (1993). Teaching children to evaluate television violence critically: The impact of a Dutch schools television project. *Journal of Educational Television, 19*, 139–152.

Vroom, V. H. (1964). *Work and motivation*. New York, NY: Wiley.

Wade, M. G. (1985). *Constraints on leisure*. Springfield, IL: Charles C. Thomas.

Wahba, M. A., & Bridwell, L. G. (1976). Maslow reconsidered: A review of research on the need hierarchy theory. *Organizational Behavior and Human Performance, 15*, 212–240.

Wahlers, R. G., & Etzel, M. J. (1985). Vacation preference as a manifestation of optimal stimulation and lifestyle experience. *Journal of Leisure Research, 17*, 283–295.

Wakefield, K. L., & Wann, D. L. (2006). An examination of dysfunctional sports fans: Methods of classification and relationships with problem behaviors. *Journal of Leisure Research, 38,* 168–186.

Walker, G. J. (2008). Motivation in everyday life: The case of ChineseCanadians. *World Leisure Journal, 50*, 116–126.

Walker, G. J. (2009). Culture, self-construal, and leisure motivations. *Leisure Sciences, 31*, 347–363.

Walker, G. J. (2010). The effects of personal, contextual, and situational factors on the facilitation of intrinsic motivation: The case of Chinese/Canadians. *Journal of Leisure Research, 42*, 43–66.

Walker, G. J., Courneya, K. S., & Deng, J. (2006). Ethnicity, gender, and the theory of planned behavior: The case of playing the lottery. *Journal of Leisure Research, 38*, 224–248.

Walker, G. J., & Deng, J. (2003/2004). Comparing leisure as a subjective experience with the Chinese experience of *rùmí. Leisure/Loisir, 28*, 245–276.

Walker, G. J., Deng, J., & Chapman, R. (2007). Leisure attitudes: A follow-up study comparing Canadians, Chinese in Canada, and Mainland Chinese. *World Leisure Journal, 49*, 207–215.

Walker, G. J., Deng, J., & Dieser, R. (2001). Ethnicity, acculturation, self-construal, and motivations for outdoor recreation. *Leisure Sciences, 23*, 263–283.

Walker, G. J., Deng, J., & Dieser, R. (2005). Culture, self-construal, and leisure theory and practice. *Journal of Leisure Research, 37*, 77–99.

Walker, G. J., Dieser, R., & Deng, J. (2005). "Whoa versus go!" A rejoinder to Mannell and Caldwell. *Journal of Leisure Research, 37*, 117–127.

Walker, G. J., Hinch, T. D., & Weighill, A. J. (2005). Inter- and intra-gender similarities and differences in motivations for casino gambling. *Leisure Sciences, 27*, 111–130.

Walker, G. J., Hull, R. B., & Roggenbuck, J. (1998). On-site optimal experiences and their relationship to off-site benefits. *Journal of Leisure Research, 30*, 453–471.

Walker, G. J., Jackson, E. L., & Deng, J. (2007). Culture and leisure constraints: A comparison of Canadian and Mainland Chinese university students. *Journal of Leisure Research, 39*, 567–590.

Walker, G. J., Jackson, E. L., & Deng, J. (2008). The role of self-construal as an intervening variable between culture and leisure constraints: A comparison of Canadian and Mainland Chinese university students. *Journal of Leisure Research, 40*, 90–109.

Walker, G. J., & Virden, R. J. (2005). Constraints on outdoor recreation. In E. L. Jackson (Ed.), *Constraints to leisure* (pp. 201–219). State College, PA: Venture Publishing, Inc.

Walker, G. J., & Wang, X. (2008). A cross-cultural comparison of Canadian and Mainland Chinese university students' leisure motivations. *Leisure Sciences, 30*, 179–197.

Walker, G. J., & Wang, X. (2009). The meaning of leisure for Chinese/Canadians. *Leisure Sciences, 31*, 1–18.

Walker, J. (1999). African Americans. In E. R. Barkan (Ed.), *A nations of people sourcebook on America's multicultural heritage* (pp. 19–47). Santa Barbara, CA: Greenwood Press.

Wang, J., & Stringer, A. (2000). Impact of Taoism on Chinese leisure. *World Leisure, 42,* 33–41.

Wang, X. (2009). *A comparison of Canadian and Chinese university students' travel motivations and the concept of face.* Unpublished doctoral dissertation, University of Alberta, Canada.

Wankel, L. M. (1985). Personal and situational factors affecting exercise involvement: The importance of enjoyment. *Research Quarterly for Exercise and Sport, 56,* 275–282.

Wankel, L. M. (1993). The importance of enjoyment to adherence and psychological benefits from physical activity. *International Journal of Sport Psychology, 24,* 151–169.

Wankel, L. M., & Berger, B. G. (1991). The personal and social benefits of sport and physical activity. In B. L. Driver, P. J. Brown, & G. L. Peterson (Eds.), *Benefits of leisure* (pp. 121–144). State College, PA: Venture Publishing, Inc.

Wankel, L. M., & Kreisel, P. S. J. (1985). Factors underlying enjoyment of youth sports: Sport and age group comparisons *Journal of Sport Psychology, 7,* 51–64.

Wankel, L. M., & Sefton, J. M. (1989a). Factors distinguishing high- and low-fun experiences in ice hockey. *World Leisure and Recreation, Fall,* 29–31.

Wankel, L. M., & Sefton, J. M. (1989b). A season-long investigation of fun in youth sports. *Journal of Sport and Exercise Psychology, 11,* 355–366.

Warner, J. (2005). *Perfect madness: Motherhood in the age of anxiety.* New York, NY: Riverhead Books.

Warr, P. B. (1983). Work, jobs, and unemployment. *Bulletin of the British Psychological Society, 36,* 305–311.

Warr, P. B., & Jackson, P. R. (1984). Men without jobs: Some correlates of age and length of unemployment. *Journal of Occupational Psychology, 57,* 77–85.

Warr, P. B., & Jackson, P. R. (1985). Factors influencing the psychological impact of prolonged unemployment and re-employment. *Psychological Medicine, 15,* 795–807.

Warren, K., Mitten, D., & Loeffler, T. A., (Eds.). (2008). *Theory and Practice of Experiential Education.* Boulder, CO: Association for Experiential Education.

Washburne, R. (1978). Black under-participation in wildland recreation: Alternative explanations. *Leisure Sciences, 1,* 175–189.

Waterman, A. S. (1990). Personal expressiveness: Philosophical and psychological foundations. *Journal of Mind and Behavior, 11,* 47–74.

Waterman, A. S. (1993a). Two conceptions of happiness: Contrasts of personal expressiveness (eudaimonia) and hedonic enjoyment. *Journal of Personality and Social Psychology, 64,* 678–691.

Waterman, A. S. (1993b). Finding something to do or someone to be: A eudaimonist perspective on identity formation. In J. Kroger (Ed.), *Discussions on Ego Identity.* Hillsdale, NJ: Lawrence Erlbaum.

Waterman, A. S., Schwartz, S., Goldbacher, E., Green, H., Miller, C., & Philip, S. (2003). Predicting the subjective experience of intrinsic motivation: The roles of self-determination, the balance of challenge and skills, and self-realization values. *Personality and Social Psychology Bulletin, 29,* 1447–1458.

Watkins, M. (2000). Ways of learning about leisure meanings. *Leisure Sciences, 22*, 93–107.

Watkins, M., & Bond, C. (2007). Ways of experiencing leisure. *Leisure Sciences, 29*, 287–307.

Watten, R. G. (1995). Sports, physical exercise and use of alcohol. *Scandinavian Journal of Medicine and Science in Sports, 5*, 364–368.

Watts, C. E., & Caldwell, L. L. (2008). Self-determination and free time activity participation as predictors of initiative. *Journal of Leisure Research, 40*, 156–181.

Wearing, B. (1990). Beyond the ideology of motherhood: Leisure as resistance. *Australian and New Zealand Journal of Sociology, 26*, 36–58.

Wearing, B. (1998). *Leisure and feminist theory*. London, UK: Sage Publications.

Wearing, S., & Wearing, B. (2000). Smoking as a fashion accessory in the 90s: conspicuous consumption, identity, and adolescent women's leisure choices. *Leisure Studies, 19*, 45–58.

Webb, H. (1969). Professionalization of attitudes toward play among adolescents. In G. D. Kenyon (Ed.), *Sociology of sport* (pp. 161–187). Chicago, IL: The Athletic Institute.

Weber, E., Hsee, C., & Sokolowska, J. (1998). What folklore tells us about risk and risk taking: Cross-cultural comparisons of American, German, and Chinese proverbs. *Organizational Behavior and Human Decision Processes, 75*, 170–186.

Wegner, L., Flisher, A. J., Muller, M., & Lombard, C. (2006). Leisure, boredom, and substance use among high school students in South Africa. *Journal of Leisure Research, 38*, 249–266.

Weiner, B. (1985). An attribution theory of achievement motivation and emotion. *Psychological Review, 66*, 297–233.

Weiner, B. (1986). *An attributional theory of motivation and emotion*. New York, NY: Springer-Velag.

Weir, L. (1928). *Parks: A manual of municipal and county parks*. New York, NY: A. S. Barnes and Co.

Weiss, P., Bialik, P., & Kizony, R. (2003). Virtual reality provides leisure time opportunities for young adults with physical and intellectual disabilities. *CyberPsychology & Behavior, 6*, 335–342.

Weiss, R. S. (2005). *The experience of retirement*. Ithaca, NY: Cornell University Press.

Weissinger, E., & Bandalos, D. L. (1995). Development, reliability and validity of a scale to measure intrinsic motivation in leisure. *Journal of Leisure Research, 27*, 379–400.

Weissinger, E., Henderson, K. A., & Bowling, C. P. (1997). Toward an expanding methodological base in leisure studies: Researchers' knowledge, attitudes and practices concerning qualitative research. *Society and Leisure, 20*, 435–451.

Weissinger, E. and Iso-Ahola, S. E. (1984). Intrinsic leisure motivation, personality and physical health. *Loisir et Société/Society and Leisure, 7*, 217–228.

Weissinger, E., & Iso-Ahola, S. E. (1987). Relationship between Type-A behavior and self-reported leisure activity patterns. *Wellness Perspectives, 4*, 9–14.

Weisz, J., Rothbaum, F., & Blackburn, T. (1984). Standing out and standing in: The psychology of control in America and Japan. *American Psychologist, 39*, 955–969.

Wells, A. J. (1988). Self-esteem and optimal experience. In M. Csikszentmihalyi and I. S. Csikszentmihalyi (Eds.), *Optimal experience* (pp. 327–341). New York, NY: Cambridge University Press.

West, P. C. (1989). Urban region parks and black minorities: Subculture, marginality, and interracial relations in park use in the Detroit metropolitan area. *Leisure Sciences, 11,* 11–28.

West, P. C., & Merriam, L. C., Jr. (1970). Outdoor recreation and family cohesiveness: A research approach. *Journal of Leisure Research, 2,* 251–259.

Westman, M., & Eden, D. (1997). Effect of respite from work on burnout: Vacation relief and fade-out. *Journal of Applied Psychology, 82,* 516–527.

Westman, M., & Etzion, D. (2001). The impact of vacation and job stress on burnout and absenteeism. *Psychology & Health. Special Issue: Burnout and Health, 16,* 595–606.

Wheeler, R. J., & Frank, M. A. (1988). Identification of stress buffers. *Behavioral Medicine, 14,* 78–89.

White, R. W. (1959). Motivation reconsidered: The concept of competence. *Psychological Review, 66,* 297–333.

Whyte, L. B., & Shaw, S. M. (1994). Women's leisure: An exploratory study of fear of violence as a leisure constraint. *Journal of Applied Recreation Research, 19,* 5–21.

Wiersma, E. C., & Dupuis, S. C. (2008). *The dual nature of leisure: Conformity and resistance.* Proceedings of the 12th Canadian Conference on Leisure Research, Montreal.

Wild, T. C., Enzle, M., Nix, G., & Deci, E. (1997). Perceiving others as intrinsically or extrinsically motivated: Effects on expectancy formation and task engagement. *Personality and Social Psychology Bulletin, 23,* 837–848.

Wilensky, H. L. (1960). Work, careers, and social integration. *International Social Science Journal, 4,* 543–560.

Wiley, C., Shaw, S., & Havitz, M. (2000). Men's and women's involvement in sports: An examination of the gendered aspects of leisure involvement. *Leisure Sciences, 22,* 19–31.

Wilkinson, I. (2001). *Anxiety in a risk society.* London, UK: Routledge.

Williams, D. (2002). Leisure identities, globalization, and the politics of place. *Journal of Leisure Research, 34,* 351–367.

Williams, D. R., Ellis, G. D., Nickerson, N. P., & Shafer, C. S. (1988). Contributions of time, format, and subject to variation in recreation experience preference measurement. *Journal of Leisure Research, 20,* 57–68.

Williams, J. M. (1978). Personality characteristics of the successful female athlete. In W. F. Straub (Ed.), *Sport psychology* (pp. 249–255). Ithaca, NY: Mouvement Publications.

Willmott, P. (1971). Family, work and leisure conflicts among male employees. *Human Relations, 24,* 575–584.

Wilson, P., Rodgers, W., Blanchard, C., & Gessell, J. (2003). The relationship between psychological needs, self-determined motivation, exercise attitudes, and physical fitness. *Journal of Applied Social Psychology, 33,* 2373–2392.

Wiltermuth, S. S., & Heath, C. (2009). Synchrony and cooperation. *Psychological Science, 20,* 1–5.

Winefield, A. H., Tiggemann, M., Winefield, H. R., & Goldney, R. D. (1993). *Growing up with unemployment: A longitudinal study of its psychological impact.* London, UK: Routledge.

Witt, P. A. (1971). Factor structure of leisure behavior for high school age youth in three communities. *Journal of Leisure Research, 3*, 213–219.

Witt, P. A., & Bishop, D. W. (1970). Situational antecedents to leisure behavior. *Journal of Leisure Research, 2*, 64–77.

Witt, P. A., & Caldwell, L. L. (2005). *Recreation and youth development.* State College, PA: Venture Publishing, Inc.

Witt, P. A., & Ellis, G. D. (1984). The leisure diagnostic battery: Measuring perceived freedom in leisure. *Loisir et Société/Society and Leisure, 7*, 109–124.

Witt, P. A., & Ellis, G. D. (1985). Development of a short form to assess perceived freedom in leisure. *Journal of Leisure Research, 17*, 225–233.

Witt, P. A., & Goodale, T. L. (1981). The relationships between barriers to leisure enjoyment and family stages. *Leisure Sciences, 4*, 29–49.

Witt, P. A., & Goodale, T. L. (1985). Barriers to leisure across family stages. In M. G. Wade (Ed.), *Constraints on leisure* (pp. 227–242). Springfield, IL: Charles C. Thomas.

Worchel, S., & Brown, E. H. (1984). The role of plausibility in influencing environmental attributions. *Journal of Experimental Social Psychology, 20*, 86–96.

World Bank. (2009). *Gross domestic product 2008.* Retrieved August 4, 2009 from http://siteresources.worldbank.org/DATASTATISTICS/Resources/GDP.pdf

World Tourism Organization. (2000). *Tourism 2020 vision: East Asia & Pacific* (Vol. 3, pp. 12–77). Madrid, Spain.

Wortman, C. B. (1975). Some determinants of perceived control. *Journal of Personality and Social Psychology, 31*, 282–294.

Wright, R. A., Wadely, V. G., Danner, M., & Phillips, P. N. (1992). Persuasion, reactance, and judgements of interpersonal appeal. *European Journal of Social Psychology, 22*, 85–91.

Wrześniewski, A., Rozin, P., & Bennett, G. (2003). Working, playing and eating: Making the most of most moments. In C. Keyes & J. Haidt (Eds.), *Flourishing: Positive psychology and the life well lived.* Washington, DC: American Psychological Association.

Wrześniewski, K., Wonicki, J., & Turlejski, J. (1988). Type A behavior pattern and illness other than coronary heart disease. *Social Science & Medicine, 27*, 623–626.

Wu, H. (2002). *Yellow: Race in American beyond Black and White.* New York, NY: Basic Books.

Yang, K., Hwang, K., Pedersen, P. B., & Daibo, I. (Eds.) (2003). *Progress in Asian social psychology: Conceptual and empirical contributions.* Westport, CT: Praeger Publishers/Greenwood Publishing.

Yarnal, C. (2006). The Red Hat Society: Exploring the role of play liminiality and communitas in older women's lives. *Journal of Women and Aging, 18*, 51–73.

Yarnal, C., Chick, G., & Kerstetter, D. (2008). "I did not have time to play growing up . . . So this is my play time. It's the best thing I have ever done for myself": What is play to older women? *Leisure Sciences, 30*, 235–252.

Yau, M. K-S., & Packer, T. (2002). Health and well-being through T'ai Chi: Perceptions of older adults in Hong Kong. *Leisure Studies, 21*, 163–178.

Yoesting, D. R., & Christensen, J. E. (1978). Reexamining the significance of childhood recreation patterns on adult leisure behavior. *Leisure Sciences, 1*, 27–38.

Yoesting, D. R., & Burkhead, D. L. (1973). Significance of childhood recreation experience on adult leisure behavior: An exploratory analysis. *Journal of Leisure Research, 5*, 25–36.

Young, R. A., & Crandall, R. (1984). Wilderness use and self-actualization. *Journal of Leisure Research, 16*, 149–160.

Yuen, F. C. (2004). "It was fun . . . I liked drawing my thoughts": Using drawings as a part of the focus group process with children. *Journal of Leisure Research, 36*, 461–482.

Yuen, F. C., Pedlar, A., & Mannell, R. (2005). Building community and social capital through children's leisure in the context of an international camp. *Journal of Leisure Research, 37*, 494–518.

Zabriskie, R. B., & McCormick, B. P. (2001). The influences of family leisure patterns on perceptions of family functioning. *Family Relations, 50*, 66–74.

Zabriskie, R. B., & McCormick, B. P. (2003). Parent and child perspectives of family leisure involvement and satisfaction with family life. *Journal of Leisure Research, 35*, 163–189.

Zajonc, R. B. (1965). Social facilitation. *Science, 149*, 269–274.

Zanna, M. P., & Rempel, J. K. (1988). Attitudes: A new look at an old concept. In D. Bar-Tal and A. Kruglanski (Eds.), *The social psychology of knowledge* (pp. 315–334). New York, NY: Cambridge University Press.

Zeijl, E., te Poel, Y., du Bois-Reymond, M., Ravesloot, J., & Meulman, J. J. (2000). The role of parents and peers in the leisure activities of young adolescents. *Journal of Leisure Research, 32*, 281–303.

Zillmann, D., & Vorderer, P. (2000). *Media entertainment: The psychology of its appeal*. Mahwah, NJ: Lawrence Erlbaum Associates.

Zimbardo, P. G. (1990). *Shyness: What is it? What to do about it?* New York: Da Capo Press.

Zimbardo, P. G. (1992). Foreword. In S. S. Brehm (Ed.), *Intimate relationships* (p. xiv–xvi). New York, NY: McGraw-Hill.

Zimbardo, P. G., & Boyd, J. (1999). Putting time in perspective: A valid, reliable individual-differences metric. *Journal of Personality and Social Psychology, 77*, 1271–1288.

Zuckerman, M. (1979). *Sensation seeking: Beyond the optimal level of arousal*. Hillsdale, NJ: LEA.

Zuckerman, M. (1994). *Behavioral expression and biosocial bases of sensation seeking*. New York: Cambridge University Press.

Zuzanek, J. (1980). The work-leisure relationship in Soviet sociological discussion. *Canadian Slavonic Papers, 22*, 122–128.

Zuzanek, J. (1982). Leisure research in North America from a socio-historical perspective. In D. Ng & S. Smith (Eds.), *Perspectives on the nature of leisure research* (pp. 170–186). Waterloo, ON: University of Waterloo Press.

Zuzanek, J. (1991). Leisure research in North America: A critical retrospective. *Loisir et Société/Society and Leisure, 14*, 587–596.

Zuzanek, J. (2005). Adolescent time use and well-being from a comparative perspective. *Loisir et Societe /Society and Leisure, 28*, 379–423.

Zuzanek, J., & Box, S. J. (1988). Life course and the daily lives of older adults in Canada. In K. Altergott (Ed.), *Daily life in later life* (pp. 147–185). Newbury Park, CA: Sage Publications.

Zuzanek, J., & Mannell, R. C. (1983). Work-leisure relationships from a sociological and social psychological perspective. *Leisure Studies, 2*, 327–344.

Zuzanek, J., & Mannell, R. C. (1993a). Gender variations in the weekly rhythms of daily behavior and experiences. *Journal of Occupational Science, 1*, 25–37.

Zuzanek, J., & Mannell, R. C. (1993b). Leisure behaviour and experiences as part of everyday life: The weekly rhythm. *Loisir et Société/Society and Leisure, 16*, 31–57.

Zuzanek, J., & Smale, B. J. A. (1992). Life-cycle variations in across-the-week allocation of time to selected daily activities. *Loisir et Société/Society and Leisure, 15*, 559–586.

Index

savoring 100, 126–127, 357, 357–360
Schachter, S. 33
Schor, J. 8–9
Schreyer, R. 121
Schwartz, G. M. 381
scientific method 5–8, 11, 17, 20
Scott, D. 118–119, 209, 235, 261, 276, 320, 437
Searle, M. S. 64, 149, 239, 304, 443, 445
selective optimization with compensation 417, 429, 434–435
self-actualization 135–136, 166, 280, 323, 355–356
self-as-entertainment 192–193, 211–212, 226
self-awareness 83, 185, 244, 362, 440
self-concept 275, 356, 364, 385, 416, 436
self-construal 330–336, 340
self-defeating personality 199
self-determination 160–164, 167, 170
    theory 156, 160–164, 171–176, 325–327
self-efficacy 122, 177, 360, 396, 408, 425, 440, 442, 444
self-esteem 135–136
self-expression 13, 89, 90, 114, 118, 120, 136, 140, 185, 190, 208, 250, 251, 253, 268, 272, 286, 298, 305, 307, 361–362, 367–368, 382–383, 409, 419, 426, 445, 451
self-identity. *See* identity
self-protection 380, 386–389
self-socialization 268, 277, 306
Seligman, M. 6, 34, 109, 149, 167, 356, 367
sensation seeking 203
serious leisure 41, 75, 91–92 116–121, 163, 168, 198, 220, 244, 273, 293, 326, 353, 355, 357, 361, 364, 382–383, 392, 407–408, 413, 418, 441, 443
service quality 9–11
Sessoms, H. D. 57
setting management 449
Shafer, C. S. 118–119, 123, 195, 437
Shamir, B. 118–119, 220, 382

Shannon, C. S. 92, 269, 283, 288
Sharp, A. 390–391, 415
Sharpe, E. 11, 360, 368
Shaw, S. M. 45–46, 80–83, 86, 92, 104, 113, 139, 245, 247, 251, 257–258, 260–261, 269, 275, 280, 283, 287–289, 292, 300–301, 307, 337–338, 352, 355, 366, 377, 383, 393, 402–403, 405, 419, 428–429, 448
Shelby, B. 418, 432–433
Sherif, M. 32, 37–38, 350, 451
Shinew, K. J. 46, 290, 304, 397, 407
Shores, K. 209
shyness 211
Sibthorp, J. 360, 386
sign value 274, 365
situationism 20–22
Skinner, B. F. 20, 164
Smith, S. L. J. 197, 353
Snepenger, D. 138
social capital 368, 406–407, 438, 451
social cognition 34, 164–167
social comparison 274–275
social exchange 33
social facilitation 31–37, 306
social influence 36–37, 267–307
social integration 278, 438
social loafing 31
social norms 215, 290, 305, 397
social perception 37–38
social psychology
    approaches 17–26, 35
    definition of 3–5
    history 30–35
    psychological 12
    social psychology of leisure 11–16, 26
    sociological 12
    treatment of leisure in social psychology 36–39
social science
    general 4–5
    study of leisure 6–9
social support 306, 329, 387–388
socialization
    adulthood 379–307

About the Authors

Douglas Kleiber is a professor in the Recreation and Leisure Studies Program of the Department of Counseling and Human Development Services at the University of Georgia where he also holds adjunct appointments in Psychology and Gerontology. After undergraduate work in psychology at Cornell University he completed a Ph.D. in educational psychology at the University of Texas in 1972. He has held faculty positions at Cornell University, St. Cloud State University and the University of Illinois before moving to Georgia in 1989. At the University of Illinois, he served as director of the Leisure Behavior Research Laboratory from 1982 to 1987, and at UGA he was the director of the School of Health and Human Performance from 2001 to 2003. Dr. Kleiber is a member and past president and treasurer of the Academy of Leisure Sciences and has received the Allan V Sapora Award, the National Recreation and Park Association's Theodore and Franklin Roosevelt Award for Excellence in Recreation and Park Research and the SPRE Distinguished Colleague Award. His research is directed primarily to the influence of leisure activity and experience on human development and adjustment across the life span. His current leisure interests include hiking and trail maintenance, biking, reading, and playing with grandchildren.

Gordon Walker is a Professor in the Faculty of Physical Education and Recreation at the University of Alberta. He received his Ph.D. from Virginia Polytechnic and State University. His research program integrates social, environmental, and cross-cultural psychology into leisure theory. He is particularly interested in how culture and ethnicity affect leisure participation (e.g., exercising, gambling, outdoor recreation) and leisure behavior (e.g., motivations for, constraints to, experiences during, and benefits from, leisure). To date, Dr. Walker's research has focused on Mainland Chinese, Chinese/Canadian, Indo/Canadian, and British/Canadian people's leisure, with funding from the Alberta Gaming Research Institute and the Social Science and Humanities Research Council of Canada. Dr. Walker was a recipient of a University of Alberta McCalla Professorship for 2008/2009. He was also invited to teach two courses on culture and leisure at Shanghai University of Sport in 2009, the same year he became an Academy of Leisure Sciences Fellow. His leisure interests include reading (histories and mysteries), adventure travel (he has visited every continent except Antarctica), and listening to music (blues, classical, and classic rock—especially "the Boss").

Roger Mannell is a psychologist and professor of leisure and health studies and gerontology at the University of Waterloo. He was Director of the Center of Leisure Studies at Acadia University in Nova Scotia, Canada before joining the University of Waterloo where he has served as Chair of the Department of Recreation and Leisure Studies and Dean of Applied Health Sciences. Currently, he is Director of the RBC Your Future by Design Retirement Research Centre. Dr. Mannell is a regular contributor to the social psychological study of leisure and his research has been funded by the Canadian Population Health Initiative, Canadian Institutes of Health Research, the Social Science and Humanities Research Council of Canada, and the Change Foundation. In particular, he is interested in social psychological factors that influence leisure and lifestyle choices and in turn how these choices affect mental and physical health. These interests have led him to study work-leisure relationships, successful aging and retirement, adolescent media use, and the role of leisure in coping with stress. Dr. Mannell is also a past president of the Academy of Leisure Sciences and has also received the Allan V. Sapora Research Award and the National Recreation and Park Association's Theodore and Franklin Roosevelt Award for Excellence in Recreation and Park Research. His leisure interests include reading, kayaking, house renovations, coaching youth sports, and recreating with his wife and five children.

Other Books by Venture Publishing, Inc.

21st Century Leisure: Current Issues, Second Edition
    by Valeria J. Freysinger and John R. Kelly
Active Living in Older Adulthood: Principles and Practices of Activity Programs
    by Barbara A. Hawkins
Activity Experiences and Programming within Long-Term Care
    by Ted Tedrick and Elaine R. Green
Adventure Programming edited
    by John C. Miles and Simon Priest
Assessment: The Cornerstone of Activity Programs
    by Ruth Perschbacher
Beyond Baskets and Beads: Activities for Older Adults with Functional Impairments
    by Mary Hart, Karen Primm, and Kathy Cranisky
Boredom Busters: Themed Special Events to Dazzle and Delight Your Group
    by Annette C. Moore
Brain Fitness
    by Suzanne Fitzsimmons
Client Assessment in Therapeutic Recreation Services
    by Norma J. Stumbo
Client Outcomes in Therapeutic Recreation Services
    by Norma J. Stumbo
Conceptual Foundations for Therapeutic Recreation
    edited by David R. Austin, John Dattilo, and Bryan P. McCormick
Constraints to Leisure
    edited by Edgar L. Jackson
Dementia Care Programming: An Identity-Focused Approach
    by Rosemary Dunne
Dimensions of Choice: Qualitative Approaches to Parks, Recreation, Tourism, Sport,
    and Leisure Research, Second Edition
    by Karla A. Henderson
Diversity and the Recreation Profession: Organizational Perspectives, Revised Edition
    edited by Maria T. Allison and Ingrid E. Schneider
Effective Management in Therapeutic Recreation Service, Second Edition
    by Marcia Jean Carter and Gerald S. O'Morrow
Everything from A to Y: The Zest Is up to You! Older Adult Activities for Every Day
    of the Year
    by Nancy R. Cheshire and Martha L. Kenney
Experience Marketing: Strategies for the New Millennium
    by Ellen L. O'Sullivan and Kathy J. Spangler
Facilitation of Therapeutic Recreation Services: An Evidence-Based and Best
    Practice Approach to Techniques and Processes
    edited by Norma J. Stumbo and Brad Wardlaw
Facilitation Techniques in Therapeutic Recreation, Second Edition
    by John Dattilo and Alexis McKenney

File o' Fun: A Recreation Planner for Games & Activities, Third Edition
   by Jane Harris Ericson and Diane Ruth Albright
Getting People Involved in Life and Activities: Effective Motivating Techniques
   by Jeanne Adams
Health Promotion for Mind, Body, and Spirit
   by Suzanne Fitzsimmons and Linda L. Buettner
Inclusion: Including People With Disabilities in Parks and Recreation Opportunities
   by Lynn Anderson and Carla Brown Kress
Inclusive Leisure Services: Responding to the Rights of People with Disabilities,
   Second Edition
   by John Dattilo
Internships in Recreation and Leisure Services: A Practical Guide for Students,
   Fourth Edition
   by Edward E. Seagle, Jr. and Ralph W. Smith
Interpretation of Cultural and Natural Resources, Second Edition
   by Douglas M. Knudson, Ted T. Cable, and Larry Beck
Intervention Activities for At-Risk Youth
   by Norma J. Stumbo
Introduction to Outdoor Recreation: Providing and Managing Resource Based
   Opportunities
   by Roger L. Moore and B.L. Driver
Introduction to Recreation and Leisure Services, Eighth Edition
   by Karla A. Henderson, M. Deborah Bialeschki, John L. Hemingway, Jan S.
   Hodges, Beth D. Kivel, and H. Douglas Sessoms
Introduction to Therapeutic Recreation: U.S. and Canadian Perspectives
   by Kenneth Mobily and Lisa Ostiguy
Introduction to Writing Goals and Objectives
   by Suzanne Melcher
Leadership and Administration of Outdoor Pursuits, Third Edition
   by James Blanchard, Michael Strong, and Phyllis Ford
Leadership in Leisure Services: Making a Difference, Third Edition
   by Debra J. Jordan
Leisure and Leisure Services in the 21st Century: Toward Mid Century
   by Geoffrey Godbey
The Leisure Diagnostic Battery Computer Software (CD)
   by Peter A. Witt, Gary Ellis, and Mark A. Widmer
Leisure Education I: A Manual of Activities and Resources, Second Edition
   by Norma J. Stumbo
Leisure Education II: More Activities and Resources, Second Edition
   by Norma J. Stumbo
Leisure Education III: More Goal-Oriented Activities
   by Norma J. Stumbo
Leisure Education IV: Activities for Individuals with Substance Addictions
   by Norma J. Stumbo
Leisure Education Program Planning: A Systematic Approach, Third Edition
   by John Dattilo

Recreation Program Planning Manual for Older Adults
    by Karen Kindrachuk
Recreation Programming and Activities for Older Adults
    by Jerold E. Elliott and Judith A. Sorg-Elliott
Reference Manual for Writing Rehabilitation Therapy Treatment Plans
    by Penny Hogberg and Mary Johnson
Service Living: Building Community through Public Parks and Recreation
    by Doug Wellman, Dan Dustin, Karla Henderson, and Roger Moore
Simple Expressions: Creative and Therapeutic Arts for the Elderly in Long-Term
    Care Facilities
    by Vicki Parsons
Special Events and Festivals: How to Organize, Plan, and Implement
    by Angie Prosser and Ashli Rutledge
Supervision and Management of Human Resources in Recreation and Sport Organizations
    by Margaret Arnold, Regina Glover, and Cheryl Beeler
Survey Research and Analysis: Applications in Parks, Recreation, and Human
    Dimensions
    by Jerry Vaske
Taking the Initiative: Activities to Enhance Effectiveness and Promote Fun
    by J. P. Witman
Therapeutic Recreation and the Nature of Disabilities
    by Kenneth E. Mobily and Richard D. MacNeil
Therapeutic Recreation: Cases and Exercises, Second Edition
    by Barbara C. Wilhite and M. Jean Keller
Therapeutic Recreation in Health Promotion and Rehabilitation
    by John Shank and Catherine Coyle
Therapeutic Recreation in the Nursing Home
    by Linda Buettner and Shelley L. Martin
Therapeutic Recreation Practice: A Strengths Approach
    by Lynn Anderson and Linda Heyne
Therapeutic Recreation Programming: Theory and Practice
    by Charles Sylvester, Judith E. Voelkl, and Gary D. Ellis
Therapeutic Recreation Protocol for Treatment of Substance Addictions
    by Rozanne W. Faulkner
The Therapeutic Recreation Stress Management Primer
    by Cynthia Mascott
The Therapeutic Value of Creative Writing
    by Paul M. Spicer
Tourism and Society: An Introduction
    by Robert W. Wyllie
Traditions: Improving Quality of Life in Caregiving
    by Janelle Sellick
Trivia by the Dozen: Encouraging Interaction and Reminiscence in Managed Care
    by Jean Vetter